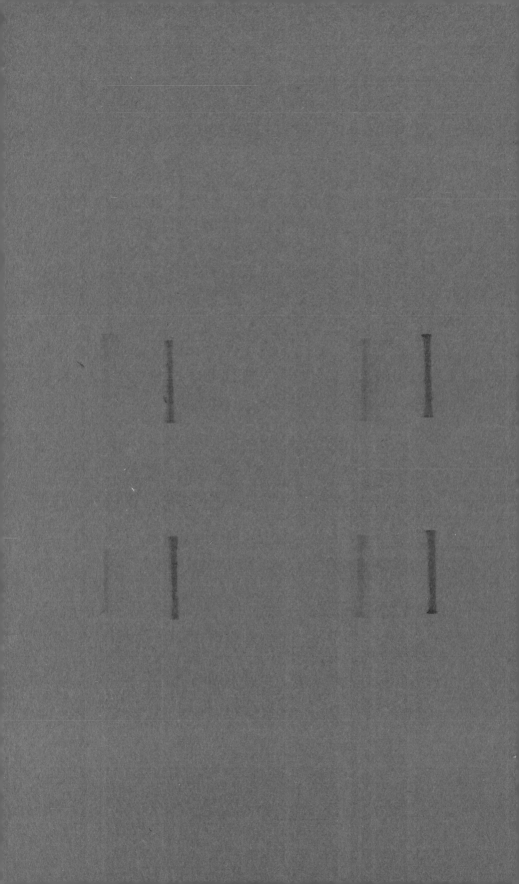

Harvard East Asian Series 46

The East Asian Research Center at Harvard University administers research projects designed to further scholarly understanding of China, Japan, Korea, Vietnam, and adjacent areas.

Hu Shih and the Chinese Renaissance

人權論集

胡適題

An example of Hu Shih's distinctive calligraphy: Title page of Jen-ch'üan lun-chi (A collection of essays on human rights), published in Shanghai, 1930

Hu Shih and the Chinese Renaissance

Liberalism in the Chinese Revolution, 1917–1937

Jerome B. Grieder

Harvard University Press
Cambridge, Massachusetts
1970

Distributed in Great Britain by Oxford
University Press, London

Preparation of this volume has been aided
by a grant from the Ford Foundation.

Library of Congress Catalog Card Number 78–106958
SBN 674–41250–8

Printed in the United States of America

To my mother and father,
Naomi Lane Babson Grieder
and Paul A. Grieder

Contents

Preface   ix

Part I   *The Education of a Chinese Intellectual*

     1   The Early Years, 1891–1910   3
     2   The American Experience, 1910–1917   39

Part II   *The Chinese Renaissance*

     3   The Literary Revolution   75
     4   The New People and the New Society   89
     5   China and the West   129

Part III *Liberalism*

     6   Peking, 1917–1926   173
     7   Shanghai, 1927–1930   217
     8   Peking Again, 1931–1937   246

Part IV   *An Epilogue and an Evaluation*

     9   The Later Years   293
    10   The Chinese Renaissance, Chinese
        Liberalism, and the Chinese Revolution   314

Appendixes   A. The Women in Hu's Life   351
           B. The Chinese Delegation to the VIII Congress
              of the International Federation of Students,
              1913   355
           C. The Chinese Communist Attack on Hu Shih   358

Bibliography   369

Glossary   399

Index   405

Illustrations

Frontispiece. An example of Hu Shih's distinctive calligraphy. Title page of *Jen-ch'üan lun-chi* (A collection of essays on human rights), published in Shanghai, 1930.

Following page 170

Hu Shih as a schoolboy. Published in *Hu Shih liu-hsüeh jih-chi*, facing p. 423.

Hu Shih in 1914. From *Leslie's Illustrated Weekly Newspaper*, June 4, 1914, p. 543.

Hu Shih in China, about 1920. From *Who's Who in China* (Shanghai: *China Weekly Review*, 1925), p. 373.

Portrait bust of Hu Shih by Lucile Swan, done in Peiping in the early 1930s. Photograph by Serge Vargassoff, published in *Asia* magazine, March 1935, p. 139.

Postwar caricature of Hu Shih by Loh Han-ying (pseud. Chang Kwong-tso). Published in Shanghai *T'ieh-pao*, reprinted in *China Weekly Review*, May 31, 1947, p. 377.

Hu Shih in Taiwan in his later years. Photograph by Li Ho-sheng, published in *Hai-wai lun-t'an*, May 1, 1962, p. 2.

Preface

This is a study of the ideas of Hu Shih (1891–1962), and of Hu's efforts to shape China's intellectual response to the modern world. It thus falls into the category of intellectual biography, a fact which I acknowledge only with some misgiving. For intellectual biography is a presumptuous undertaking. The biographer who deals in ideas must strive to tell not only what his subject said, but why; to relate word to thought, and in some measure to link thought to deed. Not only the discernible facts of a life are opened to scrutiny and judgment, but also the unseen and often unfelt threads of motive that bound these facts together into a coherent and vital whole. Even to attempt such a reconstruction presumes an encroachment by the writer upon the innermost center of his subject's being, an intimacy too great to exist without engendering in the one an emotional involvement in the life of the other. At the outset, then, it seems only fair to apprise the reader of my prejudices, insofar as I am conscious of them.

I first saw Hu Shih in the spring of 1955, when he addressed a colloquium of the East Asian Regional Studies program at Harvard University. His topic was "The Intellectual Revolution in Modern China," and even as a fledgling graduate student I knew enough about the subject to recognize its importance, and enough about Dr. Hu to acknowledge the privileged position that he had occupied in the history he proposed to discuss. I knew enough, too, to suspect in the end that he had not done justice to the subject in an hour devoted largely to a self-justifying account of the political and intellectual blunders that everyone *else* had made. I carried away from that evening an appreciation of the urbane affability of the speaker, and little desire to pursue the study of an intellectual reform movement that claimed such a self-indulgent figure as one of its leaders.

I might have dismissed Hu outright after that first encounter had it not been for the fact that the Chinese Communist attack on his life and works was just at its peak, and this suggested itself to me as a suitable topic for seminar research. Reading the anti-Hu polemics of Peking's ideologues led me inevitably back to an examination of the ideas and activities against which they aimed their

ix

criticism. As I became better acquainted with the opinions that Hu had published in China in the years 1917–1937 and with the circumstances surrounding them, my harsh first judgment of him began to soften. Later still, in Taiwan, I began to sense the dimensions of the psychological burden that rested upon Hu and others of his generation, men who had witnessed the accomplishments of a lifetime repudiated, often in a violent and highly personal fashion as was the case with Hu himself. If Hu was, at the end of his life, a disappointing figure, vaingloriously parading the reputation earned in an earlier and more propitious era, he was also, I think, a profoundly disappointed man. In that other time and setting much of what he had had to say had been perceptive, substantial, and even in an undramatic way courageous. In this book I hope that I have been able to make clear my reasons for thinking so. I should add, however, that this study is not intended merely as a defense of Hu against his critics, least of all his critics in Communist China, whose views, profusely published in the mid-1950s, I have relegated to an appendix. Hu Shih's ideas merit attention in their own right, and that is what I have tried to accord them here.

Hu Shih was a scholar — by education and vocation a philosopher, or more accurately a student of the history of philosophy, and by avocation a student of the history of Chinese literature. But he was also a man of wide-ranging interests, with opinions on the vital issues of his time that he felt obligated to share with any who might wish to listen or to read. This is not a book about Hu's scholarship or about his very considerable contributions to the development of a modern understanding of the significance of certain aspects of the Chinese tradition. I have not attempted to assess the usefulness or the validity of what Hu said concerning China's past, but rather to evaluate the manner in which he sought to mold contemporary opinion about the modern world and China's place in it. My aim has been to set forth a record of Hu's views on the great social, political, and intellectual problems that confronted the Chinese in the 1920s and 1930s, and to try to understand why he said what he did about man's relationship to his environment and his culture, about the nature of history and of cultural transformation, and about China's future in the new age into which she had been compelled to enter.

In his pronouncements on these questions of general import Hu expressed what has usually been characterized, by his enemies as well as by his friends, as a "liberal" point of view. There are sound reasons for accepting this designation, and I have done so. I refrain, however, from offering at this point a definition of what I take to be the meaning of this ambiguous and abused term. There is, I think, a sufficiently common understanding of what liberalism means (in terms of the political primacy of the individual, the rule of law, the rationality of the political process) to render superfluous any definition of the idea at this level of generality. As for what liberalism meant in the particular context of Hu Shih's ideas and times, the following pages will, I trust, offer an adequate (if tentative) answer.

Hu Shih's opinions were his own. He was not, nor did he claim to be, the spokesman for any formally constituted "liberal" faction or party, either within or outside of the political movements of his day. Often, however, his views coincided with, and perhaps influenced, the views of others whose names will appear in these pages, and it is sometimes natural to speak of the Chinese liberals as a group. Most of the men among whom Hu found intellectual companionship, especially after 1920, were similar to him in experience and occupation. Many were teachers, scholars, or publicists — not a few, like Hu himself, were all three — who had been educated in the universities of Europe and the United States. They were preeminently intellectuals, cosmopolites who felt more at home on the university campuses of China, and in her cities, than in the hinterland, sophisticated thinkers who addressed themselves not to the illiterate and intellectually passive multitudes of the peasantry but to the literate, impressionable, and articulate students in the middle schools and universities. I have tried to suggest in several places the extent to which Hu Shih's ideas were representative of the opinions of this larger group, and I have spoken occasionally of the liberals as a collectivity, without, I hope, conveying the impression that these men were more conscious of their collective identity than was in fact the case.

I certainly do not claim that the history of liberalism in modern China is, or can be, fully told in a study of Hu Shih's thought. When the full account is written, it must encompass others who were more moved than Hu was (or seemed to be) by a humanitarian concern for the misery of the Chinese people, and whose sense of outrage was consequently deeper than his. In it, too, must figure those who were themselves involved, through the mass education and rural reconstruction movements, or through the effort to establish producers' cooperatives and the like, in the day-to-day struggle against mass poverty, disease, and ignorance — malignant forces that Hu acknowledged only at the level of abstractions.

Yet as this story unfolds it will become evident, I hope, that we are in the presence of a mind sensitive to, and comprehending of, many of the values that lie close to the heart of modern liberalism, and in the company of a man who spoke consistently and thoughtfully of ideals that remain, even now, the cherished aspirations of many men. It is, on the whole, a sad story, partly because it is permeated by the greater tragedy of China's history in the first half of the twentieth century, and partly for the more personal reasons suggested earlier. Hu Shih was, at his best, an eminently reasonable man. And perhaps, as Alexander Herzen wrote a century and more ago, "Reason will always have to give way: it will always carry *less weight*. Like the Northern Lights, it shines over great distances, but it hardly exists. Reason is the final endeavor, the summit to which development seldom attains: hence it is powerful, but it cannot stand up against fists." *

In the years since I began the research that led first to a doctoral dissertation and finally to the present study I have benefited from the generous assistance of many people. It would be impossible adequately to acknowledge all my debts here, but some cannot pass without mention.

I am very pleased at last to have an opportunity to express my gratitude to Professor John K. Fairbank for all that he has done for me since I began the study of modern Chinese history, for his unfailing insight into the problems that confront a student of this frustrating and enthralling field, and especially for the persistent and invariably good-natured encouragement without which this book would not have been written. I am deeply grateful also to Professor Benjamin I. Schwartz, whose teaching and scholarship have set for me a model of perceptiveness, integrity, and modesty in the study of ideas and their place in history. To another former teacher, Professor L. S. Yang, I am indebted for sound advice on numerous points of fact and interpretation. I wish also to thank Professor C. Martin Wilbur for his kind permission to make use of

* Alexander Herzen, *My Past and Thoughts: The Memoirs of Alexander Herzen,* trans. Constance Garnett, rev. Humphrey Higgins (New York: Alfred A. Knopf, 1968), III, 1218.

unpublished materials in the archives of the Oral History Project of Columbia University, without which my understanding of the texture of Hu's life would have been much poorer.

For leading me to sources which I might otherwise have over-looked, for sharing with me their ideas on matters of mutual interest, or for offering much needed criticism of my own ideas and the expression of them, I wish to thank Dr. Dorothy Borg, Professor Chang Fo-ch'üan, Professor Chow Tse-tsung, Miss Betsy Fitzgerald, Professor Michael Gasster, Mr. Stanley Griffith, Professor Tamara Harevan, Professor John Israel, Professor Lin Yü-sheng, Professor Allen B. Linden, Professor Maurice Meisner, Professor David T. Roy, Professor Irwin J. Schulman, and Professor Yin Hai-kuang. I would like to thank Dr. Barry Keenan for making available to me some of the results of his own research on John Dewey's lectures in China.

My colleagues at Brown, Professor Lea E. Williams and Dr. Susan Han Marsh, read the entire manuscript and offered many valuable comments. Miss Dorothy Day and Mr. I-min Chiang, both of the Rockefeller Library at Brown, did much to ease the burden of research in its final stages. My father, Paul A. Grieder, subjected the manuscript to careful scrutiny, and it profits from his fine sense of the English language.

Finally, I owe more than I can express to my wife Elsa, for her patient and cheerful endurance of what threatened to become an interminable preoccupation, and for much else besides.

At various stages of the research and writing of this book I have received financial support from the Ford Foundation, the Inter-University Program for Field Training in Chinese, the Joint Committee on Modern China of the Social Science Research Council, the East Asian Research Center at Harvard University, and the Committee on Summer Stipends at Brown University, to all of which I here convey my sincere thanks.

Although this book would not exist save for the assistance of the individuals and agencies mentioned here, and many others not named but remembered, it goes without saying that none of them is in any way responsible for the opinions I have expressed, or for errors of fact or judgment that I may have committed.

Jerome B. Grieder
Providence, Rhode Island, September 1969

No doubt we should destroy all errors, but as it is impossible to destroy them all in an instant, we should imitate a prudent architect who, when obliged to destroy a building, and knowing how its parts are united together, sets about its demolition in such a way as to prevent its fall from being dangerous.

Condorcet

The speculative line of demarcation where obedience ought to end and resistance must begin is faint, obscure, and not easily definable. It is not a single act, or a single event, which determines it. Governments must be abused and deranged, indeed, before it can be thought of; and the prospect of the future must be as bad as the experience of the past. When things are in that lamentable condition, the nature of the disease is to indicate the remedy to those whom nature has qualified to administer in extremities this critical, ambiguous, bitter potion to a distempered state. Times and occasions and provocations will teach their own lessons. The wise will determine from the gravity of the case; the irritable, from sensibility to oppression; the high-minded, from disdain and indignation at abusive power in unworthy hands; the brave and bold, from the love of honorable danger in a generous cause; but, with or without right, a revolution will be the very last resource of the thinking and the good.

Edmund Burke

I possessed a passion for research, a power of suspending judgment with patience, of meditating with pleasure, of assenting with caution, of correcting false impressions with readiness, and of arranging my thoughts with scrupulous pains. I had no hankering after novelty, no blind admiration for antiquity. Imposture in every shape I utterly detested.

Francis Bacon's Proem to
The Interpretation of Nature

Part I. The Education of a Chinese Intellectual

Abbreviations Used in the Notes

CPR: C	*Chinese Press Review: Chungking*
CPR:N	*Chinese Press Review: Nanking*
CPR:P	*Chinese Press Review: Peiping*
CWR	*The China Weekly Review*
HCN	*Hsin ch'ing-nien*
HSWT	*Hu Shih wen-ts'un (1921)*
HSWT II	*Hu Shih wen-ts'un, ti-erh chi* (1924)
HSWT III	*Hu Shih wen-ts'un, ti-san chi* (1930)
HSWT IV	*Hu Shih wen-ts'un, ti-ssu chi* (1953)
HY	*Hsin yüeh*
KHYJSK	*K'o-hsüeh yü jen-sheng-kuan*
NCH	*The North China Herald*
NLCP	*Nu-li chou-pao*
TLPL	*Tu-li p'ing-lun*

Chapter 1. The Early Years, 1891–1910

Shanghai in the 1890s was a city of two worlds. There was first the old Chinese town, still walled and gated, a warren of narrow and winding alleys in the midst of which stood the Temple of Confucius and the yamen of the district magistrate and the taotai, symbols of intellectual orthodoxy and imperial authority. Beyond the old town, to the south and east, ran the Whangpoo River, along which stretched the jetties and godowns that marked Shanghai's commercial preeminence, together with a growing number of industrial enterprises. To the north and west of the Chinese City lay the French concession and the International Settlement, sheltering the homes and businesses of the foreigners whose arrival half a century earlier had so greatly altered the character of Shanghai and the destiny of China.

Between these two worlds, in a house outside the East Gate of the Chinese City, Hu Shih was born on December 17, 1891. But he would lay claim to neither. His world was China, but a China in which the city walls were crumbling and the narrow streets giving way to broad avenues, a China in which the troops of vagrant armies were quartered in the temples of Confucius, and only the memory of mandarins still lingered in the courtyards of the yamen. His world was also the West, not the circumscribed and carefully insulated West of Shanghai's foreign settlements, but the West that lay invisible beyond the ocean into which the Whangpoo emptied its muddy waters.

Hu Shih was the youngest son of Hu Ch'uan (*tzu* T'ieh-hua, 1841–1895), a minor official of the Ch'ing dynasty, who was serving, at the time of his son's birth, as inspector of the likin barriers — that is, as a collector of transit taxes — in the Shanghai area. The Hu ancestral home was the village of Shang-chuang in Chi-hsi hsien, Hui-chou prefecture, in the mountains of southeastern Anhwei province near the Chekiang border. The men of Hui-chou were famous traders, a reputation earned by necessity since much of the land was too rough and poor to sustain those who lived on it. Many families in Hui-chou depended for their livelihood on the profits sent home by fathers or brothers or sons trading in other parts the products for which the district was renowned — ink and varnish and especially tea. For several generations the Hu clan of Shang-chuang had been in the tea business.[1]

Impoverished though it was, Hui-chou was not without its illustrious sons. The most celebrated of these was the eighteenth-

1. Shang-chuang was a "one-name" village of the Hu clan located some fifty *li* north of the administrative center of Chi-hsi hsien in Hui-chou prefecture. In the middle of the nineteenth century, before the Taiping Rebellion, the population of the village was about six thousand, counting those engaged in trade in other parts and thus not in fact resident. By 1865, in the wake of the rebellion, the population of Shang-chuang had been reduced to slightly more than 1200. See Hu Shih, "Dr. Hu Shih's Personal Reminiscences" (interviews compiled and edited by Te-kong Tong, with Dr. Hu's corrections in his own handwriting, 1958; typescript in the archive of the Oral History Project of Columbia University), 9, 12, 17 (cited hereafter as Oral History).

In 1940, according to one source, the name of the village was changed to Shih-chih *ts'un*, in honor of its most illustrious son on the approach of his fiftieth birthday. See *Chi-hsi hsien-chih* (Gazetteer of Chi-hsi hsien; Taipei, 1963), 723.

century scholar and philosopher Tai Chen (1724–1777), in his day the greatest exponent of the Han Learning, a Confucian reformist movement aimed at retrieving a sense of the original meanings of Chou and Han texts which had been obscured by the thinkers of the Sung and Ming periods. Tai, though a native of Hsiu-ning, some way to the south, had studied in Hui-chou in the 1740s, and his influence continued to be felt there after his departure. Among his disciples were "the three Hus of Chi-hsi," [2] prominent purveyors of the Han Learning in the late eighteenth and early nineteenth centuries. Hu Shih's name was sometimes linked with theirs in later years after he had himself become Chi-hsi's greatest claim to fame. But in fact his own clan had sprung from different stock — it was said that its origin could be traced back to the ruling house of the T'ang dynasty[3] — and his intellectual inheritance was shaped not by the Han Learning but by his father's fondness for the philosophers of the Sung period.

Hu Ch'uan had grown up in troubled times.[4] As a boy he had been able to pick up only such education as he could come by in his travels about the country on trading expeditions that took him sometimes as far as Ch'uan-sha, just across the river from Shanghai, where the family owned a tea shop. In the early 1860s, when Hu Ch'uan was in his twenties, the Taiping rebels, their ranks swollen by bands of local brigands, repeatedly harassed the area around Chi-hsi. For several years Hu and his family lived in constant peril. His first wife died in 1864 "in defense of her honor," as the expression has it, during a sudden Taiping raid on the family's mountain

2. They were Hu K'uang-chung (*tzu* P'u-chai), Hu P'ei-hui (*tzu* Tsai-p'ing), and Hu Ch'un-ch'iao. K'uang-chung gained wide repute as a scholar in the eighteenth century, although he never rose above the rank of "Imperial student by virtue of seniority," an honorary title; among his works were several studies of the *ching-t'ien* (well-field) system. P'ei-hui, his grandson, won the *chin-shih* degree in 1819 and served officially in a number of posts; he was also a prolific scholar, his specialty being textual criticisms of various ritual texts. A cursory search in the standard collections of Ch'ing-dynasty biographies has turned up no information on the identity of Hu Ch'un-ch'iao, his relationship to the other members of the trio, or the nature of his interests or accomplishments.

3. Li Ao (Lee Ao), *Hu Shih p'ing-chuan* (A critical biography of Hu Shih; Taipei, 1964), 106, 123–124.

4. This account of Hu Ch'uan's life is largely based on Chang Huan-lun, "Hu T'ieh-hua hsien-sheng chia-chuan" (A family chronicle of Mr. Hu T'ieh-hua), an obituary essay written in the 1890s and printed in Hu Ch'uan, *Taiwan chi-lu liang-chung*, ed. Hu Shih and Lo Erh-kang (Two records of Taiwan; Taipei, 1951).

refuge south of Chi-hsi, from which Hu Ch'uan barely escaped with his own life.

Not until the rebellion had been finally suppressed in 1865 was Hu able to present himself for the prefectural examinations, where in spite of the haphazard nature of his earlier education he was successful. He thus became eligible for a scholar's stipend from the government, but though he tried repeatedly he never managed to pass the provincial examinations that would have opened to him an official career. For the next fifteen years he devoted his energies to various tasks of reconstruction in the vicinity of Chi-hsi, which had suffered cruelly during the rebellion. He supervised the rebuilding of the ancestral temple, a responsibility that occupied him for more than a decade, and he was also among the local gentry leaders who took charge of the rehabilitation of the Confucian academy. In 1866 he married again. Before her death in 1879 his second wife bore him three sons and an equal number of daughters.

In spite of his civic and domestic responsibilities Hu Ch'uan found time, in the late 1860s, to study briefly in the Lung-men Academy in Shanghai, a school founded in 1864 by Ting Jih-ch'ang as a part of the government's attempts to restore the institutions of Confucian learning in the aftermath of the rebellion. It was there that Hu came into contact with the tradition of Sung scholarship that he later transmitted to his youngest son. It was there, too, that he developed the keen interest in geography that led him in 1881, when his family obligations had somewhat eased, to set out on his own for the frontier provinces of the northeast. In Manchuria he attracted the attention of Wu Ta-ch'eng (1835–1902), the Ch'ing official in charge of the defense establishment in Kirin, to whom Hu carried a letter of introduction.[5] Through Wu's sponsorship Hu Ch'uan was at last able to embark on a career at the lower levels of the civil service.

From 1882, when he received his first official appointment, until his death in 1895 Hu Ch'uan served the empire in many and various capacities. He was engaged at one time or another in land reclamation, poor relief, census taking, map making, and the surveying of international frontiers. He served as a director of studies, as an inspector of military camps and fortifications, and as an official

5. On Wu Ta-ch'eng (1835–1902) see Arthur W. Hummel, ed., *Eminent Chinese of the Ch'ing Period* (Washington, D.C., 1943), II, 880–882.

in the Salt Bureau. He filled offices, both civil and military, at the district and departmental levels of the provincial administrations of Kirin, Kiangsu, and, finally, Taiwan. His biographer observes that wherever Hu served, the people flocked to him, and that he set such an example of generosity that the wealthy "competed with each other to give money away." Highwaymen dismounted from their horses and kowtowed as he passed; even his presence in a district was sufficient to rid it of bandits and brigands. Be that as it may, there seems no reason to doubt that Hu Ch'uan was a man of unusual vigor and resourcefulness.

In 1889, during a brief leave of absence from his duties supervising the repair of dikes in the area of Ch'engchow, Honan, Hu Ch'uan married for a third time. His bride, née Feng Shun-ti, was what the Chinese called forthrightly a "room filler" (*t'ien-fang*) — an illiterate peasant girl thirty-two years younger than her husband, a companion for his declining years, sturdy enough to survive him. Yet despite the disparity in their ages and background, their brief marriage was evidently blessed by a genuine affection and respect. Hu Shih was the only child of this union. His mother was eighteen when he was born; his father was fifty.[6]

Early in 1892 Hu Ch'uan was transferred from Shanghai to Taiwan at the request of Shao Yu-lien, the governor of the newly

6. Hu Shih's mother was born in the village of Chung-t'un, a short distance from Shang-chuang. The circumstances of her upbringing are described at length in Hu Shih, *Ssu-shih tzu-shu* (A self-account at forty; Shanghai, 1933), chap. 1 (hereafter cited as *Autobiography*; all references are to the Taipei, 1959, edition). The decision to enter into her marriage with Hu Ch'uan was her own, motivated by considerations of her parents' poverty and of the fact that she was, at seventeen, somewhat beyond the age at which a more appropriate match could be arranged.

Hu Ch'uan's first wife, also née Feng (m. 1860), died childless in 1862 during a raid by Taiping rebel forces. His second wife, née Tsao (m. 1866) bore him a son, Hung-chün, in 1871, twin sons, Hung-chui and Hung-p'i, in 1878, and three daughters whose names and birth dates are not recorded by Chang Huan-lun. She died after a lingering illness in 1879. The eldest son and at least one of the daughters were older than Hu Shih's mother. The second daughter was not a member of the household, having been given in adoption as a child. Sometime later, possibly after Hu Ch'uan's death, the younger of the twin boys was also given for adoption to continue the line of a collateral branch of the family — a circumstance that had some influence in shaping Hu Shih's youthful views on Chinese family life. In keeping with Chinese custom and family precedent, when Hu Ch'uan's youngest son was born in 1891 he was given the name Hung-hsing. Hu Shih was a name that he took for himself, adopting it permanently in 1910; see below, note 47. See Chang Huan-lun, "Hu T'ieh-hua hsien-sheng chia-chuan," and Li Ao, *Hu Shih p'ing-chuan*, chap. 1, *passim*.

created province. Hu's wife and son joined him there a year later, and the family remained together until shortly after the outbreak of the Sino-Japanese War, when Hu Shih's mother returned with the boy to the ancestral home in Chi-hsi. Hu Ch'uan remained in Taitung, on the eastern coast of the island, where he was filling the posts of departmental magistrate and garrison commander, until the end of June 1895, two months after the signing of the Treaty of Shimonoseki had turned the island over to Japanese control. By then gravely ill with beriberi, he made his way to Anping, on the western coast. There his departure from the island was further delayed by Liu Yung-fu, a Chinese soldier of fortune with a sizable private army at his command, who had proclaimed himself president of an independent republic of Taiwan in the hope of thus forestalling the Japanese. In spite of the seriousness of Hu's illness, which took the form of a progressive paralysis, Liu attempted to enlist his support in this scheme. Not until the middle of August was Hu permitted to sail for Amoy, where, too feeble to continue on his way, he died on August 22, 1895, at the age of fifty-four.

Hu Shih, referring to the circumstances of his father's death, called him "the first person to be sacrificed for a democratic state in Asia." [7] This seems, however, a peculiarly inappropriate judgment. Hu Ch'uan would more suitably be remembered as a Chinese gentleman who in energy and integrity nearly personified the Confucian bureaucratic ideal. In the imperial service he had traveled to the very frontiers of the empire, from northern Manchuria to Hainan Island in the south, and finally to Taiwan. But in the short notices we have concerning Hu Ch'uan's life and thought there is nothing to suggest that he looked beyond the horizons of the Confucian world or foresaw the changes that the next few decades would bring. His most fitting epitaph, far more traditional in tone than that bestowed upon him by his son, was uttered by his young widow when she told the boy, in a daily ritual, that his father had been "the only complete man whom I have ever known." [8]

After Hu Ch'uan's death Hu Shih's mother became, at twenty-three, the nominal head of a household that included, besides her

7. *Autobiography*, 16.
8. Hu Shih, "Hsien-mu hsing-shu" (Reflections on my late mother's life), HSWT, iv, 1108; also *Autobiography*, 28.

son, several of her husband's children by his second marriage. The eldest son, Hung-chün, was two years older than his stepmother, with a wife and son of his own. He was, moreover, something of a wastrel, an opium addict and an habitual gambler who claimed more than his share of the family's dwindling resources. It therefore fell to the second son, Hung-chui, the older of the twins born in 1878, to take over management of the small business ventures in Shanghai and Hankow on which the family depended for its living.[9] Hu Shih's mother was thus forced to rely entirely on her stepson for her own support and that of her child. To this difficult situation she brought nothing save the force of a personality which, as Hu Shih later remembered it, combined all the virtues of Chinese womanhood: modesty, integrity, forbearance, and a strong

9. Information on the economic status of the Hu family is scattered. Chang Huan-lun says only that tea had been the family business for several generations. By Hu Shih's account, his father's estate consisted of a small sum invested in a local (tea?) shop which brought in a sufficient income to support the family. It appears that Hu Ch'uan had also inherited an interest in small teashops in Ch'uan-sha, near Shanghai, and in the Chinese city of Shanghai itself, investments valued in 1880 at roughly $3000 silver. When these shops changed hands after Hu Ch'uan's death, the family reinvested in small businesses in Shanghai and Hankow, which were placed under the management of Hung-chui, the second son. For some years he was successful in these ventures, but ultimately ill luck and poor judgment combined to overwhelm him. In 1908 the Shanghai shop was taken over by creditors. In 1909, at the insistence of the older sons, the family property was divided among them: Hung-chün, the eldest, took the Hankow shop as his share, while the others received a few *mou* of land and small real-estate holdings in the vicinity of Shang-chuang. The Hankow shop was lost in 1910 during revolutionary disturbances in the city. See Oral History 17; *Autobiography*, 46, 78–79; "Hsien-mu hsing-shu," HSWT, iv, 1110; Ho Ping-ti, *The Ladder of Success in Imperial China* (New York and London, 1962), 305–307.

During the last years of his schooling in Shanghai and throughout the time he spent in the United States, Hu Shih was obliged to bear most of the responsibility for his mother's support. His student diary contains several references to the worsening financial situation at home and his own frustration at not being in a position to give more assistance. See Hu Shih, *Hu Shih liu-hsüeh jih-chi* (Hu Shih's diary while studying abroad; Taipei, 1959), 225, 229, 255, and *passim* (cited hereafter as *Diary*).

In a denunciation of his father published in 1950, Hu Shih's younger son, Hu Ssu-tu, the only member of the family who stayed on the Mainland after the Communist victory, remarked that Hu Shih came from "a fallen family of bureaucrats." The moral judgment implied is perhaps irrelevant, but the suggestion of declining fortunes seems to fit the facts of the situation with fair accuracy. See Edward Hunter, *Brainwashing in Red China* (New York, 1951), 303–307, where Hu Ssu-tu's self-criticism is reprinted from a translation that appeared in *The Hong Kong Standard*, Sept. 24, 1950.

sense of responsibility toward the family into whose keeping she had been condemned by Hu Ch'uan's untimely death. Hu Shih's childhood in Chi-hsi was spent not in poverty but in an atmosphere of chronic domestic tension and financial anxiety. Long afterwards he recalled this scene from those years: an annual crisis on the eve of the New Year, when, according to ancient and unbreakable custom, all debts must be discharged.

> Every New Year's Eve there would be a great number of people in the house, dunning us for debts. They would sit in the reception hall, each with a lantern, refusing to move. My eldest brother would disappear early in the evening. The two rows of chairs in the reception hall would fill up with the creditors and their lanterns, while my mother went in and out, busy with the preparation of the midnight meal, or thanking the kitchen god, or getting ready the money that would be distributed to the children to bring them luck in the New Year, and such occupations appropriate to the occasion. She only pretended not to see the crowd in the reception hall. When it was close to midnight, the time when we would seal the front door by pasting strips of paper over it, my mother would slip out the back way and go to beg a relative who lived in the neighborhood to come over. Then she would give each of the creditors a little money, and only then would they leave. Each putting the best face that he could upon the matter, one by one they would pick up their lanterns and depart. A moment later my eldest brother would be knocking at the gate. My mother never once berated him, and moreover, because it was New Year's Eve, she did not permit even a trace of anger to show in her face. I must have passed six or seven New Year's Eves in this manner.[10]

It is hardly surprising in these circumstances that the bond between Hu Shih and his mother was close and affectionate. He remembered her as "a paragon among women," [11] and in later years he invariably spoke of her with unabashed sentiment. "[My mother] was able to endure," he wrote, a decade after her death in 1918, "only because she had in me a bit of her own flesh and blood to

10. *Autobiography*, 30.
11. *Diary*, 252.

sustain her. She entrusted all her aspirations to my remote and unfathomable future." [12] The example which she set by her own conduct in the difficult situation of her life after Hu Ch'uan's death imparted to her son an enduring respect for moderation and compromise in personal relationships. "If I have learned a little evenness of temper, if I have learned in some slight degree an amiability that makes me helpful toward others, if I am able to forgive others and to sympathize with them I owe all my gratitude to my gentle mother." [13]

Hu Shih owed to his mother another and more onerous debt besides. After Hu Ch'uan's death it was she who supervised the boy's education, and who insisted, when he was in his early teens, that he should leave Chi-hsi to seek a "modern" education, the pursuit of which took him first to Shanghai and then to the United States. She was herself in no respect a modern woman, however, and as Hu's education revealed to him realms that his mother could never enter he found himself entangled in a profound emotional crisis. The more he came to know of Western ideas, the harder it became for him to accept the standards of social conduct to which his mother still adhered, and still expected him to conform. "There is but one truth, and it does not permit of compromise," he wrote in 1914, in the diary he kept during his student days at Cornell and Columbia. "How can I be forced to believe what I do not believe simply on account of others, or compelled to do what I do not wish to do?" Such an attitude, as Hu realized, contradicted the traditional injunctions of filiality, exemplified by the Han-dynasty scholar Mao I, who despite his distaste for public office had accepted appointment in order to please his mother. For Hu Shih the problem was more personal: it was his betrothal to an unknown girl from the village, a match arranged by his mother in the traditional manner when he was only twelve years old.

It was while Hu struggled with this dilemma that John Morley's essay *On Compromise,* to which he later attributed much significance as an influence on the development of his character, first came to his attention. "It seems to the present writer," Morley wrote, "that one relationship in life and one only justifies us in being silent where otherwise it would be right to speak. This relationship is that between child and parents . . . This, of course, only

12. *Autobiography,* 17.
13. *Ibid.,* 32.

where the son or daughter feels a tender and genuine attachment to the parent." Thus reassured, Hu was able to conclude, "When parents are old, if suddenly they lose their beliefs it is like losing their support in life, and how can the agony of that be reckoned? It is not easy for those who have reached the evening of life to change their ideas, as the young men of our generation can exchange new beliefs for old. I will follow Easterners in my family affairs, but in my ideas on society, the nation and politics I will follow Westerners." [14] Soon after he returned to China in 1917, a doctorate in philosophy from Columbia University in hand, to embark upon his remarkable career as a social critic and intellectual reformer, Hu Shih returned to Chi-hsi to marry the girl his mother had chosen for him. "If we are to lead we must obey the old conventions," he had told his friend Lewis Gannett when they were students together in America. "Ours is an intermediate generation which must be sacrificed both to our parents and to our children. Unless we would lose all influence, we must marry as our parents wish, girls selected by them for us, whom we may not see before our wedding day — and we must make society happier and healthier for our children to live in. Let that be our reward and consolation." [15]

So while his mother's bearing may have provided the model, for Hu Shih the real test of toleration and compromise was the need to reconcile his respect and affection for her with the dictates of his own new-found beliefs. His success in effecting such a reconciliation, and acting upon it, may explain in some measure the quality of his later critique of Chinese tradition, intellectually uncompromising but seldom marked by the emotional bitterness that was characteristic of the iconoclasm of many of his colleagues.

But in 1895 all this lay still far in the future.

Hu Ch'uan had begun to teach his wife and his youngest son to read during the time the family spent together in Taiwan. Shortly after he returned with his mother to Anhwei in 1895, Hu Shih entered the family school in Shang-chuang, taught by his father's younger brother. "I was very small," he later recalled, "and

14. *Diary*, 442–443; see also 448–449. The passage that Hu quotes in these entries is drawn from Morley's chapter "Religious Conformity." Although there was, in a general sense, a religious aspect to Hu's problem, the immediate issue was that of his marriage.

15. Lewis Gannett, "Hu Shih: Young Prophet of Young China," *The New York Times Magazine* (March 27, 1927), 10. On Hu's marriage see Appendix A.

I had to be lifted up and placed upon one of the high schoolroom benches; and once I was seated I could not climb down again without help. But I certainly wasn't at the bottom of the class, because I knew nearly a thousand characters before I entered school." [16] Following a practice initiated by his father, Hu's mother insisted that the boy's teachers should explain to him the meaning of the texts he studied, to which his schoolmates were introduced in the customary manner, by rote memory alone. For this additional attention she regularly paid considerably more than the usual tuition fee of two dollars a year. As a result Hu was able at an early age to supplement the standard texts of a Confucian education with other reading undertaken on his own initiative, particularly in such great historical compilations as the *Tzu-chih t'ung-chien.*

Among the first things which Hu Shih read and memorized were several texts composed by Hu Ch'uan and copied out by him shortly before his death. One of these, entitled *Poems for the Study of Manhood (Hsüeh wei-jen shih),* began with the statement that "the Way [*tao*] of manhood lies in following the good that lies within one" and closed with the following lines:

> It is unfortunate if there are changes
> Among the Five Constant Virtues.[17]
> That which concerns our relative rank
> Allows not the slightest confusion.
> One may sacrifice oneself for righteousness,
> And he who seeks and achieves benevolence
> Need feel no regrets . . .

> That which is recorded in the Classics,
> And was spoken of by the Confucian teachers,
> Is that the Way of manhood
> Has no other arts than these:
> To probe a doctrine to its depths,
> To extend one's knowledge to the utmost,
> And then to look within, and follow these
> truths in one's own conduct:

16. *Autobiography,* 18.

17. That is, the five virtues of a Confucian character: *jen* (benevolence or human-heartedness), *i* (righteousness), *li*[a] (propriety, decorum), *chih* (wisdom), and *hsin*[a] (sincerity).

To encourage study,
And to defend the Way, and never neglect it.[18]

These verses reflected Hu Ch'uan's commitment to the Confucian tradition of rational humanism. Specifically, they expressed the beliefs of a disciple of Sung-dynasty Neo-Confucianism. In China this philosophy is called the "Ch'eng-Chu School" after its first great sponsors, the brothers Ch'eng I and Ch'eng Hao and their follower Chu Hsi; or else, the *li-hsüeh* or "Study of Principle," from the central term of its metaphysics. In spite of his later reputation as a critic of the Confucian tradition, Hu Shih remained throughout his lifetime indebted to some of the insights gained from his early acquaintance with Neo-Confucian ideas.

Neo-Confucianism had arisen during the latter half of the T'ang dynasty as a movement of protest. It was a reaction both against the utilitarian exploitation of Confucian doctrine by those who sought bureaucratic advancement through the examination system, and against the otherworldliness of Buddhism, whose adherents, in the words of the great ninth-century critic Han Yü, "put themselves beyond the pale of the world and the country." [19] The collapse of the T'ang at the beginning of the tenth century, and the period of civil strife preceding the founding of the Sung dynasty in 960, lent a sense of heightened urgency to the search for the causes that might explain the obvious decadence of Confucian life. During the eleventh and twelfth centuries a procession of great thinkers emerged who took upon themselves the task of rediscovering the real significance of Confucian ideas by attempting to discern the nature of Confucian thought as it had existed before the corrupting influence of Buddhism had made itself felt.

These Neo-Confucian reformers, addressing themselves to Confucian formalists on the one hand and to Buddhist ascetics and ecclesiastics on the other, asserted the importance of real moral standards and genuine moral self-cultivation, and of a conscientious concern with the problem of human conduct in a social context. At the heart of the Neo-Confucian attack on Buddhism lay a sense of necessary involvement in life as it is lived, coupled with a typically Confucian distrust of the kind of speculation that seeks to

18. *Autobiography*, 18–19.
19. Quoted in Fung Yu-lan, *A History of Chinese Philosophy*, trans. Derk Bodde (Princeton, 1953), II, 412.

probe beyond the confines of experience. "Let us understand those things that should be understood," said Chu Hsi, echoing the sentiments of Confucius himself. "Those that cannot be understood let us set aside." [20] Both on a philosophical plane and at the level of common sense this attitude contrasted sharply with the Buddhist denial of the reality of experience, a fact that Neo-Confucian thinkers repeatedly emphasized. Sung Neo-Confucians assumed the existence and reasonableness of the external, perceived world, and they asserted the capacity of the mind to understand it. "The mind is that with which man rules his body," wrote Chu Hsi. "It . . . controls the external world instead of being controlled by it. Therefore if we observe the external objects with the mind, their principles will be apprehended." [21]

Less abstractly, Neo-Confucian thinkers accepted matter-of-factly the imperfection and suffering of human life, from which Buddhism sought a means of escape. "In the world there cannot be birth without death or joy without sorrow. But wherever the Buddhists go they want to pervert this truth and preach the elimination of birth and death and the neutralization of joy and sorrow. In the final analysis this is nothing but self-interest." [22] "How can a person escape from the world? Only when a person no longer stands under heaven or upon earth is he able to forsake the world. But while he continues to drink when thirsty and eat when hungry, he still stands under heaven and sets his feet on earth." [23]

To some extent Neo-Confucian reformers were themselves under the spell of the intellectual system they had undertaken to destroy. They introduced into their argument concepts that were clearly Buddhist in inspiration, and they responded to the Buddhist predilection for abstract speculation by constructing a metaphysical system of their own far more imposing than Confucianism had previously possessed. A central feature of this system was the concept of *li*[b], the principle which underlies the phenomenal world and manifests itself in man and in the myriad things, substantial and insubstantial, to which man is sensible. Yet even this excursion into the realm of metaphysics was prompted by typically Confucian concerns and founded on typically Confucian assumptions. It was

20. *Chu tzu ch'üan-shu*, 51/2, translated in William Theodore de Bary et al., *Sources of Chinese Tradition* (New York, 1960), 542.

21. *Ibid.*, 44/28, in de Bary, *Sources*, 553.

22. *Erh Ch'eng i-shu*, 15/7b, in de Bary, *Sources*, 533.

23. *Ibid.*

assumed, in the first place, that the natural order is constructed of harmonious elements, and secondly that social harmony must reflect the greater harmony of nature itself. The study of Principle, then, or in the terms of the Neo-Confucian argument the "extension of knowledge" (*chih-chih*) through the "investigation of things" (*ko-wu*), was justified by a mundane purpose: only an understanding of the workings of the natural order would enable men to create and maintain a harmonious social order.

The habitual Confucian concern for the condition of society provided another contrast with the attitudes of Buddhism that Sung thinkers were quick to point out: "In deserting his father and leaving his family, the Buddha severed all human relationships. It was merely for himself that he lived alone in the forest. Such a person should not be allowed in any community . . . [The Buddhists] leave these human relationships [i.e., between ruler and minister, father and son, husband and wife] to others and have nothing to do with them, setting themselves apart as a special class. If this is the way to lead the people, it will be the end of the human race." [24] A belief in the force of virtuous example was as old as Confucianism itself. In this respect the Neo-Confucian writers of the Sung did no more than reaffirm fundamental Confucian values — that the "superior man" is distinguished from the commoner not only by his intellectual accomplishments but also by his sense of social responsibility; that virtuous men must seek the means of communicating their private virtue to society at large; and, finally, that good government depends upon the moral rectitude of those who govern. Through the Neo-Confucian revival of the Sung period these essential elements of the Confucian social ethic were rescued from possible oblivion and transmitted as a mighty legacy to later generations. [25]

24. *Ibid.*, 15/5b, in de Bary, *Sources*, 533.
25. Although Neo-Confucianism as synthesized and expounded by Chu Hsi remained the orthodox and officially sponsored interpretation of Confucianism from the thirteenth through the nineteenth centuries, it did not reign unchallenged. The proto-empiricism of Sung thought was considerably offset in the Ming dynasty by a more introspective and intuitional interpretation of Confucianism associated with the school of Wang Shou-jen (Wang Yang-ming), who held that the principles of things reside in the mind and are subjectively discoverable. Wang's emphasis on an intuitive understanding of the Good, based in part on Mencius, inspired in its turn a reaction in the seventeenth and eighteenth centuries by scholars who regarded Ming Confucianism as too far removed from the world of reality and necessity. These reformers sought to redress the

Hu Shih, by his own acknowledgment, inherited from his father "a certain habitual inclination toward the rationalism of the Ch'eng-Chu School." [26] But he did not come into possession of his patrimony without a struggle. When his uncle, who shared Hu Ch'uan's convictions, was appointed to office in another district, management of the family school was turned over to a cousin. Thereafter the influence of Neo-Confucianism in the Hu household was eclipsed by the Buddhist beliefs of the womanfolk. As Hu Shih recalled it, "The strips of paper pasted on the front gates of my uncle's house and our own home, on which was written 'No affiliation with Buddhists and Taoists,' were the signboards of Neo-Confucian households . . . I remember that the notice . . . on the front gate of our new home faded from bright red to pink, then gradually turned a dull white, and finally peeled off and fluttered to the ground." [27]

The popular Buddhism which flourished in the Chinese countryside at the end of the nineteenth century was, as it had been for centuries, a superstition-ridden faith of scanty intellectual content. It appealed chiefly to the emotions of the faithful, requiring of them the fulfillment of vows made in times of illness and distress, and, with its masses and festivals and its great body of folk tales and theatricals, satisfying their taste for color and drama. The pleasures of paradise were not overlooked, but they were overshadowed by the horrors of hell, described in lavish and vivid detail, so that the fear of damnation was probably a greater spur to virtue than was the hope of salvation.

The women among whom Hu Shih spent his childhood — his mother and his maternal grandmother, his brothers' wives and his aunts — were without exception devout Buddhists, and their beliefs inspired in him a profound dread. Then, when he was ten or eleven years old, a chance encounter in the pages of a text compiled by Chu Hsi freed him from the fears thus aroused:

---

balance by returning not to Sung philosophy, in which they recognized the taint of Buddhism, but to the Confucianism of the Han dynasty, from which their school derived one of its names, *Han hsüeh* (Han Learning).

26. *Autobiography*, 34. Many years later Hu observed, "On the whole I've shown in all of my writings a fairly high respect for Confucius and his early followers such as Mencius. And I have great respect for one of the founders of Neo-Confucianism, Chu Hsi." Oral History, 263.

27. *Autobiography*, 35.

One day, while I was reviewing the *Hsiao-hsüeh* of Chu Hsi, I came to a passage consisting of the homilies of Ssu-ma Kuang, among them a discussion of Hell. One line of this read: "Substance has already decayed and been destroyed, and the spirit, too, has dissipated; although [in Hell a dead man is] sliced, burned, beaten or crushed, these [tortures] are useless [because there is nothing remaining to be mutilated]." After rereading this line I became suddenly so happy that I leaped from my seat. The horrors of Hell described in such Buddhist tales as "Mu-lien's descent into purgatory to save his mother" and "The chronicle of Yu-li" rose before my eyes, but I was no longer frightened by them. The cruelties shown in the pictures of the Ten Palaces of the King of Hell which the monks who came to celebrate the midnight masses spread out upon the altar, the images of the eighteen levels of Hell with their assorted ox-headed, horse-faced demons with iron forks pitching sinners up onto the mountain of knives or into cauldrons of boiling oil, or tossing them under the Bridge of Lost Hopes to feed ravenous dogs and poisonous vipers — all these terrors rose before me, but now they did not frighten me. Three times more I read this line . . . I was glad at heart, just as if Ti-tsang [the Buddhist Lord of Earth and Savior] had, with a flourish of his abbot's staff, broken down the gates of Hell.[28]

Before long this experience was reinforced by another. In the *Tzu-chih t'ung-chien*, the great historical compilation made by Ssu-ma Kuang in the Sung period, Hu ran across a reference to an anti-Buddhist tract written by the Confucian scholar Fan Chen at the turn of the sixth century, a time when the influence of Buddhism was very great. "Form is the substance of the soul, and the soul is the function of substance," Fan had written in his celebrated "Essay on the Extinction of the Soul" ("Shen-mieh lun"). "The soul is to form as sharpness to a knife. I have not heard of a case in which sharpness survives when the knife is no more; can we then allow that the soul should exist if the form has vanished?"[29] Hu Shih enthusiastically appropriated this argument and used it

28. *Ibid.*, 37.
29. *Ibid.*, 38. On Fan Chen see Fung Yu-lan, *A History of Chinese Philosophy*, II, 289–292; and Etienne Balazs, "The First Chinese Materialist," in *Chinese Civilization and Bureaucracy: Variations on a Theme*, ed. Arthur F. Wright (New Haven, 1964), 255–276. The latter includes a translation of "Shen-mieh lun."

repeatedly to buttress his own attack on religious superstition in the essays he wrote as a schoolboy in Shanghai a few years later. As long as he remained at home, however, he dared not reveal to his mother how far he had moved away from the gods to whom she continued to pray faithfully.

So, perched on the high benches of the village school or under his mother's watchful eye at home, Hu absorbed certain fundamental assumptions of the Confucian tradition as they were embodied in his father's writings and in the classical texts and commentaries which he read. Much of his fame in later years rested on his reputation as an opponent of the social and intellectual attitudes nurtured by the Confucian tradition broadly defined. Nevertheless, he owed a great deal to the "lesser" tradition of skeptical and humanistic critical thought which was one of the distinctions of Sung Neo-Confucianism. In the margins of the notebooks Hu Ch'uan had used as a student at the Lung-men Academy in Shanghai in the late 1860s were printed brief admonitions from the writings of the great Sung scholars, like this one from the pen of Chang Tsai: "A student should first learn how to doubt; when you can find doubt in places where no doubt had previously existed, then you are making some progress." [30] The ensuing decades brought a great change in the temper of Chinese life, but half a century later, when Hu Shih began to expound his own program for intellectual reform, he frequently expressed himself in terms very similar to these.

It was during those earliest years, too, that Hu gained the acquaintance of another aspect of China's old culture that was to assume an unusual importance for him — the illicit delights of vernacular fiction. In China under the old regime literary standards were fixed in accordance with Confucian taste. Sober Confucian opinion held the vernacular in low esteem, regarding it as stylistically worthless and morally reprehensible. Nonetheless, there were few literate Chinese whose private education had not been enhanced by hours spent surreptitiously savoring the tales of gal-

30. Oral History, 15. Hu Ch'uan was himself a confirmed skeptic in this traditional sense. See, for example, the poem he wrote in 1889 when he was stationed in Honan province, ridiculing the superstitions of the countryfolk who were repairing the dikes under his supervision. This is quoted in *Autobiography*, 33, and translated by Hu Shih in Oral History, 20. Li Ao draws attention to the fact that Hu Ch'uan, like his son, was attracted to the skepticism of Fan Chen's "Shen-mieh lun." See *Hu Shih p'ing-chuan*, 95.

lantry, intrigue, and romance, heavily flavored with eroticism and often disrepectful of the values of Confucian society, which made up the bulk of vernacular literature.

Hu's introduction to this world came accidentally when one day he happened upon a tattered fragment of *Shui-hu chuan* (The water margin) thrust into a box of rubbish in an empty room of his uncle's house. He went through it on the spot, and after that he read whatever he could borrow, devouring indiscriminately the masterpieces of Ming- and Ch'ing-dynasty fiction together with many less edifying but equally popular tales. It was only in this enterprise that Hu's ne'er-do-well eldest brother made some contribution to the boy's education, for, as Hu observed many years later, in those days "the opium lamp and the novel were often comrades." [31] What lends significance to these quite ordinary youthful diversions in Hu Shih's case is the fact that when he became, after 1917, one of the leaders of a "revolution" to overthrow the excessive formalism of orthodox Confucian literary style in favor of the more vital and vivid vernacular language, he attributed his awareness of the literary potential of the vernacular, and his sense of vernacular style, to the reading he had done as a child, and to his experience in translating the archaic prose of the stories he read into the colloquial language of Chi-hsi for the entertainment of the women of the household as they sat with their sewing and embroidery.

By the turn of the century the winds of change, blowing inland from storm centers along the coast, had penetrated even into the mountains of southern Anhwei. Hu Shih's brothers, Hung-chui and Hung-p'i, who had spent some time in school in Shanghai, advised the boy against wasting his time on the "eight-legged" essay style traditionally mastered for the examinations. By this time the examination system itself was coming under increasing attack as confidence in the classical curriculum dwindled. In the spring of 1904, when Hung-p'i returned to Shanghai to seek a cure for tuberculosis, it was decided that Hu Shih should accompany him to get a "modern" education.[32] So, at the age of twelve, he set

31. *Autobiography*, 24. The novels Hu remembered having read at this time are listed and described in some detail *ibid.*, chap. 1, part iv.

32. Hu Shih, "Shih-ch'i nien ti hui-ku" (Looking back seventeen years), HSWT II, iii, 1, gives the second month of Kuang-hsü 30 (March/April 1904) as the date of Hu's departure from home. See also *Autobiography*, 43.

out for the city, seven days away by canal and river boat, "with only a mother's love, something of a habit of applying myself, and a slight inclination to doubt." [33]

Shanghai, in that first decade of the century, was a city of close to a million inhabitants. Hu Shih later described it as a "narrow-minded commercial town," intolerant of the radical opinions of the young students who crowded into it.[34] But though it lived for trade, by the early 1900s Shanghai had become an intellectual as well as a commercial entrepôt. It was the center of China's modern publishing and journalistic enterprises, the home of the famous Commercial Press and of a growing number of newspapers — the *Shen pao* (established in 1873) and the more recent *Shih-pao* (1904) and *Shih-Shih hsin-pao* (1907), to name only the more influential. Through its port passed not only the goods that made the city rich, but also an increasing procession of young men leaving for, or returning from, the universities of Japan and the West. Students in Shanghai had easy access to such contraband publications as Liang Ch'i-ch'ao's reform paper, the *Hsin-min ts'ung-pao*, and the *Min-pao*, the propaganda organ of Sun Yat-sen's revolutionary T'ung-meng hui, both published in Tokyo and smuggled into the city in the luggage of returning travelers. These journals lent substance to the agonies of frustration and self-doubt and the stirrings of a new nationalistic consciousness that kept Shanghai's young intellectuals in a continuous state of emotional ferment.[35]

The most striking characteristic of a modern education during those years was its overriding preoccupation with the problem of China's place in the world. To a remarkable degree education, both formal and informal, had ceased to concern itself with the repetition of ancient Confucian formulas. It had become instead an endeavor to make sense out of the sequence of catastrophes which had engulfed the empire since the middle of the nineteenth century.

33. *Autobiography*, 43. See also Hu Shih's autobiographical essay, untitled, in *Living Philosophies* (New York, 1928), 246 (cited hereafter as "Credo").
34. *Autobiography*, 57.
35. *Ibid.*, 47. The Russo-Japanese War, which erupted shortly before Hu's arrival in Shanghai, provoked among China's young intellectuals a brief surge of pro-Japanese sentiment, easily converted into anti-Manchu feeling by reason of the neutrality proclaimed by the Ch'ing government. As specific instances of the kind of incidents that kept the students in such a state of patriotic enthusiasm, Hu cites the assassination of Wang Chih-ch'un, an allegedly pro-Russian official, in the International Settlement, and the killing of a Ningpo carpenter, Chou Sheng-yu, by a Russian sailor.

In September 1905 the imperial government made one of its more important, and typically belated, concessions to the times by abolishing the examination system, the venerable institution that for centuries had provided the means of entry into the bureaucracy and had in this way made a mastery of the arts of Confucian civilization much more than a polite accomplishment. Even before this final, drastic step was taken, the content of the examinations had been modified to include questions dealing with Western history and sciences, though the highest success was still reserved for those who excelled in classical studies. The need for a new and different kind of knowledge of the world was rapidly becoming evident, and it was this need that the "new" schools like those which Hu Shih attended in Shanghai, tried to meet.

Between 1904 and 1908 Hu Shih spent time in three such schools, all of which offered some courses in "Western studies" to supplement the usual classical curriculum.[36] He enrolled first in the Mei-chi School (Mei-chi hsüeh-t'ang), where his brothers had studied briefly and where the headmaster, Chang Huan-lun (tzu Ching-fu, d. 1904) had been a lifelong friend of their father. There, in addition to Chinese, he began to study English and mathematics. It is interesting to note, however, that it was not left entirely to such courses as might be found in the limited curriculum of Western studies to impart a rudimentary understanding of Western civilization. Classical studies, too, were oriented toward this compelling problem. Under the category of "interpretation of the classics" (ching-i), for example, the boys were required to discuss the ancient preference for defensive strategy as contrasted to the modern emphasis on offensive strategy, and other timely matters. One of the first assignments that Hu received at the Mei-chi School was to write an essay on "The sources of Japan's strength" — this at the time when the Japanese were waging their successful war

36. In an autobiographical account intended for an American audience, Hu was at pains to point out that none of the schools he attended in Shanghai was operated under missionary auspices; see "Credo," 247. The Mei-chi hsüeh-t'ang was a private school under the direction of its founder, Chang Huan-lun, until his death in 1904. The Cheng-chung hsüeh-t'ang had been established by Yeh Ch'eng-chung, a wealthy Ningpo merchant, originally for the purpose of providing schooling for the sons of impoverished Ningpo families; by the time Hu Shih enrolled, the school had begun to accept students from other parts of China. See Autobiography, 44, 47–48.

against imperial Russia, but when, as Hu later recalled it, "I was still not very clear on exactly where Japan was." [37]

Though Hu arrived in Shanghai with little understanding of the world, he quickly awoke to the significance of the events and ideas that enlivened that prerevolutionary decade. For the first time in his life he was exposed to news of national and international importance. He became a regular reader of the *Shih-pao* (The eastern times), a progressive daily paper established soon after his arrival in the city,[38] and he began to follow Liang Ch'i-ch'ao's arguments for reform in the *Hsin-min ts'ung-pao*. In the spring of 1905 one of his schoolmates lent him a copy of Tsou Jung's *Ko-ming chün* (The revolutionary army), a violently anti-Manchu tract by a young Szechwanese who died a martyr to his cause in a Manchu jail that same spring. *The Revolutionary Army* begins with this stirring summons:

> To sweep away the various forms of authoritarian government of the last several thousand years, to shake off the slavish nature of the last several thousand years, to exterminate the five million and more Manchus garbed in animal skins and wearing horned head-dresses, to expunge the great shame of this two hundred and sixty year torment, to make China a pure and clean land, to transform the descendants of the Yellow Emperor into Washingtons [i.e., presumably, revolutionary heroes], and thus from death to return to life . . . out of the eighteenth level of Hell to ascend to the thirty-third hall of Heaven . . . This aim worthy of the highest reverence, this unique, this greatest and most exalted aim is revolution. How imposing is revolution! How magnificent is revolution! [39]

Hu and his friends spelled each other in transcribing a copy of this inflammatory little book on the sly, since subversive literature of this kind circulated only in manuscript.[40] It failed to convert

37. *Autobiography*, 45.

38. "Shih-ch'i nien ti hui-ku," HSWT II, iii, 1–2. See also Roswell S. Britton, *The Chinese Periodical Press, 1800–1912* (Shanghai, 1933), 115.

39. Tsou Jung, *Ko-ming chün*, in Shih Chün, ed., *Chung-kuo chin-tai ssu-hsiang shih ts'an-k'ao tzu-liao chien-pien* (A survey of source materials on modern Chinese intellectual history; Peking, 1957), 628.

40. *Ko-ming chün* had been published in the revolutionary journal *Su-pao* in June 1903, resulting in the arrest and imprisonment of its author together

him wholeheartedly to the revolutionary cause, but it was at least responsible for his first rebellion against the authorities. When it was learned that Hu and several of his classmates had been selected to take an examination sponsored by the Shanghai taotai, he and one other boy withdrew from school rather than comply. As he later wrote, "How could youngsters who were just then taking turns to copy out *The Revolutionary Army* willingly present themselves at the government offices for an examination?" [41]

After his departure from the Mei-chi School, Hu enrolled in the Cheng-chung School (Cheng-chung hsüeh-t'ang), where the dean of studies was a friend of his brother Hung-chui. Its curriculum was somewhat more extensive than that of the Mei-chi School, offering courses in elementary physics and chemistry as well as in mathematics and English and, of course, Chinese (*kuo-wen*). Here, again, classical studies were turned to the purposes of reform: Hu's *kuo-wen* instructor, a man "whose thought was generally reported to be very new," set his students to writing themes on the meaning of "freedom of expression" and on terms drawn from Darwin.[42] Hu remained at the Cheng-chung School for a year and a half, being promoted rapidly as his English and mathematics improved. By 1906 he was at the head of the second form, and in this capacity he was occasionally called upon to serve as an intermediary between students and the school administration. That summer, after receiving a reprimand for protesting against what he had considered the unjust expulsion of a fellow student, Hu withdrew from school. A few months later he entered the China National Institute (Chung-kuo kung-hsüeh).

The China National Institute was by far the most unusual of the schools that Hu Shih attended in Shanghai, and politically the most radical. It had been founded early in 1906 by a group of Chinese students who had returned from Japan in protest against the Japanese government's restriction of their revolutionary activities there. Most of its first students were mature young men, many of whom had been schoolmates and friends in Japan. Hu Shih, at fourteen, was among the youngest, which earned him the Japanese

---

with Chang Ping-lin, who had contributed a laudatory introduction. See Howard L. Boorman, ed., *Biographical Dictionary of Republican China,* I (New York, 1967), 94. Thereafter it circulated only in manuscript form.

41. *Autobiography,* 47.

42. *Ibid.,* 49.

nickname *kodomo,* or "the kid." Nearly all were distinctly sympathetic to the revolutionary movement. The Institute's first director, Ma Chün-wu (Ma Ho, 1881–1940), had himself been an active member of the revolutionary student organizations that rallied around Sun Yat-sen in Japan just after the turn of the century.[43]

Ma presided over a school that offered a striking mixture of new and old. Among the teachers and students were some who came from the interior, still in old-fashioned attire and with an outlook as yet little changed by the "new thought," while those who had recently returned from abroad dressed instead in Western or Japanese style, and many had shorn their queues to mark their revolutionary dedication. In keeping with the radical views of its founders, the China National Institute made several unprecedented departures from academic tradition. Courses were taught in the "national language" (*kuo-yü* or *kuan-hua,* that is, Mandarin) rather than in the local dialect as was customary. Administratively the Institute was established in accordance with "republican" principles, as set forth in its original constitution, the administration being elected by the students themselves from among their own number and during its tenure remaining responsible to a council of student representatives.

But the wave of patriotic sentiment that had supported the establishment of the China National Institute did not last long. More and more of the students returned to Japan to resume their interrupted studies. Within a short time the Institute encountered financial difficulties from which it could extricate itself only by turning to semiofficial circles for assistance. But the Shanghai authorities, not without reason, were suspicious of the school. Its radical reputation also aroused the misgivings of the men whose patronage had now become essential to it. As a result the original constitution was revoked, and the administration was turned over to an executive committee which included such prominent political moderates as Chang Chien and Hsiung Hsi-ling. The students, of course, viewed this as an illegal infringement of their rights, and in September 1908, after many months of agitated debate, they attempted to reassert their control over school policies. Expulsions followed, and then a student strike. Finally some two hundred stu-

43. See Li Chien-nung, *The Political History of China, 1840–1928,* trans. Teng Ssu-yü and Jeremy Ingalls (Princeton, 1956), 193–194, 201. See also Li Ao, *Hu Shih p'ing-chuan,* 189–194.

dents withdrew voluntarily and established a rival institution, "The *New* China National Institute," which they contrived to keep alive until the autumn of 1909.

Hu Shih was serving as the secretary of the student association in 1908 when these events took place, and he was among those who left the China National Institute at this time. But for financial reasons he was unable to enroll in the new school. Though he remained in the city for another two years, his departure from the Institute marked the end of his formal education in Shanghai.

During the years he spent in Shanghai Hu Shih's introduction to the ways of the alien West was greatly facilitated by "extra-curricular" reading, especially Yen Fu's translations and Liang Ch'i-ch'ao's essays on Western and Chinese intellectual and political history. It is certain that Hu read Yen's translations of T. H. Huxley's *Evolution and Ethics*, Mill's *On Liberty*, and Montesquieu's *L'Esprit des lois*.[44] His only comment on Yen's translation of *On Liberty*, which he read soon after his arrival in Shanghai, was to complain that Yen's classical style was "too refined." [45] Perhaps he found fault with Yen's translation of *Evolution and Ethics* on similar grounds, but for Hu as for many others the impact of its ideas was tremendous. He has left a good description of the extraordinary vogue which this little book achieved:

> Within a few years of its publication *Evolution and Ethics* gained widespread popularity throughout the country, and even became reading matter for middle-school students. Very few who read the book could understand [the significance of] Huxley's contribution to scientific and intellectual history. What they did understand was the significance of such phrases as "the strong are victorious and the weak perish" [*yu-sheng lieh-p'ai*] as they applied to international politics . . . Within a few years these ideas spread like a prairie fire, setting ablaze the hearts and blood of many young people. Technical terms like "evolution" [*t'ao-t'ai*] and "natural selection" [*t'ien-tse*]

44. In his *Autobiography* Hu mentions only Yen's translations of *On Liberty* and *Evolution and Ethics*. He refers to *L'Esprit des lois* in an essay published in *Ching-yeh hsün-pao*; see Li Ao, *Hu Shih p'ing-chuan*, 174–175.
45. *Autobiography*, 50.

became common in journalistic prose, and slogans on the lips of patriotic young heroes.[46]

The enthusiasm for such terms extended even to the selection of personal names, and Yen's concise classical renderings fitted conveniently with the customary usage in this matter. Among Hu's schoolmates was one named Natural-selection Yang (Yang T'ien-tse), and another who called himself, even more formidably, Struggle-for-existence Sun (Sun Ching-ts'un). The character *shih* in Hu's own name was borrowed, at the suggestion of his brother, from the phrase "survival of the fittest" (*shih-che sheng-ts'un*). He used this as one of several noms de plume during his schooldays in Shanghai. He used it again in the spring of 1910 when he went to Peking to take the examination for a Boxer Indemnity scholarship, lest his failure there should make him the laughing stock of his friends in Shanghai. Thereafter he adopted it permanently.[47]

The virtually universal appeal of Darwinism to the younger generation in China just after the turn of the century is one of the more intriguing phenomena of modern Chinese intellectual history, and one that invites further study. Hu Shih was doubtless correct in assuming that its popularity stemmed initially from the ease with which Darwinist slogans could be applied to the situation in which the Chinese found themselves. But the real attraction of evolutionary thought may well have lain in the fact that it embodied a theory of historical movement closer in temper to the unhappy experience of these young intellectuals than were the discredited assumptions on which Confucian theories of history rested. Thus it imparted some kind of meaning to the grim spectacle of Chinese decline and even, perhaps, a sense of historical justification. For many it was a passing fancy, at least in its original form. Within a few years some came to find in dialectical materialism more promising answers to questions of the mechanics of history, while others moved on to an ideology founded on a belief in the achievements of the human spirit as the motivating force in historical development. But Hu Shih remained a confirmed Darwinist,

46. *Ibid.*, 49–50.
47. *Ibid.*, 50. On the names that Hu used at various times and for various purposes, see the list in Li Ao, *Hu Shih p'ing-chuan*, 289–292. See also *Diary*, 735–736.

and he drew from his later education insights that tended to strengthen rather than challenge this conviction.

The writings of Liang Ch'i-ch'ao exerted another important influence on Hu Shih's intellectual development during these years. He was particularly impressed by Liang's essays "On the New People" ("Hsin min shuo"), written soon after the turn of the century when Liang was much under the spell of eighteenth-century Western political philosophy, and published in the *Hsin-min ts'ung-pao* in 1903.[48] In these discourses on such topics as "liberty," "equality," and "popular sovereignty" the line between reform and revolution is often blurred, for they contain some of Liang's most violent denunciations of the political behavior of the Ch'ing bureaucracy ("evil, tyrannical, muddled and corrupt") and its predatory officials ("tigers, wolves, locusts . . . maggots").[49] "Time and again I have thought about this matter," Liang wrote elsewhere, "and there is almost no characteristic of present-day Chinese government which should not be utterly destroyed, the old eradicated and the new proclaimed." [50]

This was strong stuff to the mind of a youngster fresh from the provinces, and Hu Shih was suitably impressed. As he later recalled it, "It was those essays[51] which first violently shocked me out of the comfortable dream that our ancient civilization was self-sufficient and had nothing to learn from the militant and materialistic West except in the weapons of war and the vehicles of commerce. They opened to me, as to hundreds of others, an entirely new vision of the world." [52]

Liang Ch'i-ch'ao was also responsible for prompting Hu to an awareness of hitherto unsuspected aspects of the Chinese cultural tradition. Hu read with great interest Liang's summary of the his-

48. See Hsiao Kung-ch'üan, *Chung-kuo cheng-chih ssu-hsiang shih* (A history of Chinese political thought; Taipei, 1954), VI, 744–749.

49. Quoted in *Autobiography*, 51, from Liang Ch'i-ch'ao, "Lun chin-pu" (On progress). See Liang Ch'i-ch'ao, *Yin-ping-shih ho-chi* (Collected works from the Ice-drinker's studio; Shanghai, 1936), *chuan-chi* III, iv, 55–68.

50. Quoted in *Autobiography*, 51, from Liang Ch'i-ch'ao, "Hsin min i" (A discourse on the new people). See Liang Ch'i-ch'ao, *Yin-ping-shih ho-chi, wen-chi* III, vii, 104–107.

51. Hu is referring here not only to the essays "On the New People" mentioned above but also to Liang's biographical sketches of such European thinkers as Hobbes, Descartes, Bentham, Rousseau, Kant, and Darwin, also published in *Hsin-min ts'ung-pao*.

52. "Credo," 247; see also *Autobiography*, 52.

tory of Chinese thought, "General Circumstances of the Development of Chinese Scholarship" ("Chung-kuo hsüeh-shu ssu-hsiang pien-ch'ien chih ta-shih"), and later acknowledged that it was this which "caused me to know that China had learning beyond [that found in] the Four Books and the Five Classics." [53] He attributed his interest in Chinese philosophy, which a few years later led him to write his own history of the subject, employing an untraditional methodology, to his early disappointment with the "unfinished" quality of Liang's work. [54]

Liang Ch'i-ch'ao was a writer of singular emotional force. He was, moreover, despite his bitter condemnation of contemporary political and social life, profoundly attached to the culture from which he himself had sprung. "I love my fatherland, I love my fellow countrymen!" he wrote in the preface to "General Circumstances." "Born in this country and of this people, enjoying the blessings of this learning, it is then our duty to sing its praises [ko chih wu chih], to enhance it, to make it more illustrious, to extend and elevate it." [55] Though Hu Shih later paid handsome tribute to the power of Liang's style, [56] he does not disclose to the reader of his reminiscences whether as a boy he was moved by Liang's sentiment. One is left with the impression that his attitude toward the Chinese tradition was even then more detached than Liang's could ever be.

The years in Shanghai gave Hu not only a chance to learn, but also a first opportunity to develop and publish his own opinions. In 1906 a group of students at the Institute established a small newspaper which, in keeping with the spirit of the times, they called The Struggle (Ching-yeh hsün-pao). Hu was among the contributors to the first issue, and before The Struggle vanished from the scene in 1908 he had become its editor.

Like many other amateur journalistic ventures in that era, The Struggle was written for the most part in the vernacular, to facilitate the task of "instilling new ideas into the uneducated masses." [57] Its professed aims were "to stimulate education, promote popular spirit [min-ch'i], improve society and advocate political independ-

53. Autobiography, 52.
54. Ibid., 53–54.
55. Liang Ch'i-ch'ao, Yin-ping-shih ho-chi, wen-chi III, vii, 2.
56. Autobiography, 52. See also Hu Shih, The Chinese Renaissance (Chicago, 1934), 37.
57. "Credo," 249.

ence"; its real function was revolutionary political agitation.[58] Little of this revolutionary purpose, however, was reflected in Hu's contributions to the paper.[59] His first efforts were simple expositions of elementary science and geography. In an early issue he also began the serial publication of a novel, *The Island of Unchanging Reality (Chen-ju tao)*, in which he set out "to destroy superstition and enlighten popular knowledge," [60] drawing heavily on the arguments of Fan Chen and Ssu-ma Kuang that had shaken him out of the "nightmare absolutism of Karma" [61] several years earlier. Among the objects of his criticism was the concept of moral retribution. "In a general way, 'cause' and 'effect' exist," he wrote in 1908. "If a certain cause exists, a certain effect must follow from it [but] in this no man acts to control it. If there were a man acting to control it, a God or a Buddha, who could punish men who had already done wrong, why should he not be able to prevent them from doing wrong in the first place? . . . Since 'Heaven' cannot prevent men from doing evil, it cannot punish evil men." [62] Thus at seventeen Hu appears already to have accepted the idea of purely mechanistic causal relationships that, together with his

58. *Autobiography*, 60. Feng Tzu-yu lists Hu Shih, as editor of *Ching-yeh hsün-pao*, among the "revolutionary journalists" of the prerevolutionary decade, together with himself (editor of *K'ai-chih lu yüeh-k'an*), Wang Ch'ung-hui (*Kuo-min-pao yüeh-k'an*), Wu Chih-hui and Chang Shih-chao (*Su-pao*), Li Shih-tseng (*Hsin shih-chi pao*), Yü Yu-jen and Shao Li-tzu (*Shen-chou jih-pao*), Tsou Lu (*K'o-pao*), Chiang Monlin (*Ta-t'ung jih-pao*), and a number of others. See Li Ao, *Hu Shih p'ing-chuan*, 182–183 and 213, n. 54, citing Feng Tzu-yu, *Ko-ming i-shih*, 4th collection (Chungking, 1946). This places Hu in unaccustomed company. With some of the men mentioned here — Wang Ch'ung-hui, Wu Chih-hui, Chiang Monlin — Hu later developed respectful friendships; with others, notably Tsou Lu and Shao Li-tzu, he was never on friendly terms, for they represented to him the most deplorable aspect of the "revolutionary" mentality.

59. In his *Autobiography* Hu quotes at length from several essays he had published in *Ching-yeh hsün-pao*. In an interview I had with him in Nankang, Taiwan, on July 5, 1960, he remarked that his personal copies of the paper had been destroyed in Peking during the Sino-Japanese War. Li Ao lists nineteen essays contributed by Hu under various noms de plume in 1906 and 1908, which Li saw at the Kuomintang Party archive in Taichung, where apparently an incomplete file of *Ching-yeh hsün-pao* does exist. See *Hu Shih p'ing-chuan*, 178–180. I was unaware of this and unfortunately did not avail myself of the opportunity of consulting the file. Li quotes from some essays not found in the *Autobiography*, but only very briefly.

60. *Autobiography*, 62. *Chen-ju* is a Buddhist term, abbreviated from *chen-shih ju-ch'ang* (Sanskrit *Bhuthathata*).

61. "Credo," 244–245.

62. *Autobiography*, 64.

belief in evolution (from which it may have been in part derived), was a central support of his mature thought.

In these early essays, again foreshadowing the temper of many of his later writings, Hu launched a vigorous attack on the prevalence of superstition in public and private life. "It is pitiful," he wrote, "that in today's civilized world only our country, from the Emperor above to the petty officials below, is sunk in all kinds of superstition. Shanghai, now, is indeed the most enlightened. But the [officials of the] Shanghai circuit and the Shanghai district, on the occasion of the midwinter festival or the midsummer festival, or when there is an eclipse of the sun or the moon, maintain their barbarian customs as of old. Ah! such is the conduct of these scoundrels! You must not imitate them, my friends, for to imitate them is to become a scoundrel too." [63]

In pursuing this line of argument Hu was merely following in the tradition of Confucian skepticism described earlier. But in other respects he was already prepared to reject assumptions that, had he remained an orthodox disciple of the Ch'eng-Chu School, he would have been required to uphold. In his discussions of cause and effect, for example, he took for granted the moral ambivalence of human nature, in direct contradiction to the Confucian (or Mencian) premise which affirms the innate goodness of all men. Neo-Confucianism had accepted this optimistic appraisal, though in the history of Chinese thought it did not go unchallenged. Hsün-tzu, roughly a contemporary of Mencius (fourth and third centuries B.C.), held the contrary opinion, and other thinkers have stood somewhere between. Hu Shih, in a speech delivered at the Cheng-chung School in 1906 (when he was fifteen), took issue with both extremes:

> I argued against Mencius' proposition that nature is good, and neither did I approve of Hsün-tzu's theory that nature is evil. I accepted as correct Wang Yang-ming's statement that nature "is neither good nor evil, and capable of both goodness and evil." Just at that time I was reading the *English Science Readers,* and I had attained a highly superficial knowledge of science which I proceeded to use to my own purposes.

63. Hu Shih, "Lun hui-ch'ü shen-fo" (On the utter destruction of Buddha), *Ching-yeh hsün-pao,* nos. 25–28 (August–September 1908), quoted in Li Ao, *Hu Shih p'ing-chuan,* 169.

Mencius had said: "The tendency of man's nature to good is like the tendency of water to flow downwards. There are none but have this tendency to good, just as all water flows downwards." [64]

I said: Mencius did not understand science . . . he did not know the principle that water seeks its own level, nor did he know the principle of gravity . . . Water tends neither up nor down, but only to find its own level; it is, moreover, capable of going either up or down, and thus exactly resembles man's nature which is neither good nor evil, but capable of both goodness and evil.

My discourse on nature was very well received by my schoolmates, and I was delighted to think that I had really used science to prove the theories of Kao-tzu [Mencius' original disputant] and Wang Yang-ming.[65]

In spite of the childishness of this effort, it is suggestive of the direction in which Hu's mind was already moving, away from the dogmas of rationalist philosophy toward a more naturalistic and empirical viewpoint.

As it is possible to discover in these early writings the rudiments of Hu Shih's philosophical inclinations, so also one finds here the origins of his later social criticism. His point of departure, not surprisingly, was personal: the experience of his mother's unnatural and difficult situation, his eldest brother's bad habits and irresponsible ways, and the fate of his third brother, who had been adopted out of the family to continue the line of a collateral branch of the Hu clan. Some years were to pass before Hu developed an interest in the social emancipation of women, the cause to which he devoted much of his attention after 1917. But in 1908, inspired at least in part by the circumstances of his brothers' lives, he had already rejected the Confucian prejudice summed up in the dictum of Mencius that "there are three things which are unfilial, and to have no posterity is the greatest of them." [66] In an essay entitled "On the Unreasonableness of [the Custom of] Adopting an Heir," Hu expressed himself in terms clearly anticipating the "religion"

64. *Mencius*, Kao-tzu (shang ii); see James Legge, trans., *The Chinese Classics* (Hong Kong, 1960), II, 395–396.
65. *Autobiography*, 54.
66. *Mencius*, Li lou (shang xxvi); Legge, *The Chinese Classics*, II, 313.

of social immortality that he began to preach a decade later: "I now desire to recommend a most filial and well-trained heir to my four hundred million Chinese compatriots. Who is this heir? 'Society' . . . If a man can perform numerous acts which are useful and meritorious, then society as a whole becomes his filial and virtuous posterity [hsiao-tzu hsien-sun]. You must remember that sons and grandsons, whether your own or those adopted into your family, are unreliable. Only the filial and virtuous heir whom I have recommended to you is unfailingly sure." [67]

Hu Shih's youthful dedication to the cause of social reform and intellectual enlightenment was in no way extraordinary in that time and place. It seems, rather, almost the inevitable result of a "modern" education in Shanghai. But in one respect, at least, Hu's experience was unusual, for while other young students were even then embracing political revolution as the means through which to accomplish the great tasks of modernization, he remained outside the revolutionary movement from the beginning. There is no evidence to suggest that this was because of an affection on his part for the Manchu dynasty against which the revolutionaries plotted. It seems instead an early indication of the differences in temperament and objectives that later set him against the political revolutionaries of the 1920s. Despite the fact that the China National Institute was "a center of revolutionary activity" in which the great majority of students and faculty were involved,[68] Hu was never recruited to the ranks of the T'ung-meng hui (Sun Yat-sen's revolutionary party), or even required to cut off his queue as evidence of his anti-Manchu sentiment. As he recalled it, "The T'ung-meng hui members in the school had talked the matter over and reached the conclusion that I would in the future be capable of scholarly work, and as they wanted to protect me they did not urge me to take part in revolutionary activities." [69] By the late 1920s, when Hu was writing this, he had already on several occasions been moved to condemn political revolution as an enemy of the intellectual reforms which he himself sponsored; his memories may well have been colored by a sensitivity to the differences that separated him from the revolutionary movement after 1919.

67. *Autobiography*, 67.
68. "Credo," 250. See also *Autobiography*, 58–59; *Hu Shih yen-lun chi (i pien): shih-shih wen-t'i* (Hu Shih's collected speeches [b]: on current problems; Taipei, 1953), 64; Li Ao, *Hu Shih p'ing-chuan*, chap. 7, *passim*.
69. *Autobiography*, 58–59.

But this need not detract from the truth of the suggestion that his account contains of a future divergence of purpose. Several years were to elapse, however, before, toward the end of his studies in the United States, he began to work out an approach to China's problems that was explicitly critical of "revolutionary solutions." By then his Shanghai experiences had receded somewhat into the background, and he had come to think increasingly in terms acquired during the years he had spent as a student in American universities.

The crisis in the history of the China National Institute in the fall of 1908 coincided with a crisis in Hu Shih's personal affairs. The family in Chi-hsi was slowly approaching bankruptcy, and by that autumn Hu had begun to support himself in Shanghai on what little he could earn through teaching and writing, and in payment for his editorial chores on *The Struggle* until it ceased publication in the winter. He taught English for a time at the New China National Institute, and when the dispute between the rebels and the parent institution was reconciled in 1909 he secured a job teaching English and Chinese at the Hua-t'ung Public School (Hua-t'ung kung-hsüeh), supplementing his income by giving private lessons in English.[70]

Partly because of the discouraging news from home and partly, perhaps, in response to the dark mood of the times, Hu's life during his last months in Shanghai drifted toward a mild sort of dissipation. A number of his friends and associates were frustrated supporters of the revolutionary party, then at the nadir of its fortunes. In the company of these "romantics" (as he later called them),[71] Hu drank and gambled and frequented the theaters and brothels of the city, though he later observed, "Fortunately we were all without funds, and so we could only make a show of drowning our sorrows . . . During those months I truly scraped along in an atmosphere of utter darkness. Sometimes we stayed up all night playing cards; sometimes we remained drunk for days on end." [72]

---

70. Among Hu's pupils at this time were Yang Ch'üan (*tzu* Hsing-fo), a student at the Institute, and Chang Hsi-jo, whom he tutored privately in English. Both later followed Hu to the U.S. — Yang took a degree in engineering at Cornell and is frequently mentioned in Hu's *Diary*, while Chang did graduate work in government at Columbia. In later years Hu was involved in political disputes with both. See below, chap. viii.

71. *Autobiography*, 82.

72. *Ibid.*, 84.

In a poem written in 1909 he captured the dispirited mood of that period:

Wine can dispel a multitude of cares:
Before long I am drunk and like mud.
After the candle has guttered out
Only the sound of the night-watch interrupts the passing hours.
Arousing myself, bitter memories return;
Sitting up, I am at once plunged in thought.
Outside the window the east wind is harsh;
The stars grow pale and are about to set.[73]

Finally, late one rainy evening in the spring of 1910, as he was returning home alone from a drinking spree, Hu became involved in a scrape with the police and spent the night in jail. The next day, according to his recollection of the incident, as he surveyed his bruised face in the mirror a line from one of Li Po's poems in praise of wine ran through his mind: "Some use might yet be made of this material born in me!" [74] With this thought Hu resolved to reform. He abandoned his "romantic" associates and with the assistance of an uncle and several friends from Chi-hsi managed to raise enough money to pay off a few small debts and provide for his mother's support while he "closed his doors" for two months to prepare for the Boxer Indemnity scholarship examinations.

The Boxer scholarship program, financed by funds remitted to the Chinese government by the United States from its share of the Boxer indemnity of 1901, was then in its second year. Forty-seven students had been sent to America under this program in 1909, and the examinations to select the second batch were scheduled for July 1910. These examinations, administered in Peking, were formidable. Over two hundred candidates passed the qualifying rounds in Chinese and English and presented themselves for the final examinations, which tested their grasp of such subjects as higher algebra, plane and solid geometry, trigonometry, physics, chemistry, biology, geography, Latin and modern languages, and

73. *Ibid.*, 72.
74. *Ibid.*, 88. The translation is as Hu renders it in "Credo," 250. "Chiang chin chiu," the poem that inspired this reformation, hardly seems to point the moral that Hu drew from it. See *T'ang shih san-pai shou hsiang-hsi,* 2nd ed. (Taipei, 1957), 112.

ancient and modern history.[75] Hu Shih did poorly in the sciences but much better in Chinese, English, and history. When on a night in July he scanned the posted roster of successful candidates by the light of an oil lamp borrowed from his ricksha man — reading from the bottom up, since he was sure that if his name appeared it would be found far down the list — he discovered that he ranked fifty-fifth among the seventy who had been chosen.[76]

What happened next deserves to be told in the words of an English account written by two of Hu's fellow students and traveling companions.

> The seventy fortunate ones were now as gay as they were "ungay" before the announcement of their appointment. The doors of the officers of the Board of Education and the Board of Foreign Affairs were thrown wide open for them, and congratulations were tendered to them by every one of these high dignitaries. "Boys, go back to Shanghai immediately and get ready to sail for the Chinese Mecca of Education on August 16" was, however, a surprise to them all, for this meant banishment from China on short notice for a long period of time, leaving behind parents, friends, sweethearts and all. Every one departed from the Capital with a mixed sensation of joy and pain for Tientsin, where the reluctant iron horse was grudging boisterously because of the journey that he had to take. Soon the students found themselves in a boat, where they received a few attacks of the angry waves . . .
>
> Shanghai now came into view. No sooner had the ship anchored than another demonstration of joy was presented by the kinsmen and associates of the seventy passengers on the boat. Guards on the wharf had great difficulty to resume order within their jurisdiction. The tower of Babel must have fallen down in ancient times. What a medley of tongues used in greetings! After this rush, porters, drivers, tailors, and barbers had their share. So generous were they in offering us their service that we felt we were great soldiers coming back from a victorious battle. Our door-keepers soon became ill-tempered because they had

75. Ts-zun Z. Zee and Lui-Ngau Chang, "The Boxer Indemnity Students of 1910," *The Chinese Students' Monthly*, 6.1:16 (November 1910).

76. Hu Shih, "Chui-hsiang Hu Ming-fu" (Recollections of Hu Ming-fu), HSWT III, ix, 1211. Li Ao reproduces the list of successful candidates, *Hu Shih p'ing-chuan*, 271–275 and 285, n. 28.

to accept so often for their young masters the numerous invitations to dinners, tea-parties, and what not.

Time always travels faster when you need it. August 16 soon came. Willingly and yet unwillingly, we went to the tender that was to bring us to the palace of the sea. Although there was no deserter among the seventy students, we knew that their hearts were heavy. All of them, however, looked cheerful, — shouting and waving their handkerchiefs at their affectionate ones on shore.[77]

As the eighteenth-century poet Yüan Mei observed, apropos of quite a different kind of examination, "Parents, however much they love a child, have not the power to place him among the chosen few. Only the examiner can bring the youth to notice, and out of darkness carry them up to Heaven." [78] For Hu Shih it was the real beginning of a remarkable ascent.

When Hu Shih sailed from Shanghai with his companions on their "palace of the sea" — listed prosaically in the shipping news as the S.S. *China* — he was several months short of his nineteenth birthday, his queue was still uncut, and so hurried had the last weeks been that he embarked without even having had time to return to Anhwei to take leave of his mother. He departed the city greatly changed from the provincial schoolboy dressed in upcountry fashion who had arrived there in 1904. As a youngster in Chi-hsi he had lived, as he later put it, "in a women's world, so that when I set forth from home at the age of thirteen [*sui*] I was still as timid as a girl, I would blush to the tips of my ears whenever I met someone, I dared not utter a word beyond a salutation, and if questioned I would respond in the shortest possible manner." [79] He had brought with him to Shanghai only such knowledge of the West as he had been able to gain from reading a Chinese translation of Yano Fumio's *Keikoku bidan,* a political novel by a prominent Japanese liberal who argued the case for constitutionalism in the disguise of a romance based on Plutarch's life of Epaminondas.[80]

77. Ts-zun Z. Zee and Lui-Ngau Chang, "The Boxer Indemnity Students of 1910," 17.

78. Arthur Waley, *Yuan Mei: An 18th Century Chinese Poet* (New York: Grove Press, 1956), 24.

79. *Diary,* 253.

80. *Autobiography,* 25. The translation Hu read was probably the one made by Yü Ch'en-tzu, published by the Commercial Press in 1902. See Ah Ying,

Six turbulent years in Shanghai had taken away most of the provincial awkwardness and given Hu the confidence to hold his own opinions. They had given him, too, the training that enabled him to travel to the West, where, as his acquaintance with Western ideas matured into more genuine understanding, he came to accept many Western values as his own.

Yet it was in Shanghai that Hu Shih made his enduring commitment to China and to its transformation into a nation modern in intellect and spirit. Seven years abroad estranged him in some ways from the situation at home, but when he returned it was to take up again the task that he had set himself as a young man in Shanghai — the task of bringing enlightenment to the Chinese people.

Wan-Ch'ing hsi-ch'ü hsiao-shuo mu (Shanghai, 1957), 156. I am indebted to David T. Roy for assistance in tracing this work. On the popularity of the original in Meiji Japan, and for information concerning its author, see G. B. Sansom, *The Western World and Japan* (London, 1950), 421, 430; and Robert A. Scalapino, *Democracy and the Party Movement in Prewar Japan* (Berkeley and Los Angeles, 1953), 115, n. 54.

Chapter 2. The American Experience, 1910–1917

In the late spring of 1914, untroubled by any premonition of the European catastrophe that would pre-empt the world's attention at midsummer, the American press was largely preoccupied with the difficulties confronting President Wilson's Mexican policy and with problems surrounding the imminent inauguration of service through the Panama Canal. At the beginning of June, however, the editors of *Leslie's Illustrated Magazine* found space, on a page crowded with odd bits and pieces of timely trivia — the imprisonment of an American vice-consul in Mexico on charges of conspiring with Carranza's Constitutionalists, and the election to membership in the Sons of the American Revolution of the octogenarian descendant of a private in the Connecticut militia — to publish the picture of a young Chinese, accompanied by the following caption: "The strange anomaly of a Chinese student excelling all English speaking students in English is attracting wide attention to Mr. Suh Hu, the only Chinese student who has ever won first prize in English at Cornell University. In addition to this literary honor, Mr. Hu has also been awarded a scholarship in philosophy." [1]

It is a handsome and sober face that looks out at us, the eyes wide-set behind rimless glasses, the mouth straight and unsmiling, the necktie carefully knotted. It strikes one as the face of a young man who takes the world, and himself, very seriously. And so in fact it is, for Hu Shih (or Suh Hu, as he was then calling himself) had achieved his considerable academic distinction and won his first fleeting recognition in the American press by dint of diligent and studious effort.[2] The impression of seriousness of purpose is confirmed by Hu himself in a brief introspective entry in his diary made about the same time. Looking back, from the vantage point of his early twenties, over the decade since his arrival in Shanghai in 1904, he found that he had become a somewhat too intellectual young man, "possessing only a quick-witted talent, but without warmth of spirit." "The frontiers I have crossed in the last ten years have been of the intellect," he confessed. "I have neglected the emotions; meditating alone through the night, I have all but become a cold-blooded man of the world." [3]

Yet it would be wrong to conclude from this that Hu Shih's American education served only to imprison him in a rigid intellectualism. He was by nature too gregarious, possessed of too quick a curiosity and too lively an aptitude for friendship, to be trapped into austere academic seclusion. His American years were a time of wide-ranging intellectual and social experimentation. They left him more thoroughly "Westernized," better able to understand the West — or at least America — in its own terms, and more appreciative of the appeal of American aspirations than were all but a handful of his Chinese contemporaries. On the eve of his return to China in 1917 he wrote in his diary: "I often say that where my friends are, there is my home. Never have I had more

1. *Leslie's Illustrated Magazine,* 118.3065:543 (June 4, 1914).

2. The award of the Hiram Corson Browning Prize to Hu in May 1914 attracted the attention of a number of papers in upper New York State, and as far afield as New York City — e.g., *The New York Herald,* May 11, 1914.

3. *Diary,* 254, 253.

friends than in this country. Now, as I depart from this home which I have myself created, to return to the land of my forefathers, I really cannot easily decide whether my emotions are those of sorrow or joy." [4]

But although Hu's sympathetic appraisal of American civilization was born of a genuine affection, it was selective, and it was not entirely uncritical. In spite of seven years spent in American universities he remained at heart a Chinese, appreciative of the intellectual tradition that was his natural inheritance, and with an abiding concern for the problems which weighed so heavily on the spirit of his own generation.

In September 1910, immediately upon his arrival from Shanghai, Hu Shih had enrolled in the College of Agriculture at Cornell University, in accordance with "the belief, then current in China, that a Chinese student must learn some useful art, and literature and philosophy were not considered of any practical use." [5] It proved to be an unfortunate concession to the times. For a year and a half Hu pursued the study of biology and botany, plant physiology and pomology, with indifferent results and a notable lack of enthusiasm. Finally, early in 1912, aroused by the great political upheaval then taking place in China, he transferred to the College of Arts and Sciences, electing to major in philosophy.[6] Here he found himself more at home intellectually, and the change resulted in a marked improvement in his academic standing.[7] But in his own account of this move, written just before he returned to China, a suggestion still remains of the need he felt to justify his new course of study.

When I first arrived in this country, plowing and sowing were my ambition. Literature was an insignificant skill, useless to the cause of national salvation. One by one I gave away the many books I had brought with me. Often I dreamed of planting vegetables and trees.

Time passed, and suddenly I smiled at my own foolishness. Many things are necessary for the salvation of the nation, and which of them ought not be undertaken? But I am by nature

4. *Ibid.*, 1147.
5. "Credo," 251.
6. Oral History, 46.
7. I am grateful to the Office of the Registrar, Cornell University, for providing me with a transcript of Hu's work at Cornell.

suited for only one or two things. He who rebels against nature and denies his own endowments will accomplish little.

From that time forward I changed my occupation, and again argued points of scholarship and politics . . . In order to solve the difficulties of the times, study must be appropriate to the times. Who at present can question the appropriateness of an age of flourishing literature? [8]

At Cornell Hu applied himself to his studies with diligence, which was rewarded, in the spring of 1913, by his election to Phi Beta Kappa. By enrolling in the summer school for three consecutive years he was able to complete the requirements for the B.A. degree in February 1914. That autumn he entered the graduate school to pursue his study of philosophy, despite growing disenchantment with the philosophical prejudices of Professor James Edward Creighton, under whose direction the Sage School had become a stronghold of objective idealism.

During his years in Ithaca Hu's academic obligations did not prevent him from plunging vigorously into an extracurricular career as a speaker on Chinese affairs and a participant in numerous student conferences and forums at Cornell and elsewhere, activities which may well have contributed as much as did his formal studies to the shaping of his ideas and attitudes. By 1915, however, he felt that he had become overburdened by extracurricular commitments — he was, as he later recalled it, "too popular" around Ithaca — and this, together with his discovery of John Dewey's experimentalist philosophy in the summer of 1915, led him to move to Columbia in the autumn of that year, where he could be "securely hidden in a big city of millions of people" [9] and continue his graduate studies under Dewey's guidance in an intellectual environment more congenial to his own inclinations than that of the Sage School.

Hu spent two years at Columbia, completing the work for his doctorate. John Dewey's influence on him was clearly demonstrated in his dissertation, entitled "The Development of the Logical Method in Ancient China," [10] an exposition of classical Chinese

8. *Diary*, 1145. The original is in a free-verse style that I have not attempted to duplicate in this translation.

9. Oral History, 54–55; *Diary*, 686.

10. *The Development of the Logical Method in Ancient China* was published (in English) by the Oriental Book Co., Shanghai, 1922, and reprinted by

philosophy designed to uncover hitherto unrecognized applications of "pragmatic" standards of judgment, particularly in the heterodox schools. Hu defended it successfully late in May 1917, with Dewey sitting as chairman of the examining board. Early in June Hu left New York for the West Coast, stopping off briefly to pay his parting respects to friends in Ithaca, and on the twenty-first he sailed from Vancouver on the *Empress of Japan.* He arrived in Shanghai on July 10, a little over a month short of seven years after he had set forth from the same city to seek his education in America. He returned to China no longer a troubled schoolboy but, at twenty-six, an already prominent member of China's new intellectual elite — a "returned student," with two degrees from American universities,[11] a professorship in philosophy at the prestigious Peking National University awaiting him, and a firmly established reputation as a leader among the growing number of China's young intellectual revolutionaries.

It is a fact so apparent as to need no belaboring that the years which Hu Shih spent as a student in the United States, in intimate and lively contact with American ideas and institutions, contributed substantially to this remarkable transformation. The political and social ferment of that Progressive era made a lasting impression on him, and in some respects established the standards against which he was to judge Chinese political and social conditions after his return in 1917. His study of Western history, literature, and philosophy enormously enlarged his intellectual horizons and provided him with the framework around which to construct his own detached and "cosmopolitan" view of the conflict between Eastern and Western cultural values.

Yet an examination of his ideas during those years, as he expressed them in his diary and occasionally in more public forums, reveals no radical departure from the general tendency of the opinions Hu had reached during his Shanghai days. There is, indeed, some modification, as in his increasingly liberal view of the role that women should play in society, and considerable embellishment, as in his maturing interest in problems of "intellectual

---

them in 1928; it was reprinted in 1963 by Paragon, New York, with an introduction by Professor Hyman Kublin.

11. This is, in the strictest sense, inaccurate. Although Hu had satisfactorily completed all the requirements for the Ph.D. before his departure, the degree was not actually awarded until March 1927.

method." But nowhere, with the exception to be noted presently, is there evidence of a sudden and startling conversion to new beliefs, or of a fundamental revision of Hu's conception of the world. It is difficult to escape the conclusion that as a student in the United States Hu Shih responded readily and with enthusiasm to ideas for which his earlier education had prepared him, and that he assimilated those aspects of contemporary Western thought which proved most compatible with attitudes already foreshadowed, if not yet firmly held, before his arrival in this new world.

The exception has to do, initially at least, with Hu's mood rather than his mind, though in the end it profoundly altered the temper of his ideas, and hence their expression. Even more remarkable than the fact that a Chinese student should master English adequately to receive a prize in English literature — the achievement which brought Hu to the attention of the newspapers in 1914 — was the subject of the essay for which he had received the award, "In Defense of Browning's Optimism." This was the same young man who had departed China in the summer of 1910 overwhelmed by bleak uncertainty. He had not been long in this country, however, before his somber mood began to dissipate. "In letters to my friends at home I invariably urge upon them the 'optimistic viewpoint,'" he observed in his diary early in 1914. "And I believe that of the various things I have acquired since coming abroad, only this great concept is worthy to be counted." He drove the point home with some well-chosen lines from Browning:

One who never turned his back but marched breast forward,
    Never doubted clouds would break,
Never dreamed, though right were worsted, wrong would triumph,
Held we fall to rise, are baffled to fight better,
    Sleep to wake.[12]

It is certainly true that nothing Hu gained from his American experience exerted a more enduring influence on his later attitudes than this conversion from the hopelessness of his last years in Shanghai to an attitude of restrained but dogged confidence in the future. His subsequent discovery of Dewey's pragmatic methodology was of great significance to his intellectual development, but in

12. *Diary*, 175–176.

44

many respects its effect was only to confirm and strengthen ideas which he already held, and in any case his acceptance of the gradualism of Dewey's social and political philosophy would have been unlikely without a prior commitment to the optimism which gave him patience in the face of present disappointments and a strong faith in the ultimate triumph of logic and reason. Similarly, the skepticism of which he was so proud in later years — his "tough-minded" readiness to acknowledge, rather than trying to excuse, China's backwardness — was always tempered by an underlying conviction that in the end the rightminded must prevail. His "cosmopolitanism," which brought him with increasing regularity into conflict with the rising forces of nationalism in the twenties and thirties, was founded on the same conviction.

It was, then, in the creation of this new mood that the years in America affected Hu Shih most deeply and left their most enduring mark upon him. Because of it his temper was in large part free from the sense of urgency and despair, the passionate anger, which China's weak and wretched condition aroused in so many of his students and among his fellow intellectuals. And just as this sense of optimistic confidence influenced his attitude toward the many problems of social and intellectual reform in China to which he sought solutions, so also it tempered his evaluation of the worth of Western civilization, which to him always meant American civilization. Hu remained a steadfast defender and advocate of American values even when, in the aftermath of World War I and Versailles, many Chinese had abandoned their earlier faith in the promise of redemption from the liberal West. He never forgot the impression that his initial acquaintance with American life had made upon him, his admiration for "the naïve optimism and cheerfulness" of the American people, and his belief that "in this land there seemed to be nothing which could not be achieved by human intelligence and effort." [13]

In the summer of 1915, Hu Shih read, "with great eagerness, all the works of Professor [John] Dewey," whose philosophy became, after this encounter, "a guiding principle of my life and thought and the foundation of my own philosophy." [14] He thus proclaimed himself Dewey's disciple several years after he had em-

13. "Credo," 251.
14. *Diary, tzu-hsü,* 5.

45

barked on the study of philosophy, and rather late in his career as a student in America.[15] He was among the first of a sizable group of young Chinese students who came under Dewey's influence during this period, in education as well as in philosophy,[16] and after his return to China he became probably the most celebrated popularizer of Dewey's ideas there.

It may appear strange that John Dewey, in whose thought Europeans tended to identify a strikingly *American* quality — Whitehead epitomized him as "the typical effective American thinker," [17] and Russell introduced him as the inheritor of "the tradition of New England liberalism" [18] — should have elicited such a warm response from these young Chinese, burdened by problems which were peculiarly those of their own society and culture in a time of disintegration and distress. An appraisal of the degree to which the attitudes of American pragmatism were in fact adaptable to the Chinese situation, and an examination of the elements

15. The first mention of pragmatism in the *Diary* is found in the entry of May 9, 1915 (p. 629), a brief summary of the pragmatic theory of truth and its emphasis on consequences.

It is unfortunate that the *Diary* contains only brief and random references to Hu's interest in philosophy as an academic study, giving the reader no very adequate idea of the development of his opinions in this area. The omission was deliberate. In his preface to the 1936 edition Hu remarked, "In its style a diary lends itself most readily to the recording of concrete matters, but it is not the place to expound a whole philosophical system" (*tzu-hsü*, 6). In the entry of August 5, 1915, he wrote, "Since philosophy is my special study, it is not included in my diary . . . What is found here is designed to arouse the interest of the general reader. Is not the omission of philosophy just as well?" (p. 730). In an interview in 1958, Hu told Mr. Robert Muir that he wrote the *Diary* with the intention of having it read by others; see Robert Muir, "Hu Shih: A Biographical Sketch, 1891–1917" (thesis submitted in partial fulfillment of the requirements for the Certificate of the East Asian Institute, Columbia University, 1960), 8. This is substantiated both by the entry of August 5, 1915, cited above, and by the fact that excerpts from the *Diary* were published in HCN from December 1916 through September 1918, under the original title, *Ts'ang-hui-shih cha-chi* (Notes from the studio of hidden brilliance).

16. The most prominent, and the closest to Hu in later years, was Chiang Monlin (Meng-lin; 1886–1964), who also received his Ph.D. under Dewey in 1917 (his dissertation was entitled "A Study in Chinese Principles of Education"), and who later served as Minister of Education under the Nationalist government, and as chancellor of Peking National University. See Chiang Monlin, *Tides from the West* (New Haven, 1947); and Boorman, *Biographical Dictionary*, I, 347–350.

17. Alfred North Whitehead, in Paul A. Schilpp, ed., *The Philosophy of John Dewey* (New York, 1939, 1951), 478.

18. Bertrand Russell, *History of Western Philosophy* (New York, 1946), 847.

from which Hu constructed his own philosophy, can be deferred for the moment (see below, chapter 4). Here it will suffice to say that if, in the final analysis, the assumptions of Dewey's experimentalist philosophy proved more difficult to transplant to the alien Chinese environment than Hu Shih — and perhaps Dewey himself — realized would be the case, it is still not hard to uncover the reasons for Hu's early enthusiasm.

Hu Shih's interest in pragmatism arose in part as a reaction against the objective idealism preached by James Creighton and other members of the faculty at the Sage School, a philosophical persuasion to which Hu himself remained indifferent from the start. "Their problems never interested me," he wrote of the reading he had been compelled to do in Bradley and Bosanquet.[19] On the other hand, he reported in his diary as early as January 1914 that he was engaged in a search for a "practical philosophy." [20] He found it some eighteen months later in Dewey's experimentalism. The points which initially struck his fancy were, first, the experimentalist definition of Truth as a relative value, meaningful only in specific judgments and always subject to re-evaluation in the light of fresh experience; and secondly, the scientific methodology inherent in experimentalism's particularistic analysis of social and intellectual problems.[21] These were obviously highly useful concepts in the mind of an intellectual rebel already hostile to the authoritarian claims of ancient Chinese dogma but with no desire to establish in its place an intellectual system founded exclusively on Western experience. The great advantage of experimentalism was its universality. As a "scientific" methodology it transcended Western culture and was thus potentially as useful in China as it was proving itself to be in the West as a means of translating the attitudes of the scientific intellect into terms that would lend themselves to the analysis of social and political phenomena.[22]

Such, at least, was Hu Shih's understanding of experimentalism. From Dewey he took, first and foremost, a formulation of intellec-

19. "Credo," 252.

20. *Diary*, 168.

21. These aspects of pragmatism are both suggested in the only definition of the term found in the *Diary*, 629.

22. *Ibid.* Toward the end of his life Hu remarked, "I freely acknowledge my debt to John Dewey in helping me understand that there were essential steps common to all scientific research — methods of research in the West and in the East were the same. *And the reason for their fundamental likeness was their basis in the common sense of mankind.*" Oral History, 106 (emphasis added).

tual methodology. It was the methodological aspect of experimentalism that he invariably emphasized in his later expositions of the subject. On the other hand, whenever the pragmatic approach was employed in an attempt to resolve what Hu contemptuously referred to as "philosophers' problems" — as it was by C. S. Peirce in his application of pragmatic categories to epistemological problems, and by William James in his attempt to reconcile the conflict between science and religion by means of pragmatic judgments — Hu remained hostile or, at best, indifferent.[23]

Hu's acceptance of experimentalist methodology satisfied an intellectual need which he himself traced back to his student days in Shanghai. Then, speaking through one of the characters in his novel, *The Island of Unchanging Reality*, he had written: "We can only regret that we Chinese have never been willing to think, and only know how to conform, without holding opinions of our own. That our countrymen have come to their present pass is, in my view, simply the result of this unwillingness to think. So the great Confucian scholar of the Sung, Ch'eng I-ch'uan [Ch'eng I] said, 'Learning originates in thought,' and these four words are certainly the expression of an imperishable truth." [24]

Commenting on this passage twenty years after he had written it, Hu remarked, "When later I followed in the footsteps of Huxley and Dewey it was because since youth I had placed such great emphasis on intellectual method." [25] Whether or not this is accepted as an accurate interpretation of his early sentiments, Hu's diary provides several indications of an interest in intellectual method that antedates his acquaintance with Dewey's thought. In January 1914, for example, we find him writing:

What our country urgently needs today is not novel theories or abstruse philosophical doctrines, but the methods [shu^a] by means of which knowledge may be sought, affairs discussed, things examined and the country governed. Speaking from my own experience, there are three methods which are miraculous prescriptions to restore life [$ch'i$-ssu $shen$-tan]:

23. See the discussion of Peirce and James in Hu Shih, "Wu-shih nien lai chih shih-chieh che-hsüeh" (World philosophy in the last fifty years), HSWT II, ii, 245–258.
24. *Autobiography*, 66.
25. *Ibid.*

(1) the principle of inductive reasoning
(2) a sense of historical perspective
(3) the concept of progress[26]

A few months later he observed dispiritedly, "Our countrymen have no sense of logic." [27] Dewey's experimentalism provided Hu both with a logical method that he found congenial and with ideas of historical development and evolutionary progress — the "genetic" approach to intellectual problems — which he was able subsequently to turn to good use in his own scholarship.

Undeniably Hu Shih received from Dewey insights which contributed greatly to his intellectual development, as he himself insisted: "It is from Professor Dewey that I have learned that the most sacred responsibility of a man's life is to endeavor to *think well.*" [28] Yet in his later years he confessed that he "found it very hard to pin down from what place, from what book or from what teacher" he had acquired his methodological approach. He acknowledged an intellectual indebtedness to several sources, among them his early exposure to the critical tradition of Sung thought, and the courses he had taken at Cornell from Frederick Woodbridge, professor of Greek philosophy, in which much attention was paid to problems of textual reliability, and from Lincoln Burr in "auxiliary sciences of history," that is, philology, archaeology, and textual criticism.[29] It is certainly true that Hu's previous experience had made him receptive to the essential premises of Dewey's philosophy even before he read Dewey in the summer of 1915. As William James observed, "Temperaments with their cravings and refusals do determine men in their philosophies, and always will." [30] In his declaration of allegiance to the principles of Dewey's experimentalism Hu was no freer than any man can be from the promptings of his own disposition, the influences of his earlier education in China and America, and opinions of the world derived, perhaps unconsciously, from the traditional Chinese environment in which he grew up.

Here certain essentials of Neo-Confucian thought should be re-

26. *Diary*, 167.
27. *Ibid.*, 241.
28. "Credo," 255.
29. Oral History, 110, 124, 125.
30. William James, *Pragmatism* (New York: Meridian Books, 1955), 35.

called — its skepticism, its humanism, its belief that personal virtue is inseparable from a sense of social responsibility, and its acceptance of the idea that life can and must be understood in terms of human experience. Through his father's writings and the other texts he read as a boy, Hu Shih was exposed to these fundamental assumptions of the Confucian outlook, and they formed the foundation on which the structure of his thought was based. A few years later in Shanghai he added to this structure the concept of evolutionary progress, then so popular among his schoolmates. At the same time, in reaction against the superstitions of his Buddhist upbringing, he worked out for himself, starting from Chinese sources, a theory of impersonal causal relationships uninfluenced by moral judgments. These various ideas contributed to the formation of the opinions he expressed in his earliest essays, written in Shanghai. More important, they prepared him to respond positively to Dewey's thought during the final years of his residence in the United States. For Dewey's pragmatism, too, is humanistic, socially oriented, founded on ideas of change derived from evolutionary theory, and above all dedicated to the belief that experience can give men insight into their own natures and can be turned to creative purposes through an understanding of cause and effect, or, in more typically pragmatic terminology, antecedents and consequences.

This is not to say either that pragmatism is simply Confucianism modified by the idea of evolution or that Hu Shih regarded it as such. Confucianism begins the course of its reasoning from explicit and dogmatic assertions concerning the nature of man and the universe, taking the one to be good and the other harmonious, and from these assertions tends in the direction of a speculative intellectualism that would quite offend the pragmatic mind. The important thing to be noted here, however, is that on certain crucial questions the Confucian response and the pragmatic response converge closely enough to make the leap from one to the other a fairly easy matter. It was those elements of pragmatic philosophy which most nearly approximated the basic tendencies of his Confucian inheritance that Hu Shih evidently found most meaningful.

Hu mentions two courses that he took from Dewey at Columbia, one dealing with types of logical theory and the other with social and political philosophy.[31] He was fond of saying, after his return

31. Oral History, 96.

to China, that his was an "experimentalist" approach to politics. But here, as with his interest in intellectual methodology, Dewey's ideas served to confirm him in attitudes already present in his mind. Hu's vocabulary bore the impress of Dewey's political philosophy, but the opinions he articulated with an "experimentalist" turn of phrase were inspired by numerous associations made during his years in America, compatible with, but initially independent of, Dewey's influence upon him.

When Hu Shih sailed from Shanghai in the summer of 1910, the sudden and unexpected triumph of the revolutionary forces that would bring the venerable Ch'ing dynasty to its inglorious end still lay more than a year in the future. The event, when it came in the autumn of 1911, was welcomed with rapturous and, as events soon proved, misplaced enthusiasm by Chinese students in America. "Never before," proclaimed an editorial in the December issue of *The Chinese Students' Monthly*, "was there a revolution so well organized, so generally participated in by the people, army, and the scholars and gentry. Never was there a revolution in any country so peaceful, so productive of far-reaching results in such a short time." [32] Hu Shih's reaction to the news was characteristically more temperate. At the end of October he remarked despondently in his diary: "Looking homeward, the bloody war in Wuhan is not yet ended . . . Kweilin and Changsha have both become battlefields. North and south of the [Yangtze] River men are distressed and unsure at heart; what times are these!" [33] During the next six years, as he followed the unhappy course of the republican experiment from afar, his impressions of the revolution and his attitude toward it were affected as much by the distance separating him from it as by the events themselves. His idea of the role that he himself eventually should play was conditioned more by the temper of the environment in which he spent those years than by the realities of the revolution itself, of which he felt only remote reverberations.

"Wherever I live," Hu wrote in his diary in 1916, "I regard the political and social life of that place just as I would the political and social life of my own native district. Whenever there is some political activity afoot, or some social undertaking, I delight in

32. T. C. Chu, "China's Revolution," *The Chinese Students' Monthly*, 7.2:127 (December 1911).
33. *Diary*, 86.

learning of it." [34] While at Cornell he familiarized himself with the workings of American local government by attending meetings of the Ithaca Town Council,[35] and for Samuel P. Orth's course on American party politics he read the corrupt practices legislation of every state in the union. During the presidential campaign of 1912 he subscribed to three New York papers, each of which supported one of the major candidates — the *Times* (Wilson), the *Tribune* (Taft), and the *Evening Journal* (T.R.). He himself sported a Bull Moose button throughout the campaign.[36] But any disappointment he may have felt at Roosevelt's defeat was overshadowed by his chagrin when, in a straw vote taken among the members of the Cornell Cosmopolitan Club, one of his fellow Chinese students displayed unpardonable ignorance of the finer points of American phonetics by casting his ballot for "Roswell." [37]

Hu's affection for Roosevelt did not long survive Wilson's victory. Well before the end of Wilson's first term Hu had become an ardent Wilsonian, so warm in his admiration for the President's "idealistic" and "humanitarian" approach to politics that he was moved to characterize Wilson as "the supreme product of Western civilization." [38] It seems likely that Hu's image of Wilson as "a man who can make philosophical ideals the basis of politics, so that although he enters into the political arena, he maintains his uprightness and stresses humane principles [*jen-tao*] in all things" remained with him in later years, providing an example of the kind of political behavior, very Confucian in his description of it, that he strove to emulate.[39]

During those last years of peace the tide of internationalist idealism was running high, especially on American campuses. Soon after the turn of the century, as the number of foreign students studying in American universities increased, the Fédération Internationale des Etudiants, "Corda Fratres" (F.I.d.E.), founded in Italy in 1898, began attracting a following in the United States. An "Interna-

34. *Ibid.*, 1053.

35. *Ibid.*, 196–198.

36. Oral History, 36, 37.

37. *Diary*, 112–114. Wilson won handily. Eugene Debs, the Socialist candidate, received only two votes — both cast (prophetically?) by Chinese students.

38. *Ibid.*, 482. See also 301, where Hu cites, as examples of Wilson's "humanitarianism," the recent settlement of the problem of Canal tolls and the signing (in April 1914) of the U.S.-Colombian treaty which healed the breach that had existed since the Panamanian crisis of 1903.

39. *Ibid.*, 301.

tional Club" was established at the University of Wisconsin in 1903. The Cornell Cosmopolitan Club was founded the following year, the first of many similarly constituted organizations that by 1912 numbered close to thirty, scattered across the academic landscape. In 1907 the Association of Cosmopolitan Clubs was formed, and four years later it was recognized as the American affiliate of the F.I.d.E. In August 1913 the VIII International Congress of the F.I.d.E., the first to be held in the United States, convened in Ithaca, where the clubhouse of the Cornell Cosmopolitan Club was placed at the disposal of several hundred delegates from all over the world.[40]

It was in this same great, square, and ugly building, the headquarters of the Cornell Cosmopolitan Club, that Hu Shih had his rooms from 1911 to 1914. He was active in club affairs throughout that time. At the end of 1912 he was one of the club's delegates to the sixth annual convention of the Association of Cosmopolitan Clubs, in Philadelphia,[41] and in 1913 he was named as an official delegate to the VIII International Congress of the F.I.d.E. at Ithaca, representing both the Cornell Cosmopolitan Club and the Chinese Students' Alliance.[42] In 1913–1914 he served on the Central Committee of the F.I.d.E. and concurrently as president of the Cornell club,[43] and in December 1914 he again represented Cornell at the national convention of the Association of Cosmopolitan Clubs, this time in Columbus, Ohio, where he served as chairman of the resolutions committee.[44]

This record of substantial engagement in student politics stands in interesting contrast to Hu's well-known and much criticized opposition to the student movement as it developed in China, particularly after 1925. In fact, however, there was little similarity

40. For background on this development see Louis P. Lochner, *The Cosmopolitan Club Movement*, Documents of the American Association for International Conciliation, 1912, no. 61 (New York, 1912); and Efisio Giglio-Tos, *Appel pour le désarmament et pour la paix: les pionniers de la société des nations et de la fraternité internationale; d'après les archives de la "Corda Fratres," Fédération Internationale des Etudiants, 1898–1931* (Turin, 1931), 173–223.

41. *Diary*, 136–138.

42. Giglio-Tos, *Appel*, 190 and 192. According to this source, a large Chinese delegation attended the Congress, including several young men who later rose to positions of some prominence. See Appendix B.

43. *Ibid.*, 194.

44. *Diary*, 504–511.

between the kind of activities in which Hu engaged in his day and the strikes and boycotts, the street demonstrations, and campus riots which brought Chinese students in the twenties and thirties into direct confrontation with the political authorities. The organizations in which Hu participated were not intended to promote such forceful intrusion into politics. Their more detached purpose, rather, was to render intellectual and moral judgment of political conduct. What Hu took exception to in later years was not the fact that Chinese students were interested in political issues, but the nature of their involvement in political activity. He was never persuaded that the intellectual's natural concern for the quality of public life should properly find expression through public action. In this connection his account of an incident that occurred shortly after he moved to Columbia in 1915 is revealing. One October evening, as he sat reading in his room in Furnald Hall, overlooking Broadway, his attention was distracted by a commotion in the street below.

> Going to the window I looked down and saw an automobile filled with women, all of them suffragettes. In their midst was a girl playing a flute in a manner melancholy enough to move one's heart. Slowly a crowd gathered. The flute stopped and the girl arose to invite the crowd to a rally that was to be held in front of the library. I went along too. A number of women made speeches, all of them quite good. Suddenly in the crowd I caught sight of Professor John Dewey . . . the number one figure in philosophical circles in this country. I thought at first that he was perhaps only passing by, but when the speeches were over he . . . got into the car and drove off with all the women . . . and then I realized that the professor was helping them in their campaigning. Alas, a scholar of the twentieth century should not act thus![45]

Hu Shih's affiliation with the international student movement was profitable to him both intellectually and socially. Through it he was exposed to the ideas of some of the most eloquent advocates of social reform of that day — men like Lyman Abbott and Washington Gladden — either through their writings or, as in the latter

45. *Ibid.,* 809. In the Oral History (p. 39) Hu remarks only that he had been "impressed" by this experience.

case, from the lecture platform.[46] He became acquainted also with several of the younger leaders of the pacifist movement. Louis P. Lochner, who had helped to found the International Club at Wisconsin in 1903 and later served as secretary of the Central Committee of the F.I.d.E. and editor of *The Cosmopolitan Student,* counted himself a good enough friend to advise Hu to give up his "furious smoking [for] you are a rare genius [and] I think it is your duty to society to preserve your intellectual powers to their fullest extent." [47] Another and more influential friend — Hu ruefully confessed that he was unable to act on Lochner's advice — was George W. Nasmyth (1881–1920), a Cornell graduate (A.B. 1906, Ph.D. 1909) who had become a Congregational minister and an ardent pacifist. Nasmyth had developed close ties with the European student movement during a period of postgraduate study in German universities, and from 1911 to 1913 he served as president of the F.I.d.E.[48] In 1914 Nasmyth introduced Hu to Norman Angell's *The Great Illusion,* a small pacifist tract that had excited much notice in Europe and America since its publication in 1909, launching its author on a career that would win him knighthood and the Nobel Peace Prize. Hu met Angell in person in 1915 when he came to Cornell to participate in a conference on international relations jointly sponsored by the Carnegie Endowment and the World Peace Foundation of Boston, of which George Nasmyth was at the time a director. The questions discussed on that occasion ranged from "Is the Sermon on the Mount practical politics?" to "Is this war a struggle for existence?" [49] Hu Shih improved upon the opportunity by inviting various speakers to his room for tea every afternoon, having by this time removed from his room in the Cosmopolitan Club to take quarters in a house on Oak Street with a view of the Cascadilla Gorge.[50]

The common sentiments which inspired these young idealists were an intense antipathy toward nationalism narrowly conceived and belligerently expressed, and an equally fervent belief in the

46. *Ibid.,* 509. Hu was a regular reader of Abbott's magazine, *The Outlook,* and once contributed an essay to it. See below, note 77.

47. *Ibid.,* 165.

48. *National Cyclopedia of American Biography,* XVIII (1922), 246–247.

49. *Diary,* 671–684. See also Norman Angell, *After All: The Autobiography of Norman Angell* (London, 1951), 172–173 and 201–202; and *Annual Report of the World Peace Foundation, 1915* (Boston, 1915), 11–17.

50. *Diary,* 672, 678–679. Hu's move is reported in September 1914 (p. 418).

existence of universal human values that transcend national and cultural frontiers. A sense of this temper is conveyed in the closing stanza of the hymn composed in 1898 to celebrate the founding of the F.I.d.E., "Corda Fratres":

Si nous sommes séparés par des terres, des mers,
Si nous avons un langage, une religion, des moeurs, des lois et des traits différents,
Nous avons le même coeur qui nous unit tous . . . ô Frères!" [51]

The "fundamental articles" of the Federation laid upon each member the obligation "to employ without ceasing such means as are furnished him by his social position, intelligence and activity, to promote international accord among youth . . . toward the end of dissipating, in all classes of people, the prejudices, the rancor, the hatred which render states mutually hostile and always ready for war." [52] The concrete concerns of the members were at least partially reflected in the resolutions passed by the VIII International Congress of the F.I.d.E. at Cornell in 1913, advocating such measures as the adoption of Esperanto as "an official international auxiliary language" and the introduction of a worldwide penny post to facilitate international communication. They dealt also, however, with somewhat broader issues:

> The Congress congratulates the students of Finland and Russia upon their work for the uplift of their people by leading campaigns of education against illiteracy, alcoholism, tuberculosis, unsanitary living, etc. . . . It also expresses its hope that the students of the world may be fired with zeal to carry on the work of the cultural, social, political, and economic uplift of the people of their respective countries.
>
> While the Congress greatly admires those students of the European states who during the recent wars have fought so noble [sic] and died for their fatherlands, it expresses its sincere hope that in the near future the movement of internationalism may reach these countries and bring to them good tidings of understanding, good will and peace among the nations; and

51. Giglio-Tos, *Appel,* 59.
52. *Ibid.,* 84.

that it may in the future prevent the necessity for the sacrifice of the best minds of a nation.[53]

In September 1913, when a group of delegates to the Congress — Hu Shih among them — traveled to Washington to be received by President Wilson and Secretary of State Bryan, they heard from the President's lips words of approval and encouragement that can only have confirmed in them a conviction of the importance of their opinions. "I think," said Mr. Wilson, "that this little gathering represents one of the most promising things of modern life, namely, the intimate intercourse of men who are engaged in studying those things which have nothing to do with international boundaries but have only to do with the elevation of the mind and the spirit." [54]

Thus there was much in the environment of American student life during those years to lead Hu Shih toward an espousal of "cosmopolitanism." But for a young man who had lived for six years in the highly charged atmosphere of Shanghai, constantly exposed to revolutionary propaganda which depicted in bleak terms the consequences of China's traditional lack of "nationalistic sentiment," it cannot have been an entirely painless transition. Among China's young intellectuals, at home and abroad, the tendency was to view with grave foreboding China's deficiencies as a nation. Liang Ch'i-ch'ao expressed the prevailing opinion in language typical of the times, in his essay "On Patriotism": "Alas! Can such a people, standing together with the Europeans in a world where existence is a struggle in which the strong survive and the weak perish, hope for good fortune? Can they hope for good fortune? . . . The Europeans say that the Chinese lack patriotism. Oh! my four hundred million fellow countrymen, think well on these words! Expunge these words!" [55]

Hu Shih attempted always to distinguish between patriotism, as a natural affection for one's native land, and nationalism, as a perversion of this affection into a blind faith in the righteousness

53. *Ibid.*, 187.
54. *Ibid.*, 173. Although Hu Shih's *Diary* for the relevant period in 1913 is lost, his presence on this occasion is attested by photographs taken in Washington which show him in the group at the White House and with the Secretary of State; see Giglio-Tos, *Appel*, 174, 177, 178.
55. Liang Ch'i-ch'ao, "Ai-kuo lun" (1901), *Yin-ping-shih ho-chi, wen-chi* II, iii, 76–77.

of whatever course one's country might pursue. So in 1913 he was willing to concede, borrowing a phrase from Tennyson, "That man's the best cosmopolite / Who loves his native country best"; to which Hu added the comment, "In this day no one of even the slightest understanding does not know how to love his country." [56] Some months later he followed this with a quotation from Carlyle which, he said, precisely reflected his own views: "We hope there is a patriotism founded on something better than prejudice; that our country may be dear to us, without injury to our philosophy; that in loving and justly prizing all other lands, we may prize justly, and yet love before all others, our own stern Motherland, and the venerable structure of social and moral life, which Mind has through long ages been building up for us there." [57] But the distinction between a judicious patriotism and an intemperate nationalism was not easy to maintain. Frequently Hu found himself compelled to attack the latter when he might have preferred to defend the former. In 1914, for example, he became involved in a lengthy discussion of Stephen Decatur's famous motto, "My country, may she always be right, but right or wrong, my country," which appeared in abridged form at the masthead of the *Ithaca Journal*. Such sentiments, Hu insisted, implied a double moral standard, the acceptance of a degree of injustice on the part of a government in its dealings with other nations that would never be countenanced in its domestic politics. He later modified his objection slightly, in response to the suggestion that the intention of the phrase was not to condone an unjust policy but only to affirm a sense of allegiance to one's country even when its conduct departed from the path of justice. But he continued to regard the prevailing popular attitude toward international affairs as one based on hypocrisy.[58]

A few months after the outbreak of the war in Europe Hu had a long talk with George Nasmyth, just returned from England and a tour of Belgium in the wake of the German campaigns, and preaching the doctrine of nonresistance. This elicited from Hu an

56. *Diary,* 140.
57. *Ibid.,* 332.
58. *Ibid.,* 233–234, 314–315, 509. In Columbus, Ohio, for the eighth annual convention of the Association of Cosmopolitan Clubs in 1914, Hu heard Dr. Washington Gladden condemn from the lecture platform the "double standard" of political morality prevalent in international affairs, which led Hu to the satisfying conclusion that "men of intelligence tend to agree."

immediately sympathetic response.[59] He became for a time, as he later recalled it, "a zealous pacifist," [60] finding without difficulty many justifications for this position in the Chinese tradition, particularly in the *Tao te ching* with its frequent references to the compliant strength of water.[61] It was at this time, too, that his interest in the doctrines of Mo-tzu was aroused, perhaps as a result of that philosopher's pacifist views.[62] Early in 1915 Hu represented Cornell at the founding conference of the Collegiate League to Abolish Militarism (a name he claimed the honor of having proposed), organized in New York City by Oswald Garrison Villard.[63] His pacifist sentiments in the end brought about a total disillusionment with the man whose presidential candidacy he had supported in 1912. "Roosevelt says that those who talk of peace today are 'unlovely persons,' 'the most undesirable citizens.' Alas! Roosevelt is an old man! [He should] desist!" [64]

In 1915 and 1916 Hu's pacifist views underwent some modification. This was partly the result of his acquaintance with Norman Angell's arguments, which were based not so much on moral disapproval as on the conviction that war had become economically unprofitable.[65] More significantly, it was in response to two essays by John Dewey published in 1916. Dewey suggested that to call war a resort to "force" was to misunderstand it. There was "intellectual confusion" in the ranks of those who advocated a substitution of law for force, he argued, since "force is the only thing in the world which effects anything." War is inefficient and wasteful, he continued, and "must be adjudged a violence, not a use of force." He concluded that the "belief that war springs from the emotions of hate, pugnacity and greed rather than from the objective causes which call these emotions into play reduces the peace movement to the futile plane of hortatory preaching." [66] This led Hu in his turn

59. *Ibid.,* 433–435.

60. "Credo," 253. See also Oral History, 61.

61. *Diary,* 436, 465.

62. *Ibid.,* 471. See also Hu Shih (Suh Hu), "A Chinese Philosopher on War: A Popular Presentation of the Ethical and Religious Views of Mo-Ti," *The Chinese Students' Monthly,* 11.6:408–412 (April 1916).

63. *Diary,* 553–557.

64. *Ibid.,* 684.

65. See Norman Angell, *The Great Illusion — 1933* (New York, 1933), 59–62 and *passim;* and *Diary,* 432.

66. John Dewey, "Force, Violence and Law," *The New Republic,* 5:295–297 (Jan. 22, 1916), reprinted in Joseph Ratner, ed., *Characters and Events* (New

to conclude, in an essay for which he won a prize from the American Association for International Conciliation in 1916, that "what is the trouble with the world is not that force prevails, but that force does not prevail." "The real problem is to seek a more economical and therefore more efficient way of employing force: a substitute for the present crude form and wasteful use of force." [67]

This new insight did not, however, compel Hu to abandon his affiliation with the internationalist movement or to forsake his belief in the dangers of a "narrow nationalism." On this his opinions remained as he had expressed them earlier. "Patriotism is a fine thing," he had written in October 1914, "but it must be understood that above the nation there exists a higher goal, above the nation there exists a greater community, or, as Goldwin Smith says, 'Above all nations is humanity.'" [68] This phrase, borrowed from the writings of Goldwin Smith, a staunch British critic of European imperialism who had taught history at Cornell for a brief time in the 1860s, had been adopted as the motto of the Association of Cosmopolitan Clubs, and Hu used it also as the closing line of a sonnet written to commemorate the tenth anniversary of the Cornell Cosmopolitan Club early in 1915:

> "Let here begin a Brotherhood of Man,
>   Wherein the West shall freely meet the East,
>   And man greet man as man — greatest as least.
> To know and love each other is our plan."
>
> So spoke our Founders; so our work began:
>   We made no place for pleasant dance and feast,
>   But each man of us vowed to serve as priest
> In Mankind's holy war and lead the van.

York, 1929), II, 636–641; John Dewey, "Force and Coercion," *International Journal of Ethics* (April 1916), reprinted in *Characters and Events*, II, 782–789. Neither of these essays is mentioned in the *Diary*, but Hu referred to the influence that they had upon him in later writings: see Hu Shih, "Instrumentalism as a Political Concept," in *Studies in Political Science and Sociology* (Philadelphia, 1941), 4; and Oral History, 72.

67. *Diary*, 952. See also Hu Shih (Suh Hu), *Ha algum substituto efficaz que se imponha á força nas relações internacionaes?* American Association for International Conciliation, Pan-American Division, Bulletin no. 13 (New York, 1917).

68. *Ibid.*, 433.

What have we done in ten years passed away?
Little perhaps; no *one* grain salts the sea.
But we have faith that come it will — that Day —

When these our dreams no longer dreams shall be,
And every nation on the earth shall say:
"ABOVE ALL NATIONS IS HUMANITY!" [69]

The year 1915 gave Hu an opportunity to test his ideals against the harsh realities of a major international crisis that was, for Chinese students in the United States, a matter of immediate and grave concern. In January the Japanese government, seeking to secure and extend the privileged position in China it had established the year before as a result of the Japanese occupation of German concessions in Shantung, presented to the Chinese government its famous list of Twenty-One Demands. The action provoked widespread and outraged protests in China and among Chinese students in America. Many of the students urged an immediate declaration of war in spite of an obvious military advantage in Japan's favor, or suggested that at least it would be fitting to cut short one's course of study and return forthwith to China in this hour of national peril.

Against this tide of patriotic sentiment Hu stood virtually alone. His position was set forth in a "Plea for Patriotic Sanity" published in April in *The Chinese Students' Monthly. "It is pure nonsense and foolishness to talk of fighting,"* he argued, *"when there is not the slightest chance of gaining anything but devastation, and devastation, and devastation!"* He urged upon his compatriots the course of moderation:

I am afraid we have completely lost our heads, we have gone mad . . . My Brethren, it is *absolutely useless* to get excited at such a critical moment. No excitement, nor high-sounding sentiments, nor sensational suggestions, have ever helped any nation . . .

It seems to me that the right course for us students to take

69. *Ibid.*, 501–502. Several earlier versions of this sonnet, with indications of the revisions made at the suggestion of various teachers and friends, are also included in the *Diary*, together with another poem written about the same time and dedicated, defiantly, "To Mars."

at this moment and at this distance from China, is this. *Let us be calm. Let us DO OUR DUTY which is TO STUDY. Let us not be carried away by the turmoil of the newspaper from our serious mission. Let us apply ourselves seriously, calmly, undisturbedly and unshakenly to our studies, and PREPARE OURSELVES to uplift our father-land, if she [sic] survives this crisis — as I am sure she will, — or to resurrect her from the dead, if it needs be!*

My brethren, THAT is our duty and our right course![70]

The reaction to this temperate exhortation was predictably sharp. In the same issue the editor of the *Monthly* published a rebuttal considerably longer than Hu's original argument. "If you will study Japan's history of expansion of the last thirty years and her imperialistic policy, you will think your doctrine of non-resistance is after all rested on the wings [of?] philosophers' fancy and scholars' dreams . . . We are prepared to suffer 'devastation and devastation, and devastation,' but we are not prepared to be chained and bound as slaves . . . Fortunately, we are made of different materials from Suh Hu — not of wood and stone but of blood and flesh. We have senses and feelings. We do not pretend to be deaf and dumb, when the situation requires us to express what is in us." [71]

In fairness to Hu it should be noted that this attack and others in a similar vein quite missed the point he had been trying to make. He was by no means pro-Japanese in his sentiments, nor was he prepared to condone recent Japanese actions. His initial response to the Japanese occupation of the German-leased territories in Shantung in November 1914 was to remark wryly that "the tiger has been warded off and the wolves have entered." [72] In a letter to the editors of the *New Republic* written in February 1915, prompted by the suggestion put forward by "A Friend of China" in the correspondence column earlier that month that perhaps the Japanese would be able to succeed in China where the Chinese had apparently failed, Hu noted:

70. Hu Shih (Suh Hu), "A Plea for Patriotic Sanity: An Open Letter to All Chinese Students," *The Chinese Students' Monthly*, 10.7:425–426 (April 1915). See also *Diary*, 591–593.

71. H. K. Kwong, "What Is Patriotic Sanity? A Reply to Suh Hu," *The Chinese Students' Monthly*, 10.7:427–430 (April 1915).

72. *Diary*, 463.

"A Friend of China" seems to have ignored the important fact that we are now living in an age of national consciousness . . . The Chinese national consciousness has exterminated the Manchu rule, and, I am sure, will always resent any foreign rule or "direction" . . . The transformation of a vast nation like China cannot be accomplished in a day . . . The Chinese republic has been no more a failure than the American republic was a failure in those dismal days under the Articles of Confederation . . . Can we yet say, O ye of little faith! that "China as a progressive state has been tried and found wanting," and that "she is incapable of developing herself"? . . . Every nation has the right to be left alone to work out its own salvation.[73]

Yet it is difficult to escape the conclusion that Hu himself tended to minimize the significance of the fact that this was "an age of national consciousness." The disagreement reflected in the exchange of views published in *The Chinese Students' Monthly* was fundamental and enduring. Hu's statement of the intellectual's primary obligation, written when he was twenty-four, expressed convictions from which he never retreated in later years, when not infrequently they seemed, even more than in 1915, incomprehensible and reprehensible to his fellow countrymen — scholars' dreams and philosophers' fancies, if not, indeed, much worse.

It was not easy even for him to follow his own advice. Time and again "the turmoil of the newspaper" invaded his life and drew him away from the single-minded pursuit of his studies. Shortly after he had published his appeal for "patriotic sanity," for example, he confessed in a letter to an American friend, "Indeed I have been drifting — farther and farther away from my main purpose. Not without plausible pretext perhaps, — that is the worst of it . . . For a time I began to see dimly through mine own eyes this drifting, and was alarmed by it. And then this Sino-Japanese Crisis upset the whole thing and once more I found excuses for my irrelevant activities." [74] And what then was the "main purpose" from which he was so reluctantly diverted? He tells us in a self-appraisal recorded in his diary in the early summer of 1915, a few months before he left Ithaca for New York.

73. *Ibid.*, 571–572. See also p. 622, where Hu expresses his approval of the anti-Japanese boycott; and 622–623, a letter to the *Ithaca Daily News* in which Hu reiterates many of the arguments directed against "A Friend of China."
74. *Diary*, 654.

My habitual fault lies in spreading myself too thin and not bothering with detail. Whenever I look at the circumstances of our country I think that our fatherland today needs men for all kinds of things, and that I cannot but seek comprehensive knowledge and broad study in order to prepare myself to serve as a guide to my countrymen in the future — without realizing that this is a mistaken idea. Have I been studying for ten years and more without coming to understand the principle of the division of labor? My energy has its limits, I cannot be omniscient and omnipotent. What I can contribute to my society is only the occupation I choose. My duty, my responsibility toward society is only to do what I can do as well as I can do it. Will not men forgive me for what I cannot do?

From now on I must thrust everything aside and concentrate on my study of philosophy, both Chinese and Western. This is my chosen occupation.[75]

Thus, as he approached the end of his student days in the United States and as the nature of his own life's work became clearer in his mind, Hu began to look to the future and to speculate on his role in the events that were taking place in China. That he should have a part to play he never doubted — his education both in China and America had prepared him to accept the responsibilities of intellectual, if not political, leadership and to expect to stand not on the periphery of events but close to their center. In theory, at least, no conflict of taste or interest drew the Chinese philosopher away from the world of affairs. This was an attitude reinforced rather than contradicted by Dewey's belief that philosophy — and philosophers — must enter upon "the scene of human clash of social purpose and aspirations" and be concerned with "the choice of thoughtful men about what they would have life to be, and to what ends they would have men shape their intelligent activities." [76]

But things had not gone well in China during the years of Hu's absence. After 1912 the revolution had passed almost immediately into the hands of militarists who regarded republican institutions only as bothersome restraints to their ambition. Preeminent among

75. *Ibid.*, 653–654.
76. John Dewey, *Reconstruction in Philosophy*, enlarged ed. (Boston, 1948), 25–26.

them was Yüan Shih-k'ai, the Ch'ing military commander who might have used his strong northern armies to crush the revolution in 1911 had he not preferred instead to use the threat of such action to secure for himself the presidency of the new republic. Since his accession to this position early in 1912 he had enjoyed considerable success in his attempts to stamp out political opposition and turn cabinets and parliaments to his own ends. By 1914 Sun Yat-sen's revolutionary party had been expelled from the Peking government and driven underground; the few enlightened moderates, like Liang Ch'i-ch'ao and Hsiung Hsi-ling, who had thought to lead Yüan's government toward responsible republicanism by cooperating with him and participating in his administration, had again withdrawn, frustrated; Yüan had contrived, through a parliament entirely subservient to his whim, to create for himself a presidential office within the "republican" structure that was permanent, hereditary, and responsible to no one. Finally, toward the end of 1915, he decided to return to the unambiguous clarity of traditional institutions. In the middle of December, in response to a carefully cultivated "popular demand," he became the founding emperor of a new dynasty. But there, as it turned out, Yüan had overreached himself. Numerous factors — provincial discontent, an incipient military revolt in the southwest, loss of the Japanese support on which he had counted, and unrest even among his own lieutenants, who were reluctant to see Yüan secure in such an unassailable position — combined to force the new emperor to revise his plans. At the end of March 1916 he relinquished the Mandate and resumed the presidency. Early in June he died.

The failure of Yüan's attempt to restore the traditional order is perhaps the most eloquent testimony that can be found in the early history of the republic to the importance of what the revolution in 1911 had accomplished. The consequences of his ambition were nonetheless tragic. The standards of political morality and the patterns of political behavior which Yüan established survived his demise, as did men whom he raised to positions of power, like Hsü Shih-ch'ang and Tuan Ch'i-jui, who shared his contempt for republican ideals and who, by their cynical manipulations, further debased republican institutions. Though Yüan had been thwarted in his desire to recreate the empire, from the republicans' point of view the outcome could hardly have been worse had he succeeded. It was under his tutelage that armies rather than political parties became the accepted instruments for the exercise of political control, and military campaigns rather than parliamentary debates the usual means of settling disputed issues.

Much of this unhappy history lay still in the future when, during his last years in the United States, Hu Shih began to formulate his opinions of the situation in China and devise his approach to it. Many things contributed to the shaping of these opinions. There were the newspaper headlines which sketched the opening chapters of this dismal tale. There was also Hu's disagreement with the views of those Westerners who, like the "Friend of China," or Dr. Frank J. Goodnow, president of Johns Hopkins University and political adviser to Yüan Shih-k'ai, or J. O. P. Bland, the English explicator of things Chinese, regarded the republic's faltering start as positive proof of China's unfitness for progressive and democratic institutions.[77] Then too, despite the fact that he was himself far removed from the scene, Hu could not escape a sense of personal involvement. "How can I not weep for society," he wrote in 1914, lamenting the death of a friend with whom he had shared a room in Shanghai ten years earlier. "I must ask myself, and I must ask my fellow countrymen, whose fault it is that so often today our youth is cut off in midcourse . . . Is it a physical infirmity? Hereditary weakness? . . . Is it some evil social inheritance? Is it caused by the intrusion of political disaster from without? Is it that our ideas are not elevated and that we are therefore unable to struggle against evil habits and defeat? Alas! Whose fault is it?" [78]

The news from home was not reassuring. "National affairs are in a critical state, and popular feelings are confused, much the same as before I left the country five years ago," wrote a friend who had recently returned to China. "Our country falls far, far short of attaining a republican character — not one man in a hundred can

77. In an essay entitled "China and Democracy," written at the request of the editors of *The Outlook* shortly before Yüan Shih-k'ai's restoration of the monarchy — a scheme backed by Dr. Goodnow — Hu observed, "Young China believes in democracy; it believes that *the only way to have democracy is to have democracy*. Government is an art, and as such it needs practice. I would never have been able to speak English had I never spoken it. The Anglo-Saxon people would never have had democracy had they never practiced democracy." *The Outlook*, 3:27–28 (Sept. 1, 1915). See also *Diary*, 741–748. Here, in the simplest language, Hu enunciated a concept of democratic government that remained fundamental to his program for political reform throughout the years that followed.

78. *Diary*, 423.

read, you cannot speak with one in a thousand on topics of general knowledge, nor are you sure to meet one man in a million with whom to discuss foreign affairs, or who has a grasp of administrative matters. When the masses are stupid to this degree, in truth I know not with whom to talk about republicanism! If, indeed, we have achieved a republic, it is the republic of a handful of people, not a democratic republic." [79]

Yet though there was much to persuade Hu that he would be returning to a situation in which more remained to be done than had already been accomplished, his mood, while cautious, was by no means despondent. Early in 1915 he wrote: "Perhaps men will laugh at [those who] dream of accomplishing great things, believing this to be futile. But in fact it is not so. All the world's undertakings grow out of the dreams of one or two men. The great calamity of the present is that there are no dreamers . . . There is nothing in the world that cannot be done, there is no idea that cannot be realized. The telegraph, electric trams, engines, the radio, airborne flight, submarine warfare — all these things were not even dreamed of a few decades ago, and all are now accomplished fact." [80]

This was a theme to which he often returned in later years — the power of ideas in shaping events, and the conviction that men can temper their environment by the creation of new social and political forms as surely as conditions can be changed through technological innovation. Though in point of time this statement preceded Hu's acquaintance with Dewey's thought, it was certainly consonant with the attitudes he would find there.

At the same time, anticipating the gradualism of Dewey's social and political philosophy, Hu began to set forth his program for the slow and undramatic reform of China. In an essay entitled "An Adequate Defense," written as Sino-Japanese relations were becoming critical late in 1914, he remarked, "Certainly we cannot but respect the sentiments of those who at the present time desire to strengthen the military in order to save China from destruction, but [nevertheless] this is unsurpassed stupidity . . . This is not a fundamental plan." He continued:

What, then, is a fundamental plan? To make our education flourish, to release our forces of salvation [k'ai wu ti-tsang], to

79. *Ibid.*, 493–494.
80. *Ibid.*, 584–586.

promote our civilization, to bring order to our internal politics: this is the way with respect to domestic affairs. In our foreign affairs we should give our strong support to humanism [jen-tao chu-i], firmly denouncing, as individuals and as a nation, the unhuman and unchristian aggressivism [ch'iang ch'üan chu-i] of the West, and on the other hand advocating with all our might the doctrines of pacifism, and together with the United States exerting our strength to encourage international morality. Only with the progress of international morality can we really speak of progress for the world, and [only then can] our country begin to enjoy the blessings of peace.

Critics will say that this is to talk of the far distant future, and has no immediate practicality. To which I reply: This is seeking a three-year cure for a seven-year illness.[81] If we think that three years is too long a time, then we can only sit by and watch death come. I sincerely believe that a three-year cure is the *only* miraculous prescription which will restore life, and that now is the time to seek it, we cannot delay.

It is for this reason that I advocate cosmopolitanism [ta-t'ung chu-i], why I associate myself with the "pacifist group" in this country, why I do not spare myself day or night in my study of humanism. How can I speak of the distant future? I cannot do otherwise.[82]

A year later, in a letter to an American friend, Hu reviewed this position in the light of Yüan Shih-k'ai's monarchical aspirations. He introduced into his argument at this time an idea patterned on Buddhist terminology which he used often in later writ-

---

81. The phrase is drawn from *Mencius*, li lou (shang x): "*Chin chih yü wang che, yu ch'i-nien chih ping ch'iu san-nien chih ai yeh.*" Used here for the first time, it became one of Hu's favorite expressions. The general sense read into this passage by Chinese commentators (Chao Ch'i, Chu Hsi) and Western translators (Legge, Dobson) is that one must make one's preparations in advance: when the patient is at death's door, it is too late to seek a remedy that requires much time to prepare, as with the drying of mugwort grass (ai) to make it suitable for use as moxa. Dobson translates: "Those today who aspire to become the Ideal King are rather like the prescribing of a three-year-old herb for an ailment already seven years gone." (W. A. C. H. Dobson, trans., *Mencius* [Toronto, 1964], 166.) It is possible that Hu uses the phrase in this sense; but I have interpreted him to mean, as here, that a disease of long duration requires a long cure, which seems to me to fit better the various contexts in which the phrase is found in Hu's writings.

82. *Diary*, 492–493.

ings: *tsao yin,* meaning to create fundamental new causes which would serve to activate new consequences: [83]

> I have come to hold that there is no short-cut to political decency and efficiency . . . Good government cannot be secured without certain necessary prerequisites. Those who maintain that China needs a monarchy for internal consolidation and strength are just as foolish as those who hold that a republican form of government will work miracles. Neither a monarchy nor a republic will save China without what I call the "necessary prerequisites." It is our business to provide for those necessary prerequisites, — to "Create new Causes" (*tsao-yin*).
>
> I am ready to go even farther than my monarchist friends. I would not even let a foreign conquest divert my determination to "Create new Causes." Not to say the petty changes of the present! [84]

About the same time, in a letter to an old friend from Shanghai days, he set forth more explicitly what he meant by the creation of "new causes":

> Recently I have been urging others not to feel oppressed by the [matter of the] imperial system, and saying moreover that external calamities and national destruction are not worth consideration. In the event that our fatherland possesses the quality which will enable it to endure, then certainly our fatherland will not perish. In the event that it lacks this [quality], then our present confused anxiety cannot prevent it from perishing. It would be better for us to define our own aims and, starting from the very foundations, to create for our fatherland new causes which will enable it to endure . . .
>
> I believe that the proper way of creating causes at the present time lies in the cultivation of men [*shu-jen*]. This properly depends upon education. Therefore I have of late entertained no extravagant hopes, and after returning home I will seek only to devote myself to the task of social education . . . believing

83. The term *yin* connotes the conduct in one existence that determines the condition into which one will be reborn in the next — the central concept of the Buddhist doctrine of karma.

84. *Diary*, 821.

this to be the only [possible] plan for the cultivation of men over a period of one hundred years.

I am well aware that the cultivation of men is a long-range scheme, but recently I have come to understand that there is no short-cut that can be effective in national or world affairs.[85]

Hu Shih's advocacy of slow and unspectacular reform through education and the gradual transformation of popular attitudes — his willingness to seek a three-year cure for a seven-year illness — put him even at this early time at cross purposes with those who demanded quick and certain "revolutionary" solutions to China's problems. It was a fact which he himself appreciated. To one of his old professors at Cornell he wrote, in the winter of 1916:

> I do not condemn revolutions, because I believe that they are necessary stages in the process of evolution. But I do not favor premature revolutions, because they are usually wasteful and therefore unfruitful . . . It is for this reason that I do not entertain much hope for the revolutions now going on in China, although I have deep sympathy for the Revolutionists.
>
> Personally I prefer to build from the bottom up. I have come to believe that there is no short-cut to political decency and efficiency. The Revolutionists desire them, but they want to attain them by a short-cut — by a revolution. My personal attitude is: "Come what may, let us educate the people. Let us lay a foundation for our future generations to build upon."
>
> This is necessarily a very slow process, and mankind is impatient! But, so far as I can see, this slow process is the only process: it is requisite to revolutions as well as to evolutions.[86]

Thus Hu's estrangement from the revolutionary movement, foreshadowed even before his departure from Shanghai in 1910, had by 1916 been transformed into an explicit conviction that the revolutionary approach was misguided and liable to prove futile. This opinion was not the product of frustration and disillusionment experienced after his return to China. It was reached in cool deliberation far from the scene of conflict. Behind it lay the sense of cosmopolitan detachment and the persistent optimism that freed Hu

85. *Ibid.,* 832–833.
86. *Ibid.,* 842–843.

from the fearful passions on which the revolution fed. By 1916 he had enunciated the cardinal tenets of a creed to which he adhered thereafter with dogged determination: that sure progress cannot be unduly hastened, that change must come from the bottom up, that there is no quick and easy way to achieve "political decency and efficiency," that only the slow cultivation of human talent will provide a sturdy enough foundation on which to erect the new political and social order, and that the mind must not be diverted from its pursuit of this goal by the passions of the moment.

But the choice was not his to make. He was returning to a country and a people already caught up in the prolonged agony of a revolutionary cataclysm that swept everything before it, that left no part of any life untouched, no corner of any mind untroubled, that moved not by design but seemed instead to be impelled forward by some senseless inner momentum born of greed and ambition, anger, despair, cruelty, hunger, ignorance, and hope.

Shortly before Hu's departure from New York early in June 1917, Tuan Ch'i-jui, the premier of the republic during the final months of Yüan Shih-k'ai's presidency and after his death, was ousted from this office by a rival military leader, and the uneasy peace which had prevailed since Yüan's demise the year before was shattered. Now the call went out to summon armies that served no national purpose, but the contentious claims of individual militarists. The warlord period had begun in earnest. Hu Shih, reading of these events with consternation, made one of the last entries in his student diary.

In recent months I have been preparing only for the constructive labors to be undertaken after my return, in the belief that the work of destruction had in a general way been accomplished and that I could be permitted to take no part in it. What is the meaning of the confused flurry of threatening telegrams throughout the country in recent days? Strife between North and South has become a fact. The present situation, it seems, will not permit me to return to undertake the labors of reconstruction.[87]

It was a valid premonition.

87. *Ibid.*, 1147.

*The superstitious man is to the rascal what
the slave is to the tyrant. Indeed, more:
the superstitious man is ruled by the fanatic,
and turns into one . . . In a word, the
fewer superstitions, the less fanaticism; and
the less fanaticism, the fewer calamities.*

Voltaire

Part II. The Chinese Renaissance

Chapter 3. The Literary Revolution

"You shall know the difference now that we are back again!" Hu Shih wrote in his diary in March 1917, suggesting this as the motto that should be inscribed on the banner of his generation of returned students.[1] In point of fact, even before he left the United States Hu's name was already well known to readers of *Hsin ch'ing-nien* ("La Jeunesse" or *The New Youth*), China's leading journal of radical opinion. In the winter and spring of 1916–17 a number

1. *Diary*, 1106. The phrase is a line from *The Iliad*, used by Cardinal Newman; Hu discovered it in reading Canon Ollard's history of the Oxford movement. See also Hu Shih, "P'ing-Sui-lu lü-hsing hsiao-chi" (A brief record of a trip along the Peiping-Suiyuan Railroad), TLPL no. 162:13–18 (Aug. 4, 1935).

of excerpts from his student diary, "Notes from the Studio of Hidden Brilliance" (*Ts'ang-hui-shih cha-chi*) had appeared in *The New Youth*, together with several examples of his early attempts at vernacular poetry and his translations of short stories by Maupassant and Teleshëv. More important, he had published there two essays of major significance to the development of the movement in which he was to play a leading role after his return. The first, "Tentative Proposals for the Improvement of Literature" (*Wen-hsüeh kai-liang ch'u-i*), appeared in January 1917; the second, "On the Genetic Concept of Literature" (*Li-shih-ti wen-hsüeh kuan-nien lun*) followed in May. In the February issue of *The New Youth* the magazine's editor, Ch'en Tu-hsiu, had seized upon Hu's "tentative proposals" and translated them into a call for "literary revolution." The issue provoked immediate response, both critical and sympathetic. By the time Hu landed in Shanghai in July, the "literary revolution" was in full swing.

Hu Shih was lastingly proud of the part he had played as a promoter of this movement, and he is better remembered for this than for any other of his many endeavors. The discussion that follows, however, will be less concerned with the literary revolution itself than with what is revealed, in Hu's writings on the reform of literature, of his philosophy of reform in general, and of his view of the relationship between an historical tradition and the processes of evolutionary and revolutionary change.

"The literary revolution" commonly describes the sequence of events that began in 1917 with the publication of Hu Shih's "tentative proposals" and that led over the next several years to the acceptance, in the schools, in newspapers and magazines, and by the writers of a new style of literature, of a language closer than the classical written language to the usages of common speech.[2]

2. Hu Shih's original proposals included, as the eighth and final point, the injunction not to "shrink from colloquialisms" (HSWT, i, 16–17). This is a far cry from the demand for a written language exactly reproducing the spoken word. His own early models for *pai-hua* prose were drawn from the vernacular novels of the Ming and Ch'ing dynasties. Hu gave Fu Ssu-nien credit for originating the proposal that the written language should pattern itself on the spoken. See Hu Shih, *Chung-kuo hsin wen-hsüeh yün-tung hsiao-shih* (A short history of China's new literature movement; Taipei, 1958), 30. (This work comprises two brief historical accounts. The title essay was originally published as Hu's introduction to *Chung-kuo hsin wen-hsüeh ta-hsi: I: Chien-she li-lun chi* [The genesis of China's new literature: vol. I: Theoretical founda-

The revolution was, in the first instance, a movement directed only against the forms of the old written language — the "book language," as nineteenth-century Westerns aptly called it, an esoteric medium of expression far removed from the colloquial.

But as both its advocates and its adversaries knew from the start, the literary revolution carried with it far-reaching social and political implications. The classical written language had been maintained not only by the custom of centuries and, on the part of many, a genuine respect for its literary qualities, but also by significant social considerations. Initiation into the complexities of classical Chinese was arduous and painfully slow. Mastery of the language itself, of the conventions that regulated its use, and of the literature which inspired it might well be the major occupation of a lifetime. In old China the rewards had been commensurate with the cost, for literacy bestowed upon the few who possessed the leisure and the talent to pursue it a degree of social eminence and, through the examination system, a means of access to political authority denied to the illiterate majority. Thus the written language, as much as any other institution, preserved the ancient distinction between ruler and ruled in traditional China. Its survival, even after the collapse of the old political order in 1911, ensured not only the preservation of the traditional culture but also the perpetuation of traditional social attitudes. The literary revolution thus aimed far beyond the destruction of a literary style. Its opponents were defending a whole system of values.[3] Its proponents, rejecting the stiff archaisms and sterile clichés of the old literature, were repudiating an entire cultural and social inheritance.

In the late 1910s the physical and spiritual center of this vig-

tions; edited by Hu Shih, Shanghai, 1935]. The second, entitled "Pi-shang Liang-shan" [Forced into outlawry] is a chapter from Hu's autobiography, published originally in *Tung-fang tsa-chih*, 31.1 [December 1933]. This work is cited hereafter as *Short History*.) On the question of vernacular style see also Fu Ssu-nien, "Tsen-yang tso pai-hua-wen" (How to write the vernacular), *Hsin-ch'ao* (Renaissance), 1.2 (Feb. 1, 1919).

3. The most important materials concerning opposition to the *pai-hua* movement are collected in *Chung-kuo hsin wen-hsüeh ta-hsi: II: Wen-hsüeh lun-cheng chi* (Literary polemics; edited by Cheng Chen-to, Shanghai, 1935). See also Li Hui-ying, "Hsin wen-hsüeh ko-ming yün-tung chung chih fan-tui-p'ai" (The opposition party in the literary revolution), *United College Journal*, 5:63–70 (1966–67); R. David Arkush, "Ku Hung-ming (1857–1928)," *Papers on China*, 19:194–238 (1965); Leo Ou-fan Lee, "Lin Shu and His Translations: Western Fiction in Chinese Perspective," *ibid.*, 19:159–193 (1965).

orously iconoclastic movement was Peking National University (Peita), where, in the autumn of 1917, Hu Shih joined the Faculty of Letters to teach courses in Chinese and Western philosophy. Ts'ai Yüan-p'ei (1876–1940), chancellor of the university since the end of 1916, had been largely responsible for elevating Peita to its position of academic and intellectual preeminence. He desired to make of it a genuinely liberal institution, tolerant of all points of view. Since he himself was something of a radical, a classical scholar turned revolutionary, it is not surprising that under his auspices the university soon became a gathering ground for skeptics and rebels. Ch'en Tu-hsiu (1879–1942), the Japanese- and French-educated founder and editor of *The New Youth*, was appointed dean of the School of Letters in 1917. Li Ta-chao (1888–1927), who was to become with Ch'en an early Chinese convert to Marxism-Leninism, was named librarian at Peita early in 1918 and later joined the Faculty of Law. Linguistics was taught by Ch'ien Hsüan-t'ung (1887–1939), a classical philologist and disciple of Chang Ping-lin, who called himself Ch'ien the Doubter of Antiquity (Ch'ien I-ku) and came forth as one of the first and most enthusiastic supporters of the new literature. Others on the faculty included T'ao Lü-kung (*tzu* Meng-ho, L. K. Tao, 1887–1960), a British-trained sociologist, and Kao I-han (1885–   ), a political scientist educated in Japan. Also in Peking, either teaching at Peita or in close touch with the Peita group, were the writers Chou Tso-jen, an essayist of considerable note, and his more celebrated brother Chou Shu-jen (Lu Hsün). It was an extraordinary company of young men that congregated in Peking in the years between 1917 and 1920.[4] Hu Shih was, at twenty-six, one of the youngest. But his impeccable credentials as a Western-trained returned student, his position at Peita, and his connection with *The New Youth* marked him as a natural leader of this small but articulate and enormously influential avant-garde. He could be sure that whatever he said would receive an attentive and — in those early years at least — a respectful hearing.

The question of language reform was by no means a new one when Hu Shih and Ch'en Tu-hsiu made it an issue in the spring of 1917. As an aspect of the broader problem of educational modernization it had been under discussion since the early years of the

4. For information on Peita at this time see Chow Tse-tsung, *The May Fourth Movement* (Cambridge, Mass., 1960), 47–54. A full-scale study of Peita remains to be written.

century, when, spurred by Japan's victory over Russia, Chinese students had begun to give serious thought to radical proposals for the reform of the written language. Various schemes for the romanization of Chinese characters had been advanced, though always without conclusive results. At the same time the usefulness of the vernacular language as an educational medium had won increasing recognition. During the prerevolutionary decade the vernacular was commonly used in many of the student publications intended, like *The Struggle* that Hu Shih had edited in Shanghai, to "instill new ideas into the uneducated masses." It was against this background that Hu began to think in terms of a literary revolution during his years as a student in the United States.[5]

It is remarkable that a dispute which within a few short years generated such wide interest and intense feeling should have had its origin in a peculiarly trivial incident. As a Boxer Indemnity scholar Hu Shih received a monthly stipend from the Chinese Legation in Washington. The secretary responsible for mailing the checks, a Chinese Christian of elevated disposition, was in the habit of slipping into the envelope brief moral tracts and uplifting maxims: "Do not marry before the age of twenty-five," or "Plant more trees — trees are useful." One month, early in 1915, the message urged support for the introduction of a romanized script as a means of promoting popular education. Such a suggestion, coming, as Hu believed, from one who was not sufficiently educated to have the right to tamper with the language, offended Hu's sense of propriety. But after sending off a hasty and hotly worded retort Hu decided that the question was, after all, a worthy one, and that "we who were qualified ought to devote some thought to it." [6] His first analysis of the shortcomings of classical Chinese resulted from the interest thus aroused.[7]

Hu received little support from his fellow Chinese students

5. For background see Hu Shih, *Short History;* Hu Shih, "Wu-shih nien lai Chung-kuo chih wen-hsüeh" (Chinese literature in the last fifty years), HSWT II, ii, 91–213; Ch'en Tzu-chan, "Wen-hsüeh ko-ming yün-tung" (The revolutionary movement in literature), in *Chung-kuo hsin wen-hsüeh ta-hsi: X: Shih-liao, so-yin* (Historical materials and indices; edited by Ah Ying, Shanghai, 1936), 22–51; Chow, *The May Fourth Movement, passim.*

6. "Pi-shang Liang-shan," in *Autobiography,* 91–92. Liang-shan refers to the mountain stronghold of the outlawed heroes of the novel *Shui-hu chuan.* The implication is that Hu felt himself "forced beyond the law" but fighting for a righteous cause.

7. "Pi-shang Liang-shan," *Autobiography,* 94–95; *Diary,* 758–764.

when he presented these ideas to them in the summer of 1915. Their opposition, however, served only to increase his own enthusiasm.[8] The argument soon centered on the question of whether or not the vernacular style, which was generally acknowledged as suitable for the writing of such inferior things as novels and plays, could be appropriately employed in poetry and belles-lettres. Hu naturally took the affirmative and was soon experimenting with *pai-hua* poetry.[9]

Some of Hu's earliest efforts in this direction reveal clearly his awareness of the revolutionary significance of his proposals. Toward the end of the summer of 1915, for example, he wrote of his undertaking in this spirit:

China's literature has long been withered and feeble;
In the last century no robust men have arisen.
The coming of the new tide cannot be stayed:
The time is at hand for a literary revolution.
Circumstances will not permit our generation to sit and look on —
It is better for us to invite a few men
To stand in the vanguard of the revolutionary army and whip the
   horses to an even faster pace . . .
. . . To salute the new century, and enter it.
Repaying our country in this way cannot be called a trifle . . ."[10]

8. Among the few who rallied to Hu's cause were Chao Yuen-ren (Y. R. Chao), a classmate at Cornell, and Miss Ch'en Heng-che, a student at Vassar. Chao, also a Boxer Indemnity scholar of the class of 1910, was studying mathematics and physics but was already developing the interest in language that would lead him into a later career as a distinguished phonologist and linguist. Together with Hu and two other Chinese students at Cornell, Jen Hung-chün (*tzu* Shu-yung, H. C. Zen) and Yang Ch'üan (see above, chap. i, n. 70) he had helped to establish the Science Society of China in 1914, to serve as a vehicle for the promotion of scientific ideas among Chinese students at home and abroad. Ch'en Heng-che, a student of history and literature at Vassar in 1915–16, was among the first to experiment with *pai-hua* in writing short stories, some of which were published in *The New Youth*. In 1920 — the same year in which she married H. C. Zen — Ch'en Heng-che became the first woman appointed to a professorship at Peita. (See Boorman, *Biographical Dictionary*, I, 148–152 and 183–187.) One of Hu's principal adversaries in these early disputes was Mei Kuang-ti, a student at Harvard who later continued in his role as an opponent of the vernacular in the pages of the conservative magazine *Hsüeh-heng* after both Hu and he had returned to China.

9. *Diary*, 981. Hu's early *pai-hua* poetry was collected and published under the title *Ch'ang-shih chi* (A collection of experiments; Shanghai, 1920).

10. "Pi-shang Liang-shan," *Autobiography*, 96.

The following spring he expressed himself with even greater confidence:

> . . . Who can doubt the literary revolution!
> No, I am preparing to raise its banner and become its strong supporter,
> Wanting to do something never done before, to open a new millennium, to get rid of the stink of corruption, and return to our finest and best.
> To create a new literature for our great China — this is the task of our generation, and to whom would we wish to yield it? . . .[11]

This was his mood when he formulated his program for literary reform: "the eight conditions for a literary revolution," as he called them in his diary at the end of August 1916;[12] "tentative proposals for the improvement of literature," as he more modestly named them when they appeared, in somewhat modified form, in *The New Youth* the following January.[13]

The most concise and positive statement of Hu's proposals is found in his essay "On a Constructive Literary Revolution" (*Chien-she-ti wen-hsüeh ko-ming lun*), published in *The New Youth* in the spring of 1918. There Hu set forth the following points:

(1) Speak only if you have something to say.
(2) Say what you have to say, and say it as it is said.
(3) Speak your own language, not the language of others.
(4) Speak the language of your own time.[14]

To the last of these he attached particular importance, since in the final analysis his justification for promoting the vernacular lay in its historical timeliness. "Each age has its own literature,"[15] ran his argument, but the literature of any age must be a "living literature," and a "dead language cannot produce a living litera-

11. *Ibid.*, 102.

12. *Diary*, 1002–1003. See also Hu's letter to Ch'en Tu-hsiu, HSWT, i, 3.

13. Hu Shih, "Wen-hsüeh kai-liang ch'u-i" (Tentative proposals for the improvement of literature), HSWT, i, 7–23. First published in HCN 2.5 (January 1917).

14. Hu Shih, "Chien-she-ti wen-hsüeh ko-ming lun" (On a constructive literary revolution), HSWT, i, 79. First published in HCN 4.4 (April 1918).

15. Hu Shih, "Li-shih-ti wen-hsüeh kuan-nien lun" (On the genetic concept of literature), HSWT, i, 45. First published in HCN 3.3 (May 1917).

ture." [16] On this premise he based his "genetic concept of the historical evolution of literature," [17] which he called the "fundamental theory" behind the literary revolution.[18] Literature, he said, must follow an "order of precedence" in its historical evolution that necessarily originates in the liberation of form:[19]

> The history of Chinese literature is simply the history of the slow substitution of outmoded forms by new literary forms (instruments), the history of a "living literature" arising, according to the dictates of the times, to take the place of a "dead literature." The vitality of literature depends entirely upon its ability to serve as a timely and living instrument to express the sentiments and thoughts of a given period. When the instrument has become [too] rigid, a new and vital one must be substituted for it: this is "literary revolution" . . .
>
> In historical terms, "literary revolution" is solely a matter of a revolution in the instruments of literature . . . [My critics] have forgotten the great lesson to be found in the history of modern European literature! If there had not been in every country a living language to use as a new instrument . . . would modern European literature have flourished as it has? . . . The several revolutions in the history of Chinese literature have also been revolutions in the instruments of literature.[20]

On the strength of this argument Hu took a further step, asserting that "Chinese vernacular literature is the orthodox literature of China," [21] and that "*pai-hua* literature is the only literature China has possessed in the past thousand years . . . All that is not *pai-hua* literature . . . is not worthy to rank as literature of the first class." [22] This was Hu's most radical claim, and he resorted to

16. "Chien-she-ti wen-hsüeh ko-ming lun," HSWT, i, 83.
17. "Li-shih-ti wen-hsüeh kuan-nien lun," HSWT, i, 45–49.
18. *Ch'ang-shih chi, tzu-hsü* (Author's preface), HSWT, i, 270.
19. *Ibid.*, 284–285.
20. "Pi-shang Liang-shan," *Autobiography*, 99–100. Hu had in mind here such "revolutions" as the development of the *sao* form in poetry to replace the earlier forms found in the *Classic of Poetry* (in the late Chou and early Han period), and the development of the *tz'u* style in place of the more formal *shih* style (T'ang and Sung dynasties). See *Diary*, 862–867, for an early discussion of these and other "revolutions" in literary forms.
21. *Ibid.*, 100.
22. *Diary*, 943.

a variety of arguments in its defense. He discovered vernacular language where none had been seen before, in works as different and distant from each other as the *Shih-chi* and the poetry of the T'ang period — wherever clarity of expression took precedence over literary embellishment.[23] He claimed that the general popularity of vernacular literature, as opposed to that of classical texts, proved his point.[24] He intimated even that such unquestionably great classical stylists as the T'ang-dynasty essayists Han Yü and Liu Tsung-yüan had failed to write in the vernacular only because "in their day *pai-hua* had not yet arisen." [25]

Such assertions were justified, in Hu's mind, by his conviction that the literary revolution could succeed only if it was set into the context of a larger evolutionary process. Although he spoke easily enough of "revolution," he was at heart suspicious of revolutionary movements and pessimistic as to their outcome. The idea of revolution was acceptable to him only if it was viewed as a stage in the development of evolutionary change. The connection between his own literary revolution and the evolutionary history of Chinese literary forms provided a clear example. "There are two kinds of historical progress: one is completely natural change, and the other is change that accords with natural tendencies but which is enforced by human effort. The first may be called evolution, the latter may be called revolution . . . A thousand years of *pai-hua* literature has sown the seeds of the recent literary revolution [which has] only marked a brief stopping-off point in a long history. Henceforth Chinese literature will have left behind it forever the old road of blind and natural change and will travel instead upon the new road of conscious creativity." [26] It was for this reason that vernacular literature must be provided with a history of its own, and the literary revolution accepted not as a unique and violent act of rejection but rather as an act fulfilling the promise of the past.

The essence of that promise, as Hu came to understand it in the course of his American experience, was the democratization of education. As early as 1916 he was arguing that literature could no longer remain "the private possession of a minority of educated

23. Hu Shih, *Pai-hua wen-hsüeh shih, shang chüan* (A history of vernacular literature, I; Shanghai, 1928; Taipei, 1957), *tzu-hsü*, 12.
24. *Ibid., yin-tzu* (Introduction), 2.
25. "Li-shih-ti wen-hsüeh kuan-nien lun," HSWT, i, 47.
26. *Pai-hua wen-hsüeh shih, yin-tzu*, 7.

men [*wen-jen*]" but must become "something universal, lying within the competence of the great majority of our countrymen." For, he continued, literature is an instrument of change, a means to influence "the ways of the world and the hearts of men." [27] Hu was harshly critical of the reformers of earlier years for their failure to acknowledge the connection between language reform and the popularization of new ideas. Yen Fu, who employed in his translations an elegant and difficult classical style, had once observed, as Hu recalled without sympathy, "[Those] who read my translations often find them impossible to understand readily and criticize their abstruseness. Do they not know that the original works surpass this in difficulty? Principles of original subtlety certainly cannot be mixed together with language lacking in eloquence." [28] This, said Hu, was "cast-iron proof" of Yen's failure to accomplish his wider mission of intellectual reform, "the death sentence passed by the classicists upon themselves." [29] He was similarly critical of turn-of-the-century attempts to devise a phonetic script to take the place of Chinese characters. Such schemes had been foredoomed to failure, he asserted, because of the deep-seated reluctance on the part of their sponsors to acknowledge that their success must depend on the total abandonment of the traditional script. Failing this, the result would have been "to divide society into two classes: on the one side, 'we,' the gentry; and on the other side, 'they,' the common people, the masses . . . The phonetic language was [to be] no more than a beneficence bestowed upon the common people by the gentry." [30]

From the beginning, then, Hu Shih's interest in literary reform and his perception of the need for a written language that could serve to communicate with a popular audience was linked with the realization that such a language could not be employed only as an educational tool. If the chasm that separated the merely literate from the truly educated was to be bridged, the new language must possess a vitality and beauty of its own, a literary quality sufficient to justify its existence. He suggested as the slogan for this "con-

27. *Diary*, 956. See also "Pi-shang Liang-shan," *Autobiography*, 105.

28. *Short History*, 4; quoted from Yen's preface to his translation of J. S. Mill's *On Liberty*.

29. *Short History*, 4, 6. In his biography of Yen Fu, Benjamin Schwartz makes clear the fact that Yen had no intention of "popularizing" the works which he translated. See Benjamin I. Schwartz, *In Search of Wealth and Power: Yen Fu and the West* (Cambridge, Mass., 1964), 92–98.

30. *Short History*, 14.

structive literary revolution" the phrase "A literature in the national language; a literary national language."[31] For, as he repeatedly insisted, "if the national language contains no literature, then it is without value, it cannot be established, it cannot develop."[32]

In keeping with his experimentalist training, Hu Shih was disposed to remain cautious in his pronouncements concerning the eventual outcome of the literary revolution. Though he proclaimed the "orthodoxy" of *pai-hua*, he admitted in 1917 that this was "a hypothetical premise" that must await the proof offered by future generations of writers to substantiate its validity.[33] In a similar vein he observed that the correctness of his own proposals "cannot be determined overnight, nor by only one or two men. I hope that people throughout the country will show themselves able to join forces with us calmly to investigate this question!"[34]

Among Hu's earliest and most enthusiastic allies were Ch'en Tu-hsiu and Ch'ien Hsüan-t'ung. But though they made common cause with him, their attitude toward the task at hand contrasted sharply with his own. Neither Ch'en nor Ch'ien shared Hu's misgivings as to the usefulness of revolutionary change, and both were far more outspokenly antitraditional in their estimates of the purpose of their undertaking. "The toleration of divergent opinions and freedom of expression are naturally principles basic to the development of learning," Ch'en wrote to Hu in 1917. But, he continued, "in the case of the improvement of literature the theory that *pai-hua* represents the orthodox [line of development] is beyond dispute as to its correctness, and we must not give our opponents any room for discussion, but must assume the absolute truth of our own proposals."[35] In his call for a literary revolution published in *The New Youth* in February, Ch'en declared himself the "enemy of all the old-fashioned scholars in the country" and urged that the "aristocratic" literature of the past must give way to "a simple and expressive literature of the people . . . a clear and

31. "Chien-she-ti wen-hsüeh ko-ming lun," HSWT, i, 77.
32. *Ibid.,* 80. See also Hu Shih, "Hsin ssu-ch'ao ti i-i" (The meaning of the new thought), HSWT, iv, 1026–1027. First published in HCN 7.1 (December 1919).
33. "Li-shih-ti wen-hsüeh kuan-nien lun," HSWT, i, 46. See also *Ch'ang-shih chi, tzu-hsü,* HSWT, i, 285.
34. Hu Shih's letter to Ch'en Tu-hsiu (April 9, 1917), HSWT, i, 39.
35. Ch'en Tu-hsiu's letter to Hu Shih (n.d.), HSWT, i, 43.

popular social literature."[36] Ch'ien Hsüan-t'ung was, if anything, more vehement in his condemnation of the classical language as an instrument of intellectual tyranny. "Let me boldly repeat my manifesto: to the end that China may not perish and may become a civilized nation of the twentieth century, the basic task is to abolish Confucianism and annihilate Taoism. But the destruction of the Chinese written language, which has served as the repository of Confucian morality and Taoist superstition, is a prerequisite for the accomplishment of this task."[37]

Hu Shih's view of the primary purpose of the literary revolution was markedly different in emphasis. He clearly felt no affection for the "dead language" of the classics, nor for much of the tradition that it supported. But he defined the tradition more narrowly than did Ch'en Tu-hsiu and Ch'ien Hsüan-t'ung, and in keeping with his concept of revolution *within* evolution he endeavored always to look ahead rather than backward, and to draw attention to the creative potential of the reform. He acknowledged that "we who advocate literary revolution certainly cannot but start from the point of view of destruction," but he maintained that the destruction of the "false" and "dead" literature of the past would follow "naturally" from the creation of a "worthwhile and vital" modern literature. "Therefore," he wrote in reply to Ch'en, "I hope that we who advocate the literary revolution will exert our energies constructively, so that within the next thirty or fifty years we may create for China a school of new Chinese living literature."[38]

It remains open to question whether Hu's confidence in this regard has been proven justified. *Pai-hua* did indeed drive the older styles out of circulation within a relatively short time, but though the distance between the language of literature and the language of the streets grew narrower in consequence, this "liberation of forms" resulted in something less than the spontaneous generation of a vital literature. Nor was it within Hu's power to provide the initial creative inspiration, as he himself recognized.[39] As an essayist Hu

36. Ch'en Tu-hsiu, "Wen-hsüeh ko-ming lun" (On the literary revolution), *Tu-hsiu wen-ts'un* (Collected essays of [Ch'en] Tu-hsiu; Shanghai, 1922), i, 135–140. First published in HCN 2.6 (February 1917). Reprinted in HSWT, i, 24–29.

37. Ch'ien Hsüan-t'ung's letter to Hu Shih, quoted in C. T. Hsia, *A History of Modern Chinese Fiction, 1917–1957* (New Haven, 1961), 10.

38. "Chien-she-ti wen-hsüeh ko-ming lun," HSWT, i, 77–78.

39. Hu never thought of himself as a creative writer, and occasionally he expressed a sense of frustration at his deficiencies in this respect. Once, en

was the master of an uncomplicated, lucid, and lively style. But in other genres his literary output was meager: a considerable body of *pai-hua* poetry which was, as he called it, "experimental";[40] translations of short stories by a number of European writers — Daudet, Kipling, Maupassant, Strindberg, Chekov, Gorki — some of which had been made quite early in his time at Cornell and rendered into classical Chinese rather than *pai-hua*;[41] and a rather awkward one-act farce dealing with arranged marriages.[42]

The farce was intended not merely to amuse but also to serve as an example of socially responsible literature. Hu was convinced, as many modern Chinese writers have been, that literature must perform a social function, that it should not be, in content any more than in form, a private art given over to the esoteric uses of individual taste. The new literature, Hu contended, must concern itself with the urgent social and cultural issues of the moment — poverty, the living conditions of industrial workers and ricksha coolies and pedlars, the disintegration of the family system and the emancipation of women, problems of the new education and the cultural conflict between East and West.[43] A living literature might be fashioned from the forms of the new language. But what Hu called a "humanistic literature" could develop only with the introduction of fresh themes derived from new attitudes toward the writer's responsibilities and new perceptions of reality.[44] Thus while Hu

route from Peking to Shanghai by train, Hu encountered the Swedish explorer Sven Hedin, a friend of many years' standing. Hedin, a member of the Nobel Prize committee, suggested in the course of their conversation that he might nominate Hu for the prize in literature. This led Hu to reflect, privately, that if the award were made in light of his services as a promoter of literary reform he might accept, but that he could not accept the prize if it were offered him as a writer, an honor he did not believe he deserved. See Hu Shih's unpublished diaries (microfilm in the archive of the Oral History Project, Columbia University), entry for Feb. 26, 1929.

40. In Hsü Kai-yü's *Anthology of Twentieth-Century Chinese Poetry* (New York, 1963) Hu Shih is represented by only two poems — but they are the first two.

41. See Hu Shih, trans., *Tuan-p'ien hsiao-shuo ti-i chi* (Short stories, first collection; Shanghai, 1919), and *Tuan-p'ien hsiao-shuo ti-erh chi* (Second collection; Shanghai, 1933). These translations were originally published in *Hsin ch'ing-nien*, *Mei-chou p'ing-lun*, *Tu-shu tsa-chih*, *Hsin yüeh*, and other magazines.

42. Hu Shih, "Chung-shen ta-shih" (Life's great event), HSWT, iv, 1153–1172. The play was originally written in English.

43. "Chien-she-ti wen-hsüeh kuan-nien lun," HSWT, i, 93–95.

44. Hu was indebted to Chou Tso-jen for the idea of a "humanistic liter-

understood, early and clearly, the democratic potential of the literary revolution, he was less sensitive to the danger that an exclusive concern with social problems might render the new literature defenseless before the demand for conformity to an all-embracing social ideology. More than anything else, it has been this inclination to place art at the service of social and political causes of one stamp or another that has imparted to modern Chinese literature — save for a few vivid exceptions — a two-dimensional quality, an air of barren impersonality.

It was, perhaps, inevitable that this should come to pass. The literary revolution was from its inception the instrument of an intellectual reform movement much broader in scope, a tide of change so sweeping in its promise that it soon came to be known as the "New Culture Movement." For Hu Shih, *pai-hua* remained a first love down through the years, but his concerns ranged far beyond the revitalization of the written language. In the following chapters other problems that engaged Hu's interest will be discussed: his vision of the new citizen and the new society, his program for social reconstruction and intellectual regeneration, his view of China's relation to the modern West, and his attitude toward the political movements of the twenties and thirties. In his pronouncements on the literary revolution certain characteristics of his approach to these wider issues are already discernible. Where others were dogmatic, Hu tended to remain tentative. When others called for revolution as a repudiation of the past, Hu endeavored always to see it as a passage to the future. While others spoke of revolution as a sudden destructive cataclysm, Hu was disposed to think of it within the context of slower and less destructive evolutionary progress, and he remained confident that, properly guided, such "conscious evolution" would achieve the ends desired of it.

These were enduring traits of intellect and temperament, imparting to Hu's thought a character of its own, not always in agreement with the ideas of his friends nor in harmony with the temper of his times.

---

ature." This was the subject, and the title, of an essay by Chou published in *The New Youth* in December 1918.

Chapter 4. The New People and the New Society

In his eloquent "Appeal to Youth," published in the first issue of *The New Youth* in September 1915, Ch'en Tu-hsiu set a number of the themes that would dominate the intellectual revolution for the next few years. He urged his young readers to be progressive in their attitude toward change, utilitarian in their approach to new ideas and new techniques, and "cosmopolitan" (*shih-chieh-ti*) in their view of the world and China's place in it. Nothing expressed more aptly the mood of the moment than this last injunction, coupled with the characteristic warning that "when a people lack an understanding of the world, how can their nation be expected to survive in the world?" Ch'en drove his point home with a bit of proverbial Chinese wisdom: "He who builds his cart behind closed gates may find upon opening them that it will not fit the cart track." [1]

From its inception one of the primary purposes of *The New Youth* was to provide the materials out of which its readers might fashion a cosmopolitan point of view. Along with numerous interpretive essays touching upon various aspects of Western history and politics, its pages carried a steady stream of translations from Japanese and Western languages, published with a disconcerting indifference to any coherent scheme — an excerpt from *The History of Modern Civilization* by the French historian Charles Seignobos (Hsüeh-niu-po), for example, followed by a selection of pious Victorian homilies on the "Obligations of Youth," T. H. Huxley on the scientific spirit, fragments of Benjamin Franklin's *Autobiography*, a translation of "the American national anthem" (not "The Star-Spangled Banner," as it turns out, but "America"), and so on.

Throughout that first winter there also appeared, in serial form, a translation of Oscar Wilde's *An Ideal Husband,* a play set in the drawing rooms of London at the turn of the century and dealing in typical Wilde fashion with the tribulations of the socially prominent. Early in 1916, writing to Ch'en from New York, Hu criticized this translation both for its lack of artistry and its irrelevance to the Chinese situation. He was convinced of the importance of translation as one means of introducing Western ideas into the Chinese mind — several years later he listed this among the activities that to him represented "the meaning of the new thought" [2] — but he insisted that, just as literature could not be divorced from its social function, so translations must serve an instructive purpose. "If at the present time we desire to create a new literature for our fatherland, it is fitting to begin with the introduction of famous works of Europe and the West, in order to give our countrymen something to select from and turn over in their minds. Only then will they be able to speak of creating their

1. Ch'en Tu-hsiu, "Ching-kao ch'ing-nien" (Appeal to youth), *Tu-hsiu wen-ts'un*, i, 7. First published in HCN 1.1 (September 1915). Translated in Teng Ssu-yü and John K. Fairbank, *China's Response to the West: A Documentary Survey, 1839–1923* (Cambridge, Mass., 1954), 240–245.
2. Hu Shih, "Hsin ssu-ch'ao ti i-i" (The meaning of the new thought), HSWT, iv, 1021–1034. First published in HCN 7.1 (December 1919).

own literature . . . [But] in translating books, those closest to the minds of our countrymen should be translated first." [3]

It is not surprising, then, that Hu Shih's first attempt to draft a program for intellectual and social reform was made in connection with the publication in June 1918 of a special "Ibsen number" of *The New Youth* that included a translation of *A Doll's House* on which Hu had collaborated with Lo Chia-lun (then a student at Peita), and the first installment of a translation of *An Enemy of the People* by T'ao Meng-ho. It carried also a long introductory essay by Hu in which he set forth for the first time opinions concerning the qualities of genuine individualism and the relationship between the individual and society that remained of critical concern to him throughout his life.

By the time Hu Shih turned his attention in this direction, such issues were no longer entirely new to the Chinese mind. Western concepts of individualism, and Western attempts to reconcile the conflict between individual and social purposes, had attracted the particular attention of reformers ever since the end of the nineteenth century, for they had recognized this as a point at which Chinese and Western social traditions diverged radically. Confucian social theory emphasized authoritarian hierarchies and relative status within them, placing a premium on the preservation of social equilibrium and on the time-honored distinction between those who govern and those who are governed. Thus a major objective of the reformers was the destruction of these assumptions, which they viewed as impediments to the growth of a "national" consciousness based on broader popular participation in political and social life and a heightened sense of individual responsibility.

Liang Ch'i-ch'ao, in his prerevolutionary writings, clearly discerned the dimensions of the dilemma. "Treat [the people] as slaves, guard against them as against brigands, and they will come to regard themselves as slaves and brigands," he wrote in one of his sharpest indictments of the traditional attitude of Chinese rulers toward their subjects.[4] Liang early recognized the need for an awakened citizenry as the foundation on which to erect a strong national

3. *Diary*, 845.
4. Liang Ch'i-ch'ao, "Lun chin-pu" (On progress), quoted in Hsiao Kung-ch'üan, *Chung-kuo cheng-chih ssu-hsiang shih*, VI, 746–747.

state, and he perceived as well the role that the individual would have to assume in this new order. "A nation's citizenry is made up of individuals, and a nation's sovereignty consists in the gathering together of individual rights," he wrote in 1903. "Therefore, if we seek [to awaken] the thought, the consciousness, the activity of our people [as a whole], these aims cannot be achieved without [first awakening] the thought, the consciousness, the activity of each individual." [5]

For Liang, as for most who followed him, individualism remained subservient to the cause of nationalism. Writing of the relationship between individual and social (or national) purposes, Liang observed:

> Men who entertain no idea of self-benefit [li-chi] must necessarily abandon their rights, abdicate their responsibilities, and ultimately lose their independence . . . In the West there is a saying to the effect that heaven helps him who helps himself. No calamity in life is greater than failing to help oneself, hoping only for help from others . . . [But] no man can survive alone in the world, and from this [fact] arises the group. Living within the group, among one's fellows, it is of course impossible to live completely to oneself, paying no heed to the question whether something beneficial to oneself is harmful to others . . . Thus those best able to benefit themselves must first benefit the group, and from this will follow benefit to themselves. [6]

Although Liang Ch'i-ch'ao, Yen Fu, and others of their generation might call attention to China's shortcomings and urge with all the considerable eloquence at their command a program of fundamental social reform, [7] the accomplishment of such reforms was no easy task. The Revolution of 1911 swept into oblivion the visible political superstructure of imperial China, but it left virtually untouched the invisible social foundations on which the imperial edifice had rested. So it was with no feeling of being out

5. Liang Ch'i-ch'ao, "Lun ch'üan-li ssu-hsiang" (On the theory of rights), quoted in Hsiao, VI, 746.

6. Liang Ch'i-ch'ao, "Shih chung te-hsing hsiang-fan hsiang-ch'eng i, ch'i ssu: li-chi yü ai-t'a" (The complementary and antithetical significance of ten varieties of moral concepts, the fourth: self-interest and altruism), quoted in Hsiao, VI, 754-755.

7. On Yen Fu's interpretation of this problem, see Benjamin Schwartz, In Search of Wealth and Power, 69-80 and passim.

of step with the times that the writers of *The New Youth* circle turned once more to problems with which their predecessors had wrestled.

Over the several years following the publication of his essay "Ibsenism" in 1918 Hu Shih expounded, in somewhat random fashion, a design for social and intellectual reform based on a new spirit of individualism to which he afterwards adhered with remarkable persistence. If he deserves attention as a liberal thinker, this is at least as much because of his opinions concerning the intellectual and social responsibilities of the individual, and the quality of the social environment in which the individual acts, as because of his more explicitly political views which will be considered later.

In Ithaca, early in 1914, Hu Shih attended a production of Eugene Brieux's *Damaged Goods,* a melodrama dealing with the social consequences of venereal disease. He was sufficiently impressed by it to copy the program into his diary, together with a brief comparison, favoring Brieux, with Ibsen's treatment of the same subject in *Ghosts.*[8] For several months thereafter he filled his study notes with references to reading done in the "social theater" of the day, especially in the work of Hauptmann, Strindberg, and Ibsen.[9]

It was to Ibsen that Hu turned for inspiration in 1918. Though he admired the dramatic excellence of a number of Ibsen's later character studies, like *Hedda Gabler,* his exposition of "Ibsenism" was based entirely on the earlier "problem plays," for he found it much easier to draw from such works as *A Doll's House* and *An Enemy of the People* the clear social message he was seeking. The context, of course, was very different. What had originated with Ibsen as an attack on bourgeois conventionality Hu translated into an assault on the whole body of Confucian social attitudes, and especially the family system. What he was interested in was not the particular details of Ibsen's critique of European middle-class society, but Ibsen's conclusion, with which Hu heartily agreed: "No social evil is greater than the destruction of the individual's individuality." [10] Even more, he admired the spirit that had moved Ibsen

8. *Diary,* 193–195.

9. *Ibid.,* 306, 309, 310–311, 321, 332, and *passim.*

10. Hu Shih, "I-pu-sheng chu-i" (Ibsenism), HSWT, iv, 904. First published in HCN 4.6 (June 1918).

to write. Time and again Hu urged his readers to cultivate the strength of character and the intellectual honesty that would enable them to follow Ibsen's example in "speaking frankly" against social abuses:

> The underlying sickness of human life is an unwillingness to look with open eyes at the condition of the world. Clearly, ours is a government of corrupt officials and vile bureaucrats — but we perversely sing of merit and chant hymns to virtue. Clearly, ours is a sickness unto death — but we insist that no sickness exists! . . . If we desire to cure an illness, we must first acknowledge that the illness exists; if we want good government, we must first acknowledge that the present political situation is in fact bad; if we want to improve society, we must first admit that our present society is in fact a society of thieves and prostitutes! . . . Because we cannot shake off our connection with society, we cannot but speak frankly.[11]

The intellectual's first obligation, then, is to liberate himself from the bonds of thoughtlessness and self-deceit. But this is only a beginning. His duty to society is to translate his new awareness of social abuse into concrete actions designed to eradicate the social influences that stifle the growth of personality. He must, in short, "develop to the fullest his own natural ability . . . his own individuality." [12] In "Ibsenism" Hu quoted for the first time a passage from one of Ibsen's letters to the Danish critic Georg Brandes to which he frequently returned in later years: "What I most desire for you is a true and pure egoism. It will cause you at times to feel that the only things that are important in the world are those that concern yourself, and that the rest are not worth counting . . . If you desire to be of use to society, the best thing you can do is to forge yourself — this lump of material — into a finished instrument . . . At times I feel that the whole world is like a ship sinking at sea, and that the most important thing is to save oneself." [13]

11. *Ibid.*, 884–885.
12. *Ibid.*, 902.
13. *Ibid.*, 902. The passage as given here is a translation of Hu's translation into Chinese; the English version on which his translation was based reads as follows: "What I chiefly desire for you is a genuine, full-blooded egoism which shall force you for a time to regard what concerns you yourself as the only

Hu made it clear from the beginning, however, that he did not regard the development of individual personality as an end justified in itself. Though the traditional social order might force the individual into opposition against it as the price of his own salvation, the ultimate purpose behind his struggle for independence lay not in any advantage which it might have for him alone, but in its importance as a step toward the creation of a new and freer social order. In language reminiscent of Liang Ch'i-ch'ao's plea already cited Hu observed,

> Society is constituted of individuals, and . . . one more person saved is one more element prepared for the reconstruction of society. When Meng K'o [Mencius] said, "The poor attend to their own virtue in solitude," his meaning was similar to Ibsen's "Save yourself." Such egoism is in fact the most valuable kind of altruism.[14]

> A free society [tzu-chih ti she-hui] and a republican nation demand only that the individual have the power of free choice and that he bear the responsibility for his own conduct and actions. If this is not the case, then he does not possess the ability to create his own independent character. If society and the nation do not possess [men of] independent character, they are like wine without yeast, bread without leaven, the human body without nerves. Such a society has absolutely no hope of improvement or progress.[15]

The language of this appeal would undoubtedly have mystified the Confucian reformer of an earlier age, familiar enough with his beloved Mencius but at a loss for the meaning of such phrases as "a free society" and "a republican nation." Nevertheless, the Confucian critic of traditional Chinese society might well have found himself in at least partial sympathy with Hu's description of the

---

thing of any consequence, and everything else as non-existent . . . There is no way in which you can benefit society more than by coining the metal you have in yourself . . . There are actually moments when the whole history of the world appears to me like one great shipwreck, and the only important thing is to save one's self." See J. N. Laurvik and M. Morison, trans., *Letters of Henrik Ibsen* (New York, 1905), 218.

14. *Ibid.*, 902–903.
15. *Ibid.*, 906.

attributes of genuine individualism. The stalwart Confucian moralist had been as adamant in his advocacy of intellectual responsibility as was this twentieth-century rebel against the tradition. Down the long centuries of imperial history we hear the voice of the Confucian critic pleading, in the name of true Confucian values, against heedless conformity to the standards of the day and stressing the importance to society of men of uncompromising integrity and independent judgment. We cannot afford to overlook this similarity of views, for it helps to explain why it is that Hu Shih, in spite of his articulate opposition to the "tradition," appears in some lights to be arguing a very traditional case.

But if we look beyond this initial resemblance we will discover a fundamental difference separating the orthodox Confucian reformer from his latter-day counterpart: on closer inspection it becomes obvious that their ideas of what constitutes intellectual and social responsibility are not at all the same.

Confucius said: "The superior man is not an implement" (*chün-tzu pu ch'i*).[16] The sage meant this, perhaps, partly as an admonition to those who would place themselves at the service of rulers unscrupulous enough to exploit talent to their own advantage. But he was also expressing a conviction, later to become firmly embedded in the Confucian outlook, that the superior man should be no mere tool fitted to the performance of one or two narrow functions. From the Confucian point of view the key to an understanding of social organization — and on a grander scale, the whole cosmic order — was the idea of harmony, not diversity. Though the world might appear to the senses as something put together from random fragments, as Neo-Confucian thinkers conceded to their Buddhist antagonists, they insisted that this merely concealed an underlying unity which it was the purpose of the mind to discover. The formalism of the orthodox classical education, particularly its exaggerated emphasis on a mastery of the literary refinements so admired by the readers of imperial examinations, seemed to many Neo-Confucian thinkers a lamentable impediment to the realization of the true purpose of education, which was not to impart skill but to cultivate virtue. While virtue might come, following the Neo-Confucian argument, from "the extension of knowledge," such knowledge was not gained in the pursuit of

16. *Lun-yü* (The analects), II, xii. Compare Legge, *The Chinese Classics*, I, 150: "The accomplished scholar is not a utensil."

specialized competence. It was, rather, a comprehension of the fundamental harmony of all things in accordance with Principle. Virtue, or knowledge, as it showed itself in an involvement in the day-to-day affairs of public life, might be defined as a strong sense of individual integrity arising out of the civilized understanding of the world which could only be achieved after prolonged examination of the literary remains bequeathed by the founders of the tradition. Such understanding prepared one for the responsibilities of administration — meaning, in theory, maintenance of the essential harmony of the social microcosm — but it gave one neither the ability nor the license to take the social order apart and tinker with the pieces.

Yet it was precisely this ability which Hu Shih sought to encourage, and this right which he affirmed. "When I was a child in the village," he recalled in a letter written in 1915, "watching my clansmen perform the sacrifices, I used to hear the participants in the rites say, 'Let those who are managing affairs each preside over his own part of the business.' In these words is embodied an invaluable prescription for national salvation." [17] More than once he remarked of himself that, since his own talents were limited, the worthiest service he could render to society would be to do what he was capable of doing well, leaving to others the tasks which he could not accomplish. And Hu's experimentalist social philosophy, while it did not necessarily compel him to reject the idea that in a certain sense society may be regarded as a harmoniously functioning organism, convinced him of the wisdom of adopting a selective approach to the remedying of specific social problems.

There is yet another aspect of Hu's disagreement with Confucian social theory which must be noted at this point. The Confucian tradition was founded on the belief that virtue, as defined above, should not remain a private accomplishment but that it should be communicated, by the force of example, to society at large. Side by side with this tradition of social engagement, however, there existed an equally well established and honorable tradition of disengagement from concrete social situations in the interest of perfecting or protecting an allegiance to Confucian principles of righteous conduct. When the ruler proved unresponsive to the virtuous promptings of his ministerial alter ego, the strict Confucian might resign his ministry, mindful that the Master had ad-

17. *Diary*, 567.

vised his followers to hide themselves when the Way did not prevail under Heaven.[18] Even if society was beyond redemption, the self could still be cultivated, the mind kept pure and upright, and individual virtue refined. It was only in this limited but not unimportant way that the Confucian tradition made room for the individual as the final refuge of its most cherished values, though even so he remained the servant of a philosophy which assigned to him no importance in his own right.

In the politically and socially disrupted environment of the late 1910s and early 1920s the image of the righteous man who stands aside from the petty tyrannies of the moment and seeks to act upon society by improving his own character possessed a certain attraction. Hu was convinced, however, that the liberation of the individual must be accomplished not only to fulfill a social purpose but also within a social setting. Consequently he placed himself in opposition both to the new vogue of utopian or anarchistic individualism espoused by some of his friends[19] and to the revival of the ancient tradition of "self-cultivation." The individual and his society are inseparably linked, he argued. Reformation of individual character is impossible except as a result of the reformation of the social forces which shape it. In his essay "Ibsenism" he had quoted with approval Mencius' observation that "the poor attend to their own virtue in solitude," a phrase which, in its original context, describes the way of the superior man who preserves his contentment even in reduced circumstances and in the face of worldly neglect.[20] A year and a half later, in the course of a lengthy discussion of what Hu called "the anti-individualistic new life," he found it necessary to reject the implications of Mencius' advice if it was used to justify the individual's withdrawal from a

18. *Lun-yü*, VII, x, and VIII, xiii; Legge, *The Chinese Classics*, I, 197 and 212. For an illuminating discussion of this element in Confucian thinking see Benjamin I. Schwartz, "Some Polarities in Confucian Thought," in David S. Nivison and Arthur F. Wright, eds., *Confucianism in Action* (Stanford, 1959), 50–62.

19. See for example Chou Tso-jen, "Hsin-ts'un ti ching-shen" (The spirit of the New Villages), HCN 7.2:129–134 (January 1920). On this same subject see Chow Tse-tsung, *The May Fourth Movement*, 190; Maurice Meisner, *Li Ta-chao and the Origins of Chinese Marxism* (Cambridge, Mass., 1967), 56 and 275, n. 9; Olga Lang, *Pa Chin and His Writings: Chinese Youth between the Two Revolutions* (Cambridge, Mass., 1967), 55 and 296, n. 91.

20. *Mencius*, Chin hsin (shang ix); Legge, *The Chinese Classics*, II, 453. But see also W. A. C. H. Dobson, trans., *Mencius* (Toronto, 1963), 101, for a rendering of the passage which does not convey the idea of solitude.

social situation displeasing to him, whether this withdrawal took the form of religious retreat, utopian antisocial individualism, or Confucian moral cultivation:

The fundamental error of this concept lies in . . . regarding the individual as something that can be set outside of society and reformed. It is important to understand that the individual is the result of numerous and varied social forces . . . The "best elements" in society are not born that way, nor are they created by individual self-cultivation. They are the result of [the fact that] among the various forces that contribute to their creation good influences somewhat outnumber the bad . . . Ancient social and political philosophy, unwittingly hoping to reform the individual in a vacuum, advocated such methods as setting the mind in order [*cheng-hsin*], sincerity of purpose [*ch'eng-i*], and attending to one's own virtue in solitude. Actually these are not methods at all, for they provide no starting place. Modern humanistic philosophy . . . has gradually destroyed these superstitious dreams and come to the realization that the place to make a start on social reconstruction is with the improvement of the various forces that together create society — institutions, customs, thought, education, etc. When these forces have been improved, so also will men have been improved. Thus I feel that [the maxim] "social reconstruction must start with the reformation of the individual" [reflects a point of view that] has not freed itself from the influence of the old thought.[21]

The stark fact remained that within Chinese society as it still existed there was obviously little hope for the reformation of individual character. The family system especially, the institution that had served for centuries as a pillar of Confucian authoritarianism, continued to inhibit the assertion of individual personality. It was against two of the principal bulwarks of this system that Hu concentrated his attack in the months and years following the publication of "Ibsenism": the social status of women, and the doctrine of filial piety.

No social issue attracted more attention from the radical intel-

21. Hu Shih, "Fei ko-jen chu-i ti hsin sheng-huo" (The anti-individualistic new life), HSWT, iv, 1052–1053.

lectuals of the late 1910s than what was popularly known as "the women question." The social position of women was, moreover, a problem toward which Hu was likely to feel a particular sensitivity by reason of his own family experiences.[22] But while his critique of Confucian filialism can be traced to quite early origins, he was much slower in coming to a "progressive" view of women's proper social role. As late as 1914 he was still disposed to defend traditional Chinese standards of feminine conduct as against the more liberal attitudes he observed in America. "It seems to me," he wrote then, "that the position occupied by women in my country is in fact higher than that of Western women. In our country great attention is paid to the modesty and reputation of women." [23] Within the year, however, he had a change of mind, inspired, apparently, both by his increasing interest in the suffragette movement and by his close intellectual friendship with Edith Williams, the daughter of one of his professors at Cornell. He abandoned his earlier contention that women should be prepared only to become "good wives and mothers" and adopted instead the view that "the highest goal of women's education is to create women able to live free and independent." "For women have a power to move men, which they can use to inspire the weak and to arouse the timid, and in this way to change popular custom," he wrote with an uncharacteristic touch of sentimentality. "Those who love the country must recognize this capacity and seek to protect and nurture it, and put it to use." [24]

After his return to China Hu found ample evidence of the survival of traditional prejudices with which to arm himself in his assault on the old attitude toward women. Some of his most trenchant pieces were inspired by specific cases in which obedience to accepted standards of conduct had resulted in tragic sacrifice. He served, for example, as the biographer of a young student who, dying of tuberculosis in her early twenties, left behind in her correspondence with friends and family the record of a life cruelly

22. On the prevalence of this theme in the writings of the May Fourth period see Roxane Witke, "Mao Tse-tung, Women and Suicide in the May Fourth Era," *China Quarterly*, no. 31:128–147 (July-September 1967). For an account of Hu Shih's attitude toward his own marriage, see Appendix A.

23. *Diary*, 154. For an even more conservative statement see Hu Shih, "Hun-yin pien" (On marriage), *Ching-yeh hsün-pao*, nos. 24 and 25 (July-August 1908), quoted in Li Ao, *Hu Shih p'ing-chuan*, 174–176.

24. *Diary*, 806–807.

scarred by her attempts to discover an individual personality and purpose.[25] Even more dramatic were incidents regularly described in the press: a girl from Haining for example, who was permitted to starve herself to death rather than to sacrifice her reputation by outliving the man to whom she had been betrothed; or the similar case of a girl from the Shanghai area who swallowed poison and died in agony a few hours after receiving word of her fiancé's death. By traditional standards these were virtuous acts, classical examples of chaste conduct. What really angered Hu was the fact that they were still treated as such by the press and the local governments involved, and that there were laws which, recalling the imperial practice of rewarding this kind of virtue by the erection of commemorative arches, held these acts up to the public as examples to be emulated.[26] "Looking at this matter from the perspectives of contemporary humanism," Hu wrote, "there is no place for such laws in the present day." [27] The fact that they still exist, he argued, must be taken as proof of intellectual irresponsibility, the failure to define beliefs in terms of real and ultimate meanings, the uncritical acceptance of timeworn standards of morality. "If we ask a man, 'What is chastity?' or 'Why do you praise chastity?' he will most certainly reply, 'Chastity is chastity, and because it is chastity we praise it.' Such . . . reasoning is proof that present-day morality has declared itself bankrupt . . . The question of 'chastity' is by no means a matter of 'unalterable principle' [*t'ien-ching ti-i*] but rather something which can be thoroughly studied and exhaustively discussed."[28]

It is clear that Hu was seeking something more than the reform of one or another specific custom. Beyond the question of chastity, beyond the whole issue of women's social position, was the greater question of men's attitudes toward their social inheritance. In these various chronicles and commentaries the same message is invariably apparent: that the individual must assume the responsibility for his own ideas, that he must think independently, for only in this way will the new social order be realized. "A good society," said Hu in a speech delivered in the autumn of 1918 at the Peking Women's

25. Hu Shih, "Li Ch'ao chuan" (Biography of Li Ch'ao), HSWT, iv, 1077–1094.

26. Hu Shih, "Chen-ts'ao wen-t'i" (The question of chastity), HSWT, iv, 933–948. First published in HCN 5.1 (July 1918).

27. *Ibid.*, 947.

28. *Ibid.*, 945.

Normal School, in which he extolled the place of women in American society, "certainly cannot be created by men and women such as we now possess, mutually dependent and unable to 'stand alone' [*tzu-li*]. The spirit of 'independence' [*tzu-li*] of which I speak, though it may at first appear to be no more than an extreme individualism, is in fact an essential condition of the good society." [29]

Hu's belief in the crucial importance of this spirit of independence prompted his assault on another and even more pervasively influential intellectual inheritance — the concept of filial piety. His earliest attack on this cornerstone of the Confucian edifice was written while he was still in Shanghai (see above, chapter 1 at note 67). Thereafter his experiences in America served only to intensify his opposition to it,[30] until by 1914 he was ready to attribute to filialism almost the entire blame for China's deepening crisis. The unquestioning acceptance of paternal authority, Hu argued, had given rise to a system of family relationships that drew cruel strength from the weakness, the irresponsibility, and the spirit of dependence of the individuals trapped within it:

> Under our family system the father and the mother regard the son and his wife as a kind of old-age pension . . . Children regard the parents' estate as something that is sure to come to them . . . All branches of the family are mutually dependent on one another. One man becomes a Buddha and the whole family goes to heaven; one son makes a name for himself and the whole tribe puts the bite on him, like ants swarming over a bone, with no sense of shame but on the contrary thinking this quite natural — what slavishness is this! Here, indeed, is the root of the nation's downfall! Filial piety is [the principle that makes] children responsible for the care of their parents; and the parents, laying this responsibility upon their children, nurture the habit of dependence.[31]

29. Hu Shih, "Mei-kuo ti fu-jen" (American women), HSWT, iv, 931. First published in HCN 5.3 (September 1918).

30. See *Diary*, 391, 410–411, and *passim*.

31. *Ibid.*, 250–251; see also 390–393. After the birth of his first son, Hu Tsu-wang, in 1918, Hu Shih wrote: "This child did not himself freely propose to be born and live in my family. We, the parents, did not receive his agreement but casually endowed him with life . . . How can we claim any merit? How can we pretend to any particular kindness to him? . . . I want my son to know that I feel toward him only a certain contrition [*pao-ch'ien*]; cer-

The conclusion that Hu Shih had reached as a schoolboy in Shanghai, that the individual should feel responsible only to "society" as a whole, and act accordingly, was not unknown even within the Confucian tradition. A few years later Hu discovered in the *Tso chuan* commentary to the *Spring and Autumn Annals* (*Ch'un-ch'iu*) a precedent that proved very useful to him. Commenting on the phrase "To die but not to decay" (*ssu erh pu-hsiu*), the writer of the *Tso chuan* suggests that it must refer to the remembrance, even after one's death, of virtuous conduct, meritorious service, and wise words.[32] Such, Hu concluded, "is the posterity of those who have no posterity. Sakyamuni, Confucius, Lao-tzu, and Jesus did not rely on sons to perpetuate their names. Washington had no sons, yet Americans revere him as the father of his country . . . It is the works of Li Po, Tu Fu, Byron, and Tennyson that make them live on."[33] This opinion, set down in the autumn of 1914, served as the central premise of Hu's theory of "social immortality," formulated soon after his mother's death in the winter of 1918 in an essay entitled "Immortality — My Religion."[34]

This essay merits more than passing mention, since it constitutes Hu's first attempt to describe in any detail his philosophy of life, drawing together many of the ideas that had been taking shape in his mind concerning the relationship between the individual and society, and for the first time giving them systematic expression. The term *pu-hsiu* ("immortality"), used in the title, Hu had of course appropriated from the passage in the *Tso chuan* already cited. He meant by it little more than the idea that was suggested there. His theory of immortality, said Hu, "does not ask whether the soul can survive after death, but only whether a man's character, his occupation, and his works have permanent value . . . Immortality depends entirely upon a man's true worth, not upon the continuation of his family name or the survival of his soul."[35]

The individual, then, should entertain no hope of "salvation."

---

tainly I take no credit for myself, nor do I boast of my own kindness. As far as my son's conduct toward me in the future is concerned, that is his own affair." Hu Shih, "Wo-ti erh-tzu" (My son), HSWT, iv, 969–970.

32. *Tso chuan*, Hsiang-kung 24th year; see Legge, *The Chinese Classics*, V, 507, para. 1.

33. *Diary*, 410–411.

34. Hu Shih, "Pu-hsiu — wo-ti tsung-chiao" (Immortality — my religion), HSWT, iv, 975–988. First published in HCN 6.2 (February 1919).

35. *Ibid.*, 978–979.

The best he can expect — and the worst he should fear — is to be remembered. This is the immortality that society will bestow, in accordance with its judgment of the individual's merits. In the unbroken sweep of history each man is the product of everything that has gone before, and his own actions, whether he wills it or not, must affect the lives of all those who follow after. Thus, Hu observed, "the individual creates history, and history creates the individual." [36] Society and the individual — the "greater self" and the "lesser self," as Hu called them — are inseparable. The "immortality of the greater self," endowing the finite individual existence with significance beyond its own brief expectations, demands of the individual a high sense of responsibility for his own conduct, since it is by this that his "true worth" will be judged. "This present 'lesser self' of mine must bear a heavy burden of responsibility toward the limitless past of the eternal and immortal 'greater self,' and a similarly heavy burden of responsibility toward the limitless future of the eternal and immortal 'greater self.' I must constantly consider how I should endeavor to put this present 'lesser self' to good use, for only then will I discharge my responsibilities toward the past and leave no evil legacy to the future." [37]

Such was the creed, the product of an essentially skeptical intellect, that Hu Shih offered as a "religion" to take the place of Christian dogma, Buddhist superstition, and Confucian filialism.

Not until 1923 did Hu have another opportunity to express himself on questions of such consequence — in the course of the celebrated debate on "science and the philosophy of life" which preoccupied many of China's leading intellectuals during much of that year. The issues around which this dispute revolved will be examined in the following chapter; here only Hu's summary of his own views, with which he capped the debate at the end of the year, will be described.

Hu called his philosophy "a naturalistic conception of life and the universe." He thus allied himself unequivocally with those who argued that scientific knowledge is the only sure knowledge men have of their world and themselves, and that the methods of scientific inquiry are the only reliable means for obtaining such knowledge. Supporting his position with references to the appro-

36. *Ibid.*, 981.
37. *Ibid.*, 987–988.

priate branches of scientific knowledge in each instance, Hu made the following assertions:

That the world of space is "infinitely large" and that the world extends over an infinity of time.

That all phenomena follow "natural laws of movement and change — 'natural' in the Chinese sense of 'being so of themselves' — and that there is no need for the concept of a supernatural ruler or creator."

That the brutality of life, viewed as a struggle for survival, makes impossible the belief in a benevolent creator.

That man differs from other animals only in degree, not in kind.

That the laws of evolution apply with equal force to living organisms and to human societies.

That all psychological phenomena are subject to the law of cause and effect.

That morality, ethics, and religion are subject to change, the nature of which can be understood through scientific investigation.

"That the individual self is subject to death and decay, but the sum total of individual achievements, for better or worse, lives on in the immortality of the larger self; that to live for the sake of the species and posterity is religion of the highest kind; and that the religions which seek a future life either in Heaven or in the Pure Land are selfish religions." [38]

On these premises Hu drew an image of the universe and man's place in it, which, as his most sustained effort in this direction, deserves to be quoted at some length.

In this naturalistic universe, in this universe of infinite space and time, man, the two-handed animal whose average height is about five feet and a half, and whose age rarely exceeds a hundred years, is indeed a mere infinitesimal microbe. In this naturalistic universe, where every motion in the heavens has its regular course and every change follows laws of nature, where causality governs man's life and the struggle for existence spurs his activities — in such a universe man has very little freedom indeed. Yet this tiny animal of two hands has his proper place and worth in that world of infinite magnitude . . . The increase of his knowledge has extended his power, but it has also

38. KHYJSK, Hu *hsü*, 25–27; "Credo," 260–261.

widened his vision and elevated his imagination . . . He is now . . . slowly coming to a realization that the infinity of space enhances his aesthetic appreciation of the universe, the infinite length of geological and archaeological time only makes him better understand the terrific hardship his forefathers had to encounter in building up this human inheritance, and the regularity of the movements and changes in the heavens and on earth only furnishes him the key to his dominion over nature.

Even the absolute universality of the law of causality does not necessarily limit his freedom, because the law of causality not only enables him to explain the past and predict the future, but also encourages him to use his intelligence to create new causes and attain new results. Even the apparent cruelty of the struggle for existence does not necessarily make him a hardened brute; on the contrary, it may intensify his sympathy for his fellow man and make him believe more firmly in the necessity of cooperation, and convince him of the importance of conscious human endeavor as the only means of reducing the brutality and wastefulness of the natural struggles. In short, this naturalistic conception of the universe and life is not necessarily devoid of beauty, of poetry, of moral responsibility, and of the fullest opportunity for the exercise of the creative intelligence of man.[39]

From this it is easy to see why Hu believed, as he had written earlier, that "history creates the individual." But how could he couple this with the assertion that "the individual creates history"? The latter proposition can be understood only in the light of Hu's belief in "creative intelligence," the belief that critical thought is the key to freedom from the enslavement to cause and effect. Only those who perceive their situation and come to terms with it, he insisted, may hope to be rescued from the relentless mechanism of the universe.

For this reason Hu consistently assigned great importance to intelligence as a "cause" in itself. This was a point emphasized in an exchange with Ch'en Tu-hsiu arising out of the debate on science and metaphysics in 1923. Ch'en, by then firmly committed to

39. KHYJSK, Hu *hsü*, 27–29; "Credo," 262–263.

Marxism-Leninism, and arguing from the point of view of historical materialism, challenged Hu's claim to speak as a "materialist." [40] Hu in turn rejected Ch'en's narrowly Marxist definition of historical materialism. Noneconomic and particularly intellectual factors must be taken into account, he insisted, and acknowledged as "objective material causes":

> Tu-hsiu has said, "The mind [hsin[b]] is one manifestation of matter [wu] . . . It seems, in that case, that "objective material causes" ought to include all "intellectual" causes — knowledge, thought, self-expression [yen-lun], education, etc. If we explain the problem in this fashion, then Tu-hsiu's definition of historical materialism comes to read: "Only objective causes (including economic organization, knowledge, thought, etc.) can change society, explain history, and shape one's philosophy of life." This is no more than a bald view of history that need not wear a cap of any particular color . . . We who study history . . . know that the causes of historical fact are always multiple, and therefore, though we welcome the "economic view of history" most enthusiastically as an important tool for the study of history, at the same time we cannot but acknowledge that such things as thought and knowledge are also "objective causes." [41]

Hu suggested, in conclusion, that if Ch'en in fact lacked faith in the importance of such noneconomic factors, logic required him to abandon as futile his tireless efforts to foment an anticapitalist revolution by means of propaganda and agitation. [42]

To this Ch'en replied that while "within the sphere of possibilities imposed by the material conditions of society, historical materialists do not deny the effect of the activity of human effort and ability," economic factors nonetheless retain their primary importance. Making use of an example that was sure to strike home, he asserted that the literary revolution had come in response to changing economic conditions — the development of productive forces and the resultant centralization of population — and could

40. KHYJSK, Ch'en *hsü*, 10–11.
41. *Ibid.*, Hu *hsü*, 31–32.
42. *Ibid.*, 33.

not be attributed to the activity of "such men as Hu Shih-chih and Ch'en Tu-hsiu." [43]

There the argument ended, for the time being. It fell to Hu to have the last word a dozen years later, in his introduction to a collection of essays on the history of the literary revolution. Recalling Ch'en's earlier remarks, and accepting his example if not the conclusions he had drawn from it, Hu took his old friend to task for "foolishly desiring to employ a 'final cause' to explain all historical facts." In line with the importance which he attached to the search for "pluralistic" and "specific" factors to account for historical change, Hu called attention to a number of causes that had prepared the way for the literary revolution: the long history of vernacular literature in China, the gradual spread of the Mandarin dialect to encompass a wide area of the country, the end of Chinese seclusion and the stimulation provided by foreign contact in the nineteenth and twentieth centuries, and such political factors as the abolition of the examination system and the collapse of the Manchu dynasty. Moreover, he concluded, "if such men as Hu Shih and Ch'en Tu-hsiu had not become involved in the vernacular literature movement, then at the very least its appearance would have been postponed for twenty or thirty years." [44]

In Hu Shih's view, then, the individual, insignificant though he must seem when measured against the vastness of the universe, may still participate as a creative force in the life of his society — creative in the sense in which Hu had used the term when he spoke of "creating new causes," that is, new forms and ideas that will in their turn affect the shape of things to come. Possessing this ability, the individual is obliged to use it responsibly, for "we shall be judged by what humanity will be when we shall have played our part." [45] The key to creative and responsible participation in history lies in the individual's awareness of the meaning of his own ideas and the significance of his own actions. "The new life is simply meaningful life," Hu wrote in 1919[46] — a life made mean-

---

43. *Ibid.* (Ch'en's response to Hu), Hu *hsü*, 40. The most thorough study of the "materialism" of both Hu Shih and Ch'en Tu-hsiu is D. W. Y. Kwok, *Scientism in Chinese Thought, 1900–1950* (New Haven and London, 1965), esp. chaps. 3 and 4.

44. *Short History,* 19–21.

45. "Credo," 259–260.

46. Hu Shih, "Hsin sheng-huo" (The new life), HSWT, iv, 1017.

ingful by developing within oneself a conscientiously self-critical habit of mind.

> Whenever you do something without asking yourself, "Why am I doing this?" — that is meaningless life . . . The "why" of life makes it meaningful.
> The difference between men and animals lies in this "why" . . . The life of animals is muddled and obscure simply because they do not know why they act as they do. A man's actions should always turn upon a final "why" . . . Only when an answer is given is one living life as a man.[47]

> Whenever one does not ask why one acts in a certain manner, one's conduct is based on unconscious habit. That is the conduct of lower animals, shameful conduct![48]

Although in Hu's mind the ultimate purposes of this questioning attitude were constructive, its immediate function was obviously destructive. It was aimed initially against the encumbrances of the tradition which still weighed so heavily on mind and spirit. In an essay directed to a peasant audience rather than the middle-school and university students to whom he usually addressed his thoughts, Hu illustrated this aspect of the "new life" with examples drawn from familiar experience: "Suppose that, starting today, you ask yourself the 'why' of everything you do — why not cut off your queue? Why not unbind your daughter's feet? Why should your wife use so much face powder? Why, when you set out to bury someone, must you call in all those beggars, and why, when you get married, must you again call in all those beggars?[49] Why, when you curse a man, must you always curse his forebears? . . . If you will try this for a day or two you will discover that [this word] is inexhaustible in its interest and unlimited in its usefulness."[50]

47. *Ibid.*, 1018–1019.
48. Hu Shih, "Wo tui-yü sang-li ti kai-ko" (Changes that I have made in the funeral rites), HSWT, iv, 1016. First published in HCN 6.6 (November 1919).
49. It was the custom in some parts of China to hire beggars to take part as chair bearers and the like in marriage and funeral processions.
50. "Hsin sheng-huo," HSWT, iv, 1019. See also "Ta-chung-yü tsai na-erh?" (Where is the language of the masses?), HSWT IV, iv, 531–534, where Hu states that his essay on the "new life" was aimed at a peasant audience.

At a more sophisticated level of discourse Hu translated this simple "why" into a demand for the adoption of a "critical attitude" that would lead to a "transvaluation of all values." [51] (The phrase was borrowed from Nietzsche, whom Hu praised for his "fearless criticism" of traditional morals and the "destructive merit" inherent in his philosophy,[52] though he had early considered and rejected the central message of Nietzsche's thought.)[53] In 1919 he described what he meant by "the critical attitude" in the following terms:

The real significance of the new thought lies simply in a new attitude . . . "the critical attitude."

In simple language, the critical attitude can be summarized as the application to all things of a fresh judgment as to whether or not they are good. In more detailed terms, the critical attitude comprises several specific demands:

(1) Concerning institutions and customs handed down to us by habit we must ask: "Do these institutions retain at present any value to justify their existence?"

(2) Concerning the sage precepts handed down to us by antiquity we must ask: "In the present day, does this phrase still hold true?"

(3) Concerning [standards of] conduct and beliefs commonly acknowledged, in a muddled way, by society we must ask: "Must something be right because it is generally held to be so by all? If others do this, must I also do this? Can it be that there is no other way of acting that is better than this, more reasonable, more beneficial?" [54]

When Hu thus exhorted the Chinese to break the bonds that chained them to the past, he was attempting to describe an attitude that would be oriented not exclusively against the past but also toward the needs of present and future. So, for example, when Ch'en Tu-hsiu early in 1919 (still in his pre-Marxist phase) asserted that in order to support the aims of the "new thought" — at that time personified by him as "Mr. Democracy" and "Mr. Science" —

51. "Hsin ssu-ch'ao ti i-i," HSWT, iv, 1023.
52. "Wu-shih nien lai chih shih-chieh che-hsüeh," HSWT II, ii, 230.
53. Diary, 434–435.
54. "Hsin ssu-ch'ao ti i-i," HSWT, iv, 1023.

one must necessarily oppose such things as the Confucian religion, the perpetuation of traditional rites and rituals, and the whole body of classical literature,[55] Hu Shih objected to the logic of Ch'en's defense of modernism. It was, he contended, "too much of a generalization," in spite of the "simple clarity" of Ch'en's reasoning. Moreover, it was an argument addressed too much toward the disestablishment of traditional values, and not enough toward the establishment of the new values of science and democracy. Ch'en had supplied, as Hu put it, an answer to the question, "Why must we oppose the old thought and the old morality?" The real need was for an answer to the question, "Why must we oppose all those things that are opposed to democracy and science?" [56]

The value of the critical attitude, as Hu conceived of it, was thus not restricted to its obvious use as a weapon against traditional prejudices. Put to proper use it would guard against the uncritical acceptance of any idea, regardless of its origin. "Conformity" and "blind following" were intellectual sins whether the standards to which one conformed were those of traditional Confucianism or of some new and alien dogma. The critical attitude, Hu wrote in 1919, "acknowledges only right and wrong, good or bad, suitability or unsuitability — it does not acknowledge conformity to past or present, Chinese or foreign [standards]." [57]

This strikes to the heart of Hu's approach to intellectual change and the political and social reformation that must, he was confident, follow from it in due course. And here for the first time is manifested the tension that, by the end of 1919, was undermining Hu's relationship with Ch'en Tu-hsiu and other members of the Peking group who were looking already toward the brighter promises of Marxism. Before examining this rift in the leadership of the New Culture movement, however, something more must be said concerning the nature and extent of Hu's indebtedness to American pragmatism and to John Dewey.

In many of its essentials, Hu Shih's philosophy of social and intellectual reform, as it has been described in the preceding pages,

55. Ch'en Tu-hsiu, "Pen chih [Hsin ch'ing-nien] tsui-an chih ta-pien-shu" (In answer to the charges against this magazine), HCN 6.1 (January 1919); Tu-hsiu wen-ts'un, i, 361–363. See Chow Tse-tsung, The May Fourth Movement, 59.

56. "Hsin ssu-ch'ao ti i-i," HSWT, iv, 1022.

57. Ibid., 1031.

cannot truly be called either distinctive or original. It was very much the product of a particular time and situation, and many of the beliefs that went into it were held in common by others of the Peking intelligentsia in that era. Hu's concept of "social immortality," and the doctrine of individual responsibility derived from it, reflected a belief in the propriety of the intellectual's social concern that was as typical of his contemporaries as it had been, differently expressed, among his Confucian predecessors. His belief in evolutionary progress, which led him to stress the continuity of social experience even in a time of rapid and sweeping change, and which might make him appear out of place in a revolutionary milieu, was in fact quite in harmony with the temper of his circle, at least in those early years. Even the radical Ch'en Tu-hsiu, for example, observed in 1918, "Society is the collective life of individuals. If society is dissolved, there will be no memory or consciousness of the continuation of the individual after he dies. Therefore social organization and order should be respected." [58]

Where Hu Shih differed from some of his early associates — and it was a difference that became more obvious with the passage of time — was not in his espousal of liberated individualism but in his view of the qualities of intellectual independence that must be the mark of the individual's emancipation. He envisioned an individual strong enough in intellect and character to be able continuously to subject all standards of conduct and value, not excluding his own, to critical re-examination, and to deny any claim upon him to which he was unwilling to give intellectual assent. Hu was convinced that for China, as for the rest of the world, only the acceptance of this kind of "critical attitude" could prepare men to move into a more promising future. "In examining the demands of this age of ours," Hu wrote in 1922, "we must recognize that the greatest responsibility of mankind today, and its greatest need, is to apply the scientific method to the problems of human life." [59]

John Dewey's influence on Hu is clearly evident here, and so it was to Hu himself. It was Hu's habit, as noted earlier, to acknowledge that he had received from Dewey no more than an in-

58. Ch'en Tu-hsiu, "Jen-sheng chen-i" (Life's true meaning), HCN 4.2 (February 1918); *Tu-hsiu wen-ts'un*, i, 181–185, where it is dated Feb. 15, 1916. See also de Bary, *Sources*, 829–831.
59. "Wu-shih nien lai chih shih-chieh che-hsüeh," HSWT II, ii, 287.

tellectual methodology: "Dewey taught me how to think," he said,[60] or again, "It is from Professor Dewey that I have learned that the most sacred responsibility of a man's life is to endeavor to *think well.*" [61] Holding forth on the subject for his Chinese audiences, Hu invariably emphasized the methodological aspect of pragmatism, virtually to the exclusion of any other concerns: "From first to last, Dewey thought of pragmatism only as a methodology." [62] On the occasion of Dewey's departure from China in the summer of 1921, at the end of a two-year lecture tour that had taken him to many cities and provided him with innumerable platforms from which to preach his philosophy, Hu Shih epitomized his former teacher's message in these terms: "Professor Dewey has furnished us with no specific proposals concerning specific problems — such as communism, anarchism, or free love — [but] he has given us a philosophical method which enables us, through its use, to solve our own special problems." [63]

For Hu, experimentalism was no more than the methodology of doubt, a necessary (perhaps even inevitable) complement to the skeptical intellect. The purpose of the logical process that he borrowed from Dewey — the encounter with a problem, recognition of the problem, the postulation of hypothetical solutions to it, examination of the probable consequences of these hypotheses, and, finally, careful evaluation of the results attained in practice — was, as he wrote in his most detailed discussion of experimentalism, to enable men "to use their own intellectual powers to test and prove one by one the ideas and concepts gained from experience, and to maintain a critical attitude toward all institutions and customs, not using their ears instead of their eyes, nor muddleheadedly accepting the ideas of others as their own." [64] He regarded the "genetic" approach to the study of intellectual and social problems essentially as a means to a similarly skeptical end: "What is the 'genetic method'? It means simply to study the ways in which things originate, from whence they derive, and how they have come

60. Hu Shih, "Chieh-shao wo tzu-chi ti ssu-hsiang" (Introducing my own thought), HSWT IV, iv, 608.
61. "Credo," 255.
62. "Wu-shih nien lai chih shih-chieh che-hsüeh," HSWT II, ii, 289–290.
63. Hu Shih, "Tu-wei hsien-sheng yü Chung-kuo" (Mr. Dewey and China), HSWT, ii, 534.
64. Hu Shih, "Shih-yen chu-i" (Experimentalism), HSWT, ii, 478. First published in HCN 6.4 (April 1919). For Hu's discussion of the terms "pragmatism" and "experimentalism" see HSWT, ii, 409–410.

to their present form . . . For example, in studying 'the truth,' we should ask ourselves, Why does this idea enjoy the praise of men, why is it revered as 'truth'? Or in studying philosophical questions, we should ask, Why should this moral concept ('patriotism,' for example) be respected? Why should this custom ('concubinage,' for example) be commonly accepted? This kind of genetic method is a very important element in experimentalism." [65]

In Jamesian terms, Hu Shih was consistently "tough-minded": empirical, materialistic, pluralistic, and skeptical. He had no liking for James, whom he dismissed as a "propagandist for pragmatism" whose temperament was "fundamentally incompatible with pragmatism." [66] One of the few insights Hu was willing to borrow from James was the Jamesian concept of the relativity of truth. The truth, Hu proclaimed, is "man-made," "a tool of man," defined by the intellectual demands of a given situation, not a value inhering absolutely in any idea. "If perchance different realities should come into being tomorrow, rendering the concepts of former times no longer appropriate, then they would no longer be considered 'truths,' and we should proceed to seek other truths to replace them." [67] And who could deny that Chinese realities had changed?

> The ancients recognized [the Three Bonds and the Five Relationships] [68] as true, because in the clan society of antiquity such theories were useful. But now . . . the constitution of the nation has changed: of the "Three Bonds" the bond between minister and prince no longer exists, and of the "Five Relationships" the relationship between minister and prince also exists no more. Moreover, the bonds between father and son and between husband and wife can no longer be maintained [as they were formerly]. The "unalterable principles" of antiquity have become nonsense. There are many conservatives who feel that this is much to be regretted. But what, in fact, is regrettable

65. *Ibid.*, 416–417.
66. "Wu-shih nien lai chih shih-chieh che-hsüeh," HSWT II, ii, 250.
67. "Shih-yen chu-i," HSWT, ii, 435.
68. The "Three Bonds" (*san-kang*) were those connecting emperor and subject, husband and wife, and father and son; the "Five Relationships" (*wu-lun*) were those between emperor and subject (or prince and minister), father and son, husband and wife, elder brother and younger brother, and friend and friend. Taken together, "*san-kang wu-lun*" means simply the relationships essential to the preservation of Confucian society.

about it? If our clothes are ragged, we should exchange them for new . . . If this principle is no longer useful, we should exchange it. This is common sense.[69]

In Hu Shih's hands experimentalism was thus a weapon turned against the tradition. That he found it useful as such is easily understandable, for John Dewey, too, was an enemy of sterile traditionalism, of dogma, of institutions and habits that had lost their significance and purpose; he was the philosopher of a "world in process." In a sympathetic appraisal of his thought, Irwin Edman writes that Dewey "time and again reminds us . . . that government, laws, social institutions, arts both 'fine' and 'useful' are all complex active processes always in process of change . . . The key to meaningful life is growth; the constant alertness to, the freshening, the reshaping, the remaking of experience. The enemy of life (and its opposite) is rigidity and blind resistance to change. The function of intelligence is to be alertly critical of outmoded methods in society, in government, in feeling, in thought. This alertness applies also to those tendencies in human institutions and governments and laws and customs which render life more meaningful, more alive, at once more integrated and more varied." [70] Dewey himself summarized more cogently the aim of his teaching: "Not perfection as a final goal, but the ever-enduring process of perfecting, maturing, refining is the aim of living . . . Growth itself is the only moral 'end.' " [71]

It was precisely this conviction that Hu Shih endeavored to communicate to his Chinese audiences; it was to pursue this vision of the moral life that he strove to inspire a new spirit of individualism. It seems clear that, however he chose to define the extent of Dewey's influence on him, he had in fact borrowed from Dewey much more than the mere formulation of an intellectual methodology.

One of the things which undoubtedly drew Hu to Dewey in the first place was the latter's humanistic affirmation of the importance of social ethics as opposed to a transcendental morality, and the hearty antipathy with which Dewey regarded organized religion.[72] Hu could find in Dewey support for his own theory of

69. "Shih-yen chu-i," HSWT, ii, 435–436.
70. Irwin Edman, *John Dewey: His Contribution to the American Tradition* (New York, 1955), 31.
71. John Dewey, *Reconstruction in Philosophy*, 177.
72. See Oral History, 98.

social immortality, for Dewey, too, believed that the individual might discover a significance beyond his own finite existence in a sense of living within an enduring community. "There is a conceit fostered by a perversion of religion which assimilates the universe to our personal desires," wrote Dewey. "But there is also a conceit of carrying the load of the universe from which religion liberates us. Within the flickering inconsequential acts of separate selves dwells a sense of the whole which claims and dignifies them. In its presence we put off mortality and live in the universal." [73] What Dewey called the individual's "sense of the whole" was for Hu the "greater self." But with a striking difference in temper. In Hu's description of it the continuing communal existence is less a source of final spiritual consolation, as it appears to Dewey, than a tribunal privileged to sit in ultimate judgment on the "true worth" of the individual's life and works.

Hu's was the conceit of one who had taken upon himself "the load of the universe." He was unmoved by James's horrifying vision of "the utter wreck and tragedy" inherent in materialism.[74] On the contrary, he put himself forward proudly as an advocate of a "purely material and mechanistic scientific view of life." [75] Hu was equally indifferent to Dewey's admonition that "a humanistic religion, if it excludes our relation to nature, is pale and thin, as it is presumptuous, when it takes humanity as an object of worship." [76] Hu affirmed, on the contrary, that "to live for the sake of the species and posterity is religion of the highest kind."

The issue here, quite clearly, is not "religion" as Hu Shih invariably and Dewey sometimes used the term, to denote an irrelevant and superstition-ridden system of institutions and ideas. The issue, rather, is man's attitude toward himself and his world. Hu Shih might rightly claim that his conception of a "naturalistic universe" was not devoid of a sense of moral responsibility, and he could assert with some justice that it possessed a certain kind of austere beauty. What it lacked was what he lacked, an awareness

73. John Dewey, *Human Nature and Conduct* (New York, 1922), quoted in E. L. Schaub, "Dewey's Interpretation of Religion," in Schilpp, *The Philosophy of John Dewey*, 398.
74. William James, *Pragmatism*, 76.
75. KHYJSK, Hu *hsü*, 13.
76. John Dewey, *A Common Faith* (New Haven, 1934), quoted in George R. Geiger, *John Dewey in Perspective* (New York, 1958), 216.

of the vulnerability of the human spirit that had inspired James to awe and given Dewey his appreciation of humility.

The essential aim of Dewey's philosophy was to discover ways of bringing harmony out of disorganization, whether social or intellectual, through the creative understanding of experience. He thought of experience as an "interaction" or a "transaction," "a means of penetrating continually further into the heart of nature." [77] Hu Shih, though he might borrow much of Dewey's vocabulary, conceived of life in terms of a struggle against environment rather than a search for harmony with it. "Experience is life," he wrote, "and life is no more than the interrelated behavior of man and his environment, the application of thought to the guidance of all abilities" — thus far the argument is quite in keeping with the temper of Dewey's thought — but Hu concludes, "in order to *utilize* the environment, to *subdue* it, to *chain* it, to *control* it." [78] In his expositions of experimentalism Hu referred with evident approval to Dewey's assertion that reason exists only as a derivative of experience, not as "a ready-made antecedent which can be invoked at will and set into movement." [79] Yet his own thought reveals a greater debt to a kind of old-fashioned rationalism than he would have cared to acknowledge, and it is precisely such an invocation of reason that lies concealed in his vision of civilization triumphant over the forces of a hostile environment. [80]

An explanation of this difference lies, at least in part, in the fact that by the time Hu encountered Dewey's thought his own ideas were already too firmly fixed to be easily overturned. He owed more, in the formation of his intellectual disposition, to the unsophisticated skepticism of Fan Chen and Ssu-ma Kuang, and to his introduction to Spencer and Huxley through the medium of Yen Fu's translations, which stressed the elements of force, energy, and aggressiveness, than he owed to the subtler treatment of conflict that he later found in Dewey's experimentalism. [81]

77. John Dewey, *Experience and Nature*, rev. ed. (New York, 1929), x.
78. "Shih-yen chu-i," HSWT, ii, 449 (emphasis added).
79. John Dewey, *Human Nature and Conduct*, 196.
80. A very clear statement of this belief in rationalism is found in Hu Shih, "Ta Ch'en Hsü-ching hsien-sheng" (A reply to Mr. Ch'en Hsü-ching), TLPL no. 160:15–16 (July 21, 1935); see below, chap. viii at n. 115.
81. On Yen Fu's interpretation of Spencer and Huxley see Benjamin Schwartz, *In Search of Wealth and Power*, chaps. 3 and 4.

But there is more to it than this. It was possible for John Dewey to equate reason and experience because the circumstances in which he found himself did not compel him to conclude that there is a necessary antagonism between the two. Habit he regarded as an evil only if the actions inspired by it proved unsuited to the needs of the moment. "Only in a society dominated by modes of belief and admiration fixed by past custom is habit any more conservative than it is progressive . . . What makes a habit bad is enslavement to old ruts." Hence, "rationality . . . is not a force to evoke against impulse and habit," [82] because habit itself is not the enemy but the ally of experimentalist thinking.

The problem, then, is that the philosophy which Hu Shih endeavored to exploit as a rationale for cultural revolution is not, except within the domains of academic philosophy, a revolutionary creed. Experimentalism is enlivened more by the desire to conserve than by a compulsion to destroy. Its purpose, in social as in intellectual concerns, is not to cut men free from their past but to discover new and more harmonious connections between past and present. William James observed, in a discussion of his doctrine of truth, "New truth is always a go-between, a smoother-over of transitions. It marries old opinion to new fact so as ever to show a minimum of jolt, a maximum of continuity . . . The point I now urge you to observe particularly is the part played by the older truths . . . Their influence is absolutely controlling. Loyalty to them is the first principle." [83] John Dewey described the function of intelligence in very similar terms: "In its large sense, this remaking of the old through union with the new is precisely what intelligence is . . . Every problem that arises, personal or collective, simple or complex, is solved only by selecting material from the store of knowledge amassed in past experience and by bringing into play habits already formed . . . The office of intelligence in every problem that either a person or a community meets is to effect a working connection between old habits, customs, institutions, beliefs, and new conditions." [84]

Hu Shih was by no means unmindful of the essential conservatism of the experimentalist approach. As noted earlier, he was pre-

82. John Dewey, *Human Nature and Conduct*, 66, 196.

83. William James, *Pragmatism*, 51.

84. John Dewey, *Intelligence in the Modern World: John Dewey's Philosophy*, ed. Joseph Ratner (New York, 1939), 452; excerpted from *Liberalism and Social Action* (1935).

pared to go to extreme lengths to establish a historical setting for the vernacular literature movement, and the next chapter will examine his efforts, similarly motivated, to uncover in the Chinese past traces of an attitude toward the world that could be regarded as "scientific." Hu was singularly unaffected by a desire to assert China's equivalence to the West in terms of cultural or political accomplishment, and he seems to have remained remarkably immune to the psychological tensions that sometimes accompanied the realization of China's inadequacies.[85] He was, however, unalterably committed to the belief that innovation — intellectual, cultural, or political — could succeed in China only as a consciously considered stage in an ongoing evolutionary process that took its rise in past experience.

But the idea that change can be consciously promoted implies the existence of minds united in some degree in their acceptance of certain principles, aims, and methods, and consequently able to reconcile specific differences and to achieve a common understanding. A belief such as Hu's demands, in other words, a belief in the existence of a consensus. Or, as Dewey observed: "A consciously directed critical consideration of the state of present society in its causes and consequences is a pre-condition of projection of constructive ideas. To be effective, the movement must be organized; but this requirement does not demand the creation of a formal organization. It does demand that a sense of the need and opportunity should possess a sufficiently large number of minds. If it does, the results of their inquiries will converge to a common issue." [86]

85. Hu thus stands somewhat outside the mainstream of recent Chinese intellectual history, at least as the late Joseph R. Levenson has described it. In a series of stimulating studies Professor Levenson developed the thesis that a principal obstacle to intellectual reform in the period from 1840 to 1949 was the inability of would-be reformers to withstand the psychological threat of alienation from their cultural environment or, in other words, to reconcile a realization of the need for fundamental changes in the existing value structure with their need to remain "Chinese." This theory is set forth in J. R. Levenson, " 'History' and 'Value': The Tensions of Intellectual Choice in Modern China," in Arthur F. Wright, ed., Studies in Chinese Thought (Chicago, 1953), 146–194. It provides the underlying dynamic in J. R. Levenson, Liang Ch'i-ch'ao and the Mind of Modern China (Cambridge, Mass., 1953). And it is developed in dialectical fashion in J. R. Levenson, Confucian China and Its Modern Fate (Berkeley and Los Angeles, 3 vols., 1958, 1964, 1965).

86. John Dewey, Intelligence in the Modern World, 461; excerpted from Individualism Old and New (1930).

For John Dewey this may have been a reasonable expectation. Even as he struggled with the problems of a society in the process of rapid growth and change, he could feel some assurance that in America there was agreement on underlying methods and motives of action. Hu Shih, too, believed that individual minds, once informed, would "converge to a common issue." But he was soon to discover — though he was slow in comprehending the significance of the discovery — that in China no common opinion, no sense of common purpose, prevailed with respect to either immediate expediencies or ultimate aims.

Hu's faith in the experimental method rested on his belief in its universality. There were, he maintained, no a priori assumptions necessary to its effective application, no social or cultural preconditions to be met. But unquestionably Dewey *did* think in terms of certain assumptions that derived from Western, and particularly American, social experience, different in almost every important respect from the Chinese. Of crucial importance was the fact that Chinese society, even in the twentieth century, remained to a much greater degree than American society "dominated by modes of belief and admiration fixed by past custom."

Thus Hu Shih was, as Dewey was not, at war with his own past. The most he might share with Dewey was certain hopes for and expectations of the future; their views of the connection between past and future could not but be very dissimilar in temper. The Chinese were little interested in an attempt to "marry old opinion to new fact." Their aim, rather, was to use new fact to discredit old opinion, and any appeal to "experience" was necessarily an appeal to a past largely repudiated. Even Hu Shih's demand for a "transvaluation of all values" was designed not "to effect a working connection" with the past, but to serve as the justification for a new beginning.

Dewey sensed the dilemma more keenly perhaps than did his Chinese disciple. A few months before his departure from China in 1921 he observed — one is tempted to read into his thoughts the sense of bafflement so common among Westerners in China — that "the visitor spends his time learning, if he learns anything about China, *not* to think of what he sees in terms of the ideas he uses as a matter of course at home . . . It may be questioned whether the most enlightening thing he can do for others who are interested in China is not to share with them his discovery that China can be known only in terms of itself, and older European history." [87] But this was an opinion that Hu Shih could not yet permit himself to accept. All his hopes were founded on his faith in the universal applicability of reason and, equally important, in the common aspirations of reasonable men. To admit the uniqueness of Chinese conditions would be to deny to China the expectation of redemption.

This discussion of the difficulties inherent in an attempt to translate the essentials of experimentalism into terms that would make it useful in the Chinese situation should not blind us to the great appeal of the experimentalist approach in the China of the late teens and early twenties.[88] Hu Shih's essay "Experimentalism," published in *The New Youth* in April 1919, was timed to serve as an introduction for Dewey himself. The American professor found a ready audience awaiting him when he arrived in Shanghai early in May, virtually on the eve of the student demonstrations that erupted in Peking on May 4, imparting to that date its peculiar significance in the intellectual and political history of modern China. Dewey's presence, as the first Western scholar of such eminence to pay so extended a visit, undoubtedly enhanced both the popularity of his ideas and the stature of his most illustrious Chinese follower.

Conversely, Dewey's association with Hu may well have bestowed upon the American a prestige he would otherwise have lacked in this alien setting, for by this time Hu's reputation as a leading personality in the New Culture movement was firmly established. Though still under thirty, Hu was accepted by scholars of the older generation — by men like Ts'ai Yüan-p'ei and Liang Ch'i-ch'ao at least, who were themselves "modern" enough to ap-

87. John Dewey, "Is China a Nation?" *The New Republic* (Jan. 12, 1921), reprinted in *Characters and Events*, I, 240.

88. Brief appraisals of the popularity of "pragmatism" in China, especially in the 1920s, are found in Kuo Chan-po, *Chin wu-shih-nien Chung-kuo ssu-hsiang shih* (An intellectual history of China in the last fifty years; Peiping, 1935; republished in an enlarged edition, Hong Kong, 1965), 119–141, 251–255; O. Brière, *Fifty Years of Chinese Philosophy, 1898–1950* (trans. L. G. Thompson; London, 1956), 24–26; Chan Wing-tsit, "Trends in Contemporary Philosophy," in H. F. MacNair, ed., *China* (Berkeley and Los Angeles, 1951), 314–316; Chan Wing-tsit, "Hu Shih and Chinese Philosophy," *Philosophy East and West*, 6.1: 3–12 (April 1956); Homer H. Dubs, "Recent Chinese Philosophy," *Journal of Philosophy*, 35:345–355 (1938); Chow Tse-tsung, *The May Fourth Movement*, 176.

preciate his critical approach though they might argue with him on points of scholarly interpretation — as a perceptive interpreter of China's intellectual inheritance. When his first major work, *An Outline of the History of Chinese Philosophy,* was published early in 1919, it carried a flattering introduction by Ts'ai in which Hu's accomplishments as a student of Western thought were matched against his attainments as a follower of the Anhwei school of the Han Learning. (The latter compliment, at least, went wide of the mark, for it rested on the erroneous association of Hu Shih with the "Three Hus" of Chi-hsi; see above, chapter 1 at note 2.)

Among the younger generation of intellectuals Hu's reputation rested less upon his scholarly achievements than upon his image as an advocate of the literary revolution, a spokesman for the New Culture movement, and a representative of the "returned students," to whom there still clung an air of exotic glamour, not unmixed with suspicion. Many years later one such young intellectual recalled his first encounter with Hu Shih, on one of the occasions when Hu served as Dewey's interpreter at a lecture delivered in Shanghai in the early summer of 1919:

[Hu Shih] was at that time promoting the literary revolution and criticizing the traditions and customs of the past in the pages of *The New Youth,* and the young intellectuals of Shanghai all trembled at the mention of his great name, though none of us had ever seen him, or even seen photographs of him. On the tram [on the way to the lecture] we tried to imagine what kind of a person Hu Shih must be. We all assumed that he would be a model returned student, dressed in Western fashion and stiff as a ramrod [*pi-t'ing*], acting as though he were ten feet tall. But when he accompanied Dewey onto the platform he was wearing a long Chinese gown, and his manner was modest and deferential, not at all like most returned students, but rather resembling a traditional scholar.[89]

By 1919 Hu Shih's popularity was close to its zenith, and in intellectual circles at least his influence was widely felt. But his

89. Ch'eng T'ien-fang, "Wo so ch'in-chih ti Hu Shih-chih hsien-sheng" (The Mr. Hu Shih-chih for whom I mourn), in *Chi-nien Hu Shih-chih hsien-sheng chuan-chi* (A collection of memorials in honor of Mr. Hu Shih-chih; Taipei, 1962), 17. On Ch'eng T'ien-fang, who became a diplomat of some prominence, see Boorman, *Biographical Dictionary,* I, 289–291.

vision of the world and his program for social and intellectual reform did not go unchallenged. It was an exciting time. New ideas were flooding into the country. Familiar ideas were receiving new readings. With the support of such older European-trained intellectuals as Wu Chih-hui and Ts'ai Yüan-p'ei, anarchism had attained something of a following. Socialism and Marxism, discussed in desultory fashion since the turn of the century, attracted more serious interest in the wake of the Bolshevik success of 1917, and at Peita Marxist study groups had sprung up in 1918, partly under the sponsorship of Li Ta-chao. Whether as cause or effect, the student demonstrations of May and June 1919 marked a significant change in the climate of political opinion and in the temper of political activity, when for the first time the new vigor of Chinese intellectual life was translated into something at once tangible and forceful. Though it may be easier to perceive in retrospect the true dimensions of the changes that were soon to overtake the revolution, there was undeniably the prevailing sense in 1919 of a corner having been turned in China.[90]

Ever since his return from the United States Hu Shih had steadfastly refused to be drawn into discussions of explicitly political issues, in the belief, as he stated it time and time again, that the reconstruction of social institutions and the emancipation of thought must take precedence over the solution of China's immediate political problems. In the summer of 1919, however, when circumstances compelled him to assume for a time the editorship of *The Weekly Critic,* an unpretentious little review established late in 1918 by Ch'en Tu-hsiu and Li Ta-chao as an outlet for their political opinions, Hu seized upon the opportunity to unburden himself of the misgivings that the course of recent events had aroused in him.[91] In a series of essays published under the general title "Problems and Isms" he launched a frontal attack on what he chose to regard as the irresponsible fashion in which too many

90. For background on the intellectual ferment of this period see Tsi C. Wang, *The Youth Movement in China* (New York, 1927); Kiang Wen-han, *The Chinese Student Movement* (New York, 1948); Chow Tse-tsung, *The May Fourth Movement,* esp. chaps. 2, 3, 9–12; Benjamin I. Schwartz, *Chinese Communism and the Rise of Mao* (Cambridge, Mass., 1951), chaps. 1 and 2; Maurice Meisner, *Li Ta-chao and the Origins of Chinese Marxism,* esp. chaps. 2–5; Jean Chesneaux, *Le mouvement ouvrier chinois de 1919 à 1927* (Paris, 1962), chap. 1; Olga Lang, *Pa Chin and His Writings,* chaps. 2–4.

91. The rationale behind Hu's "anti-politics" position will be discussed in detail in Part III below.

of his fellow intellectuals had embraced sweeping generalizations to describe China's specific problems. "Devote more study to the solution of this or that problem," he urged them, "and indulge less in high-flown talk of the novelty of this theory or the cleverness of that one." [92] Theories — "isms," he argued, are nothing more than generalized statements of ideas that originated in a particular time and place as concrete proposals addressed to the solution of specific problems. Such proposals cannot be dissociated from their original context without first determining, through painstaking study, their applicability to new situations and conditions. But isms enjoy a dangerous vogue, Hu continued, because it is easier to speak in abstract terms than to engage in the detailed examination necessary if one is to achieve a genuine understanding of the nature of the problem.

> We don't study the standard of living of the ricksha coolie but rant instead about socialism; we don't study the ways in which women can be emancipated, or the family system set right, but instead we rave about wife-sharing [kung-ch'i chu-i] and free love; we don't examine the ways in which the Anfu Clique [the militarist power-group then in control of the Peking government] might be broken up, or how the question of [the political division between] north and south might be resolved, but instead we rave about anarchism. And, moreover, we are delighted with ourselves, we congratulate ourselves, because we are talking about fundamental "solutions." Putting it bluntly, this is dream talk . . . iron-clad proof of the bankruptcy of the Chinese intelligentsia . . . the death sentence for Chinese social reform! . . .

> The great danger of "isms" is that they render men satisfied and complacent, believing that they are seeking the panacea of a "fundamental solution," and that it is therefore unnecessary for them to waste their energies by studying the way to solve this or that concrete problem.[93]

In its tone this fusillade is reminiscent of the charge of intellectual irresponsibility that Hu had earlier leveled at those who

92. Hu Shih, "To yen-chiu hsieh wen-t'i, shao t'an hsieh 'chu-i'" (Study more problems, talk less of "isms"), HSWT, ii, 484.
93. *Ibid.*, 485–487.

defended traditional ways simply because they were traditional ("chastity is chastity"). But whereas he had previously criticized the inadequacy of such reasoning in order to expose the feebleness of traditionalist claims, his purpose now was to warn against the unthinking acceptance not of old ideas but of new ones. He was especially skeptical of the usefulness of "empty talk of 'isms' imported from abroad," [94] a stricture which seems somewhat anomalous in view of the foreign source of so much of his own inspiration and the importance that he attached to the introduction of foreign ideas. To the suggestion that in culturally stagnant societies the intellectual elite must sometimes borrow alien ideas to express their own ideals Hu responded with a lecture on the genetic method, cautioning against the appropriation of any alien theory without first arriving at an understanding of the historical context out of which it had come, the personality and circumstances of its author, the influences that had shaped his opinions, and, finally, the results already achieved in practice.[95]

What Hu was approaching here, albeit obliquely, was an attack on Marxism. Although his attitude toward Communism, especially as it was being tried in the Soviet Union, remained ambivalent for a number of years, his intellectual disagreement with Marxist doctrine as he heard it applied to the Chinese situation had crystallized by 1919 and remained constant thereafter. In Marxism he perceived all the intellectual sins that he had set himself to banish from the Chinese mind: dogmatism, adherence to arbitrary truths, an irresponsible use of terminology, and an uncritical acceptance of generalizations drawn from one historical and social context and applied to another. Moreover, Marxism offered the alluring and, in Hu's view, illusory promise of quick and all-embracing solutions to the whole range of China's problems, founded on an analysis of Chinese society that Hu did not think justified by the facts and on an interpretation of the revolutionary process with which he could not agree.[96]

It was not only for the purpose of discrediting ill-considered

---

94. *Ibid.*, 482.

95. Hu Shih, "Ssu lun wen-t'i yü chu-i" (A fourth discussion of problems and isms), HSWT, ii, 525–531. In this instance Hu was responding to criticism from Lan Chih-hsien, a member of Liang Ch'i-ch'ao's Chin-pu tang (Progressive party). See Lan's letter, reprinted in HSWT, ii, 498.

96. Hu's philosophical and political differences with the Marxists will be explored at greater length below, chap. vi.

generalizations that Hu Shih urged the study of specific problems as a first and essential step. He saw in this approach several advantages. The discussion of concrete problems would attract wider attention, Hu claimed, than could a windy theoretical dispute and would thus lead more readily to useful opposition and the resultant clarification of ideas. It would also enable men to anticipate the implications of theories as they applied to specific cases. Most important, it would nourish the capacity for critical and independent individual judgment that, more than anything else, Hu desired to encourage.[97] The study of specific and concrete problems was, in short, the key to the whole process of social and intellectual reconstruction — or, as Hu called it in more grandiose language, "the reconstruction of civilization."

> Civilization is not created in a vague and general fashion [*lung-t'ung-ti*], it is created bit by bit and drop by drop. Progress is not achieved in an evening, in a vague and general fashion, it is achieved bit by bit and drop by drop. Nowadays men are fond of talking about "liberation and reconstruction," [but] they must realize that liberation does not mean liberation at the level of vague generalities, and reconstruction does not mean reconstruction at the level of vague generalities. Liberation means liberation from this or that institution, from this or that belief, for this or that individual — it is liberation bit by bit and drop by drop. Reconstruction means the reconstruction of this or that institution, of this or that idea, of this or that individual — it is reconstruction bit by bit and drop by drop.
>
> The work which must serve as the first step in the reconstruction of civilization is the study of this or that problem. The progress of such a reconstruction of civilization means simply the solution of this or that problem.[98]

The only insight that Hu Shih borrowed from William James other than James's statement of the relativity of truth was his belief in the possibility that history may tend toward the better. For James, "meliorism" served to sanction his "right to believe." "Meliorism," he wrote, "treats salvation as neither necessary nor impossible. It treats it as a possibility, which becomes more and more

97. "Hsin ssu-ch'ao ti i-i," HSWT, iv, 1029–1030.
98. *Ibid.*, 1034.

of a probability the more numerous the actual conditions of salvation become." [99] Although Hu Shih was entirely indifferent to James's desire to justify a religious faith, he used the argument to support his own view of the future, and he spoke with less caution. "The salvation of the world is not impossible; nor is it something that we can catch sight of merely by putting our hands in our sleeves and raising our eyes. The salvation of the world is attainable, but it is necessary for each of us to set to work with all our strength. If we exert a little more effort, the salvation of the world will come a little sooner. The world is built little by little, a bit at a time. But even this little depends entirely upon the energetic contributions of you and me and the other fellow." [100]

Such, in brief, was Hu's gradualism: slow, undramatic, promising no startling results, yet for all its slowness an optimistic creed. But it placed a heavy burden of responsibility upon the individual. Hu envisioned a new breed of men, able to stand free from the prejudices of the past and to reject the false promises of the present, and prepared to move with confidence into a future made hazardous by constantly shifting and changing conditions. He sought to create a society bound together solely by a common appreciation of certain basic principles, chief among them the conviction that "growth is the only moral end." He envisioned a society in which all are leaders and none are led.

It was a benign vision, but a difficult one. And there were others upon the scene anxious to persuade China's youth to move toward different and more certain goals. Already by 1919 Li Tachao had espoused Marxism, and Ch'en Tu-hsiu was soon to follow, drawn by its incisive and uncompromising judgments of the present and its imposing image of the future. The early 1920s witnessed a dramatic growth in the popularity of Marxism and in the strength of an organized Communist movement, partly in response to the increasingly fervent nationalism of those years.

Hu Shih recognized the incompatibility between his own opinions and the Marxist point of view, and as the 1920s progressed he came more and more to sense the threat to his position inherent in the quickening of nationalist emotions. In the end it was these forces against which the liberal cause would break itself. But at the time what seemed a more serious challenge to Hu's position

99. William James, *Pragmatism*, 185.
100. "Shih-yen chu-i," HSWT, ii, 441.

came from a different quarter, from a resurgent traditionalism that sought its inspiration not in the modern civilization of the West but in China's ancient system of values. Hu might argue with Ch'en Tu-hsiu as to the meaning of material causes and take Li Ta-chao to task for oversimplifying complex issues. But after a fashion these men were, if not his natural allies, at least not his sworn enemies in a struggle against the forces of the past come back to haunt the present. For they, like him, looked not backward but ahead; their gaze, like his, was turned outward toward the world, not inward upon the mind or the spirit. And they, like him, professed a belief in the importance of scientific judgments. It was on this latter point that the new traditionalists, following the lead of Liang Ch'i-ch'ao, concentrated their attack. They denied that it was either possible or desirable to "apply the scientific method to the problems of human life," and they condemned as materialistic the culture that had given birth to so dehumanized a view of the world. The next chapter will examine the claims put forward by these neo-traditionalists and the responses that they provoked from Hu Shih and other defenders of Western civilization and scientific values.

Chapter 5. China and the West

In the middle of October 1919 Liang Ch'i-ch'ao settled down with several friends to spend the winter in a small pension in a suburb of Paris.[1] The group had come to Europe early in the year as an unofficial delegation to the peace conference from which the Chinese had expected so much and in the end received so little. They had spent the spring and summer on a whirlwind tour of European

[1]. The members of Liang's company included, besides himself, Chiang Fang-chen (*tzu* Po-li), Liu Ch'ung-chieh (*tzu* Tzu-k'ai), Ting Wen-chiang (*tzu* Tsai-chün), Chang Chia-shen (*tzu* Chün-mai), Hsü Hsin-liu (*tzu* Chen-fei), and Yang Wei-hsin (*tzu* Ting-fu). Only Chiang, Chang, and Hsü accompanied Liang to Paris in the autumn, however. By this time Ting had returned to China, Yang was in England, and Liu was in Switzerland.

capitals, a dizzying experience, "like going on horseback to view the flowers." By the time they returned wearily to Paris the weather had turned unseasonably cold. Their accommodations, intended only for summer use, afforded scant protection against the early winter chill. Outside a frost-edged wind rattled the bare branches of the chestnut trees and rustled through the withered beds of chrysanthemums and begonias in the garden, while Liang and his friends huddled wretchedly around an insufficient fire in the cramped parlor, so absorbed in their various tasks that they seldom ventured even as far as the great city that lay only twenty minutes away. "We live like students," Liang observed. "Not poor students, but still like students." He himself was studying English and using part of the time to put on paper his impressions of the year just passed.[2]

It is hardly surprising that an account of European life written under these conditions should have reflected a degree of disenchantment with the culture which had earlier inspired Liang's admiration. Nor was he alone in his pessimism. Others who were in Europe at the same time appraised the situation in similar terms, among them men like T'ao Meng-ho and Ting Wen-chiang (*tzu* Tsai-chün, V. K. Ting, 1887–1936), who were themselves European-educated and who in the end remained true to their faith in European values.[3] The importance of Liang's *Impressions of Travels in Europe* (*Ou-yu hsin-ying lu*) lay not so much in his description of the European crisis as in the conclusions that he drew from it. His indictment of science and the scientific mentality, his emphasis on a dichotomy between "material" and "spiritual" life, and his frequent references to European anxieties concerning the future of Western civilization all seemed to justify, and even to necessitate,

2. Liang Ch'i-ch'ao, preface to "Ou-yu hsin-ying lu, chieh-lu" (A condensed record of impressions of travels in Europe), *Yin-ping-shih ho-chi, chuan-chi* V, xxiii, 1–2; Ting Wen-chiang, *Liang Jen-kung hsien-sheng nien-p'u ch'ang-pien ch'u-kao* (First draft of an extended· chronology of the life of Liang Jen-kung; Taipei, 1959), 565.

3. Ting Wen-chiang's views are dealt with in the discussion that follows. For the opinions expressed by T'ao Meng-ho see "Chan-hou chih Ou-chou" (Postwar Europe), in *Meng-ho wen-ts'un* (Collected essays of [T'ao] Meng-ho; Shanghai, 1925), 65–78 (first published under the title "Yu Ou chih kan-hsiang" [Impressions of travels in Europe], HCN 7.1 [December 1919]); and "Ou Mei chih lao-tung wen-t'i" (The labor problem in Europe and America), *Meng-ho wen-ts'un*, 79–94 (first published in HCN 7.2 [January 1920]).

a radical reassessment of China's cultural and intellectual relationship to the West. Thus it was Liang who enunciated themes that were later more fully developed by others in a revitalized attack on the idea of the "westernization" of China.

Since his return to China in 1917, Hu Shih had been expounding ideas that he regarded as essential to the modernization of Chinese attitudes. The fact that these ideas were of Western origin was, to his way of thinking, a fact of only incidental significance. The important thing was that they were modern, in contrast to the old-fashioned opinions of men like K'ang Yu-wei and Lin Shu. Such earlier opponents of the New Culture had been deeply attached to the style, as it might be called, of traditional Chinese life. They decried republicanism, they bemoaned the abandonment of Confucian social standards, they denounced the vulgarity of *pai-hua,* all in the name of a political and social order that was passing but which they themselves had known.

The neo-traditionalists like Liang Ch'i-ch'ao, on the other hand, were not much interested in the style of traditional life. They were far more interested in, and concerned for, what they regarded as the substance of traditional Chinese culture. Their attempt to discredit the West in terms of contemporary and universal human values, rather than the values of a uniquely Chinese tradition, and their reliance on European self-criticism to substantiate their own claims, posed an unfamiliar challenge to the sponsors of a "new culture" founded on modern — and Western — example. Hu Shih, arguing still for reform rather than revolution, and for modernization rather than westernization, was compelled to state his case increasingly in terms of East versus West. In the process he came more and more to identify the East with reaction and the West with progress.

Liang's *Impressions of Travels in Europe* begins with a bleak description of the degradation of European life in the aftermath of World War I. The war, Liang proclaimed, had brought Europe to the brink of social and intellectual disintegration, so that even those institutions and ideals that had appealed so strongly to progressive Chinese a few years earlier now seemed dangerously infirm. Liang viewed the prospect, one suspects, with a trace of ironic satisfaction:

Who would have dared to say [before the war] that the most excellent and beautiful, the unalterable, principles of parliamentary government would today be shaken to their very foundations, so that no one is willing to guarantee their future? Who would have dared to say that England, France, and Germany, those rich old men, would in the end be talking just as poor as we are, and be forced to rely on high-interest loans to survive? Who, again, would have dared to say the day would indeed come when the flourishing nations of Europe, with their people [used to] living in comfort, would want coal, and there would be no coal; when they would want grain, and there would be none; when the very necessities of life would cause furrowed brows in every household . . . ? [4]

We, of course, are accustomed to a simple and doltish life, but for all that we have experienced all kinds of distressing discomfort. *They* have been living these many years in the shelter of their enormously wealthy and convenient material civilization. Now the rich man has money, but nowhere can he buy anything with it; the poor man who once bought something for one coin cannot now buy it for several. How can they live? [5]

Across this war-stricken landscape Liang saw "the dark tide of social revolution" sweeping in. It was, he said, the inevitable result of the nineteenth-century revolt against political and religious authority, a struggle fought in the name of individual freedom, culminating in the repudiation of all spiritual values. Instead of the bright hope of progress that had inspired him in the early years of the century, Liang now saw in Europe only a reckless waste of energy in the struggle for wealth and power and a thoughtless pursuit of militaristic and imperialistic ambition. The result, he wrote, was certain: "Social revolution is probably the only peculiar characteristic of the twentieth century. No country can avoid it: it is only a matter of whether it comes late or soon." [6]

It was against this background that Liang made his celebrated attack on the Western "dream of the omnipotence of science." Faith in science, Liang argued, had in the end destroyed man's faith in himself. As a result the confusion and uncertainties of the

4. Liang Ch'i-ch'ao, "Ou-yu hsin-ying lu," 3–4.
5. *Ibid.,* 6.
6. *Ibid.,* 8.

material world had invaded the once tranquil recesses of the human spirit. "Originally this inner life could exist as a thing apart from the external life, sustained by the authority of religion and philosophy, etc. But what of modern man? The first victim of the development of science was religion [and] speaking frankly, the philosophers have all hastened to rally to the banner of the scientists." Even the human spirit has been made subject to materialistic determinism. Hence "human free will must be denied; and if the will is not free, how can there be any responsibility for good or evil? . . . It is no longer a question of a standard of virtue, but of whether or not virtue itself can survive. The great crisis of contemporary thought lies just in this." [7]

The trouble with science, Liang continued, is that it cannot establish enduring truths in place of those it has destroyed, for scientific "truths" are constantly changing in response to new experience. So "the new authority cannot, in the end, become firmly rooted, nor can the old authority be restored. Thus the spirit of the whole society has sunk into doubt, profound depression, and fear." The Europeans live "under the leaden skies of autumn." [8]

This pessimistic analysis of the spiritual decadence of European civilization served as a preface to the second and more important part of Liang's message. He traced the development in recent European thought of ideas that held forth the promise of a regeneration of European life: a reaction against the harsh tyranny of materialism; Kropotkin's doctrine of "mutual aid" as a corrective to earlier and more brutal theories of social and political evolutionism; and, within the realm of philosophy, a reaffirmation of the possibility of a "spiritual life" in the writings of Eucken and Bergson. Liang turned to Bergson with particular enthusiasm, for he discovered in the Bergsonian idea of "creative evolution" a means of salvaging the faith in evolutionary progress that had lain close to his heart since the early days of his association with K'ang Yu-wei. "We know that the evolutionary cycle is the essential fact of the world; and we know, too, that [control over] the evolutionary process is within our power. This thought naturally imbues us with a spirit of dauntlessness." [9]

7. *Ibid.*, 10, 11.
8. *Ibid.*, 11, 14.
9. *Ibid.*, 18.

But Liang expressed grave doubt as to the ability of these temperate elements in the European mind to survive the bitter disillusionment of the postwar era unless they could be reinforced from outside. It was at this point, as Liang saw it, that a consideration of the ideals that had inspired Chinese civilization became imperative. The real dilemma of Western thought, he contended, derived from the habitual Western inclination to separate "the ideal" from "the practical." It was precisely on this point that the Chinese had never erred: no artificial distinction between ideals and practice had developed to plague Chinese thought. Despite their differences, China's sages had engaged in a common "search for consistency in ideal and practical application." If their example could be followed in the present time, Liang asserted, "I know not how many frontiers we will be able to conquer!" [10]

Liang did not define the "ideal" to which he aspired, but he left little doubt that to him it meant a system of values founded on the humane insights of Chinese philosophy, opposed in every respect to the dehumanized materialism rampant in the West. Although he ridiculed those who insisted that the West possessed nothing worthwhile that was not also intrinsic in Chinese culture, he was equally hard on those who viewed the Chinese past as a cultural desert. He conceded that in certain respects Confucianism was dated. The Confucian "aristocratic ethic," for example, could not be revived in the twentieth century. But why, Liang asked, should one therefore discard the whole body of Confucian thought, any more than one would reject the insights of Greek political thinkers merely because they had accepted as a matter of course the existence of a slave society?[11] Liang acknowledged that a "true understanding" of the Chinese past was essential, and that this could come only from an applicaion of the exacting methods of Western scholarship — so far, at least, he was willing to go in meeting the demand for a "new culture." But, he insisted, this re-examination of the Chinese tradition could only be undertaken in the spirit of genuine affection for it. Out of such an enterprise would come a new "cultural system" incorporating both Chinese and Western elements and promising spiritual redemption to all mankind. In the end Liang was moved by a truly evangelistic zeal:

10. *Ibid.*, 36.
11. *Ibid.*, 37.

The greatest goal in life is to make a contribution to the whole of humanity. Why? Because the fullest measure of "myself" is found only in the whole of humanity . . .

Our people constitute one fourth of the world's population: we should assume one fourth of the responsibility for the happiness of mankind as a whole. If we do not meet this responsibility, then we will not be able to face our ancestors, nor our contemporaries, nor, in fact, ourselves. Our beloved youth! Attention! Forward march! On the other shore of the great sea are millions of men bewailing the bankruptcy of material civilization and crying out most piteously for help, waiting for us to come to their salvation![12]

Liang Ch'i-ch'ao's *Impressions* is the product of a mind deeply attached to the culture that had nourished it. But his is a traditionalism reduced to the barest essentials. There is here no insistence on the preservation of the forms of Confucian life. What Liang proposed, rather, was an attempt to cleanse the Chinese tradition of the accumulated distortions that had gradually obscured its underlying significance and value. He aspired on the one hand to liberate his countrymen from their infatuation with ideas that had led the West into doubt and despair, and on the other to encourage them to reaffirm, in language suited to the present, the enduring ideals that he perceived at the heart of traditional Chinese civilization — ideals from which the West, too, might draw renewed strength and courage.

A similar hope inspired Liang Sou-ming, the author of a series of lectures, *The Cultures of East and West and Their Philosophies* (*Tung Hsi wen-hua chi ch'i che-hsüeh*), collected and published under that title early in 1922. Liang Sou-ming's treatise is in part an elaboration of themes already suggested by Liang Ch'i-ch'ao, but though their views coincided on certain points, Liang Sou-ming's work was more speculative in temper and more conservative in mood, and he was frequently critical of Liang Ch'i-ch'ao's conclusions.

Liang Sou-ming began with a concise statement of the question that haunted him: "Can oriental culture in the end survive?" [13]

12. *Ibid.*, 35–38.
13. Liang Sou-ming, *Tung Hsi wen-hua chi ch'i che-hsüeh* (The cultures of East and West and their philosophies; Shanghai, 1922), 4.

His conclusion, reached after tortuous and erudite reasoning, was that "in essence, the future culture of the world will be a renaissance of Chinese culture." [14] He rejected emphatically the suggestion put forward by Liang Ch'i-ch'ao, Hu Shih,[15] and others that the future "world culture" would be one of complementary association, a synthesis of Eastern and Western elements. He insisted, to the contrary, that qualitative cultural differences would render such a synthesis impossible. "If we are going to live a Chinese-style life," he contended, "it must be a completely Chinese-style life." [16] He ridiculed the attempt — which he ascribed specifically to Liang Ch'i-ch'ao — to label as Chinese those ideas that might with equal justice be credited to Europeans.[17] "If something Chinese is valued only insofar as it resembles something Western, then still it is inferior and without any value whatsoever. If Chinese culture is to be prized, it must be prized on the strength of its own particular characteristics." [18] To justify his insistence on irreconcilable cultural diversity he postulated a theory of human psychology and cultural genesis, which must be considered in order to understand his subsequent analysis of the relationship between China and the West.[19]

14. *Ibid.*, 199.

15. Hu Shih had implied as much in the preface to his *Chung-kuo che-hsüeh shih ta-kang, shang chüan* (An outline of the history of Chinese philosophy, I; Shanghai, 1919), *tao-yen*, 5–6. He made the point explicit in a number of later writings.

16. Liang Sou-ming, *Tung Hsi wen-hua chi ch'i che-hsüeh*, 8.

17. Liang Sou-ming was commenting here on Liang Ch'i-ch'ao's account of a discussion he had had with the leaders of a European socialist party, to whom he had discoursed on such Confucian maxims as "Within the four seas, all men are brothers," and, "Do not grieve that there is little, but that what little there is is unequally shared." He had spoken also of Mo-tzu's doctrine of universal love, and he capped the climax with a description of the *ching-t'ien* (well-field) system of land tenure, a system, attributed to the earliest ages of Chinese history, that had embodied, in the view of later Chinese scholars, certain elements of socialistic egalitarianism. Whereupon, Liang reported, "these gentlemen leaped to their feet and cried, 'If you possess such treasures and are content to hoard them away, without sharing a little with us, that would indeed be unforgivable!' " See Liang Ch'i-ch'ao, "Ou-yu hsin-ying lu," 36.

18. Liang Sou-ming, *Tung Hsi wen-hua chi ch'i che-hsüeh*, 14.

19. In his discussion of Liang Sou-ming's thought, Lyman van Slyke stresses the "universalism" of Liang's approach and his "denial of permanent cultural diversity." See Lyman P. van Slyke, "Liang Sou-ming and the Rural Reconstruction Movement," *Journal of Asian Studies*, 18.4:460 (August 1959). As he looked ahead to the ultimate triumph of Confucian values, Liang did perhaps

Liang equated "culture" with "a way of life." "Life" itself he defined as a continuous sequence of satisfactions and dissatisfactions, or as what he called the "unfulfilled will." [20] Culture, the way of life of a people, reflects the ends toward which the "unfulfilled will" is directed.[21] It is thus bound up with the relationship between man and his environment.

Liang rejected the Marxist-materialist view that man is merely the passive subject of "objective" forces, incapable of playing any part in the shaping of his own destiny. He recognized instead only "subjective" causes, maintaining that what is usually termed an "objective" cause is itself only the consequence of a subjective cause. Thus culture is not determined simply by (objective) geographic and economic factors, but by the (subjective) creative energies of men. Liang conceded to the materialists the validity of their contention that man is incapable of consciously controlling his environment. But he would not admit that man is impotent in his confrontation with the natural order. Into the tightly reasoned circle of materialist logic Liang introduced a factor that he called "the spirit." The spirit, he maintained, is the source of the demands that men make of their environment, and thus it is responsible for the creation of the "objective" factors that contribute directly to cultural development. In defining these objective factors Liang adhered closely to an economic interpretation of history.[22]

Liang Sou-ming was an earnest student of Buddhism, a lecturer on Buddhist and Indian philosophy at Peita in the early 1920s. His concept of the spirit rested on a view of life which owed a considerable debt to Buddhist ideas and terminology. He viewed life as a continuous sequence of causes and consequences, or, in another dimension, as a continuous sequence of questions and responses, a constant dialogue between the individual and his sur-

---

believe that eventually cultural diversity would diminish and finally vanish. But his primary concern, as I understand him, was to explain and interpret China's relationship to diverse cultural systems existing in the present time.

20. This term Liang claimed to use "approximately" in the sense in which Schopenhauer used it. It is impossible, however, to reconcile Liang's quite Confucian belief in the essential goodness of human nature with Schopenhauer's view of man as a passionate animal, and consequently it is hard to see in Liang's concept of the will (which he regards as the means through which men realize their capacity for good) any similarity to the malevolent forces represented by Schopenhauer as manifestations of the will.

21. Liang Sou-ming, *Tung Hsi wen-hua chi ch'i che-hsüeh*, 24.

22. *Ibid.*, 44, 47.

roundings, a never-ending flow of "ideas" thus stimulated.[23] In this interrogative process the individual makes use of his senses, his feelings, and his intellect. The process itself is entirely spontaneous, spurred by the unconscious demands of the "unfulfilled will."

Liang then restated this concept in terms of temporal relationships. Environment, he said, is simply the situation in which one finds oneself, the status quo or, as he called it, the "anterior self" (*ch'ien-tz'u ti wo*), the "self already formed" (*i-ch'eng ti wo*). The spirit, or the unfulfilled will, or the "present self" (*hsien-tsai ti wo*) acts upon this existing situation by making demands on it. The "present self" and the "anterior self" are essentially in conflict, and this unconscious and instinctive process of demands and responses, moment by moment, is what is meant, Liang said, by adaptation to environment.[24] It is interesting to observe in passing that in his emphasis on the process of question and response and on the importance of environment as a conditioning factor Liang seems to show a "pragmatic" bias. John Dewey was lecturing to Chinese audiences in 1920 and 1921 when Liang Sou-ming's ideas were taking shape, and one may gather that Liang knew something of Dewey from the fact that he cites Dewey — together with James, Nietzsche, Russell, Eucken, and, especially, Bergson — as evidence of the changing concerns of Western philosophers in the modern age.[25] But Liang puts himself at a great distance from pragmatic assumptions when he comes to describe the way in which human responses to environment are expressed.

Liang, then, defined "culture" as a "way of life," and "life" as the relationship between the individual and his environment. Cultural differences arise from differences in this relationship, or as Liang put it, placing his emphasis characteristically on "subjective" factors, from "differences in will." On this basis he identified three possible attitudes: first, an attitude of active struggle against the frustrations that arise in man's relationship with the world around him; second, an attitude that seeks to accommodate to the situation rather than to struggle against it; and finally, a response that escapes the frustration by denying the existence of the conflict.[26] These attitudes, Liang contended, reflect the necessary and proper

23. *Ibid.*, 48–49.
24. *Ibid.*, 49–50.
25. *Ibid.*, 176–177.
26. *Ibid.*, 54.

preoccupation of mankind at given stages in its historical development. The first is appropriate to the age in which the essential problem is still that of physical survival, when human mastery of the forces of nature is a matter of primary importance. But once man's material appetites have been satisfied such aggressiveness engenders crises in social relationships. At this point the attitude of accommodation — the second in Liang's scheme of things — comes into its own, for the crucial problem is no longer individual but social survival. Ultimately, Liang suggested, man will move on to a final stage in which he will devote attention neither to the world around him nor to his relationship with other men, but to the problem of understanding his own nature.[27]

As Liang described them, these three stages of development should not exist contemporaneously but should follow one upon the other, each supplementing its predecessor at the appropriate historical moment: "A particular kind of culture has no value until the time when it is necessary arrives." [28] What Liang envisioned was not a dialectical development but progress through distinct phases along an historico-cultural continuum.

But different cultures do exist at the same time in history: the essential issue that Liang was trying to explain was that of cultural disparity between China and the West. To this end he applied his scheme of cultural stages to the contemporary situation, attributing to European, Chinese, and Indian cultures respectively the characteristics of the cultural archetypes he had described. Western culture was obviously the prototype of the first stage: aggressive, forward-looking, absorbed in the task of asserting man's dominion over nature. To China Liang ascribed the attitude of the second stage, essentially passive and accommodating in its view of the relationship between man and his environment. In the culture of India he perceived the final stage of introspective quietism.[29]

By thus attributing to coexistent cultures the attitudes which should, in his original formulation of the idea, occur instead in sequence, Liang attempted to explain Western strength and Chinese weakness and, at the same time, to justify his contention that, in spite of appearances, in the future it would be a Chinese way of life that would attain universal ascendancy. Western superiority at

27. *Ibid.*, 166–167.
28. *Ibid.*, 200.
29. See *ibid.*, the final sections of chap. 4 and the whole of chap. 5.

the present time, he argued, is the natural consequence of the fact that the West, and only the West, had developed in ways appropriate to the conditions in which man had lived until now, struggling singlemindedly to bend nature to human purposes. "The triumph of Western culture lies simply in its adaptation to the immediate problems of mankind; the present failure of Chinese and Indian cultures cannot be attributed to their intrinsic qualities — it is only that [these cultures] have been unsuited to their times. In its initial stages human culture cannot but pursue the first course; the Chinese naturally were this way too. They did not explore this course to its end, however, but switched at the midpoint to the second course . . . Moreover, they thus forfeited their position on the first course, and in a world [dominated by] problems of the first kind they have suffered a great defeat." [30]

Liang found much to admire in the West, or so he said. He spoke of the "dazzling lights" of science and democracy, which to him as to a good many others epitomized Western accomplishment. Yet in the comparisons he drew between Western and Chinese attitudes he hardly concealed his preference for the latter. Western science, he said, is founded on "the objective recognition of true knowledge," while the Chinese view of the world is based on "a complete scorn for objective standards and regulations, and a respect for natural talent alone." [31] In the West it is regarded as essential that language should seek "clearly to define [the nature of something]," while in the East there is a preference for language that "touches upon something without defining it." [32] To put it another way, Westerners constantly strive for improvement and modernization, Chinese for the maintenance of traditional standards. On the subject of democracy Liang observed that the concepts of individualism and social spirit (she-hui-hsing) fundamental to the complex democratic institutions of the West are utterly alien to the Chinese, and that the whole intent of democratic processes seems incomprehensible and socially disruptive to a people who

30. *Ibid.*, 199–200.
31. *Ibid.*, 24, 21.
32. The well-known Japanese novelist Tanizaki Junichiro has written, "Orientals find beauty not only in the thing itself, but in the pattern of shadows, the light and the darkness, which that thing produces . . . I would call back at least for literature this world of shadows we are losing." "In Praise of Shadows," an English adaptation by Edward Seidensticker, *The Atlantic*, 195.1:144 (January 1955).

have never entertained any idea of rights as opposed to authority, or of limitations on either power or freedom.[33]

Underlying the development of science and democracy in the West Liang perceived two dominant intellectual commitments: reason and utility. From antiquity to the present day the tendency of Western philosophy has been to encourage an attitude of rational calculation and a uniquely occidental concept of the "self." "The development of modern Western culture," he wrote, "is entirely due to self-assertion [wei-wo] and the use of reason." Liang was willing to concede that the Western attitude of "labored calculation" had played a necessary part in the development of human society. He contended, however, that its final result was to give rise to the conviction that the universe is constituted of random, dead, and purposeless fragments, and that as a consequence the individual has become fearful and distrustful, sure only of himself. Western civilization has become "dehumanized." [34]

Here we approach the heart of Liang's argument, and begin to see the purpose behind it. The Chinese, Liang proclaimed, have never valued reason above intuition, or utility above sentiment. Therein has lain the fatal weakness of their civilization, and its redeeming virtue.

We have said that in the West the assertion of naturally endowed rights and the perfecting of the ideal of individualism were dependent upon the development of the concept of self. But a result of this is that the lines of demarcation between individuals must be very clearly drawn. As soon as you open your mouth, you must speak in terms of rights and obligations, legal relationships, through which everyone holds everyone else to account, even to the point of affecting the relationship between father and son or man and wife. Such life is truly unreasonable [pu-ho-li]; it is really too harsh. The Chinese attitude is the precise opposite of this: Westerners use their intellect, Chinese use their intuition, their emotions. Westerners have the "self," Chinese do not want the "self" . . . [Chinese social relationships] enable a man to take no thought of himself, but to sublimate himself to others. He draws no line separating himself from other men and does not speak of rights and obliga-

33. Liang Sou-ming, *Tung Hsi wen-hua chi ch'i che-hsüeh*, 34–43.
34. *Ibid.*, 155–158, 175, 178.

tions. The precepts of "filial piety" [hsiao], "brotherly affection" [ti], and "modesty" [li-jang] in each case exalt the emotions and contain no trace of the self. But because the spiritual ideal of Confucianism was never realized, there existed [in imperial China] only a few ancient ceremonial regulations and lifeless precepts which tended heavily in the direction of a dark and tomblike oppression and caused no little suffering. *But nevertheless* within the family and in society at large it was always possible to achieve a kind of satisfaction, not of a cold, indifferent, hostile, and calculating kind, [but of a kind] to give much vigor to the spirit of life. This cannot but be reckoned a great excellence and a great triumph.[35]

In Liang's terms, this description of traditional Chinese social values is a description of a society in the second stage of cultural development. It was this that gave Liang his faith in the historical importance of "the Chinese way." He had admitted that China turned too soon from the "first course" and had thus fallen far behind the West. But on the evidence of recent European history Liang maintained that the West had now pursued the first course to its extremity and had succumbed to economic and social crises that attested to a condition of intellectual and spiritual exhaustion. In his description of contemporary Europe, drawn at second hand from Liang Ch'i-ch'ao and others, Liang dwelt at length on the impending social catastrophes that they forecast. But always foremost in his mind was the spiritual degradation that such conditions entailed. "The current economic situation and the violence that it does to human nature — that is, to the quality of benevolence [jen] — is something that cannot be endured. No matter whether they be working men or others whose position is comparatively better — even capitalists — in each and every case their vitality has been almost completely sapped by these conditions. The unnaturalness of life, its mechanical and barren tastelessness, is the same for all." [36]

In this crisis the West must turn away, said Liang, from its aggressive past and its preoccupation with material accomplishments and must begin instead to "deal with the inner workings of the

35. *Ibid.*, 152–153.
36. *Ibid.*, 165.

minds of others." As it does so, it will find itself moving from the first to the second stage in cultural development. So Liang proclaimed that "the moment has at last arrived when the Chinese attitude, formerly unsuited to the times, has become essential." Taking his lead again from Liang Ch'i-ch'ao, he expressed confidence that such a transition was in fact discernible in recent European intellectual movements, particularly in the discovery of a "social instinct" in place of the competitive individualism of earlier times. And is this not, he asked, "a turning from the Western road to the Chinese road?" Is this not an admission of the fact that life should be based on sentiment, on "the pulse and flow of instinct and impulse," rather than on reason? Is this not an admission of the fact that a life lived in accordance with the dictates of human emotion and instinct would be "good, suitable, unsullied, and without danger?" Such would be the qualities of human existence in a culture founded on "a psychology of happiness and tranquillity," where men could lead "a lively and joyful life," "a benevolent life," "a Confucian life." [37]

So in the end Liang's vision turns out to be profoundly traditional in detail and in spirit, deeply committed to the idealized forms of Confucian culture, even to the point of arguing that, in the future, law would be replaced by rites and music as a means of disciplining man's essentially benign instincts. Thus would men reach "complete accord with the great principles of Confucianism." [38]

China's future place was secure, then, if she could but survive the present. Liang had admitted the weakness of her position. He had acknowledged that in some respects China was "far behind the West," and he admonished that "the urgent task for us today is how to go about introducing the two spirits [of science and democracy], for otherwise we will never be able to speak of character or learning." Yet the essential attributes of Chinese life must not be forfeited; China must not adopt the aggressive and self-centered values that the West was even now on the verge of abandoning, for in this respect China was not behind the West but ahead of it. Somehow Chinese deficiencies must be made good while at the same time the Chinese advantage must be safeguarded. To ac-

37. *Ibid.*, 167, 200, 170–171.
38. *Ibid.*, 195–196, 175.

complish this, Liang called for a renaissance of the "Chinese attitude" in its original and uncorrupted form: "What I want is a reconstruction of a spirit of philosophical investigation akin to that of the Sung and the Ming [dynasties], taking the philosophy of K'ung and Yen [i.e., Confucius and his favorite disciple, Yen Hui] as the means of solving the melancholy problems of life that confront our youth today . . . A man must establish his life on a firm foundation before he can move forward . . . Only with a genuine awakening of the Chinese people's attitude toward life can the oppressive atmosphere of death be completely stripped away from our vitality, and the Chinese people be brought back to life . . . Confucianism is not a way of thought; it is a way of life." [39]

Despite his repeated objections to the idea of an intercultural synthesis, and his sharp criticism of the nineteenth-century formula which advocated the importation of Western methods without modification of the underlying principles of Confucian culture (*Hsi-hsüeh wei yung, Chung-hsüeh wei t'i*), Liang Sou-ming emerged finally as a proponent of just such a synthesis: Western methods (science and democracy) and Chinese attitudes (benevolence, or *jen*). Yet he was no orthodox cultural traditionalist. The China that Liang looked back upon with such affection was not the China he had known under the late empire. His vision of the future was no less a departure from the immediate past, nor did it resemble any more closely the realities of contemporary Chinese life, than that of the thinkers who, like Hu Shih, looked ahead to an intellectually "modern" culture founded not upon Chinese values but upon the ideals and aspirations of an alien civilization.

Liang Sou-ming and Liang Ch'i-ch'ao were arguing a similar case, but they were not agreed on every point. Of the two, Liang Sou-ming was the more conservative, in his commitment to Confucian forms and in his desire to affirm China's claim to a unique spiritual heritage. He thus rejected the idea of cultural synthesis which Liang Ch'i-ch'ao openly supported. The two Liangs differed also in their assessment of the manner in which Confucian values would attain the recognition that both believed history demanded: Liang Ch'i-ch'ao promoted a kind of Chinese missionary movement to carry the glad tidings of spiritual peace to the troubled West, while Liang Sou-ming maintained that the West, having reached the end of its own road, would necessarily turn to the

39. *Ibid.*, 11, 204, 213–214.

"Chinese way" even if it remained entirely ignorant of China's intellectual and social tradition.[40]

In certain essential matters, however, the two Liangs were in accord, and taken together their ideas constituted a consistent intellectual position. They agreed, in the first place, that life is divisible into "inner" and "outer" levels of existence, separate and perhaps even mutually opposed. They shared the view that the genius of Chinese social thought lay in its treatment of the inner life, or, to put it another way, that the Chinese way of life exalted the spirit. On this account they agreed that Chinese life is morally superior to the deplorable Western obsession with material progress. And together they maintained, finally, that the West had come in recent times to a realization of the failings of its own civilization and was turning, compelled by its own inner need, to an appreciation of the values exemplified by the Chinese tradition.

Liang Sou-ming's lectures on occidental and oriental culture were delivered in Tsinan and Peking in 1920 and 1921 and were published early in 1922. Not until a year later did Hu Shih take public issue with Liang, in a long and highly critical review of *The Cultures of East and West and Their Philosophies* in which he set forth for the first time his own theory of cultural development and his own interpretation of the differences between Chinese and Western civilization. In the interval, however, another event had occurred that significantly enlarged the scope of the ensuing debate. This was the celebrated lecture delivered in February 1923 before a group of science students at Tsinghua University in Peking by a young journalist named Chang Chia-shen (*tzu* Chün-mai, Carsun Chang, 1886–   ). Chang was himself Western-trained, a graduate in political science of Waseda University in Tokyo who had gone on to postgraduate study in England and Germany during the early years of the republic. But his experiences in Europe, particularly as a student of Eucken's and later as one of Liang Ch'i-ch'ao's traveling companions in 1919, had made him sympathetic to the anti-Western cause. Whether because of the brevity and the emotional intensity of his remarks, or because Chang addressed himself directly to members of the younger generation on whom rested their own hopes for the future, Chang's Tsinghua speech aroused a wider interest among Western-oriented intellectuals, and provoked a sharper reaction from them, than had either Liang Sou-ming's

40. *Ibid.*, 203.

recondite treatise or Liang Ch'i-ch'ao's journalistic account of his European tour.

Chang's first concern was to point out to his audience what he regarded as the deficiencies in their education: "In science there are fixed theories and principles which . . . are all subject to proof . . . You have been reading textbooks for quite some time, and you must have come to believe that there are formulae for everything in the world, and that everything in the world is controlled by the law of cause and effect. In point of fact, however, . . . most problems are by no means this clear. Now problems of this [latter] kind are not at all the exalted theories of philosophy, but belong rather to the day-to-day business of living, in which there is no standard for determining the rightness or wrongness, the truth or error, of theory A or theory B."[41]

From this rather modest beginning Chang proceeded to a broad attack on the pretensions of science as the arbiter of problems that properly belong to what he called "the philosophy of life" (jen-sheng-kuan). Science, he said, is objective in its approach, and subject to universal laws, while a philosophy of life is essentially subjective, its hypotheses neither universally applicable nor universally accepted. Science is controlled by, and develops within the structure of, the laws of reason, and it must accept the limitations that this structure imposes. But a philosophy of life "is not limited by the formulae of logic and has nothing that can be called definition or method; it is put forward at the prompting of conscience . . . and hence we call it intuitive." Scientific method is analytical, whereas "a philosophy of life is a composite totality that embraces everything within itself, and if analysis is forced upon it, it must lose its true significance." Science is controlled by the law of cause and effect, but a philosophy of life moves in response to "the natural impulses of conscience." And, finally, science is founded on the assumption of an underlying "uniformity in the course of nature," while a philosophy of life is individual and must take into account the "uniqueness of personality."[42]

On the basis of these distinctions Chang defined very narrowly the area of inquiry that may legitimately be approached through scientific investigation. Since the aim of science is "to get rid of the

41. Chang Chün-mai, "Jen-sheng-kuan" (The philosophy of life), KHYJSK I, 1. See also Chow Tse-tsung, *The May Fourth Movement*, 333, note i.
42. Chang Chün-mai, "Jen-sheng-kuan," KHYJSK I, 4–9.

functions of human sentiment and to render all phenomena objective," it is the appropriate instrument for the study of the exact sciences — mathematics, physics, chemistry, biology — but it cannot be applied to any study that touches upon the spiritual aspect of human existence.[43] Having restricted the domain of science, Chang defined much more generously the legitimate concerns of a "philosophy of life." The individual's social and familial relationships, his view of human nature, his attitude toward social change, his hopes for the future, the nature of his beliefs concerning the existence of an underlying creative force in the universe, and the relationship between the individual's inner spirit and the external material world — all these are questions central to the meaning of life to which, Chang argued, science provides no answers. "No matter how science may develop, it cannot lie within its power to resolve the problems of a philosophy of life."[44]

There was, in Chang's position, more than a suggestion of mysticism. For him the incomprehensible did not constitute a challenge to human powers of understanding. It was rather a quality in life to be accepted with wonder and awe. A Confucian judgment of human nature, taken on faith, was fundamental to his creed. "Man's life lies within the limits of the spiritual and the material. That part of it which is called good — for example, such things as legal systems, religion, ethics, fine arts, and scholarship — is in every instance a manifestation of the spirit. That part of it which is called evil — for example, such things as lust and murder — arises in every case out of a conflict with the material . . . Mankind's purpose changes constantly, but though it changes it tends not toward evil but necessarily toward good. The reasons for this are most marvelous and unfathomable." [45]

Like both Liang Ch'i-ch'ao and Liang Sou-ming, Chang equated the spiritual values that he prized with the insights of traditional Chinese thought. He saw in the West only the triumph of the

43. Chang Chün-mai, "Tsai lun jen-sheng-kuan yü k'o-hsüeh, ping ta Ting Tsai-chün" (Another discussion of the philosophy of life and science, and a rejoinder to Ting Tsai-chün), KHYJSK I, 9. Chang followed Wundt's categories of *Exakte Wissenschaft* and *Geiste Wissenschaft*, the latter comprising psychology, language, history, etymology, sociology, economics, and jurisprudence (*ibid.*, 7-8). Chang denied that cause and effect play any part in the development of these areas of human experience except in certain limited contexts, as that of property in economics (*ibid.*, 25, 31).

44. Chang Chün-mai, "Jen-sheng-kuan," 2-4, 9.

45. Chang Chün-mai, "Tsai lun jen-sheng-kuan yü k'o-hsüeh," 38.

coarse materialism that he despised: a mechanistic view of life, an uncritical enthusiasm for the new at the expense of the old, acceptance of industrialism as an "ultimate policy" and the resultant commercialization of values, and a preoccupation with the struggle for national wealth and power.[46] Since the seventeenth century, Chang wrote, European emphasis on "control of the natural world by human power" had created a "materialistic civilization." The perennial Chinese concern for the "cultivation of the inner life" had, on the other hand, led to the creation of a "spiritual civilization." [47]

What hope had China of surviving the challenge of this vigorously aggressive materialistic civilization? Chang asked. "We have our culture, and the West has its culture. How are we to adopt from the West what is beneficial to us and get rid of what is injurious?" [48] The two Liangs were agreed that the solution to this problem lay, at least in part, in Western acceptance of Chinese values, which would inevitably produce a profound change in the temper of Western civilization itself. But Chang was comforted by no such assurance. He, too, referred to "the great [intellectual] reaction of the present day" in Europe,[49] but he drew little hope from it. He saw China rushing headlong after Western excesses and falling back upon the old nineteenth-century policy of "enriching the country and strengthening the army" (fu-kuo ch'iang-ping). This, Chang warned, is "the greatest danger to the future of the nation." [50] His mood was one of sorrow for the passing of an age:

> The fundamental principles upon which our nation is founded are quietism as opposed to activism, spiritual self-sufficiency as opposed to the striving for material happiness, an autarkic agricultural economy as opposed to a profit-seeking commercialism, and an actively moral brotherhood [te-hua chih ta-t'ung] as opposed to the separation of the races. In the course of several thousand years of isolation and containment [our] culture has stagnated and [our] livelihood has become barren and cold; the knowledge that brings authority has belonged to a minority, while the majority, living in rustic backwaters,

46. *Ibid.,* 78–79.
47. Chang Chün-mai, "Jen-sheng-kuan," 9–10.
48. *Ibid.,* 12.
49. Chang Chün-mai, "Tsai lun jen-sheng-kuan yü k'o-hsüeh," 66 and 9–20.
50. *Ibid.,* 80.

has remained illiterate. In a word, a nation founded on agriculture lacks a knowledge of the industrial arts, [but] it is likewise without material demands, and thus, though it exists over a long period of time, it can still maintain a standard of poverty but equality, scarcity but peace.[51]

But how will it be hereafter? Already innumerable great ships ply the estuary of the Yangtze River, and generators of tremendous power whir night and day in the markets of Tientsin, Shanghai, Canton, and Hankow; there are thousands of men who congregate and disperse at the sound of factory whistles, who, though they labor industriously all their lives, perhaps still cannot make a sufficient living; and there are thousands of business men, constantly shifting and changing . . . seeking to grab the whole trade, to monopolize the entire market, who, though they do nothing but calculate the rates of compound interest, obtain more than enough simply by standing with their hands in their sleeves. It is abundantly clear wherein the strengths and weaknesses of this situation lie . . . and therefore in the future a condition of prosperity without equality, wealth without peace, must probably prevail.[52]

Chang did not advocate a return to the ideal of equalized poverty, nor did he urge that China should remain bound to her primitive agricultural way of life. Industrialization, he conceded, could not be avoided and should not be discouraged. He was anxious, nevertheless, that economic modernization should come under the guidance of some kind of socialistic system that would save China from the misfortunes that beset contemporary Europe.

51. The phrase derives from *Lun-yü*, XVI, 10: "*pu huan kua erh huan pu chün, pu huan p'in erh huan pu an.*" Chu Hsi, and following him Legge, gives *kua* as meaning that the people are few. I prefer to follow Waley: "He is not concerned lest his people should be poor, but only lest what they have should be ill-apportioned." (Arthur Waley, trans., *The Analects*, 203.) Waley, however, gives *p'in* as "few"; here I have followed Chu Hsi's more conventional understanding of the term. This phrase was a particular favorite with the neo-traditionalists; see also note 17 above.

52. Chang Chün-mai, "Tsai lun jen-sheng-kuan yü k'o-hsüeh," 81–82. This appears as a quotation from a source that Chang identifies only as "the postface to a constitutional draft drawn up last year at Shanghai." This may be a reference to a document entitled "Pa t'uan-t'i kuo-shih hui-i hsien-fa tsao-an" (Constitutional draft of the eight-group conference on national affairs), the text of which is printed in NLCP no. 13 (July 30, 1922). Hu Shih attributed it to Chang.

But like Liang Ch'i-ch'ao and Liang Sou-ming, the best that he could hope was that a balance might be struck between the self-centered, aggressive, materialistic, and triumphant civilization of the West and the self-denying, quietistic, spiritual, and failing civilization of China. His final appeal was made not to intuition and sentiment but to reason. "Has it not been said that necessity is the mother of invention? If you contend that the human intelligence can discover no other ways [than those of the West], I will not believe it." [53]

"Metaphysics is really a worthless devil — having scraped along in Europe for something over two thousand years, until he is now coming to find himself with no place to turn and nothing to eat, suddenly he puts up a false trade mark, hangs out a new signboard, and comes swaggering along to China to start working his swindle. If you don't believe it, please just take a look at Chang Chün-mai's 'The philosophy of life.' " [54]

With these words, written a few weeks after Chang's Tsinghua speech, the first fire was returned from the Western camp. The writer was Ting Wen-chiang, who served throughout the ensuing dispute as chief spokesman for the Western cause. It was a role for which Ting was well prepared: having spent seven years as a student at the universities of London (where he worked toward a degree in medicine) and Glasgow (from which he earned degrees in biology and geology), he was both Western-trained and a scientist.[55] Ting's response to Chang Chün-mai, published in April 1923 in *The Endeavor* (*Nu-li chou-pao*), a small liberal weekly that he and Hu Shih had established in Peking a year earlier, signaled the start of a debate that spread and flourished during the following months in typically Chinese fashion, becoming in short order a full-scale "war of words" (*lun-chan*) as others rallied to the support of the major protagonists and the exchange of opinion became increasingly heated and diffuse.[56] It was perhaps inevitable

53. Chang Chün-mai, "Tsai lun jen-sheng-kuan yü k'o-hsüeh," 84.
54. Ting Wen-chiang, "Hsüan-hsüeh yü k'o-hsüeh" (Metaphysics and science), KHYJSK I, 1.
55. Hu Shih, *Ting Wen-chiang ti chuan-chi* (Biography of Ting Wen-chiang; Taipei, 1956), 11.
56. At the end of 1923 a number of the more significant essays inspired by this polemic were collected and published, in two substantial volumes, under the title *K'o-hsüeh yü jen-sheng-kuan* (Science and the philosophy of life), with prefaces contributed by Hu Shih and Ch'en Tu-hsiu. In this collection Chang's

that the issues in dispute should lack very precise definition; Hu Shih complained that the whole argument had been carried on at the level of generalities, a failing he attributed to the vague formulation of Chang Chün-mai's opening charges.[57] Nevertheless, the fundamental issues were clear enough.

Hu Shih was absent from Peking during much of 1923, recuperating in the mountains of Chekiang from a physical breakdown suffered at the end of 1922. But although he contributed little to the controversies that raged that year, there was no question where his allegiance lay. "The greatest need of mankind today is to apply the scientific method to the problems of human life," he had written in 1922; it was this proposition that Chang Chün-mai directly challenged: "No matter how it may develop, it cannot lie within the power of science to resolve the problems of a philosophy of life." On this question the adversaries were irreconcilably divided. Even Liang Ch'i-ch'ao, who hastened to disavow the claim (which he was generally credited with having initiated) that "science is bankrupt," and who dissociated himself from Chang's narrow definition of the function of science — even Liang would admit only that matters lying within the "realm of reason" were properly the subject of scientific study, and he still maintained that everything pertaining to the "feelings" must remain "above science." [58]

One point of general agreement among the neo-traditionalists was the conviction that human life is separable into distinct and, to a certain degree, autonomous levels of existence, which they referred to variously as "internal" and "external," or "spiritual" and "material." Hu Shih's counterargument, set forth in his critique of Liang Sou-ming's *The Cultures of East and West and Their Philosophies* in 1923 and in several later essays, turned on a denial of the validity of this premise. Spiritual and material achievements, he maintained, are coordinate aspects of a single living experience, individual or historical. Spiritual qualities are no more than a reflection of the level of material accomplishments. He rejected categorically the contention that the material aspect

---

original lecture takes up only twelve pages, while Ting's rebuttal runs to thirty, and Chang's rejoinder three times that. Wu Chih-hui, coming to the defense of science in a series of articles published in the autumn, wrote what amounted to a small book in itself, covering 165 pages in the larger collection.

57. KHYJSK, Hu *hsü*, 10.

58. Liang Ch'i-ch'ao, "Jen-sheng-kuan yü k'o-hsüeh" (The philosophy of life and science), KHYJSK I, 9.

of life is in some way inferior to the spiritual aspect: "Raising the level of man's enjoyment of material objects and increasing his material advantages and security . . . leads toward the liberation of mankind's abilities and enables men to do more than dedicate their every energy and thought to survival alone; [it] furnishes men with a reservoir of strength which allows them to seek the satisfaction of their spiritual demands." [59]

As an avowed "materialist" Hu had tolerated without difficulty the idea that repelled Liang Ch'i-ch'ao and his fellow spirits, the vision of the individual imprisoned within the meshes of a relentless determinism. He found fault, indeed, even with those who hastened to the defense of science in the debates of 1923, because, with the exception of Wu Chih-hui, none were prepared to go as far as he thought they should in acknowledging that the scientific view is "purely materialist and purely mechanistic." [60] He maintained that it was the function of intelligence to rescue the individual from the more brutal implications of this materialistic view of the universe. For him reason was the key to human freedom and creativity — the same reason that the neo-traditionalists joined forces to attack. Liang and his disciples condemned the West for its obsession with material progress and its insensitivity to the spiritual dimensions of human existence. Hu insisted, to the contrary, that Western civilization was more genuinely concerned with the spiritual aspect of life than were the impoverished and backward civilizations of the East, precisely because of its greater emphasis on the importance of material well-being. "The level at which modern Western culture is able to satisfy the spiritual demands of mankind is far away beyond the dreams of the old civilization of the Orient . . . Modern Western civilization is not at all a materialistic civilization; it is, rather, idealistic, it is spiritual." [61]

Proof of this, he continued, lay on every hand: candid appraisal of the conditions of Chinese life must discredit any claims made in its name to "spiritual superiority" over the West. On a trip to Europe in 1926 — his first to that shore of the Atlantic — Hu stopped off in Harbin, the Manchurian city where passengers from China boarded the Trans-Siberian Railroad for the long journey westward across the Soviet Union. The area of Harbin that before

59. Hu Shih, "Wo-men tui-yü Hsi-yang chin-tai wen-ming ti t'ai-tu" (Our attitude toward modern Western civilization), HSWT III, i, 6.
60. KHYJSK, Hu hsü, 13.
61. "Wo-men tui-yü Hsi-yang chin-tai wen-ming ti t'ai-tu," HSWT III, i, 8.

the Bolshevik Revolution had comprised the Russian concession was no longer under extraterritorial jurisdiction, but it retained a "special" status, and several of the earlier regulations remained in force, including a prohibition against the use of rickshas within its boundaries. "When I saw . . . the difference between the District and the areas outside it, I could not suppress a sigh," Hu wrote later. "I thought to myself, '. . . The line of the demarcation between the civilizations of East and West is simply the line of demarcation between ricksha civilization and motor-car civilization.' " The moral was obvious: no civilization that uses men in place of beasts of burden or machines can pride itself on its spiritual accomplishments, and no civilization that employs "the mind and intelligence of man to create machines to take the place of man-power" can be denounced as materialistic.[62] Hu's enormous enthusiasm for "motor-car civilization" was matched by a derisive scorn for China's material and intellectual backwardness. "The peasants of the Chinese countryside often stand rooted in fear when they see an automobile, not knowing enough even to get out of the way. You can toot your horn with all your might, but they hear nothing." [63] "Others were long ago flying across the oceans, while we are still scrambling along the ground." [64]

So much for China's pretensions to spiritual supremacy. But the great question remained to be answered: why were the Chinese still scrambling along the ground, and why in China were men still harnessed as beasts of burden? How could the all-too-obvious disparity between Chinese and Western achievements be explained?

Liang Sou-ming had suggested that the answer lay in the nature of the Chinese response to environment in the course of China's long historical development. Hu Shih was willing to agree, at least in part. In his critique of Liang's work he asserted, "We take the particular characteristics manifested by the cultures of different races at certain periods to be only the consequences of environment and time." [65] But he rejected Liang's opinion that qualitative differences in the level of cultural accomplishment derive from

62. Hu Shih, "Man-yu ti kan-hsiang" (Impressions of ramblings), HSWT III, i, 52.

63. Ibid., 56–57.

64. Hu Shih, "Ch'ing ta-chia lai chao-chao ching-tzu" (Please let us look in the mirror), HSWT III, i, 42.

65. Hu Shih, "Tu Liang Sou-ming hsien-sheng ti *Tung Hsi wen-hua chi ch'i che-hsüeh*" (On reading Mr. Liang Sou-ming's The cultures of East and West and their philosophies), HSWT II, ii, 82.

significant differences in the nature of human responses to the problems posed by environment. It was nonsense, in other words, to say that Chinese values had been shaped by an intuitive response to the natural world, while European values were the product of a rational approach to fundamentally similar problems. "The human mind, whether occidental or oriental, cannot differ greatly by reason of differences in kind," Hu insisted, and he maintained further that what he called "the theory of limited possibilities" in human development made it impossible to attribute varying degrees of cultural accomplishment to basic differences in racial attitudes.[66] All peoples, not only the Europeans, have striven to master environment by means of reason and intelligence. All have followed throughout their histories what Liang Sou-ming had called "the first road" of life. "If we examine culture in the light of history, we see simply that every race is following 'the original road of life.' But because of environmental difficulties or the lack of them and because of the [differing degrees of] urgency involved in the problems [facing them], there are differences in the speed with which they travel and differences in the order in which they reach their destination." [67]

Environment itself, then, not man's attitude toward it, is the controlling factor. Within certain natural limitations, it may impose differing conditions on various races, but man's essential nature is such that he will invariably seek to devise rational solutions to whatever problems arise in his relationship with the world around him. It is thus that cultures are born and civilizations made. China and India have indeed fallen behind the West, not because their peoples are afflicted by "an unhealthy tendency toward harmoney or retrogression," but rather because they have never been confronted by "coercive and compelling" environmental problems.[68] Since cultures develop along a single line of progress, and in accordance with the theory of limited possibilities, the disparity between East and West must be one of degree, not kind. And since cultural differences cannot be construed as evidence of talents or capabilities unique to one or another race, in the final analysis they must be acknowledged as indications of relative achievement

66. *Ibid.*, 73–74, 79.
67. *Ibid.*, 82–83.
68. *Ibid.*, 83–84.

or, in harsher terms, as proof of success or failure in meeting the challenge of history.

In his review of Liang Sou-ming's *The Cultures of East and West and Their Philosophies*, written in 1923, Hu accepted, or at least did not take issue with, Liang's contention that human responses to environment are instinctive rather than calculated. Though he denied that such responses might arise from intuition rather than reason, he appeared to believe that the use of reason in this way was spontaneous and natural, having nothing to do with conscious attitudes. Within a short time, however, he began to reconsider this position. In an important and widely read essay published in 1926, entitled "Our Attitude toward Modern Western Civilization" (*Wo-men tui yü Hsi-yang chin-tai wen-ming ti t'ai-tu*), he repeated his earlier definition of civilization as "the general achievement of a people in response to its environment." He re-affirmed, too, his belief that to stigmatize any civilization as material-istic, in the sense in which apologists for China used the term, was meaningless and unjustified, since all cultures contain both material and spiritual elements.[69] But whereas he had earlier attempted to explain cultural diversity strictly in terms of differ-ences in the impact of environment on certain races at various times in their development, he now acknowledged that the attitude of a given people toward the natural order might affect their response to it. Thus he conceded a point that the neo-traditionalists had insisted upon throughout their argument: that the Chinese view of life was in some respects uniquely Chinese. Unlike them, how-ever, Hu did not find it praiseworthy on this account. He acknowl-edged that the Chinese temperament was characterized by the qualities that the neo-traditionalists attributed to it: "satisfaction with one's lot in life, contentment in poverty, acceptance of the will of heaven, quietism, and the acceptance of suffering." But these, he insisted, were its vices rather than its virtues. That the passive acceptance of suffering and deprivation should become the

69. "Wo-men tui-yü Hsi-yang chin-tai wen-ming ti t'ai-tu," HSWT III, i, 4–5. An English translation of this essay by Lucius C. Porter, entitled "Two Wings of One Bird: A Chinese Attitude toward Eastern and Western Civiliza-tion," was published in *Pacific Affairs*, 1.1:1–8 (May 1928). Hu's own English version is "The Civilizations of the East and the West," in Charles A. Beard, ed., *Whither Mankind: A Panorama of Modern Civilization* (New York, London, Toronto, 1928), 25–40.

central feature of a civilization's social and political philosophy was, he proclaimed, a greater tragedy than the fact of suffering itself. "Such a civilization [as the Chinese], which endures the bonds and the coercive power of the material environment and cannot free itself from them, which cannot use man's reason and intelligence to temper his environment and improve his condition — this is the civilization of a lazy and retarded race. This is truly a material-istic civilization, [which] can only restrain man's spiritual demands but never satisfy them." [70]

The West, as Hu described it, was dedicated to very different principles. In contrast to oriental passivity and resignation, the Western temperament was characterized by "discontent with one's lot, dissatisfaction with poverty, an unwillingness to suffer, [respect for] hard work . . . and [the desire for] continuous improvement of the environment." This explained to Hu's satisfaction the re-markable record of European material accomplishment. It attested also to the fact that in the West there prevailed a better under-standing of the spiritual dimensions of life. For the essence of spiritual freedom is not, as the apologists for China would have it, contentment and quietism, but the active pursuit of truth. It is knowledge, and only knowledge, that enables one "to break the bonds of environment . . . and fearing neither heaven nor hell, with all dignity to be a man." So, Hu concluded, "the quest for knowledge is a naturally endowed spiritual demand of human life. The ancient civilizations of the East not only did not attempt to satisfy this demand but, on the contrary, often sought to keep it in check . . . Here, truly, is a fundamental difference between the cultures of East and West. On the one hand, unthinking blindness to one's own interests; and on the other, an endless search for truth." [71]

Hu Shih was naturally inclined to minimize the significance of those Western dissatisfactions with Western civilization which gave the neo-traditionalists such comfort in their own arguments. This self-doubt was, it should be noted, more European than American in origin. Liang Ch'i-ch'ao, though he had at best a traveler's acquaintance with Europe, had spent time there on

70. "Wo-men tui-yü Hsi-yang chin-tai wen-ming ti t'ai-tu," HSWT III, i, 19, 6–7, 20.
71. Ibid., 19, 7, 9–10.

several occasions since the turn of the century, and in the course of his tour in 1919 he had called upon Bergson and Eucken. A few years earlier Chang Chün-mai had studied under both men. Hu Shih's education and experience were by contrast entirely American, and when he spoke of the West it was America that he had in mind, for to him it represented a "third way." [72] As a student at Cornell during the early years of the war, much under the influence of his pacifist associations, he too had condemned the "unhuman and unchristian aggressivism of the West." In the 1920s he was willing to concede, privately, that the war had probably signaled the beginning of the irreversible decline of European culture. But he cherished the hope that modern civilization might find a permanent refuge in the great nations bordering upon the Pacific — America and China.[73] In public he dismissed Western soul-searching as no more than a reflection of "the pathological mentality of war-stricken Europe,"[74] and he denounced Bergson and Eucken as "reactionary philosophers who, in the course of things, have eaten to repletion of the delicacies of science, and then casually grumble a bit, like the rich man who has eaten his fill of meat and fish and then wishes to taste a little salted vegetable or beancurd." [75]

In the West, where by long tradition an appreciation of the importance of scientific method was firmly grounded, Hu thought that the reaction against science need cause little concern. But in China this was not the case. "At the present time," he wrote in 1923, "China has not yet enjoyed the blessings of science — how much the less, then, can we speak of the 'catastrophes' that science brings with it." [76] In this Hu seconded a point made some months earlier by Ting Wen-chiang. Ting was gravely concerned lest the younger generation be persuaded by Chang Chün-mai to believe that political and social problems "do not come under the control of reason . . . and that all they need do to solve them is to apply a subjective . . . and free-willed philosophy of life." Were such an attitude to gain a following, Ting warned, "there would be

72. "Man-yu ti kan-hsiang," HSWT III, i, 62–63.
73. See for example Hu Shih's unpublished diaries, entry for July 3, 1922, for his account of a conversation with Chiang Monlin, who had recently returned from attending the Washington Conference, and the bleak conclusions that Hu drew from it.
74. "The Civilizations of the East and the West," *Whither Mankind*, 25.
75. KHYJSK, Hu *hsü*, 7.
76. *Ibid.*

no need to study nor to seek learning; knowledge and experience would come to be [regarded as] futile, and one would need only 'to advocate what one's own conscience ordains' . . ." [77] Ting compared the situation to the reaction of the early Ch'ing thinkers against the speculative metaphysics of the Ming period. He turned against his own enemies Ku Yen-wu's indictment of those "who abandon further study and take learning to be the search for a comprehensive system," and "who set aside the hardships of the world and speak not of them, but spend whole days discoursing on theories lofty and increasingly abstruse." Ku had lamented the intellectual follies of his own times in these words: "Ambitious young men who wish quickly to make a name for themselves in the world — if you speak to them of the Five Classics they are unwilling to study them; but speak to them of the recorded conversations of [Ch'en] Po-sha and [Wang] Yang-ming and they will be overjoyed!" Ting Wen-chiang, addressing himself to the young Chinese intellectuals of the 1920s, paraphrased Ku's sentiments thus: "The gentlemen of today, wishing quickly to make names for themselves in the world — if you speak to them of science they are unwilling to study it; but speak to them of the metaphysics of Bergson and Dreisch and they will be overjoyed!" [78]

For both Ting Wen-chiang and Hu Shih the great importance of scientific education lay in the mental discipline and objectivity that it would presumably inculcate. Their advocacy of the scientific attitude was not an advocacy of science for its own sake. As Ting summed up the case, "[Science] is the best instrument available for education, because the daily search for truth, the constant desire to banish preconceptions, not only gives the student of science an ability to seek truth, but, moreover, it inspires in him a sincere love of truth. No matter what he may encounter, he can always proceed to analyze and examine it with detachment and candor, seeking simplicity out of complexity and order out of confusion, using reason to discipline his thinking and thus increasing his power to think, using experience to guide his intuition and thus enlivening his intuitive powers." [79]

Perhaps because he was himself European-educated, or perhaps as a consequence of his own firsthand experiences in Europe im-

77. Ting Wen-chiang, "Hsüan-hsüeh yü k'o-hsüeh," KHYJSK I, 18.
78. *Ibid.*, 27–29.
79. *Ibid.*, 20–21.

mediately after the war — he too had accompanied Liang Ch'i-ch'ao on his tour in 1919 — Ting Wen-chiang was more inclined than was Hu Shih to take a serious view of the postwar crisis in European values. He was, consequently, anxious to dissociate Western science from the commercialism and militarism that many Chinese found so repugnant. Chang Chün-mai was wrong, said Ting, when he lumped the scientist and the industrialist together in assigning the blame for the recent European debacle. *"A laboratory and a factory are absolutely two different things* . . . The laboratory is the place where truth is sought, and the factory is the instrument for making money . . . The great industrialists of Europe and America are for the most part men like our military governors and inspectors-general, of inferior birth and without scientific knowledge." It was not the scientists who had been responsible for the war, Ting argued, but the "politicians and educators . . . who are still for the most part unscientific" in their attitudes and convictions.[80]

Hu Shih felt no such compulsion to hedge his acceptance of Western values, and he took a more sanguine view of Western prospects, founded on a sympathetic appraisal of the general tendency of Western history since the Renaissance. He admitted that "when we look collectively at modern Western industrial arts, sciences, and laws, [we see] among them, certainly, implements of human death and institutions of aggression and plunder." But he insisted that "we cannot fail to acknowledge the fundamental [Western] spirit of attending to the well-being of the masses." [81] He perceived in the history of the West the slow growth of a "new morality" based on man's increasing confidence in the authority of reason and on his deepening sense of kinship with others — the

80. *Ibid.,* 22. To substantiate this claim Ting cited Gladstone's attacks on Darwin, David Balfour's book *The Foundations of Belief: Being Notes Introductory to the Study of Theology,* and William Jennings Bryan's opposition to the theory of evolution (the Scopes trial was still two years in the future). On this basis Ting asserted: "We need only look at those men who, never having studied science, have served as British and American parliamentarians, prime ministers, and presidents [*sic*] to know that science has never directly influenced politics." *Ibid.,* 25.

81. "Wo-men tui-yü Hsi-yang chin-tai wen-ming ti t'ai-tu," HSWT III, i, 8. The phrase "attending to the well-being of the masses" (*li-yung hou-sheng*) is drawn from the *Shu ching;* see Legge, *The Chinese Classics,* III, 56. It appears in the context of an injunction to the ruler to promote the useful arts in order to provide for the people's convenience and comfort.

same authority, be it noted, that Liang Ch'i-ch'ao and his intellectual followers repudiated, and the very sense of sympathy that they failed to find in the Western mind. The danger Hu saw in neo-traditionalist opinion was that it turned the Chinese away from the West and its culture, "which is fast becoming the world civilization," [82] and by giving comfort to the forces of sinocentric conservatism encouraged them to contemplate the imaginary — or at least highly idealized — accomplishments of their own tradition. Since the publication of Liang Ch'i-ch'ao's *Impressions of Travels in Europe*, Hu complained, "most of the old men who have never been outside the country have been crying happily, 'Science is bankrupt! Liang Jen-kung has said so!' " [83] Thus Liang and his followers were "gratifying the vanity of Oriental apologists and thereby strengthening the hand of reaction in the East." [84]

Although to all appearances Hu Shih was better able to withstand the emotional attraction of the past than were many of his contemporaries, he was neither insensitive nor indifferent to the psychological dilemma that had sprung from the unequal conflict with Western arms and ideas. As early as 1917 he had stated the problem perceptively:

> How can we Chinese feel at ease in this new world which at first sight appears to be so much at variance with what we have long regarded as our own civilization? For it is perfectly natural and justifiable that a nation with a glorious past and a distinctive civilization of its own making should never feel quite at home in a new civilization, if that new civilization is looked upon as part and parcel imported from alien lands and forced upon it by external necessities of national existence. And it would surely be a great loss to mankind at large if the acceptance of this new civilization should take the form of abrupt displacement instead of organic assimilation, thereby causing the disappearance of the old civilization. The real problem, therefore, may be restated thus: How can we best assimilate modern civilization in such a manner as to make it congenial and congruous and continuous with the civilization of our own making?

82. "The Civilizations of the East and the West," *Whither Mankind,* 25.
83. KHYJSK, Hu *hsü,* 6.
84. "The Civilizations of the East and the West," *Whither Mankind,* 25.

> . . . The solution to this great problem . . . will depend solely on the foresight and the sense of historical continuity of the intellectual leaders of New China, and on the tact and skill with which they can successfully connect the best in modern civilization with the best in our own civilization.[85]

Hu Shih's approach to China's "distinctive civilization" was thoroughly critical but by no means contemptuous. He did not believe that the past had nothing of value to give to the present, for he was convinced of the importance of finding Chinese precedents that might make the introduction of "modern" attitudes and methods easier and more natural. He did insist, however, that the past must be properly understood, and that such an understanding could come only from a dispassionate re-evaluation of every aspect of the traditional culture. He had no sympathy for those who appealed to the tradition to sanction ideas that would serve no useful purpose in the new age in which China must make a place for herself, and he was unrelentingly scornful of those whose defense of the tradition was emotional rather than reasoned — men like Lin Shu, the translator of Dumas and Dickens, who argued against the abolition of the classical language but confessed, "Although I understand the principle, I cannot express in words why this is so!"[86] The attitude of the new thought toward the old culture, Hu wrote in 1919, should be one of opposition to such "blind following and conformity" to ancient standards, taking as its principal aim the introduction of the scientific method which alone could provide the unprejudiced understanding of the past on which depended China's survival in the future.[87] After his return from the United States in 1917 Hu soon became an acknowledged leader in the movement to "systematize the national heritage" (*cheng-li kuo ku*).[88] In the next few years he contributed to it, among other things, a history of classical philosophy, a partial

85. Hu Shih, *The Development of the Logical Method in Ancient China* (Shanghai, 1922), introduction, 6–7. No similar statement appears in the preface to *Chung-kuo che-hsüeh shih ta-kang*, the Chinese revision of Hu's work on the logical method; nor have I found so lucid an analysis of the problems discussed here in any of Hu's writings in Chinese.

86. Quoted in Hu Shih, "Hsin ssu-ch'ao ti i-i," HSWT, iv, 1033.

87. *Ibid.*, 1032–1034.

88. As far as I can determine, the term *cheng-li* (accompanied by the translation given here) first appears in Hu's writings in some random jottings made while he was en route to China in 1917. *Diary*, 1166.

history of *pai-hua* literature and numerous long critical essays dealing with the authorship and lineage of the great vernacular novels, several scholarly studies of the methods and motives of Ch'ing-dynasty thinkers, and a series of essays on the influence of Buddhism on Chinese intellectual and social history.

The originality of Hu's approach to this vast scholarly undertaking stemmed in part from his exploitation of new sources to shed fresh light on old controversies. A good example of this was his research on the origins of *The Dream of the Red Chamber* (*Hung-lou meng*), the great eighteenth-century novel by Ts'ao Chan that describes the decline of a prosperous and powerful clan. When Hu turned his attention to it in 1921 — taking advantage of the leisure afforded by a student strike — he dispatched two of his most talented students, Ku Chieh-kang and Yü P'ing-po, to search through local gazetteers and histories, collections of contemporary poetry, and the archival collections of the Peking Metropolitan Library for references to the Ts'ao family that might substantiate Ts'ao Chan's claim (generally dismissed by later critics as a literary device) that the novel was essentially autobiographical in inspiration and not, as had been widely believed, a veiled attack on the ruling Manchu house.[89]

In other instances the importance of Hu's scholarship derived not so much from his use of new materials as from his application of new standards of judgment to traditional problems. He reread the history of Chinese intellectual development in the light of certain ideas fundamental to the evolution of Western civilization, measuring Chinese accomplishments against these alien achievements — though again it was not what was Western but what seemed modern that attracted his attention. His doctoral dissertation, *The Development of the Logical Method in Ancient China*, was a first attempt in this direction, and it set the pattern for much of his later work. In the introduction he observed, "The emphasis on experience as against dogmatism and rationalism, the highly developed scientific method in all its phases of operation, and the historical or evolutionary view of truth and morality, — these which I consider the most important contributions of modern philosophy

89. For background on this study see Ku Chieh-kang, *The Autobiography of a Chinese Historian*, trans. Arthur W. Hummel from the author's preface to *Ku-shih pien* (Leyden, 1931); and Jerome B. Grieder, "The Chinese Communist Critique of *Hung-lou meng*," *Papers on China*, 10:142–168 (1956).

in the Western world can all find their remote but highly developed precursors in those great non-Confucian schools [i.e., among such thinkers as Mo-tzu, Hui-tzu and Kung-sun Lung, Hsün-tzu and Han Fei] of the fifth, fourth and third centuries B.C." [90]

Hu hastened to disclaim any intention of begging for China the satisfaction of superiority over the West in this development: "Mere priority in invention or discovery without subsequent efforts to improve and perfect the original crudities can only be a matter for regret, certainly not for vainglory." But he expressed "the strongest desire to make my own people see that these methods of the West are not totally alien to the Chinese mind," for "when the philosophies of Ancient China are reinterpreted in terms of modern philosophy, and when modern philosophy is interpreted in terms of the native systems of China, then, and not until then, can Chinese philosophers and students of philosophy truly feel at ease with the new methods and instrumentalities of speculation and research." [91]

In keeping with this conviction, Hu was inclined to treat Chinese history in terms of European historical development, though frequently the comparisons he drew were less than flattering from the Chinese point of view. He did not hold with Liang Sou-ming's contention that "if Chinese culture is to be prized, it must be prized on the strength of its own particular characteristics." In refutation of Liang's description of the Chinese as intuitive rather than rational, Hu had insisted that they, no less than any other race, had brought reason to bear upon the problems that confronted them. But the comparison did not end there. In China, Hu argued, as in the West, reason had been compelled to wage a secular struggle against the forces of religious dogmatism and ecclesiastical authority:

It has been said that the Chinese people are the least religious among the civilized races, and that Chinese philosophy has been most free from the domination of religious influences. Both of these observations are not true in the light of history. A study of history will convince us that the Chinese people were capable of highly religious emotions; . . . and that Chi-

90. *The Development of the Logical Method in Ancient China,* introduction, 9.
91. *Ibid.*

nese philosophy has always been so much conditioned by the religious development of the different periods that the history of Chinese thought cannot be properly understood without being studied together with that of the Chinese religions. If our people today do not appear as religious as the other races of the world, it is only because our thinkers, our Voltaires, and our Huxleys, had long ago fought hard against the forces of religion. And if China has so far failed to achieve a truly humanistic civilization, it is only because the rationalistic and humanistic tendencies of Chinese thought have been more than once frustrated by the too great powers of religion.[92]

In briefest outline, Hu's theory of the evolution of rationalism in Chinese thought may be summarized as follows:

The founders of the tradition of humanistic philosophy in China — Confucius himself, and Mencius, Hsün-tzu and his Legalist student Han Fei, and somewhat later the skeptic Wang Ch'ung — had been able to temper, but never to eradicate, a pervasive religiosity inherited from the pre-Confucian age and subsequently incorporated into the conglomeration of superstitions that formed the state cult of the Han period. Later still, with the advent of Buddhism, the Chinese succumbed to an infatuation with religious forms and metaphysical speculation that Hu branded as "opposed to all the best traditions of China" and "most foreign to the simple and straightforward ways of thinking of the native Chinese" [93] — but which, he admitted, had been persuasive enough to hold sway over the Chinese mind for a thousand years. It was in reaction to this "Indianization of China" [94] that Neo-Confucianism developed in the late T'ang and Sung period, a return to "reason and humanity" [95] and an attempt to retrieve something of the earlier tradition of skeptical naturalism.

It was to this movement that Hu traced the origins of the Chinese "renaissance." Its "historic mission was comparable to the

92. Hu Shih, "Religion and Philosophy in Chinese History," in Sophia H. Chen Zen (Ch'en Heng-che), ed., *Symposium on Chinese Culture* (Shanghai, 1931), 31.

93. *Ibid.*, 50.

94. Hu Shih, "The Indianization of China: A Case Study in Cultural Borrowing," in *Independence, Convergence and Borrowing* (Cambridge, Mass., 1937), 219–247.

95. Hu Shih, "Chinese Thought," in H. F. MacNair, ed., *China,* 227.

Renaissance in Europe": the secularization of life and the liberation of the mind from the authority of religion.[96] Its method, based on the injunction to "extend knowledge to the utmost" through "the investigation of things," was scientific in its original inclination. But the impetus toward the development of a genuine scientific methodology had been blunted by an unscientific desire to achieve "enlightenment" in terms of absolute principles, by an entrenched anti-utilitarian bias on the part of the principal sponsors of the movement, and by their continuing commitment to the authority of the Classics, which inhibited them from proclaiming a creed of intellectual freedom such as would have been necessary to the development of a genuinely scientific approach to the world. These defects, coupled with an inherited diffidence toward the tasks of scientific investigation and the handicap of insufficient and inadequate instruments and equipment, effectively turned the Neo-Confucian movement back upon itself, making it the instrumentality through which many of the abuses it had been designed to destroy were in fact perpetuated.[97]

Only with the rise of the *Han-hsüeh* scholarship of the seventeenth and eighteenth centuries, Hu maintained, did there emerge attitudes worthy of being called "scientific" in the true sense of the term. The textual researches of such scholars as Ch'ien Ta-hsin, Ku Yen-wu, Wang Nien-sun and Wang Yin-chih, Yen Jo-chü, and Tai Chen had demonstrated, according to Hu, the requisite combination of inductive and deductive reasoning, a boldness in making hypotheses and a careful regard for objectivity in seeking proofs, and an enthusiasm for active scholarship, epitomized in Tai's admonition, "The only suitable thing to do is to investigate — do not sit stupidly by, waiting for results to come to you." [98] Though Hu acknowledged certain shortcomings of the *Han-hsüeh* movement — the narrowness of its interests, its lack of a comprehensive aim, and its indifference to the formulation of general principles — he was willing nevertheless to link his own attempts to "system-

96. "The Indianization of China," 247.

97. This is the thesis put forward in several historical surveys, including "The Indianization of China" and "Ch'ing-tai hsüeh-che chih chih-hsüeh fang-fa" (The scholarly methodology of Ch'ing-period scholars), HSWT, ii, 539–579.

98. See "Ch'ing-tai hsüeh-che chih chih-hsüeh fang-fa," *passim*. For background on these scholars see Liang Ch'i-ch'ao, *Intellectual Trends in the Ch'ing Period*, trans. Immanuel C. Y. Hsü (Cambridge, Mass., 1959); and the pertinent biographies in Hummel, *Eminent Chinese of the Ch'ing Period*.

atize the national heritage" with the scholarly movement that had begun three centuries before, claiming that the modern techniques that he espoused would supplement the attitudes of the Ch'ing scholars rather than discredit their endeavors. On this point he won the support of Ting Wen-chiang, who maintained that "the authority of science, its universality and pervasiveness, derive not from its materials [i.e., the objects of study] but from its methods." The methodology of Ch'ing scholarship and Western scientific methodology were "one and the same," he continued, and thus those who condemned science as alien to China were in error.[99]

The *Han-hsüeh* movement thus provided Hu with a natural opportunity to demonstrate the relationship between Chinese experience and modern attitudes, and to establish the sense of "historical continuity" that would render the values of "modern" civilization "continuous," "congruous," and "congenial" with the Chinese past. But there was, perhaps inevitably, a certain ambiguity in his attitude toward this linking of the present with the past. He was critical of others who made similar attempts, however progressive their motives might be, if he found their scholarship wanting in objectivity. In 1919, for example, he took issue with Hu Han-min and Liao Chung-k'ai, Kuomintang intellectuals and socialists of sorts, in a dispute concerning the significance in Chinese economic history of the *ching-t'ien* system of land distribution. Mencius had made much of the institution, an orderly arrangement of eight fields around a common central plot tilled for the benefit of the prince, which drew its name from a resemblance to the Chinese character meaning "a well." Mencius attributed it to the Golden Age of high antiquity; for later reformers, including twentieth-century socialists, it was attractive because it suggested a native tradition of primitive social and economic egalitarianism. Hu Han-min and Liao Chung-k'ai may have regarded the system less as an historical reality than as a Chinese ideal that coincided closely enough with certain contemporary aspirations to provide legitimacy for the claim to an indigenous socialist tradition. But from Hu Shih's point of view they were abusing history. He dismissed the *ching-t'ien* system as no more than "a utopia of the Warring States period." [100] What he objected to, however, was only

99. Ting Wen-chiang, "Hsüan-hsüeh yü k'o-hsüeh," KHYJSK I, 20, 27.
100. Hu Shih, "Ching-t'ien pien" (Making distinctions concerning the well-field [system]), HSWT, ii, 583. On this controversy see also J. R. Levenson, "Ill-

the example that Hu and Liao had used; it did not occur to him that the term "socialism" — descriptive of European intellectual development and burdened with European connotations — might itself be difficult to apply to the Chinese situation, past or present. He had his own theory concerning the origins of socialism in China, centering on the figure of Wang Mang, the reformist emperor whose short-lived dynasty separated the Former Han from the Later Han in the first century A.D.[101]

Yet it is obvious that Hu Shih was himself interpreting the tradition in ways that suited his own purposes. His persistent efforts "to connect the best in modern civilization with the best in our own civilization" were not always compatible with the kind of rigorous scientific objectivity that he advocated, and his conviction that such linkages could be made was in itself a prejudice. In the minds of some, for example, Hu and Ting were guilty, in drawing their facile comparison between Ch'ing scholarship and Western science, of precisely the same kind of intellectual irresponsibility that they condemned in others. Chang Tung-sun, a philosopher well versed in Western thought, a disciple of Kant and translator of Plato and Bergson, took Ting to task on just this point. Science, Chang said, is unified not in its method, as Ting had maintained, but in its aim, which is to generalize from particulars and to define forms and relationships. Insofar as science possesses a method common to all its branches it is the method of logic. But the techniques developed to such a high degree by Ch'ing scholars could be said to disclose no more than "a little of the scientific spirit"; their methods were particularly suited to the tasks of their interest, philological and textual research, and could not be applied to other areas with comparable results. They showed, moreover, little desire to formulate general propositions on the basis of their discoveries.[102]

Wind in the Well-Field: The Erosion of the Confucian Ground of Controversy," in A. F. Wright, ed., *The Confucian Persuasion* (Stanford, 1960), 268–287.

101. Hu Shih's views on Wang Mang were set forth in "I-ch'ien chiu-pai nien ch'ien ti i-ko she-hui-chu-i-che: Wang Mang" (A socialist of nineteen centuries ago: Wang Mang), HSWT II, i, 31–42; "Tsai lun Wang Mang" (Another discussion of Wang Mang), HSWT III, vii, 885–890; and "Wang Mang, the Socialist Emperor of Nineteen Centuries Ago," *Journal of the North China Branch of the Royal Asiatic Society*, 59:218–230 (1928). See also unpublished diary, entry for April 28, 1922.

102. See Chang Tung-sun's comment appended to Liang Ch'i-ch'ao, "Jen-sheng-kuan yü k'o-hsüeh," KHYJSK I, 10–14. For biographical information on Chang Tung-sun, see Boorman, *Biographical Dictionary*, I, 129–133.

Chang Tung-sun was also among those who found fault with Hu Shih on a broader issue. Soon after Hu published "Our Attitude toward Modern Western Civilization" in 1926, Chang reproached him for his failure to sense fully the emotional and intellectual perplexities of the situation in which the Chinese found themselves. Opposition to westernization might be a losing cause, Chang admitted, but the reasons for it should not be misinterpreted. The West had not brought peace and security to China but chaos and social unrest, and the "new men" created in accordance with Western concepts of moral conduct were in no way superior to the old. "In this distorted situation," Chang observed, "everyone who is dissatisfied with the present state of affairs because of a lingering affection for what is past makes slanderous statements concerning the material civilization of the West. Though what they say may be in error, their motives may be forgiven . . . Under present circumstances, the importation of Western civilization is not without its problems." [103]

At the time of his return to China Hu had been very much alive to the implications of these problems, and for a number of years he remained optimistic concerning their eventual solution. "The future scientification and democratization of China and India is beyond doubt," he predicted confidently in 1923, at the conclusion of his critique of Liang Sou-ming's book.[104] But as time went on his mood began to change, though his habitual optimism did not entirely forsake him. The persistence of neo-traditionalist sentiment and, even more important, the quickening temper of political nationalism shook his conviction that China in the future would indeed display the qualities of intellectual independence and honesty he hoped for. "Today China is pervaded by an atmosphere of boastful madness!" he complained in 1928 soon after the Nationalist armies had occupied Peking, thus extending the victorious revolution to all of China; and he called again for "a new awakening" and for the creation of "a new attitude." [105]

It was, really, no more than he had been demanding ever since his return from the United States: that the Chinese should look at their situation realistically, that they should be wary of acting on

103. Chang Tung-sun, "Hsi-yang wen-ming yü Chung-kuo" (Western civilization and China), *Tung-fang tsa-chih*, 23.24:93–94 (1926).
104. "Tu Liang Sou-ming hsien-sheng ti *Tung Hsi wen-hua chi ch'i che-hsüeh*," HSWT II, ii, 83.
105. "Ch'ing ta-chia lai chao-chao ching-tzu," HSWT III, i, 48.

beliefs that had not been critically examined, that they should learn to think independently. But by the end of the 1920s his tone was sharper:

> *We must acknowledge our own mistakes.* We must acknowledge that in a hundred ways we are inferior to others, and that it is not only in the material way and with respect to mechanization that we are not equal to others, but that politically, socially, and morally as well we are not equal to others . . .
>
> We have never once repented of our past misdeeds, or thoroughly reproached ourselves, or fully acknowledged our errors.
>
> [We must] *give up all hope, and go to study others.* Speaking frankly, we must not be afraid of imitating.[106]

The moving spirit of the decade born of the May Fourth movement in 1919 was an articulate and ardent nationalism that brought together in a common revolutionary cause Nationalists, Communists, and a growing number of intellectuals and students with no formal political affiliation. For some of these nationalism meant that the encumbrances of China's "feudal" past must be destroyed; for others it justified a reaffirmation of traditional standards. For nearly all it meant that China must throw off the political and economic burden of Western imperialism and regain her independence as a sovereign state.

In whatever guise, it was a movement that Hu Shih regarded with profound distrust, partly because he disagreed with the ideological assumptions that provided the rationale for the revolutionary cause, and partly because the cause itself was promoted primarily as a political movement. Hu clung to the view that China's fundamental problems were not political but social and intellectual, and that therefore cultural regeneration must take precedence over political reconstruction. And he was apprehensive of political activity, lest those who must bear the responsibility for intellectual leadership should dissipate their energies and compromise their integrity in wasteful political bickering. But throughout much of the 1920s, and later, the Chinese temper was little suited to Hu Shih's purposes. And even he found it impossible to stand against the current as his country was drawn deeper into the maelstrom of the revolution.

106. *Ibid.,* 48–49.

Hu Shih as a schoolboy, from a photograph taken shortly before his departure from Shanghai in 1910

Hu Shih in 1914, at the time of his graduation from Cornell

Hu Shih in China,
about 1920

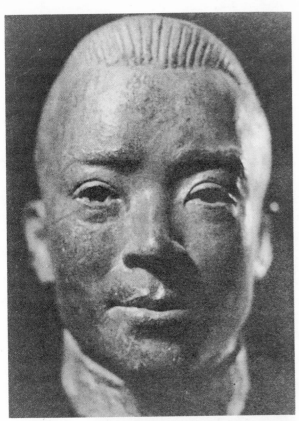

A portrait bust of Hu Shih by Lucile Swan, done in Peiping in the early 1930s

教育第一

△胡　適

五四運動，早露鋒鋩；獨立評論
，亦曾風行；一度出使，；瞬成黃粱；
不是依舊，猢猻稱王。

A postwar caricature by Loh Han-ying (pseud. Chang Kwong-tso). The inscription on the blackboard says, "Education first." The verse at left remarks upon the decline in Hu's reputation since the beginning of his affiliation with the Nationalist government.

Hu Shih in Taiwan in his later years

I try to keep neutral, so as to help the revival of learning as much as I can. And it seems to me that more is accomplished by civil modesty than by impetuosity.

Erasmus to Martin Luther

Part III. Liberalism

Chapter 6. Peking, 1917–1926

On the first of July, 1917, a restoration of the Manchu imperial house was proclaimed in Peking. The Hsüan-t'ung Emperor (P'u-i), deprived of his throne in 1912 at the age of six, again assumed the imperial title. Court robes long locked away were unpacked, and for a few days horsehair queues enjoyed a brisk sale on the streets of the ancient capital. K'ang Yu-wei, by then an old man, and older in spirit than in body, emerged from retirement in the south to give his benediction to the restoration and serve as an imperial adviser.

K'ang's presence imparted to the movement its closest link with the tradition of Confucian monarchy. For in fact this revival of the institutions of dynastic government was no more than a rather bizarre episode in the long struggle among various warlord factions for control of the "central" government of China which remained still in Peking, more from habit than by reason of effective control exercised over the rest of the country. With the emperor as his instrument, Chang Hsün, the military governor of Anhwei, strove to break the power of Tuan Ch'i-jui and the northern militarists who had risen to prominence after Yüan Shih-k'ai's death a year earlier. But Tuan, fighting on home ground, raised an anti-restoration army in the countryside around Peking, and by mid-July he was again in command of the city. The republic was saved, though its saviors, the victorious warlords, soon showed themselves to be no more deeply attached to republican ideals than their monarchist rivals had been moved by genuine loyalty to the young emperor whose cause they had proclaimed and who was now for a second time dispossessed of his imperial patrimony.

While this brief drama was being played out in Peking, Hu Shih was on his way home aboard the *Empress of Japan*. He learned of Chang Hsün's coup only when the ship docked in Yokohama on July 5. From the first Hu was confident that Chang would fail. What worried him instead was the willingness of Liang Ch'i-ch'ao and other "moderate" politicians, in whom Hu had placed great faith, to ally themselves with Tuan and his cohorts in common opposition to the restoration. He was convinced that there could be no genuine sharing of political interests between the warlords on the one hand and the advocates of responsible government on the other. "The militarists today, though nominally opposed to the restoration of imperial government, are in fact themselves at the root of these catastrophes. The moderates [*wen-chien-p'ai*] evidently hope to utilize the opposition of the militarists as a means of disposing of the Chang Hsün clique; but though they may temporarily come together, in the end they will fall out. If the current disorders continue as of old and this opportunity for reconstruction is let slip, there may not come another." [1]

1. *Diary*, 1165. In mid-July 1916, shortly after the death of Yüan Shih-k'ai, Hu wrote: "[When] people ask about the general trend of events at home, I reply that there are grounds for great hope. This is because the central figures of the present revolution are not of the radical party but rather of the moderate party, that is, the conservative party of former days . . . The reactionary bureaucratic party and the extremist radical party have both lost out at the same time, and it is the personalities of the moderate party upon whom all

Hu was essentially correct in his estimate of the viability of such an alliance, though it is difficult to perceive in the confused events of that July the "opportunity for reconstruction" of which he spoke, or to imagine how the moderates might have turned the affair to their own purpose as he had hoped they would. For men of such political scruples were then, as they remained throughout the following years, at a disadvantage in the tumultuous upheavals of warlord politics — armed only with vaguely defined standards of political conduct, which they sought to impose on governments that were founded on force and remained indifferent at best to the principles espoused by their critics. Hu himself was before long to feel the awkwardness of their situation.

After an absence of seven years Hu Shih returned to Shanghai in the summer of 1917 to find that the city's once stimulating intellectual life had become sterile and stifling. "I realized then," he wrote some years later, "that the restoration had been an entirely natural phenomenon." What he saw in China confirmed the opinion he had reached before he left the United States: he became even more convinced that intellectual and cultural regeneration must take precedence over political reform, and that new social values must supersede the old before a satisfactory political settlement could be effected. From his initial sense of shock and disappointment came Hu's resolve "to refrain from talking politics for twenty years," in the hope that in that time "a new foundation for Chinese politics" might be laid.[2]

In the end it proved an impossible resolution to keep. Time and again in the following years Hu was prompted to publish his political views, though invariably he did so with a certain diffidence. His public role, however, was always that of an observer, a political critic. In an era when revolutionary agitation engulfed the streets of China's cities and filtered even into the narrow alleys of hinter-

are relying. The conservative thought of these men has been destroyed by the above-mentioned extremists of both kinds, and they have progressed from conservatism to moderation. Moreover, since the reputation of the members of the extremist parties (like Huang Hsing among the new [men] and Yüan Shih-k'ai among the old) has already declined, there remain only such moderates as Liang Ch'i-ch'ao and Chang Chien, whose reputations are still good, in whom men can put their faith." (*Diary*, 960–961.)

2. Hu Shih, "Wo-ti ch'i-lu" (My crossroads), HSWT II, iii, 96 and 108; first published in NLCP no. 7 (June 18, 1922). See also Hu Shih, "Kuei-kuo tsa-kan" (Random reflections on returning home), HSWT, iv, 871–882; first published in HCN 4.1 (January 1918).

land villages, Hu clung stubbornly to his belief that such political activity was, for an intellectual, wasteful of energies that might better be devoted to more constructive causes.

The course of events from 1917 to 1919 could well have encouraged Hu to hope that his apolitical approach to problems of social and intellectual reform was destined to prevail. Possibly out of deference to his views, and certainly with his wholehearted approval, *The New Youth* adhered to a policy of noninvolvement in politics during these years.[3] But 1919 marked a turning point that made such a preoccupation with literary and cultural concerns appear to many only peripheral to the vital issues of the moment. Frustrated by the outcome of the Paris Peace Conference, which had supported Japan's claim to former German concessions in Shantung, and infuriated by their government's supine acceptance of the Treaty of Versailles, the students of Peking took to the streets on May 4 to vent their anger. In the course of the ensuing protests the students realized for the first time their power as a political force. One immediate result of the unfamiliar sense of purpose and importance thus engendered was an extraordinary proliferation of student-sponsored periodicals and magazines to serve as vehicles for the dissemination of the "new thought."[4] The May Fourth movement served in this fashion to broaden the basis of participation in the discussion of new ideas. At the same time, however, the events of 1919 established a tradition of active political engagement as an honorable, and even necessary, expression of the intellectuals' public concern and encouraged the very kind of activity of which Hu Shih was so profoundly apprehensive.

At the end of his life Hu described the May Fourth movement as "a most unwelcome interruption" of the work initiated in 1917

3. In an interview at Nankang, Taiwan, on July 5, 1960, Hu Shih told me that *The New Youth* group adhered to its apolitical stand out of deference to his opinions. It should be pointed out, however, that the policy had been laid down originally by Ch'en Tu-hsiu, though it is probably true that Hu Shih's strong views on this subject served to maintain the policy after Ch'en began to feel that it imposed an artificial restraint. See Maurice Meisner, *Li Ta-chao*, 38 and 273, n. 19 and n. 20. See also *Tu-hsiu wen-ts'un*, iii, 11–12 and 125–126.

4. Estimates of the number of new periodicals published in 1919 vary considerably, due partly to the ephemeral quality of many of the student publications of that year. Hu Shih set the figure at about four hundred; see Hu Shih, "Intellectual China in 1919," *The Chinese Social and Political Science Review*, 4.4:348 (December 1919). See also Chow Tse-tsung, *The May Fourth Movement*, 178–180, and *Research Guide to the May Fourth Movement* (Cambridge, Mass., 1963), 43–68.

and 1918, a blow from which the New Culture movement never fully recovered.[5] But at the time he took a very different view of the matter. In a summary of the year's activities written (in English) in December 1919 he praised the movement as an indication of the growing awareness of the importance of nonpolitical reform, and he spoke with confidence of its intellectual significance. The rapidity of the "intellectual transformation" in recent months, he wrote, had "even astounded those who have entertained the wildest hopes for its final triumph." Ever since 1898, the year of K'ang Yu-wei's abortive reform program, Chinese intellectuals "had staked all their hopes on the political, at the expense of neglecting the nonpolitical. They were bound to be disappointed, and great indeed was their disappointment!" [6] But the events of 1919, Hu continued, had offered "a new lesson":

> It was the nonpolitical forces — the students, the merchants, the demonstrations and street orations, and the boycott — that did the work and triumphed. This was a great revelation and produced a new optimism.
>
> . . . Let alone the Anfu Club [i.e., Tuan Ch'i-jui's faction, still in control of the Peking government]; let alone the internal peace conference at Shanghai [a warlord conference convened early in 1919 in an unsuccessful attempt to negotiate the reunification of north and south]; let alone the petty political intrigues in Peking and elsewhere — we still have the masses to educate, the women to emancipate, the schools to reform, the home industries to develop, the family system to reshape, the dead and antiquated ideas to combat, the false and harmful idols to dethrone, the many, many social and economic wrongs to redress. It is in these new channels of activity that Young China, with reawakened hope and vigor, is now working slowly but steadily to rebuild a new foundation for Chinese democracy.[7]

The view set forth here of what constitutes "political" activity

5. Vincent Shih, "A Talk with Hu Shih," *China Quarterly*, no. 10:163 (April–June 1962). This is an account of a conversation that Professor Shih had with Hu Shih in the spring of 1959. Hu told me virtually the same thing when I interviewed him in July 1960. See also Oral History, 188–189.

6. "Intellectual China in 1919," 345, 350.

7. *Ibid.*, 350–351.

is significant. When Hu Shih spoke of "politics," he had in mind the cynical intrigues of warlord governments. To him, "participation in politics" meant dealing with these corrupt regimes on their own terms, and a "political solution" meant a settlement reached by accommodation with rascals. Real reform could not be achieved by such means, he contended, for it was not, in this sense, a political problem, but a much broader complex of social and intellectual problems. Hu regarded democracy — the ultimate goal toward which he strove — less as a concrete system of political institutions than as a state of mind conducive to the maintenance of a particular social condition. It followed logically that the creation of a democratic society would be essentially an intellectual rather than a political accomplishment. One of the happy results of 1919, he wrote at year's end, had been an awakening to "a better understanding of the meaning of democracy." "Eight years of bitter failure under a nominal republic has gradually brought young China to the realization that democracy cannot be secured through political changes alone . . . Democracy . . . is no more and no less than the sum total of all the democratized and democratizing forces, social, economic, moral, and intellectual. It is this realization which constitutes one of the guiding principles of the new movements in China." [8]

At the end of 1919 Hu had some reason to entertain such confident expectations. The prevailing mood of exalted intellectualism was vividly reflected in the declarations of principles set forth by many of the new periodicals that sprang up in the wake of the May Fourth demonstrations: "To reform the nation and society, physically and socially" — "To introduce new thoughts to the citizen and uplift his personality while promoting home industries" — "To bring about a development of learning so as to apply the idea of research and criticism to the reform of society" — "To introduce new thoughts to the world, and to apply an optimistic but critical attitude to the reconstruction of society." [9] For Hu Shih it must have been both satisfying and reassuring to find such sentiments in general circulation and expressed in language so close to his own.

In his interpretation of the significance of the May Fourth movement, Hu enjoyed, moreover, the concurrence of his American mentor. John Dewey had arrived in China in time to witness

8. *Ibid.*, 350.
9. Chow Tse-tsung, *The May Fourth Movement*, 180.

at first hand the crisis of May and June, and he had been greatly impressed. "This is the first time that students have taken any organized part in politics," he wrote at midsummer. "The spell of pessimism seems broken. An act has been done, a deed performed."[10] Before the end of the year, however, Dewey observed with satisfaction that the movement had been "diverted from breaking against the political and militaristic dam" and had instead been "drawn into a multitude of side streams and is now irrigating the intellectual and industrial soil of China . . . The students' organizations have gone into popular education, social and philanthropic service and vigorous intellectual discussion. China has never been anything but apathetic towards governmental questions. The Student Revolt marked a temporary exception only in appearance . . . The more the so-called political revolution exhibits itself as a failure, the more active is the demand for an intellectual revolution which will make some future political revolution a reality . . . When most political in its outward expression, [the Student Revolt] was not a political movement. It was the manifestation of a new consciousness, an intellectual awakening in the young men and young women who through their schooling had been aroused to the necessity of a new order of belief, a new method of thinking."[11]

Yet if this was true, it was only a partial truth, even in 1919. As Hu Shih finally acknowledged, the attitudes engendered in 1919 were not apolitical either in inspiration or direction. The government of Tuan Ch'i-jui that Hu dismissed so lightly was the first object of the students' resentment; its collapse in early June was the movement's first concrete accomplishment. Over the next several years, moreover, the forces that Hu had confidently labeled "nonpolitical" lent themselves increasingly to obviously political uses. Both the reorganized Nationalist Party of Sun Yat-sen and the nascent Communist Party drew much of their strength and vitality from their ability to harness the energies released in 1919 to the promotion of their own political programs. Hu Shih had badly misjudged the situation, and he approached the turbulent decade of the 1920s with an imperfect understanding of the forces that would shape the course of events.

10. John Dewey, "The Student Revolt in China," *The New Republic*, 20.248: 18 (Aug. 6, 1919).

11. John Dewey, "The Sequel of the Student Revolt," *The New Republic*, 21.273:380–382 (Feb. 25, 1920).

Even before the May Fourth movement Hu Shih's insistent demand that intellectuals should shun political discussions had been the cause of dissension among the members of the "New Youth group" in Peking. As early as July 1918 Ch'en Tu-hsiu had complained, in the pages of *The New Youth,* "My associates on this magazine, and its readers, frequently take exception to my speaking of political matters. Some contend that the important thing for our generation of youth is to cultivate learning and reconstruct society from its foundations, and question the need to talk of politics. Others say that this magazine once declared that its purpose is to guide the youth, rather than to comment on the political happenings of the moment, and ask why we should now engage in discussions of the events cast up by politics. Alas! such talk is all wrong . . . I am speaking now not of the problems of common politics, nor of the problems of political administration, but of the fundamental political problems that concern the survival of the nation and the race." [12] By placing such emphasis on the need for the discussion of "fundamental" political problems Ch'en underscored a point of basic disagreement with Hu Shih. Hu consistently denied that it was possible to treat fundamental problems in meaningful terms. When he reluctantly permitted himself to be drawn into political debate, it was to what Ch'en had called the problems of "common politics" that he addressed himself: civil service reforms, bureaucratic reorganization, constitutional revision. This difference of opinion as to the proper definition of political concerns proved, in the end, irreconcilable.

Although Hu was generally successful in his endeavor to keep *The New Youth* free from political entanglements, he could not curb the desire of his friends to speak out. When his mother died, late in November 1918, and he returned to Anhwei for the funeral, several of the more restive members of the New Youth group — Ch'en Tu-hsiu, Li Ta-chao, Kao I-han, and Chang Wei-tz'u — took advantage of Hu's absence from Peking to establish a small magazine, *The Weekly Critic (Mei-chou p'ing-lun),* expressly as a forum for political debate. The manifesto published to mark its inauguration at the end of December is revealing of the mood of the moment and the temper of the men.

12. Ch'en Tu-hsiu, "Chin-jih Chung-kuo chih cheng-chih wen-t'i" (China's present political problems), *Tu-hsiu wen-ts'un,* i, 221–225. First published in HCN 5.1 (July 1918).

Since the defeat of Germany, the phrase "Right triumphs over might" has become almost a platitude.

Do you want to know what right is, and what might is? In simple terms, right means everything which is in accord with equality and freedom, and might means to rely on one's own strength to encroach upon the equality and freedom of others . . .

The fact that "Right triumphs over might," as the people of every nation of the world should clearly understand, [means] that might is unreliable, and that we must speak instead of right, with regard both to internal and external affairs . . .

Our purpose in publishing *The Weekly Critic* is also summed up in the words "To advocate Right and oppose Might," in the hope that in the future might shall not triumph over right. Long live mankind! Long live this paper! [13]

Hu was presented with this fait accompli when he returned to Peking early in 1919. In response to Ch'en's invitation he contributed a few translations of short stories to *The Weekly Critic*,[14] and an occasional poem, but otherwise he stood aloof from it for several months. In June, however, Ch'en was arrested by Tuan Ch'i-jui's gendarmes — he had been caught at one of Peking's popular teahouses passing out handbills denouncing the government's attempts to suppress the student demonstrations — and at this juncture Hu agreed to assume editorial responsibility for *The Weekly Critic*.[15] In July and August his essays on "Problems and Isms," al-

13. "*Mei-chou p'ing-lun* fa-k'an tz'u" (Inaugural statement of The weekly critic), reprinted in *Chung-kuo hsin wen-hsüeh ta-hsi*, X, 190.

14. According to one account, written in 1932, Hu Shih contributed only two translations to *Mei-chou p'ing-lun;* see Chow Tse-tsung, *The May Fourth Movement,* 57. But according to the preface to *Tuan-p'ien hsiao-shuo ti-i chi* (1919), at least three of the short stories in that collection had appeared originally in *Mei-chou p'ing-lun:* Hu's translations of Strindberg's "Love and Bread," Castelnuevo's "An Unsent Letter," and Gorki's "Her Lover."

15. In the interview I had with him in July 1960, Hu recalled that on the day of the arrest (June 11, 1919) Ch'en Tu-hsiu had invited Hu and Kao I-han to have tea with him at one of Peking's more popular teahouses — Hu could not remember whether it was the Ta shih-chieh (Great world) or the Hsin shih-chieh (New world). No sooner had Hu and Kao arrived than Ch'en produced a great wad of handbills demanding action against the government for its mistreatment of the students; as Ch'en began to distribute these among the patrons, Hu and Kao took their leave. That evening Hu was informed by a mutual acquaintance, a Peking journalist, of Ch'en's arrest. This account differs slightly from other versions of what happened on that June 11; see, for

ready referred to, were published in its pages, together with lengthy
rebuttals from Li Ta-chao and Lan Chih-hsien. These essays, Hu
remarked some years later, constituted "the introduction to my
political theory," but because *The Weekly Critic* was finally shut
down by the government early in September, "I never had the opportunity to get on to the 'text' itself." [16] Still he felt compelled
to offer a retrospective justification even for this brief excursion
into the forbidden realm of politics. In 1922, in an essay entitled
"My Crossroads" ("Wo-ti ch'i-lu"), Hu recalled the circumstances
of that earlier day: "It was just at that time that the Anfu Clique
was at the height of its power, and the spoils-sharing Shanghai
peace conference had not yet dissolved.[17] But as far as concrete
political problems were concerned, the 'new' elements within the
nation kept their silence, though they talked expansively of such
things as anarchism and Marxism. I could not bear the sight of
this, I could no longer tolerate it — because I am an experimentalist — and my indignation drove me to speak out about politics." [18]

In "Problems and Isms," however, Hu was "talking politics"
only in a rather particular sense. Without himself engaging in a
detailed analysis of specific issues, he appealed to his fellow intellectuals to deal with concrete political problems, and he warned
them against the dangers of abstractions and vague generalizations.
"There is no abstract noun in the world," he argued, "which can
encompass the proposals of a given man or group." Abstractions,

---

example, Maurice Meisner, *Li Ta-chao,* 103. Ch'en had edited *Mei-chou p'ing-
lun* in his own home, and after his arrest the magazine remained without an
editor until Hu Shih agreed to assume the responsibility — the implication being, in Hu's telling of the story, that no one else dared to take the job. A similar
account is given in Oral History, 189–190. A contradictory version of the story
is given by the Communists, who, in line with their characterization of Hu as
a political reactionary, accuse him of trying to seize control of *The Weekly
Critic* in order to subvert its revolutionary policies. See Li Lung-mu, "I-ko
'Wu-ssu' shih-ch'i ti cheng-chih k'an-wu — *Mei-chou p'ing-lun*" (A political
publication of the May Fourth era: *The weekly critic*), in Chang Ching-lu, ed.,
Chung-kuo hsien-tai ch'u-pan shih-liao (Materials on the history of contemporary Chinese publishing; Peking, 1954–1959), IV, 40–43.

16. "Wo-ti ch'i-lu," HSWT II, iii, 97.

17. Hu's memory seems to have deserted him on this point: the peace conference had collapsed in mid-May. See Li Chien-nung, *The Political History of
China*, 388–393.

18. "Wo-ti ch'i-lu," HSWT II, iii, 96.

however, tend to make men "satisfied and complacent, in the belief that they are seeking the panacea of a 'fundamental solution,'" and thus imperil the future course of the reform movement as a whole.[19] The issue of "fundamental solutions" as opposed to gradualist reforms rose to the surface repeatedly in Hu's disputes with his friends of more revolutionary inclinations. His reference to it in the summer of 1919 was an indication of the growing ideological tension within the leadership of the New Culture movement.

The rift did not become final, however, until the winter of 1920–21. In the autumn of 1919, after Ch'en Tu-hsiu's release from prison, a reconciliation of conflicting attitudes seemed to have been achieved. The December issue of *The New Youth* carried a manifesto signed by Hu, Ch'en, Li, and a number of others, the purpose of which was to reaffirm the magazine's identification with the cultural revolution. Although Li Ta-chao was already well on the way to a full commitment to Marxism-Leninism, and Ch'en Tu-hsiu's conversion was imminent, the manifesto reflected little or nothing of their new enthusiasm. It was, rather, an expression of Hu Shih's opinions, embodying only minimal concessions on his part. So, for example, the sponsors of the statement acknowledged that "although we do not believe in the omnipotence of politics, yet we recognize that politics is an important aspect of public life." But they continued, "We believe it is requisite for the progress of our present society to uphold natural science and experimentalist philosophy and to abolish superstition and fantasy."[20] In the same issue of *The New Youth* appeared the first installment of a translation (by Kao I-han) of Dewey's recent lectures on social and political philosophy, together with Hu's survey of "The Meaning of the New Thought" ("Hsin ssu-ch'ao ti i-i"), in which he returned briefly to his attack on "isms" and outlined his own gradualist program of social and intellectual regeneration.[21] Finally, in that same December number, Ch'en Tu-hsiu published an essay entitled "The Basis for the Realization of Democracy" ("Shih-hsing min-chih ti chi-ch'u"), accepting — if only temporarily — Dewey's (and Hu's) particularistic approach and stressing the necessity for thinking in

19. "Wen-t'i yü chu-i," HSWT, ii, 483, 487.

20. *"Hsin ch'ing-nien tsa-chih* hsüan-yen" (Manifesto of The new youth magazine), HCN 7.1 (December 1919). I follow, with slight modifications, the translation given in Chow Tse-tsung, *The May Fourth Movement*, 175.

21. HSWT, iv, 1021–1034.

terms of slow and piecemeal reforms rather than all-embracing solutions.[22]

It was the last occasion on which Hu and Ch'en spoke with a common understanding. That winter Ch'en moved from Peking to Shanghai, at the same time resuming full editorial responsibility for *The New Youth*.[23] Thereafter the magazine served more and more as an outlet for the Marxist views of Ch'en and others, though several members of the original Peking group continued to publish in it for some time. Hu Shih contributed nothing of general significance to *The New Youth* after the end of 1919 and was represented in its pages only by a few articles on literary reform and an occasional poem. His personal break with Ch'en Tu-hsiu came in the winter of 1920–21, chronicled in an exchange of letters between Ch'en on the one side and Hu and a number of his colleagues in Peking on the other.

In mid-December 1920 Ch'en wrote to Hu and Kao I-han from Shanghai, informing them of his imminent departure for Canton at Sun Yat-sen's invitation. *The New Youth*, he said, would henceforth be edited by Ch'en Wang-tao, an avowed Marxist[24] — as,

22. *Tu-hsiu wen-ts'un*, i, 373–389. On Ch'en's intellectual condition at the end of 1919 see also Chow Tse-tsung, *The May Fourth Movement*, 230–232; Benjamin I. Schwartz, *Chinese Communism and the Rise of Mao*, 19–20; and Maurice Meisner, *Li Ta-chao*, 112–113.

23. Since January 1918 *The New Youth* had been edited by a committee that included, besides Ch'en Tu-hsiu, Hu Shih, Ch'ien Hsüan-t'ung, Li Ta-chao, Liu Fu, and Shen Yin-mo (with others later joining this group); see Chow Tse-tsung, *The May Fourth Movement*, 44, note d. According to Hu Shih (in the interview I had with him in July 1960 and also in the Oral History, 191–192), Ch'en Tu-hsiu was paroled from prison in September 1919 "in the old way," i.e., through the intervention in his behalf of Hu Shih and other natives of Anhwei, which was also Ch'en's native province. Ch'en had been on leave of absence from Peita since the spring of 1919, but he continued to receive his salary. In January 1920, however, Ch'en went to Wuhan, substituting at a speaking engagement for Hu Shih, who was busy translating for John Dewey in Peking. He thus in effect broke parole. The Peking police discovered his absence, and soon after he returned to Peking he was forced to flee the city, together with Li Ta-chao, in whose house he had sought refuge. At this point his Peita salary was stopped, and since he had no other means of support it was agreed that he should resume sole editorial responsibility for *Hsin ch'ing-nien* and be paid a salary for his services. Ch'en settled in Shanghai and within a few months announced his conversion to Marxism.

24. Ch'en Wang-tao was a Japanese-educated journalist and scholar. He was active in the organizational meetings that led to the founding of the Chinese Communist Party, and it was he who made the first complete translation of *The Communist Manifesto* into Chinese, published in April 1920.

indeed, was Ch'en Tu-hsiu himself by this time — and, what was probably just as disturbing to Hu, a stranger to the Peking group. In the same letter, apparently in response to earlier criticism, Ch'en Tu-hsiu expressed his own "disagreement" with the "new style" of *The New Youth* in recent months, adding that Ch'en Wang-tao was also anxious to "change the contents slightly" and "henceforth to emphasize philosophy and literature, as of old." But, he continued, "this makes it imperative that our associates in Peking should write more articles. If the content of our recent issues has changed . . . one important reason is that our associates have sent us too few essays." [25]

To this rebuke Hu Shih retorted that, in spite of Ch'en's expressed desire to reform *The New Yorth,* "this is already no easy matter. The skill of the Peking associates in washing clean is no match for the lightning-quick methods of the Shanghai group in besmirching." He suggested that if *The New Youth* was allowed to continue as "a particular and partisan journal," a new magazine should be established to be devoted exclusively to literature and philosophy, "small in size but unadulterated in content." If, on the other hand, Ch'en genuinely hoped to avoid an open rift in the New Youth group, Hu insisted that this could be accomplished only by returning editorship of the magazine to Peking and publishing another manifesto, similar in temper to that of the year before but explicitly disavowing political discussions.[26]

Ch'en Tu-hsiu objected vehemently to the idea of returning *The New Youth* to Peking, which in effect would have taken the magazine out of his hands. Even more strongly he rejected Hu's demand for a public declaration of disengagement from politics. On the latter point he was supported by several of Hu's friends in Peking — T'ao Meng-ho, Chou Tso-jen, and Lu Hsün. "I think it quite unnecessary," Lu Hsün wrote to Hu early in January 1921. "This is, of course, partly because of 'not wanting to appear weak in the eyes of others'; but in fact everything that the New Youth group writes, no matter what we may proclaim, gives officialdom a head-

25. Ch'en Tu-hsiu's letter to Hu Shih and Kao I-han, dated Dec. 16, 1920; reprinted in Chang Ching-lu, ed., *Chung-kuo hsien-tai ch'u-pan shih-liao,* I, 7. According to Hu Shih (interview of July 5, 1960) this and the following letters were among the documents that Hu left at Peita when he fled Peking in December 1948; they were on display as part of an exhibition commemorating the university's fiftieth anniversary.

26. Hu Shih's letter to Ch'en Tu-hsiu, undated, *ibid.,* 8.

ache for which they can't forgive us." [27] Bowing to such opposition, Hu abandoned the idea of a new manifesto, but he remained adamant in his insistence that *The New Youth* should again be edited in Peking.

In the end the dispute was unwittingly resolved in Ch'en's favor by the intervention of the French police, who at the prompting of the Shanghai authorities confiscated the plates for the February issue of *The New Youth* just prior to publication. In the middle of February Ch'en wrote to Hu that the only way out of the situation was to transfer the magazine to Canton, where it might prosper in an environment more friendly to its revolutionary aims. His conviction that *The New Youth* should not be returned to Peking had arisen, he said, from his belief that, "speaking quite frankly, . . . the atmosphere at the University has not been good recently." He welcomed the idea of a new journal devoted to scholarship but rejected in advance any suggestion that he contribute to it. Finally he appended this admonition: "You urge me not to entertain too many doubts about my friends, and I acknowledge this as advice that I ought never to forget. But I am constantly fearful lest my good friends, in their ivory tower, should let themselves be used by the politicians." [28]

Publication of *The New Youth* was in fact resumed in Canton in April, with Ch'en still in control of the magazine he had founded six years earlier. In effect Hu Shih's association with both came to an end.[29] Two and a half years later he wrote with regret, "The

27. Lu Hsün's letter to Hu Shih, dated Jan. 3, 1921, *ibid.*, 12. This is reprinted in *Lu Hsün ch'üan-chi* (Complete works of Lu Hsün; Peking, 1958), IX, 301.

28. Ch'en Tu-hsiu's letter to Hu Shih, dated Feb. 15, 1921, in Chang Ching-lu, ed., *Chung-kuo hsien-tai ch'u-pan shih-liao*, I, 13. Ch'en's apprehension in this regard was shared by Li Ta-chao, who wrote to Hu about this time: "Of late we university people are rather in the situation of a young virgin — the Communications Clique [Chiao-t'ung hsi], the Research Clique [Yen-chiu hsi], and the Political Study Clique [Cheng-hsüeh hsi] all want to compromise our virtue, and, frustrated in this, they spread rumors about us. And then there's the Nationalist Clique [Kuo-min hsi], which, seeing these others pant and drool over us, inevitably becomes a little jealous and begins to make a nuisance of itself!" (*Ibid.*, 12.) The various cliques referred to here were bureaucrat-militarist factions jockeying for influence within, or ranged against, the Peking government.

29. There is a notable difference in the nature of Hu Shih's attitudes toward, and relationships with, the two most celebrated first-generation converts to Marxism-Leninism in China, Li Ta-chao and Ch'en Tu-hsiu. With Li, who was the first to declare his allegiance to Marxism, Hu remained on terms of

destiny of *The New Youth* lay with the revolution in literature and thought. Unfortunately this destiny was cut short in mid-course . . . Had *The New Youth* continued to the present day, dedicating itself without interruption over the past six years [i.e., since 1917,

---

intimate and affectionate friendship, terminated only by Li's execution in 1927. Hu later mourned Li's death in the dedication of the third series of his *Collected Essays* (*Hu Shih wen-ts'un, san chi;* Shanghai, 1930). The warmth of this friendship is the more interesting because Li Ta-chao was in many respects Hu's polar opposite: fervently nationalistic, anti-Western to an unusual degree for a member of *The New Youth* group, mass-oriented in his thinking even before his conversion to Marxism, and from an early age strongly inclined to political activism. Maurice Meisner, on whose excellent biography of Li Ta-chao I have relied in making these evaluations, remarks upon "the quality of amiability that marked his [Li's] personal relations" and observes that "Li took particular pains to prevent political differences from degenerating into personal quarrels" (p. 220). This could be said with equal justice of Hu Shih.

With Ch'en Tu-hsiu, on the other hand, Hu maintained a respectful, but hardly cordial, relationship despite the fact that Ch'en's views prior to 1920 were closer to his own than were Li's. Temperamentally Ch'en was quite differently constituted: "combative, fearlessly individualistic, and impatient of convention or authority of any sort," with "a penchant for polemic" and "a taste for violent partisanship" (Boorman, *Biographical Dictionary,* I, 248). It is worth noting, in passing, that both Hu Shih and Li Ta-chao were content to be married in the traditional fashion; Ch'en Tu-hsiu, in a comparable situation, is believed to have abandoned his wife. After Ch'en's departure from Peking in the winter of 1919–1920, of course, physical as well as intellectual separation made it unlikely that Hu and Ch'en could maintain a close relationship. The last sustained dialogue between them seems to have been the exchange on "materialism" provoked by the 1923 debate on science and the philosophy of life. On more than one occasion Hu interceded with the authorities on Ch'en's behalf: in 1919, as noted above; again in 1922, following Ch'en's arrest in the French Concession in Shanghai, when Hu urged his friend Ku Wei-chün (V. K. Wellington Koo), the Foreign Minister of the Peking government, to have a word with the French lest student opinion should become inflamed or Ch'en be denied the sanctuary of the Concession (see Hu Shih's unpublished diaries, entries for Aug. 16 and 19, 1922); and again, indirectly, in 1932 after Ch'en's arrest by the Nationalist government. In this last instance *Tu-li p'ing-lun* (The independent critic), the liberal weekly that Hu Shih edited in Peking during the 1930s, rose to Ch'en's defense, though it was not Hu Shih but Fu Ssu-nien who outlined the position, in strikingly mild terms: "The government, with its responsibility for the maintenance of law and order, cannot casually set men free, [but] at the same time the Kuomintang has not the right, in a time when the forces of reaction are gathering strength, to extinguish this fiery, long-tailed comet of the Chinese revolution!" (See Fu Ssu-nien, "Ch'en Tu-hsiu an" [The case of Ch'en Tu-hsiu], TLPL no. 24 [Oct. 30, 1932].)

Ch'en Tu-hsiu died in 1942; Hu Shih outlived him by twenty years and had the privilege of passing posthumous judgment on his old comrade-in-arms: in the preface to a slender collection of Ch'en's last essays, published after World War II, Hu welcomed him back (with perhaps just a trace of condescension) to the ranks of those who struggle for democracy and individual freedom.

when Hu himself had joined it] to the business of literary and intellectual revolution, its influence would certainly not have been slight." [30]

The "new magazine" of which Hu Shih had spoken in his correspondence with Ch'en Tu-hsiu did not make its appearance until the spring of 1922. It turned out to be something quite different from the "unadulterated" scholarly journal that Hu had originally envisioned.[31] It was called, symbolically, *The Endeavor* (*Nu-li chou-pao*). In the first issue, published in Peking on May 7, Hu set the theme of the new enterprise with a poem entitled "The Song of Endeavor" ("Nu-li ko"):

"This situation can't last long."
My friends, you are wrong.
Unless you and I do something about it
This situation can last a long time.

Nothing in the world is impossible
Unless you and I, who call ourselves good men,
Should say, "It is impossible to do anything."
Then, indeed, it would become impossible.[32]

True to the promise of these lines, in *The Endeavor* Hu Shih assumed for the first time the role of a commentator on the passing political scene. The person chiefly responsible for this abrupt change in Hu's attitude toward politics was Ting Wen-chiang, the British-educated geologist already mentioned as a defender of science in the disputes of 1923. *The Endeavor* was as much Ting's undertaking as it was Hu's. But of those most closely associated with this new venture only he had had no connection with *The New Youth*, and he utterly scorned the self-conscious attempts that Hu and his friends had made to remain above the political strug-

30. Hu Shih's letter to Kao I-han, Chang Wei-tz'u, and others, dated Oct. 9, 1923, HSWT II, iii, 141–144.

31. It should be noted that Hu Shih was busy at this same time with preparations for the publication of another journal, *Kuo-hsüeh chi-k'an* (Sinological quarterly), as an outlet for the growing body of modern critical scholarship. Volume I, number 1 was published in January 1923, with Hu serving as editor-in-chief. *Kuo-hsüeh chi-k'an* was one of the most prestigious academic journals of the prewar years; it survived until 1937.

32. NLCP no. 1 (May 7, 1922); reprinted in *Ting Wen-chiang ti chuan-chi*, 37.

gle. Ting dismissed as "a kind of fantasy" Hu's belief that politics could be relegated to a subordinate position, and he scoffed at "Hu Shih-chih's trick of saying that political reform must start from [a revolution in] thought and literature." [33]

Thus stung, Hu acquiesced to Ting's argument that social reform can succeed only in a politically progressive environment. For the time being he was fully committed to this new belief, refusing to be dissuaded even by those friends who held up before him the example of Liang Ch'i-ch'ao's unfortunate associations with the governments of Yüan Shih-k'ai and Tuan Ch'i-jui. Liang's mistake, in Hu's view, was to accept public office under the warlords; he himself was trying only to live up to his responsibilities as a disinterested commentator on public issues, and he would never succumb to the lure of official position. [34]

Nevertheless, Hu was at pains to demonstrate that his position had changed less than it might appear. His primary concern, he said, was still what it had been in 1919 when he wrote "Problems and Isms." He had waited, he remarked in an early issue of *The Endeavor*, for "two years and eight months" (that is, since the publication of the manifesto of the New Youth Society at the end of 1919) for a "new public opinion" to make itself felt, until "now I can stand it no longer. If I come out at the present juncture to speak of politics, although in part I am driven to it by the corruption of domestic politics, in fact I am compelled to speak in large part by the 'new public opinion' of recent years, which 'talks a great deal of isms, but does not study problems.' In talking politics now I am only putting into practice my own proposal to 'study more problems and talk less of isms' . . . I am greatly dissatisfied with present-day thought and art, for though the slaves of Confucius and Chu Hsi are fewer now, a new breed of slaves of Marx and Kropotkin has sprung up. The rotten old orthodoxies have been overthrown, but in their place are various wretched new orthodoxies." [35]

The front page of the second issue of *The Endeavor*, published on May 14, was entirely given over to a manifesto entitled "Our Political Proposals." He had drafted it originally to serve only as a

33. *Ting Wen-chiang ti chuan-chi*, 35–36.
34. See, for example, Hu Shih's unpublished diaries, entry for Feb. 7, 1922.
35. "Wo-ti ch'i-lu," HSWT II, iii, 99–102; see also unpublished diary, entry for Feb. 7, 1922.

statement of editorial policy, but in its final form it incorporated revisions suggested by Li Ta-chao and Ts'ai Yüah-p'ei, and it carried the signatures of Ting Wen-chiang, Kao I-han, T'ao Meng-ho, Liang Sou-ming, and a number of other scholars and public figures.[36] "Our Political Proposals" was the first systematic summary of opinions that can be identified as "liberal," and it constituted the platform of what came to be called, for reasons that will shortly be obvious, the "good government group."

Perhaps the most striking impression conveyed by "Our Political Proposals" arises from what it reveals of the environment of public life in warlord China. The specific recommendations put forward by its sponsors, concerning such issues as the reunification of northern and southern governments, the re-establishment of a "legitimate" parliamentary organ, the drafting of a permanent constitution, disarmament, bureaucratic reforms, and the introduction of systems of public budgeting and accounting, reflect the whole range of abuses inflicted upon China's nominally republican institutions by successive warlord regimes: large "private" armies maintained by foreign loans and burdensome domestic levies, swollen bureaucratic structures in which office was held regardless of merit or ability, parliamentary processes designed to suit the convenience of men strong enough to impose their ambitions by force or bribery, the absence of any fundamental law against which

36. Hu Shih, "Wo-men-ti cheng-chih chu-chang" (Our political proposals), HSWT II, iii, 27–34. First published in NLCP no. 2 (May 14, 1922), signed by Ts'ai Yüan-p'ei (Chancellor of Peita), Wang Ch'ung-hui (Professor at Peita), Lo Wen-kan (Professor at Peita), T'ang Erh-ho (M.D.), T'ao Chih-hsing (Chairman, Department of Education, Tung-nan University [Nanking]), Wang Po-ch'iu (Chairman, Department of Law and Economics, Tung-nan University), Liang Sou-ming (Professor at Peita), Li Ta-chao (Librarian at Peita), T'ao Meng-ho (Chairman, Department of Philosophy, Peita), Chu Ching-nung (Professor at Peita), Chang Wei-tz'u (Professor at Peita), Kao I-han (Professor at Peita), Hsü Pao-huang (Professor at Peita), Wang Cheng (Secretary, New American Consortium), Ting Wen-chiang (Former Director, Geological Survey Institute), and Hu Shih (Dean, Peita). Hu's unpublished diary establishes him as the principal author of this manifesto; see entries for April 22 and 27, and May 11 and 14, 1922. Hu apparently drafted "Our Political Proposals" at the prompting of Ts'ai Yüan-p'ei, to whom, in turn, the idea of such a document had been suggested by Lin Ch'ang-min (tzu Tsung-meng), a member of Liang Ch'i-ch'ao's so-called "Research Clique" (Yen-chiu hsi). Lin and Liang envisioned it as a joint manifesto to be signed by them and by others prominent in education or public life. This idea did not appeal to Hu because of the somewhat unsavory reputation for political opportunism that clung to Liang and his party. Much to the chagrin of Liang and his friends Hu did not consult them, and "Our Political Proposals" was published without their signatures.

to measure political conduct, and, most irksome of all, the total indifference of such governments to the opinions of their critics and the people whom they claimed to govern. It is against this sordid background that the manifesto of May 1922 must be judged.

The significance of "Our Political Proposals" goes beyond the circumstances of the time in which it was published, however. In its prefatory paragraphs, translated *in extenso* below, were set forth assumptions and objectives that remained for many years central features of the liberal approach to politics.

"In order to provide everyone with a basic starting point for discussion, we here first raise our own proposals concerning Chinese politics, inviting all to criticize, discuss, or express their approval.

"I. The objectives of political reform: We hold that, while it is permissible to refrain from political discussions today, if we do talk politics we should have [before us] an effective and clear objective which all can understand. We also contend that the outstanding elements of the nation, no matter what may be their ideal of political organization (government by all the people [*ch'üan-min cheng-chih chu-i*], guild socialism, anarchism), should all now openly acknowledge, frankly and without passion, the objective of 'good government' as the minimum demand for the reform of Chinese politics. United in mind and spirit, we should take this common objective and with it wage war against the evil forces within the country.

"II. The minimal significance of 'good government': What we call 'good government' is, in its negative aspect, the existence of proper organs to oversee and protect against all illegal, self-seeking, and madly corrupt officials. On the positive side, we raise two points:

(1) Fully to utilize the instruments of politics to plan for the total welfare of the whole society.
(2) Fully to tolerate the freedom of the individual, and to love and protect the development of individuality [*ko-jen-hsing*].

"III. Three fundamental principles of political reform: We have three basic demands to make concerning subsequent political reforms.

"First, we demand a 'constitutional government,' because this is the first step in setting politics on the right track.

"Second, we demand a 'public government' [*kung-k'ai ti cheng-fu*], including such things as the publication of fiscal policies and the use of men in accordance with some form of public examination system, because we firmly believe that 'publicity' [English in text] is the only weapon with which to combat all hidden works of darkness.

"Third, we demand a 'government with a plan,' because we firmly believe that China's great malady is unplanned and aimless drifting, because we firmly believe that planning is the source of efficiency, and because we firmly believe that [even] a commonplace plan is better than blind groping!

"IV. The only way to initiate the work of political reform: We firmly believe that the reason that China has fallen to its present condition is without doubt because 'good men pride themselves on their purity and loftiness,' 'good men put their hands in their sleeves and are carried on the shoulders of the wicked.' Therefore, we firmly believe that the first step toward political reform at the present time is that good men must have a fighting spirit. All the superior elements of the society ought to plan for self-defense and for society and the nation, and come out to do battle with the forces of evil. We should call to mind: in the early days of the Republic, was not the new climate of opinion a result of the fact that the superior elements of China entered into the political movement? Many members of the [old] bureaucracy then scurried off to Tsingtao, Tientsin, and Shanghai, where they took out funds to go into business and refused to serve as officials any longer. It is said that Ts'ao Ju-lin [Vice-Minister of Foreign Affairs at the end of the Ch'ing dynasty; later Minister of Communications in Tuan Ch'i-jui's cabinet at the time of the May Fourth incident and very unpopular because of his pro-Japanese leanings; and in 1922 Commissioner of Industry] during that time closed the doors of his house every day and studied the Constitution [i.e., as the bureaucrats of former days were supposed to have studied the Confucian Classics]. Then, gradually, the good men wearied of politics. Some fled, and some retired, and so Ts'ao Ju-lin laid aside his copy of the Constitution and opened his doors again; and thus also the old bureaucrats in Tsingtao, Tientsin, and Shanghai came scurrying back one after another to become the chairmen and vice-chairmen of political advisory councils. Since the fifth or sixth year of the Republic [1916–1917], good men have stood by with their hands in their sleeves watching China being torn apart, watching the punishment of the southwest, watching the establishment of the Anfu Clique and all its rapacious violence, watching the loss of Mongolia, watching the sellout of Shantung, watching the outrageous behavior of the warlords, watching the nation go bankrupt and lose face until it has reached its present condition! Enough! Now the good men, those chief offenders, those ringleaders of calamity, must arise! It is not enough to be a good man — it is necessary to be a good man who can fight. Negative public opinion is not enough — it is necessary to have a militant and decisive public opinion. This is the first labor of political reform."

On the question of strong government, "government with a plan," Hu Shih's convictions had long been fixed. As early as 1914 he had remarked with satisfaction, "The tendency of modern Western political theory is away from laissez-faire and toward intervention by the state [kan-she chu-i], away from individualism and toward socialism . . . The evils of the laissez-faire attitude maintained by eighteenth-century scholars are slowly coming to be understood." [37] Well before his return to China he was writing in terms that clearly anticipate the verdict brought against warlordism in "Our Political Proposals": "The greatest need at present is to fix one's purpose and to establish a fundamental policy . . . and, when this has been done, to work steadily for a period of twenty or fifty years without faltering. Only then can there be some hope for national salvation. In recent years the government of our country has been without ideas, plans, or policies, like a ship adrift without a compass, at the mercy of wind and waves. Such drifting is a great calamity." [38] It was a theme to which he returned with dogged persistence over the following years. "Our first demand of any government, no matter who organizes it, is that it 'have a plan,'" he wrote in The Endeavor in the summer of 1922. "A nation is a great instrument, and politics is a great undertaking . . . Men without a plan are not worthy to engage in politics." [39]

37. Diary, 396.
38. Ibid., 960.
39. Hu Shih, "Che-i chou" (This week), HSWT II, iii, 156. First published in NLCP no. 7 (June 18, 1922).

Four years later, on his first trip to Europe, Hu had an opportunity to examine both positive and negative examples of this proposition at first hand. A glimpse of life in the Soviet Union greatly excited his admiration and laid the basis for an infatuation with "the Soviet experiment" that lasted until after World War II. He wrote to Chang Wei-tz'u enthusiastically from Moscow in the summer of 1926, describing the sense of dedication that he discovered among the Russians. Their ideals, he admitted, might not be those of which "we who love freedom can approve completely," but he insisted that "we must respect their seriousness of purpose. Here they are conducting a political experiment of unprecedented magnitude. They have ideals, plans, and an absolute faith, and these alone are enough to make us die of shame . . . How are our drunk and dreaming people worthy to criticize the Soviet Union?" [40]

Hu's impressions of England, where he arrived for a more leisurely tour a few weeks later, were just as emphatically critical. That was a troubled autumn, with memories of the general strike of May still fresh and the miners still out of the pits in many places. In a letter to his Cambridge-educated friend, the poet Hsü Chih-mo, Hu denounced with unusual vehemence the "muddling through" policies of the Baldwin ministry. "England is not worth studying," he concluded. "I am utterly opposed to this kind of negligent government. It is permissible to take no interest in politics, but if we want to have a hand in politics we must have a plan, and proceed according to that plan. This is method. Everything else is nonessential." [41]

The best government is not the least government, then, but rather the government that shapes its policies in full consciousness of the purposes it hopes to accomplish and then pursues them with forceful efficiency. Hu viewed the doctrines of laissez-faire liberalism not as an affirmation of principles right or desirable in themselves but merely as a negative response to the administrative incompetence of the governments of the eighteenth and nineteenth centuries. In any case, he contended, the crucial political problem of the twentieth century "is not how to limit the range of governmental authority, but how to use this important instrument to plan

---

40. Hu Shih's letter to Chang Wei-tz'u, undated (but written in 1926), "Ou-yu tao-chung chi-shu," HSWT III, i, 74–75.

41. Hu Shih's letter to Hsü Chih-mo, dated Oct. 4, 1926, HSWT III, i, 87.

for the welfare of the greatest number." This he called, for the first time in 1923, the theory of "political instrumentalism." [42]

Hu did not find it inconsistent to link this belief in the necessity for a strong political power with an acceptance of the idea that national government should be based on a federative structure that would grant to the provinces a substantial measure of autonomy. Federalism was one of the mildly popular causes of the early 1920s, favored in particular by intellectuals who saw in the idea a possible solution to the dual problems of warlordism: undisciplined regionalism and a central government reduced virtually to impotence. *The Endeavor* lent itself wholeheartedly to the cause. Chinese history, Hu contended, offers ample proof that China is too large and too diverse to be successfully governed as a centralized political entity. The tradition of unity appealed to by the revolutionaries Hu dismissed as a "misguided dream" (*mi meng*) — even at its best it had been, he insisted, a unity established and maintained only by force. The desire once more to impose a centralized government on a country vastly unfit for it was, in his view, the root cause of the schisms of the warlord era. Conversely, federalism held the answer to warlordism: "To encourage the development of genuine regional authority and thus to enable the various regions to develop the strength that lies latent there, in order to wage war on the warlords and to overthrow them — this is the meaning of provincial self-government and the purpose of the federalist movement." [43] To argue, as did the opponents of federalism, that the irresponsible behavior of the warlords attested to the danger of a decentralization of political authority was, in Hu's opinion, to confuse cause and effect.

This is not the place to weigh the merits of the case for and against federalism. It was a feeble and a losing cause, discredited in part by the support it received, for reasons that are not hard to understand, from various of the warlords themselves.[44] Hu Shih's enthusiasm for it may perhaps be explained as an expression of his

42. "Wu-shih nien lai chih shih-chieh che-hsüeh," HSWT II, ii, 303.

43. Hu Shih, "Lien-sheng tzu-chih yü chün-fa ko-chü" (Federative provincial self-government and warlord separatism), HSWT II, iii, 115. First published in NLCP no. 19 (Sept. 10, 1922).

44. A brief but excellent discussion of this movement is Jean Chesneaux, "Le mouvement fédéraliste en Chine (1920–1923)," *Revue historique*, 236:347–384 (October–December 1966).

tendency to seek American solutions to Chinese problems. It seems questionable, in retrospect, whether such a formal decentralization of authority could have been effected without incurring the danger of a complete fragmentation of political power, as those who opposed the idea argued at the time. Yet it should be noted, in defense of the proponents of federalism, that the tradition of centralized government against which they set themselves had involved an excessive degree of control from the center and had made little or no provision for the representation of local interests within the formal political structure. What Hu was urging, perhaps, was only that a balance should be struck that would take into account local and regional interests.[45] Although the federalist movement never became anything more than academic, this was a demand that Hu continued to make against the governments that came to power in the 1920s and 1930s.

Despite Hu's emphasis on the responsibility of the political authorities to keep in mind "the welfare of the greatest number," and his concern for the representation of local interests in the affairs of government, there was nothing inherently democratic in his insistence on the need for "a government with a plan." There is, on the contrary, a marked strain of potentially antidemocratic elitism evident in his thinking. His approach to politics, as to the broader issues of social reform, was essentially intellectual. He assigned extraordinary significance to ideas as the agents of change, and he laid a heavy burden of responsibility upon the shoulders of the enlightened minority whose duty it must be to express the "militant and decisive public opinion" on which reform depended. In this he was not alone. Writing in one of the last issues of *The Endeavor* in 1923, Ting Wen-chiang summarized in the clearest possible terms the elitist view generally prevalent among the liberals:

> The confusion of Chinese politics stems not from the immaturity of our people, nor from the corruption of our officials, nor from the fact that the law is laid down by militarists and warlords — it is the result, rather, of the fact that the "minority" lacks a sense of responsibility, and lacks, moreover, the ability to assume responsibility . . .

45. "Che-i chou," HSWT II, iii, 223–226. First published in NLCP no. 30 (Nov. 26, 1922).

We need only a few men of unbending resolution, [men] with the courage to climb mountains and leap over oceans, [men] with ability as well as knowledge, and with a desire to work in addition to virtue. When their influence is abroad, then the spirit [of the times] will change . . .

If we have even a minority of the minority, the most outstanding of the outstanding, who will be unwilling to wait for death with folded hands, then we need not fear that we will be unable to manage the affairs of the world . . . The most fearful thing is to have men of knowledge and virtue who will not enter into the political struggle! [46]

It was only to such a "minority of the minority" that the liberals' appeal for intellectual individualism could be truly relevant. And it was only through the acts of a government sympathetic to the standards held by this public-spirited elite that there could be created the conditions necessary to the slow nurturing of a capacity for self-government in the people as a whole.

Yet Hu Shih was firmly committed to a belief in democracy, not merely as an institutional complex but as a social and intellectual environment that would make certain institutions viable. He could not bring himself to accept the political backwardness of the Chinese people as sufficient justification for the perpetuation of an undemocratic system of government. He argued, in consequence, that democratic institutions are essential to the educative process that will ultimately lead to the realization of democracy in its fullest sense. In *The Endeavor* he put his case in these terms:

Looking at the matter in the light of the experience of the democratic nations, we must recognize that democratic institutions are an important instrument for the training of good citizens . . . The reason that democratic institutions can be adopted by other nations is simply because of the fact that the institutions themselves perform an educative function. The principle behind this is not, really, particularly startling. The Chinese, accustomed to using vegetable-oil lamps, can now use electric lights; the Chinese, who formerly did not know how to organize large-scale commercial enterprises, can now organize

46. Ting Wen-chiang, "Shao-shu-jen ti tse-jen" (The responsibility of the minority), NLCP no. 67 (Aug. 12, 1923).

large banks and great companies. Although political life is not so simple a thing as electricity and the telephone, it is in actuality only a kind of organized life. This kind of organized life can be learned . . .

Any nation which has experienced training through democratic institutions over a long period of time will possess a higher level of civic knowledge and morality than other nations . . . The spread of civic knowledge is an important condition for the cultivation of civic morality.[47]

For the time being Hu could let the matter rest there. Not until the end of the decade, in response to the argument that democracy could be established in China only as the product of a period of party dictatorship and "political education," was Hu forced to express his belief in the educative usefulness of democratic institutions as an explicit affirmation of the innate political wisdom of the people. And not until the 1930s did circumstances compel him to acknowledge the difficulty of reconciling this view with his continuing belief in the crucial role of an intellectually enlightened elite.

If institutions are the proper instruments of change, they must be responsive to the need for change. But if adequately responsive institutions do not exist, how are they to be created? It was on this question that Hu Shih parted company with those of his friends who advocated a revolutionary course of action. Though he expected little from warlord governments, he remained unwilling to demand the destruction of their authority by revolutionary means. An analysis of the reasoning which underlay this attitude may be deferred for the moment, since in Hu's mind the issue did not become critical until after the establishment of an avowedly revolutionary regime in 1927. Here it suffices to note that Hu's aim was never more than the reform of the government in power, and that in consequence his demands of the authorities were tempered by his estimate of what might reasonably be demanded of them. "We should lay aside, for the time being, our great political hopes," he wrote in *The Endeavor* in June 1922, "and be content to 'take what we can get.' Then we will be prepared dispassionately to lay

47. Hu Shih, "*Cheng-chih kai-lun* hsü" (Preface to [Chang Wei-tz'u's] Outline of politics), HSWT II, iii, 19–23.

our plans for actual political change." [48] The fact remained, however, that what Hu and his fellow liberals could get from governments controlled by militarists and bureaucrats who scorned their criticism and resented their attempts to interfere was little enough. And public opinion, the only weapon of which the proponents of "good government" were willing to avail themselves, proved both too weak and too disorganized to accomplish the task they had assigned to it.

The purpose of "Our Political Proposals" was to stimulate debate, and in this its sponsors were not disappointed. Its publication did in fact provoke considerable discussion, much of it addressed not to the specific issues broached by Hu and his associates but to their intent and the usefulness of their endeavor. Some readers agreed that in a country like China, burdened by an illiterate, inarticulate, and unenlightened population, reform was properly the business of "good men" whose purpose should be only to establish the general principles on which all might reach agreement.[49] But others questioned the effectiveness of such an approach. "Sometimes propaganda can arouse the popular spirit," wrote one young skeptic, "and it is an essential element in mass movements. But to rely only on propaganda seems to me still the attitude of scholars, and not sufficiently thoroughgoing . . . Why not form yourselves into a 'Good Government Party'? If there are only proposals, but no concrete organization, then I fear that these suggestions are merely empty talk and will never be realized in fact." [50]

Hu Shih's response to this suggestion is significant in what it reveals of his position on the question of political organization. He was not unmindful of the role that political parties should play in a properly ordered political system. In 1916, for example, before he had become disillusioned with Liang Ch'i-ch'ao as a politician, Hu had entertained optimistic expectations for China's future with men like Liang and Chang Chien occupying influential positions. "As for future hopes," he observed, "it will be necessary to have an enlightened and unyielding opposition party to serve as the overseer of this moderate party, so that today's moderates do not become tomorrow's reactionaries." [51]

48. "Che-i chou," HSWT II, iii, 146. First published in NLCP no. 7 (June 18, 1922).

49. Letter from Mei Tsu-fen, HSWT II, iii, 41–45.

50. Letter from Ch'eng Chen-chi, *ibid.*, 66.

51. *Diary*, 1165.

The idea of partisan factionalism was abhorrent to him, however, and he was ever reluctant to cross the line from critical detachment to active political involvement. The manifesto of the New Youth Society, published at the end of 1919, had straddled the issue neatly: "We . . . recognize [political parties] as a necessary device for the practice of politics, but we will never tolerate membership in parties which promote the interests of a few, or of one class, rather than the happiness of the whole society." [52] By 1922 Hu had retreated from even this cautious approval. Not without reason, he laid much of the blame for the disappointments of the early republic on the "narrow attitudes," the "mutual intolerance," and "constant bickering" of the political parties and cliques of the time. In answer to his critics, he set forth his own view in the following terms:

> I personally believe that at present we can only hope that everyone will maintain a sense of historical perspective . . . and with a penitent attitude work together toward the common objective of "good government." The greatest need at the present time is to propagandize this commonplace and general aim, to make the people recognize clearly that our common enemy is the bad government of the forces of evil, and that our responsibility is to wage war against it. This, then, is our great party. After the restoration of the parliament the old political parties will, of course, revive. Now, and in the near future, we should all occupy the position of mediators, impartial men, judges, and overseers. In the future, after politics have got on the right track, differences in concrete proposals will perhaps force us to organize a political party, but that is another question.[53]

In another essay published in *The Endeavor* about the same time Hu attacked the issue from a slightly different perspective. Political critics (*cheng-lun-chia*), he wrote, fall into three categories. First, there are those who remain subservient to the leadership of a particular political party. Second, there are those who themselves exercise leadership within a party. Finally, there are some — and

52. HCN 7.1 (December 1919); cited in Chow Tse-tsung, *The May Fourth Movement*, 175.

53. Hu Shih, "Ta Ch'eng Chen-chi" (Reply to Ch'eng Chen-chi), HSWT II, iii, 67–68.

obviously it was in this category that Hu saw himself — who remain unaffiliated with any party, in order to supervise the conduct of all. Such men are, as Hu put it, "transcendent and independent. They recognize only society and the nation, not parties and cliques. They take a statesmanlike view [cheng-chien], not a partisan view [tang-chien]. Perhaps by temperament and ability they are not fitted to organize a political party. They can comprehend matters, but not necessarily manage affairs; they can plan, but not necessarily ex-ecute; they can criticize men, but they don't necessarily know how to deal with them. They should, of course, exploit their strong points, and certainly they should not try to do what they cannot do well."

But, Hu was asked, is it possible to have effective political in-fluence without participating directly in the exercise of power? Hu replied that "independent critics" such as he described have at their disposal two important means of making their judgments count. The first is, of course, the role that they play in shaping public opinion. The second is their role in the creation of an independent electoral majority. "Independent political critics have no party, yet sometimes it can be said that they have a party. Their party con-sists of the innumerable unaffiliated independent voters. In nations where the political situation is clear and education well developed there is always a part of the electorate that belongs to no party or group; their support is given according to the excellence of policies and personalities." [54]

The mark of Hu's American experience is perhaps nowhere more evident than in this attempt to define his own role in the un-settled political life of China in terms of what he had seen in the United States. Even John Dewey, whose influence is particularly apparent here and who shared with Hu — or borrowed from him — many opinions concerning the nature of China's crisis and its solution, entertained strong reservations on this score. He observed of the events of 1919 that, in spite of appearances, "it would be . . . unsafe to argue for the existence of a persistently influential minority from the fact of the thousands of telegrams sent to Paris in protest against signing [the Versailles Treaty], or from the fact that a cabinet dominated by pro-Japanese politicians and in control

54. Hu Shih, "Cheng-lun-chia yü cheng-tang" (Political critics and political parties), NLCP no. 5 (June 4, 1922). (The title is misprinted to read "Cheng-lun-chia cheng yü tang.")

of finances and the army, simply did not dare enter into negotiations with Japan about Shantung. In a crisis there may be a minority so substantial as to be dominating. But only in a crisis." [55]

For Hu Shih the bitter lesson of the 1920s was that even in a crisis the dissident minority tended increasingly to phrase its protests in language with which he could not agree, and to expend its energies in ways of which he could not approve.

The life of *The Endeavor* coincided with one of the dreariest periods of warlord history. It was born almost at the moment when one of the many shifts in power that marked those strife-filled years occurred with the victory, in the Chih-Feng War of April and May 1922, of Wu P'ei-fu and Ts'ao K'un over the forces of their erstwhile ally Chang Tso-lin, the master of Manchuria. Initially, the prospects for significant reform may well have appeared brighter to the advocates of good government after the Chihli victory. Wu P'ei-fu was, perhaps, a cut above the average for a warlord; in any case, he espoused a number of the causes to which the "good government group" was committed. In the early summer of 1922 Hsü Shih-ch'ang, who had been elected to the presidency of the Republic in 1918 with the backing of Tuan Ch'i-jui and the Anfu Clique and had contrived to survive Tuan's fall from power two years later, was replaced by Li Yüan-hung. Li was Wu P'ei-fu's man, but his claim to the presidential office derived in theory from the fact that he had been vice-president at the time of Yüan Shih-k'ai's death in 1916 and thus enjoyed a rather tenuous connection with the earliest republican administration. At the same time, again as a result of Wu's initiative, the so-called "Old Parliament" was reconvened in Peking, charged with the task of drafting a new and permanent constitution. This was the body — or what remained of it — elected in 1913 and soon thereafter dissolved by Yüan Shih-k'ai, recalled in 1916 after Yüan's demise, and dispersed again a year later by Tuan Ch'i-jui. The government thus provisionally constituted in 1922 conveyed a sense of legitimacy that recent warlord regimes had lacked, and the hope flickered briefly that, by bringing together political elements that traced their descent from the days before the rupture between north and south had taken place, it might be pos-

55. John Dewey, "Is China a Nation?" *The New Republic*, Jan. 12, 1921; reprinted in *Characters and Events*, I, 237–238.

sible to turn history back and to achieve through "legal" means the unification that arms could not impose.[56]

This was the political situation that Hu Shih and *The Endeavor* confronted in 1922. Shortly before the parliament convened in August Hu put forth his hopes for it:

> The parliament should devote its full energy to the matter of establishing the constitution. Its only duty is to establish a formal government [*cheng-shih-ti cheng-fu*] on the foundation of a fixed constitutional system . . .
>
> Most important, the parliament should recognize the present government of Li Yüan-hung and Yen Hui-ch'ing [the acting premier] as the defacto provisional government which will remain in office until the constitution has been enacted and the formal government established.
>
> In this manner the parliamentarians will be able to devote their entire attention to the matter of the constitution . . . We hope that their political conscience will enable them to approve of these suggestions.[57]

In September three of the men who had signed the "good government manifesto" in May were appointed to cabinet posts. Wang Ch'ung-hui (*tzu* Liang-ch'ou, 1882–1956), an American- and British-trained lawyer and politician, replaced Yen Hui-ch'ing as acting premier. Lo Wen-kan (*tzu* Chung-jen, 1888–1941), another British-educated lawyer, was named Minister of Finance. And T'ang Erh-ho (1877–1943), a medical doctor schooled in Japan, became Minister of Education. Hu Shih was on friendly terms with all three, as he was also with the new Foreign Minister, Ku Wei-chün (*tzu* Shao-ch'uan, V. K. Wellington Koo, 1887–   ).

For Wang and his colleagues the much-publicized connection with the "good government group" proved to be more of an embarrassment than an asset. They soon found themselves subjected to ridicule in the press, and taken to task by their friends who remained on the sidelines, for their conspicuous failure to come up

56. For background on these events see Li Chien-nung, *The Political History of China*, 419–422.

57. "Che-i chou," HSWT II, iii, 182. First published in NLCP no. 11 (July 16, 1922).

with a program — a "plan." [58] Even worse, the new government never received the support of Ts'ao K'un, with whom Wu P'ei-fu was linked in uneasy alliance. What had seemed momentarily a triumph for the cause of good government rapidly turned into a disorderly retreat. In November Lo Wen-kan was accused by the speaker of the House of Representatives, Wu Ching-lien — one of Ts'ao's stalwarts — of having accepted a bribe in connection with the signing of a treaty with Austria. At this crucial juncture Wu P'ei-fu deserted the liberal cause, and without his support the "Good Men Government" collapsed. Lo was relieved of office and imprisoned. The resignation of Wang's entire cabinet followed inevitably. Ts'ao K'un, whose great ambition was to be elected to the presidency, was served thereafter by cabinets more amenable to his purposes. The confidence that Hu had expressed in the political conscience of the parliament was utterly betrayed. By the beginning of 1923 he was complaining that "a constitution is a fundamental law; the laws of a democratic nation certainly cannot be established by the kind of shameless politicians who cannot themselves obey the law. We can predict that if the parliament of Wu Ching-lien does in the end put forward a constitution, it can-

58. From June through October 1922 Hu Shih was a participant in an informal and irregular series of "tea parties" (*ch'a-hua-hui*), held for the most part at Wellington Koo's residence, which brought together a number of European- and American-educated "returned students" for discussions of political issues of moment. Other members of the group included Ts'ai Yüan-p'ei, Wang Ch'ung-hui, Lo Wen-kan, Ting Wen-chiang, Chiang Po-li, Lin Ch'ang-min, T'ao Meng-ho, Li Shih-tseng, Yeh Ching-hsin (*tzu* Shu-heng), Chou I-ch'un (*tzu* Chi-mei, Y. T. Tsur), Wang Ch'ang-hsin, Chang Chün-mai, Kao Lu, and others. After the formation of the Wang cabinet these social gatherings became increasingly tense, partly because of Hu's demand (publicized in *The Endeavor*) that the new government must come up with a "plan." Confronted by this criticism, Wang Ch'ung-hui grew more and more morosely defensive until, at the end of October, the "tea parties" were discontinued at the suggestion of Ts'ai Yüan-p'ei, on the ground that further meetings would not be productive so long as Wang and Lo remained in the government. See Hu Shih, "Che-i chou," NLCP no. 15, Aug. 13, 1922 (HSWT II, iii, 192), NLCP no. 20, Sept. 17, 1922 (HSWT II, iii, 198), and NLCP no. 22, Oct. 1, 1922 (HSWT II, iii, 206–208); and Hu's unpublished diary, entries for Sept. 9 and 22, and Oct. 27, 1922. In November, when Lo Wen-kan was charged with corruption, Hu observed editorially: "Our ideal of 'good men' has at least two aspects. One is personal reliability and the other is resourcefulness . . . We have certainly been less than satisfied with the Wang-Lo group with respect to their political resourcefulness, but we retain confidence in their unsullied personal integrity." ("Che-i chou," HSWT II, iii, 220–221; NLCP no. 30 [Nov. 26, 1922].)

not in the future have the effect of a constitution: it will be only another scrap of waste paper!" [59]

The Endeavor set itself firmly against Ts'ao K'un's presidential aspirations, and Hu waxed eloquent in his editorial denunciations of the parliament as it tended increasingly to submit to Ts'ao's ambitions. But to no avail. The final draft of the Constitution of 1923 provided for the election of the president by parliament sitting as an electoral body, and early in October Ts'ao was elevated to the presidency in this manner — an honor for which he paid to various politicians, according to one estimate, the sum of fifteen million silver dollars.[60]

Hu Shih's health had broken at the end of 1922, and in December he received a one-year leave of absence from his duties at Peita. In May 1923 he departed from Peking, turning *The Endeavor* over to Ting Wen-chiang, T'ao Meng-ho, Kao I-han, and Chang Wei-tz'u. He spent the summer and autumn recuperating at Yen-hsia-tung, a Buddhist retreat in the mountains of Chekiang. From there, on October 9, four days after Ts'ao's election and on the eve of his inauguration and the promulgation of the new constitution, Hu wrote to his friends in Peking concerning the future of their joint enterprise. On the advice of his doctors, he said, he had postponed his return to the north until the expiration of his leave. He suggested that, in the interim, publication of *The Endeavor* should be "temporarily suspended." Acknowledging the hopelessness of the situation in which he and his colleagues had found themselves, he wrote with some bitterness: "At the present time it is utterly futile to talk politics. If you attack men, you merely add one curse to the nationwide chorus of vilification, and what is the point of that? If you steer clear of personalities and speak instead of problems and proposals, like the parliament, disarmament, or the constitution, then inevitably you incur the misunderstanding of others; while presenting a clear and well-reasoned petition to bandits is not something that we have any desire to do."

Hu interpreted the misfortunes that had befallen *The Endeavor* as a vindication of his earlier opposition to political engagement. "Henceforth," he wrote, "I believe that we should expand *The*

59. "Che-i chou," HSWT II, iii, 249; NLCP no. 41 (Feb. 11, 1923).
60. H. F. MacNair, *China in Revolution: An Analysis of Politics and Militarism under the Republic* (Chicago, 1931), 53–54.

Endeavor to the point at which it can carry forward the unfulfilled mission of *The New Youth,* and, by struggling without interruption for another twenty years, we should lay a firm foundation in literature and thought for Chinese politics." As he had launched *The Endeavor* eighteen months earlier with a poem calling upon "good men" to come forth to battle, so now he bestowed an epitaph upon it in poetic form.

> The leaves are touched with the air of autumn
> But most still hold fast against the autumn wind.
> Only the plum trees along the road at the foot of the mountain
> Have long since withered to ugliness.
> We dare not mock them for fading so soon;
> Let them rest well
> And next year they will blossom before all the others! [61]

But *The Endeavor* was never revived, and Hu's career as a "political critic" was temporarily at an end. In 1924 a group of Peita professors established *The Contemporary Review (Hsien-tai p'ing-lun)* as an outlet for liberal opinion. Hu Shih used the new magazine to publish poetry, short scholarly pieces, and essays on the broader issues of cultural reconstruction. He held his silence on political questions. Not until 1928, five years after *The Endeavor* had succumbed in the harsh climate of warlord politics, did Hu again undertake a sustained presentation of his political opinions, in the pages of *The Crescent (Hsin yüeh),* published in Shanghai. In the interval profound and stirring changes had taken place in China, and with the establishment of a new government in Nanking the revolution had entered a fresh phase in its development. Hu Shih's reaction to this changed situation, and his relations with the Nationalist government, will be the subject of a separate chapter. First, however, something more must be said about the nationalistic aspirations that helped to bring the revolutionary movement to power, and about Hu Shih's view of these sentiments.

When Hu Shih announced his decision to refrain from political activity in order to devote his energies to the creation of a "new public opinion," he looked for support, as has been noted, to the

61. Hu Shih, letter to Kao I-han, Chang Wei-tz'u, and others, Oct. 9, 1923, HSWT II, iii, 141–144.

numerically small but crucially important class of modernized intellectuals: the middle-school and university students, the writers, journalists, and professional men, the teachers and the scholars. Only among such as these did he have any hope of finding individuals who could understand what he had to say or act upon it. Yet he had always to compete for this audience with the spokesmen for other forces that took shape in the early 1920s. The Chinese Communist Party (CCP), foreshadowed in the Marxist study groups founded in Peking and elsewhere in 1918 and 1919, was formally established in 1921, with Ch'en Tu-hsiu as its first secretary-general. Partly in response to the same quickening of Soviet and Comintern interest in China, Sun Yat-sen's Nationalist Party (Kuomintang, KMT) was reorganized in 1923 and 1924 along Leninist lines to make it a more efficient instrument of revolutionary aims. Unlike Hu Shih, neither CCP nor KMT leaders entertained any doubts as to the necessity of political organization, nor did they reject the use of force as a means of attaining their objectives. Their appeal for support, moreover, was expressed in language that betrayed — or so it seems in retrospect — a keener sensitivity than his to the frustrations and discontents of their audience: citizens of a nation that was not a nation, members of a race that had lost its self-esteem and seemed, not unrealistically, in danger ultimately of losing its political identity.

Both the CCP and the KMT were in part created by, and in part the creators of, the ardent nationalism that swept across China in the 1920s. To it they gave a stridently anti-imperialist expression, placing the blame for China's unhappy plight upon the Western encroachments which since the middle of the nineteenth century had undermined the nation's capacity to resist economic and political subjugation. During the period of the KMT-CCP alliance, from 1923 to 1927, revolutionary ideology blended anti-imperialism together with anti-feudalism (the term used to describe, with more emotion than precision, the manifold abuses of the past — the social inequities, the political oppression and corruption, and the moral decadence of Chinese life). This is the fashion in which the *First Manifesto of the Chinese Communist Party on the Current Situation,* published in June 1922, put the case:

> The result of the revolution's defeat has been a strengthening of the world imperialist yoke in China and of the reac-

tionary regime of her own militarists. The so-called republican rule is in the hands of militarists, who, under conditions of a semi-feudal economy, use it to join their own actions with those of the world imperialists . . . The foreign states are making use of the opportunity to invest their capital in China, thus acquiring, by means of a system of financial enslavement, "spheres of influence" in China and special rights and privileges.

But the maintenance of civil war in China is of first importance to the world imperialists, for it delays China's progress, prevents China from developing her own industry, saturates the Chinese market with goods of their own foreign manufacture, and also prevents the Chinese bourgeoisie from utilizing the country in the interests of domestic exploitation.[62]

From such an analysis of the Chinese situation Hu Shih was divided by differences in both sentiment and opinion. Where others felt resentment at China's degradation, he felt scorn for China's backwardness. He was less disposed to anger over the wretchedness of China's swarming millions than to be grateful that he lived in an age that commanded the means of alleviating their misery, at least in theory. Watching the sweaty exertion of his ricksha boy moved him not to a condemnation of the economic system that made such inhuman labor necessary, but rather "to give thanks to the great sage who discovered electricity, and to the great sage who discovered the steam engine," and "to bless those great sages who created steamships and automobiles . . . for using their minds and their intelligence to save human energy and destroy human suffering." [63] These views, it might be argued, reflected the "cosmopolitanism" of Hu's student days carried to its logical extreme. They made of him, in an angrily nationalistic era, a more comfortable citizen of his century than of his country.

Hu's differences with the revolutionary nationalists thus stemmed in part from his sense of detachment from the passions that moved so many of his countrymen. There were intellectual considerations as well. Hu was skeptical of revolutionary promises inspired by the hope of securing, through revolution, a radical improvement in China's condition. In the language of his dispute with Li Ta-chao

62. Conrad Brandt, Benjamin I. Schwartz, and John K. Fairbank, *A Documentary History of Chinese Communism* (Cambridge, Mass., 1952), 56.
63. "Man-yu ti kan-hsiang," HSWT III, i, 53.

in 1919, Hu rejected as impractical the vision of a "fundamental solution" to the complex problems that the Chinese confronted. Li, while acknowledging that "a considerable amount of preparatory work is necessary" before a "fundamental solution" can be attempted, had nonetheless insisted, "In a society [like China's] which lacks organization and vitalizing principles, all the faculties are already impaired, and even if you possess the instrument, you will have no opportunity to put it to use. At such a time there must probably be a fundamental solution before there can be any hope of solving various concrete problems one by one." Li had cited the example of Russia by way of illustration. No remedies to specific problems had been feasible in Russia, he asserted, until after the fall of the Romanovs and the reorganization of the economy by the Bolsheviks, "whereas now [in 1919] everything has been resolved." [64]

To Hu Shih, Li's argument represented precisely the kind of oversimplified generalization that, as an "experimentalist," he had vowed to root out of the Chinese mentality. "Experimentalism is, of course, also a kind of ism," he admitted, "but experimentalism is only a method for the study of problems. Experimentalism emphasizes concrete facts and problems, and consequently it does not acknowledge [that there can be] any fundamental solutions. It recognizes only that kind of progress which is achieved bit-by-bit — each step guided by intelligence, each step making provision for automatic testing — only this is true progress." Even the Bolsheviks, Hu insisted, had not been able to achieve a fundamental solution: the new regime in Russia, if it hoped to survive, must surely "respond to problems that appear slowly, one at a time." [65]

Hu reaffirmed his convictions on this point in laying down the editorial policy of *The Endeavor* in 1922: "Because we put no faith in talk of fundamental reconstruction and believe only in bit-by-bit

64. Li Ta-chao, "Tsai lun wen-t'i yü chu-i" (Another discussion of problems and isms), *Mei-chou p'ing-lun*, no. 35 (Aug. 17, 1919); reprinted in *Li Ta-chao hsüan-chi* (Selected works of Li Ta-chao; Peking, 1962), 233. A discussion of Li's position in this dispute is found in Maurice Meisner, *Li Ta-chao*, 105–114. Meisner translates the final sentences of Li's statement to read: "If the Romanoffs had not been overthrown and the economic organization not reformed, no problems could have been solved. Now they are all *being* solved" (p. 107; emphasis added). This reading casts Li's beliefs in a somewhat different light. The original text of the last sentence is "*Chin tse ch'üan tou chieh-chüeh le.*" I interpret the final particle *le* as indicative of perfective action.

65. "Wo-ti ch'i-lu," HSWT II, iii, 99.

reconstruction, we do not speak of isms but only of problems, we entertain no great hopes, nor can we be gravely disappointed. As we look at the present age, when the causes of evil are so numerous, and good men so few, and education in such a state of confusion, there is certainly no great revolution that can completely satisfy men." [66]

To the revolutionaries the attitude represented by *The Endeavor* and the measures advocated in "Our Political Proposals" appeared, at best, unrealistic. "Democratic power in China can triumph only through the revolutionary seizure of power," proclaimed the *First Manifesto of the Chinese Communist Party on the Current Situation* in June 1922. It went on to accuse the sponsors of "Our Political Proposals," published in Peking a few weeks earlier (and signed, it might be noted, by Li Ta-chao, the leading Communist in north China) of "bourgeois pacifism" and "opportunism," and to ridicule them for their political naïveté:

> Do you really believe that a "good government" can be organized under the existing conditions? Do you count on carrying out your three principles and the six concrete aims of your programme under military dictatorship?
>
> "The government opposition game, played by the bourgeoisie, the intelligentsia and the politicians, cannot be trusted . . .
>
> "The concrete aims of the present political struggle cannot be limited to a fight for the publication of data on government finances or for surveillance over the activity of parliament." [67]

Hu Shih did his best to talk away the disagreement. "They differ with us only on questions of sequence and priorities," he remarked in his editorial reaction to the CCP manifesto. But though he insisted that "there is no point on which there is absolute incompatibility" between the CCP position and his own,[68] it is impossible to conclude that even he believed it. On the contrary, on nearly every important point Hu was out of sympathy with the revolutionaries' description of the present and the past, and with their program for the future. To his mind "imperialism," "capitalism," "feudalism" were merely the kind of catchwords that tended to obscure rather than clarify the genuine issues.

66. "Che-i chou," HSWT II, iii, 145–146; NLCP no. 7 (June 18, 1922).
67. Brandt, Schwartz, and Fairbank, *Documentary History*, 56–62.
68. "Che-i chou," HSWT II, iii, 168; NLCP no. 10 (July 9, 1922).

This was, however, much more than a semantic squabble, though Hu did not spell out his differences with the Communists until the end of the decade. He rejected not only the terms employed by the Communists and their nationalist revolutionary allies, but also the phenomena these terms were intended to describe. In China, he maintained, "we are not yet qualified to speak of capitalism . . . We have at most a few moderately wealthy men — how can we have a capitalist class?" As for feudalism, it had "disappeared from [China] two thousand years ago." [69] Hu found fault, moreover, with the whole mechanism of Marxist historiography to which the Communists endeavored to make Chinese realities conform. Dialectical materialism was rendered invalid, he insisted, by its "unscientific" conception of the evolutionary process, by its reliance on pre-Darwinian dynamics, and by its belief that the ceaseless movement of the dialectic could, at a given point — that is, after the victory of the proletarian revolution — be held in check. "Such a simplification of the complex, such a fundamental denial of the continuity of evolution, is 100 percent pre-Darwinian thought, more conservative than the conservative Hegel himself. Experimentalism developed from Darwinism and consequently can recognize only gradual and constant reform as true and dependable progress." [70]

Finally, and perhaps most significantly, Hu refused to accept the Communist-nationalist view of China's situation because it was founded on what he regarded as a misrepresentation of contemporary Western society. Not the least of the diverse emotions which nourished Chinese nationalism after 1919 was a prevalent sense of disillusionment with the West. One consequence of this was that the Marxist-Leninist critique of European values gained a popularity in China in the early 1920s far beyond the still small circle of committed Marxists or proto-Communists — a vogue in some ways reminiscent of that enjoyed by Social Darwinism just after the turn of the century. Cultural conservatives like Liang Ch'i-ch'ao and his kindred spirits enthusiastically promoted the impression of European society debased by social inequalities and rent by class antagonisms. Even British-educated scholars like Ting Wen-chiang

69. Hu Shih, "Wo-men tsou na-i-t'iao lu?" (Which road shall we follow?), HSWT IV, iv, 432. First published in HY 2.10 (Dec. 10, 1929).

70. Hu Shih, "Chieh-shao wo tzu-chi ti ssu-hsiang" (Introducing my own thought), HSWT IV, 609. First published in HY 3.4 (n.d.).

and T'ao Meng-ho, though generally sympathetic to the West, acknowledged the gravity of the postwar crisis in Europe.[71]

Although Hu Shih took a different view of Western development, he, too, was at times inclined to accept uncritically the Marxist description of European conditions.[72] But to him America was always a case apart, and American prospects were infinitely brighter. "America will not have a social revolution," he wrote after his return from the United States in 1927, "because America is in the middle of a social revolution every day . . . In America in recent years, while capital has become concentrated, ownership has been distributed among the people . . . Everyone can be a capitalist, and consequently agitation for class war is ineffective." [73]

If America was different, however, it was not so, Hu insisted, by reason of conditions that should be regarded as peculiar to the American situation. It was, rather, that America had inherited from Europe, and given new expression to, an intellectual and social tradition tracing its origins to the Renaissance: America had become the refuge of "the spiritual civilization of the West" and of "a new morality" founded on the realization of the power of human reason and on a mutual sympathy of man for man arising out of an awareness of the dignity of human life.[74] This Hu called "the religion of Democracy." [75] He regarded the principles of socialism as its contemporary articles of faith:

> The ideals of Socialism are merely supplementary to the earlier and more individualistic ideas of democracy. They are historically a part of the great democratic movement. By the middle of the nineteenth century, the laissez-faire policy was no longer sufficient to achieve the desired results of equality and liberty under the highly organized and centralized economic system . . . Hence the rise of the socialistic movements, which, when freed from their distracting theories of economic determinism and class war, simply mean the emphasis on the neces-

71. See above, chap. v, n. 2.
72. See for example "Wu-shih nien lai chih shih-chieh che-hsüeh," HSWT II, ii, 300–303.
73. "Man-yu ti kan-hsiang," HSWT III, i, 58–59.
74. "Wo-men tui-yü Hsi-yang chin-tai wen-ming ti t'ai-tu," HSWT III, i, 18–19 and *passim*.
75. "The Civilizations of the East and the West," *Whither Mankind*, 37.

sity of making use of the collective power of society or of the state for the greatest happiness of the greatest number . . .

This religion of Democracy, which not only guarantees one's own liberty, nor merely limits one's liberty by respecting the liberty of other people, but endeavors to make it possible for every man and every woman to live a free life; which not only succeeds through science and machinery in greatly enhancing the happiness and comfort of the individual, but also seeks through organization and legislation to extend the goods of life to the greatest number — this is the greatest spiritual heritage of Western civilization.[76]

It was with this spiritual heritage, Hu insisted, that the Chinese must strive to identify themselves. He called it, in a letter to Hsü Chih-mo written in 1926, "the New Liberalism" (*hsin-tzu-yu chu-i*) or "Liberal Socialism" (*tzu-yu ti she-hui chu-i*). It was one of the few occasions on which he made use of the term, and he was anxious to distinguish this from the classical laissez-faire liberalism for which he entertained so little sympathy: "My friends in the Communist party say to me, 'Liberalism is the political philosophy of capitalism.' This . . . cannot be historically substantiated. The trend towards liberalism is something that has grown broader gradually. In the seventeenth and eighteenth centuries only the aristocracy fought for liberty. The twentieth century should be the age when the people as a whole struggle for liberty. What conflict is there between this concept and [that of] liberalism? Why must [the CCP] insist on handing liberalism over to capitalism?" [77]

If Hu Shih's exposition of Western history is open to the charge of "simplification of the complex" that he had himself leveled against Li Ta-chao, it seems nevertheless unjust to label him, on the basis of these views, an advocate of capitalist-imperialist exploitation, as the Communists have consistently done. Yet apart from the ideological inspiration behind such an accusation, there was, in the perspectives of that era, a kind of justice to it. Some months after the publication of the *First Manifesto of the Chinese Communist Party on the Current Situation* Hu had taken issue with its major premise in these terms:

76. *Ibid.*, 38–40. See also "Wo-men tui-yü Hsi-yang chin-tai wen-ming ti t'ai-tu," HSWT III, i, 16–19.

77. Hu Shih's letter to Hsü Chih-mo, undated [1926], HSWT III, i, 85–86.

We should know that *the hopes of the foreign capitalists for peace and unity in China are in no way less than the hopes of the Chinese themselves for peace and unity in China* . . . Foreign capital has become a problem simply because the country in which the capital is [invested] is not at peace, not stable, and cannot protect the well-being and security of the capitalists . . . Speaking frankly, China is no longer in any great danger from foreign aggression . . . We need no longer fear the nightmare of foreign aggression. The most important thing at present is to work together to get our country on the right track politically . . . My friend Ch'en Tu-hsiu and others have published in Shanghai in their *Hsiang-tao chou-pao* [Guide weekly] two major aims: first, a democratic revolution, and second, opposition to international imperialist aggression. We can, of course, agree with the first of these. As for the second, we feel that it should properly be subsumed under the first. For we feel that once the democratic revolution has succeeded, and when politics has got on the right track, international imperialist aggression will in large part naturally have disappeared. [78]

This is certainly as friendly an interpretation of the motives of foreign interests in China as one could hope to find from the pen of a Chinese writer. It was not hard to cast Hu as an apologist for imperialism, though his purpose was not so much to defend the imperialists as it was to warn his readers against the dangers inherent, as he believed, in nationalist ideology. In his student days Hu had echoed Carlyle's invocation of "a patriotism founded on something better than prejudice" and shared with him the hope "that our country may be dear to us, without injury to our philosophy." But Chinese patriotism in the 1920s — at least in Hu's view of it — was both founded on prejudice and injurious to the philosophy that he espoused and advocated. Thus by 1925, a year second in importance only to 1919 in the history of the nationalist movement, Hu had become a spokesman for moderation.

On May 30, 1925, a student-led demonstration in Shanghai, organized to protest Japanese treatment of Chinese workers in a local textile mill, was fired upon in the International Concession by police under British command. Three weeks later, on June 23,

78. Hu Shih, "Kuo-chi ti Chung-kuo" (China among the nations), HSWT II, iii, 128a–i *passim*. First published in NLCP no. 22 (Oct. 1, 1922).

students in Canton marching to protest the Shangahi incident were themselves fired upon by British and French guards as they passed the foreign concessions on the island of Shameen. These tragedies, resulting in a number of deaths among the demonstrators and many wounded, blew the fires of nationalist passion to a white heat. "The trouble won't end here," promised one young student in Shanghai. "We are determined to resist foreign imperialism to the last man." [79]

This was by no means the kind of thing that Hu Shih had had in mind in 1922 when he issued his call for "a militant and decisive public opinion." His reaction to the events of 1925 was predictably cool and reasonable. Writing at the end of that tempestuous summer, he admitted that the students could hardly be blamed for their outbursts at a time "when many men of mature years can no longer contain themselves, and when old gentlemen of sixty are hotly advocating a declaration of war." But, he cautioned, "national salvation is not something that can be achieved in a short period of time: imperialism cannot be overthrown with naked fists, nor can the 'English and Japanese bandits' be shouted to death by a million voices." He summarized his own views in language that must have struck his audience as oddly familiar. "In this period when the praises of patriotism are loudly sung, we wish to point out in all earnestness that what Ibsen called 'true egoism' is the only road that will lead us to [true] patriotism. *The salvation of the nation must begin with the salvation of you yourself!* In a time of ferment and chaos, you cannot consider that you have discharged your patriotic duty simply by chasing after others, running and shouting. Over and above this you have another more difficult and more precious obligation: to be able, in the very midst of the shouting, to plant your feet firmly on the ground, to make your plans, to save yourself, to struggle to turn yourself into something useful!" [80]

When Hu Shih had first summoned forth the spirit of "Ibsenism" in 1918, the idea had embodied a revolutionary appeal: in urging his readers to have the courage to stand alone against the crowd, he was calling them to battle against the tyranny of tradi-

79. Quoted in Kiang Wen-han, *The Chinese Student Movement* (New York, 1948), 87.
80. Hu Shih, "Ai-kuo yün-tung yü ch'iu-hsüeh" (The patriotic movement and getting an education), HSWT III, ix, 1146, 1149, 1150–1153. First published in *Hsien-tai p'ing-lun*, 2.39:5–9 (Sept. 5, 1925).

tional society. If Hu's motives were valid in 1918, they were no less so in 1925. But by then the same message carried a very different meaning: to argue the case for "pure egoism," to speak out against conformity in the name of intellectual individualism, was, in the context of this explosively tense situation, a call not for battle but for retreat.

The mood of the moment was not one of retreat. The tide of nationalist revolution was at full flood from 1925 to 1927. In July 1926 Kuomintang and Communist troops and cadres marched northward from their base in Kwangtung to pursue by force of arms and revolutionary agitation the first aim of their revolution: reunification. Two weeks later, on July 22, Hu Shih boarded a train in Peking, enroute to Harbin and thence across Russia, bound for London to attend a meeting of the British Boxer Indemnity committee. He was not in China to witness the steady advance of the revolutionary armies, and by the time he returned to Shanghai in the spring of 1927 a crucial turning point in the history of the revolution had been passed, and a new era was dawning.

Chapter 7. Shanghai, 1927–1930

When Hu Shih boarded the Peking-Mukden express on that July day in 1926, escorted to the station in Chinese fashion by a throng of friends and well-wishers, he left a life to which he never returned. Never again would what he had to say engage the attention of his audience in quite the same way as during the lively and productive years in Peking that were now behind him, nor again would he appear so luminous an embodiment of what was modern in intellect and hopeful in spirit. The events then stirring in the south that would, in time, transform China's political landscape would alter, too, the shape and dimensions of the world to which Hu Shih returned.

This was Hu's first trip abroad since his homecoming in 1917. It abounded in new experiences and fresh inspirations. During the autumn, while in China the revolutionary armies pitted their strength against the forces of Wu P'ei-fu in Hunan and Sun Ch'uan-fang in Kiangsi, Hu divided his time between Paris and London, stopping to pay his respects at the great centers of European sinological research, poring for long hours over the Tun-huang manuscripts in the Bibliothèque Nationale, and lecturing at Cambridge, Dublin, and other British universities. In January he sailed for America, where he found himself in considerable demand as a speaker to audiences whose concern with events in China mounted steadily as the revolutionary forces approached the great citadels of Western enterprise along the Yangtze. In April Hu set out for home, to discover for himself the nature of the new order that had been established during the ten months of his absence.

So long an interruption of normal routines, and so many hours of solitary travel, gave Hu unaccustomed time for reflection. To his friend Hsü Chih-mo he wrote from Paris in an uncommonly introspective mood:

In the final analysis, what have I done in the nine years since I returned to China? Where are the achievements? I see with my own eyes the politics of the nation going from bad to worse; this, in truth, is hard to bear . . . We may, of course, shift the responsibility by saying that this is the evil result of [the actions of] our predecessors and has nothing to do with us. But where, then, are the consequences of our own actions? Periodicals dealing with the "new art and literature" are everywhere. Everywhere one finds shallow and foolish discussions of art and literature and politics — can these be the source of fresh consequences? Did *The Endeavor* that a few of us edited for a year or so inspire new results?

. . . In Peking these last few years we have in truth been too comfortable, too indolent, too unconscientious. Two years ago [Jen] Shu-yung said that our life in Peking was a bit frivolous, and at that time, perhaps, we congratulated ourselves on this score . . . But as I think of it now, our life in Peking was . . . totally frivolous.

. . . I believe that we must stir things up a bit, and whip up a little of the spirit to undertake great things. *We must be individuals with all dignity, and we must do things conscientiously.* Only then can we face our present situation.[1]

To outward appearances the years on which Hu looked back with such sentiments had been less frivolous than endlessly busy, crowded with opportunities to promote or defend one or another of the innumerable causes to which he was committed. He was interested in everything, and he had ideas on nearly every subject. He numbered among the acquaintances of the past decade not only the most celebrated representatives of the new intelligentsia and many of the men who stood on the periphery of the political arena, but also most of the foreigners of note who came to Peking in that era of easy access to and increasing interest in China. He translated for Margaret Sanger when she lectured on birth control in Peking; he dined with Sherwood Eddy, the evangelist; and at Li Ta-chao's invitation he endured a dreary dinner party in honor of Adolf Joffe, the newly appointed Comintern representative in China. He talked archaeology with J. G. Anderson, fresh from the new excavations in Honan, and discussed questions of mutual scholarly interest with one after another of the international procession of sinologists that passed through Peking: Siren, des Rotours, Latourette, Franke. The Swedish explorer Sven Hedin, off for a prowl in Sinkiang, entrusted his library to Hu. Even the twice-deposed emperor, P'u-yi, hardly more than a prisoner in his ancestral palace, invited Hu in to bring him news of the manner in which his former realm was changing.[2]

For diversion there were the pleasures of Peking's secondhand bookstores, and the occasional delight of discovering a long-sought Ming edition. There were family weekend excursions to the Western Hills outside the city to escape the heat of a Peking summer, and frequent dinners with friends — T'ao Meng-ho, Kao I-han, Chang Wei-tz'u — one or another of the city's better restaurants, with sometimes an evening of cards to follow. Every

1. "Ou-yu tao-chung chi-shu," HSWT III, i, 77–79. See also unpublished diary, entry for Aug. 23, 1926, concerning an exchange of letters with Lewis Gannett touching upon this same subject.

2. See Hu Shih, "Hsüan-t'ung yü Hu Shih" ([The] Hsüan-t'ung [emperor] and Hu Shih), NLCP no. 12 (July 23, 1922). For the ex-emperor's account of this incident, which he passes off as nothing more than a lark provoked by the desire to try out a newly installed telephone, see Aisin-Gioro Pu Yi, *From Emperor to Citizen*, I (Peking, 1964), 127–128.

Sunday, in an informal but enduring ritual, Hu opened his study to all who might wish to come — old friends or new acquaintances, Chinese or foreigners, eminent scholars or fledgling students — to argue politics and scholarship, to trade academic or political gossip, or perhaps merely to lay claim to having been there.

And always, of course, there was work to be done: lectures on Chinese philosophy and the methodology of thought at Peita, committee meetings of one kind or another, editorial responsibilities to be discharged, a voluminous correspondence to maintain, and a prodigious amount of writing. Hu's history of classical philosophy, destined to remain unfinished, was published in 1919, followed by the famous Oriental series of *pai-hua* novels carrying Hu's long critical prefaces. Throughout these years, moreover, an unending stream of essays flowed from Hu's brush, some hardly more than notes, others substantial enough to be counted as small books, periodically gathered together into collected works, four volumes of which were published in 1921, and a second series, even bulkier, in 1924.

Such had been the life to which Hu looked back in 1926. In the years ahead many of the same concerns would continue to occupy his attention, and many of the same people would still come to his Sunday open house. But life would not be the same, for by the time Hu returned to Shanghai late in the spring of 1927 the Nationalists had established themselves in power in the Yangtze valley. Thenceforth it would be the Kuomintang government that would dictate, by what it did and failed to do, the terms in which the debate concerning China's future must be conducted.

The Kuomintang had come to power as one element of a revolutionary coalition whose aim was the destruction of Chinese militarism and foreign imperialism. Even after the unstable Kuomintang-Communist alliance collapsed in April 1927, the KMT government that established itself in Nanking remained — in its own estimate, at least — a revolutionary regime, dedicated to the consummation of the revolution as Sun Yat-sen had conceived of it.

In one respect the new government was the kind that Hu Shih and his liberal friends had long hoped for. It was, or claimed to be, a government with a plan. On his death in 1925 Sun had bequeathed to his party a considerable clutter of ideas concerning the problems that still confronted the revolution: military and political unification, social and economic reconstruction, the preparation of the people for the responsibilities of citizenship, the establishment of governmental institutions and the separation of political functions, and, eventually, the implementation of constitutional and democratic rule.

In spite of its revolutionary ideals, however, or perhaps because of them, under the new regime intellectual life was less venturesome than it had been during the preceding years of political cynicism and near anarchy. At the height of the warlord era, in 1921, John Dewey had aptly observed, "Intellectually China has the advantage of a weak and corrupt government. The uniform attitude of the educated class toward their government . . . is critical . . . Every thinker, every writer, every articulate conscious influence is liberal." [3] The warlords, in other words, had not been much interested in ideas. The Nationalists very definitely were. They quickly translated the often vague and sometimes contradictory opinions of their late *Tsung-li* (Party leader) into an ideology to which they demanded dogmatic allegiance, and against which they would tolerate no dissent.

After eighty years "under the yoke of political and economic imperialism," the Kuomintang argument proclaimed, China must accept the leadership of the party in her struggle for liberation from semicolonial enslavement. To achieve this end, political authority must be entrusted to the tutelary dictatorship of the party. The thoughts of the people must be "solely guided" by Sun's famous "Three People's Principles" of nationalism, democracy, and livelihood, enunciated in lectures given in the early 1920s and by his *Plans for National Reconstruction*, a final summary of his ideas written the year before his death. Just as the revolutionaries of an earlier era had argued that the collapse of dynastic institutions would lead of itself to the establishment of a viable republican government, so now Kuomintang ideologues insisted that with the destruction of imperialism all else would follow naturally. "After all the unequal treaties will have been terminated," ran the official line, "China will become a strong and wealthy nation and, as a matter of course, occupy an important position in the family of nations." [4]

3. John Dewey, "Public Opinion in Japan," *The New Republic* (Nov. 16, 1921); reprinted in *Characters and Events*, I, 178.

4. "Resolution Adopted by the Third National Congress of the Kuomintang with Regard to China's Foreign Relations," March 23, 1929. Text in Arthur N.

The logic of this argument ran directly contrary to Hu Shih's analysis of the situation. His contention (noted earlier) was that "once the democratic revolution has succeeded, and when politics has got on the right track, then international imperialist aggression will in large part naturally have disappeared." [5] But in the China to which Hu returned in 1927, political revolution, virulently nationalistic in its temper, had clearly taken precedence over the unhurried intellectual change in which he had placed his hopes for the regeneration of Chinese politics and the ultimate success of the democratic revolution.

Homeward bound in April 1927, Hu Shih arrived in Yokohama to find a letter from Ting Wen-chiang awaiting him. In view of the unsettled political situation in China, Ting wrote, Hu would be well advised to prolong his stay in Japan, taking this opportunity to gain an acquaintance with a people who would soon play, as Ting rightly foresaw, a preeminent role in the lives of the Chinese. But Hu had no personal ties in Japan and spoke no Japanese. His funds, moreover, were nearly exhausted. So after a three-week excursion that took him along the usual tourist's itinerary to Lake Hakone, Kyoto, and Nara, he sailed from Kobe on a small Japanese ship and a few days later disembarked in Shanghai.[6]

The political situation that he confronted was indeed fraught with uncertainty. In mid-April the uneasy Kuomintang–Communist Party coalition had come to a violent and bloody end; throughout the spring and summer the Yangtze provinces lay under the harassment of Chiang Kai-shek's "White Terror." The Kuomintang was divided even against itself, with a radical faction in Wuhan still trying to maintain political and ideological ties with the Left, in the face of mounting pressure from the militarily dominant and politically conservative wing of the party that controlled Nanking and Shanghai. In the north, Peking remained in the hands of Chang Tso-lin, the pro-Japanese warlord of Manchuria. Not until the summer of 1928 would the revolutionary banner be hoisted above the old capital. But already the center of political interest had

Holcombe, *The Chinese Revolution: A Phase in the Regeneration of a World Power* (Cambridge, Mass., 1931), 382.

5. "Kuo-chi ti Chung-kuo," HSWT II, iii, 128i.

6. Hu Shih, *Ting Wen-chiang ti chuan-chi,* 82.

shifted to the new capital that the Nationalists were laying out in the south, at Nanking.

Peking had by this time lost not only its political preeminence but also much of its intellectual luster. Many of the men whose names had made the city famous a decade earlier had departed from it, in divers directions. Ts'ai Yüan-p'ei was in Nanking in the spring of 1927, endeavoring, in his capacity as one of the party's elder statesmen, to influence the educational policies of the new government. Lu Hsün, expelled from Peking by Tuan Ch'i-jui's government in 1926, and disillusioned by what he had seen of the revolution in Canton over the following winter, was soon to return to Shanghai to spend his remaining years in embittered and embattled opposition to the Nationalists. Ch'en Tu-hsiu, of course, had been among the first to leave, pursuing the revolutionary cause that would turn on him in the summer of 1927 — holding him responsible for the disasters that had befallen the Communist movement — and cast him from the leadership of the party he had helped to found. And even while Hu Shih was en route home, in April, his old friend and indefatigable ideological disputant, Li Ta-chao, had been seized and summarily executed by Chang Tso-lin's gendarmes in the famous raid on the Soviet Legation in Peking.

At the end of 1922, when Hu Shih had requested leave from his duties at Peita in the wake of the debacle of the "Good Men Government," unfriendly rumors had circulated to the effect that the illness he claimed was no more than a matter of political convenience. "How *is* Mr. Hu Shih?" inquired Shao Li-tzu, editor of the revolutionary *Min-kuo jih-pao* (Republican daily news), published in Shanghai. Could it be, Shao had asked, that Hu had discovered wisdom in the proverbial saying, "Of the thirty-six stratagems, the best is to run?" From his bed in the Peking Union Medical College hospital Hu had retorted with unwonted fury: "When we see the many men in the foreign concessions with their breezy talk and grandiloquent theories, and the many notable little politicians chasing about from here to there, then we realize what kind of sons of harlots this debased psychology [of escape] gives rise to. I don't run. Never in my life have I followed the fashions of the day, or avoided danger. In the eyes of a responsible political critic, a paper closed down or a time in jail cannot be counted a danger. But 'to run,' especially 'to run' off to a foreign concession from which to talk down to others — that is shameful, that is something I would never do!" [7]

In the spring of 1927, however, Hu elected not to return to Peking. Instead he took a house on Jessfield Road in the International Concession and settled down to spend three and a half somewhat restless years in Shanghai. But it soon became apparent that escape was not what he had in mind.

In such chaotic times Shanghai had much to make it an attractive stopping place. Most important, perhaps, was the refuge offered in the foreign concessions to men of independent opinions. Then, too, Shanghai was nearer than Peking to the seat of the new government and in closer touch with the comings and goings of the world beyond. It was still the center of the largest publishing enterprises. And if none of its universities could quite match the renown of Peita and Tsinghua, it boasted a number of reputable private institutions. One of these was Kuang-hua University, established in 1925 by students who had withdrawn for patriotic reasons from various mission-operated colleges. Another was the China National Institute, Hu's old school, which had survived the vicissitudes of its early years to attain the status of a private university with a campus situated in Woosung, on the outskirts of Shanghai. Hu Shih taught philosophy at Kuang-hua during much of the time he spent in Shanghai, and in 1928 he accepted, without particular enthusiasm, the presidency of the China National Institute.[8] In view of the uncertainty that still prevailed as to the educational policies that the Nanking regime would pursue, and the role that it would assign to the government universities in its ongoing revolution, it was prudent of Hu to associate himself with institutions not directly subject to Nanking's control. For his relations with the Nationalist government started off very badly indeed.

Hu Shih brought back something of the "new inspiration" that had come to him on his trip through Russia and Europe, the desire to "stir things up a bit." The spirit of *The Endeavor* period had been rekindled. In place of *The Endeavor* Hu now had at his disposal a monthly review called *The Crescent (Hsin yüeh)*, the

7. Hu Shih, " 'Hu Shih hsien-sheng tao-ti tsen-yang?' " (How *is* Mr. Hu Shih?), NLCP no. 36 (Jan. 7, 1923).

8. On Hu Shih's attitude toward his duties at Chung-kuo kung-hsüeh see the unpublished diary, entries for June 17 and 25, 1928.

creation of a handful of Western-educated intellectuals of essentially literary inclinations, that began publishing in Shanghai in March, 1928. The magazine's first editorial board consisted of Hsü Chih-mo, Wen I-to, and Jao Meng-k'an, romantic poets of the "Crescent group" established in the early twenties, who had little interest in politics. There were others associated with the new venture, however, who were concerned with public issues, men like the literary critic Liang Shih-ch'iu, and the Columbia-educated sociologist P'an Kuang-tan (Quentin Pan), and Lo Lung-chi, who held a Ph.D. in government from Columbia, and Hu Shih himself. Under their influence *The Crescent* became, particularly in 1929 and 1930, a notable forum for the discussion of politics.

Whether they were writing poetry, or literary criticism, or political commentaries, the writers who published in *The Crescent* addressed themselves to a highly selective audience. They wrote only for that sophisticated, urbane, and largely Western-educated minority which could appreciate the opinions of men whose literary tastes had been cultivated on Wordsworth and Byron and the Pre-Raphaelites, who read Katherine Mansfield and Virginia Woolf and knew something about Bloomsbury, and who discussed politics in terms borrowed from Harold Laski and the Fabians. Despite a common antipathy to the Kuomintang, the views of the Crescent group found little favor among left-wing intellectuals. Lu Hsün, who engaged Liang Shih-ch'iu in a running feud concerning the "class character" of literature, denounced Liang and his friends as shadows "skulking in the twilight of bourgeois culture." [9] Agnes Smedley, similarly prejudiced but more polite, described them merely as "decent and respectable men of letters . . . the intellectual aristocrats of a dying and decadent social order." [10] Nevertheless, some of the most pointed and pertinent criticism ever directed against the Nationalists and their government was published in *The Crescent*. For this Hu Shih was in no small part responsible.

Hu's contributions to *The Crescent* spanned the wide range of his interests. In it he published essays on the history of Buddhism in China (in part the result of his study of the Tun-huang manu-

9. Lu Hsün, " 'Hard Translation' and the 'Class Character of Literature,' " *Selected Works of Lu Hsun*, III (Peking, 1959), 79.
10. Agnes Smedley, "Chinese Poets and Professors," *New York Herald Tribune Books*, vol. XC, no. 30,499 (May 18, 1930), sect. xi, p. 9.

scripts in Paris in 1926) and on various questions pertaining to the *pai-hua* movement; his autobiography in serial form; book reviews and a few translations of European and American short stories; and, finally, the several forceful critiques of Kuomintang ideology discussed below.

Hu accepted the Nationalist government, even as he had tolerated its warlord predecessors, as the de facto ruling power. He strove to enlighten, but never to overthrow, the new authority. He sought only reform. Of China's new rulers he demanded only some assurance that they would heed the voice of responsible criticism, and profit from it.[11] Among his friends were men who stood high in the government's councils: Ts'ai Yüan-p'ei, Wang Ch'ung-hui, Chiang Monlin, Wu Chih-hui, and T. V. Soong. Hu himself remained apart from it, in a position, as he liked to think, of loyal opposition. He was to discover in 1929, however, that the Nanking authorities did not share his belief in either the necessity or the usefulness of criticism, regardless of the spirit in which it was offered.

Hu's differences with the Kuomintang began at the level of basic premises. He was affronted both by the Kuomintang's habit of blaming China's problems exclusively on the effects of imperialism and by the "revolutionary" solutions proposed by KMT propagandists. As evidence of the shallowness of this analysis Hu pointed to the example of Japan. "Why were the unequal treaties unable to hinder the free development of Japan?" he asked. "Why is it that we, having knelt, cannot rise to our feet again?" [12]

The answer, Hu insisted, lay deeper than the anti-imperialist slogans pasted on every available wall or chanted in angry chorus by students as they marched past the foreign concessions in Shanghai, Hankow, and Canton. Such nationalistic catechisms, Hu declared, were no more than the modern expression of China's age-old enslavement to "the religion of names" — a superstitious faith in the mystical power of language. "Let me ask," he wrote in 1928, "what difference is there between pasting 'Down with imperialism!' on a wall and pasting . . . 'May you see happiness when you raise your head!' [*t'ai-t'ou chien-hsi*] on a wall? Is this an inheritance passed down from our forefathers or isn't it?" [13]

11. See, for example, Hu's unpublished diary, entry for July 2, 1929.

12. "Ch'ing ta-chia lai chao-chao ching-tzu," HSWT III, i, 47.

13. Hu Shih, "Ming chiao" (The religion of names), HSWT III, i, 98. First published in HY 1.5 (July 1928).

Hu could not deny that a reaction against what he himself labeled "a history of some eighty years of insult and oppression" was to be expected.[14] He insisted time and time again, however, that the unequal treaties, the foreign concessions, extraterritorial jurisdiction — the whole edifice of imperialist privilege against which the students hurled their fury — was only the visible facade concealing more fundamental problems, problems to which no solutions could be sought by revolutionary means. His distrust of revolutionary methods was, as has been noted, an essential and persistent element in his intellectual outlook. As early as 1916 he had argued that while revolution may in some instances be "a necessary stage of evolution," nevertheless "premature revolutions . . . are usually wasteful and therefore unfruitful." [15] Urged to define his views on this subject in 1922 by some young and skeptical readers of "Our Political Proposals," he had replied with studied ambiguity: "For those things which can be reformed it will do no harm to begin with reform, bit by bit. For those things that are too bad, and incapable of being reformed, or if the powers of evil are determined not to tolerate bit-by-bit reform, then we must adopt revolutionary measures. Destruction and construction are not fundamentally opposed to each other . . . Sometimes destruction is construction, and sometimes construction is destruction; sometimes destruction must come first, sometimes it follows naturally in the wake of construction, and sometimes both are carried out simultaneously." [16]

In 1929 Hu was prepared to deal with the problem more fully. In an important and widely read essay entitled "What Road Shall We Follow?" he asserted that "revolution" and "evolution" must not be understood as mutually exclusive processes. Revolution, he wrote, is simply "forced evolution." Specific revolutions are inevitably absorbed into the evolutionary flow of history. But revolution is a conscious act, while evolution is on the whole unseen and unfelt. For this reason evolution is "slow" and "ungovernable" and "frequently results in the retention of antiquated institutions and conditions." [17]

14. Hu Shih, "Chin-jih chiao-hui chiao-yü ti nan-kuan" (The difficulties facing religious education today), HSWT III, ix, 1162.

15. *Diary*, 842.

16. Correspondence concerning "Wo-men ti cheng-chih chu-chang," HSWT II, iii, 39. First published in NLCP no. 4 (May 28, 1922), a special issue given over to this discussion.

17. Hu Shih, "Wo-men tsou na-i-t'iao lu?" (Which road shall we follow?),

Hence, Hu continued, unconscious evolution is inferior to "conscious revolution." He was careful, however, to distinguish between violent and nonviolent revolutionary approaches, and to make it clear that he advocated only the kind of "revolution" which achieves its ends by means of education, legislation, and constitutional political processes. His enduring belief in the importance of *controlled* change was nowhere better expressed:

> We are all dissatisfied with the present state of things, and we are all opposed to the lazy inclination to "let things take their own course." But if we look attentively into China's real needs and China's present position in the world, we cannot fail to oppose as well what is presently called the "revolutionary" method. We earnestly declare: China's need today is not for that kind of revolution which is created by a violent despotism. Nor does China need that kind of revolution which fights violence with violence. Nor does China need that kind of revolution which fabricates imaginary enemies of the revolution in order to stir up a revolution. It is better to accept the epithet "counterrevolutionary" than to accept these various kinds of revolution, for they are in every case capable only of wasting our energy, instigating a foolish and cruel pettiness of spirit, disrupting the peace of society and the nation, and sowing the seeds of mutual destruction and killing. Such revolutions will permit our real enemies to go their own way unmolested . . . And such revolutions will allow us to stray farther and farther from our true path in establishing the kind of nation we ought to establish.
>
> Our genuine enemies are poverty, disease, ignorance, greed, and disorder. These five evil spirits are the real opponents of the revolution, but they are not the kind that we can overthrow by resorting to violent methods. The real revolution against these five enemies has only one road to follow: Clearly to recognize our enemies, clearly to recognize our problems, and then to gather together [those of] ability and intelligence in the

HY 2.10 (Dec. 10, 1929); reprinted in Hu Shih, ed., *Chung-kuo wen-t'i* (China's problems; Shanghai, 1932), and in *Hu Shih lun-hsüeh chin-chu* and HSWT IV. A translation entitled "Which Road Are We Going?" was published in *Pacific Affairs*, 3.10:933–946 (October 1930). Quotation used here is from *Chung-kuo wen-t'i*, 11–13.

country at large, to adopt the knowledge and methods of the world's science, and step by step to undertake conscious [*tzu-chüeh*] reforms, under conscious leadership, and thus little by little to harvest the results of constant reforms . . .

This method is very difficult, but we do not acknowledge any simpler or easier method. This method is very slow, but we know of no other, quicker road." [18]

No aspect of Hu's thought is more important, or more consistently expressed, than the conviction summarized here that change must come not blindly but consciously, in pursuit of aims that have been critically examined, to meet genuine needs.

But though Hu urged moderation, his purpose was not to impede change. His whole philosophy was predicated on the assumption that change is the central fact of individual and historical experience. His endeavor, as he saw it, was to encourage change in proper sequence and direction. "The fundamental significance of the New Culture movement," he wrote in 1929, "lies in the recognition that the old culture of China is not suitable to a modern situation, and in the advocacy of the complete acceptance of the new civilization of the world." [19]

On this count Hu was bitterly critical of the Kuomintang, which in its search for an ideology was betraying increasing hostility to the "new culture." The Nationalist movement had its origins in turn-of-the-century anti-Manchu organizations that were, intellectually and politically, only partially Western-oriented. Moreover, although the reorganized Kuomintang owed a considerable debt to Leninist principles of party organization and, ideologically, to the Leninist description of imperialism, Sun Yat-sen had never acknowledged the applicability of Marxist social theory to China, or taken to heart its internationalist doctrine. The 1927 coup had signaled not only the KMT's retreat from social revolution but also its repudiation of the internationalist implications of Marxism-Leninism. Thereafter the party turned more and more to a kind of conservative culturalism as the basis for its world view, reaffirming

18. *Chung-kuo wen-t'i*, 19–21.

19. Hu Shih, "Hsin wen-hua yün-tung yü Kuomintang" (The new culture movement and the Kuomintang), HY 2.6–7 (September 1929); reprinted in Hu Shih, with Liang Shih-ch'iu and Lo Lung-chi, *Jen-ch'üan lun-chi* (A collection of essays on human rights; Shanghai, 1930). Quotation here is from *Jen-ch'üan lun-chi*, 125–126.

the unique wisdom enshrined in China's intellectual and social traditions. This revival of Confucian values was not formally acknowledged until 1934, when the Nationalists inaugurated what they hopefully called "The New Life Movement" and reinstituted official observances of Confucius' birthday. The disposition to move toward the past was already clearly evident by the late 1920s, however, in the public pronouncements of Chiang Kai-shek and other Kuomintang leaders.[20]

Hu Shih regarded this intellectual retrogression as a betrayal of the most significant accomplishments of the last several decades, fully justifying his habitual distrust of nationalism. "All narrowly nationalistic movements are to some degree conservative, tending to praise traditional culture and resist the incursions of alien cultures," he wrote in 1929. To this general rule the Kuomintang was no exception: "At bottom, the Kuomintang movement is a kind of extreme nationalist [or racist: *min-tsu chu-i*] movement, which from its inception has possessed a conservative character . . . These ideas have become the basis for various kinds of reactionary conduct and thought since it has achieved power." [21] Among the counts listed in his indictment of the Nanking regime were its notable lack of enthusiasm for the *pai-hua* movement, its uncritical view of Confucian virtues, and the idealized vision of the accomplishments of pre-Ch'ing China that its ideologues promoted.

An even more ominous indication of the intellectual temper of the new government, in Hu's view, was its increasingly vehement insistence on loyalty to the "thought of Sun Yat-sen." Its demand for conformity to intellectual and political orthodoxy ran directly counter to the principles of criticism that Hu Shih had been preaching ever since 1917. He could lay no more serious charge than this against the Nationalists: "One of the great undertakings of the New Culture movement was the liberation of thought. When we criticized Confucius and Mencius, impeached Ch'eng I and Chu Hsi, opposed the Confucian religion and denied God, our purpose was simply to overthrow the canons of orthodoxy, to liberate Chinese thought, and to encourage a skeptical attitude and

20. See, for example, Chiang Kai-shek's address on "Double Ten," 1929, commemorating the eighteenth anniversary of the revolutionary uprisings of October 10, 1911. Text in CWR 50.6:250 (Oct. 12, 1929).

21. "Hsin wen-hua yün-tung yü Kuomintang," *Jen-ch'üan lun-chi*, 127.

a critical spirit. But out of the alliance between the Communist Party and the Kuomintang grew an absolute authoritarianism which has brought about the total loss of freedom of thought and opinion. [Now] you may deny God, but you may not criticize Sun Chung-shan. You need not go to church, but you must not fail to read the Tsung-li's *Last Will and Testament,* nor to observe the weekly memorial service." [22]

The grip of ideology was tightening.

Sun Yat-sen had been sincere enough in his commitment to democracy to establish democratic constitutionalism as the ultimate goal toward which his party should aim. He had been, however, by no means a consistent democrat, and especially toward the end of his life he had expressed a concern that China should be spared what he called "the confusions of Western democracy." [23] In 1928–1929, therefore, China was in the first years of a period of "political tutelage," intended, as Sun put it, to train the people "in the exercise of their political rights" and to accustom them "to the performance of their civic duties according to the principles of the revolution." [24] During this tutelage period, as the KMT policy that was laid down in October 1928 specified, it must be the party which "guides the people in the exercise of political authority." Legislative and judicial powers, as well as administrative, "are entrusted in toto to the National Government for execution." [25] The party professed its desire to have done with the period of tutelage at the earliest opportunity, "so that the constitutional powers may ultimately be delegated to the people." [26] But the existence of an identity of interests between the governed and the governing authority — a crucial asumption on Sun's part — was in question from the beginning. The Kuomintang did not view its educative responsibilities as the primary condition for progress; other considerations — political unification, the expulsion of imperialism, the

22. *Ibid.,* 124.

23. Sun Yat-sen, *San Min Chu I,* trans. F. W. Price (Shanghai, 1928), 318.

24. Sun Yat-sen, "Fundamentals of National Reconstruction" (1924). Text in Holcombe, *The Chinese Revolution,* 353.

25. "General Principles Governing the Period of Political Tutelage," promulgated by the Central Executive Committee of the Kuomintang, Oct. 3, 1928. Text in Holcombe, *The Chinese Revolution,* 371.

26. "Manifesto of the Second Plenary Session of the Central Executive Committee of the Kuomintang," June 18, 1929. Text in Holcombe, *The Chinese Revolution,* 388.

suppression of "counterrevolution" — took precedence over the task of political education.[27] It soon became apparent that the doctrine of tutelage served only to justify and maintain a one-party dictatorship.

"I do not believe in dictatorship," Hu Shih had written to Hsü Chih-mo shortly after his brief visit to Moscow in 1926. "People nowadays who dream of dictatorship can well be compared to T'ang Ming-tsung of the Five Dynasties period [907–960], who every night burned incense and prayed to heaven to send down a sage to pacify China. Such a shortcut is unthinkable." Even Hu's enthusiasm for the "great experiment" going on in the Soviet Union did not convince him that authoritarian methods offered a way out for the Chinese. He did not believe, in the first place, that power alone would suffice to insure capable leadership. "Lenin and men of his caliber all had great learning and experience — they did not drop from heaven," he wrote to Hsü. He knew, too, that the authoritarian spirit was incompatible with the intellectual values that he prized. "Under a dictatorship the only distinction drawn is between obedience and disobedience, not between right and wrong . . . There would be no place under such a system for independent thinkers like ourselves." [28] Finally, and fundamentally, Hu rejected authoritarianism because of his still firm belief in the educative function of democratic institutions — the same faith he had so often expressed in his critiques of warlord governments,

27. The elliptical quality of Kuomintang reasoning in this regard was vividly revealed in the "Manifesto of the Second Plenary Session of the Central Executive Committee of the Kuomintang," published in June 1929: "Without peace, it is really impossible to mitigate the sufferings of the people in China today. But in order to attain peace, we must have unification, it is impossible to attain real unification without removing all the obstacles which the regime of militarism has chosen to cast upon the nation. In order to prevent the militarists from having their way, however, we must do all we can to show something constructive and to train the people in real political democracy. But again when we speak of constructive schemes, nothing can be accomplished without mustering all the forces of the nation into an organized unit. The causal relations between these factors are indeed irrefragable, so that the only way to remove all the difficulties whatsoever is to continue our struggle and our endeavour. It is only when all the Party members and all the people in the nation coöperate to the fullest extent in pushing forward with the guidance of the principles of the Party and show willingness to sacrifice and a firm determination to complete the educative period [i.e., the period of political tutelage] in an orderly manner that we shall be able to remove the sufferings of the people." Text in Holcombe, *The Chinese Revolution*, 389.

28. "Ou-yu tao-chung chi-shu," HSWT III, i, 88.

and which he would be compelled to reaffirm once more in the 1930s in the face of a coherently articulated theoretical defense of dictatorship.

In *The Crescent*, as earlier in *The Endeavor*, Hu repeatedly stressed the importance of ruling through "the proper organs of government." His specific demands remained much the same as those put forward in "Our Political Proposals" in 1922, but he gave even greater emphasis to the need for a fundamental law. "If we truly desire to guarantee human rights and to establish the basis for lawful government, the first thing we must do is to draw up a constitution for the Republic of China," Hu wrote in April 1929. "At the *very least* we must draw up a provisional constitution for the so-called period of political tutelage." [29] And again, two months later: "We want to ask what inconsistency there is between training the people and having a constitution . . . We do not believe that without a constitution there can be a tutelage government. Without a constitution there can be only a dictatorship." [30]

Hu attributed the Kuomintang's blindness on this issue to the failing vision of Sun Yat-sen himself. Despite his early enthusiasm for democracy, Hu declared, Sun had come toward the end of his life to harbor "strong doubts as to the ability of the common people to participate in political affairs." [31] This was indeed the case. During the years of bitter frustration and uncertain expectations that followed the initial failure of republicanism in 1912 and 1913, Sun had become convinced that his cause had been betrayed not only by Yüan Shih-k'ai and the militarists but also by his own comrades-in-arms, who, in his words, "themselves became the slaves of the theory of the difficulty of action and the easiness of knowledge, [and] began to look on my plan as a Utopia and empty words, and renounced responsibility for the reconstruction of China." [32] Living in semi-exile in Shanghai in the winter of 1918, his fortunes

29. Hu Shih, "Jen-ch'üan yü yüeh-fa" (Human rights and the provisional constitution), HY 2.2:5–7 (April 1929). Reprinted in *Jen-ch'üan lun-chi*. An English version appears in *China's Own Critics* (Tientsin, 1931), a selection of essays by Hu Shih and Lin Yü-t'ang, with commentaries by Wang Ching-wei.

30. Hu Shih, "Wo-men shen-mo shih-hou ts'ai k'o yu hsien-fa?" (When *can* we have a constitution?), HY 2.4:3 (June 1929). Reprinted in *Jen-ch'üan lun-chi*; English version in *China's Own Critics*.

31. *Ibid.*, 5.

32. Sun Yat-sen, *Memoirs of a Chinese Revolutionary* (London, 1918; Taipei, 1953), vii.

at their lowest ebb, Sun undertook to refute this defeatist psychology. The result, cast in the form of a memoir, was a collection of arguments, some of which can only be called ludicrous, intended to prove Sun's thesis that "knowledge is difficult, while action is easy." [33] What Sun meant was that it is incomparably more difficult to understand the significance of action than to act. Thenceforth the belief that only a few — the foreknowers, as Sun called them, those with "prevision" — may lead, while the multitude must be content to follow, became imbedded in Kuomintang ideology, serving, among other things, to rationalize the existence of the party dictatorship.

The problem of striking a balance between knowledge and action was an old one for the Chinese. Sun's point of departure was the thesis of the Ming-dynasty philosopher and statesman Wang Yang-ming (Wang Shou-jen, 1472–1529), that knowledge and action are, or should be, united into one (*chih hsing ho-i*). Wang's aim had been to demonstrate that knowledge of a principle is genuine only if it finds expression in action — for example, that there is no principle of filialism that can be understood apart from filial conduct. His correlative proposition that all knowledge is innate, awaiting only discovery by a perceptive intuition, led subsequently to the development of an introspective school of Confucianism quite at odds with the *engagé* attitudes of Sung-dynasty thinkers. Wang was, nevertheless, a participant in an ongoing Neo-Confucian dialogue. But Sun Yat-sen, endeavoring to refute what he took to be the irresponsible implications of Wang's doctrine, and Hu Shih, who supported Wang in order to refute Sun, were not much in-

33. The following excerpt (*ibid.*, 83) is a not untypical example of the manner in which Sun developed his argument:

In China there is the custom of calling an adopted son "the son of a caterpillar," as it is supposed that a wasp has not its own young, but, as the popular story has it, always has a caterpillar in its nest. In reality this is not so: the wasp first takes a caterpillar into its nest, then, by letting a certain poisonous fluid into the head of the caterpillar, makes it motionless but does not kill it. Then it lays its eggs in the body of the caterpillar . . . We see that the wasp invented this anaesthetic many thousands of years before our doctors. The wasp required it to prevent the caterpillar from crawling away, and at the same time to prevent the decay of the body it needed for the welfare of its young. This circumstance may also help us to convince ourselves that "action is easy but knowledge is difficult," since the wasp is quite ignorant, but acts; so that we see that the theory is justified in application, not only to men, but also to insects.

terested in the traditional debate from which they drew their terms.[34]

Sun was searching for an ideology of leadership. His purpose was to persuade his followers that "in the building up of a country it is easy to find men of action, but very difficult to find people who can work out plans of reconstruction." [35] Consequently, men of the latter mold — and Sun left no doubt that he was speaking of himself — are greatly to be valued, and they must be listened to.

Hu Shih's purpose, in turn, was not to reinstate the doctrine of Wang Yang-ming[36] but to expose the authoritarian implication of Sun's theory and to reaffirm the persistent premise of China's liberals that government should be the business of men whose authority derives not from the ascription to them of ideological infallibility but from their proven competence in administrative matters. Although he did not make a point of it, his insistence on the inseparability of knowledge and action echoed not only Wang Yang-ming but John Dewey. "The more you act, the greater your knowledge," Hu wrote in connection with the issue of constitutionalism and political education. "Knowledge is the result of action, and the function of knowledge is to assist action, to guide and improve action." [37] In similar circumstances Dewey would undoubtedly have said the same thing.

The gravest of Hu's objections to Sun's theory of knowledge and action stemmed from his fear that it would encourage the men on whom rested the burden of administration to take too casual a view of the complex and difficult problems with which they must deal. Behind this fear lay the conviction, as Hu had enunciated it in 1923, that the crucial problem of modern politics is not the extent of power but the manner in which power is exercised (see above, chapter 6 at note 44). He rejected authoritarianism, not because authoritarian attitudes exaggerate the importance of gov-

34. For background on this question see David Nivison, "The Problem of 'Knowledge' and 'Action' in Chinese Thought since Wang Yang-ming," in Arthur F. Wright, ed., *Studies in Chinese Thought* (Chicago, 1953), 112–145.

35. Sun Yat-sen, *Memoirs*, 88.

36. For Hu's view of Wang Yang-ming's place in China's intellectual history see Hu Shih, "Ch'ing-tai hsüeh-che ti chih-hsüeh fang-fa" (The scholarly methodology of Ch'ing-period scholars), HSWT, ii, 539–579, esp. sect. 3.

37. Hu Shih, "Chih nan, hsing i pu-i" (Knowledge is difficult, but action is not easy either), HY 2.4:11 (June 1929). Reprinted in *Jen-ch'üan lun-chi*; English version in *China's Own Critics*.

ernment, but because authoritarian methods are unsuited to the complexities of the modern political process.

During the Shanghai years Hu received support in this view from Lo Lung-chi, chairman of the department of political science at Kuang-hua and a regular contributor to *The Crescent*. Lo had returned to China in 1928 from seven years spent at the University of Wisconsin, the London School of Economics, and Columbia, where he had earned his doctorate in government. At the L.S.E. in 1925 and 1926 he had studied under Harold Laski. His own opinions, expressed in a series of trenchant political commentaries published in *The Crescent* in 1929 and 1930,[38] clearly reflected Laski's preoccupation with problems of political administration, and his belief that governments must finally be judged not by their ideological claims but by the nature of their administrative processes.[39] Prompted by Lo's interest in Laski and the Fabians, a few of the Crescent group came together in an informal study society and began to turn out essays modeled on the Fabian Tracts.[40]

38. Of Lo Lung-chi's numerous contributions to *Hsin yüeh* the most interesting from the standpoint of political theory are: "Lun jen-ch'üan" (On human rights), HY 2.5 (July 1929); "Wo-men yao shen-mo-yang ti cheng-chih chih-tu?" (What kind of a political system do we want?), HY 2.12 (February 1930); "Lun kung-ch'an chu-i: kung-ch'an chu-i li-lun-shang ti p'i-p'ing" (On communism: a critique of communist theory), HY 3.1 (September [?] 1930); "Tui hsün-cheng shih-ch'i yüeh-fa ti p'i-p'ing" (A critique of the provisional constitution for the period of political tutelage), HY 3.8 (n.d.); "Shen-mo shih fa-chih" (What is the rule of law?), HY 3.11 (n.d.). In "Kao ya-p'o yen-lun tzu-yu che" (A word to those who suppress freedom of expression), HY 2.6–7 (September 1929), Lo comes to Hu Shih's defense in his confrontation with the Kuomintang.

39. See Harold Laski, *A Grammar of Politics* (New Haven, 1925), esp. pp. 35–240.

40. In the spring of 1929 several members of the Crescent group (including Hu Shih, Hsü Chih-mo, Liang Shih-ch'iu, Lo Lung-chi, Yeh Kung-ch'ao, and Ting Hsi-lin) assembled to discuss the possibility of publishing another magazine, tentatively entitled *P'ing-lun*, presumably as an outlet for political criticism. Apparently this scheme came to naught; instead, as noted in the text below, the editorial policy of *Hsin yüeh* was liberalized in April 1929 to make that magazine a more suitable vehicle for the publication of political opinions. The informally constituted "P'ing society" (P'ing she) remained in existence, however, and out of it came a series of essays, on various social, economic, and political issues, which were published in *Hsin yüeh*, and some of which were later collected in *Chung-kuo wen-t'i*. It seems likely that this undertaking was inspired by the example of the Fabians. At a meeting of the P'ing she in May, Lo Lung-chi read a paper giving a brief historical account of the Fabian Society and its concerns, which prompted Hu Shih to suggest that the members of their own group should address themselves in similar fashion to

Although it is difficult to assess the extent of direct or indirect influence that Lo may have had on Hu Shih's thinking, the emphasis on administrative competence and "government by experts" that Lo borrowed from Laski certainly conformed to Hu's restrictive definition of what "politics" is all about (as he had been arguing it ever since his early dispute with Ch'en Tu-hsiu) and served to reinforce his suspicion of political discussions conducted at the level of abstract generalizations. Nor was it difficult, measuring the Nationalists against such standards, to condemn their government as the embodiment of a theory of what Laski called the "intangible state," [41] dedicated to the promotion of an image of power but indifferent to the processes of administration. In his major rebuttal of Sun's thesis, entitled "Knowledge Is Difficult, But Action Is Not Easy Either," [42] Hu summarized his views in the following terms:

Governing a country is a most difficult and important art. Knowledge and action should go side by side. Vague theories on paper cannot be considered to constitute knowledge, nor can rough and ready doings be mistaken for action. One may easily plunge the people into misery, and the nation into calamity, if one does not execute efficiently the plans that have been so carefully laid . . . How difficult it is to govern!

The great danger of the present time is that the political leaders do not know how to act when confronted by important and difficult problems. Is there anything more difficult than to administer a country as vast as this one with men who possess no understanding of the modern world? If this great undertaking is to be dealt with properly, it is essential to call upon eminent experts for advice, and to utilize modern knowledge. "Action is easy" can serve as a prescription only to poorly edu-

---

an examination of specific Chinese problems. See Hu Shih's unpublished diary, entries for March 25 and 29 and May 11 and 19, 1929. A list of the participants in the group and of the projected topics for study is given in the entry of May 19. It should be noted, finally, that while Lo Lung-chi may have been responsible for stimulating this interest in Laski and the Fabians, Laski's name was not unknown before this time: he had figured prominently in an essay by Chang Wei-tz'u entitled "Pluralism" (*To-yüan-ti chu-ch'üan lun*) published in NLCP no. 19 (Sept. 10, 1922).

41. Harold Laski, *A Grammar of Politics*, 430.

42. "Chih nan, hsing i pu-i;" the translation given here follows, with some modification, that found in *China's Own Critics*, 57–58.

cated militarists and politicians. But if this theory . . . is not discarded, China can never hope to be well administered.

Hu Shih's quarrel with the ideological heirs of Sun Yat-sen on the question of knowledge and action throws into sharp relief the contradictory elements in his thought that have already been considered, the one democratic, the other elitist. His desire to discredit Sun's thesis that "knowledge is difficult" led him to place, at least by implication, considerable trust in the native wisdom of the people. His case against the concept of political tutelage, as he developed it in 1929, was based on the unstated premise that the masses, once provided with institutions of self-government, would know how to make responsible use of them. Yet he could not be fully confident of the progressive instincts of the majority. Writing on the subject of popular attitudes toward cultural innovation, he observed, also in 1929, "A civilization by its very magnitude affects necessarily the vast majority of the people who are invariably conservative . . . It is, therefore, gratuitous and absolutely unnecessary that the thinkers and leaders of a nation should worry about traditional values being lost. Let them move forward a thousand steps and the masses will probably be carried no further than ten steps away from the traditional position. But if the leaders should hesitate and waver in their advances, the masses will surely stand still and no progress result." [43] Moreover, Hu's refutation of Sun's conclusion that "action is easy" involved him inescapably in the defense of an explicitly elitist position, emphasizing the difficulty of the tasks of government and the importance of utilizing expert knowledge in administration. Hu's conflicting commitments to a popularly based system of political institutions, on the one hand, and to the dominance of a highly trained and forward-looking political leadership, on the other, remained unreconciled until, in the 1930s, he worked out in tentative fashion a theory of a dichotomous political structure within which both might coexist.

43. Hu Shih, "Conflict of Cultures," in *The China Christian Yearbook* (Shanghai, 1929), 114–115. Virtually the same argument is reiterated in Hu Shih, "Shih-p'ing so-wei 'Chung-kuo pen-wei chih wen-hua chien-she'" (A critique of so-called "cultural reconstruction on a Chinese base"), TLPL no. 145:4–7 (April 7, 1935).

When Hu Shih complained, in the autumn of 1929, that "you may deny God, but you may not criticize Sun Chung-shan," he was speaking from unhappy personal experience. His relations with the Nanking regime had reached a low point a few weeks earlier. The ostensible cause of the trouble was Hu's disparagement of Sun in his essays on constitutionalism published in *The Crescent*. There were also, however, more personal issues dividing him from the conservative faction in Nanking, growing out of the government's desire to exert tighter control over higher education.

From the first, Hu had been skeptical of the Kuomintang's intentions toward intellectuals and the educational establishment, and he had resisted any attempt to enlist his support and cooperation. Not until May 1928, nearly a year after his return to China, did he travel for the first time to Nanking, to attend, out of deference to Ts'ai Yüan-p'ei, the National Education Conference convened by Ts'ai in the capital. On that occasion Hu responded to the invitation extended to the assembled educators to participate in the tasks of revolutionary reconstruction with the observation that the government's only responsibility to intellectuals was to provide money, peace, and the freedom to think their own thoughts. He was predictably unimpressed by the assurance given in return that Sun Yat-sen had bequeathed peace and freedom, and that money would be found.[44] In the conference itself, and in the dispute that erupted later in the summer between Ts'ai Yüan-p'ei on the one side and Ch'en Kuo-fu, representing the interests of the Organization and Training Departments of the party on the other, Hu supported Ts'ai's attempt to restrain the Kuomintang from exploiting the student movement for political purposes, and to minimize the impact of its demand for political indoctrination in the guise of "party education." [45]

Although Hu's positions at the China National Institute and Kuang-hua rendered him immune from Nanking's direct control, the government was not without means of interfering with his activities. Since its inception in 1924 Hu had been a member of the Board of the China Foundation for the Promotion of Education

44. Unpublished diary, entry for May 19, 1928.

45. See Allen B. Linden, "Politics and Education in Nationalist China: The Case of the University Council, 1927–1928," *Journal of Asian Studies*, 27.4:763–776 (August 1968).

and Culture, an agency established to administer the remaining portion of the American Boxer Indemnity fund remitted to China in that year. The Board, consisting of ten Chinese members and five Americans, was by the provisions of its charter a self-perpetuating body. Vacancies in its membership were supposed to be filled through election by the remaining members, a procedure designed to keep the Board free of political manipulation. In July 1928, however, the Nanking government abolished the old Board and named a new group to replace it. All of the Americans were retained, together with some of the original Chinese members, but several, including Hu Shih, were dropped in favor of Kuomintang appointees of more certain loyalties, among them Sun Fo and Wang Ching-wei. The American government retaliated by suspending remittance to the Foundation. Finally, at the end of the year, a compromise was reached whereby the Kuomintang candidates were "properly" elected to their new positions by the Board which they displaced. Hu declared himself entirely satisfied by this arrangement,[46] though it is doubtful that the government shared his belief that it had been a victory for the principle of the separation of education and politics. In any case, Hu's difficulties with the Nanking authorities were just beginning.

In Shanghai the principal agent of Hu's discomfiture was Ch'en Te-cheng, director of the special Kuomintang headquarters in the city and of its propaganda department, a man of unswervingly dogmatic ideological loyalties. Late in March 1929 Ch'en promulgated an official warning against "counterrevolutionary" activities, counterrevolutionaries being defined for his purposes as "all who oppose the Three Principles of the People." Hu was provoked to write an open letter to his old acquaintance Wang Ch'ung-hui, then serving as president of the Judicial Yuan, in which he protested this expression of the party's willingness to subvert established legal procedures and definitions. The letter was stopped by the censor, but it did not go unnoticed.[47] Ch'en Te-cheng made his displeasure public a few days later with a bit of

46. Hu Shih, "Hu Shih Sees China Foundation Free of Political Interference," *The Peking Leader,* Jan. 23, 1929.

47. On this incident see I-jan (pseud.), "Cheng tzu-yu yü Hu Shih ti hu-shuo" (The struggle for freedom and Hu Shih's nonsense), *Pai-hua san-jih-k'an* (Vernacular three-day journal), June 6, 1929; *The North China Daily News,* editorial for June 21, 1929; and Hu Shih's unpublished diary, entry for March 26, 1929.

doggeral printed in the *Min-kuo jih-pao*. The title of the piece, "Hu-shuo" (meaning "nonsense"), was an obvious enough pun on Hu's name, but it was made even more pointed in the closing lines:

To oppose the precious teaching of the Tsung-li
Is to oppose the law;
Opposition to the law
Brings judgment by the law of the land.
This is a fixed principle
That does not permit Dr. Nonsense [*Hu-shuo po-shih*] to talk nonsense about it.[48]

Hu and his colleagues ignored the hint. In April — the same month in which Ch'en Te-cheng assumed, in addition to his other responsibilities, those of director of education for the Shanghai municipality — *The Crescent* proclaimed editorially its intention to "publish more in the area of [political] thought and criticism." "We welcome all articles that may be submitted," the editorial statement continued, "for if we know that . . . we do not stand entirely alone, then naturally we will be most willing to step forward to struggle for freedom and to march on the great freedom road." [49] Hu Shih's essay "Human Rights and the Provisional Constitution" was published in the April issue of *The Crescent,* followed in June by two even sharper indictments of the Nationalists, "When *Can* We Have a Constitution?" and the essay on knowledge and action already referred to.

In August Ch'en Te-cheng struck back. At a meeting on August 24 the Executive Committee of the Shanghai Kuomintang Headquarters heard a resolution adopted earlier in the month by the Shanghai Third District Party Bureau demanding Hu's dismissal from the China National Institute on grounds of "false opinions." [50] Several days later the Executive Committee dealt with the matter in its own fashion: "As proposed by the propaganda department of the Shanghai District Headquarters, that Dr. Hu Shih . . . having publicly insulted our late Leader and the Party, and having de-

48. Ch'en's "poem" was published in *Min-kuo jih-pao hsing-ch'i p'ing-lun* (Republican daily news weekly review), 2.46 (April 1, 1929).

49. "Pien-chi hou-yen" (Editorial notes), HY 2.2 (April, 1929).

50. A newspaper clipping to this effect, from an unidentified source, is pasted into Hu's diary under the date of August 13, 1929.

structively criticized his ideology, which must be considered as
treason against the Government and the people, he should be
recommended for severe punishment . . . It is hereby resolved that
the proposal of the propaganda department be submitted to the
Central Party Headquarters for its consideration." [51] In mid-September the Executive Committee of the Kiangsu provincial Kuomintang headquarters officially demanded Hu's arrest on charges
of subversion. When, however, at the end of the month the case
finally came before the State Council (the supreme governmental
organ, indistinguishable in membership from the highest organs
of the party, the Central Executive Committee and the Political
Council), the action taken was less drastic. The Council accepted
the judgment of the Training Department of the Central Party
Headquarters to the effect that Hu's criticism of Sun was "meaningless quibbling," revealing a total ignorance of "the nature of
the present society." Citing the recommendation of the Training
Department, the State Council concluded:

> The ideology of our Party is all-embracing, and it does not
> grudge the study and examination of the members of the Party
> or those who are not members, as only in this way can it be
> better understood and disseminated.
>
> But Hu Shih, although he is the President of a University,
> not only has misinterpreted the ideology of our Party, he has
> also violated the limit of scholarly discussion by incorporating
> unwarranted attacks of a vicious character. It is certainly an
> undignified action on the part of a university president and it
> has the evil effect of misleading such of our people as have not
> yet gained a firm belief in our ideology. This cannot pass un-
> corrected, lest it should give encouragement to similar con-
> duct.[52]

Hu was accordingly reprimanded by the Ministry of Education,
headed at that time, ironically, by Chiang Monlin (Meng-lin, 1886–
1964), an old friend of Hu's, like him a former student of Dewey's,
and a colleague at Peita in the early 1920s. Hu was subjected also
to less formal rebukes. Sun Fo, speaking in Nanking on September
9, reaffirmed the official view that a constitution granted before the

51. NCH 171.3238:321 (Aug. 31, 1929).
52. NCH 173.3243:4 (Oct. 5, 1929).

people had been "properly trained to exercise their political rights" would be "no more than a piece of paper." Suggestions to the contrary, Sun declared, are "academic and impractical." "If anyone thinks that the work of the revolutionary movement is over, he is greatly mistaken," Sun concluded. "This is not the end of the revolution. This is only the start." [53] A few weeks later, on the eve of the eighteenth anniversary of the 1911 Revolution, Chiang Kai-shek himself added a warning against the "opportunism" of those who promoted the cause of freedom of opinion in order to "spread rumors and create disturbances." [54]

Though there were reports that a warrant had been issued against Hu, and even that he had been arrested, tried *in camera,* and sentenced to summary execution,[55] these direct and indirect expressions of disapprobation were apparently the only substantive action that the government took against him. Some supporters had rallied to his defense. An editorial published late in August in the influential Shanghai newspaper *Shih-shih hsin-pao* (The China times) pointed out that Hu's ideas, which the government regarded as such dangerous radicalism, had been common currency in the

53. NCH 172.3240:397 (Sept. 14, 1929).

54. NCH 173.3244:42 (Oct. 12, 1929).

55. CWR 50.3:127 (Sept. 21, 1929) reprints a *Kuo-wen* report, dated September 13, to the effect that the Executive Committee of the Kiangsu Provincial Party Headquarters had decided to issue a warrant for Hu's arrest. Hallett Abend, China correspondent for *The New York Times,* asserted that Hu had been arrested, secretly tried and condemned to death, and the date for his execution set late in August, whereupon Abend himself intervened in the case by prevailing upon the *Times* to come to Hu's defense. An editorial entitled "Muzzling China's Truth-teller," strongly supporting Hu's character and motives and sharply critical of the Kuomintang, was published in the *Times* on August 31, 1929. Abend had this circulated, in Chinese and Japanese translations as well as in English, throughout China, Japan, and southeast Asia. "Four days later," Abend writes, "Hu Shih was unconditionally released and resumed his lecturing and his writing without any curb on his criticism of the Kuomintang." See Hallett Abend, *My Life in China* (New York, 1943), 141–145. I am of the opinion that a good reporter's sense of the dramatic led Abend astray on this matter. Hu Shih's diary is of only limited assistance in untangling the mystery, since there are almost no entries in his own hand after the middle of August. There are, however, many press clippings concerning his troubles with the party pasted in under various dates, and none of these substantiates Abend's dire tale. Furthermore, at the time when, according to Abend, Hu Shih was in prison under sentence of death, *The North China Herald* (171.3238:321 [Aug. 31, 1929]) noted that one of its reporters had interviewed Hu to find out whether he had any comment to make on the resolution adopted by the Shanghai District Party Headquarters on August 28.

West since the eighteenth century. Unless the Kuomintang desired to be judged by the same standards as those applied to the Bolsheviks and the Fascists, the editorial continued, it must show itself more tolerant of freedom of expression. Yet even the *Shih-shih hsin-pao* was not unequivocal in its support of Hu. "We do not oppose Mr. Hu's plain speech," the editorial concluded. "But we can only regret the attitude that underlies his words . . . His criticism inevitably inspires ill feeling and scorn for the government." [56]

The Western press, in China and abroad — notably *The North China Herald* and *The New York Times*[57] — was less reserved in its commendation of Hu's outspokenness and its condemnation of Nanking's attempt to silence him. It may have been, as an editorial writer for *The North China Herald* suggested, that Hu was "too great an international figure to be suppressed by petty censorship." [58] It seems equally probable, however, that what saved him from more stringent punishment was not public expressions of sympathy and outrage but private intercession on his behalf by his friends in the more moderate councils of the Kuomintang, like Ts'ai Yüan-p'ei and Chiang Monlin, or Wang Ch'ung-hui, or even the Generalissimo's brother-in-law, T. V. Soong.[59]

56. Editorial by Ch'eng Ts'ang-p'o, *Shih-shih hsin-pao*, Aug. 27, 1929.

57. NCH 172.3242:480 (Sept. 28, 1929); *The New York Times*, Aug. 31, 1929, 14.

58. NCH 172.3242:480 (Sept. 28, 1929).

59. Hu's acquaintance with T. V. Soong dated back to their student days in the United States, and the friendship revived after the Nationalists' rise to power. T. V. Soong (Soong Tzu-wen, 1894–) emerges from the accounts of contemporary witnesses as one of the more enigmatic and unhappy personalities of the late 1920s, a man torn between the humanitarian and progressive opinions of his older sister, Ch'ing-ling (Mme. Sun Yat-sen, 1890–) and the overwhelming political ambition of his younger sister, Mei-ling (Mme. Chiang Kai-shek, 1896–). In 1929 he was serving as Vice-President of the Executive Yuan and concurrently as Minister of Finance, positions that gave him an opportunity to initiate a number of important economic reforms. During the summer Hu Shih was in touch with T. V. Soong on several occasions (see, for example, Hu's unpublished diary, entries for July 2 and August 6, 1929), urging upon him in private the same reforms that Hu was demanding publicly in the pages of *Hsin yüeh*: the promulgation of a constitution, bureaucratic reforms of several kinds, the subordination of party to government organs at all levels of administration. At the beginning of August, however, as a result of chronic intraparty disputes, Soong suddenly resigned from his positions at Nanking and retired to Shanghai. It may not have been entirely coincidental that Hu Shih's difficulties with the Kuomintang became serious shortly thereafter, during this temporary eclipse in the authority of the man who was probably his most influential contact within the councils of the Nanking government.

In any case, the government's admonitions did not have the intended effect. Two of Hu's most forthright attacks on the ideological shortcomings of the Kuomintang were published in *The Crescent* during and immediately after the crisis. In one of these Hu expressed this bleak prophecy: "Who does not know that intellectual conformity means that thought will become rigid and dead rather than changing with the times? . . . The Kuomintang has now lost popular confidence, partly because its political programs cannot satisfy the people's hopes and partly because [its] moribund ideology cannot win the sympathy of the progressive intellectuals. On the day when the sympathy of the progressive intellectuals is completely forfeited, the Kuomintang will have reached the end of its tether." [60] In 1929, when the Nationalists were at the zenith of their power, it was a warning to which few paid heed. But twenty years later, as their authority crumbled beneath them, there may have been those within the party who recalled Hu's words with new understanding.

Although the Nanking regime failed to silence Hu in 1929, it was successful in unseating him from the presidency of the China National Institute the following year, when it secured his resignation in return for official accreditation of the university by the Ministry of Education. It was reported in the press that Hu would be leaving shortly for the United States to lecture at Yale and Chicago. He had indeed received such an invitation two years earlier, but the trip was not in fact undertaken until 1933. Instead Hu remained in Shanghai until the end of the year. Then, shortly before his thirty-ninth birthday, he returned once more to Peking, to head the recently established Compilation and Translation Committee of the China Foundation. A few weeks later he went back again to Peita, as dean of the College of Arts, at the invitation of Chiang Monlin, who, having resigned from the Ministry of Education in October 1930, was the newly appointed chancellor of the university.

Hu Shih was in Peking in September 1931, when Japanese troops marched into Mukden, launching the conquest of Manchuria and opening a new and tragic chapter in China's modern history.

60. "Hsin wen-hua yün-tung yü Kuomintang," *Jen-ch'üan lun-chi*, 141–142.

Chapter 8. Peking Again, 1931–1937

"It is snowing hard in Peking today," Hu Shih wrote in December 1935 to the Japanese journalist Murobushi Kōshin. "The branches of the pines in my garden are bowed beneath fluffy silver quilts . . . The tiles that mark the boundaries in the garden are souvenirs from the Summer Palace. The marble threshold at the gate was also brought by my landlord from the ruins of the Summer Palace. As I stand at the threshold, seeing the tiles barely visible above the snow, I cannot help recalling the history of the sack of the Summer Palace by the Anglo-French expeditionary forces seventy-five years ago. Yet though there are many things before my eyes to prompt my memory, somehow it seems to me that this tale is now a bit vague, no longer clear. My gaze moves on to newer things. One of your esteemed country's airplanes drones overhead, east to west, painting a black shadow across the clean snow. The shadow passes; the snow is pure again. But in my heart it lingers vividly. I recall the saying of the ancient Chinese philosopher: 'The shadow of a flying bird never moves.' " [1]

China lay in the unmoving shadow of Japanese aggression from the night in September 1931 when peace departed until the July night six years later when war finally came. Throughout this time men moved and spoke in a half-light, their meanings and motives oddly distorted. New issues arose out of the gathering darkness, and old questions were argued with a new urgency. The threat of imminent destruction compelled the Chinese to probe once more into the causes of their national vulnerability, and to set a value on the achievements of recent decades. The years of Hu Shih's second sojourn in Peking were a time of doubt and anger.

It was during these years that Hu Shih attained his greatest prominence as a spokesman for liberal opinions. From its inception in May 1932 until it vanished beneath the avalanche of war in the summer of 1937, Hu edited a weekly review of politics called *The Independent Critic* (*Tu-li p'ing-lun*). In its pages, against the darkening background of foreign invasion and civil strife, Hu continued to argue the case for constitutionalism, to weigh the feasibility of democracy for a country like China, to warn against the dangers of authoritarianism, to demand the willingness to seek a "three-year cure" for a "seven-year illness," and to urge adherence to the spirit of the new individualism. In the midst of events that seemed often to resist reasonable analysis and to belie optimistic appraisal, Hu struggled to make the voice of reason heard and to dispel the sense of frustration that threatened at times to cloud even his habitual optimism.

Like *The Endeavor* and *The Crescent* before it, *The Independent Critic* was a private journalistic enterprise, the creation of a small group of liberal intellectuals — "eight or nine friends" — who wrote for it without compensation and, during the early years, moreover, contributed to its support out of their own pockets. By 1934, however, the magazine had begun to attract a sufficient readership to pay its own way. In 1935 it had a circulation of around seven thousand, which grew to nearly double that number a year later. Meas-

1. Hu Shih, "Ta Shih-fu Kao-hsin hsien-sheng" (A reply to Mr. Murobushi Kōshin), TLPL no. 180:5–8 (Dec. 8, 1935).

ured against the immensity of China's population it was a tiny figure, but it comprised a significant fraction of the educated and urbane minority toward which *The Independent Critic* directed its appeal. The magazine may not have been, as Hu once proudly claimed, unique in the annals of journalism.[2] Through five troubled years, however, it succeeded admirably in preserving the temper with which it was launched in the anxious months after the Manchurian Incident. "We are calling this magazine *The Independent Critic* because we hope always to maintain an independent spirit," proclaimed the editorial announcement in the first issue. "An independent spirit means: favoring no party or faction; blindly subscribing to no preconceptions; and employing responsible language to express the conclusions drawn from individual reflection . . . We ask of our readers only what we demand of ourselves: . . . criticism and discussion that is fair-minded and based on the realities of the situation." [3]

For the Chinese in the 1930s "the realities of the situation" meant, first and foremost, the Japanese presence in Manchuria and Japanese designs upon the rest of China. There were, broadly speaking, two schools of thought on the question of how the Chinese should respond to this challenge. The official government position was that the nation must be unified — politically, militarily, and ideologically — before effective action against Japan would be pos-

---

2. This information on the establishment and growth of *Tu-li p'ing-lun* is drawn from the following sources: Hu Shih, *Ting Wen-chiang ti chuan-chi*, 83–90;"*Tu-li p'ing-lun* yin-yen" (Introductory statement of The independent critic), TLPL no. 1:2 (May 22, 1932); Hu Shih's anniversary editorials in TLPL nos. 51 (May 21, 1933), 151 (May 19, 1935), and 201 (May 17, 1936); "Pien-chi hou-chi" (Editor's notes), TLPL nos. 150 (May 12, 1935), 183 (Dec. 29, 1935), and 188 (Feb. 16, 1936).

I have not found a list of the members of the so-called Tu-li p'ing-lun she, about a dozen in all according to Hu Shih (TLPL no. 51). Over the first four years of publication these "insiders" contributed 483 articles to the magazine, as opposed to 588 contributed by "outsiders" (TLPL no. 201). Hu later attributed *Tu-li p'ing-lun's* success in large part to the willingness of its readers to submit manuscripts for which they received no remuneration. Initially the members of the "society" contributed 5 percent of their incomes to defray the magazine's costs; this was subsequently reduced to 2.5 percent, until in 1934 such subsidies were no longer needed (TLPL no. 151). Editorial chores, proofreading and the like, were performed gratis by Hu Shih, Lo Erh-kang, and Chang Hsi-lü. Accounts were kept, also gratis, by friends in one of the Peking banks.

3. "*Tu-li p'ing-lun* yin-yen," TLPL no. 1.

sible. This view was founded in part, perhaps, on a realistic appraisal of the disparity between Japan's offensive capacity and China's ability to defend itself. In part, however, it reflected attitudes inherited from earlier years, political enmities deeply etched into the minds of Nanking's leaders during the long history of factional rivalry that had marked the party's ascent to power and, almost without interruption, the years since the establishment of its authority. In the cause of unity the Nationalists — belying their name, as some came to think, and forsaking their revolutionary heritage — waged war against ill-defined enemies within while putting up only token resistance to the easily identifiable enemy without.

To a growing number of Chinese, and especially to the students and young intellectuals who had so often been at the forefront of the nationalist movements of the 1920s, Nanking's attitude seemed unreasonable at best, treasonable at worst. The early 1930s were a period of dazed confusion within the ranks of the student movement, but in the deepening crisis the students became increasingly outspoken in their demands for an end to the civil war and for the adoption of stronger measures against the Japanese. The government's response was predictable: as criticism became more vehement and articulate, official tolerance, never in abundant supply, diminished nearly to the vanishing point. By 1935 and 1936 a substantial number of Chinese students and intellectuals were divided from their government by a chasm of suspicion and not-always-suppressed hostility.[4] The fact that the Chinese Communists, from their remote strongholds in Kiangsi and later in the northwest, enlisted the sympathy of many frustrated patriots by demanding the creation of a united front against a common enemy only enhanced the Kuomintang's distrust of its critics and exacerbated relations between the government and the intellectuals.

It was fortuitous that on the two overriding issues of the day Hu Shih's adherence to long-standing views placed him, at least superficially, on the side of the government. He opposed the idea of a militant response to Japan until very late, hoping still on the eve of the war that a negotiated settlement might be reached. He opposed, too, the involvement of intellectuals in the kinds of activities to which they resorted in their effort to influence the Nanking regime. No one familiar with Hu's opinions could have been sur-

4. The fullest account of the student movement in these years is John Israel, *Student Nationalism in China, 1927–1937* (Stanford, 1966).

prised by either position. On the question of Japan his attitude was remarkably like that expressed in 1915, at the time of the crisis engendered by the Twenty-One Demands. His views on the student movement remained much as they had been throughout the 1920s. Yet amidst the tensions of the 1930s it appeared to some that Hu had made an expedient and dishonorable peace with the government he had so sharply criticized a few years earlier.[5] This impression is not borne out, however, by a reading of Hu's published attacks on the party's continuing pretensions to ideological omniscience, on its claim to broader political powers, and on the conservative culturalism to which it increasingly turned for ideological nourishment. What *is* revealed in Hu's writings of this period is the confusion of a mind which shunned violence in a violent age and clung in a time of duplicity to a naïve faith in good will, and which stubbornly prized reasonableness above all else in a deranged world.

These several qualities of intellectual bewilderment marked Hu's approach to the problem of Japan. It was a country he knew little about at first hand, and for which he had long felt a considerable respect. In the past, and even still in the 1930s, he had used Japan on more than one occasion as the example of a nation that had succeeded where China had failed. The Japanese had moved with speed and purpose to remake themselves in the image of modernity. In his admiration for Japanese energy Hu seemed at times almost to concede that the Japanese had earned the right to behave as they did toward their lethargic Chinese neighbors. His dilemma was compounded by the fact that the official Japanese description of China as a nation that must be saved from self-inflicted anarchy and destruction — the justification for Japan's presence on the continent — tallied on a number of points with Hu's own opinions of his native land.[6]

5. A fair idea of this interpretation of Hu's activities in the 1930s is conveyed by Y. C. Wang in *Chinese Intellectuals and the West, 1872–1949* (Chapel Hill, 1966), 406–421 and *passim*. Wang makes extensive use of the defamatory literature published in Communist China in the course of the 1955 attack on Hu Shih, accepting uncritically the evidence offered and the interpretation given to it. His account must be read in this light, and used with extreme caution.

6. See, for example, Hu Shih, "Ts'an-t'ung ti hui-i yü fan-hsing" (Grievous recollections and reflections), TLPL no. 18:8–13 (Sept. 18, 1932); Hu Shih, "T'ung-i ti lu" (The road to unification), TLPL no. 28:2–6 (Nov. 27, 1932); Hu Shih, "Hsin-hsin yü fan-hsing" (Faith and reflection), TLPL no. 103:2–6 (June 3, 1934).

Yet Hu was by no means sympathetic to Japan's aggressive course of action. He held more hope, however, for Japanese self-restraint, and the restraining influence of world opinion as it was expressed through the League of Nations and the U.S. Department of State, than for China's ability to turn back by force this threat to her existence. The choice, Hu said, rested with the Japanese as to whether they would have "nine generations of enmity or a century of friendship" with China.[7] It was up to them to decide whether they would fulfill the promise of their recent history of progress, or pursue instead the road to self-destruction,[8] whether they would have Japan become the England of Asia, or another Weimar Germany,[9] whether "this most hopeful nation" would become "one of the most feared nations in the world." [10]

Hu brought to his understanding of political relations among nations the same ill-founded trust in the existence of common values and aspirations that marked his views on the conduct of domestic political life. "International politics functions essentially on the same principle as domestic politics," he wrote in one of his hopeful pieces on the League resolutions condemning Japan. "A government is of course established on a certain kind of power, but this power is not derived entirely from military strength. In large part a government must still depend on social habit and the influence of public opinion. Putting it a little more simply, political authority may be compared to a paper tiger, animated only by such intangible forces as ideas, beliefs, and custom." [11]

In this spirit Hu doggedly awaited Japan's awakening to a realization of the damaging effect that her policies must inevitably have on world opinion. His belief in the restraining influence of the international agreements to which Japan was a party, and the admonitions addressed to the Japanese by the League of Nations, remained firm long after grounds for optimism had all but disappeared. Typi-

7. Hu Shih, "Jih-pen-jen ying-kai hsing-hsing le!" (The Japanese must wake up!), TLPL no. 42:2–4 (March 19, 1933).

8. Hu Shih, "Kuo-chi wei-chi ti pi-chin" (The approaching international crisis), TLPL no. 132:2–4 (Dec. 23, 1934).

9. Hu Shih, "Chung-Jih t'i-hsi: ta k'o-wen" (Sino-Japanese reconciliation: an interview), TLPL no. 143:2–3 (March 25, 1935). These are Hu's answers to questions put by the Peking correspondent of the Japanese United Press agency.

10. Hu Shih, "Tung-ching ti ping-pien" (The military coup in Tokyo), TLPL no. 191:2–5 (March 8, 1936).

11. Hu Shih, "Chiu-ching na-i-ko t'iao-yüeh shih fei-chih?" (Which treaty is after all a scrap of waste paper?), TLPL no. 19:2–7 (Sept. 25, 1932).

cal of this attitude was Hu's positive reaction to the Lytton report, published in the autumn of 1932. "If this kind of serious restraint exercised by world opinion still cannot, even at the moment of gravest crisis, make a drunken people sober up a bit, then our country and the whole civilized world must prepare to live through ten years of hell!" [12]

Hu did not advocate peace with Japan at any price, though he was willing to envision a more costly peace than many of his countrymen would contemplate. From the beginning he rejected Japan's claim that the Manchukuo regime should be regarded as an independent and sovereign political entity, and he steadfastly demanded Japan's withdrawal from the northeast as a precondition to any negotiated settlement.[13] But he did not take exception to the recommendation of the Lytton commission that, once the Japanese had been evicted, Manchuria should be granted a large measure of autonomy from Chinese control. Such a solution was entirely in keeping with the view that China is too large and too diverse to be governed by a tightly centralized political authority, as Hu had maintained in the discussion of federalism in the 1920s and still believed.[14] Even more remarkably, Hu's was virtually the only voice raised in public support of the unpopular Tangku truce, by which hostilities were suspended in north China in the spring of 1933. Since the Chinese stood no chance of gaining a military victory, he argued, the only alternative to a peace dictated by the Japanese would be the military occupation of the whole of north China. In that event the international situation in the Pacific would deteriorate, perhaps even to the point of a general war. But, Hu contended, a world conflict would not profit China's cause.[15]

To his compatriots Hu could only recommend forbearance, self-discipline, and, most important, repentance. "The fortunes of a

12. Hu Shih, "I-ko tai-piao shih-chieh kung-lun ti pao-kao" (A report that represents world public opinion), TLPL no. 21:2–6 (Oct. 9, 1932).

13. See for example Hu Shih, "Wo-men k'o-i teng-hou wu-shih nien!" (We can wait fifty years!), TLPL no. 44:2–5 (April 2, 1933); and Hu Shih, "Wo-ti i-chien yeh pu-kuo ju-tz'u" (My ideas are simply these), TLPL no. 46:2–5 (April 16, 1933).

14. "I-ko tai-piao shih-chieh kung-lun ti pao-kao," TLPL no. 21. For Hu's views on the question of unification by force see also "T'ung-i ti lu," TLPL no. 28, and Hu Shih, "Cheng-chih t'ung-i ti t'u-ching" (The path to political unification), TLPL no. 86:2–7 (Jan. 21, 1934).

15. Hu Shih, "Pao-ch'üan Hua-pei ti chung-yao" (The importance of defending North China), TLPL nos. 52–53:2–6 (June 4, 1933).

nation are not accidental, or free from the iron law of cause and effect," he admonished the university graduates of 1932. "Our present suffering and shame are the evil results of evil causes sown in the past . . . We must firmly believe that today's defeats are a consequence of the fact that in the past we exerted too little effort." [16] Though he depended on foreign pressure to stay the Japanese, he insisted that ultimately China's salvation could come only through her own doing. "A nation which cannot save itself cannot earn the sympathy and support of others," he observed somewhat sententiously;[17] and again, "Good fortune . . . never lights upon the head of the man who is incapable of helping himself." [18]

In Hu's view the path to "salvation" lay not in a short and inevitably catastrophic test of arms with the aggressor, but, as might be expected, in the patient nurturing of human and material resources to the point at which aggression would no longer be possible. He offered his audience only the comfort provided by a sense of history: "We must not be pessimistic. Look! In the very midst of our silent endurance of this suffering, a new people [and] nation has gradually taken form. If, in such a situation as this, we can preserve silence, tranquillity, and order, this is the beginning of strength . . . The old saying that nations flourish on hardship [*to nan hsing pang*] states an historical fact about which there is no deception." [19] "Our final victory is beyond the shadow of a doubt! . . . In the long life of a nation, of what importance are four or five, or forty or fifty, years?" [20]

Such admonitions seem now, as they did to many then, to reveal little comprehension of the capacity of the Chinese to absorb without complaint the humiliations heaped upon them by Japan, or to contemplate with equanimity the threat that confronted them. The Chinese of the 1930s wanted heroics, not homilies. Yet it must still be said for Hu that he foresaw, as many then did not or would not, the dreadful consequences of war. More than anything else it was the prospect of "ten years of hell" that moved Hu to counsel half a

16. Hu Shih, "Tseng-yü chin-nien ti ta-hsüeh pi-yeh-sheng" (An offering to this year's university graduates), TLPL no. 7:2–5 (July 3, 1932).

17. Hu Shih, "Nei-t'ien tui shih-chieh ti t'iao-chan" (Uchida's challenge to the world), TLPL no. 16:2–3 (Sept. 4, 1932).

18. "Kuo-chi wei-chi ti pi-chin," TLPL no. 132.

19. Hu Shih, "Ch'en-mo ti jen-shou" (Silent endurance), TLPL no. 155:2–3 (June 16, 1935).

20. "Wo-men k'o-i teng-hou wu-shih nien!" TLPL no. 44.

century of humiliation. The pacifism of his student days flickered briefly to life again:

> . . . I cannot go against my conscience by coming out for war [he wrote in the spring of 1933]. This is not to say that all who advocate war are unconscionable; it is to say only that my own intellect and training do not permit me to advocate war . . .
>
> I have the greatest respect for the heroes who have dared to risk their lives in the fight for their fatherland, but my conscience will not allow me to use my pen for the purpose of urging others to use their flesh and blood, risking their lives in the face of the most cruel and merciless modern weapons.
>
> "To war!" is only two words, yet few of us have really thought through their meaning.[21]

The Japanese, of course, did not conduct themselves with the restraint or the sense of responsibility that Hu had hoped for. By the end of 1935 Japanese pressure, both military and diplomatic, had so effectively impaired the ability of Nanking to exercise control over large areas of north China that Peking existed in a kind of political no-man's-land. In the autumn of that year the Japanese took the penultimate step of demanding the creation of an "autonomous area" that would comprise five northern provinces, over which Nanking would no longer be able even to claim jurisdiction. At this juncture Hu Shih finally came to the conclusion, as he expressed it to a member of the American embassy, that the Chinese had no alternative but to fight "for self-preservation." The American ambassador, Nelson T. Johnson, found Hu's conversion to this opinion significant enough, as an indication of the hardening temper of the Chinese, to make it the subject of a dispatch to the State Department, noting Hu's warning that the war would be the worst in history and that China would unquestionably make every effort to involve other Pacific powers in the fight. "He also said," Johnson concluded, "that it should be realized that for some time the Chinese would be fighting alone against the Japanese, with the result that there would be appalling destruction of Chinese life and property." [22]

21. "Wo-ti i-chien yeh pu-kuo ju-tz'u," TLPL no. 46.

22. *Foreign Relations of the United States, Diplomatic Papers, 1935,* III (Washington, D.C., 1953), 400–401 (793.94/7473, dated Nov. 6, 1935). I am indebted to Dorothy Borg for calling this reference to my attention.

About this same time, and in response to the same provocation, the uneasy relationship between the Kuomintang government in Nanking and the students in north China reached the point of crisis. While Nanking talked of peace throughout the autumn of 1935, Sung Che-yüan, commander of the only effective Chinese military force in the Peking area, gave indications of being compelled to submit to Japanese pressure. In December the students of Tsinghua, Peita, and Yenching, supported by those from other middle-schools and colleges in the city, seized the initiative. There were massive student demonstrations in the streets of Peking on December 9 and 16, and a strike paralyzed the city's universities. The authorities responded by placing the universities virtually under a state of siege, and many of the demonstrators were roughly handled by the civilian and military police. Undaunted, bands of student activists set off at year's end on walking trips through the north China countryside to arouse the peasants against the Japanese menace and the policies of their own government.[23]

These events were of concern to Hu Shih not only in his capacity as dean at Peita but for familiar reasons as well. He shared the opinion expressed with typical bluntness by Ting Wen-chiang in the early 1930s: "In China today very few men over the age of forty are capable of building a new China. Our only hope lies in the young people who are now receiving higher education."[24] Yet it was these same young men and women who were abandoning their classrooms and laboratories in that anxious winter to march through the city and trek off to the villages — following an uncertain cause when they should instead have been learning how to lead. Such, at least, was Hu's view of the situation. He was not insensitive to the problems confronting the students. He wrote with feeling of the economic hardships and uncertainties under which they labored; he condemned the government's inclination to politicize the universities by appointing party men rather than educators to preside over them; he regretted the fact that private influence was still more

23. These events are described in detail in John Israel, *Student Nationalism*, chap. 5. See also Hubert Freyn, *Prelude to War: The Chinese Student Rebellion of 1935–1936* (Shanghai, 1939), the account of a foreigner who witnessed the demonstrations and took part in some of the subsequent educational movement.

24. Ting Wen-chiang, "K'ang Jih ti hsiao-neng yü ch'ing-nien ti tse-jen" (The feasibility of resisting Japan, and youth's responsibilities), TLPL no. 37: 2–8 (Feb. 12, 1933).

useful than educational accomplishment when it came to getting a job.[25] He acknowledged, moreover, the legitimacy of the students' role as the voice of public conscience. Young people are natural radicals, Hu observed, and he charged that the government had filled its prisons with youngsters arrested on the grounds of childish opinions childishly expressed.[26] "In any country where politics is not on the right track, and where institutions for the peaceful transfer of political authority and organs for the legal representation of the popular will are lacking, the responsibility for encouraging political reform always falls on the shoulders of the young intellectuals . . . Since young people are easily stirred and do not have to think of wives and families, they dare to brave the battle in pursuit of their beliefs; their political activity, as a result, commonly arises from very pure motives, or we may at least say from very natural motives." [27]

Nevertheless, Hu reacted equivocally to the events of December 1935. He denounced the Japanese scheme for the creation of a north China "autonomous area" and urged Nanking to "do its duty" in defense of the north.[28] He praised the spirit of self-sacrifice in which the students acted, and he condemned as "unforgivably barbaric" the measures to which the police resorted in dealing with the demonstrators. He lamented the government's inability to understand young men and women who sought only to stand vigil over the conduct of the nation. The December 9 demonstration was "a most happy event" (Hu wrote), signaling an awakening to danger in the midst of a conspiracy of silence. As he watched the students marching south from the Tung-an Gate, he had heard, he said, the welcome sound of "footsteps in an empty valley."

Yet he opposed the strikes that followed — "a weapon too often used" since 1919 — and he warned the students that to continue in this fashion would lose them the sympathy they had already earned.

25. "The government should awaken to the fact that a Wu Nan-hsien can provoke student demonstrations and that a Weng Wen-hao can pacify student demonstrations." Hu Shih (writing under the pseudonym Ts'ang-hui), "Lun hsüeh-ch'ao" (On the student movement), TLPL no. 9:6–9 (July 17, 1932). Weng Wen-hao, a European-trained geologist and a regular contributor to Tu-li p'ing-lun, was at that time acting president of Tsinghua University.

26. Hu Shih, "Wang Chiang t'ung-tien-li t'i-ch'i ti tzu-yu" (On the freedom discussed in the Wang-Chiang telegram), TLPL no. 131:3–6 (Dec. 16, 1934).

27. "Lun hsüeh-ch'ao," TLPL no. 9.

28. Hu Shih, "Hua-pei wen-t'i" (The question of North China), TLPL no. 179:2–3 (Dec. 1, 1935).

Their function, he lectured them, was only to serve as "supervisors." They must beware of direct action, lest they should be misled by an extreme minority. (If Hu meant the Communists, he did not say so.) Even in these turbulent times they must exercise the intellectual restraint and uphold the standards of individual integrity of which, as students, they should be the prime exemplars. Most important, they must strive to maintain a sense of perspective, for if the situation is bad today, Hu warned, it will be incalculably worse tomorrow. He left them with an injunction set forth in language that was, perhaps, only too familiar: "The students' fundamental obligation is to endeavor unceasingly to develop their knowledge and talents. Social progress is bit-by-bit progress, and the strength of the nation depends upon the strength of individuals." [29]

In Hu Shih's view, in short, the gravest peril confronting China in the 1930s was not the threat of Japanese aggression. It was, rather, that in their anxiety the Chinese might resort to methods of resistance that would jeopardize both the material and the intellectual achievements of the last several decades.

Hu's assessment of these achievements varied according to the particular audience he was addressing, and whether he was comparing China to the West or to its own former self. He was ever prepared to remind the leaders of the political revolution that the disparity between the ideals of an earlier generation and the accomplishments of the present mocked any pretension to real progress. In 1934, on the anniversary of the 1911 Revolution, he wrote dispiritedly: "They [the revolutionaries of 1911] envisioned a free and egalitarian, a glorious and flourishing nation. Twenty-three years have passed, and we are still a third-rate nation that cannot hold up its head. They dreamed of creating a free people living under a

29. Hu Shih, "Wei hsüeh-sheng yün-tung chin i-yen" (A word to the student movement), TLPL no. 182:4–7 (Dec. 22, 1935), reprinted from *Ta-kung-pao hsing-ch'i lun-wen* (Dec. 12, 1935); Hu Shih, "Tsai lun hsüeh-sheng yün-tung" (Another discussion of the student movement), TLPL no. 183:2–4 (Dec. 29, 1935). These views gained little support from either extreme. Leftist students denounced Hu as "a running dog of imperialism and the traitorous government, a criminal who swindles the masses" (cited in John Israel, *Student Nationalism,* 133); the Japanese, on the other hand, suspected Hu Shih and Chiang Monlin of having had a hand in instigating the demonstrations (see *Foreign Relations of the United States, 1935,* III, 476 and 483). In the first instance, of course, the judgment is a matter of opinion. In the second, Hu Shih's diary for December 1935 makes abundantly clear (if, indeed, it was necessary to make the issue clearer than Hu's published statements did) the improbability of the Japanese suspicion.

democratic constitution, but twenty-three years later there are still not a few who imagine that they have fixed their gaze even higher, who sneer at popular rights and freedom but sing the praises of autocracy and dream of creating a new slavery under despotism!" [30]

More typically, however, Hu was disposed to encourage those whose spirits flagged by affirming the "real and genuine" advances that had been made in recent years. "The greatest pessimists today are those who were formerly excessive optimists," he remarked only a few days after penning the despondent sentiments cited above. Only those who had underestimated the difficulty of China's problems and overestimated the effectiveness of her response have been discouraged by the course of events — and, as Hu had observed of himself a decade earlier, he entertained no great hopes, and so anticipated no great disappointments.[31] If the aspirations of earlier years remained unfulfilled, much of importance had been accomplished nonetheless: imperial institutions were a thing of the past; education had been revolutionized in form and content; social institutions and habits had begun to change, especially in the area of family life and with regard to the status of women.[32] "The China before our eyes is no longer something that can be described by the term 'old society' . . . To say that we are not yet sufficiently modern is irrefutable. To say that this is still the 'old society' . . . is to deny reality." [33]

Most important of all, wrote Hu, a start had been made on the difficult task of transforming the Chinese people into a united citizenry imbued with ideals appropriate to the modern age. How much greater, he declared, than even the greatest of traditional martyrs to the cause of virtuous government, the Tung-lin group of the late Ming period, are the present-day martyrs to the revolutionary cause: those who died in the struggle against the Manchus, and in the revolutionary battles of 1926 and 1927; those who have

30. Hu Shih, "Shuang-shih-chieh ti kan-hsiang" (Impressions on Double Ten), TLPL no. 122:2–4 (Oct. 14, 1934).

31. Hu Shih, "Pei-kuan sheng-lang-li ti lo-kuan" (Optimism in the midst of a wave of pessimism), TLPL no. 123:15–18 (Oct. 21, 1934). This is the gist of a speech delivered at Yenching University on October 9, reprinted in Ta-kung-pao on October 14.

32. Hu Shih, "Hsieh tsai K'ung-tzu tan-ch'en chi-nien chih hou" (Written after the celebration of Confucius' birthday), TLPL no. 117:2–6 (Sept. 9, 1934). See also "Pei-kuan sheng-lang-li ti lo-kuan," TLPL no. 123.

33. Hu Shih, " 'Chiu-p'ing pu-neng chuang hsin-chiu' ma?" (Can't you put new wine in old bottles?), TLPL no. 87:15–17 (Jan. 28, 1934).

died fighting the Japanese; those who have laid down their lives for the cause of the communist revolution. For Hu the conclusion to be drawn was obvious and reassuring: "The character of those who have been most influenced by the New Culture is incomparably better than that of the sages of any age." [34]

So, in a sense, Hu made his peace with the revolution — though not, as he soon made clear, with the revolutionary party. In a 1934 essay entitled "Optimism in the Midst of a Wave of Pessimism" (*Pei-kuan sheng-lang-li ti lo-kuan*) he wrote: "Revolution is, after all, revolution, and it is inevitable that there should be unscrupulous and evil forces created by it; but at the same time it can destroy old institutions and forces that should be destroyed . . . If in all fairness we reckon up the accounts of the last twenty years and more, in the end we must acknowledge that in the republican period we have made great progress, nor can we fail to recognize that this progress is in large part a result of the blessings bestowed upon us by the liberation effected by the revolutionary trends since 1911. If we clearly acknowledge the achievements secured by the endeavors of the last two decades, we can overcome pessimism and find the courage we need to move forward . . . Pessimism and disillusionment can never help us to bear our heavy burden down the long road that lies ahead!" [35]

It was not without reason that Hu Shih worried lest the circumstances in which the Chinese found themselves should persuade some to abandon the "long road" toward which he pointed, to explore instead one or another shortcut. His criticism of those who "sing the praises of autocracy" had been aimed not only at the Kuomintang but also at some notable defectors from the democratic cause among the members of his own circle — men who, under the compulsion of events, acquiesced to the argument that extraordinary times demand a government armed with extraordinary powers.

The debate was sparked by Chiang T'ing-fu (T. F. Tsiang, 1895–1965), the talented American-educated chairman of the Tsinghua history department,[36] in an essay, "Revolution and Authoritarianism" (*Ko-ming yü chuan-chih*), published in *The Independent Critic* of December 10, 1933. "China seems now to have reached the

34. "Hsieh tsai K'ung-tzu tan-ch'en chi-nien chih hou," TLPL no. 117.
35. "Pei-kuan sheng-lang-li ti lo-kuan," TLPL no. 123.
36. On Chiang T'ing-fu see Boorman, *Biographical Dictionary*, I, 354–358.

point at which there is no way out except revolution," Tsiang wrote, "while revolution itself is not a way out." The problem, as Tsiang analyzed it, was that the revolution had come to China before its time. A genuine revolution, like the French, requires as a first step "the creation of a nation," and this, Tsiang argued on the basis of European example, had been the historical function of autocracy. In its present condition China is comparable only to France before the Bourbons, England before the Tudors, Russia before the Romanovs — "capable only of civil war, not true revolution." Only the establishment of a political power strong enough to impose national unity, regardless of the cost in terms of "enlightenment" (too abstract a quality in any case to serve as the criterion of political legitimacy)[37] could prepare China for the necessary second step: a revolution that would effect the democratization of political authority and create a government capable of promoting the general welfare. In the present time, Tsiang concluded, "our government promotes only the welfare of an individual, his family and friends. Eight or nine out of every ten so-called revolutionaries are frustrated politicians or ambitious militarists." China, in other words, far from being the progressive revolutionary nation that its leaders claimed it to be, could not even pass muster as an old-fashioned autocracy.[38]

Tsiang's semischolarly historical generalizations served to crystallize issues already present in the intellectual discourse of the 1930s and provoked a dispute that continued, in one form or another, throughout the remaining years of peace. The issues were difficult and nebulous ones: the legitimacy of China's historical claim to nationhood; the degree to which political centralization was feasible or even desirable in so diverse a society; the price that must be paid for political order. Hu Shih, defending the democratic position — and finding himself, to his dismay, deserted even by such old comrades-in-arms as Ting Wen-chiang — put forward two major propositions, in support of which he marshaled arguments that required him to revise or even to forsake long-cherished opinions. The first of these propositions, aimed primarily at discrediting the view that strong government is synonymous with good govern-

37. Chiang T'ing-fu, "Lun chuan-chih ping ta Hu Shih-chih hsien-sheng" (On authoritarianism, in reply to Mr. Hu Shih-chih), TLPL no. 83:2–6 (Dec. 31, 1933).

38. Chiang T'ing-fu, "Ko-ming yü chuan-chih" (Revolution and authoritarianism), TLPL no. 80:2–5 (Dec. 10, 1933).

ment, he called the theory of "*wu-wei* politics," or, roughly, "government by non-action." The second was the idea that democracy is the least sophisticated form of political life — "kindergarten government" (*yu-chih cheng-chih*) Hu called it — and consequently the best suited to a politically inexperienced people like the Chinese.

The term *wu-wei*, variously translated as "quiescence," "non-action," "inaction," or "taking no action," has a venerable lineage in the history of Chinese thought. It was used in classical times by Taoists, Legalists, and even Confucians — proponents of very different political viewpoints in many respects — to describe a quality of wise rulership on which they all agreed: the virtue of leaving well enough alone, the wisdom to refrain from helping life along, as the Taoist Chuang-tzu put it.[39] In Burton Watson's apt phrase, *wu-wei* describes "not a forced quietude, but a course of action that is not founded upon any purposeful motives of gain or striving." [40] As expounded by Taoist mystics the concept enshrined a paradox. "*Tao* never does, yet through it all things are done," says the *Tao-te ching: wu-wei erh wu-pu-wei.*[41] Practical Confucian scholar-officials in later centuries interpreted this as advice to the ruler to delegate administrative functions to his ministers, and to beware the lure of overreaching ambition.

There is something of this latter sense in Hu Shih's use of the term. His turn to the idea of "non-active" government is startling, not because the idea itself is so freighted with traditional connotations, but because of the change it marks both in his view of the proper function of government and in his appraisal of China's position vis-à-vis the West.

Hu had, of course, always acknowledged a disparity between Chinese and Western levels of accomplishment. But this had never prevented him from insisting that China's salvation lay in the application of the methods of "modern" civilization to Chinese problems, under the sponsorship of an enlightened and purposeful government. In his essays on *wu-wei* government, however, Hu wrote as if the distance between Chinese backwardness and Western progress was in fact all but insurmountable. "We are only poor children," he declared in the spring of 1933. "How can we dream of imitating the great show of a rich family? We are but a babe in

39. Burton Watson, trans., *Chuang-tzu: Basic Writings* (New York, 1964), 72.
40. *Ibid.*, 6.
41. Fung Yu-lan, *A History of Chinese Philosophy*, I, 178.

arms. How can we dream of accomplishing the work of a strong and healthy young man?" The difference between the West and China, he continued, is the difference between wealth and poverty, between an abundance of educated men and women and a complete lack of such talented human resources, between stable political systems on the one hand and anarchy on the other. With this unpromising comparison in mind Hu drew the following conclusion: "The political philosophy that China needs now is certainly not the positive, activist political philosophy popular in Europe and America since the nineteenth century. What is needed today is a political philosophy that advocates non-action. When the philosophers of ancient times preached non-action, [their purpose] was not to instruct men to refrain from all activity but merely to urge men not to act blindly and wildly — to open their eyes and examine the situation to determine whether or not, given certain objective material conditions, action was possible." [42]

At the present time such a candid examination of China's "objective material conditions" must inevitably lead, Hu contended, to the conclusion that the government's grandiose plans for modernization should be abandoned. "Reconstruction," he argued, must be limited first to the relief of existing abuses, especially to some improvement in the deplorable conditions of rural life. Hu's essays on *wu-wei* government are one of the few places in which he treated, even in general terms, the problems of the peasantry: "The sufferings of the villages in the interior at the present time are the result of too heavy taxes, too many soldiers to support, too many officials to maintain. Taxes are collected to provide for officials who can do nothing whatever to benefit the people . . . and to maintain troops who can in no way fulfill their responsibility to protect the people . . . Beset by such hardships, if the people do not run away, or resist, or become Communists or bandits, then indeed they are a worthless breed!" [43]

A decade earlier Hu had observed with satisfaction, in tracing the recent development of Western political thought, that the doctrines of laissez-faire liberalism had lost ground in Europe and the United States since the end of the nineteenth century. But in

42. Hu Shih, "Ts'ung nung-ts'un chiu-chi t'an-tao wu-wei ti cheng-chih" (From rural relief to a discussion of *wu-wei* government), TLPL no. 49:2–6 (May 7, 1933).

43. *Ibid.*

1933 he recalled approvingly Spencer's dictum that the only legitimate function of government is to exercise the police power. It had been, he admitted, an already outmoded idea in the England of Spencer's time. But in China, "backward in every respect," it still merited careful consideration,[44] especially by a government which was unable to discharge even this minimal civic obligation within its domains.[45]

It is improbable that Hu intended this latter recommendation very seriously. "I am not opposed to reconstruction," he wrote later. "What I am opposed to is reconstruction that injures the people." [46] He took as his example the construction of motor roads, then much in vogue as an index of economic progress. To build roads city walls were demolished, land was taken out of cultivation, taxes were increased, and peasants were conscripted to work on road gangs. Once built, however, the highways remained in a state of chronic disrepair, and the peasants, unable to pay the higher costs of motor transport, discovered that the river and canal routes on which they had formerly depended had been allowed to fall into ruin. Finally, as an ironic climax to this tale of ineptitude, the city walls so lately dismantled must hastily be rebuilt as a defense against banditry.[47] It was against such expensive exercises in futility that Hu counseled when he urged the Kuomintang to discard its modernization programs. "The real aim of *wu-wei* government is to give the people rest," he wrote, in much the same manner in which the Confucian statesman of an earlier age might have admonished his prince to abandon the construction of some monument to imperial grandeur. "The rulers remain ignorant of the political principle that 'it is better to get rid of one abuse than to bestow one benefit,' with the result that every benefit produces another hardship and adds to the people's burden." [48]

With the theory of non-active government Hu was attempting to accomplish several things. He wanted, first of all, to dramatize his opposition to the entrepreneurial style of the Kuomintang, and to

44. *Ibid.*

45. Hu Shih, "Tsai lun wu-wei ti cheng-chih" (Another discussion of *wu-wei* politics), TLPL no. 89:2–6 (Feb. 25, 1934).

46. Hu Shih, "Chien-she yü wu-wei" (Reconstruction and *wu-wei*), TLPL no. 94:2–5 (April 1, 1934).

47. "Tsai lun wu-wei ti cheng-chih," TLPL no. 89; "Chien-she yü wu-wei," TLPL no. 94.

48. "Tsai lun wu-wei ti cheng-chih," TLPL no. 89.

emphasize the need for policies that would reconcile political power with popular welfare. He desired also to point up the government's failure to preserve the degree of stability and public security necessary to even the most modest kind of "progressive" enterprise. Most important of all, he wanted to underscore as forcefully as possible his conviction that politicians, militarists, and party men had neither the skill nor the wisdom to manage the great affairs attendant upon China's transformation into a modern nation. It was a point that he had scored against every government that had come to power since 1917:

> Political leaders must understand very clearly that reconstruction is an undertaking that calls for specialized knowledge [*chuan-men hsüeh-shu*], not something they can accomplish by dispatching telegrams to a dozen or so provinces and fixing a time limit of so-and-so-many months. They must be very clear on the fact that they themselves are not worthy to talk about reconstruction, and even more clearly should they understand that the reconstruction they are now engaged in is not genuine and permanent reconstruction, but only the kind of jobbery that enables political headmen to keep their ricebowls full. When they have realized their own unworthiness . . . they can relax into inactivity, and practice a bit of the benevolent policy of giving the people rest [*yü min hsiu-hsi ti jen-cheng*]. When the sufferings of the people have been somewhat eased, and when national vigor has been revived to some extent, and when the investigations and studies [conducted] by experts have borne results, only then can action be undertaken.[49]

If China's self-proclaimed leaders were thus unfit for their self-appointed task (a presumption on which the liberal intellectuals were generally agreed), and if the nation lacked "men of talent" in sufficient number to promote a transition to modernity from the bottom up (as again the liberal intellectuals conceded), the obvious conclusion was that progress must be encouraged by other means, and in accordance with other principles. This was, of course, an important point in the case put forward by the proponents of dictatorship. Their enthusiasm for authoritarian methods reflected little admiration for the Kuomintang tutelary dictatorship as it was

49. "Chien-she yü wu-wei," TLPL no. 94.

then constituted. On the contrary, they regarded it as self-seeking, inefficient, unprincipled, and old-fashioned.[50] In their view, however, the alternative to the kind of "old-style" dictatorship represented by the Kuomintang could not be a democratic system, for which the Chinese were unprepared and which, to judge by the recent history of the Western democracies, might well prove no more efficient, no more purposeful, and no more enlightened than the existing regime. "What China needs," asserted Ch'ien Tuan-sheng, a Harvard-educated political scientist, "is a capable and principled dictatorship." [51]

What Ch'ien and others had in mind when they spoke of a "new-style" dictatorship was perhaps best expressed by Ting Wen-chiang, who came forth in strong support of the idea. The advantage of such a government, Ting claimed, would be that it would possess a clear understanding of the nature of a "modern" state, and it would be correspondingly eager to make the best use possible of the expert knowledge that the educated elite could place at its disposal. It could rid itself of the distracting factionalism that sapped the vitality of the Nationalist regime, and its leadership, by placing the national interest above all else, would be able to exploit China's present troubles as a rallying point around which to gather all those able to participate in the processes of modernization.[52] Survival itself was the most important matter of business for China, Ting argued. Viewed in this light, the mark of the Kuomintang's inadequacy was its inability to stand firm in the face of popular pressure and make peace with Japan at almost any cost. "I would rather be an American or English workingman than a member of the Soviet intelligentsia," Ting concluded. "Nevertheless, I would rather be a

50. Some advocates of autocracy did express the hope that the Kuomintang could be made over into a more efficient instrument of authoritarian rule. See Ch'en Chih-mai, "Cheng-chih kai-ko ti pi-yao" (On the need for reform of the political system), and Ch'ien Tuan-sheng, "Tui-yü liu chung ch'üan hui ti ch'i-wang" ([Our] hopes for the sixth plenary sessions), both in TLPL no. 162 (Aug. 4, 1935).

51. Ch'ien Tuan-sheng, "Min-chu cheng-chih hu? Chi-ch'üan kuo-chia hu?" (Democratic government [or] a unified nation?), Tung-fang tsa-chih, 31.1:17–27 (Jan. 1, 1934); cited in Hu Shih, "Chung-kuo wu tu-ts'ai ti pi-yao yü k'o-neng" (On the necessity and the feasibility of China's remaining nonautocratic), TLPL no. 130:2–6 (Dec. 9, 1934). On Ch'ien Tuan-sheng see Boorman, Biographical Dictionary, I, 376–379.

52. Ting Wen-chiang, "Min-chu cheng-chih yü tu-ts'ai cheng-chih" (Democratic government and autocratic government), TLPL no. 133:4–7 (Dec. 30, 1934).

Soviet technician than a White Russian émigré." [53] Ting Wen-chiang was prepared to admit that a dictatorship such as he envisioned was "not yet feasible" in China. But, he insisted, "we must strive to make it feasible within the shortest possible time. A first step in this direction is to abandon the advocacy of democracy." [54]

Hu Shih's disagreement with his old friend was based in part on his conviction that the kind of "idealistic" dictatorship proposed by Ting and Ch'ien Tuan-sheng and T. F. Tsiang would *never* be feasible in China. He denied that there existed in China "a man, or a party, or a class capable of autocratic rule." Moreover, he added, "I do not believe that at the present time China has any vital problem of sufficient fascination to engage the emotions and intelligence of the people generally and enable the country as a whole to follow the leadership of any individual or party or class toward the creation of the conditions necessary for a new-style dictatorship." China, he said, is not like Russia, Turkey, Italy, or Germany — though he left it unclear whether it was China's problems that were different, or the responses that the Chinese were capable of making.[55]

In greater part, however, Hu's opinions on this issue were shaped more by his continuing faith in democracy than by his reservations concerning the practicality of dictatorship. Starting from the same premises with respect to the qualifications of the Kuomintang leadership and the political inexperience of the Chinese people, he argued to the contrary conclusion. He did not minimize the difficulty of the problems that the Chinese must solve in order to attain the modern status to which they aspired. But while Ting, Ch'ien, and Tsiang used this to justify a monopoly of political authority by a small group of "experts" in the interests of efficiency, Hu took a different view. His point of departure was his long-standing confidence — a "mad prejudice" he confessed — in the usefulness of democratic institutions in educating a politically uninstructed people in the ways of self-government. Democratic government, he insisted, is simply "government by common sense" (*ch'ang-shih ti*

53. Ting Wen-chiang, "Tsai lun min-chu yü tu-ts'ai" (Another discussion of democracy and autocracy), TLPL no. 137:19–22 (Jan. 27, 1935).

54. Ting Wen-chiang, "Min-chu cheng-chih yü tu-ts'ai cheng-chih," TLPL no. 133.

55. Hu Shih, "Tsai lun chien-kuo yü chuan-chih" (Another discussion of national reconstruction and authoritarianism), TLPL no. 82:2–5 (Dec. 24, 1933).

cheng-chih), while despotism, at least enlightened despotism, demands "government by especially outstanding men" (*t'e-pieh ying-chieh ti cheng-chih*). Hence, "in a country like ours, poor in human talent, the best political training is democratic constitutionalism, which can gradually broaden [the base of] political authority." [56] National unity, whether physical or spiritual, cannot be imposed from above, or by force. It must come, rather, from below, through the use of political institutions designed "gradually to cultivate a centripetal force throughout the nation, and gradually to create a 'public loyalty' [*kung chung*] in place of the 'private loyalties' [*ssu chung*] of the present time." [57]

Hu's theory of "kindergarten" democracy was a logical extension of this line of thought. Democracy, he maintained, is not, as some would have it, the most sophisticated and burdensome form of political life and hence the most difficult to appropriate. On the contrary, it is the least demanding, and the easiest to understand and use, even by a people as poorly equipped as the Chinese to function politically. The "muddling through" psychology of the British that he had so roundly condemned in 1926 appeared to Hu eight years later as reassuring evidence of the "common sense" basis of democracy. "Democratic government requires only that a qualified electorate be able to exercise its civic rights to good effect; training of this kind is not difficult." [58]

It was an arresting proposition, and an easy one to attack. Hu's critics would not concede that democracy is either as simple or as reliable as Hu had made it out to be.[59] Even if the Chinese possessed the characteristics of a "qualified electorate," wrote Ting Wen-chiang — and it was to his way of thinking an absurd presupposition — the effective use of democratic institutions would require of them a higher degree of political involvement than had been achieved even in countries where democratic traditions were deeply rooted. Ting charged that neither the British nor the Americans participate

56. *Ibid.*

57. "Cheng-chih t'ung-i ti t'u-ching," TLPL no. 86.

58. "Chung-kuo wu tu-ts'ai ti pi-yao yü k'o-neng," TLPL no. 130.

59. See, for example, Chang Hsi-jo, "Min-chu cheng-chih tang-chen shih yu-chih ti cheng-chih ma?" (Is democracy truly kindergarten government?), TLPL no. 239:3–6 (June 20, 1937); Chang Hsi-jo, "Wo wei-shen-mo hsiang-hsin min-chih" (Why I believe in democracy), TLPL no. 240:2–5 (June 27, 1937); Wu Ching-ch'ao, "Ko-ming yü chien-kuo" (Revolution and national reconstruction), TLPL no. 84:2–5 (Jan. 7, 1934).

fully in the political processes of democracy, and, he asked, if this is the case with well-educated citizens, what could the Chinese expect of democracy? [60]

Hu's defense was to turn the vices of the democratic system as Ting described it into its virtues. His opinions were not the "poor joke" that his friends dismissed them as, he said, but "the conclusion drawn from scrupulous study of democratic constitutionalism in practice during seven years in the United States." [61] In the presidential elections of 1912 and 1916, he recalled, he had witnessed men of "low intelligence" exercising their rights of American citizenship.[62] It was this that had convinced him that democracy could work in China too, for it is the genius of a democratic system to engage the energies of the unenlightened majority in the political process, albeit only momentarily and occasionally. Since democracy is founded on a realistic appraisal of the limited political interest of the greater part of the people, it does not demand of them the intensive and continuous involvement in political life that authoritarian regimes insist upon. But to the degree that the citizens of a democratic society do participate in politics, Hu continued, their participation expresses genuine support, inasmuch as those who wish to remain disengaged may do so without fear of reprisals.[63] So, Hu concluded, constitutional democracy "is not an unattainable ideal system, but a system of government by common sense that can, given room to develop, gradually improve and broaden the base of political authority." [64]

In earlier years Hu had invariably spoken of democracy as the final destination toward which the Chinese must set their course. But if, as he argued in the 1930s, democracy is the "natural" political form of immature societies, one possible conclusion was that a fully developed, or "modern," nation must inevitably rely increasingly on elitist (and at least potentially undemocratic) political forms.

60. Ting Wen-chiang, "Min-chu cheng-chih yü tu-ts'ai cheng-chih," TLPL no. 133.

61. Hu Shih, "Tsai t'an-t'an hsien-cheng" (Talking again about constitutional government), TLPL no. 236:5–7 (May 30, 1937).

62. "Chung-kuo wu tu-ts'ai ti pi-yao yü k'o-neng," TLPL no. 130.

63. Hu Shih, "Ta Ting Tsai-chün hsien-sheng lun min-chu yü tu-ts'ai" (In reply to Mr. Ting Tsai-chün's discussion of democracy and autocracy), TLPL no. 133:7–9 (Dec. 30, 1934). There is a play on words here, involving the English "no" and the Chinese no, meaning "to respond," "to answer," or (as here) "to go along."

64. "Tsai t'an-t'an hsien-cheng," TLPL no. 236.

This was, indeed, the view of some of Hu's adversaries, who suggested that the extent to which a government adopts elitist principles of leadership (that is, government by experts) depends not upon an a priori decision for or against democracy, but upon the breadth of the functions that the government accepts as its responsibility.[65]

For a time Hu was himself trapped in the logic of this argument. He acknowledged that governmental functions, and hence governmental powers, had increased enormously in the West in the wake of the war and the depression. He admitted, too, that with this development had come a greater dependence on "experts" in government, represented in his mind by the role of the Fabians in England and Roosevelt's "brain trust" in the United States. He had always believed, of course, that men of such high qualifications should be engaged in public life. But if modern governments were in fact becoming too powerful and too complex to be directed by any but the most highly trained intellects, did this mean that the day of "youthful" democracy was passing even in those lands where it had seemed so secure and so promising?[66] For one who had always insisted, as Hu had, that China must create political institutions suited to the times, this was an unsettling prospect. Conceivably it was for this reason that he came to the view that China and the West were running by different clocks, and for a time argued so vigorously in favor of *"wu-wei* government," reasoning that if democracy were to succeed in China the government must not assume responsibilities that lay beyond the capacity of a democratic government to discharge.

Eventually Hu discovered other grounds on which to defend his theory of kindergarten democracy without condemning the Chinese to march always at the end of the line of human progress. Writing in the late spring of 1937, only a few weeks before the dispute was drowned out by the roar of Japanese artillery, Hu accused his critics of having misunderstood him by failing to distinguish (as, in truth, he himself had not distinguished earlier) between political systems (*cheng chih*) and governments (*cheng-fu*). The distinction, as Hu drew it, was between a political culture on the one hand and an administrative organization on the other. There is no reason, Hu

65. See, for example, Ch'en Chih-mai, "Min-chu yü tu-ts'ai chih t'ao-lun" (The debate on democracy and autocracy), TLPL no. 136:4–11 (Jan. 20, 1935); Chang Hsi-jo, "Min-chu cheng-chih tang-chen shih yu-chih ti cheng-chih ma?" TLPL no. 239.

66. "Chung-kuo wu tu-ts'ai ti pi-yao yü k'o-neng," TLPL no. 130.

maintained, why a democratic political culture cannot support a government staffed and directed by expertly trained administrators, whose importance he readily acknowledged.[67]

This was as far as Hu went toward effecting a reconciliation of the persistent elitist-democratic tension in his thinking. The difficulty lay in his indecision as to whether political institutions may in fact be relied upon as the agents of political regeneration, as he insisted in his criticism of the theory of political tutelage, or whether, as he argued at other times, they are merely mechanical devices controlled as to direction and effect by the intentions of the men who use them.[68]

The latter view was one that could easily be read from the disastrous history of republican institutions after the 1911 Revolution. It seems to have been, essentially, the opinion of Sun Yat-sen, and it was for this reason (among others) that Sun came to attach such great importance to the need for unquestioning commitment to "the principles of the revolution." In his description of the ultimate stage of democratic rule for which China was being prepared by the party tutelage, Sun had drawn a sharp distinction between political rights (*ch'üan*) and administrative ability (*neng*). He had therefore discriminated also between the right to exercise political authority, which he regarded as belonging properly only to the administrative elite, and the right, reserved to the people as sovereign, to extend or withdraw support of the government. According to Sun's theory, the people control the government by means of certain mechanical checks, comparable to the switches that activate a machine. These he enumerated as election, recall, petition, and referendum. So long as the switches remain open — that is, so long as the government operates under popular sanction — the people have neither the ability nor the right to interfere in the workings of the machine they have animated.[69]

Hu Shih's belief in the compatibility of a democratic political society and an elitist governing authority suggests a comparable distinction, though he never made so detailed an analysis of the connection between governmental and popular powers. Had he

67. Hu Shih, "Pien-chi hou-chi" (Editor's notes), TLPL no. 239:18 (June 20, 1937).

68. Hu Shih, "Hsien-cheng wen-t'i" (The question of constitutional government), TLPL no. 1:5–7 (May 22, 1932).

69. Sun Yat-sen's theory of "rights" and "ability" (*ch'üan* and *neng*) is set forth in *San Min Chu I*, lectures 5 and 6.

done so, he might have felt compelled to confront a problem that Sun had never dealt with adequately: the problem of representation. The only way in which the essential link between a genuinely democratic base and an administrative elite can be forged is by the interposition of representatives whose connection with the people is intimate and vital, and whose relationship to those in positions of administrative authority is clearly defined. What both Sun and Hu failed to account for in sufficient measure, though for different reasons, was this representational nexus.

The difference between them was the result of differing time schedules and priorities. When Sun spoke of democracy for China, it was always in the future tense, when, presumably, the period of "political education" would have yielded its intended harvest: an informed and public-spirited citizenry competent to the responsibilities of its newly acquired status. Eventually, then, the people as a whole would exercise control over the governmental machine, within the limits of Sun's understanding of the substance of popular control. In the meantime, however, until such control became feasible, they would live under a frankly dictatorial regime. Sun could not or would not foresee the tendency of this regime to become self-perpetuating.

Hu Shih was painfully sensitive to this danger, however. For him, consequently, democracy was a present necessity. But he knew as well as any other the impediments that stood in the way of broadly representative institutions in a nation that remained as backward as China in the elementary skills of citizenship. He argued, therefore, that democracy must come at once, while tacitly acknowledging that it could involve directly only the minority capable of becoming significantly engaged in political life. On the infrequent occasions when Hu offered concrete proposals for the reform or establishment of representative institutions, he said nothing of the peasant majority. Instead he stressed the role that must be played by the modernized urban constituencies: chambers of commerce, university faculties and educational associations, bar associations and banking and finance groups, the general labor unions, and, finally, the party.[70] The Kuomintang's habitual reluctance to allow for the free par-

70. For example, see Hu Shih, "Chung-kuo cheng-chih ch'u-lu ti t'ao-lun" (A discussion of the way out for Chinese politics), TLPL no. 17:2–6 (Sept. 11, 1932); and Hu Shih, "Kuo-min ts'an-cheng-hui ying-kai ju-ho tsu-chih" (How the National People's Assembly should be organized), TLPL no. 34:2–5 (Jan. 8, 1933).

ticipation of groups such as these in the councils of government remained one of Hu's principal objections to its rule. He called repeatedly for an "opening up of political power" (*k'ai-fang cheng ch'üan*), and he rejected as "nonsensical" the Kuomintang's slogan, "Party power above all." "My common sense tells me: the welfare of the people above all, the life of the nation above all . . . In the interests of justice, and in order to marshal national support, the Kuomintang should make political power public, and permit the people of the whole nation freely to organize political parties and groups." [71]

The problem of trying to adjust a belief in popular sovereignty to a realization of the need for, or even the stark fact of, elitist leadership had, of course, been recognized and described in the literature of political theory long since. Yet even if Hu had been familiar with the ideas of theorists in the tradition of Michels, Mosca, and Pareto — and there is no evidence to suggest that he was — he would not have found the concept of organized competition among leadership elites compatible with his own sentiments. His aversion to partisanism remained as strong as ever, as did his distrust of a political process based on the representation of conflicting interests. He confessed that he would have been unable to bring himself to join a political party even had the opportunity presented itself.[72] He insisted, moreover, that constitutional parliamentary government need not be organized on the principle of partisan representation, an assurance designed partly to allay the misgivings of those who feared a return to the sham parliaments of the early republican period:

According to my outsider's view, such fears are groundless. The strange drama of the early years of the Republic was the result of the superstitious belief of the men of that time that democratic government must necessarily be party government; it was thus that there occurred the odd situation of trying to draw a tiger and winding up with the picture of a dog instead. In the last twenty years the general tendency of politics throughout the world has considerably diminished men's superstitious faith in party politics, especially in this country, basically hostile to [the idea of] party politics. We may anticipate that in the future

71. Hu Shih, "Cheng-chih kai-ko ti ta lu" (The great road toward the reform of political institutions), TLPL no. 163:2–9 (Aug. 11, 1935).
72. *Ibid.*

China under constitutional rule will not experience very sharp partisan struggle. If we examine the national crisis of the last four years, we see that as national consciousness increases, partisanism declines; this is not only a Chinese phenomenon, for the "national governments" throughout the world (including Germany) point to the same conclusion. Farsighted statesmen should seize upon this tendency to create a national, supraparty politics.[73]

If the Kuomintang moved in this direction, Hu asserted, it would fulfill the intentions of Sun Yat-sen's "Five-Power Constitution." Under the provisions of this constitutional scheme, regarded by Sun as his great contribution to political theory, certain functions traditionally discharged by the legislative and executive branches were to be turned over to separate branches of the government: investigation and impeachment to the Control Yuan and the staffing and supervision of the civil service to the Examination Yuan. Hu endorsed the idea without reservation: deprived of its right of patronage, and relieved of the responsibility of supervision of the administration, the legislative branch would be free, he contended, to devote its full attention to the "specialized art of establishing and amending the laws, which of course can be done on a nonpartisan basis." Thus, he concluded, "to move from one-party government to nonpartisan government, and in this fashion to create political institutions in China that might serve as a model to the world — this seemingly was Mr. Sun Chung-shan's intention." [74]

Hu's insistence that the government should formulate its policies on the basis of a coherently articulated concept of the common interest can hardly be quarreled with, nor, under the circumstances, is his distrust of partisanism difficult to understand. The dismal example of unprincipled partisan wrangling provided by China's recent history did not inspire confidence in a system of political relationships incorporating partisanship at the level of institutional principles. Yet at the same time it must be noted that the acceptance of divided interests is one of the hallmarks of the liberal approach to politics. The conciliation of conflicting definitions of the "common" interest provides the dynamic of political life, in the liberal

73. Hu Shih, "Ts'ung i-tang tao wu-tang ti cheng-chih" (From one-party to nonpartisan politics), TLPL no. 171:10–12 (Oct. 6, 1935).
74. *Ibid.*

view of it. Seen in this light, Hu's demand for the creation of a "supraparty politics" and his insistence on the need for unanimity of purpose expressed an illiberal, and even an incipiently authoritarian, bias. For, as has already been observed, there existed in China no possibility of a consensus at any level of political activity. The masses of the Chinese people were politically too unsophisticated to express opinions relevant to the major issues of political and social reorganization, while the informed minority remained too deeply divided on fundamentals to adhere in any constructive way to a common system of political and social values. Thus in China any assessment of the common interest was bound to reflect the attitudes and aspirations of only a few, to be imposed by them (given the opportunity) upon the masses and upon dissident members of the elite as well.

This was a realization that Hu did not grasp as fully as did his friends who argued the case in favor of authoritarianism. Persuaded of the need for a sense of national purpose, they were prepared to pay a high price in terms of the values of political "enlightenment." Hu Shih thought the cost exorbitant. Yet even his own eloquent and sincere defense of the right to dissent seems, in the context of his political ideas as a whole, less an affirmation of the usefulness of divided opinion for its own sake than a rejection of the authority of the Kuomintang to determine the limits of consensus according to priorities and prejudices with which Hu was in basic disagreement.

Hu's essays in *The Independent Critic* deal more respectfully with Sun Yat-sen than had his earlier writings. True, he remained skeptical of the wisdom of trying to follow Sun's teachings slavishly,[75] and he still scoffed at the notion that so voluminous and disparate a body of ideas could be treated as a single "legacy." [76] But whereas in the Shanghai years his criticism of the Kuomintang had been in substantial measure an attack on the logic and motives of Sun's thought, his inclination now was to question instead the degree to which Sun's heirs were living up to the Tsung-li's expectations. In contradiction to his previous assessment of Sun's intellectual aspirations, Hu insisted that the founder of the party *had* been genuinely

75. Hu Shih, "Lun hsien-fa ch'u-kao" (On the draft constitution), TLPL no. 96:2–6 (April 15, 1934).

76. Hu Shih, "Pien-chi hou-chi," TLPL no. 232:18 (May 2, 1937).

influenced by the traditions of Anglo-Saxon liberalism and fully committed to democracy for China.[77] Therefore, Hu concluded, "unless the Kuomintang repudiates the teachings bequeathed to it by Mr. Sun Chung-shan, it must sooner or later take the road toward democratic constitutional government. As it does so . . . the Kuomintang can count on the sympathy and assistance of those outside the party who are concerned with national affairs." [78]

This was, at best, a conditional endorsement of the party. It is typical, however, of the ambivalence with which Hu approached the prickly question of the Kuomintang's proper political role. On the one hand he was perpetually resentful of the party's monopoly of power. He vigorously condemned its suppression of legitimate dissent, its mastery of "the techniques of Fascist intolerance," [79] and its reliance on what he called "the psychology of terror." [80] With similar persistence he derided the party's pretensions to unify the nation, when in fact it could not maintain unity even within its own ranks.[81]

Yet on the other hand Hu remained, as he had always been, a reformer. Feeling neither trust nor affection for the Kuomintang, he was nevertheless still disposed to "take what we can get" in the way of a modification of the party's dictatorship, rather than to strive for its overthrow by revolutionary means. Any parliament would be better than none, he asserted. Even the warlord-dominated parliaments of the 1920s, hollow forms though they had been, had served to remind men of the importance of the parliamentary principle, as the Kuomintang was unwilling to do.[82] In this spirit Hu was prepared to welcome any institutional reforms that held even a promise of democratic potential as indications that the party was moving in

77. Hu Shih, "Ko-jen tzu-yu yü she-hui chin-pu: tsai t'an Wu-ssu yün-tung" (Individual freedom and social progress: more on the May Fourth movement), TLPL no. 150:2–5 (May 12, 1935).

78. Hu Shih, "Ts'ung min-chu yü tu-ts'ai chih t'ao-lun-li ch'iu-te i-ko kung-t'ung cheng-chih hsin-yang" (A common political faith derived from the debate concerning democracy and autocracy), TLPL no. 141:16–18 (March 10, 1935).

79. "Ko-jen tzu-yu yü she-hui chin-pu," TLPL no. 150.

80. Hu Shih, "Min-ch'üan ti pao-chang" (The defense of popular rights), TLPL no. 38:2–5 (Feb. 19, 1933).

81. "Cheng-chih t'ung-i ti t'u-ching," TLPL no. 86; "Cheng-chih kai-ko ti ta lu," TLPL no. 163.

82. "Cheng-chih t'ung-i ti t'u-ching," TLPL no. 86. Hu was recalling here a remark once made to him by Ma Chün-wu. For the original account of their conversation see Hu's unpublished diary, entry for April 26, 1929.

the right direction.[83] He continued doggedly to demand the promulgation of a permanent constitution as the necessary first step toward the creation of a stable political order. It was a recurrent theme: his first essay in *The Independent Critic* dealt with the question of constitutionalism, and so also, five years later, did his last contribution to the magazine, published a few days after the outbreak of fighting around Peking in July 1937. He was always careful, however, to make it clear that this was not a *revolutionary* demand. Constitutionalism, Hu maintained, "means only that the government must be according to law, and that the government must be responsible in its dealings with the people." [84] Since in the final analysis constitutional government comes down to the willingness of the government to abide by the law, the laws in question must therefore be "practical" — that is, they must be laws that the government will be prepared to accept as binding upon its conduct.[85] Interpreted in this fashion, the establishment of the rule of law would be no more than a minimal concession on the part of the ruling party that would not significantly diminish the substance of its authority. Far from jeopardizing the Kuomintang's political position, Hu contended, the promulgation of a constitution would establish it on a firmer foundation by making it legitimate.[86]

This was a precarious position: Hu was walking a thin line between open opposition and unconditional surrender to the existing order. His demand for a constitution could be read as a challenge to the Kuomintang to submit to the rule of law as evidence of its right to govern. Still, his habitual respect for the principle of acknowledging the existing authority compelled him to defend the Kuomintang's right to rule despite its indifference to his standards of legality. In the 1920s Hu had argued that only a government established in accordance with constitutional principles could be acknowledged as legitimate. The conclusion that emerges from the essays of the 1930s, on the other hand, is that the promulgation of a constitution would suffice to legitimize any government. The shift

83. "Kuo-min ts'an-cheng-hui ying-kai ju-ho tsu-chih," TLPL no. 34; "Ts'ung min-chu yü tu-ts'ai chih t'ao-lun-li ch'iu-te i-ko kung-t'ung cheng-chih hsin-yang," TLPL no. 141.

84. "Hsien cheng wen-t'i," TLPL no. 1.

85. Hu Shih, "Wo-men neng hsing ti hsien-cheng yü hsien-fa" (The constitutional government and the constitution that we can implement), TLPL no. 242:12–13 (July 11, 1937); reprinted from *Ta-kung-pao hsing-ch'i lun-wen,* July 4, 1937.

86. "Cheng-chih kai-ko ti ta lu," TLPL no. 163.

of emphasis was a subtle one, so slight as to go unmarked at the time. But it prepared the way for Hu's unqualified acceptance of the Kuomintang constitution that was eventually enacted a decade later.

The difficulty of Hu's attempt to define the limits of "reasonable" demands upon the government was clearly illuminated in the course of his brief and stormy affiliation with the Chinese League for the Protection of Civil Rights (*Chung-kuo min-ch'üan pao-chang t'ung-meng*). The League, patterned on the model of the American Civil Liberties Union, was established late in 1932, primarily to seek justice for the growing numbers of political prisoners incarcerated by the Kuomintang. Ts'ai Yüan-p'ei was the organization's titular president. Its guiding spirit, however, was Soong Ch'ing-ling, the widow of Sun Yat-sen and sister-in-law of Chiang Kai-shek, long estranged from the Nationalist government and a bitter critic of Nanking. The League's secretary was a young scholar named Yang Ch'üan (*tzu* Hsing-fo), who had been Ts'ai's assistant in the University Council in 1927–1928 and had subsequently moved with Ts'ai to the Academia Sinica, becoming secretary-general of that organization when Ts'ai assumed its presidency in 1928.

Hu Shih served as chairman of the League's Peking branch from its inception at the end of 1932 until he resigned (or was expelled) from membership in February 1933. There were several reasons for this rupture, both personal and intellectual. The immediate cause was Hu's belief, publicly expressed, that Yang and the radical Shanghai faction had distorted the findings of an investigation into prison conditions in which Hu had also participated. Behind this charge lay Hu's distrust of Yang's character and his motives. The two had known each other for many years — Yang had been, in fact, among Hu's first students when he taught English in Shanghai in 1909, and a few years later they had studied together at Cornell. But Yang was too radical in his political views to suit Hu's more moderate temper, and too unscrupulous in his associations, particularly in light of the influence he exerted as Ts'ai Yüan-p'ei's protégé. Hu differed with Yang also in his view as to the proper purpose for an organization like the League for the Protection of Civil Rights.

The issue, as Hu interpreted it, concerned the function of law in an evolving political order. The law can define rights, Hu argued, but it cannot of itself guarantee them. The protection of rights requires a proper understanding of their significance and the cultivation of "a habit of mind that refuses to forsake" the freedoms defined by law. Generally speaking, however, and certainly in China where the whole concept of rights and freedom is alien to the traditional mentality, "the ordinary man's knowledge and ability are limited. We cannot hope that everyone will understand what his rights are, nor that everyone will be able to defend his own rights." Hu readily admitted, therefore, that the League had an important educative function to perform.

Nevertheless, Hu continued, the League had erred by trying to turn a legal problem into a political cause. Its demand for the immediate and unconditional release of all political prisoners had not been intended to promote an understanding of civil liberty, Hu declared. It was, rather, "a demand upon the government for freedom to revolt. In order to survive, a government must, of course, restrain all activities aimed at overthrowing it or opposing it. To demand from the government the right to revolt, is this not to take a tiger by the tail? If you take a tiger by the tail, you must be prepared to be devoured by the tiger — this is the responsibility that those who engage in political movements take upon themselves."

The most that Hu was willing to require of the government was that the law should be as carefully defined and scrupulously observed in political cases as in criminal cases: that arrests should not be made without firm evidence; that political prisoners should receive "just legal protection," including quick arraignment, public trial, and an opportunity for the accused to confront his accuser; and that, upon conviction, political prisoners should be accorded "the most humane treatment" possible. "Beyond this we can only take to the barricades," Hu concluded. "But that could not be considered a movement for the protection of civil rights." [87]

Hu's narrowly legalistic approach was intolerable to Yang's faction. At a meeting of the League in Shanghai, Hu was dismissed from membership. Mme Sun accused him of pursuing a "reactionary and

[87]. "Min-ch'üan ti pao-chang," TLPL no. 38. This stand conformed closely to the position taken by *Tu-li p'ing-lun* when Ch'en Tu-hsiu was arrested in the autumn of 1932; see Fu Ssu-nien, "Ch'en Tu-hsiu an" (The case of Ch'en Tu-hsiu), TLPL no. 24 (Oct. 30, 1932). It is interesting to note, however, that a year and a half later Hu was forced to repeat, in strong language, his demand that the government should be more tolerant of radical opinion, especially among students, and that it should do more than had been done to guarantee just treatment in political cases; see "Wang Chiang t'ung-tien-li t'i-ch'i ti tzu-yu," TLPL no. 131.

dishonest" course designed to make the League "an appendix to the system of Kuomintang rule." "The League should congratulate itself for having got rid of such a 'friend,' " she declared.[88] Yet Hu had judged the government's temper accurately. Within a few months his warning as to the perils of political involvement assumed the character of prophecy: on June 18 Yang Ch'üan was shot to death as he emerged from the headquarters of the Academia Sinica in the French Concession in Shanghai. It was generally believed, though never proved, that the assassins were Kuomintang hirelings, and that Yang's death was the price exacted for his League activities. Certainly the Kuomintang profited as a result, at least in the short run. Despite Mme Sun's vow to carry on the fight, in effect the League for the Protection of Civil Rights died with Yang that Sunday morning in the Avenue du Roi Albert.[89]

Late in the evening of that same June Sunday, Hu Shih embarked in Shanghai, bound for America to head the Chinese delegation to the Banff conference of the Institute of Pacific Relations and to deliver the Haskell lectures at the University of Chicago. In his Chicago lectures, later published as *The Chinese Renaissance*, Hu spoke confidently of China's progress toward modernity through the "slow permeation" of Western influence. To his American listeners he remarked upon the popularity of leather shoes and bobbed hair in China as indications of Chinese acceptance of modern ways, and

88. Soong Ching Ling, *The Struggle for New China* (Peking, 1952), 34–35. There are certain inconsistencies with respect to the dating of several of the documents here collected that induce reservations as to the reliability of this source. The statments in question here, however, parallel closely enough statements cited or referred to at the time in *The China Weekly Review* and elsewhere to justify taking them as genuine expressions.

89. Information on the League is scarce and scattered. See, for example, Lin Yutang, *A History of the Press and Public Opinion in China* (Chicago, 1936), 172–174; Edgar Snow, *Journey to the Beginning* (New York, 1958), 87; CWR 63.5:231 (Dec. 31, 1932), 65.4:146–147 (June 24, 1933), and 65.5:200 (July 1, 1933). Lin Yutang (Yü-t'ang) was himself a member of the League. Edgar Snow was a good friend of Mme Sun's and sympathetic to her opinions. Hu Shih's attitude toward Yang Ch'üan is suggested in his diary entries for June 1928 (especially June 14 and 15), at the time of the University Council crisis, and for June 16 and 18, 1933. He accepted as a matter of fact the supposition that Yang was murdered by KMT agents in reprisal for his League activities. T. F. Tsiang, who assumed editorial responsibility for *The Independent Critic* while Hu was abroad in 1933, published a sharp but very brief editorial comment on the incident — two weeks after the event, and without mentioning Yang by name. See "Che-i hsing-ch'i" (This week), TLPL no. 57:2 (July 2, 1933).

he held forth the promise that the Chinese would in the course of time create "a new civilization not incompatible with the spirit of the new world." [90] On his return to Peking in November, however, Hu's first concern was to remind his Chinese audience of the enormous chasm that still separated China from the modern civilization of the West: "The peoples of European nations are not faced with the great problem of the establishment of the nation because their nations were long ago established on firm foundations. Thus they have energy to spare for the discussion of social problems, problems of production and distribution, and the like. But in this country of ours, this nation that is not yet a nation, this government that is not a government . . . how are we worthy to discuss changes in the system of production and distribution! I am not saying that [such questions] are unimportant. I am only saying that, in China's present circumstances, such problems are without a means of solution until there is some way of insuring the survival of the nation itself." [91]

In his Chicago lectures a few months earlier Hu had once more expressed his admiration for "the great Soviet experiment." He had praised the Russian leaders as "most ardent champions of science and technological progress"; socialism and communism, he had suggested, should be regarded as "an integral part" of Western civilization, "the logical consequence in the fulfillment of its democratic ideal," "merely supplementary to the earlier and more individualistic ideas of democracy." [92] In the essay cited above, however, entitled "An Introduction to the Question of National Reconstruction" ("Chien-kuo wen-t'i yin-lun"), Hu vigorously renewed his attack on "isms" as a substitute for critical thought, making it very clear that his aversion to the analysis of Chinese problems in Marxist terms had not diminished with the passage of time. Despite this recurrence of a familiar theme, it is perhaps more significant that by the end of 1933 Hu was willing to concede that in a society as decadent as China's there must be fundamental change before there can be useful solutions to problems of detail. In this respect he seemed to have come around to the view outlined by Li Ta-chao in the debate on problems and isms in 1919. Although Hu did not argue, as Li had, that any single "fundamental solution" might con-

90. Hu Shih, *The Chinese Renaissance* (Chicago, 1934), 26.
91. Hu Shih, "Chien-kuo wen-t'i yin-lun" (An introduction to the question of national reconstruction), TLPL no. 77:2–7 (Nov. 19, 1933).
92. *The Chinese Renaissance*, 42–43.

stitute a remedy to all of China's ills, he appeared more ready than he had earlier been to recognize the importance of underlying social and political conditions to the success of his program of piecemeal reform.

Hu Shih's analysis of "the question of national reconstruction" appeared in *The Independent Critic* several weeks before the publication of T. F. Tsiang's "Revolution and Authoritarianism," mentioned earlier. Hu thus anticipated Tsiang's conclusion that China could claim none of the attributes of modern nationhood. The point at issue between them was the manner of accounting for this deficiency: Tsiang attributed it to political factors, Hu to certain peculiarities of China's social development. The Chinese, Hu insisted, do not need to have a sense of political unity thrust upon them by a despotic autocracy, as Tsiang argued. They have possessed an awareness of common cultural and political identity ever since the imperial unification of the Han period.[93] What would make China's transformation into a modern nation "incomparably more difficult than in the case of Europe, America, or Japan" was the absence, in the Chinese situation, of a class around which a new political order could take form.[94] This Hu saw as a result of the fact that Confucian society had at an early point ceased to evolve in such a way as to generate new centers of elite control. This, in turn, Hu attributed to a number of factors: the leveling process encouraged over a long period by the examination system; the fact that traditional methods of economic organization and attitudes toward economic enterprise had forestalled the development of a class comparable in its social and political function to the European bourgeoisie;[95] and the fact that, long before the 1911 Revolution administered the coup de grace to imperial institutions, the traditional ruling class, the old "gentry" (*shih-ta-fu*), had succumbed to the intellectual regimentation that was the price demanded for imperial sponsorship of Confucian learning.[96]

93. Hu Shih, "Chien-kuo yü chuan-chih" (National reconstruction and authoritarianism), TLPL no. 81:2–5 (Dec. 17, 1933). Ever ready to argue two points at once, Hu constructed quite an elaborate case for the view that the Han unification was made effective in large part because of the wise implementation of *wu-wei* policies prior to the reign of Han Wu-ti; see "Ts'ung nung-ts'un chiu-chi t'an-tao wu-wei ti cheng-chih," TLPL no. 49.

94. "Chien-kuo yü chuan-chih," TLPL no. 81.

95. "Ts'an-t'ung ti hui-i yü fan-hsing," TLPL no. 18.

96. Hu Shih [Shih-chih], "Ling-hsiu jen-ts'ai ti lai-yüan" (The sources of leadership talent), TLPL no. 12:2–5 (Aug. 7, 1932).

But, Hu asserted, "each age has its own 'gentry.'" For the Chinese, deprived of a natural elite by historical circumstance, the problem was to *create* a class that could provide the intellectual and social leadership necessary to the establishment of a new political order. For Hu, there was no question as to where to begin: only in the centers of modern thought, the universities, could the intellectual attitudes required of this "new gentry" be cultivated and refined.[97]

The issue that divided Hu Shih from the Kuomintang most bitterly, and made its rule all but intolerable to him, was the party's hostility to intellectual innovation and to the values that should shape the character and conduct of China's "modern" gentry. It seems probable, indeed, that Hu could have accommodated to life under the Nationalists without undue strain, despite his sensitivity to the political shortcomings of the regime, had the party shown itself more willing to live, in mind and spirit, in the modern age. Hu's restrictive interpretation of politics might well have enabled him to compartmentalize "political" demands upon the government, had the Kuomintang dictatorship not used its authority to impose a moribund system of values in areas that far exceeded the range of what Hu regarded as its legitimate political concerns.

The Nationalists' inclination to refurbish the image of the Confucian past, in evidence almost from the moment of the establishment of the Nanking government, reached something of a climax in the first half of 1934 with the inauguration of the "New Life" movement and, some months later, a return to the practice of official observance of the birthday of the Sage. The New Life movement was launched in mid-February by Chiang Kai-shek himself, in a speech to a mass rally in Nanchang, the capital of Kiangsi province. The location was undoubtedly selected with strategic considerations in mind: it lay close to the soviet areas in southern Kiangsi which had been for several years the stronghold of the Chinese Communist movement, and it was against the appeal of Communist ideology that the New Life movement was primarily directed, as a sort of ideological adjunct to the military "extermination campaigns" waged by Nanking against the Communist bases in the Kiangsi border area. In place of revolutionary promises the New Life movement offered tips on personal hygiene, and it extolled frugality and

97. *Ibid.*

the simple life and the excellence of traditional Confucian moral values.[98]

Hu Shih responded to the New Life movement without enthusiasm, as might be expected, but also without particular rancor. He observed mildly that the movement could hardly be expected to accomplish what the government hoped for it; to tell the people to button their jackets, brush their teeth, and stop spitting in public was all very well, but genuine progress should not be confused with such efforts to bring the Chinese up to "minimal standards of human behavior." On the contrary, "national salvation and the revitalization of the race . . . depend entirely on knowledge and skill of the highest order." Moreover, Hu added, "the government must clearly understand what it can and what it cannot do." Political propaganda cannot improve public morals. Proper habits can be cultivated only in an adequate material environment, and consequently the government's first responsibility should be to promote the welfare of the people.[99]

This last injunction has a remarkably traditional ring to it: generation upon generation of Confucian statesmen schooled in Mencius had addressed themselves in virtually the same language to the rulers of their own day. It is true that in the spring of 1934 Hu was in an unusually old-fashioned mood, propounding his theory of *wu-wei* government and, in his own terms, extolling the virtue of simplicity. But this did not suffice to make him receptive to the kind of retrogressive cultural nationalism espoused by the Kuomintang and vigorously expounded in the speech delivered by Wang Ching-wei, president of the Executive Yuan, in Nanking on the occasion of the first official celebration of Confucius' birthday late in August. Wang said, in part:

It is a Chinese custom to spill wine on the ground during a sacrificial worship as a token of thanks to the ancestors, who first made food. Since Confucius has passed down such a grand civilization to us, should we not hold the same thankful attitude toward him? Should we not try our utmost to better what Con-

98. On the New Life movement see John Israel, *Student Nationalism*, 96–100; Samuel Chu, "The New Life Movement, 1934–1937," in John E. Lane, ed., *Researches in the Social Sciences on China* (New York, 1957).

99. Hu Shih, "Wei Hsin sheng-huo yün-tung chin i-chieh" (A word on the New Life movement), TLPL no. 95:17–20 (April 8, 1934).

fucius has handed down to us? Confucius has again and again advised us to promote virtue with the advancement of time. The same attitude holds good in other respects. We should above all take up the responsibility to make greater achievements in Chinese civilization, and not lay the blame upon our great teacher for the present backwardness of China.

. . . On this present occasion, when we all rejoice in celebrating the birthday of the great master, we should among other things think deeply how to keep China in a position of equality and freedom in the modern world by dint of the teachings of Confucius.[100]

Not everyone rejoiced with Wang, however. Hu Shih, viewing this Confucian revival as a repudiation of the intellectual accomplishments won at great cost in recent decades, reacted furiously. The Kuomintang's effort to prop up the tattered figure of Confucius, Hu declared, was an act of cowardice unpardonable in the leaders of a modern state: "Pitiful and despairing old revolutionary party! You wanted a revolution, but now that the revolution has achieved these twenty years of unprecedented progress, you disown it. What progress there has been in these two decades was not a gift from Confucius, but the result of a common revolutionary struggle, the result of a common acceptance of the new civilization of a new world. Our only hope lies in moving forward." [101]

It is not difficult to understand the bitterness of Hu's sentiments on this score. He had argued tirelessly, ever since his return from the United States in 1917, that the Chinese could hope for no improvement in their condition until they had assessed with critical candor the nature of their inheritance. Now the Kuomintang's invocation of Confucius as a deus ex machina offered, to Hu's way of thinking, incontrovertible evidence that time had not brought to the Chinese a sufficient capacity for honest self-examination. "Our people know no sense of shame," he wrote in 1934, "because they have never once reflected on their past." [102]

In view of their reluctance to take this responsibility upon themselves, Hu passed along to his countrymen his own cheerless con-

100. For the text of Wang's speech see *The China Yearbook, 1935* (Shanghai, 1935), 92–93.
101. "Hsieh tsai K'ung-tzu tan-ch'en chi-nien chih hou," TLPL no. 117.
102. "Hsin-hsin yü fan-hsing," TLPL no. 103.

clusions. He rehearsed once more the dreary catalog of China's "unique treasures": a sterile literature, bound feet, eunuchs, concubinage, five-generation households, memorials erected to honor "chastity," hellish prisons, and the time-honored practice of flogging high officials of state in the imperial presence.[103] As for those virtues which some claimed for the Chinese alone — "loyalty and filiality" (chung-hsiao), "benevolence and compassion" (jen-ai), "sincerity and righteousness" (hsin-i), and pacifism (ho-p'ing) — these, Hu maintained, are sentiments common to mankind generally. He conceded only that in different cultures one might find differences in the manner of giving expression to such ideals — and, he inquired mockingly, how much "benevolence and compassion" might really have been involved in the "private meditations" of Chinese monks following the scriptural injunction to "think on all living creatures" while urinating? [104]

The dispute thus had its fatuous aspect. Hu was not above solemnly debating the question of whether bound feet were any worse than chastity belts, or memorial arches indicative of a more reprehensible mentality than the *droit de seigneur*.[105] But this was really beside the point. Hu was quite willing to agree with Chou Tso-jen's observation that "there are bedbugs in the West, too." [106] What was important was not the evidence on one side of the case or the other, but the conclusion: China's cultural tradition, Hu proclaimed, is "as useless in real life as the silvered wax spears used on the stage." [107] "If our old culture were worthy of being revived," he wrote elsewhere, "then we would not be in the predicament we are in today." [108]

It was only natural that such opinions, publicly expressed and widely circulated, should have won for Hu a reputation as the most extreme spokesman of the demand for "total" westernization. He said nothing to contradict this interpretation of his position,[109] and

103. *Ibid.*

104. Hu Shih, "Tsai lun hsin-hsin yü fan-hsing" (Another discussion of faith and reflection), TLPL no. 105:2–6 (June 17, 1934).

105. Hu Shih, "San lun hsin-hsin yü fan-hsing" (A third discussion of faith and reflection), TLPL no. 107:2–6 (July 1, 1934).

106. Chou Tso-jen, "Hsi-yang yeh yu ch'ou-ch'ung" (There are bedbugs in the West, too), TLPL no. 107:12 (July 1, 1934).

107. "Hsin-hsin yü fan-hsing," TLPL no. 103.

108. "Tsai lun hsin-hsin yü fan-hsing," TLPL no. 105.

109. See for example Hu Shih, "Pien-chi hou-chi," TLPL no. 142:24 (March 17, 1935); "Chung-Jih t'i-hsi," TLPL no. 143; Hu Shih, "Ta Ch'en Hsü-ching

on more than one occasion he came under fire from Nationalist patrons of the conservative revival on this account. The most dramatic instance, and the best publicized, occurred early in 1935 when Hu took his first trip to south China to receive an honorary degree from the University of Hong Kong. While in the colony he made several speeches outspokenly critical of the provincial administration of neighboring Kwangtung for its tradition-bound educational policies.[110] His reception in Canton, the provincial capital, a few days later was predictably inhospitable. The lectures he had been scheduled to give at Sun Yat-sen University were canceled, and he was publicly rebuked by Tsou Lu, the president of the university and an old Kuomintang stalwart. He was also privately called to account by Ch'en Chi-t'ang, the governor, a militarist of profoundly conservative views who was the chief sponsor of the policies to which Hu had taken exception. His interview with Ch'en (who behaved, by Hu's account, in a startlingly unConfucian manner, shouting and threatening, while Hu remained throughout the very model of the equable Confucian gentleman) cast into sharp relief the issue that divided Hu from the cultural traditionalists. It was, essentially, the same dusty issue over which the Chinese had been wrangling since the 1880s: the question of whether the "practical" aspects of Western civilization could be appropriated without damage to the "fundamentals" of the Confucian social ethic. Ch'en was quick enough to acknowledge the usefulness of Western armaments and industrial technology, even as the "self-strengtheners" of the last half of the nineteenth century had hoped to stay the encroachment of the West by importing "ships and guns." Men of Ch'en's type, Hu remarked sourly, were not trying "blindly to return to the past in its entirety; they buy airplanes and guns, and of course they drive the latest 1935-model cars. It is only in shaping human character that they want to rely upon the sage prescriptions of twenty-five hundred years ago." [111] This was indeed the gist of Ch'en's position: in "teaching men to be men" (*tso-jen*), he insisted, only Chinese

hsien-sheng" (A reply to Mr. Ch'en Hsü-ching), TLPL no. 160:15–16 (July 21, 1935). The last piece is Hu's response to Ch'en Hsü-ching, "Ch'üan-p'an hsi-hua ti pien-hu" (In defense of total westernization), TLPL no. 160.

110. Hu Shih, "Nan yu tsa-i: (1) Hsiang-kang" (Random impressions from southern travels: [1] Hong Kong), TLPL no. 141:11–16 (March 10, 1935).

111. Hu Shih, "Shih-p'ing so-wei 'Chung-kuo pen-wei chih wen-hua chien-she'" (A critique of so-called "cultural reconstruction on a Chinese base"), TLPL no. 145:4–7 (April 7, 1935).

"roots" (*pen*), that is, the principles of Confucian moral education, should be employed.[112]

Hu's demand for total westernization was intended to discredit this kind of dogged intellectual reaction. Yet the end he had in view was by no means the annihilation of every vestige of traditional Chinese culture. Despite his profound distrust of nationalistic emotions, Hu was in his own fashion as much a nationalist as were the men whose intellectual prejudices and political strategies he deplored. He was deeply concerned for the fate of China, both as a nation and as a civilization. Over the years such terms as "national salvation" and "the revival of the race" recurred too often in his writings to be dismissed as empty rhetoric. Though he could never bring himself to march under the banner of nationalism, he never lost the sense of commitment to China's deliverance that he carried with him from Shanghai in 1910. To Hu, however, modernization meant something different from what it signified to cultural nationalists like Ch'en Chi-t'ang. To Hu it meant, first and foremost, the modernization of values and attitudes, a far more important and difficult thing than the modernization of the economy and the military establishment — the point at which the latter-day self-strengtheners stopped short, overwhelmed by the dread of becoming strangers in an alien world. Hu did not share their misgivings, partly because to him that world was less alien, but also because he thought their fears unfounded. "Modernization" was not, in his view, synonymous with "westernization," nor could it be. He saw the interaction of civilizations as an enormously complex process, taking place simultaneously at several levels, conscious and unconscious, rational and irrational.[113] In this process human intervention is difficult, but essential. Insofar as possible the irrational responses inevitably generated in the confrontation of conflicting values must be subdued by rational judgments. "It is always reason that plans and directs," Hu wrote in 1935, "it is reason that governs the unbridled passions and disciplines the inclination to laziness, fear, and indifference." And he continued: "Our ideal of 'complete cosmopolitanization' [*ch'ungfen shih-chieh-hua*] means to use reason to define our aims [and to] persuade men to an acceptance of these aims; to expend our strength

112. Hu Shih, "Nan-yu tsa-i: (2) Kuang-chou" (Random impressions from southern travels: [2] Canton), TLPL no. 142:16–23 (March 17, 1935). On Ch'en Chi-t'ang see Boorman, *Biographical Dictionary*, I, 160–163.
113. "The Indianization of China," 219–223 and *passim*.

in the fullest measure to overcome all conservative and antiquarian sentiments [and to] lead the nation as a whole in the direction we have chosen — this and nothing more. Beyond this, if there are still a few in private life who like to read the eight-legged essays of Jen Tsai-t'ang, or to write *wu-t'i shih* in the style of Li I-shan, or to eat snake meat, or to listen to ancient music, in such matters our reason 'has no power to act.' " [114]

In both the common and the technical senses of the term, Hu was enough of a pragmatist to recognize utility as the sole criterion by which to judge the value of specific aspects of a cultural tradition and concrete proposals for reform. Such a judgment, he believed, must be based on a careful examination of the results achieved in practice. No abstract standard — not even that of "the scientific method," he admitted in 1935 — could be trusted as an entirely reliable guide to cultural change. [115] Too many invisible filaments bind a people to its traditional ways, too many unrecognized forces act to conserve the old or shape the form in which the new may be accepted. The final effect of any effort at innovation will be limited by the natural conservatism of the recipient culture.

It was this belief in cultural inertia that both provoked Hu's anger against men like Ch'en Chi-t'ang and, at the same time, permitted him to feel a degree of confidence in the survival of Chinese civilization as an identifiable entity. The demand for total westernization or complete cosmopolitanization was no more than stratagem designed to offset the danger that, given the least encouragement, such latent cultural conservatism would overwhelm any endeavor to escape the burden of outmoded attitudes. It was not the West to which the Chinese must accommodate themselves, but the modern world. "At the present time there is no other road to follow except the complete acceptance of the civilization of the new world," Hu wrote. "If we who are destined to be leaders speak emptily of compromise and selectivity, the result can only be the cherishing of useless remnants and the preservation of our shortcomings." [116] Therefore the Chinese must "humbly accept" the "scientific-industrial world culture and the spiritual civilization on which it rests." But, Hu continued, they could do so with the assurance that the

114. "Ta Ch'en Hsü-ching hsien-sheng," TLPL no. 160.

115. "Shih-p'ing so-wei 'Chung-kuo pen-wei chih wen-hua chien-she,' " TLPL no. 145.

116. Hu Shih, "Pien-chi hou-chi," TLPL no. 142.

eventual product "will be, as a matter of course, a culture built on Chinese foundations." [117] He looked ahead with equanimity, firm in the belief that the birthright of his people would remain secure: "What pessimistic observers have lamented as the collapse of Chinese civilization, is exactly the necessary undermining and erosion without which there could not have been the rejuvenation of an old civilization. Slowly, quietly, but unmistakably, the Chinese Renaissance is becoming a reality. The product of this rebirth looks suspiciously occidental. But, scratch its surface and you will find that the stuff of which it is made is essentially the Chinese bedrock which much weathering and corrosion have only made stand out more clearly — the humanistic and rationalistic China resurrected by the touch of the scientific and democratic civilization of the new world." [118]

The ordeal of the 1930s demanded courage of the Chinese, a demand that was met in varying measure and in different ways: the boldness of the students who invaded Peking's streets, the desperate resolution of those who harbored the revolutionary cause in the hinterland, the audacity of individuals like Yang Ch'üan. Hu Shih's courage was of a kind harder to discern, and perhaps too easy to dismiss when measured against the vastness of the tragedy that engulfed his country. His was the courage of patient hopefulness. Mindful that China's transition to modernity would be difficult, painful, and not without its perils, he was still able to face the prospect uncomforted by dogmatic belief, yet unafraid. The luminous promise of the modern world and the benign hope it held for China dispelled from his mind the shadow of doubt. "Faith is simply the courage to dare to confront an unknowable future," he wrote in 1934.[119] Few were as steady as he in such faith.

Early in July 1937 Hu Shih left Peking to attend a series of "summer conversations" convened by the government, in the spirit of the "united front" proclaimed at the end of 1936, to bring together intellectuals, educators, officials, and party men for discussions of the national crisis. Nine years were to pass before Hu returned again to the old city. On July 7, even as the leaders of China's

117. "Shih-p'ing so-wei 'Chung-kuo pen-wei chih wen-hua chien-she,'" TLPL no. 145.
118. *The Chinese Renaissance,* preface.
119. "Hsieh tsai K'ung-tzu tan-ch'en chi-nien chih hou," TLPL no. 117.

intellectual and political elite converged on Kuling, the mountain resort in Kiangsi where Chiang Kai-shek maintained his summer residence, armed clashes broke out between Chinese and Japanese troops at the Marco Polo Bridge near Peking. By the end of the month the city was under Japanese occupation; within a few weeks the fighting had spread to Shanghai, and Japanese bombs were falling on Nanking. As the Japanese advanced, systematically laying waste the universities of north China and driving before them a flood of refugee students and intellectuals, Hu Shih's gravest apprehensions were realized. Institutions built by long and arduous effort were destroyed with terrible swiftness — tiny islands of enlightenment submerged beneath the onrushing tide of war. Just as surely, though less visibly, the confidence so patiently nurtured was destroyed: Hu Shih's serene faith that ultimately reason, and reasonable men, would shape the course of history could not survive the bitter years of war, political collapse, civil conflict, and social revolution upon which the Chinese entered in the summer of 1937.

Wandering between two worlds, one dead,
The other powerless to be born,
With nowhere yet to rest my head . . .

For the world cries your faith is now
But a dead time's exploded dream . . .

Matthew Arnold's *Stanzas*
from the Grande Chartreuse

Part IV. An Epilogue and an Evaluation

Chapter 9. The Later Years

With all hope for a less costly settlement with Japan shattered in the summer of 1937, Hu Shih lost no time in proclaiming his allegiance to the Nationalist government in the cause for which it was now fighting. In such times, he declared at Kuling, the preservation of the state must be the first concern of all.[1] In this spirit Hu left China in mid-September as a semi-official envoy to plead China's case in the United States and Europe. Of the twenty-five years that remained to him, he was destined to spend all but seven abroad, watching from afar China's descent into war and revolution. It is thus not without reason that his departure from China in 1937

1. CWR 81.8:270 (July 24, 1937).

should be taken to mark the end of Hu's effective involvement in the struggle for social and intellectual reform. China's history during the turbulent quarter century that followed was shaped by forces that Hu little understood, leaving him at the end of his life bereft of the optimism that had sustained him through so many earlier difficulties.

Hu spent several months in the United States in the autumn and winter of 1937 before proceeding to Geneva to observe at first hand the deliberations of the League of Nations, in whose influence he had placed such high and unavailing trust throughout the 1930s. He was still in Geneva in September 1938, when Chiang Kai-shek named him to replace C. T. Wang (Wang Cheng-t'ing) as the Chinese ambassador to Washington. So, for the first time, Hu found himself in the employ of the Nationalist government. He assumed his new responsibilities at an inauspicious moment: unexpectedly easy Japanese victories at Hankow and Canton in September and October had deprived the Nationalists of their remaining outlets to the sea and imprisoned them deep in the interior. At a time when the Chinese were still fighting alone, in desperate need of American sympathy and support, Hu Shih was in many respects an ideal representative of China's cause. He was singularly well liked and respected in the United States. *The New York Times* commented editorially that "Americans who know Dr. Hu Shih will rejoice" at the news of his appointment. "Few of Dr. Shih's [sic] countrymen are so thoroughly representative of the best of the new and the old China," the editorial continued. "Few are so well qualified to explain China to the United States and the United States to China." [2] In *Inside Asia*, published a few months later, John Gunther introduced the new ambassador to a wider public as "beyond doubt the single most distinguished living Chinese, from any point of view not narrowly political . . . a mental giant . . . the best type of discriminating Chinese nationalist." [3]

Hu did not disappoint the confidence expressed in *The New York Times* that he would "do much to strengthen the warm ties of sympathy which already unite the Chinese and American peoples." [4] "Explaining China to the United States" seems to have been, indeed, the chief effort of his mission. He lectured widely to academic and

2. *New York Times,* Sept. 20, 1938, 22.
3. John Gunther, *Inside Asia* (New York and London, 1939), 260–262.
4. *New York Times,* Sept. 20, 1938, 22.

civic groups, speaking usually not only of the heroism of China's beleaguered defenders but also of the natural affinity that should bind the democratic American people to the democratically inclined Chinese.[5] Along the way he garnered an imposing number of honorary degrees from American universities anxious to demonstrate their esteem for him and for the people he represented. Meanwhile, much of the crucially important business of negotiating for American economic and, ultimately, military assistance was conducted on the Chinese side by the Generalissimo's brother-in-law, T. V. Soong, who was virtually in residence in Washington from 1940 onward, first as Chiang's "personal representative" to President Roosevelt and subsequently as Foreign Minister.

In August 1942 Hu Shih was unexpectedly recalled by his government. Stanley Hornbeck, Adviser on Political Relations in the Department of State, immediately concluded that the ambassador had somehow trespassed upon the foreign minister. He received assurances from the embassy that in fact Hu and Soong had worked out a mutually satisfactory division of functions. Chiang Kai-shek's displeasure with Hu, it was hinted, stemmed from his belief that Hu had been trying harder to justify American policy to Chungking than to argue China's case in Washington. Hu had become, in other words, a casualty of the growing distrust between the Chinese and American allies.[6] His dismissal did nothing to ease the strain. *The New York Times* registered "shock" at the news. "Unless some higher post is reserved for him at home," warned the *Times*, "his recall is a mistake." [7] Conceding something to such American criticism, the Generalissimo appointed Hu to serve as a special adviser to the Executive Yuan, on the same day that Wei Tao-ming was confirmed by that body as Hu's successor in Washington.[8] Hu discharged this new responsibility in absentia, very likely in the spirit in which the appointment had been made. He had been suffering for several years from an intermittent heart condition, and now, pleading ill health, he elected to remain in the United States, lec-

5. See, for example, Hu Shih, "Historical Foundations for a Democratic China," in *Edmund J. James Lectures on Government*, 2nd series (Urbana, Ill., 1941), 53–64; Hu Shih, "The Struggle for Intellectual Freedom in Historic China," *World Affairs*, 105.3:170–173 (September 1942).

6. *Foreign Relations of the United States, Diplomatic Papers, 1942: China* (Washington, D.C., 1956), 132–134, 135–139.

7. *New York Times*, Sept. 3, 1942, 18.

8. *New York Times*, Sept. 9, 1942, 12. See also *Foreign Relations of the United States, 1942: China*, 157.

turing at Harvard and Columbia, acting as a consultant to the Oriental division of the Library of Congress, and pursuing his study of *Shui-ching chu* (Commentary on the Book of waterways), a sixth-century work on geography that would remain his principal scholarly preoccupation for the rest of his life. He did not completely sever his connections with the Nationalist government, however. In 1945 he was a member of the Chinese delegation to the founding conference of the United Nations at San Francisco, a duty which, in view of his lifelong interest in international organization, must have given him considerable satisfaction. Later that year he served as acting head of the Chinese delegation to the UNESCO conference in London, in the absence of Chu Chia-hua, the Minister of Education. When Chiang Monlin was appointed secretary-general of the Executive Yuan in June 1945, Hu was named to succeed his old friend as chancellor of Peita. So began his last brief and troubled affiliation with the institution where he had spent his most productive and, probably, his happiest years.

By the time Hu returned to China to assume his new post in the summer of 1946 Peita had emerged from its wartime exile in the southwest and was once again established in its accustomed location, adjacent to the old Imperial City in Peking. Despite the familiarity of these surroundings, Hu discovered that little else remained the same. The problems of the 1930s paled to insignificance beside the crises of the late 1940s. Corruption spread like cancer through the body politic. Inflation raged unchecked, making paupers of many who before the war had enjoyed a modest security, and condemning the poor of city and countryside to starvation. The civil war sputtered and flared. Chinese life was militarized to a far greater degree than it had been a decade earlier. In the words of a manifesto signed by nearly six hundred professors from Peita, Tsinghua, Yenching, Nankai, and other north China universities in June 1947, China "is on the verge of political, military, economic, and cultural collapse. Disaster is at our very door . . . The situation is no less critical than that in France on the eve of the French Revolution, or that in Russia just preceding the October Revolution." [9]

In the years of Hu's absence, moreover, political loyalties had become increasingly divided. Some of his old friends, especially those who had served the Nationalists in the prewar years, had maintained their connections with the government during and after the war.

9. CWR 106.2:36 (June 14, 1947).

T. F. Tsiang, who had left his duties at Tsinghua to become China's ambassador to the U.S.S.R. in 1936 and had served as director of the Political Affairs Department of the Executive Yuan throughout the war, was director-general of the Chinese National Relief and Rehabilitation Administration when Hu returned to China in 1946. In 1947 he became the permanent Chinese representative to the United Nations. Weng Wen-hao, a Western-educated geologist and, like Tsiang, a former member of *The Independent Critic* coterie, had served as secretary-general of the Executive Yuan in 1935–36 and as Minister of Economic Affairs during the war; he was destined to fill a brief and unhappy term as the first premier under a "constitutional" government in the summer of 1948. Chiang Monlin, as noted earlier, had left Peita to become the secretary-general of the Executive Yuan in 1945. And then there was Wellington Koo, that indefatigable and indestructible public servant, who replaced Wei Tao-ming as the Chinese ambassador to Washington in 1946.

But many of Hu's colleagues of former days, men who, unlike him, had remained in China throughout the war, were by its end implacably hostile to the Nationalist regime. Some were involved in active opposition to it, as members of a loose confederation of anti-Kuomintang groups known as the Democratic League, established in 1944 and outlawed at the end of 1947.[10] In July 1946, only a few days after Hu disembarked from the *President Taft* in Shanghai, his old friend Wen I-to, transformed by the war from the apolitical scholar-poet of *The Crescent* era into a passionate opponent of the party dictatorship, was assassinated as he emerged from the offices of the *Democratic Weekly* (*Min-chu chou-k'an*), the League newspaper he had edited in Kunming.[11] Lo Lung-chi, another of Hu's friends since the days of *The Crescent*, and never enamoured of the Nationalist cause, was a leading spokesman for the League in 1946 and 1947, for which he paid the price of constant harassment by the secret police.[12] Ch'ien Tuan-sheng, with whom Hu had debated

10. On the Democratic League see Melville T. Kennedy, Jr., "The Chinese Democratic League," *Papers on China*, 7:136–175 (1953). Kennedy states that Hu Shih joined the League in August 1945, citing a news item to this effect published in *Hsin-hua jih-pao* (Chungking), Aug. 27, 1945, datelined Chengtu. In the absence of corroborating evidence I am inclined to doubt the accuracy of this report.

11. See Hsü Kai-yü, "The Life and Poetry of Wen I-to," *Harvard Journal of Asiatic Studies*, 21:173–179 (December 1958).

12. CWR 102.8:177 (July 20, 1946), 102.9:204 (July 27, 1946), and 104.5:143 (Jan. 4, 1947). See also *United States Relations with China, with Special Refer-*

the issue of democracy vs. dictatorship in the 1930s, was in the post-war period an outspoken, if somewhat more academic, critic of Chiang Kai-shek's militarization of Chinese politics.[13]

Inevitably, the younger generation was both the agent and the victim of political unrest. Student demonstrations and strikes were endemic in the postwar years, provoked by the all-but-impossible economic condition in which the students found themselves, or by specific cases of bureaucratic mismanagement of the universities, and, most important, by a growing sense of frustration and outrage as corruption spread and the civil war dragged on at great cost in blood and wealth. The Kuomintang's increasingly brutal efforts to silence its critics served, needless to say, only to hasten the drift toward radicalism among the students. All in all, China in the years from 1946 to 1949 afforded an unpromising setting in which to play the role that Hu Shih was accustomed to playing, that of the detached and dispassionate critic.

The position that Hu would take on the great issue of those years, the deadly problem of civil war, was foreshadowed in rather strange fashion well before he himself reappeared upon the scene. From New York City, in the late summer of 1945, Hu dispatched a telegram to Mao Tse-tung, the text of which was carried in the Chinese press as follows:

> Mr. Mao: From the newspapers I have learned that you so kindly told Mr. Fu Shih-nien [Fu Ssu-nien, acting chancellor of Peita in 1945–46] to convey your greetings to me, and I am grateful to you for this kindness. On the night of August 22 I had a long talk with Mr. Tung Pi-wu [Chinese Communist representative to the San Francisco Conference], to whom I expressed the hope that the Chinese Communist leaders, in consideration of the international situation and China's future, should strive to forget what is past and look forward to what is coming, and be determined to build up a second major party in China not dependent on armed strength by laying down their arms. If you are so determined, then the eighteen years of internal conflicts will be settled, and your efforts through the past twenty-odd

ence to the Period 1944–1949 (Washington, D.C., 1949), 836–838 (cited hereafter as White Paper). Lo had been a good friend of Wen I-to since the days, thirty years earlier, when they had been classmates at Tsinghua.

13. See Chalmers A. Johnson, "An Intellectual Weed in the Socialist Garden: The Case of Ch'ien Tuan-sheng," _China Quarterly_, no. 6:29–52 (1961).

years will not be nullified by civil war. Jefferson fought peacefully for more than ten years in the early days of the United
States, finally succeeding in bringing the Democratic Party, of
which he was the founder, to power in the fourth presidential
election. The British Labor Party polled only 44,000 votes fifty
years ago, but as a result of peaceful struggle, got 12,000,000
votes this year and becomes the major party. These two instances
should furnish much food for thought. The Chinese Communist
Party, today the second major party in China, has a great future
if peacefully developed. It should not destroy itself through
intolerance. This was the gist of my talk with Mr. Tung Pi-wu,
to which I particularly call your attention. Hu Shih. August
24th, 1945.[14]

The sentiments expressed here are more remarkable in retrospect
than they would have appeared in the context of that particular
moment. Mao Tse-tung was just then in Chungking, where he and
Chiang were exploring, with superficial cordiality, the possibilities
for an accommodation of the interests that each represented. More
than a year would pass before the futility of this effort became
clearly apparent, and in the interim Hu was not the only one who

14. *Ta kung pao* (Chungking), Sept. 2, 1945; CPR:C no. 238:6 (Sept. 4,
1945). In his introduction to J. Leighton Stuart's autobiography Hu recalled
this incident in the following terms: "I, too, was just as naïve a tyro [as Ambassador Stuart] in national and international politics in those days of ex-
pansive idealism. So naïve, indeed, was I that shortly after V-J Day I sent a
lengthy radiogram to Chungking to be forwarded to my former student Mao
Tse-tung . . . My Chungking friend radioed me that my message had been
duly forwarded to Mr. Mao in person. Of course, to this day I have never received a reply." (John Leighton Stuart, *Fifty Years in China* [New York, 1954],
xix.) Mao might have been surprised to have Hu lay claim to him as a
"former student" in this fashion. He acknowledged to Edgar Snow in 1936 that
at the time of his graduation from Changsha Normal School in 1918 Hu Shih
and Ch'en Tu-hsiu had been among his heroes. "At that time," he said, "my
mind was a curious mixture of ideas of liberalism, democratic reformism, and
Utopian Socialism. I had somewhat vague passions about 'nineteenth-century
democracy,' Utopianism and old-fashioned liberalism, and I was definitely anti-
militarist and anti-imperialist." (Edgar Snow, *Red Star Over China* [New York,
1938], 132.) During his brief sojourn in Peking over the following winter,
however, when he worked for a time as an assistant in the Peita library and
came under the influence of Li Ta-chao, Mao felt that with the exception of
Li the great figures of the New Culture movement were little interested in
the ideas of a young man from the provinces. He was, by one account, particularly snubbed by Hu Shih. (Stuart Schram, *Mao Tse-tung* [New York, 1966],
42.)

clung to the hope for a peaceful settlement of the conflict. His telegram to Mao reflects, certainly, a naïve understanding of the kind of historical precedent that was likely to impress its recipient and, in this way, reveals a remarkable misjudgment of the social and political forces that were to bring the Communists to power a few years later. But in this, too, Hu was not alone. The most interesting and significant aspect of this appeal lies in the suggestion which it contains that no cause is just if it seeks change outside the framework of the institutions available to it. This was, of course, no more than a restatement of opinions that Hu had expressed often enough in the twenties and thirties. But in the postwar period this view carried an ominous corollary: that any government which professed its desire to maintain the institutional structure intact was thereby rendered deserving of support, regardless of its moral or political deficiencies. This clearly meant support for the government in power; and, in the China to which Hu Shih was returning, this meant, in turn, support for a failing regime.

After his return in 1946 there were still some who urged Hu to assume again the "nonpartisan" stance of the prewar years, to avoid the snare of "politics," to resurrect *The Independent Critic*.[15] He regretfully rejected the last suggestion: "The golden age of pamphleteering journalism has passed," he wrote. "The value of money changes from day to day, and scholars who are compelled to wait for rice to put in the pot write to sell, in order to eat, and must be paid for their efforts. Moreover, labor costs have risen to the point where it costs more to set a thousand characters in print than one is paid for writing a thousand characters. There is no way for us to undertake to publish a truly 'independent' journal."[16]

In any case, genuine nonpartisanism, difficult enough in the 1930s, was virtually impossible after the war. For a man of Hu's persuasion, there was no longer any middle ground. One could side with the government, with the hope — a hope that grew ever fainter — of exerting a modifying influence upon its policies. Or one could side with those who challenged the government, at least to the extent of demanding (as probably a majority of Chinese intellectuals did, in private if not in public, by 1947) an end to the civil war and the

15. See for example "What We Expect of Dr. Hu Shih," *Yi shih pao* (Tientsin), July 31, 1946; CPR:P no. 109:1 (July 31, 1946); and C. Y. W. Meng, " 'New Revolutionary Movement,' " CWR 103.12:364–365 (Nov. 23, 1946).

16. Hu Shih, *Ting Wen-chiang ti chuan-chi*, 84.

establishment of some kind of coalition government, however detrimental this might be to the interests of the Kuomintang. On the one side: order, albeit an order imposed by coercion and intimidation; freedom, even though severely circumscribed, and made possible more by the ineffectiveness of the government than by its willingness to tolerate criticism; and most important, the hope for progressive change, even in the face of continued intransigeance in some quarters. On the other side, destruction in the name of revolution, and the tyranny of dogmatic belief.

Such, at least, are the terms in which Hu Shih seems to have judged the choices open to him. As the balance tipped from unstable dictatorship to open insurrection in 1947 and 1948, he came increasingly to identify with those who sought to bolster the diminishing authority of the Nationalist regime. As chancellor of the country's most illustrious university he found himself unenviably situated between the anvil of student unrest and the hammer of police repression. Hu's stand on the student movement in the postwar years is open to varying interpretations, depending in some measure on the political color of the lens through which one views the subject. He said little that he had not said on many previous occasions in the 1920s and 1930s, but now he was compelled to speak not in detached and general terms but in response to specific incidents of student protest and governmental harassment. When Peita opened in October 1946, Hu voiced his hope that the university would be, in spirit and in fact, an institution where free inquiry and independent thinking could flourish. The students, he suggested, were there to study.[17] Throughout 1947, however, and especially after the collapse of the Marshall mission and the final breakdown of KMT-CCP negotiations, relations between the Kuomintang and its academic critics (both students and teachers) deteriorated rapidly. As reports of student arrests came in from around the country, Hu tried to reassure his own students: such things could never come to pass at Peita, he told them, and he promised personally to stand bail for any Peita students arrested.[18] Before many months had gone by, it was a promise that Hu had to keep.[19]

It is possible, however, that the weight of Hu's still considerable

17. *Hsin min pao* (Peiping), Oct. 11, 1946; CPR:P no. 167:8 (Oct. 11, 1946).
18. *Shih-chieh jih-pao* (Peiping), Feb. 9, 1947; CPR:P no. 264:5 (Feb. 10, 1947).
19. *Peiping shih pao* (Peiping), June 4, 1947; CPR:P no. 360:4 (June 4, 1947).

prestige and the esteem in which he was held abroad, especially in the United States, saved Peita from feeling the full force of the government's suppression of political dissent, at least for a time.[20] Although every student strike or demonstration estranged him further from the radical strain infiltrating Chinese intellectual life, Hu continued to insist, as he had in the prewar years, that intellectuals in general, and students in particular, had a legitimate "supervisory" function to perform. Repeatedly he warned the government that it must adhere scrupulously to established legal procedures in dealing with its student critics. On at least one occasion he denounced in unequivocal language Chiang Kai-shek's habit of blaming all student unrest on Communist subversion; most of the students, Hu said, were merely expressing an entirely natural and praiseworthy concern for China's condition.[21]

But if he could sympathize with their motives, even as he had in the 1930s, Hu still could not approve of the students' methods. Time and again he urged them, in tones that varied from gentle reproof to stern admonition, to have done with demonstrations and strikes and to return to the business of getting an education. And he told them that those whose convictions drove them, in spite of everything, to active political protest must be prepared to accept the responsibility for their actions and face up to the penalties that might be laid against them: the law is the law, and universities cannot serve as asylums for lawbreakers.[22] By the late summer of 1948, as time began to run out for the Nationalists in north China, whatever security Peita might once have afforded was gone. With the university virtually under a state of siege by KMT police and gendarmes — part of a nationwide, last-minute drive to root out subversion and bring the intellectuals to heel — Hu informed the Peita students that those of them summoned before the special criminal courts established to try "subversives" must surrender or face expulsion.[23]

Hu Shih's view of the general political situation reflected a similarly legalistic bias. He stated his position clearly in July 1947, commenting on the State Council's order for general mobilization to prosecute the war against the Communists:

20. This is suggested by James P. Speer III, "Liquidation of Chinese Liberals," *Far Eastern Survey*, 16.14:160–162 (July 23, 1947).

21. *Ching shih jih-pao* (Peiping), May 20, 1947; CPR:P no. 348:3 (May 20, 1947).

22. *Peiping jih-pao* (Peiping), Oct. 28, 1947; CPR:P no. 459:5 (Oct. 28, 1947).

23. CWR 110.13:358 (Aug. 28, 1948) and 111.1:4–5 (Sept. 4, 1948).

Political parties competing for political power should follow the legal way of winning the support of a vast majority of the people. To overthrow the Government by force of arms is not a legal way but a revolution. For the sake of self-defense, the Government is duty-bound to suppress the Communist rebellion. All communications have been cut, most of the mines have been destroyed, and the chimneys of how many factories are [still] spitting smoke? Tsichihsien [Chi-hsi hsien], Anhwei, my home town, stood intact during the war of resistance and was destroyed by the Communists last month. Difficulties which did not exist during the war of resistance have now come into being, and what was spared during the war of resistance has now been destroyed. Therefore the Communist rebellion must be suppressed. After eight years of war . . . poor and weak China has risen to the rank of one of the Big Four in the world. Certainly President Chiang hopes to maintain this international prestige.[24]

Hu Shih was by no means alone in lamenting the devastation wrought by continued fighting. But in view of the fact that the Communist party had been outlawed since March, and that in its order for general mobilization the State Council proclaimed the Communists to be in open rebellion against the government (a not inaccurate assessment of the situation), Hu's statement had about it an air of fantasy.[25] To acknowledge the Nationalists' right to defend themselves at all cost was one thing, though by this time there were many who would have questioned whether in so doing the regime truly represented either the interests or the desires of the people. But to rebuke the Communists because they would not press their claims by "legal" means — presumably Hu still had in mind the salutary examples of Thomas Jefferson and the British Labor party — was, under the existing circumstances, perilously close to sophistry. The Communists, weighing the probability of their being permitted to avail themselves of "legal" means of winning support in light of the history of their relations with the Nationalist regime, were unlikely to find such an argument persuasive. Nor did they feel any need to rely upon institutions that they did not trust; it

24. *Ho-p'ing jih-pao* (Nanking), July 7, 1947; CPR:N no. 457:5 (July 7, 1947). See also *Hsin min pao* (Peiping), July 6, 1947; CPR:P no. 382:4–5 (July 7, 1947).

25. Text of the resolution on general mobilization passed by the State Council on July 4, 1947, is given in White Paper, 476–478.

soon became devastatingly apparent that the Communists had discovered sources of political energy that could be translated by means of new institutions into an authority conformed to their own aspirations. As the revolutionary struggle reached its climax in 1947 and 1948, Hu Shih remained remarkably unaware of — or indifferent to — the dynamic forces at work in the Communist "rebellion."

Although Hu Shih had chosen the side on which he would stand in this conflict, he was as reluctant as always to abandon the semi-privacy of academic life to enter actively into politics. Reports of his imminent appointment to one post or another — Ambassador to the United States,[26] Minister of Education,[27] even Premier[28] — were a staple item in the press almost from the moment that Hu set foot again on Chinese soil. Invariably such reports were followed by more or less emphatic denials on Hu's part of any interest in or talent for political office.[29] In 1946, however, he did stand successfully for election to the Constituent National Assembly that convened in Nanking in November–December for the purpose of drafting the long-awaited "permanent" constitution. The promulgation of that document on the first day of 1947 officially brought to an end the period of political tutelage. Despite the fact that the Assembly had been dominated from first to last by the Kuomintang (neither the Communist party nor the Democratic League had participated in its deliberations), the very act of constitution-making provided, in Hu's view, a sufficient legitimization of Nationalist rule. He declared himself perfectly satisfied as to the "sincerity" of the government's intention to "return political power to the people and enforce constitutional administration," and thereafter he cited China as evidence of the slow but steady worldwide victory of democracy over totalitarianism.[30] In November, running as a nonparty candidate

26. *Chi shih pao* (Peiping), July 19, 1947; CPR:P no. 392:4 (July 21, 1947).

27. *Hsin min pao* (Nanking), March 7, 1947; CPR:N no. 347:1 (March 6–7, 1947); *Ching shih jih-pao* (Peiping), Oct. 15, 1947; CPR:P no. 451:4 (Oct. 15, 1947).

28. *Peiping shih pao* (Peiping), Aug. 31, 1947; CPR:P no. 422:2 (Sept. 2, 1947); *Yi-shih pao* (Peiping), March 19, 1948; CPR:P no. 564:4–5 (March 19, 1948).

29. For example, concerning the ministry of education, *Hsin min pao* (Nanking), March 21, 1947; CPR:N no. 359:5 (March 21, 1947); and concerning the ambassadorship, *Hsin min pao* (Nanking), July 21, 1947; CPR:N no. 469:6 (July 21, 1947).

30. CWR 106.12:357 (Aug. 23, 1947), reprinting the report of a speech that Hu had made at a political rally in Peking, from *Sin Wan Pao (Hsin-wen pao,* Shanghai). See also Hu Shih, "Yen-ch'ien shih-chieh wen-hua ti ch'ü-hsiang"

representing "educational circles," Hu was elected to the National Assembly created by the new constitution. Due to the fact that no further elections to the Assembly were held after the Nationalist government was expelled from the Mainland in 1949, Hu retained his seat in the Assembly until his death fifteen years later.

Among the constitutional duties of the National Assembly was the election of a president and vice-president to head the new government. Shortly before the Assembly convened in Nanking at the end of March 1948, there was speculation that Hu Shih would place himself in candidacy for the vice-presidency; Hu immediately disclaimed any such intention.[31] A few days later events took a more interesting turn when Chiang Kai-shek announced that he would not seek the presidency of a disunited nation. The presidential nominee, said the Generalissimo, should be "a person outside our Party," and he went on to describe in some detail his preferences: "a person who comprehends the essentials of the Constitution . . . a person inspired by the ideals of democracy and imbued with a democratic spirit . . . one who has a profound understanding of our history, culture, and national traditions . . . one who follows world trends and has a rich knowledge of contemporary civilization."[32] Informed sources confirmed the impression that this description had been drawn to fit Hu Shih's qualifications, and there is evidence to suggest that Chiang did indeed try to persuade Hu to accept the office.[33] If so, he was unsuccessful. It came as no real surprise when Chiang himself was elected to the presidency in mid-April. The vice-presidential election did produce unexpected results, however, when the Generalissimo's personal choice, Sun Fo, was defeated by the independent-minded old warlord Li Tsung-jen, a man distrusted by the party's ruling cliques and generally regarded as the candidate of disaffected "liberals" inside and outside the party organization. In May Hu Shih, who had played a substantial role in

(The direction in which contemporary world culture is tending), a radio talk delivered in the summer of 1947, printed in Hu Shih, *Wo-men pi-hsü hsüan-tse wo-men-ti fang-hsiang* (We must choose our course; Hong Kong, 3rd printing, 1957), 11.

31. *Peiping jih-pao* (Peiping), March 18, 1948; CPR:P no. 563:4 (March 18, 1948). Hu's denial: *Hsin min pao* (Peiping), March 19, 1948; CPR:P no. 564:4 (March 19, 1948).

32. Text of Chiang Kai-shek's speech to the Central Executive Committee of the KMT, April 4, 1948, is given in White Paper, 847–848.

33. White Paper 849, 851. See also CWR 109.6:170 (April 10, 1948); *New York Times*, April 5, 1948, 1.

the organizational meetings of the Assembly, and who may have had a hand in Li's election, retired once more to Peking and Peita.[34]

There are several possible explanations for this somewhat bizarre effort to elevate Hu Shih to such high office. The American ambassador, Dr. J. Leighton Stuart, surmised that Chiang might genuinely have preferred to forsake the presidency, an office without broad executive powers under the new constitution, in favor of the premiership, where he would exert a more immediate influence on the conduct of government.[35] It is also possible that Chiang was responding directly to pressure from Stuart himself: shortly before the National Assembly was scheduled to meet, the ambassador had taken the unusual step of publicly rebuking the Kuomintang leadership for not making better use of enlightened and liberal intellectuals.[36] Certainly the same considerations which had made Hu an attractive choice as China's emissary in Washington a decade earlier — his intimate associations with America over the years, his thorough understanding of the American scene, and the respect in which he was held in the United States — must have seemed just as important in the postwar years, when to an ever greater degree the survival of the Nationalist government was contingent upon American economic and military assistance.

But if these qualifications recommended Hu to the Generalissimo and his American advisers, they served to do irreparable injury to his reputation among Chinese students and intellectuals, for whom the American presence in China and American partisanship in Chinese politics provided inflammatory issues throughout the postwar period.[37] The Communists, of course, had identified Hu as the

34. On Hu's role in the National Assembly see White Paper, 846, 854, and 907.

35. J. Leighton Stuart, *Fifty Years in China*, 193. Hu Shih may have suggested this idea to Stuart; see White Paper, 846. In this connection it is interesting to note that the National Assembly invested the presidential office with broad "emergency powers" the day before Chiang finally accepted the position.

36. The text of Stuart's "personal message to the people of China," issued on the occasion of the presentation of the China Aid Bill to the U.S Congress in February 1948, is given in White Paper, 985–987.

37. On the rise of anti-Americanism see Thurston Griggs, *Americans in China: Some Chinese Views* (Washington, D.C., 1948), a survey of the Peking press in 1947; and Dorothy Borg, "America Loses Chinese Good Will," *Far Eastern Survey*, 18.4:37–45 (Feb. 23, 1949). Two or three particularly unpleasant issues thrust themselves above the generally troubled surface of Sino-American relations in the postwar years. The first of these was the celebrated "Peiping rape case," the alleged molestation of a Peita girl student by American Marines

servant of imperialistic interests long before.[38] In 1947 and 1948, as the United States came to seem more and more the only prop to an increasingly unpopular government and hence implicated in its shortcomings, it became common, especially among the radical younger generation, to associate Hu Shih with the "imperialist" designs of the Americans. As one Western observer noted, in assessing the potential political role of the liberal, Western-trained intellectuals, Hu Shih and others like him were better known abroad than in the hinterland of China where the real revolutionary struggle was being waged. Moreover, the same writer continued, "some American-educated scholars who are thought much of in the States stand very low in the eyes of the Chinese students." [39] The students themselves put it in blunter terms: Hu Shih behaves "like a man with a Chinese body but an American brain," proclaimed a student editorial commemorating the twenty-ninth anniversary of the May Fourth movement in 1948. "Some people say that he is actually the American ambassador stationed in Peiping . . . He has changed. Excuse us for our impoliteness, he is no longer a bourgeois scholar.

---

on Christmas Eve, 1946, which provoked protests and demonstrations that lasted throughout the first half of 1947. The second was General Wedemeyer's mission to China in the summer of 1947 and the criticism of the Nationalist government that Wedemeyer was believed to have expressed after his return to the United States. The third crisis grew out of the U.S. policy of assisting in the rehabilitation of the Japanese economy, which inspired great bitterness on the part of Japan's recent victims, especially in the spring and summer of 1948. Hu Shih was compelled to take a stand on each of these issues. In the first instance he was directly involved inasmuch as the victim had been a Peita student, and the university was thus her legal guardian. Hu expressed sympathy with the students and confidence that the American authorities would see justice done. (*Hsin min pao* [Peiping], Dec. 31, 1946; CPR:P no. 232:3 [Dec. 31, 1946]; *Hsin min pao* [Peiping], Jan. 7, 1947; CPR:P no. 237:3 [Jan. 7, 1947].) The defendant, a Marine corporal, was found guilty and sentenced to ten years imprisonment at the first trial in January; he was subsequently cleared of all charges by a naval board of review in June. With respect to the Wedemeyer report, Hu was mildly critical. (*Ho-p'ing jih-pao* [Nanking], Sept. 5, 1947; CPR:N no. 507:3 [Sept. 5, 1947].) On the Japan issue Hu did his best to justify American policy to a skeptical public. Without economic aid, he argued, the distress of the Japanese people would drive them toward Communism; and surely the United States would never permit the Japanese to rearm themselves with aggressive intent. (*Hsin min pao* [Peiping], May 26, 1948; CPR:P no. 622:4 [May 26, 1948]; *Hsin min pao* [Nanking], May 29, 1948; CPR:N no. 706:11 [June 1, 1948]. See also CWR 110.1:26–27 [June 5, 1948], and 110.2:59 [June 12, 1948].)

38. See Appendix C.

39. Charles J. Canning, "What Can China's Liberals Do?" CWR 109.5:135 (April 3, 1948).

He has become a compradore scholar." [40] Thus even before the establishment of the Communist regime and the promulgation of an official line on Hu Shih and his kind, the label had been put on the particular purgatory to which he would be consigned.

Throughout these ruinous years Hu Shih struggled to keep alive the "sense of historical perspective" which in the past he had so often urged upon his young audiences as a source of comfort and strength. "I am a student of history," he wrote in 1947. "If we look at the tendency of world culture from an historical point of view, we see that it is tending in the direction of democratic liberalism [*min-chu tzu-yu*] — that over the last three or four centuries this has been its great objective, its clear aim. The illiberal, antidemocratic totalitarian movements of the last thirty years are, in my own view, only a slight ripple, a slight adverse current. We need not negate the great democratic tide of the last three hundred years merely because of this slight adverse current within it." [41] A little later he wrote again, "Today we Chinese must clearly recognize the tendency of world culture, and we must choose the direction in which we will proceed. Only with freedom can we liberate the spirit of our race, only under democratic government can we bring the strength of our whole people to bear upon the hardships that beset us, only under a liberal democracy will we be able to cultivate a humanistic, civilized society." [42]

But events rapidly outstripped Hu's sense of history. It had fallen upon others to devise the means of liberating the protean energies of the Chinese people and to define the democracy under which they would live — the "New Democracy" of Mao Tse-tung. By the autumn of 1948 the Nationalist cause was lost, at least in north China. In October and November the Communists expelled the last Nationalist armies from Manchuria. By December the cities of the north were no more than isolated Nationalist garrisons, all but engulfed in the rising revolutionary tide. On December 15 Hu Shih flew out of the besieged city of Peking in a plane dispatched by the Generalissimo's personal order. He left behind him his personal library, together with many manuscripts and letters, some parts of

40. Chow Hwa, "Hu Shih and the May Fourth Movement," *Yenching News* (Journalism Department of Yenching University, Peiping, May 3, 1948); CPR:P no. 608:3–4 (May 10, 1948).

41. "Yen-ch'ien shih-chieh wen-hua ti ch'ü-hsiang," 11.

42. Hu Shih, "Wo-men pi-hsü hsüan-tse wo-men-ti fang-hsiang" (We must choose our course), *Wo-men pi-hsü hsüan-tse wo-men-ti fang-hsiang*, 17.

his diaries, and other mementos of the past — and, one may conjecture, a litter of broken hopes. A few days later, on December 17 to be exact, his fifty-seventh birthday, he paid a call on the American ambassador in Nanking. The two men were friends of many years' standing, reaching back into the early twenties when Hu Shih was a young professor at Peita and Stuart was the first president of the newly created Yenching University — happier days for both. Stuart reported to the Secretary of State:

> The conversation with Hu was especially saddening because he represents [the] finest type of patriotic idealism in his attempt to be loyal to [the] Chiang Government. Hu's argument is that Communism is so implacable and intolerant, so diabolically thorough in its indoctrination and so ruthless in enforcing its totalitarian control even in China that Chiang Kai-shek should be supported despite his shortcomings because he alone sees this and has been uncompromising in resisting it, also because he almost alone among KMT leaders has been free from [the] taint of avarice or other typical vices of Chinese officialdom . . . Tears came to his eyes when he asked me, on the basis of our long friendship, to tell him what he should say to President Chiang and what else he could do now that he had determined to give up [his] academic career for service to [the] nation. I told him that [the] primary weakness of [the] Chiang Government was moral rather than military, in [the] sense that troops had lost fighting spirit and people had lost confidence in [the] Government's ability to provide for them as well as in [the] cause for which they were being asked to suffer. America was powerless under these conditions. I had repeatedly urged upon President Chiang [the] supreme importance of rallying public opinion behind him but had failed. I wondered if Hu could lead in another "new thought movement" or "literary revolution" on [the] issues of freedom and democracy as he had done with brilliant success thirty odd years ago. He said he bitterly regretted not having used [his] talents in this field since V-J Day rather than selfishly returning, as he had, to more congenial academic activities.[43]

43. White Paper, 898–899. Ambassador Stuart confided further to the Secretary of State: "This lengthy comment is to prepare [the] way for discussion of our policy if coalition Government will in course of time be formed. Presumably C[ommunist] P[arty] will dominate at [the] outset . . . [But there will be a] necessity for CP to adopt [a] tolerant course at [the] beginning because of

It is not difficult to believe that Hu was genuinely distressed by the spectacle of political and military collapse that he saw around him in the winter of 1948. Nevertheless, his declaration of a determination to sacrifice himself in the Nationalists' cause must be taken at something less than face value. Only a few weeks before his conversation with Ambassador Stuart he had once more declined to accept the premiership, vacated by Weng Wen-hao in the wake of the catastrophic failure of the currency reforms on which he had counted to stabilize the regime. Hu had demurred, reportedly, on the grounds that a scholar who could not even keep his desk in order had no business trying to manage a government. At the end of December Hu again refused an invitation to join the government, this time as Foreign Minister.[44]

In early April 1949, a few weeks before the battle for Shanghai began in earnest, Hu Shih sailed once more from the city of his birth, the city from which he had embarked nearly forty years earlier on his first adventure into the great world beyond and so many times in the intervening years, the city to which he had always returned. He would not return again.

The Communist victory left Hu Shih deeply shaken. He found it easy enough to accept the Nationalists' image of their triumphant adversaries as mindless agents of Soviet imperialism, and he was even willing to exploit his privileged position to convey this view in an article entitled "China in Stalin's Grand Strategy," published in *Foreign Affairs* in October 1950.[45] The refusal of the United States to offer Chiang Kai-shek unconditional and unlimited support in the final crisis had been, in Hu's eyes, a bitter betrayal of historic friendship and righteousness. "The United States was not 'innocent of the blood' of fallen China," Hu intoned, recalling the ceremonial

---

their own limitations. This would doubtless be nothing more than temporary tactics but in that period inter-action between their own ideology and more liberal ideas might have permanent effects." It was an idle dream. The magnitude of the Communist victory then in the making dashed any hope that they might find it expedient to participate in a coalition regime. Even if this had not been the case, it is difficult to imagine either that Hu Shih would have been prepared to serve in such a government or that the Communists would have tolerated his presence.

44. CWR 112.1:18 (Dec. 4, 1948).

45. This view contrasts interestingly with Hu's insistence, fifteen years earlier, that the Chinese Communists were Chinese first and Communists second. See "Pien-chi hou-chi," TLPL no. 142:24 (March 17, 1935).

ablutions of Pontius Pilate.[46] For the most part, however, Hu stood aloof from the rancorous debate on the "China question" that raged in America in the early 1950s.[47] During the nine years that he spent in semi-exile in the United States he remained primarily the scholar, serving for a time as the curator of the Gest Oriental Collection at Princeton University and living otherwise in retirement in New York City, in an apartment piled high with books and manuscripts, the genteel clutter of the life of letters and learning. In 1952–53 he paid a brief visit to Taiwan, where the Nationalists had ensconced themselves after the debacle on the Mainland. He went to Taiwan again in 1954, to attend the sessions of the National Assembly at which Chiang Kai-shek was elected to his second term in the presidency. Then in 1958 Chiang named Hu to the presidency of Academia Sinica, and for once Hu acquiesced to the Generalissimo's wishes. He returned to the island in April and, in the four years that were left to him, exerted himself to improve the facilities for scientific education in Taiwan and to encourage Sino-American scholarly cooperation.

In these last years Hu Shih was without doubt "Free" China's most conspicuous intellectual ornament, the most prestigious survivor of the May Fourth generation on the island, a visible link with the hopeful era of the twenties. He played this role with his

46. J. Leighton Stuart, *Fifty Years in China*, xx.

47. See Charles Wertenbaker and Philip Horton, "The China Lobby," *The Reporter*, 6.8,9 (April 15 and 29, 1952). Hu is referred to as Chiang Kai-shek's "trusted informant on U.S. developments" and is mentioned as an occasional participant in the discussions held by interested parties in New York (6.9:4,7). But his connection with the "Lobby" is not firmly established. Several of his old friends, however, figure prominently in this exposé. Ch'en Chih-mai, Minister Counsellor of the Chinese Embassy, who had been a regular contributor to *Tu-li p'ing-lun*, emerges as one of the more unsavory villains of the piece; T. F. Tsiang, Chinese representative to the U.N., is accused of using his position to channel funds to the "Lobby" — a charge firmly denied by Tsiang a few weeks later (see his letter to the editor, *The Reporter*, 6.12:3–4 [June 10, 1952]); and T. V. Soong, living in exile in Scarsdale, N.Y., is depicted as one of the principal parties involved. In a speech delivered in April 1951, entitled "How to Understand a Decade of Rapidly Deteriorated Sino-American Relations," Hu Shih dissociated himself from one of the fundamental contentions of the China lobbyists, that the "loss of China" to Communism should be attributed primarily to Communist subversion of the U.S. Department of State; rather, Hu argued, the decline of the Nationalists was the result of China's physical and psychological inability to rise to the position of full partnership assigned to her as one of the "Big Four." See *Proceedings of the American Philosophical Society*, 95.4:457–460 (August 1951).

customary grace, urbanity, and good humor. But he could say nothing that he had not said on countless earlier occasions. He could only stir the embers of old antagonisms;[48] he could not kindle a fire to warm the hearts and minds of Taiwan's younger intellectuals. It was not that the battles of an earlier day had been won: there were still some who derided Hu's vision of the spiritual supremacy of modern civilization; there was still ample cause to remind the Nationalist government of the need for the toleration of legitimate dissent; there was still reason to invoke the spirit of "Ibsenism" and to emphasize the importance of independent critical thought. Yet somehow Hu's entry into the lists in behalf of such familiar and beloved causes could not dispel the sense of anachronism.[49] He remained respected by some, as always, and as always there were some who denounced him; but for the most part he was ignored, a peripheral figure despite his eminence. Not even the Communists' sedulous campaign to discredit his life and works, conducted with scrupulous thoroughness and a massive mobilization of intellectual talent in 1955, could cast Hu in an heroic light or lay about his shoulders the mantle of martyrdom.[50]

He was an old man now, in poor and failing health. His heart

48. The most interesting example of this was the publication, a short time before Hu Shih returned to Taiwan in 1958, of a little book entitled *Hu Shih and the Nation's Destiny* (*Hu Shih yü kuo-yün*), a violent attack on Hu's role in discrediting traditional Chinese values. The book appeared anonymously. Subsequent government investigations revealed it to be the work of several hands, among them that of one Hsü Tzu-ming, a man in his seventies, a graduate of the University of Wisconsin and, at one time, a colleague of Hu's at Peita. A typical example of the opinions expressed in this little polemic is found below, Chap. x at n. 9.

49. In 1949 Hu had been one of the founders of the fortnightly magazine *Tzu-yu Chung-kuo* (*Free China*), which served throughout the 1950s as an outlet for the opinions of liberal thinkers in Taiwan and Hong Kong, and which was often cited as evidence of the KMT's willingness to tolerate criticism. In the late summer of 1960, however, the magazine's editor, Lei Chen, himself a one-time confidant of the Generalissimo's, was arrested on insubstantial treason charges, condemned to ten years imprisonment, and deprived of his rights of citizenship. Lei was accused of having associated with Communists many years earlier; the real problem, however, was that Lei and several others connected with *Tzu-yu Chung-kuo* had tended increasingly to couple their demands for the creation of an opposition party with suggestions that the Taiwanese should be granted a greater role in provincial and national politics. Hu Shih, who was abroad at the time of Lei's arrest, protested the act upon his return — but privately, in muted tones, and with no effect whatever.

50. See Appendix C for a brief account of the Communist attack on Hu Shih.

was giving out. Death came quickly and kindly, late in the afternoon of February 24, 1962. After presiding at a reception for newly elected fellows of the Academia Sinica, Hu Shih collapsed and died of a heart attack as he was bidding his guests goodby. His last hours had been fittingly spent in the sociable company of friends and scholars, men who could appreciate him for what he was, and some, perhaps, who could appreciate him also for what he had tried to be. He was accorded an impressive funeral, though more traditional in tone than he might have desired. The flags of Peking National University and the Republic of China were draped over his coffin, and Chiang Kai-shek himself came at the head of numberless mourners to pay his final respects. A tomb was constructed overlooking the low, sprawling buildings of the Academia Sinica in Nankang, some ten miles east of Taipei, and there amidst the green and rugged hills of northern Taiwan, in a setting perhaps not too unlike the mountainous Anhwei countryside he had known as a boy, Hu Shih was laid to rest. So ended a life that had begun, seventy years earlier, in a time so remote in mind and custom that the stages of Hu's journey must be measured not in decades but in centuries.

Chapter 10. The Chinese Renaissance, Chinese Liberalism, and the Chinese Revolution

At the head of the editorial published in the first number of *The Crescent* in March 1928, setting forth the attitude of the sponsors of this new venture, appeared two literary embellishments, in English. The first was from Genesis: "And God said, Let there be light: and there was light." The second was from Shelley: "If Winter comes, can Spring be far behind?" Nothing could express more vividly the temper of the men or of their undertaking than the themes struck here: enlightenment and rebirth. This was the spirit of the Chinese Renaissance.

Looking back over the record of Hu Shih's thoughts and hopes, one is more likely, perhaps, to be reminded of the European Enlightenment than of the Renaissance. Indeed, if it is possible to speak of the Chinese liberals of the 1920s and 1930s as an identifiable group, this is in part because of the degree to which, consciously or unconsciously, this small band of Western-educated scholars, educators, publicists, and professional men reflected certain of the characteristic attitudes of the Enlightenment and embraced some of the values of that age. In Peter Gay's deftly etched "collective portrait" of the European philosophes it is easy to discern an image of the Chinese liberals of the prewar decades. The philosophe, as Gay describes him, "was a cosmopolitan by conviction as well as by training. Like the ancient Stoic, he would exalt the interest of mankind above the interest of country or clan." And again, "The typical philosophe . . . was a cultivated man, a respectable scholar and scientific amateur, . . . rarely ponderous and generally superbly articulate." Nor does the comparison stop there. "Such a type could flourish only in the city," Gay observes, "and in fact the typical philosophe was eminently, defiantly, incurably urban . . . The best of the urban spirit — experimental, mobile, irreverent — was in the philosophes' bones." [1]

Not only in matters of personal and intellectual style may the "enlightened" Chinese of the twentieth century be likened to the purveyors of enlightenment in eighteenth-century Europe, but in their intellectual concerns as well. Like the great figures of the European Enlightenment, the Chinese liberals of Hu Shih's generation tended to be historians — not necessarily in any narrowly technical sense, but in their general inclination to frame an understanding of the present in terms of the past and in their desire to locate their own place along history's progressive march. They shared, too, a specific interest in the condition of the mind as the key to an assessment of any age. "Whatever history the Enlightenment historians pursued," Gay observes, "they focused their attention on the rise and decline of the philosophic party, on the fortunes of criticism." [2] In their prejudices, even, there is a common element. The touch of arrogance that Gay perceives as a flaw in the intellect of the Enlightenment finds its reflection in the self-conscious "tough-mindedness" of China's liberals: "They never wholly discarded that final, most

1. Peter Gay, *The Enlightenment: An Interpretation. The Rise of Modern Paganism* (New York, 1967), 13–16.
2. *Ibid.*, 34.

stubborn illusion that bedevils realists — the illusion that they were free from illusions." [3]

Even the most informative analogy, however, has its limits. Despite a common appreciation of the function of skeptical criticism, a common urbanity and cosmopolitanism, a common self-assurance, the men who made the Chinese Renaissance cannot be fully understood in terms of the European Enlightenment. The first reservation that one must enter is, of course, the most obvious: Europe in the eighteenth century and China in the first half of the twentieth century present vastly different spectacles. The philosophe moved in an environment more congenial to his purposes than was the fortune of his Chinese epigone. The philosophes, Gay tells us, "preached to a Europe half prepared to listen to them . . . The war they fought was half won before they joined it." [4] No such happy verdict is in order with respect to the endeavors of the liberal Chinese intellectuals of the twenties and thirties. When they enlisted to fight on the side of reasonable and orderly change, the final issue of the struggle was still much in doubt; and the victory they sought seemed to them closer when they stepped to the fore invigorated by the spirit of the May Fourth era than it did when they retired, their ranks thinned by death and defection, a generation later.

This is not to say, of course, that the Chinese were unprepared to heed voices that called for change. It was the nature of that change which divided them — its dimensions, its purpose, the price that should be paid to bring it into being. On these issues there was bitter difference of opinion, only superficially masked by the agreement within the ranks of the innovators that China's traditional culture was unfit to survive in a changed world or to insure the survival of the nation itself. It was generally conceded that China must become "modern." But there was little agreement on a definition of "traditional culture" — whether to construe the term broadly or narrowly, whether to eradicate the tradition root and branch or only to prune away the deadwood. Nor was there agreement concerning the changing nature of the world beyond China to which the Chinese must reconcile themselves — whether this promised the liberation of mankind or threatened its enslavement under a new tyranny, economic, political, or spiritual. Nor, finally, was there agreement on the significance of "modernity" — whether to define it in terms of national

3. *Ibid.*, 27.
4. *Ibid.*, 21–23.

power or individual dignity, or how to balance these values against each other. Only Hu Shih and some of his liberal friends, striving to unfetter the spirit of criticism, to emancipate the individual, and to set China's problems against the wider horizons of human progress, were disposed to equate modernization with enlightenment.

In another and even more significant way the Enlightenment provided no parallel to China. Wittingly or no, the philosophes ushered in a revolutionary age. But the enterprise of the Enlightenment had been, in part, to refurbish a structure still regarded as admirable in many of its essentials. In this respect it was an undertaking closer in spirit to the great reform movements that had from time to time swept through the Confucian world than to the post-Confucian Renaissance promoted by Chinese liberals. For the philosophes, as for Confucian reformers, classical antiquity remained a source of inspiration, "the useful and beloved past," in Peter Gay's apt phrase.[5] The enlightened intellectuals of the May Fourth era in China, on the contrary, entangled in the emotional and intellectual crises of a revolution in process, were compelled partly by conviction and partly by circumstance to cut themselves off from China's classical tradition and from much of their own history. Picking their way amongst the rubble of institutions and beliefs that had been purposefully destroyed or had fallen under their own weight as other buttresses to the traditional edifice were demolished, the Chinese liberals found little to salvage. Historical-minded they were, but they sought *their* place on a universal scale of human progress. So, of course, had the philosophes — but they had not felt constrained to discriminate too carefully between what was natural to mankind in general and what was natural only to Europeans. Thus while the philosophes, for all their cosmopolitanism, remained essentially Westerners, the Chinese liberals were Westernizers, even though the designation rankled at times; and while the philosophes were early moderns without being aware of the fact, their Chinese counterparts were self-consciously modernizers.

Even more than the Enlightenment, the European Renaissance offered an inspiration which the intellectuals of the May Fourth era consciously exploited. The theme of rebirth runs like a silver thread through the literature of those years, though often the appeal was emotive rather than analytical. Hu Shih was more careful than many of his contemporaries to use the term in a strict historical con-

5. *Ibid.*, book one, *passim*.

text, for he attached particular significance to it. As a pragmatist he was committed to the belief that the new could flourish only if it were grafted onto a living historical experience. Motivated less by a lingering affection for any part of China's past than by a concern for the survival of what must come in its stead, he tried to sift out from China's vast historical inheritance those elements that he believed would prove compatible with the modern attitudes he desired to see established in China. His belief that the future must come not as a rupture with the past but as a fulfillment of its promise encouraged him to discover numerous parallels between China's modern experience and the European Renaissance. The Chinese Renaissance, he wrote in 1933, was a "conscious movement to promote a new literature in the living language of the people to take the place of the classical literature of old"; "a movement of conscious protest against many of the ideas and institutions in the traditional culture, and of conscious emancipation of the individual man and woman from the bondage of the forces of tradition"; "a movement of reason versus tradition, freedom versus authority, and glorification of life and human values versus their suppression." "And lastly," he concluded, "strange enough, this new movement was led by men who knew their cultural heritage and tried to study it with the new methodology of modern historical criticism and research. In that sense it was also a humanist movement." Thus Hu was led to the confident prediction that the Chinese Renaissance "promised and pointed to the new birth of an old people and an old civilization." [6]

Yet it is precisely on this last point that the validity of Hu's comparison comes into question. The same sense of disjunction from the past which distinguishes the spirit of the Chinese Renaissance from that of the Enlightenment limits also the acceptability of the European Renaissance as a model for the Chinese. "The new birth of an old people" was indeed the end Hu sought, not through the rebirth of an old civilization in any but a rhetorical sense, but through the creation of a new civilization. His own early understanding of the idea of the European Renaissance underlines this perception of its significance. The term "Renaissance," he noted in his diary in 1917, "has been translated in the past as 'the period of a revival in arts and letters' [wen-i-fu-hsing shih-tai], but I think this inadequate to convey the full significance, and not as good as a

6. *The Chinese Renaissance*, 44.

318

direct translation of the original meaning." The translation Hu proposed, therefore, was *tsai-sheng shih-tai,* meaning literally "the period of being born again." [7] From the moment of his return he devoted his energy to the task of introducing into China a *new* thought, a *new* spirit of individual and social responsibility, a *new* culture. Despite his profound temperamental and intellectual aversion to violent change and his enduring hope to conserve wisely rather to destroy indiscriminately, his own demand for "a transvaluation of all values" was, as noted earlier, a declaration of emancipation from the past in its entirety.

Rejection of the past, then, is a pervasive element in Hu Shih's thought and in the temper of Chinese liberalism generally, constituting its closest link with the radicalism of the May Fourth period. It is this that has inspired an attack on the liberal position by those who can explain the misfortunes that have befallen China only as a result of the abandonment of traditional values and virtues. Among the foremost of such critics has been the man whose political wisdom Hu Shih so often challenged in the 1920s and the 1930s, Generalissimo Chiang Kai-shek. Chiang's critique of the liberal position conveys concisely a sense of the conservative reaction that helped to undermine the liberal cause. In *China's Destiny,* written in the early 1940s, Chiang observed:

> After the May 4th Movement, the ideas of Liberalism [Democracy] and Communism spread throughout the country. But those that advocated these ideas had no real knowledge of the enduring qualities of Chinese culture; they were simply looking for something new. Moreover, they merely endeavored to copy the superficial aspects of Western civilization without attempting to adopt its basic principles for the benefit of the Chinese econ-

7. *Diary,* 1155–1156. This observation was prompted by Hu's reading of Edith Sichel's *The Renaissance,* Home University Library of Modern Knowledge, no. 87 (New York and London, 1915), the book with which he whiled away the hours as his train made its slow way from Portal, N.D. across the Canadian Rockies toward Vancouver in June 1917. Most of his attention was directed toward the literary movements of the Renaissance. But undoubtedly his interest was caught also by Miss Sichel's evocation of the Renaissance as "the time when man was, as it were, re-created more glorious than before, with a body naked and unashamed, and a strong arm, unimpaired by fasting, outstretched towards life and light" (p. 7), and by her salute to the passing of that age: "Yet nothing that has lived can live in vain. From the chaotic decay of the great creative period came forth, at first unrecognized, the new-born spirit of the modern world — the spirit of criticism and of science" (p. 162).

omy and the people's livelihood. As a result, the educated classes and scholars [i.e., the remnants of the traditional gentry] generally lost their self-respect and self-confidence. Wherever the influence of these ideas prevailed, the people regarded everything foreign as right and everything Chinese as wrong . . . [The liberals'] ideas circulated widely and disturbed the people. But . . . their ideas and proposals did not coincide with our nation's psychology and character . . . The struggle between Liberalism and Communism . . . was merely a reflection of the opposition of Anglo-American theories to those of Soviet Russia . . . The people that promoted them forgot that they were Chinese and that they should study and apply foreign theories for the benefit of China. As a result their copying [of Western theories] only caused the decay and ruin of Chinese civilization, and made it easy for the imperialists to carry on cultural aggression.[8]

Similar criticism, more personal in intent and far more abusive in tone — in obvious consequence of the catastrophes that had befallen the conservative cause in the postwar years — greeted Hu Shih upon his return to Taiwan in 1958. In the spring of that year a slender, anonymous pamphlet appeared mysteriously on the bookstalls of Taipei, bearing the title *Hu Shih and the Nation's Destiny (Hu Shih yü kuo-yün)*. The following is not untypical of the sentiments expressed therein: "Hu Shih . . . by destroying our national thought [*min-tsu ssu-hsiang*] threw open our frontiers and let the Communist bandits hand over the broad expanses of China to the Russian big-noses as a satellite . . . With no weapons save his pen and a few foreign phrases he was able within the short span of thirty or forty years . . . to arrange matters in such a way that the descendants of the Yellow Emperor will soon disappear from the face of the earth, leaving no trace behind them." [9]

Despite great differences in ideological inspiration and political motivation, such assessments of the liberal position and of Hu Shih's role in the intellectual reform movement share much with Chinese Communist attacks on Hu made in the 1950s, in which he was de-

8. Chiang Kai-shek, *China's Destiny*, with notes by Philip Jaffe (London, 1947), 98–100.

9. Chu Kuang-han, "Ch'ing k'an k'ung-ch'ien-ti Hu Shih po-shih ho wo tsen-yang p'ei-fu t'a ti li-yu" (Please look at the unprecedented Dr. Hu Shih and my reasons for respecting him as I do), in *Hu Shih yü kuo-yün* (Hu Shih and the nation's destiny; Taipei, 1958), 11–12.

nounced as a "cultural compradore" and "an accomplice in the slaughter of our cultural and intellectual elements." [10] By the 1950s the Chinese Communists had left the cosmopolitanism of the May Fourth era far behind them. What had survived after a quarter of a century in the wilderness was not the sweeping iconoclasm of Ch'en Tu-hsiu but a brand of cultural nationalism intellectually foreshadowed, perhaps, in the thought of Li Ta-chao[11] and nourished through the perilous years of exile. The regime triumphantly established in Peking still claimed an alien doctrine as its inspiration and paid respectful homage to the foreign prophets of this creed. But the Communists were no more open than the Nationalists had been to the suggestion that China's past was useful primarily as a negative example. "China is a great nation," wrote Mao Tse-tung in 1939, "with an immense population, a long history, a rich revolutionary tradition and a splendid historical heritage." [12] Whereas the Kuomintang had based its cultural nationalism on the discredited values of Confucianism and the gentry culture of the vanished empire, however, the Chinese Communists linked their movement to the "popular" culture that had flourished — they asserted — unrecognized or despised beneath the surface of the "feudal" culture of imperial China.[13] Ironically, in their discovery of a reputable tradition to serve as an alternative focus of loyalty, the Communists owed a considerable debt to the "systematization of the national heritage" in which Hu Shih had played such a prominent role in the twenties and thirties. For it had been Hu, in his tireless search for Chinese antecedents that might ease the strain of cultural innovation, who had first suggested the existence of a submerged tradition of greater historical significance than the Confucian tradition itself. If the Communists recognized their debt to Hu, they repaid it only in abuse, castigating him as an agent of American cultural imperialism and a traitor to Chinese culture.

There would be little to be gained from a study of the liberal position in China if the conclusion could so easily be reduced to the verdict of "cultural treason." But the facts are otherwise. Despite the antitraditionalism of the liberal viewpoint, despite the cosmopoli-

10. Tientsin *Chin-pu jih-pao,* Dec. 27, 1951; *Current Background,* no. 167 (March 25, 1952).

11. Meisner, *Li Ta-chao,* 263.

12. Mao Tse-tung, "The Chinese Revolution and the Chinese Communist Party," *Selected Works* (Peking, 1965), II, 307.

13. J. R. Levenson, *Confucian China and Its Modern Fate,* I, 134–145.

tanism that set Hu Shih in dogged opposition to the official nationalism of his time, despite his sometimes uncritical admiration for much that was western, Hu never forgot that he was a Chinese nor abandoned the belief that his own particular "foreign theories" would prove beneficial to his people. Though his diagnosis of China's infirmities differed from theirs in almost every detail, he was no less committed than were the most fervent self-proclaimed nationalists to the search for a remedy that would restore the patient to health. What set Hu Shih apart from both the conservative and the radical practitioners of nationalism, then, was not an indifference on his part to China's fate, though it must be conceded that the dispassionate reasonableness of his attitude could be, and often was, mistaken for indifference. One senses a hostility to China's liberals, especially on the part of the radical Left, that brings to mind Bernard Shaw's wry commentary on the responses of revolutionary socialists toward the British Fabians, a group whose intellectual style Hu greatly admired. "Our preference for practical suggestions and criticisms," wrote Shaw, "and our impatience of all general expressions of sympathy with working-class aspirations, not to mention our way of chaffing our opponents in preference to denouncing them as enemies of the human race, repelled from us some warmhearted and eloquent Socialists, to whom it seemed callous and cynical to be even commonly self-possessed in the presence of the sufferings upon which Socialists make war." [14]

What divided Hu from so many of his contemporaries was an irreconcilable difference of opinion as to how best to insure China's survival as a nation and as a culture. This disagreement colored every aspect of Hu's thinking. Of primary importance to the history of liberal ideas in China, however, is the influence that this had on Hu Shih's understanding of politics and the political process. For not the least striking of his accomplishments was the enunciation of a "modern" theory of politics consonant with the values of individual dignity and intellectual independence which were, in his view, the indispensable components of national and cultural regeneration.

This claim may seem at first sight unwarranted. Despite Hu's insistence that he had cherished throughout his life "a disinterested

14. *Fabian Tract No. 41,* cited in A. M. McBriar, *Fabian Socialism and English Politics, 1884–1918* (Cambridge, Eng., 1962), 12.

interest in politics as a civic duty of an educated man," [15] it is difficult not to interpret his consistent disparagement of "political" problems and his narrow definition of "political" action as indications of a distaste for politics that led him to misjudge the political demands and opportunities of his time. It has frequently been said that liberalism was inoperative as a system of political beliefs and a guide to political action in China — or, in the language of the charge that Hu once laid against the utopian anarchists, that liberalism "offered no starting place." Hu and the liberals have been condemned as intellectual elitists who attached too great an importance to the definition of "problems" through rigorous intellectual analysis and remained insensitive to the greater and more nebulous "fundamental" issues of their times. The liberals, it has further been argued, were blinded, by their preference for dealing with the "specific" and the "concrete," from perceiving the true dimensions of China's agony and putting forward a reform program adequate to the need. The liberals' attitude toward political movements has been interpreted as a reflection of an underlying distrust of the "masses," and a contempt for the intellectual waywardness of the common people. So, for example, it has been suggested that the program of gradual reform promoted by Hu Shih and John Dewey was "neither conservative nor radical but largely irrelevant" in the context of "the total crisis of Chinese society." [16] And it has been argued that by their failure to communicate with the masses the westernized liberal intellectuals yielded "their moral and political leadership [and] promoted, by default, the rise of totalitarian rule in China." [17] This pervasive sense of the irrelevance of the liberal prescription for China was more cogently expressed in the acid comment, made as long ago as the early 1930s, that Hu Shih "never scratched where it itched." [18]

These are serious criticisms in that they touch upon genuine weaknesses of the liberal position. The problems posed by the liberals' reluctance to engage in political activity and the shortcomings of the liberal analysis of China's condition will be dealt with shortly. But first the ground must be cleared by assessing the contribution

15. Oral History, 42.
16. Meisner, Li Ta-chao, 107–108.
17. Y. C. Wang, Chinese Intellectuals and the West, 420–421, 502–503.
18. Yeh Ch'ing, Hu Shih p'i-p'an (A critique of Hu Shih; Shanghai, 1933), 863.

that Hu Shih and his circle made to a new understanding of the nature of political life.

"Politics," writes Bernard Crick, "are the public actions of free men. Freedom is the privacy of men from public actions." [19] The distinction suggested here reduces to the briefest possible expression an issue that has been one of the most persistently perplexing to Western political thinkers since the decline of the Greek city-states: the problem of defining the relationship between what is legitimately within the realm of public concern, relevant to the life of the community as a whole and hence subject to the jurisdiction of those in positions of political authority, and what remains private and within the realm of individual judgment and the dictates of individual conscience. Such a distinction is virtually absent from the great body of traditional Chinese political literature. On the contrary, Confucian theory implicitly denied the propriety of discriminating between public and private values: the same moral qualities that were presumed to inform the character of the superior man were attributed to the virtuous ruler and became by extension the public values of the well-governed state. In practice, moreover, no claim to "privacy from public actions" could stand against the awful authority of the imperial sovereign. The Confucian-educated bureaucrat-scholar possessed no status as a private person, protected by right or custom from the demands his imperial master might lay upon him. Those centers of social organization and activity that remained outside the formal structure of governmental authority — for example, family and clan organizations and the local gentry groups which bore some of the responsibilities of local government — were by long tradition expected to discharge certain functions of social control compatible with the maintenance of imperial order. "Private loyalties" (*ssu-chung*), that is, loyalty to clan above emperor, or to province above empire, were by definition subversive of that order. The only acceptable alternative to the kind of political engagement expected of the Confucian elite was retreat into a life of scholarly or contemplative seclusion; but this was clearly a means of escape, a tacit acknowledgment of the unchallengeable pervasiveness of imperial power in the world at large.

If the distinction between public and private is one of the essential conditions of politics, then the government of Confucian China, for all its imposing administrative accomplishments, must be ad-

19. Bernard Crick, *In Defence of Politics* (Baltimore, 1964), 18.

judged to have constituted something other than a political order. Turn-of-the-century reformist literature lends credence, at least obliquely, to this seemingly improbable conclusion. A consideration of the qualities of the modern state quickly led Liang Ch'i-ch'ao and Yen Fu and the propagandists of the T'ung-meng hui into extended discussions of the relationship between public and private interests, for the sense of common purpose on which depended, in their view, China's survival as a nation required a clearer definition of what must be the public concern than Confucian literature provided. These early writers, however, remained largely preoccupied with the sphere of public action; private interests existed for them more as a logical corollary than as a social or political value to be given systematic expression. Individualism was attractive to them because it offered a means to the desired end of "wealth and power" — that is, national survival.

It was left to the intellectuals of Hu Shih's generation to shift the emphasis from public action to freedom — to conclude, in other words, that political systems must be evaluated not only in terms of the ends ascribed to them but also in terms of the processes that maintain them. Only with the emergence of this awareness of politics as a process may one begin to speak of liberalism in China in specific and meaningful fashion. It was their attachment to means rather than ends that made Hu Shih and his fellow liberals "republicans" and "democrats" in a manner in which the men who had engineered the republican revolution in 1911, or subsequently laid claim to it, had not been, since for the revolutionaries the end of nation-building always remained more important than the republican means they had chosen to achieve it. Similarly, it was this attachment that gave the liberals their typically utilitarian and instrumentalist view of political institutions, whether borrowed from Dewey or from Laski or from J. S. Mill, or rooted in other, less easily identifiable sources. And, finally, it was this that prompted them to equate individualism with skepticism, with the capacity for critical thought, in order that the individual might be enabled to steer clear of philosophies that made more of ends than of means.

The guiding principle behind Hu Shih's whole system of beliefs was unquestionably this capacity for criticism, the importance of intellectual independence. It may be useful to pause here long enough to review the fundamental tenets of that creed.

Hu Shih believed, first of all, that the world, the workings of nature, environment, the very universe itself are comprehensible because they can be understood by reason. He believed that it is possible for men to achieve an ever-deepening understanding of the mechanisms that bind the universal order together, and that, once it has yielded its secrets to the inquiring mind, environment can be controlled and directed by human intelligence. Man, Hu believed, is endowed with the power of rational response that will enable him to shape his world to his own purposes, becoming more than the servant of events and environment — the creator of a civilization that will allow him to give expression to the finest talent that is within him.

History, Hu asserted, is but the record of this accomplishment, of the changes wrought by human endeavor. History is, in Hu's view, purposive if not rigidly deterministic, its purpose being the realization of man's capacity for rational thought and the consequent maturing of a civilization founded on the complementary principles of "science" and "democracy." The first of these terms Hu took to mean, in a general way, a constant alertness to the fluid movement of ideas and beliefs and a perpetual willingness to abandon one view of the "facts" for another that might, in the light of altered circumstances, prove more useful. He was disposed to think of democracy less as a specific institutional system than as a state of mind, an extension into the sphere of political and social life of the tolerant and critical spirit of science, though he did not slight the importance of democratic institutions as a means of preventing political abuse and insuring the preservation of sufficient standards of political, social, and intellectual liberty.

These were the components of Hu Shih's essentially optimistic world view. It was this steady optimism, in turn, that gave him the courage to advocate an approach to China's problems promising no quick and certain solutions but looking ahead to a time generations hence when China would achieve the means of creating and maintaining a genuinely free society. Freedom, in this sense, was for Hu the precondition of modernity; it was also synonymous with it.

Seeking to ally himself with the purpose of history as he understood it, Hu set himself resolutely against all arbitrary intellectual authority, against the claims of dogma and orthodoxy, ancient and contemporary, that would impede the free movement of the mind. "Blind following" and "conformity" were, in his view, patently evil, the real enemies of progress. His tireless advocacy of criticism had as

326

its ultimate justification the desire to enable the Chinese to move with the times in which they must live, to comprehend the nature of the momentous changes that were taking place in China and in the world beyond, to become the masters of their history, not, as in the disastrous century just behind them, its slaves.

Hu Shih was not alone in assigning primacy to intellectual reform as a first step toward the creation of a new political and social order. When Sun Yat-sen wrote, "Mind is the beginning of everything that happens in the world," [20] he expressed an opinion that had been deeply imbedded in the Confucian mentality and that remained, implicitly or explicitly, a principle of all Chinese reformers, even the most antitraditional. Indeed, perhaps the most distinctive feature of the Chinese revolutionary experience as a whole has been the preoccupation of the men who have led it at various times with the problem of recasting individual moral character in conformity with new visions of ultimate social good. Liang Ch'i-ch'ao's concern for the creation of a "new people," Chiang Kai-shek's enthusiasm for the archaic principles of the New Life movement, and Mao Tse-tung's attempts to forge a revolutionary personality on the anvil of the Cultural Revolution — all these have reflected a common conviction that men's minds must be made over before the conditions of their lives can change.

Where Hu Shih differed, then, was not in placing greater emphasis on the importance of intellectual change but in the substance of the change that he encouraged. Hu's vision of the new individual — critical, tolerant, creative, intellectually his own master, seeking to mold his natural and cultural surroundings to suit his own benign purposes, and thus moving ever toward richer and more satisfying life experiences — gave expression to an ideal that had no precedent in the traditions of Chinese social thought and found no echo among Hu's adversaries of the radical extremes. It is, however, a vision that lies close to the heart of modern liberal theory. Hobhouse stated it eloquently in 1911 in his classic definition of the "new" liberalism: "Liberalism is the belief that society can safely be founded on this self-directing power of personality, that it is only on this foundation that a true community can be built, and that so established its foundations are so deep and so wide that there is no limit that we can place to the extent of the building. Liberty then becomes not so much a right of the individual as a necessity of society. It rests not on the

20. Sun Yat-sen, *Memoirs of a Chinese Revolutionary*, vii.

claim of A to be let alone by B, but on the duty of B to treat A as a rational being . . . The rule of liberty is just the application of the rational method. It is the opening of the door to the appeal of reason, of imagination, of social feeling; and except through the response to this appeal there is no assured progress of society." [21] It is not beyond the bounds of possibility that Hu Shih encountered this statement at some point during his years at Cornell or Columbia. In any case, he found in Dewey a similar inclination to speak of liberalism as a state of mind, an intellectual discipline conducive to the maintenance of democratic social structures. Dewey, as might be expected, gave particular emphasis to the dynamic potential of liberalism. For him, the liberal habit of mind was itself the key to an understanding of social change: "As a social philosophy, 'liberalism' runs the gamut of which a vague temper of mind — often called forward-looking — is one extreme, and a definite creed as to the purposes and methods of social action is the other. The first is too vague to afford any steady guide in action; the other is so specific and fixed as to result in dogma, and thus to end in an illiberal mind. Liberalism as a method of experimentation based on insight into both social desires and actual conditions, escapes this dilemma. It signifies the adoption of the scientific habit of mind in application to social affairs." [22]

This statement embodies the essentials of Hu Shih's conception of liberalism — or, as he was more apt to call it, "democracy." And this leads to a final aspect of Hu's understanding of politics: the belief that politics cannot be dissociated from a specific context, or, in other words, the belief that politics must involve not only the institutions and processes of government but also the social and cultural environment in which institutions exist and processes operate. Here once again a tenuous continuity links the modern iconoclast with the tradition that he strove to discredit. The fundamental assumption of Confucian social theory was that the people's response to government will be conditioned by environment: it was the obligation of the Confucian monarch, therefore, to create an environment of virtue that would allow the people to live in accordance with their benign social instincts. But the parallel is deceptive. Confucians had emphasized especially the importance of material cir-

---

21. L. T. Hobhouse, *Liberalism* (London, 1911), 123.

22. John Dewey, "Justice Holmes and the Liberal Mind," cited in George Raymond Geiger, *John Dewey in Perspective*, 171.

cumstances: "If [the people] have a secure livelihood, they will have a secure mind," said Mencius.[23] Chinese liberals, on the other hand, typically stressed the influences that contribute to the shaping of a free intellectual environment: education, the right to hold one's own opinions, the right to dissent, the need for toleration. For Hu, as for Dewey, the final test of the value of social and political institutions is "the extent to which they educate every individual into the full stature of his possibility." [24] But Hu, and the liberals generally, rejected as firmly as Dewey did the claim of government to set the limits of this possibility. It was the business of government to maintain institutions useful to the individual in his effort to realize his own potential, but not to define the standards by which individual excellence, individual virtue, would be judged. Thus Hu and the liberals affirmed the legitimacy of *private* opinion, and the importance of "freedom from public action." Hu's indefatigable efforts to nurture what Hobhouse referred to as "the appeal of reason, imagination, and social feeling," his enduring belief in the ultimate trustworthiness of individual opinion, and his steadfast refusal to equate "loyalty" and "conformity" thoroughly justify his claim (a claim made more often for him than by him) to stand as a representative of liberal aspirations.

Liberalism, however, for all its concern with social attitudes and its interest in the individual, is primarily an approach to the solution of political problems — that is, a manner of conducting public life. In light of this, what was the significance of Hu Shih's consistent inclination to minimize the importance of "politics," to restrict the range of "political" issues, and to remain, in his activities and associations, "above politics"? To many this has seemed a fatal flaw in Hu's position, at best an overly fastidious detachment from "reality," at worst (as in the Communists' view of the matter) a deliberate attempt to obscure and falsify "reality." With considerable justification these critics point out that the governments to which Hu and his fellow liberals offered their high-minded and unsolicited advice remained manifestly unreceptive to the standards of conduct thus urged upon them, and that the "public opinion" on which the liberals relied so heavily was neither forceful enough nor sufficiently articulate to accomplish the supervisory function they assigned to it.

23. *Mencius,* T'ang wen-kung (shang iii); the translation here follows Wing-tsit Chan, *A Source Book in Chinese Philosophy* (Princeton, 1963), 66.
24. John Dewey, *Reconstruction in Philosophy,* 186.

The liberals thus condemned themselves to the frustrations of perpetual powerlessness, this argument concludes, and courted inevitable defeat.

It is indisputable that Hu and his group were men without power in any real sense in a time when power was computed almost exclusively in terms of physical force. And it is true that although Hu's vision of China's future condition transcended China's present no less than did the vision of the most idealistic revolutionaries, Hu remained, in sharp contrast to the revolutionaries, dependent for the realization of his vision upon the functioning of the very institutions that were to be transcended. It must be conceded, moreover, that in China liberalism provided slight impetus to social action: it failed, by and large, despite a transitory intellectual following, to excite an emotional commitment to solutions sought in the liberal (or pragmatic) fashion, and it offered an insufficient sense of direction, at least in the short run — which was, after all, what the Chinese became more and more concerned with as conditions degenerated to the point of total confusion and despair.

Several questions arise inescapably at this juncture. Was the frailty of the liberal cause, and the vulnerability of the liberals themselves, the result of a misunderstanding on their part of some essential element of liberal doctrine? Did Hu Shih misrepresent the liberal approach, thus robbing it of an efficacy it might otherwise have had? Or was the weakness of liberalism and the liberals inherent in the creed itself, a flaw magnified in significance, perhaps, by the extraordinary conditions that prevailed in China and the awesome handicaps against which the liberals struggled? Was Hu Shih, then, the victim of his own beliefs and of his age? Or, finally, if (as seems likely) an answer to these questions cannot be given in terms of alternatives that exclude each other, how may a proper balance be struck between them?

Liberalism, as suggested earlier, may be conceived of as a certain kind of response to political problems, a response based on characteristic values and predicated on a characteristic conception of the problems themselves and of the processes that will be employed in their solution. Politics, in the liberal view of it, is the process of easing the conflicts that are presumed inevitably to exist in society through a continuous adjustment of contending interests. Behind this seemingly simple proposition lurks a subtle and problematical notion, a paradox well expressed by Rousseau: "For if the establishment of societies has been made necessary by the antagonism that exists between particular interests, it has been made possible by the conformity that exists between these same interests. The bond of society is what there is in common between these different interests, and if there were not some point in which all interests were identical, no society could exist." [25] In the tradition out of which Rousseau came and to which he gave further impetus, the great problem of politics — or of political theorists — has been the problem of how to discover the point at which interests converge, the point at which the common good assumes precedence over individual goods. To a significant degree, liberal values are no more than a reflection of liberal methods in seeking to determine this point. Thus, for example, the liberal values moderation because he is accustomed to thinking in terms of problems that are amenable to moderate solutions, that is, solutions achieved by the reconciliation of interests that are not fundamentally divergent. The liberal values freedom because to his way of thinking freedom — especially the freedom of the mind — serves most reliably to lead men toward the discovery of the grounds of such reconciliation. The liberal values law, or the rule of law, because he believes that it provides the most satisfactory means of structuring the process of reconciliation. An attachment to liberal values, then, suggests a corrresponding acceptance of liberal presuppositions concerning the nature of political problems and the functioning of the political process. Liberalism as a value system is largely empirical in its origins: liberal principles are essentially statements of expectation based on common social and political experience, statements of what it is possible to achieve by certain means under certain circumstances. As circumstances change, so too will the expectation of what can and should be achieved through the processes of politics.

Nothing was more important in Hu Shih's mind than the idea of *change*. He exalted change, movement, growth, the evolution of institutions, ideas, and aspirations. It was the responsiveness of liberalism to social and intellectual change that persuaded Hu of its usefulness in China: what China needed was a political system that could accommodate to, and at the same time give direction to, the sweeping transformation of Chinese life. Yet, oddly and un-

25. J.-J. Rousseau, *du Contrat Social*, book II, chap. 1, in *Social Contract: Essays by Locke, Hume and Rousseau*, with an introduction by Sir Ernest Barker (London: Oxford University Press, 1947), 269.

happily, liberalism in the Chinese context conveys an impression of immobility, and Hu Shih stands as the spokesman for ideals that are static and lifeless.

Why? The answer lies partly, perhaps, in the aversion to politics already referred to. If one desires to bring about change, one must pay the price of involvement, a price that Hu always regarded as exorbitant. Behind his studied diffidence with respect to political activity one may sense a degree of the intellectual's superciliousness and, perhaps, a certain timidity not of mind but of person. Yet if Hu erred in thinking that politics is indeed a risky and sordid enterprise, he only shared a prejudice common enough to liberals who find themselves in situations where this is less evidently true than it was in the China of Hu's time. There is, as Bernard Crick well says, a type of liberal who "likes to honor the fruit but not the tree" of politics, who "wishes to pluck each fruit — liberty, representative government, honesty in government, economic prosperity, and free general education, etc. — and then preserve them from further contact with politics." And there is, as Crick writes further, a kind of naïve liberal who, even as Hu did, "overestimates the power of reason and the coherence of public opinion; he underestimates the force of political passions and the perversity of men in often not seeming to want what is so obviously good for them. He is not fond of political parties . . . He tends to think in terms of an enlightened public opinion working on clear and simple representative institutions." [26] It may be conjectured that Hu was disposed toward such opinions by influences that shaped his earliest understanding of politics — that is, by the somewhat simplistic republicanism of the prerevolutionary decade in China. His subsequent exposure to American Progressivism, with its sweeping condemnation of political corruption, and to Wilsonian idealism would hardly have counteracted this predisposition. And his acquaintance with Dewey's social philosophy might well have served to encourage the inclination to think of the "fruits of politics" as the products of broad social and intellectual forces and to see politics as the beneficiary rather than the prime agency of reform.

It must be recalled, however, that Hu was anything but indifferent or unresponsive to the idea of government. With the exception of the brief and anomalous *wu-wei* interlude in the 1930s, he was a consistent advocate of strong and purposeful government. Recog-

26. Bernard Crick, *In Defence of Politics*, 123.

nition of the importance of "the active power or force necessary for the working of [political] institutions," Hu wrote, was one of the great insights of the "instrumentalist" (that is, Deweyan) theory of politics, emphasizing an element of political life "which has often been neglected by most liberals and radicals." In this vein Hu described government as "the public agency or sum of public agencies for the realization of definite public ends by the use of organized energies or forces." It was not the thought that governments should pursue "ends" that Hu found objectionable, then, but the idea that governments should pursue the wrong ends, or worse still, should come to regard their own survival as in itself a sufficient end. And what he feared was not the concentration of force in the hands of government but its improper use: "The danger of a machine lies not in the stupendous amount of power it generates, but in the weakness of its controls . . . With effective and conscious methods of democratic control, a modern government machinery can greatly enhance its positive usefulness and efficacy without the danger of becoming despotic and dictatorial." [27]

Hu Shih's dilemma lay in the disparity between this view of the potential of government and the possibility, in China, of exercising "effective and conscious methods of democratic control" over it. At one level his refusal to become involved in politics revealed an entirely realistic appraisal of his probable effectiveness in influencing governments whose authority was legitimized by arbitrary force alone. He was, perhaps, excessively sensitive to the importance of environment in conditioning political habits of mind and behavior, a Confucian inheritance enhanced by acquaintance with Dewey's ideas. After his return to China in 1917, finding himself imprisoned in a social environment that was fundamentally inhospitable to the values that he prized, Hu might well have felt compelled to make a strenuous effort to refrain from assessing present needs in terms of what was politically feasible. Viewed in this light, his reluctance to be drawn into political debate—which meant, for him, debating within the context of the situation that existed at any given moment, not arguing at the level of abstract principle — need not be taken as an indication of an immutable antipathy to politics; it may equally well be construed as evidence of the hope that he

27. Hu Shih, "Instrumentalism as a Political Concept," in *Studies in Political Science and Sociology* (Philadelphia: University of Pennsylvania Press, 1941), 4–6.

could in this manner protect the good name of politics, in preparation for a time and setting better suited to the functioning of proper political processes.

At another level, however, Hu's approach to politics reveals an underlying misapprehension of liberal theory. He had a clear and enduring vision of government as the instrument for the accomplishment of public ends, without a comparably clear understanding of how such ends should be determined by means consonant with his democratic inclinations. He embraced the view that government exists to serve the interests of those whom it governs. But he was never able to strike a balance, in his own thinking, between interests that were common and interests that were diverse and individual, nor was he able to accept the proposition that a diversity of interests is fundamental to social organization and, properly disciplined, a source of political freedom. Surveying the unfortunate spectacle of a people in whom "the bond of society" had seemingly dissolved, Hu was inclined, not without reason, to emphasize the underlying conformity of interests that he presumed *must* unite a divided people. He based this presupposition on the belief that because all men are reasonable creatures they must, once informed, come to a common understanding, a common opinion. Implicit in Hu's gradualist and moderate program of reform was the assumption that both the means and the ultimate aims of intellectual, social, and political regeneration (in that order) would be accepted by all men of good will and sincere purpose: the means being the conscious and uncoerced transformation of intellectual premises, social patterns, and political forms and habits; the end being the creation of an intellectually liberated society, tolerant of change, capable of progress, necessarily and inevitably democratic in its social and political institutions.

This prejudice on Hu's part led him, in turn, both to misjudge the situation in which he found himself in China and to overestimate the capacity of liberal methods to engender liberal values. His belief that the universality of reason implies a corresponding universality of aspirations and expectations among men encouraged him to believe, in turn, that the Chinese must, as a natural right, share the ideals which served to inspire the liberal democracies of the West — that the Chinese, no less than the Americans, were heir to a common political legacy. He was sustained in these beliefs, certainly, by the cosmopolitan idealism that had so profoundly moved him during his student days, and also by John Dewey. Yet such beliefs were founded on the illusion that men are free to act outside of an historical context, to shape, unencumbered by the burden of their past, the political instruments that will serve them. Hu recalled with admiration what Thomas Paine had said of the American revolution: "We are brought at once to the point of seeing Government begin, as if we had lived in the beginning of time." And Thomas Jefferson: "Our revolution presented us an album on which we were free to write what we pleased." [28] If these expressions had been, in their proper time and place, something more than revolutionary rhetoric, their application to China's condition was nevertheless highly problematical. The Chinese stood not at the beginning of time but poised between a troubled past and an uncertain future; and the page on which they sought to sketch the outline of new institutions and beliefs was already closely written over by many hands.

Strange thoughts these, in any case, in the mind of an avowed "experimentalist," bound by conviction to affirm the importance of experience, of history. John Dewey was better able to draw the obvious, if disheartening, lesson. "One realizes," he wrote after his first year in China, "how the delicate and multifarious business of the modern state is dependent upon knowledge and habits of mind that have grown up slowly and that are now counted upon as a matter of course." [29] The viability of pragmatic liberalism depends — as Dewey saw more clearly as a result of his experience in China — upon the existence of certain values as a precondition. Or as George Santayana succinctly put it, "In a hearty and sound democracy all questions at issue must be minor matters; fundamentals must have been silently agreed upon and taken for granted when the democracy arose." [30]

This is only to say what has often been said before: that the functioning of a democratic system presumes the existence of an unsystematic and largely unarticulated agreement on basic social and political values. But whence does such agreement arise? From pure reason? Or from experience? For Hu Shih an answer to this question was extremely difficult. He was sensitive enough to the temper of American life, and to the main thrust of Dewey's philosophy, to

28. *Ibid.,* 3.

29. John Dewey, "The New Leaven in Chinese Politics," *Asia,* April 1920; reprinted in *Characters and Events,* I, 253.

30. Cited in Giovanni Sartori, *Democratic Theory* (New York, Washington, and London, 1965), 243. Sartori's work contains an extended and lucid analysis of the "empirical" foundations of Anglo-American democracy.

perceive as early as his student days that democratic values could not flourish in the absence of democratic processes of government or, in other words, a democratic experience. *"The only way to have democracy is to have democracy,"* he wrote in 1915, stating a view that he never abandoned.[31] What hope was there, then, for China, where neither democratic values nor the processes that might encourage their growth existed? In such circumstances Hu could only argue that the advocacy of liberal and democratic aspirations must be the particular responsibility of an enlightened minority — men to whom reason had revealed truth. It is not to challenge the honor or the honesty of Hu's beliefs to say that his adamant defense of the right to dissent was at heart a demand that he and others like him should be accorded the hearing they deserved. For Hu, no less than for the Nationalists and the Communists (and for similar reasons, though with far different intent), a definition of the common good was properly and necessarily the task of a progressive elite.

That this should be so is hardly surprising. Elitist inclinations were a natural, perhaps even an inescapable, inheritance that Chinese intellectuals in the twentieth century received from the hands of their Confucian forebears. Often this legacy was recast in modern form in the course of early education, when almost without exception China's young intellectuals accepted, even as Hu Shih did as a schoolboy in Shanghai, the conviction that the salvation of their nation was their particular privilege and obligation. Carrying such sentiments with him to America in 1910, Hu found much there to confirm and strengthen them in the following years. The currents of reform that coursed through American public life in that era were shaped and channeled by an enlightened minority; Progressivism was not a grass-roots movement but the product of the efforts of a fairly small number of civic-minded academics, journalists, social workers, and politicians. In a more personal way, Hu's long and intimate involvement with the international student movement undoubtedly encouraged the tendency to regard himself as among the select few whose responsibility it was to uphold the standards against which public conduct should be measured. And, finally, there was the example set by Woodrow Wilson and the Wilsonian vision of the New Freedom. In 1914 Hu noted in his diary, sum-

31. *Diary*, 746–747. Bernard Crick writes, along this same line, that consensus, in the meaning of the term used here, "is more likely to be a *product* of politics than a condition." *In Defence of Politics,* 177.

marizing remarks recently made by Wilson and Theodore Roosevelt in the course of Independence Day celebrations: "Which shall it be? Mr. Roosevelt, at Pittsburgh: 'We must supervise and direct the affairs of the people.' Mr. Wilson, at Philadelphia: 'We must establish conditions under which the people will be free to manage their own affairs.' This is the pivotal question on which turn all present arguments concerning free government. Between the two, I follow Mr. Wilson." [32] This casual observation attests Hu's genuine and enduring trust that "the people" will ultimately prove competent to the responsibilities of self-government. But the crucial phrase is still, "*We* must establish . . ." It is tempting to surmise that as he browsed through the volume of Henrik Ibsen's letters from which he later draw his call for "a true and pure egoism," Hu's eye fell also on these lines from another of Ibsen's letters to Georg Brandes: "[Björnstjerne] Björnson says: 'The majority is always right.' And as a practical politician he is bound, I suppose, to say so. I, on the contrary, must of necessity say: 'The minority is always right' . . . I mean that minority which leads the van, and pushes on to points which the majority has not yet reached. I mean: That man is right who has allied himself most closely with the future." [33]

In any time and place the dissident intellectual, the social critic and would-be reformer, the man who has allied himself with the future, at least in his vision of it, is a lonely figure. In Hu Shih's case the inevitable sense of isolation was enhanced by the particular circumstances in which he found himself after his return to China in 1917. Throughout the next two decades he waged a battle on two fronts. On the one hand he acknowledged, indeed he tirelessly denounced, the tyranny of society over the individual, whose intellectual emancipation was always Hu's greatest concern. In the struggle against the authority of traditional social values, moreover, Hu demanded the assistance of those who wielded political power: progress would be impossible, he repeatedly insisted, without the purposeful intervention of "a government with a plan." On the other hand, however, Hu relied heavily on the society itself — or on public opinion, which comes to the same thing — to supervise the manner in which the government discharged its responsibilities. Hu thus made government and society each the guardian of the

32. *Diary*, 300.
33. J. N. Laurvik and M. Morison, trans., *Letters of Henrik Ibsen*, 350.

other's virtue. But the individual, in Hu's vision, transcended both: he stood beyond the reach of the government, which earned his loyalty only in proportion to the adequacy with which it served his needs; and he stood above the society, which claimed his talent but could lay no claim to his mind. Such would be the community of free intellect, in which, as Hu once remarked, all would be leaders and none be led.

There is thus implicit in Hu's conception of the highest form of individualism an air of almost utopian detachment from reality, an intellectual prejudice strengthened by the temperamental aloofness that made it possible for Hu to remain emotionally uninvolved in the tragedy that had descended upon his country and his people. The coolness of Hu's response to the tumult that shook his world strikes one as being symptomatic of a moral blindness to the dimensions of the suffering that afflicted his countrymen. The sound of strife seldom penetrated Hu's study, nor did the violence that stalked the land distract him from his meditations. Reading his essays, even those provoked by what he once referred to as "the turmoil of the newspaper," one recalls often only with conscious effort that beyond Hu's gate, beyond the exquisite garden with its mementos of departed imperial splendor, men were caught up in the agonies of this cruel century's longest, cruelest, and most costly revolution.

Yet Hu sought only for fair-minded, dispassionate understanding, for moderation. Such was not the temper of his age, admittedly; but must he be condemned for that? His was the personal and public dilemma that seems with grim certainty to confront men of compromise and common sense overtaken by a revolutionary deluge — when, as Crane Brinton observes, "the normal social roles of realism and idealism are reversed," and "the wisdom and common sense of the moderate are not wisdom and common sense, but folly." [34] If Hu Shih's message was incomprehensible to his people, alien to them and hence unable to move them, as his detractors charge, this was not because (as his conservative enemies would have it) what he said derived in good part from foreign sources, nor because (as his radical critics have maintained) he strove to uphold an order that others had already rejected. Rather, it was because Hu was by nature, by experience, and by education prepared to claim the liberties he prized. Thus he was almost infinitely estranged from the mute and miserable existences of men and women blinded

34. Crane Brinton, *The Anatomy of Revolution* (New York, 1957), 153–154.

still by ignorance, struck dumb by indifference to any fate save their own, and crippled by the social lethargy of unnumbered generations.

Yet he was in fact no freer than they were. It was his fate to be, from the moment of his return to China in 1917, the prisoner of a revolution that he understood only imperfectly. He did not acknowledge his servitude until very late; but again, we must not too hastily condemn him. It is far easier for us now to see the chains that weighed him down, to attribute meanings to the seemingly random events of that era, to perceive a drift through time that might have been imperceptible to one living moment by moment through the passing years. We realize better than Hu did — or could, perhaps — how little time there was; we sense the appalling urgency with which events were building toward some sort of climax. It is easy for us, therefore, to disparage as beguilingly naïve nonsense Hu's hope that the Chinese would be restrained and wise enough to seek "a three-year cure for a seven-year illness." And, knowing what we are privileged to know, we may too lightly dismiss Hu's lifelong statement of first principles as insufficient because it offers little in the way of concrete social analysis.

Whatever Hu's shortcomings in this last regard — and they were substantial — he deserves credit at least for a keen appreciation of the importance of the specific and the concrete. Although he did not see the Chinese revolution as what we now take it for, although he did not grasp its implications to the fullest nor gauge its tempo accurately, still Hu urged his young audiences in evident good faith to go out and grapple with the issues of this vast upheaval. Forsake the false gods of the revolution, he implored them time and again, and turn to a studious and passionless examination of *real* problems. No conviction ran deeper in Hu than the belief that China's eventual salvation depended upon such study and the knowledge of particulars that it would generate. Reflecting a concern generally shared by his liberal acquaintances, Hu consistently emphasized the importance of recruiting men of specalized training and expert knowledge to the public service. It was, of course, only natural for men who had been educated to think of themselves as academic or professional specialists in the modern sense to regard government as the proper business of their own kind, and to contend that neither general competence in the arts of civilization (in the Confucian pattern) nor mere ideological fervor (as the revolutionaries maintained) prepared one adequately to manage the complexities of a modern political administration or to assume the responsibilities of decision-making. Government, the liberals insisted, must become the joint enterprise of many minds addressing themselves to the painstaking examination of specific problems from different points of vantage and competence, converging ultimately in the formulation of policies that would rest on the unchallengeable authority of expert opinion.

Such was the belief that, together with his aversion to Marxist abstractions, propelled Hu to the position that he took in the celebrated debate on "problems and isms" in 1919, and which he defended for the rest of his life. Behind it lay, certainly, something of the American enthusiasm for expertise that Hu had acquired abroad, and something, too, of the Deweyan faith in the efficacy of intellectual analysis. Large questions have been raised concerning the viability of Dewey's faith in this regard, questions as to whether a social philosophy that eschews ends can provide a sufficient sense of purpose and direction, whether liberalism conceived of as a methodological "mediator of transitions" can generate the enthusiasm necessary to the accomplishment of great social undertakings, and whether liberalism so construed can in fact move from analysis to action.[35] If such questions arise from a consideration of the place of Dewey's thought in its native American setting, they present themselves even more insistently and with greater force in application to a social context where, as in China, men have lost their bearings completely.

But if pragmatic liberalism as it was exemplified in China conveys the sense of irrelevance that its critics rightly find there, the whole blame cannot be put on whatever intellectual abstractness is inherent in the doctrine itself. Dewey speaks pointedly of the need for "insight into both social desires and actual conditions" as the necessary foundation for a liberal approach to social change. It is on this point that his Chinese disciples, Hu Shih more than others, seem most conspicuously to have misunderstood him. Hu's values and aspirations reflected little real understanding of the "social desires" of his people or the "actual conditions" of their lives. He could never reconcile himself fully to the knowledge that for them "freedom" meant not the eventual freedom to hold their own

---

35. See, for example, George Raymond Geiger, "Dewey's Social and Political Philosophy," in Paul Schilpp, ed., *The Philosophy of John Dewey*. Geiger, it is worth noting, is by no means an unfriendly critic.

opinions but immediate freedom from the scourge of hunger, conscription, and pillage — neither more nor less. The "problems" that engaged Hu's attention, meanwhile, were for the most part the kind of intellectual riddles likely to provoke the leisurely curiosity of the professional scholar. This was, of course, the occupation for which Hu had prepared himself with great care, and it was always the role in which he preferred to think of himself. For reasons suggested in the Preface, little has been said of Hu's scholarship in this book, despite the fact that his most easily discernible and perhaps, at least in an indirect sense, his most durable contributions to the shaping of a modern Chinese intellect were the result of his scholarly and academic concerns. Although much of Hu's scholarship in the fields of Chinese philosophy and literary history was rather quickly superseded, it was in its time startling, original, and provocative enough permanently to change the perspectives in which these subjects are viewed. Moreover, during his long association with China's modern institutions of higher learning and research — Peita, Academia Sinica, the China Foundation — Hu did much to broaden the horizons of scholarly opportunity. In his own scholarship he served as preceptor and inspiration for many younger men, opening to them wide and inviting new vistas. Among those who have recorded their debt to Hu are Ku Chieh-kang, the historian and folklorist; Yü P'ing-po, literary critic and historian; and Lo Erh-kang, a specialist in the history of the Taiping Rebellion, to name only a few of the more eminent.[36]

Unquestionably, this was worthwhile and useful work. But Hu claimed too much for it, perhaps. It is difficult to share, in retrospect, his conviction that this sort of scholarly endeavor provided an adequate demonstration of the relevance of his principles to Chinese circumstances, or that it could, as he believed, affect in compelling fashion the destiny of his nation in a critical age. Of the several studies of vernacular fiction that absorbed much of Hu's attention in the May Fourth era he later remarked that such research "is only the intellectual method of Huxley and Dewey given practical application. My textual examination of these novels, running to several tens of thousands of characters, are simply 'profound and

36. See Lo Erh-kang, *Shih-men wu-nien chi* (A record of five years at my teacher's door; privately printed in Taiwan, December 1958); Ku Chieh-kang, *The Autobiography of a Chinese Historian;* Yü P'ing-po, "Resolutely Demarcate Boundaries with the Reactionary Hu Shih Ideology," translated from *Hsüeh-hsi* (Peking, March 15, 1955), in *Current Background*, no. 325 (April 5, 1955).

clear' examples to teach men how to think." [37] Yet at a time when survival itself was a brutal, and too often a losing, gamble for millions of Chinese, the "problem" of who had written which chapters of an eighteenth-century novel was, at best, of marginal significance. Without disputing the superficial truth of Hu's interpretation of the importance of his own work, must we not still conclude that he had tragically misjudged the needs of his times — and misread Dewey into the bargain?

Dewey would almost certainly have thought so. As early as 1921, even while he applauded the inclination of China's young intellectuals to promote democracy as an educational rather than a political movement, Dewey expressed the hope that they would not "permanently foreswear" an interest in "detailed" and "practical" social analysis.[38] Otherwise, he warned, intellectual reform would degenerate into "a cultural and literary sideshow." [39] Yet it may well be that in some measure Hu Shih's preoccupation with scholarship was subtly dictated by his acceptance of Dewey's emphasis on the function of experience in controlling change. Perhaps Hu devoted himself to the history of philosophy and literature because in these areas he could fashion a credible case for transformation on the basis of Chinese experience. He could argue persuasively that *pai-hua* literature would flourish because it came as the outgrowth of the long evolution of vernacular forms. He could assert that precedents derived from Chinese experience made it possible for the Chinese to appropriate the modern scientific method. But Hu could hope to establish the *evolutionary* context essential to reform on experimentalist principles only in isolated and peripheral areas like these that could be detached from the requirement for *revolutionary* change. He could not affirm with comparable conviction that the spirit of emancipated individualism he summoned into being had lain immanent within the despotism of the traditional social order. Or that the intellectual lethargy of peasant life had nurtured, unseen and unfelt, a capacity for critical and independent thought.[40]

37. Hu Shih, "Chieh-shao wo tzu-chi ti ssu-hsiang," HSWT IV, 621.

38. John Dewey, "New Culture in China," *Asia,* July 1921; reprinted in *Characters and Events,* I, 270–284.

39. John Dewey, "The Sequel of the Student Revolt," *The New Republic,* 21.273:381 (Feb. 25, 1920).

40. In a few of his later essays, especially those written in English for American consumption, Hu did argue in very general terms that a "democratic" tradition had existed in pre-imperial China and, further, that the enlightened

Chinese society demanded revolutionary liberation. This Hu acknowledged. But it was not within his power, because it lay beyond the power of his principles, to devise a strategy of revolution.

If such considerations played some part in shaping Hu's interests, it can only have been unconsciously. His decision to devote himself to scholarship, to the "systematization of the national heritage," however, was consciously taken. He acted on the premise that a solution to the problem of national survival could emerge only from an understanding of why the problem had arisen in the first place, and that this understanding must take into account *all* the historical factors that had contributed to the present crisis. His own scholarly work enriched this understanding only in limited fashion, perhaps — but he himself recognized the limitation. All his life he believed in a "division of labor." He never presumed, however extravagant his claims may have sounded at times, that a solution to China's problems could be the product of a single mind, or even of a single generation. "My duty to society is only to do what I can do to the best of my ability," he wrote in 1915. "Will not men forgive me for what I cannot do?" [41]

In their insistence that government must be the particular responsibility of an ideologically neutral, technically specialized elite, Chinese liberals sounded a strikingly modern note. In another way, however, they remained, albeit only half consciously, much closer to the spirit of Confucian elitism. Imbedded in the liberal mentality were vestiges of the venerable Confucian conviction that knowledge is virtue, that intellectual attainment carries with it civic responsibility and, more generally, the responsibility to set in one's own conduct a moral example to be followed by others. The only ethical norm that one may rely upon in any circumstance, he wrote in 1914, is the principle expressed in the Chinese term *i-chih* ("integrity," or as Hu translated it, "consistency"). He discovered here the best of every ethic, Western and Eastern — from the Christian Golden Rule and Kant's categorical imperative enjoining the individual's act of will to assume universal significance, to the Confucian idea of "reciprocity" (*shu*[b]) and the age-old Chinese ideal of the virtuous ruler as one whose "movements . . . constitute an example to the world for ages" and whose acts "are for ages a law

(Confucian) minority in China, like its European counterpart, had always voiced the demand for toleration and intellectual freedom. See above, chap. ix, n. 5.

41. *Diary*, 654.

to the kingdom." [42] Throughout his life Hu tried to follow this maxim in his own conduct; it was the steady sincerity of his commitment to it that elevated above the level of mere rhetoric his frequent admonitions to the students of new China to remember, even in times of overwhelming emotional distress, that theirs was a special privilege and a special responsibility, that in them resided the values of candor, reflectiveness, and seriousness of purpose that should be upheld at all cost.

We must then speak, in the end, not only of "liberalism in China" but also of "*Chinese* liberalism." Liberalism in China, on the one hand, meant much the same thing that liberalism has meant elsewhere: a belief in popularly based institutions of government, in the rule of law, in political processes that are made legitimate by the manner in which they function rather than by the ends ascribed to them; and, uniting all these elements, a belief in the creative and benign power of free intelligence. Liberalism in China remained, in the context of Chinese conditions, essentially an abstraction. *Chinese* liberalism, on the other hand, meant something more concrete in the Chinese mind: a pattern of personal values reminiscent of the values of the Confucian "superior man," an ideal that had existed virtually unchanged through the long centuries of imperial history. Hu Shih and his liberal friends, modern men in so many ways, with modern aspirations, underwent in the grotesque decades of the 1920s and 1930s a strange sea change. They became, as it were, latter-day literati. By education endowed with the privilege and the obligation of offering advice to their rulers, by moral scruple prevented from serving a corrupt and corrupting political authority, they remained "good men" very much in the Confucian sense of these words: conscientious, humane, pensive, responsible, speaking for what they believed to be right even at considerable peril, mindful of the public weal but speaking for the people rather than to them, making no effort to establish an alternate center of loyalty or to put forward a political program of their own, ever hopeful that by remonstrance alone they might transform the minds and hearts of their rulers and in this fashion benefit the lives of their people. Chiang Kai-shek wrote better than he knew, perhaps, when on Hu's death he penned the obituary scrolls that were sent to honor the man who had been, at times, his most perceptive critic.

42. *Ibid.,* 437–438. For the passage from the *Chung-yung* (chap. 29, sect. v) see Legge, *The Chinese Classics,* I, 426.

Intending only to flatter, he inadvertently described with fair accuracy the anomalous role that his old adversary had found thrust upon him. Hu Shih, wrote the Generalissimo, had been "a model of old moral values within the New Culture — an example of the new thought within the framework of ancient principles." [43]

Liberalism failed in China in its time. Its time was brief — a few years, a decade or two at the most rather than the half a century that Hu hoped for. It failed not because the liberals themselves failed to grasp an opportunity afforded them, but because they could not manufacture the opportunity they needed. Liberalism failed because China was in chaos, and liberalism requires order. It failed because in China the common values which liberalism assumes to exist did not exist, and liberalism could provide no means to bring such values into being. It failed because the lives of the Chinese were shaped by force, while liberalism requires that men should live by reason. Liberalism failed in China, in short, because Chinese life was steeped in violence and revolution, and liberalism offers no answers to the great problems of violence and revolution.

The failure of liberalism in China seems, at this close point in time, dictated by the creed itself. China's liberals might have been more effective critics of the existing order had they been more willing to work against it rather than through it. They might have been more persuasive advocates of radical change had revolution not seemed to them so ambiguous and perilous a prescription. But had they argued another case they could not have remained liberals. And some, indeed, did not. Hu Shih did, with cheerful patience. There is thus an element of personal defeat involved in the defeat of liberalism that brings us, finally, to speak not in terms of the failure of a cause but of the tragedy of a man.

"It is unfortunate for men of talent to be born in China today," Hu Shih remarked with uncanny presentiment to his friend Lewis Gannett in the mid-1920s, at a time when his powers and his reputation were close to their zenith. And he continued: "They get too far too easily; they are pushed rapidly to responsibilities beyond their powers — and they are done. Wellington Koo would have been a splendid permanent under-secretary of the Foreign Office — he becomes prime minister; Wu Pei-fu an excellent division commander — he has to try to be a generalissimo; two years after I

43. See Feng Ai-ch'ün, *Hu Shih-chih hsien-sheng chi-nien chi* (A collection of memorials honoring Mr. Hu Shih-chih; Taipei, 1962), 189.

345

returned from America a newspaper straw ballot declared me one of the greatest living Chinese! When you have made a reputation you have to do one of two things: live up to it or live on it. In the first case, you are ruined physically; in the second, you are ruined morally and intellectually. You try to be a great man; you try to do too many things — and you break." [44] It was Hu Shih's misfortune to make his reputation early, to become when he was still a young man a symbolic figure in the eyes of men who watched him with admiration or with distrust. He was an intellectual, in a culture which had always attached particular significance to intellectualism; an educator in a society which assigned to educators special prestige and responsibility. He was a returned student, in a time when the Chinese were still enthusiastically searching abroad for the means of salvation, and a spokesman for radical intellectual innovation in an era when this was a compelling cause. But he was also, and just as consistently, the spokesman for moderate means, at a time when such a program seemed less and less feasible or justified. Throughout his life Hu Shih was revered by some, and by others despised, not for what he was but for what he represented; for the manner in which he met, or failed to meet, the confused, changing, and ever more burdensome demands of his age.

It would be neither kind nor just to say that Hu Shih only strove for greatness. He attained it, in some measure. For China was, as he repeatedly insisted, poor in men of talent — the kind of talent, at least, that Hu esteemed and regarded as essential to the transformation of an ancient culture into a modern civilization. And Hu was talented and sufficiently conscious of it to aspire greatly. From time to time he stopped, discomforted momentarily by doubts as to where it might all be leading; then, spurred by his sense of the need and by a great confidence in his own powers, he would reach out once more. Finally, after much had been accomplished, when still more was demanded, his understanding of the need proved insufficient. "Poverty," "disease," and "ignorance" no longer seemed to many as meaningful definitions of China's physical and spiritual

44. Lewis Gannett, *Young China* (New York, 1927), 11. Hu's reference is to a poll conducted by *Millard's Review* (later *The China Weekly Review*) in 1919. The readership of this English-language publication was presumably either foreign or foreign-educated in large part. Gannett, whom Hu had known since his student days in the United States, was in China for several months in the winter of 1925–1926, reporting on the Chinese revolution for *The Nation*, of which he was an associate editor.

ills as "imperialism" and "feudalism," the catchwords Hu detested; the revolutionaries, for all their ideological cant, appeared just as anxious as he to curb ignorance and eradicate disease, just as scornful of political corruption, and more sensitive than he to the misfortunes of the Chinese people. Hu Shih, having claimed more for his principles than was allowable, found them rejected and himself neglected. Men did not forgive him what he could not do: charity is not a revolutionary virtue.

And some would say Hu broke — or was broken by implacable circumstance. What once had been a clarion call to freedom from the dead burden of the past became itself anachronistic rhetoric. The demand for political justice became a justification for political ineptitude. Self-confident enthusiasm became a windy and defensive vanity.

But we must remind ourselves once more than Hu Shih lived through momentous times, through years of anguish that could all too easily and early exhaust physical and spiritual vitality, voracious years that devoured the substance of sympathy and imagination and left only the husk of abstract beliefs. In the end even he was no longer able to derive much warmth from the optimistic faith in man's innate dignity and reasonableness that had so long sustained him. Yet even at the last the capacity for candor had not entirely deserted him. Little more than a year before his death he wrote despondently to an old friend: "My birthday [the sixty-ninth] is nearly here. As I look back upon the labors of the last forty or fifty years, it seems to me that everything has been utterly ruined, utterly destroyed, as by some irresistible force." [45]

It would be a cruel irony if this should stand as the final verdict upon the life of a man who trusted history enough to proclaim that "we shall be judged by what humanity will be when we shall have played our part." It is not yet time, perhaps, to render such a judgment on Hu Shih. But as citizens of the "modern civilization" that he sought so earnestly to establish in China, we cannot forget that much of what he strove to accomplish was what we ourselves might have hoped to see done. Even while we recognize the imperfection of his understanding of things close at hand, we cannot overlook the clarity of his vision of things far off, his vision of the future. The frustration of his hopes, the clouding of that bright

45. Hu Shih's letter to Chang Fo-ch'üan, dated Dec. 11, 1960. I am indebted to Professor Chang for providing me with a photostat of the original.

promise, may rightly prompt us to ask again what may be the fate of the ideals of moderation, tolerance, intellectual freedom, individual liberty, and the rule of law and reason in a world rent by immoderate and brutal revolutions.

Appendixes   Bibliography   Glossary   Index

Appendix A. The Women in Hu's Life

A psychoanalytical study of Hu Shih's relationship to the two women in his life, his mother and his wife, might yield provocative conclusions if properly handled, and if informed by sufficient (and sufficiently revealing) data. Unfortunately, I am not equipped by training or inclination to press such an investigation, nor is the material that I have used in the writing of this book especially conducive to insights into this sequestered realm. The tone of Hu's autobiography is generally rather bland and sentimental, while his student diary is too much an assortment of random fragments of experience to support sustained speculation concerning the psyche of its author. One may wonder, certainly, how the absence of paternal discipline from the home — in a culture that exalted patri-

351

archal influence — might have affected Hu's attitude toward authority; and one may conjecture that his disposition toward his mother might have been different, though not necessarily less deferential, had she not been compelled to serve as sole guardian and mentor of her child's moral character as well as bearing the full burden of responsibility for his physical welfare. The environment in which Hu spent his early years was unusual in a number of respects, and this undoubtedly left its mark upon his temperament in later life.

On the question of his marriage, Hu's student diary does afford some disjointed but nonetheless revealing glimpses of intense inner conflict. For a long time he argued with himself the question of whether marriage should be based on intellectual compatibility, and there is reason to suppose that his theory of "social immortality" (see above, chapter 4) derived at least in part from a personal need for reassurance: in 1914 he compiled a list of "great men of modern times who remained unmarried" (Descartes, Spinoza, Kant, Hobbes, Locke, Herbert Spencer, Newton, Adam Smith, Voltaire, William Pitt, Cavour, Gibbon, and others.)[1] There is evidence to suggest that Hu was strongly attracted to, perhaps even in love with, Edith Williams, the daughter of one of his professors at Cornell. Miss Williams was studying art in New York City during the last year of Hu's residence in Ithaca, and she tried with some success to cultivate his taste for modern art. It was she, too, ironically, who sent Hu the copy of Morley's *On Compromise* that helped to reconcile him to an acceptance of his mother's wishes. Some months after he had made his decision to "follow the ways of the East" in his private life, he wrote to his mother:

> Everything I said [in an earlier letter] concerning Tung-hsiu's education . . . was expressed in the emotions of the moment, with no intention of rebuking Tung-hsiu, much less of placing any blame on my mother. In the matter of my marriage I harbor no grievances whatever. I know full well that in [this matter] my mother has indeed expended much effort to arrange for me a completely happy married life; were I still to cherish resentment, then certainly I would be a hopeless creature, without a true understanding of the situation, nor an appreciation of the feelings of others, unable to tell good from bad . . . Nowadays, if a woman can read and write, this is of course a good thing; but if not, it is no great failing. The learning that one

1. *Diary*, 441–442.

gets from books . . . is only one of many [kinds of knowledge]. I have seen many who can read and write, but who have not the capacity to be good wives and mothers; and how could I reprimand [one who] seeks to perfect [herself]? [If] a married couple can be at the same time teacher and friend [*k'ang-li erh chien shih yu*], this is indeed one of life's greatest joys. But genuine equality in learning between husband and wife is not often found even in this country — how much the less in our country where there is no education offered to women? If I were to hold up the standard of "intellectual equality" [*chih-shih p'ing-teng*] in seeking a mate, there is no doubt that I would live a solitary existence to the end of my days.[2]

In the end Hu's marriage to Chiang Tung-hsiu proved to be an enduring and evidently affectionate match despite the disparity in education and experience that made it impossible for her to share directly in much of his later activity. His unpublished diaries make frequent mention of her role in the home, and of informal social occasions in which she had a part. Two poems, one written before the marriage and the other shortly after that event (which took place at the end of 1917), are suggestive of Hu's attitude toward his bride:

Receiving a Letter from Tung-hsiu While I Am Ill [3]

Her letter comes while I am ill —
Fewer than eight lines of quite unimportant chatter,
Yet it makes me happy!

I do not know her,
Nor does she know me.
Why, then, do I think so often of her?

Is it not that we are destined to share
A relationship from which affection grows,
And so we are not strangers?

Do you not love freedom?
This is an idea that no one understands.
To consent to being unfree
Is also freedom!

2. *Ibid.*, 647–648; letter dated May 9, 1915.
3. Ch'ien Chi-po, *Hsien-tai Chung-kuo wen-hsüeh shih* (A history of contemporary Chinese literature; enlarged ed., Hong Kong, Lung-men, 1965), 425.

Newly Married [4]

Today it is over, the thirteen years of thinking of each other with
never a glimpse of each other.
We will speak of every one of the moments of heartbreak, from the
beginning.
You must not apologize to me, nor will I apologize to you.
Hold fast instead to the memory of the bright moon in the sky on
this thirtieth night of December.

In the summer of 1918, in a lecture entitled "American women"
delivered at the Peking Women's Normal School, Hu spoke dis-
paragingly of the "returned students of recent days who, having
breathed a bit of the air of enlightenment, get divorced first thing
upon returning home — not stopping to think that their own civilized manner was bestowed upon them by good fortune, and paid
for with a good deal of money; and that if their wives had enjoyed
similar opportunities they too could have breathed the air of civilization, rather than suffering such derision!" [5]

Finally, it is interesting, and perhaps significant, to note that
when Hu's mother died at the end of 1918 Hu used the occasion
to make a number of startling and well publicized departures from
the time-honored proprieties of the funeral ceremony.[6] Thus did
the woman whose attachment to the old ways had proved too strong
to sever in life serve her son in death as a symbol of the attack on
traditional customs.

4. Hu Shih, "Hsin-hun tsa-shih wu-shou" (Five poems in various styles on
being newly married), HCN 4.4:311 (April 1918).
5. Hu Shih, "Mei-kuo ti fu-jen" (American women), HSWT, iv, 924.
6. Hu Shih, "Wo tui sang-li ti i-tien i-chien" (Some of my ideas on [a reform
of] funeral rites), HCN 6.6 (November 1919); HSWT, iv, 997–1016, retitled "Wo
tui-yü sang-li ti kai-ko" (Changes that I have made in the funeral rites).

Appendix B. The Chinese Delegation to the VIII Congress of the International Federation of Students, 1913.

Research is only just beginning on the impact of American education, and American life in general, on the Chinese students who studied in the U.S. in the years immediately preceding and during World War I. To what I hope will someday be a full-scale history of this important subject I offer the following as a footnote. The vagaries of transliteration make positive identification in many cases problematical, and in some impossible. Nor is there any way of knowing how many of the Chinese listed as members of the Chinese delegation actually attended the congress or were active in the Federation. For what it is worth, however, I have listed below the members of the Chinese delegation as given in Giglio-Tos (p. 192) and compared this list with that found in the "Directory of American Returned Students" published as an appendix to *Who's Who in China,* 3rd edition (Shanghai, 1925). As nearly as I can ascertain, all of the men listed in the right-hand column were in the United States in 1913 and might therefore have attended the meetings at Ithaca. Superscript letter "a" indicates a biographical entry in the 1925 (3rd) edition of *Who's Who in China*; superscript letter "b" indicates a biographical entry in the 1936 (5th) edition of *Who's Who in China.*

Giglio-Tos, *Appel*	"Directory of American Returned Students" (Wade-Giles romanization)
Chang Loy	–
Chang Pung C.	Chang P'eng-ch'un[b]
Chen Cheng-Sze	Ch'en Cheng-shih
Chen Y. T.	? Ch'eng I-tsao
Chiu Chong Y.	Chiu Ch'ang-yün
Chow Hou-Kun	Chou Hou-k'un
Chow Tse Ki	Chou Tse-ch'i
Chu Che C.	Chu Ch'i-chih
Hou Mao C.	Hou Mao-ch'ing
Hsu Y. F. Jabin	Hsü Chien-p'ing (Jabin Hsu)[a,b]
Hu Suh A. B.	Hu Shih[a,b]
Jen Carl	–
King Pang C.	–
Lau Wai Ming	–
Lind D. Y.	? Ling Tao-yang[a,b]
Lind K. Z.	–
Ling Tsoe-run L.	–
Lo T. S.	–
Mei Yu C.	? Mei I-ch'i[b]
Pan Wen Huan	P'an Wen-huan
Soong Tze V.	Sung Tzu-wen (T. V. Soong)[b]
Tong Yoehliang	T'ang Yüeh-liang[b]
Tsao Sik K.	–
Tsen Mao Kung	Ch'en Mao-k'ang
Wang Cheng Fu E. M.	Wang Cheng-fu[a,b]
Wang Hung C.	Wang Hung-cho

Wang Ing Tso	–
Wang K.	Wang Keng[a,b]
Wei Wen P.	Wei Wen-pin
Wo Sun P.	–
Wong Parkin	–
Woo Sien Ming	Hu Hsüan-ming[b]
Yui David Z. T.	Yü Jih-chang (David Yui) [a,b]

Chang Loy, although not listed in the "Directory of American Returned Students," was almost certainly the same Chang Loy who later served as Chinese Commissioner of Customs. Chang P'eng-ch'un became a teacher and educational administrator associated with Tsinghua and Nankai universities, the latter founded by his older brother, Chang Po-ling. Jabin Hsu worked as a journalist in Shanghai in the 1920s; he later became H. H. Kung's confidential secretary and held several posts in the Kuomintang government. Mei I-ch'i (Y. C. Mei) rose to prominence both as a scientist and as an educational administrator. T. V. Soong needs no introduction, but it is worth noting that Hu Shih's acquaintance with him may have begun at this time. T'ang Yüeh-liang pursued a colorful career as a diplomat and as the brother-in-law of the "Christian general," Feng Yü-hsiang. David Yui was for twenty years the general secretary of the Chinese YMCA. Many of the other men listed here were connected with the "modern establishment" in China after their return — in the Ministry of Foreign Affairs, in the employ of modern industrial, mining, and railroad enterprises, or in the fields of education, agriculture and forestry, or public health.

Appendix C. The Chinese Communist Attack on Hu Shih

Hu Shih's sudden death in February 1962 was the occasion for a massive outpouring of sentiment on Taiwan. In Mainland China, on the contrary, the event passed not only without mourning but without any official notice whatever. On the Mainland, his obituary had been written prematurely: in the 1950s Hu was the object of a campaign of renunciation and defamation conducted under the sponsorship of the Peking government and waged with all the thoroughness, all the marshaling of intellectual talent and political invective, that such sponsorship entails. Still there must have been some to whom the news of Hu's death brought memories of a distant and different time. Many of Hu's old friends, many of his

358

former colleagues and students, had stayed behind in 1949, choosing the uncertainties of the new regime over the all-too-familiar liabilities of the old. Kao I-han, T'ao Meng-ho, Chou Tso-jen, Ch'ien Tuan-sheng, Liang Sou-ming, Lo Erh-kang, Ku Chieh-kang, Yü P'ing-po, Chang Hsi-jo, Lo Lung-chi — these and many others whose lives had touched upon Hu's in some fashion over the years remained in China after he departed, as did his younger son, Hu Ssu-tu. On a few of them, at least, the burden of this old acquaintanceship fell with almost unbearable weight.

The disfavor in which Hu Shih was held by the Communists was not, of course, a new thing after 1949. As early as 1922, when Hu had used *The Endeavor* to support the "good men cabinet" of Wang Ch'ung-hui, he had been attacked in the official Communist party organ *Hsiang-tao chou-pao* (*The guide weekly*) as a "petit-bourgeois pacifist" for his willingness to compromise with the warlord regime.[1] The ridicule to which the Peking liberals were treated by their friends on the Left in the early twenties has been mentioned elsewhere in this book (see above, chapter 6 at note 67). Throughout the twenties and thirties, as the rift between moderation and radicalism widened to become an unbridgeable chasm, Communist criticism of Hu's class outlook, his political affiliations, and his connections with the westernized educational establishment grew sharper. Kuo Mo-jo, a prominent Marxist historian and litterateur, summed up the Communists' perception of Hu's position in these terms in the 1930s: "Mr. Doctor, I will tell you something quite frankly: You, old man, you are yourself one of the viruses that have made China sick. You are the bastard offspring of feudal forces and foreign capitalism . . . You demand proof? Very well, take as examples the crowd of disciples pressing around you: that is your feudal power. And the British and American governments that hold you in such high esteem, they are the very ones whom we call imperialists."[2]

In an exhaustive critique of Hu's scholarship and philosophy published in 1933, Yeh Ch'ing, a Marxist writer of somewhat unorthodox views, observed that only three intellectuals in modern China were widely enough acclaimed to merit critical attention

1. (Chang) Kuo-t'ao, "Wo-men tui-yü hsiao-tzu-ch'an chieh-chi ho-p'ing-p'ai ti ch'üan-kao" (Our advice to the petit-bourgeois peacemakers), *Hsiang-tao chou-pao*, no. 13:105 (Dec. 23, 1922).

2. Kuo Mo-jo, *Ko-ming ch'un-ch'iu* (Annals of the revolution; Shanghai, 1956), 155–156.

from the Communists: Liang Ch'i-ch'ao, Ch'en Tu-hsiu, and Hu Shih. Of these Hu was the most dangerous, Yeh wrote, since Liang was already dead and Ch'en, though still alive, had entered upon a decline following his expulsion from the Communist party. Only Hu's influence was still growing, Yeh contended; and he estimated that at least ten million young people had read Hu's works and fallen under his spell.[3] In fact, however, it seems probable that by the time Yeh Ch'ing published his criticism of Hu, the latter's hold on the mind of the younger generation in China was already weakening. The Communist party, from its beleaguered refuge in the northwest, apparently did not regard Hu as sufficiently important to make a special point of its distaste for his principles. He, for his part, paid little attention to the Communists during the thirties. His very occasional references to them in *The Independent Critic* were invariably respectful, and sometimes downright decorous — as when, after the inauguration of the United Front in 1936, he referred to Chou En-lai in super-honorific terms as "Chou *chün*," "Gentleman Chou," an epithet I have found nowhere else in his writings.[4]

In the postwar years the Communists dismissed Hu easily enough as a mere agent of the "corrupt and desperate reactionary ruling class" and its American backers, a willing pawn in their plot "to deceive the Chinese people."[5] It was thus not until after the Communists' accession to power in 1949 that Hu became, in absentia, a personage of sufficient importance to elicit from China's new rulers a full-scale attempt to set the record straight.

The first criticism of Hu Shih to appear after the establishment of the Communist regime was indicative of the line that would later be followed, though in itself it was of only peripheral significance to the subsequent campaigns against him. In the fall of 1950 Hu Ssu-tu wrote a self-criticism that received wide publicity in the Mainland press, not because of the prominence of its author but because it served as a vehicle for an attack on the elder Hu. Hu Ssu-tu wrote of his father as the scion of "a fallen family of bureaucrats," a pliant personality who had been "dazzled" and "swiftly conquered" by insidious American influences during his student

3. Yeh Ch'ing, *Hu Shih p'i-p'ing*, 1–2.
4. Hu Shih, "Pien-chi hou-chi," TLPL no. 237:18 (May 7, 1937).
5. New China News Agency editorial, "An Old China Is Dying, a New China Is Marching Ahead," May 1948; White Paper, 862–863.

days and thus transformed into "a bourgeois." After his return to China he "wandered among the rulers of those days, hoping his evolutionism would be adopted by them . . . The weak capitalist intellectuals never dared resist the 'government.' He, like all the other members of his class, bowed his head to the reactionary government, and turned to Chiang K'ai-shek to practice his doctrine of reform." As a "docile tool of the imperialists" Hu promoted cultural aggression against China. As Chiang's ambassador to Washington he secured the arms that Chiang then turned against the Communists. In the final denouement, Hu Ssu-tu wrote, his father, seeing that "victory was about to descend to the people," chose exile and the life of a "White Chinese." "Today," the son concluded, "in my determination to rebel against my own class, I feel it important to draw a line of demarcation between my father and myself . . . I must establish close relations with the working and farming class." [6]

As these last lines clearly reveal, the primary function of Hu Ssu-tu's attack on his father was his own ideological and political rehabilitation. Similar motives probably inspired some of the participants in the anti-Hu campaign that took place during the winter of 1951–1952. But in this case other considerations were also involved. The Communists, standing much in need of the services of the American-educated intellectuals it had inherited from the old regime, needed no less to discover some means of rendering this potentially unsympathetic group politically innocuous. Hu Shih, who had been a friend to some, and certainly known to all, provided a convenient minatory example. At forums convened for the special purpose of discussing Hu's baleful influence on Chinese intellectual life — one such meeting was arranged under the auspices of the Shanghai *Ta-kung pao*, formerly a highly respected liberal-independent newspaper, and another was held at Peita — a number of his friends of former days came forth to repent publicly the esteem in which they had once held him. Shen Yin-mo, who had taught Chinese at Peita in the May Fourth era and had shared with Hu editorial responsibilities for *The New Youth*, recalled him now as an "exhibitionist" and a "show-off," "always ready to yield and to iden-

6. A translation of Hu Ssu-tu's self-criticism appeared in the *Hong Kong Standard*, Sept. 24, 1950; it was reprinted in Edward Hunter, *Brainwashing in Red China* (New York: Vanguard, 1951), 303–307, from which these excerpts are taken.

tify himself with authority"; a man of vast conceit, "good at propaganda, particularly for himself," who had tried to take the credit for many undertakings in which he had played only a minor role. The *pai-hua* movement, according to Shen, was one example of this — it had been, in fact, Ch'en Tu-hsiu's idea in the first place.[7] Ku Chieh-kang, who had been one of Hu's first and favorite students, now reprimanded his old teacher for having turned him into a "revisionist," for trying to stifle his "revolutionary consciousness," and for attempting to indoctrinate him with the view that "the masses are both ignorant and dangerous." "He had absolutely no understanding of the people and was completely estranged from them," wrote Ku. "He was doomed to oppose the people and the revolution."[8]

This first campaign against Hu Shih was short-lived. It was carried out in conjunction with mass campaigns aimed at bureaucratic reforms (the so-called "Three-anti" and "Five-anti" movements) and in an environment highly charged with "Hate America, aid Korea" propaganda. It centered at Peita, which is not surprising, given the duration and intimacy of Hu's association with that institution; and it involved only a relatively small number of people, most of whom had had some connection with Hu.

In 1954 and 1955, however, the Communists launched another attack on Hu, far more sweeping in its implications and more impressive in its leadership. Its underlying purpose remained much the same, nevertheless. Despite all the regime's earlier efforts, intellectuals who had received their education in America, or from American-educated teachers in China, remained "incapable of fostering hatred for America," as an editorial in the *Ta-kung pao* complained. The "returned-students' dream" persisted still: " 'fame' and 'position' are used as an enticement to turn students into bourgeois 'scholars' . . . [They] are corrupted by the preoccupation with personal fame and gains."[9] And so the already battered figure of the archetypical returned student was once more propped up as a target.

The second campaign against Hu Shih rapidly assumed awesome proportions. It originated, however, in peculiarly oblique fashion.

7. Shen Yin-mo, "This man Hu Shih," *Ta-kung pao*, Dec. 16, 1951; *Current Background*, no. 167:3–5 (March 25, 1952).

8. Ku Chieh-kang, "The Way I Look at Hu Shih," *Ta-kung pao*, Dec. 16, 1951; *Current Background*, no. 167:6.

9. *Ta-kung pao*, March 27, 1952; *Current Background*, no. 182:5–9 (May 15, 1952).

In September 1954 two obscure graduates of Shantung Provincial University published, in the literary magazine of that institution, an essay entitled "On *A Short Dissertation on Hung-lou meng* and other matters." The object of their criticism was a study by Yü P'ing-po of the great eighteenth-century novel of manners *Hung-lou meng* (The dream of the red chamber). Yü had, in his younger days, collaborated with Hu Shih in the latter's early research on the authorship of the novel, and he had since written several studies of it himself. He was now taken to task for having overlooked, or misrepresented, the social significance of the story, which describes the decline of a wealthy and privileged family: clearly, from the Communists' point of view, *The Dream of the Red Chamber* was a protest against the decadence of feudal society. Yü P'ing-po was in some measure pardoned for his negligence in not having brought this to light, the presumption being that he had acted out of ignorance. His old mentor was not let off so lightly. The re-evaluation of *The Dream of the Red Chamber* quickly moved to an attack on Hu's scholarship, involving a number of the regime's leading literary lights: Cheng Chen-to, director of the Department of Classical Literature of the Union of Chinese Writers; Chou Yang, vice-minister of cultural affairs and vice-chairman of the All-China Federation of Literary and Art Circles; Lao She, bearer of the honorary title "People's Artist" and chairman of the Peking Art and Literature Association (and familiar to American readers as the author of *Rickshaw Boy* and *The Yellow Storm*).[10]

By the end of 1954 any interest that the Communist leadership might have had in the literary or social significance of *The Dream of the Red Chamber* had receded very much into the background, and Hu Shih himself had become the principal object of their concern. In December a "Committee for the Investigation and Criticism of Hu Shih's Ideology" was established, under the joint sponsorship of the Union of Chinese Writers and the Academy of Sciences. Included among its members were Kuo Mo-jo, president of the academy; Mao Tun, president of the Union of Chinese Writers and concurrently Minister of Culture; Ai Ssu-ch'i, a veteran theoretician and editor of *Hsüeh-hsi* (*Study*), the party's theoretical journal; and, in addition, the chancellor of Peita, the editor of the Peking *Jen-min*

10. For a brief account of the reappraisal of *The Dream of the Red Chamber* and allied matters, see Jerome B. Grieder, "The Chinese Communist Critique of *Hung-lou meng*," *Papers on China*, 10:142–168 (1956).

jih-pao, and several other cultural luminaries of comparable stature. Various subcommittees were created to deal with the political, literary, philosophical, and educational aspects of the investigation, and in the early months of 1955 forums convened under the auspices of these groups served to publish the results of their findings. The major journals such as *Li-shih yen-chiu* (Historical research) and *Hsüeh-hsi* gave prominent place to attacks on Hu throughout the first half of 1955. In July, as final proof of the importance attached to the campaign by its sponsors, an account of it by Ai Ssu-ch'i appeared in *Kommunist,* the theoretical journal of the Central Committee of the Communist Party of the Soviet Union.[11] The Peking regime was obviously prepared to go to whatever lengths might prove necessary in order to demolish Hu's reputation and obliterate the last vestige of his claim to the admiration of the Western-trained intellectuals.

This massive assault on the life and works of a single individual left no part of that life untouched, nor any aspect of that work unchallenged. Hu's philosophy, his scholarship, his career as a teacher and as an educational administrator, his political views and associations — all these were subjected to close and critical scrutiny. Many of the arguments were ad hominem, and much of the criticism did not rise above the level of journalistic hack work. There were, however, a few exceptions: some theoretical discussions, clearly written with serious intent, in which Hu's pragmatism was linked to bourgeois culture in terms drawn from Lenin's polemic against Ernst Mach in *Materialism and Empiro-Criticism,* published in 1909;[12]

11. Ai Ssu-ch'i, "Bor'ba protiv burzhuaznoi ideologii v narodnom Kitae," *Kommunist,* no. 11:86–96 (July 1955).

12. Marxist-Leninist philosophers have generally equated Mach's "scientific positivism" with "pragmatism." See M. Rozental' and P. Yudin, eds., *Kratkii filosofskii slovar'* (Moscow, 1952), 402; Chang Ju-hsin, *P'i-p'an Hu Shih ti shih-yung-chu-i che-hsüeh* (A critique of Hu Shih's experimentalist philosophy; Peking, 1955), esp. chap. 4.

Marxist-Leninist philosophical objections to pragmatism revolve around what Marxists take to be "the denial of an objective reality existing independent of any and all human experience," and "the consequent denial of any objective necessity . . . that given such-and-such events and processes something else necessarily follows"; "the denial of any objective knowledge or truth and hence of any real possibility of either prediction or control of natural and social phenomena"; and "the assertion that the successful fulfillment of given aims . . . is the only test of the validity of any ideas or principles and constitutes the sole meaning of their 'truth.'" Given the dogmatic nature of Marx's social hypotheses, rebuttal of the "pragmatic" definition of truth is perhaps the central issue involved; the Marxist philosopher contends that "although the test of the

and some attempts to provide biographical treatments that were, though fearfully biased, nonetheless consistent and carefully documented.[13] The attack on Hu's politics concentrated at least as much on the unsavory nature of his political friendships as it did on the theoretical shortcomings of liberalism. A great deal of attention, of course, was given to his American connections, to his "worship America" inclination, and to his position as a "compradore scholar" and an agent of American "cultural imperialism." His accommodation to Kuomintang rule, however belated, was by no means forgotten, and his political importance was exaggerated beyond all reason — Kuo Mo-jo went so far as to set Hu up as "the civil counterpart of Chiang Kai-shek." [14] At the same time, his positive contributions to the New Culture movement were consistently disparaged and he was made to appear at best a secondary figure standing in the reflected light of such brilliant personalities as Li Ta-chao and Lu Hsün. (It is interesting to note that the Communists subsequently redressed the balance slightly. In a collection of materials on nineteenth- and twentieth-century intellectual history, published in 1957, Hu's "Tentative Suggestions for the Improvement of Literature" and his essays on "Problems and Isms" were included, together with a brief biographical notice conceding that, despite his deplorable political views, he had performed "a somewhat useful educational function in the context of the New Culture movement and its times.") [15]

In many of its aspects the campaign against Hu Shih conveys the impression, to an outsider at least, that the Communists were using their heaviest cudgels to beat a dead horse. But in one respect the

---

truth of our ideas is found solely in practice, they work, in the long run, only insofar as they are true and not as pragmatism holds that they are true because they work." H. K. Wells, *Pragmatism, Philosophy of Imperialism* (New York: International Publishers, 1954), 9–10.

13. See, for example, Hou Wai-lu, "Chieh-lu Mei ti-kuo-chu-i nu-tsai Hu Shih ti fan-tung mien-mao" (Uncovering the reactionary visage of Hu Shih, the slave of American imperialism), in *Hu Shih ssu-hsiang p'i-p'an* (A critique of Hu Shih's thought; Peking, 1955), III, 17–83. This account purports to be based in good part on manuscripts, letters, and documents that Hu left behind when he departed from Peking in December 1948.

14. Quoted in Fan Wen-lan, "K'an-k'an Hu Shih ti 'li-shih-ti t'ai-tu' ho 'k'o-hsüeh-ti fang-fa'" (Let's look at Hu Shih's "historical attitude" and "scientific method"), *Li-shih yen-chiu* (Historical research), no. 3:18 (1955).

15. Shih Chün, ed., *Chung-kuo chin-tai ssu-hsiang shih ts'an-k'ao tzu-liao chien-pien* (A survey of source materials on modern Chinese intellectual history; Peking, 1957), 1273–1274.

attack was immediately relevant to contemporary realities. Throughout the course of the campaign great attention was paid to Hu's
scholarship, not so much to discredit his conclusions as to cast doubt
upon his motives. He was repeatedly indicted for having submerged
himself in scholarly pursuits in order to "elevate the prestige of
Peita, to meet the ornamental needs of the reactionary ruling class,
and to extend his own influence as an educational boss." [16] Some
perceived an even more sinister purpose: "Hu Shih's plot was to
cause young people to lose themselves in textual criticism [for] only
in this way could the young people be forced to abandon Marxism,
to reject the viewpoint of historical materialism; only thus could
they be forced to discard reality, to discard the revolution." [17] For
the Communists, committed by conviction and necessity to the view
that education must "serve the revolution," the pernicious evil of
Hu's scheme could hardly be too strongly emphasized.

By the summer of 1955 the second campaign against Hu Shih had
run its course; new victims were found for the continuing war
against "bourgeois ideology." [18] What the invisible effect of the
campaign may have been remains a question open to speculation.
If the Communists sought only to diminish Hu's stature as an individual, they may well have succeeded. If, as I believe, their principal
aim was to bring the Western-educated intellectuals to heel and to
extirpate once and for all the professional and private values which
this group had been educated to accept — and which, in some degree, Hu Shih represented — then the success of the campaign
seems more problematical. In the course of the Hundred Flowers
movement that began in the winter of 1955–1956, many of these
men voiced criticisms of the regime which eloquently attested the
survival of these values — though, needless to say, none of the embattled intellectuals of 1956 invoked Hu Shih's name in their cause.

16. The quotation given here dates in fact from the 1951–52 campaign
against Hu Shih; see Tientsin *Chin-pu jih-pao,* Dec. 13, 1951; *Current Background,* no. 167:11. Similar views were frequently expressed in the course of
the 1954–55 attack.

17. Chou I-liang, "Hsi-yang 'Han-hsüeh' yü Hu Shih" (Western "sinology"
and Hu Shih), *Li-shih yen-chiu,* no. 2:1–2 (1955).

18. The attack on Hu Shih merged into a full-scale campaign against Hu
Feng, a writer and long-time Communist sympathizer; by the summer and fall
of 1955, the latter attack had pre-empted the attention of the regime's cultural
leadership. See Merle Goldman, "Hu Feng's Conflict with the Communist
Literary Authorities," *China Quarterly,* no. 12:102–137 (1962).

The concrete results of the campaign are easier to weigh: they take the form of several books and a great sheaf of essays and articles, only a portion of which, collected and published in 1955 under the general title *Hu Shih ssu-hsiang p'i-p'an* (A critique of Hu Shih's thought), fill eight fair-sized volumes.

It was Hu Shih's custom, in his last years, to point with pride to this small library of defamatory literature, and to remark amiably that no greater honor had ever been paid him, nor any more convincing evidence of his enduring influence assembled. If Hu believed that the Communist attack upon him somehow proved, retrospectively, the fitness of his philosophical principles, he was, I think, deceived. But in a wider sense he may have been right. The campaign against him had served primarily as a means for the Communists to enforce their view that intellectuals are the servants of politics, not its masters — a view that Hu Shih and his liberal circle had consistently challenged in the twenties and thirties. The attempt to discredit Hu suggests a continuing tension between the claims of ideology on the one hand and those of technical competence on the other: in Communist terminology, a tension between "Red" and "expert" which, to judge by the convulsive history of the Cultural Revolution, has yet to be resolved.

The Chinese Communists celebrated Hu Shih's decease before the fact. Having dispatched him at their convenience, they were at liberty to resurrect him when it suited their purposes. In the spring of 1966, as the Cultural Revolution gathered momentum, Hu's shadow fell again across the life of an old friend. Among the first victims of this purge was the historian Wu Han, author of a play entitled *The Dismissal of Hai Jui,* which concerns the attempt of a righteous official of the Ming dynasty to bring justice to the peasants of his district. Wu's critics accused him of exploiting the past "to ridicule the present"; and as the case against him was constructed it was discovered that, among his other crimes, Wu had been guilty of admiring Hu Shih. Wu had, in fact, been a student at the China National Institute in the late twenties when Hu was the school's president; and in the early 1930s, after Hu had returned to Peita and Wu had embarked on graduate study at Tsinghua, the two had corresponded from time to time. Excerpts from their correspondence were published in *Jen-min jih-pao* in 1966, offered as "iron-clad evidence" of Wu's subservience to Hu's baleful influence. The letters dealt largely with nothing more subversive than some of the finer points in the study of Ming history, but that made little difference.[19] Any excuse will serve a tyrant.

19. See Shih Shao-p'in, "Hu Shih yü Wu Han" (Hu Shih and Wu Han), *Jen-min jih-pao*, April 13, 1966; and Shih Shao-p'in, "Wu Han t'ou-k'ao Hu Shih ti t'ieh-cheng" (Iron-clad proof that Wu Han relied upon Hu Shih), *Jen-min jih-pao*, June 3, 1966. See also Stephen Uhalley, Jr., "The Cultural Revolution and the Attack on the 'Three Family Village,'" *China Quarterly*, no. 27:149–161 (1966).

Bibliography

The following is a selective list of works cited in the text or of particular interest and significance to this study.

Works by the same author are listed chronologically by date of original publication wherever possible. When the location and date of original publication are unknown, entries are made according to the dating of the text if this information is given. Otherwise, works are listed according to the date of publication of collections in which they appear.

Abend, Hallett. *My Life in China.* New York: Harcourt, Brace and Company, 1943.
Ai Ssu-ch'i. "Recognize Clearly the Reactionary Nature of the Ideology of the Bourgeois Class," *Current Background,* no. 179 (May 6, 1952).

———— "Bor'ba protiv burzhuaznoi ideologii v narodnom Kitae," *Kommunist*, no. 11: 86–96 (July 1955).

Aisin-Gioro Pu Yi. *From Emperor to Citizen: The Autobiography of Aisin-Gioro Pu Yi*. 2 vols. Peking, 1964–1965.

Angell, Sir Norman. *The Great Illusion*. New York and London, 1911.

———— *After All: The Autobiography of Norman Angell*. London, 1951.

Arkush, R. David. "Ku Hung-ming (1857–1928)," *Papers on China*, 19: 194–238 (1965). Harvard University, East Asian Research Center.

Autobiography, see Hu Shih, *Ssu-shih tzu-shu* (1933).

Bachrach, Peter. *The Theory of Democratic Elitism: A Critique*. Boston and Toronto, 1967.

Berry, Thomas, C. P. "Dewey's Influence in China," in John Blewett, S. J., ed., *John Dewey: His Thought and Influence*. New York, 1960.

Boorman, Howard L., ed. *Biographical Dictionary of Republican China*, I. New York and London: Columbia University Press, 1967.

Borg, Dorothy. "America Loses Chinese Good Will," *Far Eastern Survey*, 18.4: 37–45 (Feb. 23, 1949).

Brandt, C., B. I. Schwartz, and J. K. Fairbank. *A Documentary History of Chinese Communism*. Cambridge, Mass.: Harvard University Press, 1952.

Brière, O., S. J. "Un maître de la pensée en Chine: Hou Che," *Bulletin de l'université l'Aurore*, 3rd series, no. 5: 871–893 (1944), and no. 6: 41–73 (1945).

———— *Fifty Years of Chinese Philosophy, 1898–1950*, trans. L. G. Thompson. London, 1956.

Brinton, Crane. *The Anatomy of Revolution*. New York: Vintage Books, 1957.

Britton, Roswell S. *The Chinese Periodical Press, 1800–1912*. Shanghai, 1933.

Canning, Charles J. "What Can China's Liberals Do?" *The China Weekly Review*, 109.5: 135 (April 3, 1948).

Chan Lien. "Chinese Communism vs. Pragmatism: The Criticism of Hu Shih's Philosophy, 1950–1958," *Journal of Asian Studies*, 27.3: 551–570 (May 1968).

Chan Wing-tsit. "Trends in Contemporary Philosophy," in H. F. MacNair, ed., *China*, 312–330.

———— "Hu Shih and Chinese Philosophy," *Philosophy East and West*, 6.1: 3–12 (April 1956).

———— *A Source Book in Chinese Philosophy*. Princeton, N. J.: Princeton University Press, 1963.

Chang Ch'in-nan 張琴南. "Wu-ssu ch'ien-hou Hu Shih ti fan-tung mien-mu" 五四前後胡適的反動面目 (Hu Shih's reactionary visage before and after May Fourth), in *Wu-ssu yün-tung wen-chi*, 61–66.

Chang Ching-lu 張靜廬 ed. *Chung-kuo hsien-tai ch'u-pan shih-liao* 中國現代出版史料 (Materials on the history of contemporary Chinese publishing). 4 vols. Peking, 1954–1959.

———— *Chung-kuo chin-tai ch'u-pan shih-liao* 中國近代出版史料 (Materials on the history of modern Chinese publishing). 2 vols. Peking, 1957.

———— *Chung-kuo ch'u-pan shih-liao pu-pien* 中國出版史料補編 (Supplementary materials on the history of Chinese publishing). Peking, 1957.

Chang Chün-mai 張君勱. "Jen-sheng-kuan" 人生觀 (The philosophy of life), in KHYJSK I.

—— "Tsai lun jen-sheng-kuan yü k'o-hsüeh, ping ta Ting Tsai-chün" 再論 人生觀與科學並答丁在君 (Another discussion of the philosophy of life and science, and a rejoinder to Ting Tsai-chün), in KHYJSK I.

—— "Tao Shih-chih hsien-sheng" 悼適之先生 (Mourning Mr. Shih-chih), Hai-wai lun-t'an (World forum), 3.5: 3 (May 1, 1962).

Chang Fo-ch'üan 張佛泉. "Wo-men chiu-ching yao shen-mo yang ti hsien-fa?" 我們究竟要什么樣的憲法 (What kind of a constitution do we want after all?), TLPL no. 236: 2–4 (May 30, 1937).

Chang Hsi-jo 張熙若. "Kuo-min jen-ko chih p'ei-yang" 國民人格之培養 (The cultivation of civic character), TLPL no. 150: 14–17 (May 12, 1935).

—— "Tsai lun kuo-min jen-ko" 再論國民人格 (Another discussion of civic character), TLPL no. 152: 2–5 (May 26, 1935).

—— "Min-chu cheng-chih tang-chen shih yu-chih ti cheng-chih ma?" 民主政治當眞是幼稚的政治嗎 (Is democracy truly kindergarten government?), TLPL no. 239: 3–6 (June 20, 1937).

—— "Wo wei-shen-mo hsiang-hsin min-chih" 我爲什么相信民治 (Why I believe in democracy), TLPL no. 240: 2–5 (June 27, 1937).

Chang Huan-lun 張煥綸. "Hu T'ieh-hua hsien-sheng chia-chuan" 胡鐵花先生 家傳 (A family chronicle of Mr. Hu T'ieh-hua), in Hu Ch'uan, Taiwan chi-lu liang-chung.

Chang Ju-hsin 張如心. P'i-p'an Hu Shih ti shih-yung-chu-i che-hsüeh 批判胡適的實 用主義哲學 (A critique of Hu Shih's experimentalist philosophy). Peking, 1955.

(Chang) Kuo-t'ao 張國燾. "Wo-men tui-yü hsiao-tzu-ch'an chieh-chi ho-p'ing-p'ai ti ch'üan-kao" 我們對于小資產階級和平派的勸告 (Our advice to the petit-bourgeois peacemakers), Hsiang-tao chou-pao, no. 13: 105–106 (Dec. 23, 1922).

Chang Tung-sun 張東蓀. "Hsi-yang wen-ming yü Chung-kuo" 西洋文明與中 國 (Western civilization and China), Tung-fang tsa-chih, 23.24: 93–94 (1926).

Chang Wei-tz'u 張慰慈. "To-yüan-ti chu-ch'üan lun" 多元的主權論 (Pluralism), NLCP no. 19 (Sept. 10, 1922).

Ch'en Chih-mai 陳之邁. "Min-chu yü tu-ts'ai chih t'ao-lun" 民主與獨裁之討 論 (The debate on democracy and autocracy), TLPL no. 136: 4–11 (Jan. 20, 1935).

—— "Cheng-chih kai-ko ti pi-yao" 政制改革的必要 (On the need for reform of the political system), TLPL no. 162: 2–5 (Aug. 4, 1935).

Ch'en Hsü-ching 陳序經. "Kuan-yü ch'üan-p'an hsi-hua, ta Wu Ching-ch'ao hsien-sheng" 關於全盤西化答吳景超先生 (Concerning total westernization, in reply to Mr. Wu Ching-ch'ao), TLPL no. 142: 2–9 (March 17, 1935).

—— "Tsai t'an 'ch'üan-p'an hsi-hua'" 再談 "全盤西化" (Another discussion of "total westernization"), TLPL no. 147: 4–9 (April 21, 1935).

—— "Ts'ung hsi-hua wen-t'i ti t'ao-lun li ch'iu-te i-ko kung-t'ung hsin-yang" 從西化問題的討論裏求得一個共同信仰 (A common faith derived from the discussion of the question of westernization), TLPL no. 149: 9–13 (May 5, 1935).

—— "Ch'üan-p'an hsi-hua ti pien-hu" 全盤西化的辯護 (In defense of total westernization), TLPL no. 160: 10–15 (July 21, 1935).

Ch'en Te-cheng 陳德徵. "Hu shuo" 胡說 (Nonsense), *Min-kuo jih-pao hsing-ch'i p'ing-lun* (Republican daily news weekly review), 2.46 (April 1, 1929).

Ch'en Tu-hsiu 陳獨秀. "Ching-kao ch'ing-nien" 敬告青年 (Appeal to youth), HCN 1.1 (September 1915); *Tu-hsiu wen-ts'un*, i, 1–10.

—— "Wen-hsüeh ko-ming lun" 文學革命論 (On the literary revolution), HCN 2.6 (February 1917); *Tu-hsiu wen-ts'un*, i, 135–140.

—— "Jen-sheng chen-i" 人生眞義 (Life's true meaning), HCN 4.2 (February 1918); *Tu-hsiu wen-ts'un*, i, 181–185.

—— "Chin-jih Chung-kuo chih cheng-chih wen-t'i" 今日中國之政治問題 (China's present political problems), HCN 5.1 (July 1918); *Tu-hsiu wen-ts'un*, i, 221–225.

—— "Pen chih [*Hsin ch'ing-nien*] tsui-an chih ta-pien-shu" 本誌[新青年]罪案之答辯書 (In answer to the charges against this magazine), HCN 6.1 (January 1919); *Tu-hsiu wen-ts'un*, i, 361–363.

—— "Shih-hsing min-chih ti chi-ch'u" 實行民治的基礎 (The foundations for the realization of democracy), HCN 7.1 (December 1919); *Tu-hsiu wen-ts'un*, i, 373–389.

—— *Tu-hsiu wen-ts'un* 獨秀文存 (Collected essays of [Ch'en] Tu-hsiu). 3 *chüan* in 4 vols. Shanghai, 1922.

—— "*K'o-hsüeh yü jen-sheng-kuan* hsü" 科學與人生觀序 (Preface to Science and the philosophy of life), KHYJSK I.

—— *Ch'en Tu-hsiu ti tsui-hou tui-yü min-chu cheng-chih ti chien-chieh* 陳獨秀的最後對于民主政治的見解 (Ch'en Tu-hsiu's last thoughts on democratic government), 3rd ed. Taipei, 1959.

Ch'en Tung-hsiao 陳東曉, ed. *Ch'en Tu-hsiu p'ing-lun* 陳獨秀評論 (A critique of Ch'en Tu-hsiu). Shanghai, 1933.

Ch'en Tzu-chan 陳子展. "Wen-hsüeh ko-ming yün-tung" 文學革命運動 (The revolutionary movement in literature), in *Chung-kuo hsin wen-hsüeh ta-hsi*, X, 22–51.

Ch'eng T'ien-fang 程天放. "Wo so ch'in-chih ti Hu Shih-chih hsien-sheng" 我所親炙的胡適之先生 (The Mr. Hu Shih-chih for whom I mourn), in *Chi-nien Hu Shih-chih hsien-sheng chuan-chi*, 17–19.

Chesneaux, Jean. "Le mouvement fédéraliste en China (1920–1923)," *Revue historique*, 236: 347–384 (October-December 1966).

Chi-hsi hsien-chih 績溪縣志 (Gazetteer of Chi-hsi hsien). Taipei: Chi-hsi t'ung-hsiang-hui, 1963.

Chi-nien Hu Shih-chih hsien-sheng chuan-chi 紀念胡適之先生專集 (A collection of memorials in honor of Mr. Hu Shih-chih). Taipei, 1962.

Chi Wen-fu 嵇文甫. "P'i-p'an Hu Shih ti to-yüan li-shih-kuan" 批判胡適的多元歷史觀 (A critique of Hu Shih's pluralist historical view), *Li-shih yen-chiu* (Historical research), no. 4: 9–17 (1955).

Chiang Kai-shek. *China's Destiny*, with notes by Philip Jaffe. London: Dennis Dobson Ltd., 1947.

Chiang Meng-lin 蔣夢麟 (Monlin). *Kuo-tu shih-tai chih ssu-hsiang yü chiao-yü* 過度時代之思想與教育 (Thought and education in a transitional period). Shanghai, 1933.

———— *Tides from the West.* New Haven, 1947.

Chiang T'ing-fu 蔣廷黻. "Chih-shih chieh-chi yü cheng-chih" 知識階級與政治 (The intelligentsia and politics), TLPL no. 51: 15–19 (May 21, 1933).

———— "Ko-ming yü chuan-chih" 革命與專制 (Revolution and authoritarianism), TLPL no. 80: 2–5 (Dec. 10, 1933).

———— "Lun chuan-chih ping ta Hu Shih-chih hsien-sheng" 論專制並答胡適之先生 (On authoritarianism, in reply to Mr. Hu Shih-chih), TLPL no. 83: 2–6 (Dec. 31, 1933).

Ch'ien Tuan-sheng 錢端升. "Tui-yü liu chung ch'üan hui ti ch'i-wang" 對於六中全會的期望 ([Our] hopes for the sixth plenary sessions), TLPL no. 162: 5–9 (Aug. 4, 1935).

———— *The Government and Politics of China.* Cambridge, Mass., 1950.

China Christian Yearbook. Shanghai: Christian Literature Society, 1926, 1929.

The China Weekly Review (formerly *Millard's Review*). Shanghai, 1917–1949.

The China Yearbook, ed. H. G. W. Woodhead. Shanghai, 1928, 1931–32, 1933–1937.

Chinese Press Review. U.S. Embassy, Chungking and Nanking, U.S. Consulates in Peiping, Shanghai, and elsewhere, 1945–1949.

Chinese Social and Political Science Review. Peking, 1917–1937.

The Chinese Students' Monthly. Published by the Chinese Students' Alliance in the U.S.A., 1910–1917.

Ching Yuan. "What Kind of a Man Is Hu Shih?" *Current Background*, no. 167 (March 25, 1952).

Cho Hua 灼華. "Hu Shih so chu 'Jen-ch'üan yü yüeh-fa' chih huang-miu" 胡適所著人權與約法之荒謬 (The absurdities of Hu Shih's "Human rights and the provisional constitution"), *Min-kuo jih-pao* (Republican daily news), Aug. 9–10, 1929.

Chou I-liang 周一良. "Hsi-yang 'Han-hsüeh' yü Hu Shih" 西洋 "漢學" 與胡適 (Western "sinology" and Hu Shih), *Li-shih yen-chiu* (Historical research), no. 2: 1–14 (1955).

Chou Tso-jen 周作人. "Hsin ts'un ti ching-shen" 新村的精神 (The spirit of the New Villages), HCN 7.2: 129–134 (January 1920).

———— "Hsi-yang yeh yu ch'ou-ch'ung" 西洋也有臭虫 (There are bedbugs in the West, too), TLPL no. 107: 12 (July 1, 1934).

Chow Hwa. "Hu Shih and the May Fourth Movement," *Chinese Press Review* (Peiping), 608: 3–4 (May 10, 1948).

Chow Tse-tsung. "The Anti-Confucian Movement in Early Republican China," in A. F. Wright, ed., *The Confucian Persuasion*, 288–312.

———— *The May Fourth Movement: Intellectual Revolution in Modern China.* Cambridge, Mass.: Harvard University Press, 1960.

———— 周策縱. "Hu Shih-chih hsien-sheng ti k'ang-i yü jung-jen" 胡適之先生的抗議與容忍 (Mr. Hu Shih-chih's protestation and toleration), *Hai-wai lun-t'an* (World forum) 3.5: 21–38 (May 1, 1962).

———— *Research Guide to the May Fourth Movement.* Cambridge, Mass., 1963.

Chu Kuang-han 朱光漢. "Ch'ing k'an k'ung-ch'ien-ti Hu Shih po-shih ho wo tsen-yang p'ei-fu t'a ti li-yu" 請看空前的胡適博士和我怎樣佩服他的理由 (Please look at the unprecedented Dr. Hu Shih and my reasons for respecting him as I do), in Hsü Tzu-ming et al., *Hu Shih yü kuo-yün*, 5–19.

Chu, Samuel. "The New Life Movement, 1934–1937," in John E. Lane, ed., *Researches in the Social Sciences on China*. New York, 1957.

Chu, T. C. "China's Revolution," *The Chinese Students' Monthly*, 7.2: 127–140 (December 1911), 7.3: 207–210 (January 1912), 7.4: 289–292 (February 1912), *et seq.*

Chui-ssu Hu Shih-chih hsien-sheng chuan-chi 追思胡適之先生專集 (Memorial essays in honor of Mr. Hu Shih-chih). Tainan: Ch'en-kuang ch'u-pan she, 1962.

Chung-Hsi lun-chan yü Hu Shih 中西論戰與胡適 (Hu Shih and the debate on China vs. the West). Tainan: Wen-hua ch'u-pan she, 1962.

Chung-kuo hsin wen-hsüeh ta-hsi 中國新文學大系 (The genesis of China's new literature). 10 vols. under the general editorship of Chao Chia-pi 趙家璧. Shanghai, 1935–1936. Vol. I: *Chien-she li-lun chi* 建設理論集 (Theoretical foundations), ed. with intro. by Hu Shih; vol. II, *Wen-hsüeh lun-cheng chi* 文學論爭集 (Literary polemics), ed. with intro. by Cheng Chen-to 鄭振鐸; vol. X, *Shih-liao so-yin* 史料索引 (Historical materials and indices), ed. with intro. by Ah Ying 阿英.

"Credo," see Hu Shih, "My Credo and Its Evolution" (1931).

Crick, Bernard. *In Defence of Politics*. Baltimore: Penguin Books, 1964.

Current Background. Publication of the Press Monitoring Service of the American Consulate-General, Hong Kong, 1950–   .

de Bary, William Theodore et al., eds. *Sources of Chinese Tradition*. New York, 1960.

de Francis, John. *Nationalism and Language Reform in China*. Princeton, 1950.

de Ruggiero, Guido. *The History of European Liberalism*, trans. R. G. Collingwood. Boston: Beacon Press, 1959.

Dewey, John. *Essays in Experimental Logic*. Chicago, 1916.

———— "Force, Violence and Law," *The New Republic*, 5: 295–297 (Jan. 22, 1916); *Characters and Events*, II, 636–641.

———— "Force and Coercion," *International Journal of Ethics*, 26: 359–367 (April 1916); *Characters and Events*, II, 782–789.

———— "On the Two Sides of the Eastern Sea," *The New Republic*, 19: 346–348 (July 16, 1919); *Characters and Events*, I, 170–176.

———— "The Student Revolt in China," *The New Republic*, 20: 16–18 (Aug. 6, 1919).

———— "Militarism in China," *The New Republic*, 20: 167–169 (Sept. 10, 1919).

———— "Liberalism in Japan," *The Dial*, 67: 283–285 (Oct. 4, 1919), 333–337 (Oct. 18, 1919), 369–371 (Nov. 1, 1919); *Characters and Events*, I, 149–169.

———— "Transforming the Mind of China," *Asia*, 19: 1103–1108 (November 1919); *Characters and Events*, I, 285–295.

———— "Chinese National Sentiment," *Asia*, 19: 1237–1242 (December 1919); *Characters and Events*, I, 222–236 (retitled "The Growth of Chinese National Sentiment").

——— "The American Opportunity in China," *The New Republic*, 21: 14–17 (Dec. 3, 1919); *Characters and Events*, I, 296–311 (retitled "America and China").

——— "The Sequel of the Student Revolt," *The New Republic*, 21: 380–382 (Feb. 25, 1920).

——— "The New Leaven in Chinese Politics," *Asia*, 20: 267–272 (April 1920); *Characters and Events*, I, 244–254 (retitled "Justice and Law in China").

——— "What Holds China Back," *Asia*, 20: 373–377 (May 1920); *Characters and Events*, I, 211–221 (retitled "Chinese Social Habits").

——— "Is China a Nation?" *The New Republic*, 25: 187–190 (Jan. 12, 1921); *Characters and Events*, I, 237–243 (retitled "Conditions for China's Nationhood").

——— "Old China and New," *Asia*, 21: 445–450, 454, 456 (May 1921); *Characters and Events*, I, 255–269 (retitled "Young China and Old").

——— "New Culture in China," *Asia*, 21: 581–586, 642 (July 1921); *Characters and Events*, I, 270–284.

——— "Federalism in China," *The New Republic*, 28: 176–178 (Oct. 12, 1921).

——— "Public Opinion in Japan," *The New Republic*, 28: 15–18 (Nov. 16, 1921); *Characters and Events*, I, 177–184 (retitled "Japan Revisited: Two Years Later").

——— *Human Nature and Conduct*. New York, 1922, 1957.

——— "As the Chinese Think," *Asia*, 22: 7–10, 78–79 (January 1922); *Characters and Events*, I, 199–210 (retitled "The Chinese Philosophy of Life").

——— "America and Chinese Education," *The New Republic*, 30: 15–17 (March 1, 1922); *Characters and Events*, I, 303–309 (retitled "America and China," part 2).

——— *Experience and Nature*. Chicago and London, 1925; rev. ed., New York: Open Court Publishing Co., 1929.

——— *Characters and Events: Popular Essays in Social and Political Philosophy*, ed. Joseph Ratner. 2 vols. New York: Henry Holt and Co., 1929.

——— *Intelligence in the Modern World: John Dewey's Philosophy*, ed. Joseph Ratner. New York: Modern Library, 1939.

——— *Reconstruction in Philosophy*, enlarged ed. Boston: Beacon Press, 1957.

Diary, see Hu Shih, *Hu Shih liu-hsüeh jih-chi* (1959).

Dobson, W. A. C. H., trans. *Mencius*. Toronto: University of Toronto Press, 1963.

Dubs, Homer. "Recent Chinese Philosophy," *Journal of Philosophy*, 35: 345–355 (1938).

Edman, Irwin. *John Dewey: His Contribution to the American Tradition*. New York: Bobbs Merrill Co., 1955.

Fairbank, John King. *The United States and China*. Cambridge, Mass., 1948; rev. ed., 1958.

——— ed. *Chinese Thought and Institutions*. Chicago, 1957.

Fan Wen-lan 范文瀾. "K'an-k'an Hu Shih ti 'li-shih-ti t'ai-tu' ho 'k'o-hsüeh-ti fang-fa' " 看看胡適的 "歷史的態度" 和 "科學的方法" (Let's look at Hu Shih's "historical attitude" and "scientific method"), *Li-shih yen-chiu* (Historical research), no. 3: 1–30 (1955).

Feng Ai-ch'ün 馮愛羣, ed. *Hu Shih-chih hsien-sheng chi-nien chi* 胡適之先生紀念集 (A collection of memorials honoring Mr. Hu Shih-chih). Taipei: Hsüeh-sheng shu-chü, 1962.

Foreign Relations of the United States, Diplomatic Papers, 1935, vol. III: *The Far East*. Washington, D.C., 1953.

Foreign Relations of the United States, Diplomatic Papers, 1942: China. Washington, D.C., 1956.

Freyn, Hubert. *Prelude to War: The Chinese Student Rebellion of 1935–1936*. Shanghai: China Journal Publishing Co., Ltd., 1939.

Friedman, Maurice. *To Deny Our Nothingness: Contemporary Images of Man*. New York, 1967.

Fu Ssu-nien 傅斯年. "Ch'en Tu-hsiu an" 陳獨秀案 (The case of Ch'en Tu-hsiu), TLPL no. 24: 2–7 (Oct. 30, 1932).

Fukui Kōjun 福井康順. *Gendai Chūkoku shisō* 現代中國思想 (Contemporary Chinese thought). Tokyo: Waseda University, 1956.

Fung Yu-lan. *A History of Chinese Philosophy*, trans. Derk Bodde. 2 vols. Princeton, N.J.: Princeton University Press, 1953.

Gannett, Lewis S. *Young China*, rev. ed. New York: *The Nation*, 1927.

——— "Hu Shih: Young Prophet of Young China," *The New York Times Magazine*, March 27, 1927, 10 and 20.

Gay, Peter. *The Enlightenment: An Interpretation. The Rise of Modern Paganism*. New York: Alfred A. Knopf, 1967.

Geiger, George Raymond. *John Dewey in Perspective*. New York: Oxford University Press, 1958.

Giglio-Tos, Efisio. *Appel pour le désarmement et pour la paix: les pionniers de la société des nations et de la fraternité internationale; d'après les archives de la "Corda Fratres," Fédération Internationale des Etudiants, 1898–1931*. Turin: Tipografia A. Kluc, 1931.

Gray, J. "Historical Writing in Twentieth-Century China," in W. G. Beasley and E. G. Pulleyblank, eds., *Historians of China and Japan*, pp. 186–212. London, 1961.

Grieder, Jerome B. "The Chinese Communist Critique of *Hung-lou meng*," *Papers on China*, 10: 142–168 (1956). Harvard University, East Asian Research Center.

Griggs, Thurston. *Americans in China: Some Chinese Views*. Washington, D.C.: Foundation for Foreign Affairs, 1948.

Gunther, John. *Inside Asia*. New York and London: Harper and Brothers, 1939.

HCN, see *Hsin ch'ing-nien*.

Ho Ping-ti. *The Ladder of Success in Imperial China: Aspects of Social Mobility, 1368–1911*. New York and London, 1962.

Hobhouse, Leonard T. *Liberalism*. Home University Library of Modern Knowledge, no. 16. London: Williams and Norgate, 1911.

Holcombe, Arthur N. *The Chinese Revolution: A Phase in the Regeneration of a World Power*. Cambridge, Mass.: Harvard University Press, 1931.

Hou Wai-lu 侯外盧. "Chieh-lu Mei ti-kuo-chu-i nu-tsai Hu Shih ti fan-tung mien-mao" 揭露美帝國主義奴才胡適的反動面貌 (Uncovering the reactionary visage of Hu Shih, the slave of American imperialism), in *Hu*

Shih ssu-hsiang p'i-p'an, III, 17–83.

Hsia, C. T. *A History of Modern Chinese Fiction, 1917–1957*. New Haven: Yale University Press, 1961.

Hsiao Kung-ch'üan 蕭公權. *Chung-kuo cheng-chih ssu-hsiang shih* 中國政治思想史 (A history of Chinese political thought). 6 vols. Taipei, 1954.

Hsien-tai p'ing-lun 現代評論 (Contemporary review). Peking, 1924–1927; Shanghai, 1927– . Weekly.

Hsin ch'ing-nien 新青年 (The new youth). Peking and Shanghai, 1915–1921; Canton, 1921– . Monthly, with occasional lapses.

"*Hsin ch'ing-nien tsa-chih* hsüan-yen" 新青年雜誌宣言 (Manifesto of the New youth magazine), HCN 7.1: 1–4 (December 1919).

Hsin yüeh 新月 (The crescent). Shanghai, 1928– . Monthly.

"*Hsin yüeh yüeh-k'an* ching-kao tu-che" 新月月刊敬告讀者 (An announcement to readers of the Crescent monthly), HY 2.6, 7 (September 1929).

Hsü Kai-yü. "The Life and Poetry of Wen I-to," *Harvard Journal of Asiatic Studies*, 21: 134–179 (December 1958).

Hsü Tzu-ming 徐子明 et al. *Hu Shih yü kuo-yün* 胡適與國運 (Hu Shih and the nation's destiny). Taipei: Taiwan Hsüeh-sheng shu-chü, 1958.

HSWT, see Hu Shih, *Hu Shih wen-ts'un* (1921, 1924, 1930, and 1953).

Hu Ch'uan 胡傳. *Taiwan chi-lu liang-chung* 台灣紀錄兩種 (Two records of Taiwan), ed. Hu Shih and Lo Erh-kang. Taipei: Taiwan sheng wen-hsien wei-yüan-hui, 1951.

Hu Shih (Hu Suh). "The International Student Movement," *The Chinese Students' Monthly*, 9.1: 37–39 (November 1913).

———— "The Confucianist Movement in China: An Historical Account and Criticism," *The Chinese Students' Monthly*, 9.7: 533–536 (May 1914).

———— "Japan and Kiao-chau," *The Chinese Students' Monthly*, 10.1: 27 (October 1914).

———— "History of the German Leased Territory of Kiao-chau," *The Chinese Students' Monthly*, 10.2: 68–69 (November 1914).

———— "Letter to the Editor of The New Republic," reprinted in *The Chinese Students' Monthly*, 10.6: 389–390 (March 1915).

———— "A Plea for Patriotic Sanity: An Open Letter to All Chinese Students," *The Chinese Students' Monthly*, 10.7: 425–426 (April 1915).

———— "China and Democracy," *The Outlook*, 111: 27–28 (Sept. 1, 1915).

———— "A Philosopher of Chinese Reactionism [Dr. Frank J. Goodnow]," *The Chinese Students' Monthly*, 11.1: 16–19 (November 1915).

———— "A Chinese Philosopher on War: A Popular Presentation of the Ethical and Religious Views of Mo-Ti," *The Chinese Students' Monthly*, 11.6: 408–412 (April 1916).

———— 胡適. "T'ung-hsin: chih Tu-hsiu" 通信：致獨秀 (Letter to [Ch'en] Tu-hsiu), HCN 2.2 (October 1916); HSWT, i, 1–6.

———— "Wen-hsüeh kai-liang ch'u-i" 文學改良芻議 (Tentative proposals for the improvement of literature), HCN 2.5 (January 1917); HSWT, i, 7–23.

———— "Li-shih-ti wen-hsüeh kuan-nien lun" 歷史的文學觀念論 (On the genetic concept of literature), HCN 3.3 (May 1917); HSWT, i, 45–50.

—— "T'ung-hsin: chih Tu-hsiu" 通信：致獨秀 (Letters to [Ch'en] Tu-hsiu), HCN 3.3 (May 1917) and 3.4 (June 1917); HSWT, i, 51–76.

—— *Ha algum substituto eficaz que se imponha á força nas relações internacionaes?* American Association for International Conciliation, Pan-American Division, bulletin no. 13. New York, 1917.

—— "Kuei-kuo tsa-kan" 歸國雜感 (Random reflections on returning home), HCN 4.1 (January 1918); HSWT, iv, 871–882.

—— "Lü ching tsa-chi" 旅京雜記 (Miscellaneous notes on a trip to the capital), HCN 4.3: 248–254 (March 1918).

—— "Chien-she-ti wen-hsüeh ko-ming lun" 建設的文學革命論 (On a constructive literary revolution), HCN 4.4 (April 1918); HSWT, i, 77–102.

—— "Hsin-hun tsa-shih wu-shou" 新婚雜詩五首 (Five poems in various styles on being newly married), HCN 4.4: 311 (April 1918).

—— "I-pu-sheng chu-i" 易卜生主義 (Ibsenism), HCN 4.6 (June 1918); HSWT, iv, 883–908.

—— "Chen-ts'ao wen-t'i" 貞操問題 (The question of chastity), HCN 5.1 (July 1918); HSWT, iv, 933–948.

—— "Mei-kuo ti fu-jen" 美國的婦人 (American women), HCN 5.3 (September 1918); HSWT, iv, 909–932.

—— "Wen-hsüeh chin-hua kuan-nien yü hsi-chü kai-liang" 文學進化觀念與戲劇改良 (The concept of progress in literature and the reform of drama), HCN 5.4: 308–321 (October 1918).

—— "Wu-li chieh-chüeh yü chieh-chüeh wu-li" 武力解決與解決武力 (Resolving problems by force, and resolving the problem of force), HCN 5.6: 571–574 (December 1918).

—— *Chung-kuo che-hsüeh shih ta-kang, shang chüan* 中國哲學史大剛，上卷 (An outline of the history of Chinese philosophy), I. Shanghai: Commerical Press, 1919. Republished, with a new preface by Hu Shih, under the title *Chung-kuo ku-tai che-hsüeh shih* 中國古代哲學史 (A history of ancient Chinese philosophy). Taipei: Commercial Press, 1958.

—— trans. *Tuan-p'ien hsiao-shuo ti-i chi* 短篇小說第一集 (Short stories, first collection). Shanghai: Ya-tung t'u-shu kuan, 1919.

—— "Pu-hsiu" 不朽 (Immortality), HCN 6.2 (February 1919); HSWT, iv, 975–988.

—— "Chung-shen ta-shih" 終身大事 (Life's great event), HCN 6.3 (March 1919); HSWT, iv 1153–1172.

—— "Shih-yen chu-i" 實驗主義 (Experimentalism), HCN 6.4 (April 1919); HSWT, ii, 409–480.

—— "To yen-chiu hsieh wen-t'i, shao t'an hsieh 'chu-i'" 多研究些問題，少談些"主義" (Study more problems, talk less of 'isms'), *Mei-chou p'ing-lun*, no. 31 (July 20, 1919); HSWT, ii, 481–487.

—— "Wo-ti erh-tzu" 我的兒子 (My son), *Mei-chou p'ing-lun*, no. 33 (Aug. 3, 1919); HSWT, iv, 965–974.

—— "Hsin sheng-huo" 新生活 (The new life), *Hsin sheng-huo tsa-chih*, no. 1 (Aug. 24, 1919); HSWT, iv, 1017–1020.

—— "San lun wen-t'i yü chu-i" 三論問題與主義 (A third discussion of problems and isms), *Mei-chou p'ing-lun*, no. 36 (Aug. 24, 1919); HSWT, ii, 511-524.

—— "Ssu lun wen-t'i yü chu-i: lun shu-ju hsüeh-li ti fang-fa" 四論問題與主義：論輸入學理的方法 (A fourth discussion of problems and isms: on the methods of importing theories), *Mei-chou p'ing-lun*, no. 37 (Aug. 31, 1919); HSWT, ii, 524-531.

—— "Wo tui sang-li ti i-tien i-chien" 我對喪禮的一點意見 (Some of my ideas on [a reform of] funeral rites), HCN 6.6 (November 1919); HSWT, iv, 997-1016, retitled "Wo tui-yü sang-li ti kai-ko" 我對於喪禮的改革 (Changes that I have made in the funeral rites).

—— "Ching-t'ien pien" 井田辨 (Making distinctions concerning the well-field [system]), dated Nov. 8, 1919, Jan. 9, 1920, and July 4, 1921; HSWT, ii, 581-618.

—— "Intellectual China in 1919," *The Chinese Social and Political Science Review*, 4.4: 345-355 (December 1919).

—— "Li Ch'ao chuan" 李超傳 (Biography of Li Ch'ao), dated December 1919; HSWT, iv, 1077-1094.

—— "Hsin ssu-ch'ao ti i-i" 新思潮的意義 (The meaning of the new thought), HCN 7.1 (December 1919); HSWT, iv, 1021-1034.

—— *Ch'ang-shih chi* 嘗試集 (A collection of experiments). Shanghai: Ya-tung t'u-shu-kuan, 1920; rev. ed., 4th printing, 1922.

—— "Fei ko-jen chu-i ti hsin sheng-huo" 非個人主義的新生活 (The anti-individualistic new life), dated Jan. 26, 1920; HSWT, iv, 1043-1060.

—— and Chiang Monlin. "Wo-men tui-yü hsüeh-sheng ti hsi-wang" 我們對于學生的希望 (Our hopes for the students), *Tung-fang tsa-chih*, 17.11: 117-122 (June 6, 1920). Reprinted in Chiang Monlin, *Kuo-tu shih-tai chih ssu-hsiang yü chiao-yü*, 156-171.

—— "Yen-chiu she-hui wen-t'i ti fang-fa" 研究社會的問題方法 (The method of studying social problems), *Tung-fang tsa-chih*, 17.13: 113-121 (July 10, 1920).

—— "Hsien-mu hsing-shu" 先母行書 (Reflections on my late mother's life), dated June 25, 1921; HSWT, iv, 1107-1113.

—— *Hu Shih wen-ts'un* 胡適文存 (Collected essays of Hu Shih). 2 vols., 4 chüan. Shanghai: Ya-tung t'u-shu-kuan, 1921.

—— "Tu-wei hsien-sheng yü Chung-kuo" 杜威先生與中國 (Mr. Dewey and China), dated July 11, 1921; HSWT, ii, 533-537.

—— "Shih-ch'i nien ti hui-ku" 十七年的回顧 (Looking back seventeen years), dated Oct. 3, 1921; HSWT II, iii, 1-8.

—— "Ch'ing-tai hsüeh-che ti chih-hsüeh fang-fa" 清代學者的治學方法 (The scholarly methodology of Ch'ing-period scholars), dated Nov. 3, 1921; HSWT, ii, 539-579.

—— Unpublished diaries, 1921-1935. Microfilm in the archive of the Oral History Project, Columbia University. 6 reels.

—— *The Development of the Logical Method in Ancient China*. Shanghai: Oriental Book Co., 1922. Reprinted, with intro. by Hyman Kublin; New York: Paragon Book Company, 1963.

—— "Nu-li ko" 努力歌 (A song of endeavor), NLCP no. 1 (May 7, 1922).

———— "Wo-men-ti cheng-chih chu-chang" 我們的政治主張 (Our political proposals), NLCP no. 2 (May 14, 1922); HSWT II, iii, 27–34.

———— "Ta-chia ch'i-lai chien-tu ts'ai-cheng" 大家起來監督財政 (Let everyone supervise public finance), NLCP no. 3 (May 21, 1922).

———— "Hou nu-li ko" 後努力歌 (A second song of endeavor), NLCP no. 4 (May 28, 1922).

———— "Kuan-yü 'Wo-men-ti cheng-chih chu-chang' ti t'ao-lun" 關於 "我們的政治主張" 的討論 (Discussion of "Our political proposals"), NLCP no. 4 (May 28, 1922) et seq.; HSWT II, iii, 35–90.

———— "Cheng-lun-chia yü cheng-tang" 政論家與政黨 (Political critics and political parties), NLCP no. 5 (June 4, 1922).

———— "Che-i chou" 這一週 (This week), NLCP no. 7 (June 18, 1922) to NLCP no. 48 (April 1, 1923); HSWT II, iii, 145–272.

———— (signing himself "QV"). "Cheng-chih yü chi-hua" 政治與計畫 (Politics and planning), NLCP no. 7 (June 18, 1922).

———— "Wo-ti ch'i-lu" 我的岐路 (My crossroads), NLCP no. 7 (June 18, 1922); HSWT II, iii, 91–108.

———— "Hsüan-t'ung yü Hu Shih" 宣統與胡適 ([The] Hsüan-t'ung [emperor] and Hu Shih), NLCP no. 12 (July 23, 1922).

———— "Wu P'ei-fu yü lien-sheng tzu-chih" 吳佩孚與聯省自治 (Wu P'ei-fu and federalism), NLCP no. 15 (August 13, 1922).

———— "Fa-ch'i Tu-shu tsa-chih ti yüan-ch'i" 發起讀書雜誌的緣起 (The reasons for publishing Reading magazine), Tu-shu tsa-chih, no. 1 (Sept. 3, 1922); HSWT II, i, 29–30.

———— "I-ch'ien chiu-pai nien ch'ien ti i-ko she-hui-chu-i-che: Wang Mang" 一千九百年前的一個社會主義者：王莽 (A socialist of nineteen centuries ago: Wang Mang), Tu-shu tsa-chih, no. 1 (Sept. 3, 1922); HSWT II, i, 31–42.

———— "Lien-sheng tzu-chih yü chün-fa ko-chü" 聯省自治與軍閥割據 (Federative provincial self-government and warlord separatism), NLCP no. 19 (Sept. 10, 1922); HSWT II, iii, 109–119.

———— "Kuo-chi ti Chung-kuo" 國際的中國 (China among the nations), NLCP no. 22 (Oct. 1, 1922); HSWT II, iii, 128a–i.

———— "Chi ti-pa-chieh ch'üan-kuo chiao-yü-hui lien-ho-hui t'ao-lun hsin hsüeh-chih ti ching-kuo" 記第八屆全國教育會聯合會討論新學制的經過 (A record of the proceedings of the eighth plenary meeting of the National Education Association to discuss the new educational system), NLCP no. 25 (Oct. 22, 1922).

———— "Wo-men hai chu-chang chao-chi ko-sheng hui-i" 我們還主張召集各省會議 (We still advocate the calling of provincial assemblies), NLCP no. 28 (Nov. 12, 1922).

———— "Shei shih Chung-kuo chin-jih ti shih-erh-ko ta jen-wu?" 誰是中國近日的十二個大人物？ (Who are China's twelve leading personalities today?), NLCP no. 29 (Nov. 19, 1922).

———— "Literary Revolution in China," The Chinese Social and Political Science Review, 6.2: 91–100 (1922).

———— "Social Message in Chinese Poetry," The Chinese Social and Political

Science Review, 7.1: 66–79 (January 1923). Paper read before the "Things Chinese" Society, Peking.

———— " 'Hu Shih hsien-sheng tao-ti tsen-yang?' " "胡適先生到底怎樣？" (How *is* Mr. Hu Shih?), NLCP no. 36 (Jan. 7, 1923).

———— "Tu Liang Sou-ming hsien-sheng ti *Tung Hsi wen-hua chi ch'i che-hsüeh*" 讀梁漱溟先生的東西文化及其哲學 (On reading Mr. Liang Sou-ming's The cultures of East and West and their philosophies), dated March 28, 1923; HSWT II, ii, 57–85.

———— "Wu-shih nien lai Chung-kuo chih wen-hsüeh" 五十年來中國之文學 (Chinese literature in the last fifty years), in *Tsui-chin wu-shih nien: Shen-pao-kuan wu-shih chou-nien chi-nien* (The last half century: Commemorating the fiftieth anniversary of *Shen-pao;* Shanghai, 1923); also in HSWT II, ii, 91–213.

———— "Wu-shih nien lai chih shih-chieh che-hsüeh" 五十年來之世界哲學 (World philosophy in the last fifty years), in *Tsui-chin wu-shih nien: Shen-pao-kuan wu-shih chou-nien chi-nien;* also in HSWT II, ii, 217–303.

———— "Yü I-han teng ssu-wei ti hsin" 與一涵等四位的信 (Letter to [Kao] I-han and others), dated Oct. 9, 1923; HSWT II, iii, 141–144.

———— "Sun Hsing-che yü Chang Chün-mai" 孫行者與張君勱 (The king of the monkeys and Chang Chün-mai), KHYJSK I; HSWT II, ii, 53–56.

———— "*K'o-hsüeh yü jen-sheng-kuan* hsü" 科學與人生觀序 (Preface to Science and the philosophy of life), KHYJSK I; HSWT II, ii, 1–52.

———— "*Cheng-chih kai-lun* hsü" 政治概論序 (Preface to Outline of politics [by Chang Wei-tz'u]), dated Nov. 17, 1923; HSWT II, iii, 19–23.

———— *Hu Shih wen-ts'un, erh-chi* 胡適文存二集 (Collected essays of Hu Shih, second collection). 2 vols., 4 *chüan.* Shanghai: Ya-tung t'u-shu-kuan, 1924.

———— "A Chinese Declaration of the Rights of Women," *The Chinese Social and Political Science Review*, 8.2: 100–109 (April 1924). Paper read to the Tientsin Rotary Club, February 1924.

———— "Ai-kuo yün-tung yü ch'iu-hsüeh" 愛國運動與求學 (The patriotic movement and getting an education), *Hsien-tai p'ing-lun*, 2.39: 5–9 (Sept. 5, 1925); HSWT III, ix, 1145–1154.

———— Reply to Liu Chih-hsi 劉治熙, *Hsien-tai p'ing-lun*, 2.42: 20–21 (Sept. 26, 1925).

———— "Chin-jih chiao-hui chiao-yü ti nan-kuan" 近日教會教育的難關 (Problems facing mission education today), dated March 9, 1926 (draft of a speech delivered at Yenching University in 1925); HSWT III, ix, 1159–1170.

———— "Wo-men tui-yü Hsi-yang chin-tai wen-ming ti t'ai-tu" 我們對於西洋近代文明的態度 (Our attitude toward modern Western civilization), *Hsien-tai p'ing-lun*, 4.83: 3–11 (July 10, 1926); HSWT III, i, 3–13.

———— "Cheng-li kuo-ku yü 'ta-kuei' " 整理國故與 "打鬼" (Systematizing the national heritage and 'fighting ghosts'), *Hsien-tai p'ing-lun*, 5.119: 13–15 (March 19, 1927); HSWT III, ii, 207–220.

———— "Man-yu ti kan-hsiang" 漫遊的感想 (Impressions of ramblings), *Hsien-tai p'ing-lun*, 6.140: 9–12 (Aug. 13, 1927), 6.141: 11–13 (Aug. 20, 1927), and 6.145: 12–15 (Sept. 17, 1927); HSWT III, i, 51–72.

——— *Pai-hua wen-hsüeh shih, shang chüan* 白話文學史上卷 (A history of vernacular literature), I. Shanghai, Hsin-yüeh shu-tien, 1928. Reprinted in Taipei, 1957.

——— "The Civilizations of the East and the West," in Charles A. Beard, ed., *Whither Mankind: A Panorama of Modern Civilization*, 25–42. New York, London and Toronto: Longmans, Green and Co., 1928.

——— "Two Wings of One Bird: A Chinese Attitude toward Eastern and Western Civilization," *Pacific Affairs*, 1.1: 1–8 (May 1928). Translation by Lucius C. Porter of "Wo-men tui-yü Hsi-yang chin-tai wen-ming ti t'ai-tu."

——— "Wang Mang, the Socialist Emperor of Nineteen Centuries Ago," *Journal of the North China Branch of the Royal Asiatic Society*, 59: 218–230 (1928).

——— "Jen-sheng yu ho i-i?" 人生有何意義? (What is the meaning of life?), dated Jan. 27, 1928; HSWT III, ix, 1143–1144.

——— "Chi-ko fan-li-hsüeh ti ssu-hsiang-chia" 幾個反理學的思想家 (Some anti-rationalist thinkers), dated Feb. 7, 1928 (revised draft); HSWT III, ii, 111–185.

——— "Chui-hsiang Hu Ming-fu" 追想胡明復 (In memoriam for Hu Ming-fu), dated March 17, 1928; HSWT III, ix, 1211–1222.

——— "Tsai lun Wang Mang" 再論王莽 (Another discussion of Wang Mang), dated April 19, 1928; HSWT III, vii, 885–890.

——— "Ch'ing ta-chia lai chao-chao ching-tzu" 請大家來照照鏡子 (Please let us look in the mirror), dated June 24, 1928; HSWT III, i, 39–50.

——— "Ming chiao" 名教 (The religion of names), HY 1.5 (July 1928); HSWT III, i, 91–110. Also reprinted in *Jen-ch'üan lun-chi*.

——— "Chih-hsüeh ti fang-fa yü ts'ai-liao" 治學的方法與材料 (The methods and materials of scholarship), HY 1.9 (November 1928); HSWT III, ii, 187–206.

——— "Conflict of Cultures," *The China Christian Yearbook*, 112–121. Shanghai, 1929.

——— "The Establishment of Confucianism as a State Religion during the Han Dynasty," *Journal of the North China Branch of the Royal Asiatic Society*, 60: 20–41 (1929).

——— "Hu Shih Sees China Foundation Free of Political Interference," *The Peking Leader*, Jan. 23, 1929.

——— "Jen-ch'üan yü yüeh-fa" 人權與約法 (Human rights and the provisional constitution), HY 2.2 (April 1929). Reprinted in *Jen-ch'üan lun-chi*.

——— "Wo-men shen-mo shih-hou ts'ai k'o yu hsien-fa?" 我們什么時候才可有憲法? (When *can* we have a constitution?), HY 2.4 (June 1929). Reprinted in *Jen-ch'üan lun-chi*.

——— "Chih nan, hsing i pu-i" 知難, 行亦不易 (Knowledge is difficult, but action is not easy either), HY 2.4 (June 1929), reprinted from *Wu-sung yüeh-k'an*, no. 2: 1–10 (May 1929). Reprinted in *Jen-ch'üan lun-chi*.

——— "'Jen-ch'üan yü yüeh-fa' t'ao-lun" "人權與約法" 討論 (Discussions of 'Human rights and the provisional constitution'), HY 2.4 (June 1929). Reprinted in *Jen-ch'üan lun-chi*.

———— "Hsin wen-hua yün-tung yü Kuomintang" 新文化運動與國民黨 (The new culture movement and the Kuomintang), HY 2.6–7 (September 1929). Reprinted in *Jen-ch'üan lun-chi.*

———— "Wo-men tsou na-i-t'iao lu?" 我們走那一條路？(Which road shall we follow?), HY 2.10 (Dec. 10, 1929); HSWT IV, iv, 429–443. Also reprinted in *Chung-kuo wen-t'i.*

———— "*Hu Shih wen-hsüan* tzu-hsü: chieh-shao wo tzu-chi ti ssu-hsiang" 胡適文選自序：介紹我自己的思想 (Author's preface to Selected works of Hu Shih: Introducing my own thought), *Hu Shih wen-hsüan* 胡適文選. Shanghai: Ya-tung t'u-shu-kuan, 1930. Reprinted in HY 3.4 (1930?), and in HSWT IV, iv, 607–624.

———— *Hu Shih wen-ts'un, san chi* 胡適文存，三集 (Collected essays of Hu Shih, third collection). 4 vols., 9 *chüan.* Shanghai: Ya-tung t'u-shu-kuan, 1930.

———— "Ou-yu tao-chung chi-shu" 歐遊道中寄書 (Letters written enroute through Europe), HSWT III, i, 73–90. Three letters to Chang Wei-tz'u, undated; two letters to Hsü Chih-mo, dated Aug. 27 and Oct. 4, 1926.

———— with Liang Shih-ch'iu and Lo Lung-chi. *Jen-ch'üan lun-chi* 人權論集 (A collection of essays on human rights). Shanghai: Hsin-yüeh shu-tien, 1930.

———— and Liang Sou-ming. "Kuan-yü 'Wo-men tsou na-i-t'iao lu?' i-wen ti t'ao-lun" 關於 "我們走那一條路？" 一文的討論 (A discussion of the essay 'Which road shall we follow?'), HY 3.1 (1930?). Liang's letter dated June 3; Hu's reply dated July 29, 1930.

———— "Letter to the Editor of the North China Daily News," Aug. 28, 1930.

———— "Which Road Are We Going?," *Pacific Affairs,* 3.10: 933–946 (October 1930). Translation of "Wo-men tsou na-i-t'iao lu?"

———— with Lin Yutang, commentaries by Wang Ching-wei. *China's Own Critics.* Peiping: China United Press, 1931.

———— "The Literary Renaissance," in Sophia Zen, ed., *Symposium on Chinese Culture,* 129–141.

———— "Religion and Philosophy in Chinese History," in Sophia Zen, ed., *Symposium on Chinese Culture,* 31–58.

———— "My Credo and Its Evolution," in *Living Philosophies,* 235–263. New York: Simon & Schuster, 1931.

———— ed. *Chung-kuo wen-t'i* 中國問題 (China's problems). Shanghai: Hsin-yüeh shu-tien, 1932.

———— "Hsien-cheng wen-t'i" 憲政問題 (The question of constitutional government), TLPL no. 1: 5–7 (May 22, 1932).

———— "Tseng-yü chin-nien ti ta-hsüeh pi-yeh-sheng" 贈與今年的大學畢業生 (An offering to this year's university graduates), TLPL no. 7: 2–5 (July 3, 1932); HSWT IV, 505–511.

———— (signing himself "Shih-chih" 適之). "So-wei chiao-yü ti fa-hsi-ssu-ti-hua" 所謂教育的法西斯蒂化 (The so-called fascistization of education), TLPL no. 8: 14–15 (July 10, 1932).

———— (signing himself "Ts'ang-hui" 藏暉). "Lun hsüeh-ch'ao" 論學潮 (On the student movement), TLPL no. 9: 6–9 (July 17, 1932).

———— (signing himself "Shih-chih"). "Ling-hsiu jen-ts'ai ti lai-yüan" 領袖人

才的來源 (The sources of leadership talent), TLPL no. 12: 2–5 (Aug. 7, 1932); HSWT IV, 494–499.

——— "Wang Ching-wei yü Chang Hsüeh-liang" 汪精衛與張學良 (Wang Ching-wei and Chang Hsüeh-liang), TLPL no. 13: 2–4 (Aug. 14, 1932).

——— "Nei-t'ien tui shih-chieh ti t'iao-chan" 內田對世界的挑戰 (Uchida's challenge to the world), TLPL no. 16: 2–3 (Sept. 4, 1932).

——— "Chung-kuo cheng-chih ch'u-lu ti t'ao-lun" 中國政治出路的討論 (A discussion of the way out for Chinese politics), TLPL no. 17: 2–6 (Sept. 11, 1932).

——— "Ts'an-t'ung ti hui-i yü fan-hsing" 慘痛的回憶與反省 (Grievous recollections and reflections), TLPL no. 18: 8–13 (Sept. 18, 1932); HSWT IV, 450–457.

——— "Chiu-ching na-i-ko t'iao-yüeh shih fei-chih?" 究意那一個條約是廢紙? (Which treaty is after all a scrap of waste paper?), TLPL no. 19: 2–7 (Sept. 25, 1932).

——— "I-ko tai-piao shih-chieh kung-lun ti pao-kao" 一個代表世界公論的報告 (A report that represents world public opinion), TLPL no. 21: 2–6 (Oct. 9, 1932).

——— "T'ung-i ti lu" 統一的路 (The road to unification), TLPL no. 28: 2–6 (Nov. 27, 1932).

——— trans. *Tuan-p'ien hsiao-shuo, ti-erh chi* 短篇小說第二集 (Short stories, second collection). Shanghai: Ya-tung t'u-shu kuan, 1933.

——— "Kuo-min ts'an-cheng-hui ying-kai ju-ho tsu-chih" 國民參政會應該如何組織 (How the National People's Assembly should be organized), TLPL no. 34: 2–5 (Jan. 8, 1933).

——— "Min-ch'üan ti pao-chang" 民權的保障 (The defense of popular rights), TLPL no. 38: 2–5 (Feb. 19, 1933).

——— "Jih-pen-jen ying-kai hsing-hsing le!" 日本人應該醒醒了! (The Japanese must wake up!), TLPL no. 42: 2–4 (March 19, 1933).

——— "Wo-men k'o-i teng-hou wu-shih nien!" 我們可以等候五十年! (We can wait fifty years!), TLPL no. 44: 2–5 (April 2, 1933).

——— "Wo-ti i-chien yeh pu-kuo ju-tz'u" 我的意見也不過如此 (My ideas are simply these), TLPL no. 46: 2–5 (April 16, 1933).

——— "Ts'ung nung-ts'un chiu-chi t'an-tao wu-wei ti cheng-chih" 從農村救濟談到無爲的政治 (From rural relief to a discussion of *wu-wei* government), TLPL no. 49: 2–6 (May 7, 1933).

——— "Chih hsien pu-ju shou-fa" 制憲不如守法 (Making a constitution is not so good as staying within the law), TLPL no. 50: 2–4 (May 10, 1933).

——— "*Tu-li p'ing-lun* ti i-chou-nien" 獨立評論的一週年 (The first anniversary of the Independent critic), TLPL no. 51: 2–5 (May 21, 1933).

——— "Pao-ch'üan Hua-pei ti chung-yao" 保全華北的重要 (The importance of defending North China), TLPL nos. 52–53: 2–6 (June 4, 1933).

——— "Chien-kuo wen-t'i yin-lun" 建國問題引論 (An introduction to the question of national reconstruction), TLPL no. 77: 2–7 (Nov. 19, 1933).

——— "Fu-chien ti ta pien-chü 福建的大變局 (The great revolt in Fukien), TLPL no. 79: 2–4 (Dec. 3, 1933).

——— "Chien-kuo yü chuan-chih" 建國與專制 (National reconstruction and authoritarianism), TLPL no. 81: 2–5 (Dec. 17, 1933).

———— "Tsai lun chien-kuo yü chuan-chih" 再論建國與專制 (Another discussion of national reconstruction and authoritarianism), TLPL no. 82: 2–5 (Dec. 24, 1933).

———— *The Chinese Renaissance.* Chicago: University of Chicago Press, 1934. Reprinted, with intro. by Hyman Kublin; New York: Paragon Book Company, 1963.

———— "Types of Cultural Response," *The Chinese Social and Political Science Review,* 17.4: 529–552 (January 1934). Also published as chap. 1 of *The Chinese Renaissance.*

———— "Wu-li t'ung-i lun" 武力統一論 (On unification by force), TLPL no. 85: 2–7 (Jan. 14, 1934).

———— "Cheng-chih t'ung-i ti t'u-ching" 政治統一的途徑 (The path to political unification), TLPL no. 86: 2–7 (Jan. 21, 1934).

———— " 'Chiu-p'ing pu-neng chuang hsin-chiu' ma?" "舊瓶不能裝新酒"嗎? (Can't you put new wine in old bottles?), TLPL no. 87: 15–17 (Jan. 28, 1934).

———— "Tsai lun wu-wei ti cheng-chih" 再論無爲的政治 (Another discussion of *wu-wei* politics), TLPL no. 89: 2–6 (Feb. 25, 1934).

———— "Chien-she yü wu-wei" 建設與無爲 (Reconstruction and *wu-wei*), TLPL no. 94: 2–5 (April 1, 1934).

———— "Chin-jih k'o-tso ti chien-she shih-yeh" 今日可做的建設事業 (The reconstruction that can be undertaken today), TLPL no. 95: 2–4 (April 8, 1934).

———— "Wei Hsin sheng-huo yün-tung chin i-chieh" 爲新生活運動進一解 (A word on the New Life movement), TLPL no. 95: 17–20 (April 8, 1934).

———— "Lun hsien-fa ch'u-kao" 論憲法初稿 (On the draft constitution), TLPL no. 96: 2–6 (April 15, 1934).

———— "Chin-jih chih wei-chi" 今日之危機 (The present-day crisis), TLPL no. 99: 2–4 (May 5, 1934).

———— "Hsin-hsin yü fan-hsing" 信心與反省 (Faith and reflection), TLPL no. 103: 2–6 (June 3, 1934); HSWT IV, iv, 458–464.

———— "Tsai lun hsin-hsin yü fan-hsing" 再論信心與反省 (Another discussion of faith and reflection), TLPL no. 105: 2–6 (June 17, 1934); HSWT IV, iv, 465–472.

———— "San lun hsin-hsin yü fan-hsing" 三論信心與反省 (A third discussion of faith and reflection), TLPL no. 107: 2–6 (July 1, 1934); HSWT IV, iv, 473–479.

———— "Ta-chung-yü tsai na-erh?" 大衆語在那兒? (Where is the language of the masses?), dated Sept. 4, 1934; HSWT IV, iv, 531–534.

———— "Hsieh tsai K'ung-tzu tan-ch'en chi-nien chih hou" 寫在孔子誕辰紀念之後 (Written after the celebration of Confucius' birthday), TLPL no. 117: 2–6 (Sept. 9, 1934); HSWT IV, iv, 486–493.

———— "Cheng-cheng san-nien le!" 整整三年了! (Just three years ago!), TLPL no. 119: 2–4 (Sept. 23, 1934).

———— "Shuang-shih-chieh ti kan-hsiang" 雙十節的感想 (Impressions on

Double Ten), TLPL no. 122: 2–4 (Oct. 14, 1934).

———— "Cheng-chih t'ung-i ti i-i" 政治統一的意義 (The meaning of political unification), TLPL no. 123: 2–4 (Oct. 21, 1934).

———— "Pei-kuan sheng-lang-li ti lo-kuan" 悲歡聲浪裏的樂觀 (Optimism in the midst of a wave of pessimism), TLPL no. 123: 15–18 (Oct. 21, 1934); HSWT IV, iv, 480–485. Theme of a lecture delivered at Yenching University on Oct. 9, 1934.

———— "Chung-kuo wu tu-ts'ai ti pi-yao yü k'o-neng" 中國無獨裁的必要與可能 (On the necessity and the feasibility of China's remaining nonautocratic), TLPL no. 130: 2–6 (Dec. 9, 1934).

———— "Wang Chiang t'ung-tien-li t'i-ch'i ti tzu-yu" 汪蔣通電裏提起的自由 (On the freedom discussed in the Wang-Chiang telegram), TLPL no. 131: 3–6 (Dec. 16, 1934).

———— "Kuo-chi wei-chi ti pi-chin" 國際危機的逼近 (The approaching international crisis), TLPL no. 132: 2–4 (Dec. 23, 1934).

———— "Ta Ting Tsai-chün hsien-sheng lun min-chu yü tu-ts'ai" 答丁在君先生論民主與獨裁 (In reply to Mr. Ting Tsai-chün's discussion of democracy and autocracy), TLPL no. 133: 7–9 (Dec. 30, 1934).

———— "Pi-shang Liang-shan: wen-hsüeh ko-ming ti k'ai-shih" 逼上梁山：文學革命的開始 (Forced into outlawry: The origins of the literary revolution), *Tung-fang tsa-chih*, 31.1: 15–31 (1934).

———— *Hu Shih lun-hsüeh chin chu, ti-i chi* 胡適論學近著，第一集 (Hu Shih's recent writings on scholarship). Shanghai: Commercial Press, 1935. Republished as *Hu Shih wen-ts'un, ti-ssu chi*, Taipei, 1953 (see below).

———— "An Optimist Looks at China," *Asia*, 35.3: 139–142 (March 1935).

———— "Nan yu tsa-i: (1) Hsiang-kang" 南遊雜憶：(一)香港 (Random impressions from southern travels: [1] Hong Kong), TLPL no. 141: 11–16 (March 10, 1935).

———— "Ts'ung min-chu yü tu-ts'ai chih t'ao-lun-li ch'iu-te i-ko kung-t'ung cheng-chih hsin-yang" 從民主與獨裁之討論裏求得一個共同政治信仰 (A common political faith derived from the debate concerning democracy and autocracy), TLPL no. 141: 16–18 (March 10, 1935).

———— "Nan yu tsa-i: (2) Kuang-chou" 南遊雜憶：(二)廣州 (Random impressions from southern travels: [2] Canton), TLPL no. 142: 16–23 (March 17, 1935).

———— "Pien-chi hou-chi" 編輯後記 (Editor's notes), TLPL no. 142: 24 (March 17, 1935).

———— "Chung-Jih t'i-hsi: ta k'o-wen" 中日提携：答客問 (Sino-Japanese reconciliation: an interview), TLPL no. 143: 2–3 (March 25, 1935).

———— "Shih-p'ing so-wei 'Chung-kuo pen-wei chih wen-hua chien-she'" 試評所謂"中國本位之文化建設" (A critique of so-called "cultural reconstruction on a Chinese base"), TLPL no. 145: 4–7 (April 7, 1935); HSWT IV, iv, 535–540.

———— "Wo-men chin-jih hai pu-p'ei tu-ching" 我們今日還不配讀經 (Today we are not yet qualified to read the Classics), TLPL no. 146: 2–5 (April 14, 1935); HSWT IV, iv, 525–530.

———— "Chi-nien 'Wu-ssu'" 紀念"五四" (Commemorating May Fourth),

TLPL no. 149: 2–8 (May 5, 1935).

—— "Ko-jen tzu-yu yü she-hui chin-pu: tsai t'an Wu-ssu yün-tung" 個人自由與社會進步：再談五四運動 (Individual freedom and social progress: more on the May Fourth movement), TLPL no. 150: 2–5 (May 12, 1935).

—— "Yu ta i-sui le" 又大一歲了 (Another year older), TLPL no. 151: 2–4 (May 19, 1935).

—— "Chin-jih ssu-hsiang-chieh ti i-ko ta pi-ping" 今日思想界的一個大弊病 (A great malady among intellectuals today), TLPL no. 153: 2–5 (June 2, 1935).

—— "Lüeh-ta T'ao Hsi-sheng hsien-sheng" 略答陶希聖先生 (A brief reply to Mr. T'ao Hsi-sheng), TLPL no. 154: 14 (June 9, 1935).

—— "Ch'en-mo ti jen-shou" 沈默的忍受 (Silent endurance), TLPL no. 155: 2–3 (June 16, 1935).

—— "Ta Ch'en Hsü-ching hsien-sheng" 答陳序經先生 (A reply to Mr. Ch'en Hsü-ching), TLPL no. 160: 15–16 (July 21, 1935).

—— "P'ing-Sui-lu lü-hsing hsiao-chi" 平綏路旅行小記 (A brief record of a trip along the Peiping-Suiyuan Railroad), TLPL no. 162: 13–18 (Aug. 4, 1935).

—— "Cheng-chih kai-ko ti ta-lu" 政制改革的大路 (The great road toward the reform of political institutions), TLPL no. 163: 2–9 (Aug. 11, 1935).

—— "Su-o ko-ming wai-chiao-shih ti yu i-yeh chi ch'i chiao-hsün" 蘇俄革命外交史的又一頁及其教訓 (Another page from the history of Soviet Russian international relations, and what it teaches us), TLPL no. 163: 15–18 (Aug. 11, 1935).

—— "Ts'ung i-tang tao wu-tang ti cheng-chih" 從一黨到無黨的政治 (From one-party to nonpartisan politics), TLPL no. 171: 10–12 (Oct. 6, 1935).

—— "Ching-kao Jih-pen kuo-min" 敬告日本國民 (An appeal to the Japanese people), TLPL no. 178: 10–14 (Nov. 24, 1935).

—— "Hua-pei wen-t'i" 華北問題 (The question of North China), TLPL no. 179: 2–3 (Dec. 1, 1935).

—— "Ta Shih-fu Kao-hsin hsien-sheng" 答室伏高信先生 (A reply to Mr. Murobushi Kōshin), TLPL no. 180: 5–8 (Dec. 8, 1935).

—— "Wei hsüeh-sheng yün-tung chin i-yen" 爲學生運動進一言 (A word to the student movement), TLPL no. 182: 4–7 (Dec. 22, 1935).

—— "Tsai lun hsüeh-sheng yün-tung" 再論學生運動 (Another discussion of the student movement), TLPL no. 183: 2–4 (Dec. 29, 1935).

—— "Ting Tsai-chün che-ko jen" 丁在君這個人 (This man Ting Tsai-chün), TLPL no. 188: 9–15 (Feb. 16, 1936).

—— "Hu Shih's Appeal to Japan with the Reply by Takanobu Murobushi [Murobushi Kōshin]," *Asia*, 36.3: 166–170 (March 1936). English version of "Ching-kao Jih-pen kuo-min," in TLPL no. 178.

—— "Tung-ching ti ping-pien" 東京的兵變 (The military coup in Tokyo), TLPL no. 191: 2–5 (March 8, 1936).

—— "*Tu-li p'ing-lun* ti ssu-chou-nien" 獨立評論的四週年 (The fourth anniversary of the Independent critic), TLPL no. 201: 3–5 (May 17, 1936).

—— "Ching-kao Sung Che-yüan hsien-sheng" 敬告宋哲元先生 (An appeal to Mr. Sung Che-yüan), TLPL no. 204: 2–3 (June 7, 1936).

———— "Reconstruction in China," *Asia*, 36.11: 737–740 (November 1936).

———— "The Indianization of China: A Case Study in Cultural Borrowing," in *Independence, Convergence and Borrowing in Institutions, Thought and Art,* 219–247. Cambridge, Mass.: Harvard University Press, 1937.

———— "The Changing Balance of Forces in the Pacific," *Foreign Affairs*, 15.2: 254–259 (January 1937).

———— "Jih-pen pa-ch'üan ti shuai-lo yü T'ai-p'ing-yang ti kuo-chi hsin hsing-shih" 日本霸權的衰落與太平洋的國際新形勢 (The decline of Japanese hegemony and the new international situation in the Pacific), TLPL no. 230: 2–8 (April 18, 1937). Modified Chinese version of the preceding item.

———— "Pien-chi hou-chi" 編集後記 (Editor's notes), TLPL no. 232: 18 (May 2, 1937).

———— "Tsai t'an-t'an hsien-cheng" 再談談憲政 (Talking again about constitutional government), TLPL no. 236: 5–7 (May 30, 1937).

———— "Pien-chi hou-chi" 編輯後記 (Editor's notes), TLPL no. 239: 18 (June 20, 1937).

———— "Wo-men neng hsing ti hsien-cheng yü hsien-fa" 我們能行的憲政與憲法 (The constitutional government and the constitution that we can implement), TLPL no. 242: 12–13 (July 11, 1937).

———— "The Westernization of China and Japan," *Amerasia*, 2.5: 243–247 (July 1938). Book reviews.

———— "What Can America Do in the Far Eastern Situation?" *Amerasia*, 2.6: 293–295 (August 1938). Radio address delivered over the Columbia network, June 24, 1938.

———— "The Political Philosophy of Instrumentalism," in *The Philosopher of the Common Man: Essays in Honor of John Dewey to Celebrate His Eightieth Birthday*, 205–219. New York: G. P. Putnam's Sons, 1940.

———— "Historical Foundations for a Democratic China," in *Edmund J. James Lectures on Government*, 2nd series, 53–64. Urbana: University of Illinois Press, 1941.

———— "Instrumentalism as a Political Concept," in *Studies in Political Science and Sociology*, 1–6. Philadelphia: University of Pennsylvania Press, 1941.

———— "The Struggle for Intellectual Freedom in Historic China," *World Affairs*, 105.3: 170–173 (September 1942). Address delivered to the Institute on World Organization, May 12, 1942.

———— "Yen-ch'ien shih-chieh wen-hua ti ch'ü-hsiang" 眼前世界文化的趨向 (The direction in which contemporary world culture is tending), radio lecture on Peiping radio, Aug. 1, 1947; *Wo-men pi-hsü hsüan-tse wo-men-ti fang-hsiang*, 5–12.

———— "Wo-men pi-hsü hsüan-tse wo-men-ti fang-hsiang" 我們必須選擇我們的方向 (We must choose our course), August 1947, reply to criticism of the preceding item; *Wo-men pi-hsü hsüan-tse wo-men-ti fang-hsiang*, 13–17.

————"Tzu-yu-chu-i shih shen-mo?"自由主義是什么？(What is liberalism?) [1948]; *Wo-men pi-hsü hsüan-tse wo-men-ti fang-hsiang*, 25–28.

———— "*Tzu-yu Chung-kuo* ti tsung-chih" 自由中國的宗旨 (The mission of Free China [magazine]), dated at sea, April 14, 1949; *Wo-men pi-hsü hsüan-tse wo-men-ti fang-hsiang*, 29.

388

———— "China in Stalin's Grand Strategy," *Foreign Affairs*, 29.1: 11–40 (October 1950).

———— "Chinese Thought," in H. F. MacNair, ed., *China*, 221–230.

———— "How to Understand a Decade of Rapidly Deteriorated Sino-American Relations," *Proceedings of the American Philosophical Society*, 95.4: 457–460 (August 1951).

———— "The Natural Law in the Chinese Tradition," *Natural Law Institute Proceedings*, 5: 119–153 (1953).

———— *Hu Shih wen-ts'un, 1–4 chi* 胡適文存, 1-4 集 (Collected essays of Hu Shih, collections 1–4). 4 vols. Taipei: Yüan-tung t'u-shu kung-ssu, 1953. A reset and re-edited edition. Volume II, corresponding to *Hu Shih wen-ts'un, erh chi* (1924), is severely expurgated, and there are minor excisions from the other volumes as well. Volume IV corresponds to *Hu Shih lun-hsüeh chin-chu* (1935).

———— *Hu Shih yen-lun chi: chia pien: hsüeh-shu chih pu; i pien: shih-shih wen-t'i* 胡適言論集：(甲編) 學術之部；(乙編) 時事問題 (Collected speeches of Hu Shih: [a] on scholarship; [b] on current problems). 2 vols. Taipei: Hua-kuo Ch'u-pan-she, 1953.

———— "Authority and Freedom in the Ancient Asian World," in *Man's Right to Knowledge*, 1st series: *Tradition and Change*, 40–45. New York: Columbia University Press, 1954.

———— *Wo-men pi-hsü hsüan-tse wo-men-ti fang-hsiang* 我們必須選擇我們的方向 (We must choose our course), 3rd printing. Hong Kong: Tzu-yu Chung-kuo she, 1957. First published 1949.

———— "Dr. Hu Shih's Personal Reminiscences." Interviews compiled and edited by Te-kong Tong, with Dr. Hu's corrections in his own handwriting, 1958. Typescript in the archive of the Oral History Project, Columbia University.

———— *Chung-kuo hsin wen-hsüeh yün-tung hsiao-shih* 中國新文學運動小史 (A short history of China's new literature movement). Taipei: Ch'i-ming shu-chü, 1958.

———— *Hu Shih liu-hsüeh jih-chi* 胡適留學日記 (Hu Shih's diary while studying abroad). 4 vols. Taipei: Commercial Press, 1959. Originally published under the title *Ts'ang-hui-shih cha-chi* 藏暉室劄記. Shanghai: Ya-tung t'u-shu-kuan, 1939.

———— *Ssu-shih tzu-shu* 四十自述 (A self-account at forty). Taipei: Yüan-tung kung-ssu, 1959. First published, Shanghai: Ya-tung t'u-shu-kuan, 1933.

———— "Jung-jen yü tzu-yu" 容忍與自由 (Toleration and freedom), *Tzu-yu Chung-kuo* (Free China), 20.6: 179–180 (March 16, 1959).

———— "Tu-wei tsai Chung-kuo" 杜威在中國 (Dewey in China), *Tzu-yu Chung-kuo* (Free China), 21.4: 104–107 (Aug. 16, 1959). Lecture at University of Hawaii, Honolulu, July 16, 1959; trans. Hsia Tao-p'ing 夏道平.

———— *Ting Wen-chiang ti chuan-chi* 丁文江的傳記 (Biography of Ting Wen-chiang). Taipei: Ch'i-ming shu-chü, 1960. First published 1956.

———— "The Scientific Spirit and Method in Chinese Philosophy," in Charles A. Moore, ed., *Philosophy and Culture—East and West*, 199–222. Honolulu: University of Hawaii Press, 1962.

———— *Hu Shih shu-chien* 胡適書簡 (Hu Shih's correspondence). Taipei: Shih-tai wen-hua ch'u-pan-she, 1962.

———— "The Right to Doubt in Ancient Chinese Thought," *Philosophy East and West*, 12.4: 295–300 (January 1963). Paper read at sixth annual meeting of Far Eastern Association, 1954.

———— *Hu Shih ti i-ko meng-hsiang* 胡適的一個夢想 (One of Hu Shih's dreams). Taipei-Nankang: Hu Shih chi-nien-kuan ch'u-pan, 1966.

"Hu Shih chuan" 胡適傳 (Biography of Hu Shih), in *Chi-hsi hsien-chih*, 723–747.

Hu Shih ssu-hsiang p'i-p'an 胡適思想批判 (A critique of Hu Shih's thought). 8 vols. Peking: San-lien shu-tien, 1955.

Huang Sung-k'ang. *Lu Hsün and the New Culture Movement of Modern China.* Amsterdam: Djambatan, 1957.

Hughes, E. R. *The Invasion of China by the Western World.* London, 1937.

Hummel, Arthur W. "What Chinese Historians Are Doing with Their Own History," *American Historical Review*, 34.4: 715–724 (July 1929).

Hung, William. "Main Tendencies in Literary Circles," *China Christian Yearbook*, 1926, 364–369.

HY, see *Hsin yüeh.*

I-jan 衣然. "Cheng tzu-yu yü Hu Shih ti hu-shuo" 爭自由與胡適的胡說 (The struggle for freedom and Hu Shih's nonsense), *Pai-hua san-jih-k'an* (Vernacular three-day journal), June 6, 1929.

Israel, John. *Student Nationalism in China, 1927–1937.* Stanford, 1966.

James, William. *Pragmatism, and Four Essays from The Meaning of Truth.* New York, Meridian Books, 1955.

Johnson, Chalmers A. "An Intellectual Weed in the Socialist Garden: The Case of Ch'ien Tuan-sheng," *China Quarterly*, no. 6: 29–52 (1961).

Kao Chung-ju. *Le mouvement intellectuel en Chine et son rôle dans la revolution chinoise.* Aix-en-Provence, 1957.

Kennedy, Melville T., Jr. "The Chinese Democratic League," *Papers on China*, 7: 136–175 (1953). Harvard University, East Asian Research Center.

KHYJSK, see *K'o-hsüeh yü jen-sheng-kuan.*

Kiang Wen-han. *The Chinese Student Movement.* New York: King's Crown Press, 1948.

K'o-hsüeh yü jen-sheng-kuan 科學與人生觀 (Science and the philosophy of life). 2 vols. Shanghai, 1923.

Ku Chieh-kang 顧頡剛. *The Autobiography of a Chinese Historian.* Author's preface to *Ku-shih pien* 古史辯 (A symposium on ancient history), trans. A. W. Hummel. Leyden, 1931.

———— "The Way I Look at Hu Shih," *Current Background*, no. 167 (March 25, 1952).

Kuo Chan-po 郭湛波. *Chin wu-shih-nien Chung-kuo ssu-hsiang shih* 近五十年中國思想史 (An intellectual history of China in the last fifty years). Peiping, 1935; enlarged ed., Hong Kong, 1965.

Kuo Mo-jo 郭沫若. *Ko-ming ch'un-ch'iu* 革命春秋 (Annals of the revolution). Shanghai, 1956.

Kwok, D. W. Y. *Scientism in Chinese Thought, 1900–1950.* New Haven and London, 1965.

Kwong Hsu Kun. "What is Patiotic Sanity? A Reply to Suh Hu," *The Chinese Students' Monthly*, 10.7: 427–430 (April 1915).

Lang, Olga. *Chinese Family and Society*. New Haven, 1946.

—— *Pa Chin and His Writings: Chinese Youth between the Two Revolutions*. Cambridge, Mass., 1967.

Laski, Harold J. *A Grammar of Politics*. New Haven: Yale University Press, 1925.

—— *The Rise of European Liberalism*. London, 1936.

Laurvik, J. N., and M. Morison, trans. *Letters of Henrik Ibsen*. New York: Fox, Duffield and Co., 1905.

Lee, Leo Ou-fan. "Lin Shu and His Translations: Western Fiction in Chinese Perspective," *Papers on China*, 19: 159–193 (1965). Harvard University, East Asian Research Center.

Legge, James, trans. *The Chinese Classics*. 5 vols. Hong Kong: Hong Kong University Press, 1960.

Levenson, Joseph R. " 'History' and 'Value': The Tensions of Intellectual Choice in Modern China," in A. F. Wright, ed., *Studies in Chinese Thought*, 146–194.

—— *Liang Ch'i-ch'ao and the Mind of Modern China*. Cambridge, Mass., 1953.

—— *Confucian China and Its Modern Fate*. 3 vols. Berkeley and Los Angeles, 1958–1965.

—— "Ill-Wind in the Well-Field: The Erosion of the Confucian Ground of Controversy," in A. F. Wright, ed., *The Confucian Persuasion*, 268–287.

Li Ao (Lee Ao) 李敖. *Hu Shih p'ing-chuan*. 胡適評傳 (A critical biography of Hu Shih). Taipei, 1964.

—— *Hu Shih yen-chiu*. 胡適研究 (Studies of Hu Shih). Taipei, 1964.

Li Chien-nung. *The Political History of China, 1840–1928*, trans. Teng Ssu-yü and Jeremy Ingalls. Princeton: van Nostrand, 1956.

—— 李劍農. *Chung-kuo chin pai-nien cheng-chih shih* 中國近百年政治史 (The political history of China in the last hundred years). 2 vols. Taipei, 1957.

Li Lung-mu 李龍牧. "I-ko 'Wu-ssu' shih-ch'i ti cheng-chih k'an-wu—*Mei-chou p'ing-lun*" 一個 "五四" 時期的政治刊物—每週評論 (A political publication of the May Fourth era: The weekly critic), in Chang Ching-lu, ed., *Chung-kuo hsien-tai ch'u-pan shih-liao*, IV, 40–43.

Li Shu-hua 李書華. "Hu Shih-chih hsien-sheng sheng-p'ing chi ch'i kung-hsien" 胡適之先生生平及其貢獻 (The life and the contributions of Mr. Hu Shih-chih), *Ta-lu tsa-chih* (The continent magazine), 26.10: 301–317 (May 1962).

—— "Hu Shih-chih hsien-sheng tsui-chin chi-tuan pi-chi ho chi-feng hsin" 胡適之先生最近幾段筆記和幾封信 (Some recent notes and letters of Mr. Hu Shih-chih), *Hai-wai lun-t'an* (World forum), 3.5: 4–8, 11–14 (May 1, 1962).

Li Ta 李達. *Hu Shih fan-tung ssu-hsiang p'i-p'an* 胡適反動思想批判 (A critique of Hu Shih's reactionary thought). Hankow: Hupeh Jen-min ch'u-pan she, 1955.

Li Ta-chao 李大釗. "Tsai lun wen-t'i yü chu-i" 再論問題與主義 (Another discussion of problems and isms), *Mei-chou p'ing-lun*, no. 35 (Aug. 17, 1919);

Li Ta-chao hsüan-chi, 228–234.

—— *Li Ta-chao hsüan-chi* 李大釗選集 (Selected works of Li Ta-chao). Peking, 1962.

Liang Ch'i-ch'ao 梁啟超. "Ai-kuo lun" 愛國論 (On patriotism), *Yin-ping-shih ho-chi, wen-chi*, II, iii, 65–77.

—— "Hsin min shuo" 新民說 (On the new people), *Yin-ping-shih ho-chi, chuan-chi*, III, iv, 1–162.

—— Introduction to "Chung-kuo hsüeh-shu ssu-hsiang pien-ch'ien chih ta-shih" 中國學術思想變遷之大勢 (General circumstances of the development of Chinese scholarship), *Yin-ping-shih ho-chi, wen-chi*, III, vii, 1–4.

—— "Ou-yu hsin-ying lu, chieh-lu" 歐遊心影錄節錄 (A condensed record of impressions of travels in Europe), *Yin-ping shih ho-chi, chuan-chi*, V, xxiii, 1–162.

—— "Jen-sheng-kuan yü k'o-hsüeh" 人生觀與科學 (The philosophy of life and science). KHYJSK I.

—— *Yin-ping-shih ho-chi* 飲冰室合集 (Collected works from the Ice-drinker's studio). 40 vols. Shanghai, 1936.

—— *Intellectual Trends in the Ch'ing Period*, trans. Immanuel C. Y. Hsü. Cambridge, Mass., 1959.

Liang Sou-ming 梁漱溟. *Tung Hsi wen-hua chi ch'i che-hsüeh* 東西文化及其哲學 (The cultures of East and West and their philosophies). Shanghai, 1922.

Liang Ts'ung-chieh 梁從誡. "Hu Shih pu-shih yen-chiu li-shih, erh-shih wai-ch'ü ho nieh-tsao li-shih" 胡適不是研究歷史而是歪曲和捏造歷史 (Hu Shih does not study history but perverts and fabricates history), *Li-shih yen-chiu* (Historical research), no. 3: 45–51 (1955).

Lin Yutang. *A History of the Press and Public Opinion in China*. Chicago, 1936.

Linden, Allen B. "Politics and Education in Nationalist China: The Case of the University Council, 1927–1928," *Journal of Asian Studies*, 27.4: 763–776 (August 1968).

Liu Chun-jo. *Controversies in Modern Chinese Intellectual History: An Analytical Bibliography of Periodical Articles, Mainly of the May Fourth and Post-May Fourth Era*. Harvard East Asian Monographs, no. 15. Cambridge, Mass., 1964.

Lo Erh-kang 羅爾綱. *Shih-men wu-nien chi* 師門五年記 (A record of five years at my teacher's door). Taipei: published for private distribution by Hu Shih, December 1958.

Lo Lung-chi 羅隆基. "Lun jen-ch'üan" 論人權 (On human rights), HY 2.5 (July 1929).

—— "Kao ya-p'o yen-lun tzu-yu che" 告壓迫言論自由者 (A word to those who suppress freedom of expression), HY 2.6, 7 (September 1929).

—— "Wo-men yao shen-mo-yang ti cheng-chih chih-tu?" 我們要什么樣的政治制度？ (What kind of a political system do we want?), HY 2.12 (February 1930).

—— "Tui hsün-cheng shih-ch'i yüeh-fa ti p'i-p'ing" 對訓政時期約法的批評 (A critique of the provisional constitution for the period of political tutelage), HY 3.8 (n.d.).

—— "Shen-mo shih fa-chih?" 什么是法治？ (What is the rule of law?),

HY 3.11 (n.d.).

Lochner, Louis P. *The Cosmopolitan Club Movement.* Documents of the American Association for International Conciliation, no. 61 (1912). New York, 1912.

Lu Hsün. " 'Hard Translation' and the 'Class Character of Literature,' " *Selected Works*, III, 65–86.

———— *Selected Works of Lu Hsun.* 4 vols. Peking, 1956–1960.

———— 魯迅. *Lu Hsün ch'üan-chi* 魯迅全集 (Complete works of Lu Hsün). 10 vols. Peking, 1958.

MacNair, Harley Farnsworth. *China in Revolution: An Analysis of Politics and Militarism under the Republic.* Chicago, 1931.

———— ed. *China.* Berkeley and Los Angeles: University of California Press, 1951.

"*Mei-chou p'ing-lun* fa-k'an tz'u" 每週評論發刊詞 (Inaugural statement of The weekly critic), *Mei-chou p'ing-lun*, no. 1 (Dec. 22, 1918); *Chung-kuo hsin wen-hsüeh ta-hsi*, X, 190; *Chung-kuo hsien-tai ch'u-pan shih-liao*, ed. Chang Ching-lu, I, 3–4.

Meisner, Maurice. *Li Ta-chao and the Origins of Chinese Marxism.* Cambridge, Mass.: Harvard University Press, 1967.

Meng, C. Y. W. " 'New Revolutionary Movement,' " *The China Weekly Review*, 103.12: 364–365 (Nov. 23, 1946).

Meng Sen 孟森. "Ch'iu yu-wei wu-wei chih chieh-shuo" 求有爲無爲之界說 (Seeking a definition of *yu-wei* and *wu-wei*), TLPL no. 94: 5–7 (April 1, 1934).

Moore, E. C. *American Pragmatism: Peirce, James, and Dewey.* New York, 1961.

Morley, John Viscount. *The Works of Lord Morley*, vol. III: *On Compromise.* London: Macmillan and Co. Ltd., 1921.

Muir, Robert. "Hu Shih: A Biographical Sketch, 1891–1917," thesis for the certificate of the East Asian Institute, Columbia University, 1960.

Murobushi Kōshin 室伏高信. "Ta Hu Shih-chih shu" 答胡適之書 (A reply to Hu Shih-chih), TLPL no. 180: 8–12 (Dec. 8, 1935).

———— "Tsai ta Hu Shih-chih shu" 再答胡適之書 (Another reply to Hu Shih-chih), TLPL no. 192: 15–19 (March 15, 1936).

"Muzzling China's Truth-teller," *New York Times*, Aug. 31, 1929, 14.

Nivison, David. "The Problem of 'Knowledge' and 'Action' in Chinese Thought since Wang Yang-ming," in A. F. Wright, ed., *Studies in Chinese Thought*, 112–145.

———— and A. F. Wright, eds. *Confucianism in Action.* Stanford, 1959.

NLCP, see *Nu-li chou-pao.*

Nu-li chou-pao 努力周報 (The endeavor). Peking, 1922–1923. Weekly.

Oral History Project of Columbia University, see Hu Shih, "Dr. Hu Shih's Personal Reminiscences" (1958).

"Pa t'uan-t'i kuo-shih hui-i hsien-fa ts'ao-an" 八團體國是會議憲法草案 (Constitutional draft of the eight-group conference on national affairs), NLCP no. 13 (July 30, 1922).

P'an Kuang-tan 潘光旦. "I-pen yu-ch'ü ti nien-p'u" 一本有趣的年譜 (An interesting life chronology), HY 3.5, 6 (n.d.).

Roy, A. T. "Liang Shu-ming and Hu Shih on the Intuitional Interpretation of Confucianism," *The Chung Chi Journal*, 1.2: 139–157 (July 1962).

Sartori, Giovanni. *Democratic Theory*. New York, Washington, and London: Praeger, 1965.

Scalapino, R. A., and H. Schiffrin. "Early Socialist Currents in the Chinese Revolutionary Movement: Sun Yat-sen versus Liang Ch'i-ch'ao," *Journal of Asian Studies*, 18.3: 321–342 (May 1959).

———— and George Yü. *The Chinese Anarchist Movement*. Berkeley, 1961.

Schilpp, Paul A., ed. *The Philosophy of John Dewey*. New York: Tudor Publishing Co., 1939, 1951.

Schwartz, Benjamin I. "Ch'en Tu-hsiu and the Acceptance of the Modern West," *Journal of the History of Ideas*, 12: 61–74 (1951).

———— "Some Polarities in Confucian Thought," in D. Nivison and A. F. Wright, eds., *Confucianism in Action*, 50–62. Stanford, 1959.

———— "The Intelligentsia in Communist China: A Tentative Comparison," *Daedalus*, 89.3: 604–622 (Summer 1960).

———— *In Search of Wealth and Power: Yen Fu and the West*. Cambridge, Mass., 1964.

Shen Yin-mo. "This man Hu Shih," *Current Background*, no. 167 (March 25, 1952).

Shih Chün 石峻. ed. *Chung-kuo chin-tai ssu-hsiang shih ts'an-k'ao tzu-liao chien-pien* 中國近代思想史參考資料簡編 (A survey of source materials on modern Chinese intellectual history). Peking, 1957.

Shih Shao-p'in 史紹賓. "Hu Shih yü Wu Han" 胡適與吳晗 (Hu Shih and Wu Han), *Jen-min jih-pao*, April 13, 1966.

———— "Wu Han t'ou-k'ao Hu Shih ti t'ieh-cheng" 吳晗投靠胡適的鐵證 (Iron-clad proof that Wu Han relied upon Hu Shih), *Jen-min jih-pao*, June 3, 1966.

Shih, Vincent. "A Talk with Hu Shih," *China Quarterly*, 10: 149–165 (April–June 1962).

Shih Yao 史垚, ed. *Hu Shih ai-jung chi* 胡適哀榮集 (A collection lamenting and honoring Hu Shih). Kaohsiung: Tse-chung ch'u-pan she, 1962.

Short History, see Hu Shih, *Chung-kuo hsin wen-hsüeh yün-tung hsiao-shih* (1958).

Sichel, Edith. *The Renaissance*. Home University Library of Modern Knowledge, no. 87. London and New York: Henry Holt and Co., 1915.

Smedley, Agnes. "Chinese Poets and Professors," *New York Herald Tribune Books*, vol. XC, no. 30, 499 (May 18, 1930), sect. xi, p. 9.

———— *Battle Hymn of China*. New York, 1945.

Snow, Edgar. *Red Star Over China*. New York: Random House, 1938.

———— *Journey to the Beginning*. New York, 1958.

Soong Ching Ling. *The Struggle for New China*. Peking, 1952.

Speer, James P., III. "Liquidation of Chinese Liberals," *Far Eastern Survey*, 16.14: 160–162 (July 23, 1947).

Stuart, John Leighton. *Fifty Years in China: The Memoirs of John Leighton Stuart, Missionary and Ambassador*. New York: Random House, 1954.

Sun Yat-sen. *Memoirs of a Chinese Revolutionary*. London, 1918; Taipei, 1953.

———— *San Min Chu I*, trans. F. W. Price. Shanghai, 1928.

Takeuchi Yoshimi 竹内好 et al. *Chūgoku kakumei no shisō* 中國革命の思想 (The thought of the Chinese revolution). Tokyo, 1954.

T'an T'ien 譚天. *Hu Shih yü Kuo Mo-jo* 胡適與郭沫若 (Hu Shih and Kuo Mo-jo). Shanghai, 1933.

T'ang Yung-t'ung. "Remarks on Hu Shih," *Current Background*, no. 167 (March 25, 1952).

T'ao Hsi-sheng 陶希聖. "Wu-wei hai-shih yu-wei?" 無爲還是有爲？ (*Wu-wei* or *yu-wei?*), TLPL no. 91: 4–7 (March 11, 1934).

———— "Min-chu yü tu-ts'ai chih cheng-lun" 民主與獨裁之爭論 (The dispute over democracy or autocracy), TLPL no. 136: 11–12 (Jan. 20, 1935).

———— "Ssu-hsiang-chieh ti i-ko ta jo-tien" 思想界的一個大弱點 (A great weakness among intellectuals), TLPL no. 154: 10–14 (June 9, 1935).

———— "Lun k'ai-fang tang-chin" 論開放黨禁 (On lifting the proscriptions against [opposition] parties), TLPL no. 237: 9–11 (June 6, 1937).

———— "Pu-tang-che ti li-liang" 不黨者的力量 (The strength of the nonpartisans), TLPL no. 242: 9–11 (July 11, 1937).

———— "Hu Shih-chih hsien-sheng erh-san shih" 胡適之先生二三事 (One or two matters concerning Mr. Hu Shih-chih), in Shih Yao, ed., *Hu Shih ai-jung chi*, 52–55.

T'ao Meng-ho 陶孟和. "Yu Ou chih kan-hsiang" 遊歐之感想 (Impressions of travels in Europe), HCN 7.1 (December 1919); reprinted as "Chan-hou chih Ou-chou" 戰後之歐州 (Postwar Europe), *Meng-ho wen-ts'un*, 65–78.

———— "Ou Mei chih lao-tung wen-t'i" 歐美之勞動問題 (The labor problem in Europe and America), HCN 7.2 (January 1920); *Meng-ho wen-ts'un*, 79–94.

———— *Meng-ho wen-ts'un* 孟和文存 (Collected essays of [T'ao] Meng-ho). 3 *chüan*. Shanghai, 1925.

Teng Ssu-yü. "Chinese Historiography in the Last Fifty Years," *Far Eastern Quarterly*, 8.2: 131–156 (February 1949).

———— and J. K. Fairbank, eds. *China's Response to the West: A Documentary Survey, 1839–1923*. Cambridge, Mass.: Harvard University Press, 1954.

T'ien Shih-ch'ing 田食慶. "Ch'ing-ch'u Hu Shih ssu-hsiang tsai li-shih k'ao-chü-chung ti o-lieh ying-hsiang" 清除胡適思想在歷史考據中的惡劣影響 (Eradicate the vile influence of Hu Shih's thought in the field of historical research), *Li-shih yen-chiu* (Historical research), no. 2: 15–35 (1955).

Ting Wen-chiang 丁文江. "Hsüan-hsüeh yü k'o-hsüeh" 玄學與科學 (Metaphysics and science), KHYJSK I.

———— "Hsüan-hsüeh yü k'o-hsüeh, ta Chang Chün-mai" 玄學與科學答張君勱 (Metaphysics and science, a rejoinder to Chang Chün-mai). KHYJSK I.

———— "Shao-shu-jen ti tse-jen" 少數人的責任 (The responsibility of the minority), NLCP no. 67 (Aug. 12, 1923).

———— "Chung-kuo cheng-chih ti ch'u-lu" 中國政治的出路 (The way out for Chinese politics), TLPL no. 11: 2–6 (July 31, 1932).

———— "K'ang-Jih ti hsiao-neng yü ch'ing-nien ti tse-jen" 抗日的效能與青年的責任 (The feasibility of resisting Japan, and youth's responsibilities), TLPL no. 37: 2–8 (Feb. 12, 1933).

——— "Min-chu cheng-chih yü tu-ts'ai cheng-chih" 民主政治與獨裁政治 (Democratic government and autocratic government), TLPL no. 133: 4–7 (Dec. 30, 1934).

——— "Tsai lun min-chu yü tu-ts'ai" 再論民主與獨裁 (Another discussion of democracy and autocracy), TLPL no. 137: 19–22 (Jan. 27, 1935).

——— "Hsien-tsai Chung-kuo ti chung-nien yü ch'ing-nien" 現在中國的中年 與青年 (The middle-aged and the youth in China today), TLPL no. 144: 8–11 (March 31, 1935).

——— *Liang Jen-kung hsien-sheng nien-p'u ch'ang-pien ch'u-kao* 梁任公先生年譜長 編初稿 (First draft of an extended chronology of the life of Liang Jen-kung). 3 vols. Taipei, 1959.

TLPL, see *Tu-li p'ing-lun.*

Tong Te-kong (T'ang Te-kang) 唐德剛. "Ch'ien-shih k'o-hsüeh min-chu, chui-tao Hu Shih-chih hsien-sheng" 淺釋科學民主追悼胡適之先生 (Some simple thoughts on science and democracy, in memory of Mr. Hu Shih-chih), *Hai-wai lun-t'an* (World forum), 3.5: 15–18 (May 1, 1962).

Tsiang, T. F., see Chiang T'ing-fu.

Tsou Jung 鄒容. *Ko-ming chün* 革命軍 (The revolutionary army), in Shih Chün, ed., *Chung-kuo chin-tai ssu-hsiang shih ts'an-k'ao tzu-liao chien-pien*, 626–661.

Tsui Shu-chin. *From Academic Freedom to Brainwashing: The Tragic Ordeal of Professors on the Chinese Mainland.* Taipei: China Culture Publishing Foundation, 1953.

Tu-li p'ing-lun 獨立評論 (The independent critic). Peking, 1932–1937. Weekly, with occasional lapses.

"*Tu-li p'ing-lun* yin-yen" 獨立評論引言 (Introductory statement of the Independent critic), TLPL no. 1: 2 (May 22, 1932).

United States Relations with China, with Special Reference to the Period 1944–1949. Washington, D.C.: Department of State, 1949.

van Boven, Père Henri. *Histoire de la littérature chinoise moderne.* Schent editions, series I, Critical and Literary Studies, vol. II. Tientsin: The Chihli Press, 1946.

van Slyke, Lyman P. "Liang Sou-ming and the Rural Reconstruction Movement," *Journal of Asian Studies*, 18.4: 457–474 (August 1959).

Waley, Arthur, trans. *The Analects of Confucius.* London: George Allen and Unwin, 1938.

Wang, Tsi C. *The Youth Movement in China.* New York: The New Republic, 1927.

Wang, Y. Chu. "Intellectuals and Society in China, 1860–1949," *Comparative Studies in Society and History*, 3.4: 395–426 (July 1961).

——— *Chinese Intellectuals and the West, 1872–1949.* Chapel Hill: University of North Carolina Press, 1966.

Washburne, Carleton. *Remakers of Mankind.* New York, 1932.

Watson, Burton, trans. *Chuang-tzu: Basic Writings.* New York and London: Columbia University Press, 1964.

Wertenbaker, Charles, and Philip Horton. "The China Lobby," *The Reporter*, 6.8: 4–24 (April 15, 1952) and 6.9: 5–22 (April 29, 1952).

White Paper, see *United States Relations with China, with Special Reference to the*

Period 1944–1949.

Witke, Roxane. "Mao Tse-tung, Women and Suicide in the May Fourth Era," *China Quarterly*, no. 31: 128–147 (1967).

World Peace Foundation Annual Report, 1915. Boston: World Peace Foundation, December 1915.

Wright, Arthur F., ed. *Studies in Chinese Thought.* Chicago, 1953.

—— ed. *The Confucian Persuasion.* Stanford, 1960.

Wright, Mary C. *The Last Stand of Chinese Conservatism.* Stanford, 1957.

Wu Ching-ch'ao 吳景超. "Ko-ming yü chien-kuo" 革命與建國 (Revolution and national reconstruction), TLPL no. 84: 2–5 (Jan. 7, 1934).

—— "Yü-lun tsai Chung-kuo ho-i pu fa-ta" 輿論在中國何以不發達 (Why public opinion is not developed in China), TLPL no. 87: 2–5 (Jan. 28, 1934).

—— "Chien-she wen-t'i yü Tung Hsi wen-hua" 建設問題與東西文化 (The problem of reconstruction and Eastern vs. Western culture), TLPL no. 139: 2–6 (Feb. 24, 1935).

—— "Ta Ch'en Hsü-ching hsien-sheng ti ch'üan-p'an hsi-hua lun" 答陳序經先生的全盤西化論 (In response to Mr. Ch'en Hsü-ching's discussion of total westernization), TLPL no. 147: 2–4 (April 21, 1935).

Wu-ssu shih-ch'i ch'i-k'an chieh-shao 五四時期期刊介紹 (An introduction to the periodicals of the May Fourth era), I. Peking, 1958.

Wu-ssu yün-tung wen-chi 五四運動文輯 (Essays on the May Fourth Movement). Wuhan: Hupeh Jen-min ch'u-pan she, 1957.

Yeh Ch'ing 葉青. *Hu Shih p'i-p'an* 胡適批判 (A critique of Hu Shih). Shanghai: Hsin-k'en shu-tien, 1933.

Yeh Shu-heng 葉叔衡. "Min-chu yü tu-ts'ai ti cheng-lun yü t'iao-chieh" 民主與獨裁的爭論與調解 (The dispute concerning democracy and autocracy, and its settlement), TLPL no. 140: 5–12 (March 3, 1935).

Yin Hai-kuang 殷海光. "Hu Shih ssu-hsiang yü Chung-kuo ch'ien-t'u" 胡適思想與中國前途 (Hu Shih's thought and the future of China). *Bulletin of the Institute of History and Philology, Academia Sinica*, no. 28: 883–888. Taipei, 1957.

—— "Hu Shih lun 'Jung-jen yü tzu-yu' tu-hou" 胡適論 "容忍與自由" 讀後 (After reading Hu Shih on "Toleration and freedom"), *Tzu-yu Chung-kuo* (Free China), 20.7: 219–220 (April 1, 1959).

—— "Hu Shih yü kuo-yün" 胡適與國運 (Hu Shih and the nation's destiny), *Tzu-yu Chung-kuo* (Free China), 20.9: 277–283 (May 1, 1959).

Yü P'ing-po. "Resolutely Demarcate Boundaries with the Reactionary Hu Shih Ideology," *Current Background*, no. 325 (April 5, 1955).

Yüan T'ung-li 袁同禮. "Hu Shih hsien-sheng chu-tso mu-lu" 胡適先生著作目錄 (A bibliography of Mr. Hu Shih's Chinese writings). *Bulletin of the Institute of History and Philology, Academia Sinica*, no. 28: 889–907. Taipei, 1957.

Zee, Ts-zun Z., and Lui-Ngau Chang. "The Boxer Indemnity Students of 1910," *The Chinese Students' Monthly*, 6.1: 16–19 (November 1910).

Zen, Sophia H. Chen (Ch'en Heng-che), ed. *Symposium on Chinese Culture.* Shanghai: China Institute of Pacific Relations, 1931.

Glossary

Ai Ssu-ch'i 艾思奇
ch'a-hua-hui 茶話會
Chang Chia-shen 張嘉森
Chang Chien 張謇
Chang Ching-fu 張經甫
Chang Hsi-lü 章希呂
Chang Hsün 張勳
Chang P'eng-ch'un 張彭春
Chang Ping-lin 章炳麟
Chang Shih-chao 章士釗
Chang Tsai 張載
Chang Tso-lin 張作霖
ch'ang-shih ti cheng-chih 常識的政治

Chao Ch'i 趙岐
Chao Yüan-jen 趙元任
Chen-ju tao 眞如島
chen-shih ju-ch'ang 眞實如常
Ch'en Cheng-shih 陳承栻
Ch'en Chi-t'ang 陳濟棠
Ch'en Heng-che 陳衡哲
Ch'en Kuo-fu 陳果夫
Ch'en Mao-k'ang 陳茂康
Ch'en Po-sha 陳白沙
Ch'en Wang-tao 陳望道
Cheng Chen-to 鄭振鐸
cheng-chien 政見

cheng chih 政制
Cheng-chung hsüeh-t'ang 澄衷學堂
cheng-fu 政府
cheng-hsin 正心
Cheng-hsüeh hsi 政學系
cheng-li kuo-ku 整理國故
cheng-lun-chia 政論家
cheng-shih-ti cheng-fu 正式的政府
Ch'eng Chen-chi 程振基
Ch'eng Hao 程顥
Ch'eng I (I-ch'uan) 程頤 (伊川)
ch'eng-i 誠意
Ch'eng I-tsao 程義藻
Ch'eng Ts'ang-p'o 程滄波
ch'i-ssu shen-tan 起死神丹
"Chiang chin chiu" 將進酒
Chiang Fang-chen (Po-li) 蔣方震 (百里)
Chiang Kai-shek 蔣介石
Chiang Sung Mei-ling 蔣宋美玲
Chiang Tung-hsiu 江冬秀
ch'iang-ch'üan chu-i 強權主義
Chiao-t'ung hsi 交通系
Ch'ien Hsüan-t'ung (I-ku) 錢玄同 (疑古)
Ch'ien Ta-hsin 錢大昕
ch'ien-tz'u ti wo 前此的我
chih 智
chih-chih 致知
Chih-Feng 直奉
chih hsing ho-i 知行合一
chih-shih p'ing-teng 智識平等
"chin chih yü wang che, yu ch'i-nien chih ping ch'iu san-nien chih ai yeh" 今之欲王者，猶七年之病求三年之艾也.
Chin-pu tang 近步黨
chin-shih 進士
chin tse ch'üan tou chieh-chüeh le 今則全都解決了
ching i 經義
ching-t'ien 井田
Ching-yeh hsün-pao 兢業旬報
Chiu Ch'ang-yün 裘昌運
Chou chün 周君
Chou Hou-k'un 周厚坤
Chou I-ch'un (Chi-mei) 周詒春 (寄梅)
Chou Sheng-yu 周生有
Chou Shu-jen 周樹人
Chou Tse-ch'i 周澤岐
Chou Yang 周揚
Chu Ch'i-chih 朱起蟄
Chu Chia-hua 朱家驊
Chu Ching-nung 朱經農
Chu Hsi 朱熹
Chu-tzu ch'üan-shu 朱子全書
chuan-men hsüeh-shu 專門學術
Ch'uan-sha 川沙
ch'üan 權
ch'üan-min cheng-chih chu-i 全民政治主義
Chuang-tzu 莊子
chün-tzu pu ch'i 君子不器
Ch'un-ch'iu 春秋
chung-hsiao 忠孝
Chung-kuo kung-hsüeh 中國公學
Chung-kuo min-ch'üan pao-chang t'ung-meng 中國民權保障同盟
Chung-t'un 中屯
ch'ung-fen shih-chieh-hua 充分世界化
Erh Ch'eng i-shu 二程遺書
Fan Chen 范縝
Feng Shun-ti 馮順弟
Feng Tzu-yu 馮自由
Feng Yü-hsiang 馮玉祥
fu-kuo ch'iang-ping 富國強兵
Han Fei 韓非
Han-hsüeh 漢學
Han Wu-ti 漢武帝
Han Yü 韓愈
ho-p'ing 和平
Hou Mao-ch'ing 賀懋慶
Hsi hsüeh wei yung, Chung hsüeh wei t'i 西學爲用，中學爲體
Hsiang-tao chou-pao 嚮導週報
hsiao 孝
Hsiao-hsüeh 小學
hsiao-tzu hsien-sun 孝子賢孫
hsien-tsai ti wo 現在的我
hsin[a] 信
hsin[b] 心
Hsin-ch'ao 新潮

hsin-i 信義
Hsin-min ts'ung-pao 新民叢報
Hsin shih-chi pao 新世紀報
Hsin shih-chieh 新世界
hsin tzu-yu chu-i 新自由主義
Hsiu-ning 休寧
Hsiung Hsi-ling 熊希齡
Hsü Chien-p'ing 許建屏
Hsü Chih-mo 徐志摩
Hsü Hsin-liu (Chen-fei) 徐新六（振飛）
Hsü Pao-huang 徐寶璜
Hsü Shih-ch'ang 徐世昌
Hsüan-t'ung (P'u-i) 宣統（溥儀）
Hsüeh-heng 學衡
Hsüeh wei-jen shih 學為人詩
Hsün-tzu 荀子
Hu Ch'un-ch'iao 胡春喬
Hu Feng 胡風
Hu Han-min 胡漢民
Hu Hsüan-ming 胡宣明
Hu Hung-chui 胡洪雕
Hu Hung-chün 胡洪駿
Hu Hung-hsing 胡洪骍
Hu Hung-p'i 胡洪駓
Hu K'uang-chung (P'u-chai) 胡匡衷（樸齋）
Hu P'ei-hui (Tsai-p'ing) 胡培翬（載平 [屏]）
Hu Shuo po-shih 胡說博士
Hu Ssu-tu 胡思杜
Hu Tsu-wang 胡祖望
Hua-t'ung kung-hsüeh 華同公學
Huang Hsing 黃興
Hui-chou 惠州
Hui-tzu 惠子
"Hun-yin p'ien" 婚姻篇
Hung-lou meng 紅樓夢
i 義
i-ch'eng ti wo 已成的我
i-chih 一致
Jao Meng-k'an 饒孟侃
jen 仁
jen-ai 仁愛
Jen Hung-chün (Shu-yung) 任鴻雋（叔永）
jen-sheng-kuan 人生觀

jen-tao 人道
jen-tao chu-i 人道主義
Jen Tsai-t'ang 仁在堂
K'ai-chih lu yüeh-k'an 開智錄月刊
k'ai-fang cheng-ch'üan 開放政權
k'ai wu ti-tsang 開吾地藏
kan-she chu-i 干涉主義
k'ang-li erh chien shih yu 伉儷而兼師友
K'ang Yu-wei 康有為
Kao I-han 高一涵
Kao Lu 高魯
Kao-tzu 告子
Keikoku bidan 經國美談
ko-chih wu-chih 歌之舞之
ko-jen-hsing 個人性
Ko-ming i-shih 革命逸史
ko-wu 格物
K'o-pao 可報
Ku Wei-chün (Shao-ch'uan) 顧維鈞（少川）
Ku Yen-wu 顧炎武
kuan-hua 官話
Kuang-hua 光華
kung-ch'i chu-i 公妻主義
kung-chung 公忠
kung-k'ai ti cheng-fu 公開的政府
Kung-sun Lung 公孫龍
Kuo-hsüeh chi-k'an 國學季刊
Kuo-min hsi 國民系
Kuo-min-pao yüeh-k'an 國民報月刊
Kuomintang 國民黨
kuo-wen 國文
kuo-yü 國語
Lan Chih-hsien (Kung-wu) 藍志先（公武）
Lao She (Shu Ch'ing-ch'un) 老舍（舒慶春）
Lao-tzu 老子
Lei Chen 雷震
li[a] 禮
li[b] 理
li-chi 利己
li-hsüeh 理學
Li I-shan 李義山
li-jang 禮讓
Li Po 李白

Li Shih-tseng 李石曾
Li Tsung-jen 李宗仁
Li Yüan-hung 黎元洪
li-yung hou-sheng 利用厚生
Liang Shih-ch'iu 梁實秋
Liao Chung-k'ai 廖仲凱
Lin Ch'ang-min (Tsung-meng) 林長
民（宗孟）
Lin Yü-t'ang 林玉堂
Ling Tao-yang 凌道楊
Liu Ch'ung-chieh (Tzu-k'ai) 劉崇傑
（子楷）
Liu Fu 劉復
Liu Tsung-yüan 柳宗元
Liu Yung-fu 劉永福
Lo Chia-lun 羅家倫
Lo Wen-kan (Chün-jen) 羅文幹（鈞
任）
lun-chan 論戰
"Lun hui-ch'u shen-fo" 論毀除神佛
Lung-men shu-yüan 龍門書院
lung-t'ung-ti 攏統的
Ma Chün-wu (Ma Ho) 馬君武（馬
和）
Mao I 毛義
Mao Tse-tung 毛澤東
Mao Tun (Shen Yen-ping) 茅盾（沈
雁冰）
Mei-chi hsüeh-t'ang 梅溪學堂
Mei Kuang-ti 梅光迪
Mei Tsu-fen 梅祖芬
Mei I-ch'i 梅貽琦
Mencius (Meng-tzu, Meng K'o) 孟
子，孟軻
mi meng 迷夢
Min-chu chou-k'an 民主週刊
min-chu tzu-yu 民主自由
Min-kuo jih-pao 民國日報
Min-pao 民報
min-tsu chu-i 民族主義
min-tsu ssu-hsiang 民族思想
Mo-tzu 墨子
neng 能
no 諾
pai-hua 白話
P'an Wen-huan 潘文煥
pao-ch'ien 抱歉

Peita 北大
pen 本
pi-t'ing 筆挺
P'ing she 評社
pu-ho-li 不合理
"pu huan kua erh huan pu chün, pu
huan p'in erh huan pu an" 不患寡
而患不均，不患貧而患不安
san-kang wu-lun 三綱五倫
San Min Chu I 三民主義
sao 騷
Shang-chuang 上莊
Shao Li-tzu 邵力子
Shao Yu-lien 邵友濂
she-hui-hsing 社會性
Shen-chou jih-pao 神州日報
"Shen mieh lun" 神滅論
Shen-pao 申報
Shen Yin-mo 沈尹默
shih 詩
shih-che sheng-ts'un 適者勝存
Shih-chi 史記
shih-chieh-ti 世界的
Shih-chih ts'un 適之村
Shih-pao 時報
Shih-shih hsin-pao 時事新報
shih-ta-fu 士大夫
shu[a] 術
shu[b] 恕
Shu ching 書經
shu-jen 樹人
shu-min 庶民
Shui-ching chu 水經注
Shui-hu chuan 水滸傳
Soong Ch'ing-ling 宋慶齡
Soong Tzu-wen 宋子文
ssu chung 私忠
ssu erh pu-hsiu 死而不朽
Ssu-ma Kuang 司馬光
Su-pao 蘇報
Sun Ching-ts'un 孫兢存
Sun Ch'uan-fang 孫傳芳
Sun K'o (Sun Fo) 孫科
Sun Yat-sen (Chung-shan) 孫逸仙
（中山）
Sung Che-yüan 宋哲元
Ta-kung pao 大公報

Ta shih-chieh 大世界
ta-t'ung chu-i 大同主義
Ta-t'ung jih-pao 大同日報
Tai Chen 戴震
t'ai-t'ou chien-hsi 抬頭見喜
tang-chien 黨見
T'ang Erh-ho 湯爾和
T'ang Ming-tsung 唐明宗
T'ang Yüeh-liang 唐悅良
tao 道
Tao te ching 道德經
T'ao Chih-hsing 陶知行
T'ao Lü-kung 陶履恭
t'ao-t'ai 陶汰
te-hua chih ta-t'ung 德化之大同
t'e-pieh ying-chieh ti cheng-chih 特別英傑的政治
ti 弟
Ti-tsang 地藏
t'ien-ching ti-i 天經地義
t'ien-fang 添房
t'ien-tse 天擇
Ting Hsi-lin 丁西林
Ting Jih-ch'ang 丁日昌
to nan hsing pang 多難興邦
tsai-sheng shih-tai 再生時代
Ts'ai Yüan-p'ei 蔡元培
tsao yin 造因
Ts'ao 曹
Ts'ao Chan 曹霑
Ts'ao Ju-lin 曹汝霖
Ts'ao K'un 曹錕
Tso chuan 左傳
tso-jen 做人
Tsou Lu 鄒魯
Tsung-li 總理
Tu Fu 杜甫
Tu-shu tsa-chih 讀書雜誌
Tuan Ch'i-jui 段棋瑞
Tun-huang 敦煌
Tung-lin 東林
Tung Pi-wu 董必武
T'ung-meng hui 同盟會
tzu-chih ti she-hui 自治的社會
Tzu-chih t'ung-chien 資治通鑑
tzu-chüeh 自覺
tzu-li 自立

Tzu-yu Chung-kuo 自由中國
tzu-yu-ti she-hui-chu-i 自由的社會主義
tz'u 詞
Wang Ch'ang-hsin 王長信
Wang Cheng 王澂
Wang Cheng-fu 王正輔
Wang Cheng-t'ing 王正廷
Wang Chih-ch'un 王之春
Wang Ching-wei 汪精衞
Wang Ch'ung 王充
Wang Ch'ung-hui (Liang-ch'ou) 王寵惠 (亮疇)
Wang Hung-cho 王鴻卓
Wang Keng 王賡
Wang Mang 王莽
Wang Nien-sun 王念孫
Wang Po-ch'iu 王伯秋
Wang Yang-ming (Shou-jen) 王陽明 (守仁)
Wang Yin-chih 王引之
Wei Tao-ming 魏道明
Wei Wen-pin 魏文斌
wei-wo 爲我
wen-chien-p'ai 穩健派
wen-i fu-hsing shih-tai 文藝復興時代
Wen I-to 聞一多
wen-jen 文人
Weng Wen-hao 翁文灝
wu 物
Wu Chih-hui 吳稚暉
Wu Ching-lien 吳景濂
Wu Han 吳晗
Wu Nan-hsien 吳南軒
Wu P'ei-fu 吳佩孚
Wu Ta-ch'eng 吳大澂
wu-t'i shih 無題詩
wu-wei erh wu-pu-wei 無爲而無不爲
Yang Ch'üan (Hsing-fo) 楊銓 (杏佛)
Yang T'ien-tse 楊天擇
Yang Wei-hsin (Ting-fu) 楊維新 (鼎甫)
Yeh Ch'eng-chung 葉成忠
Yeh Ching-hsin (Shu-heng) 葉景莘 (叔衡)
Yeh Kung-ch'ao 葉公超

Yen-chiu hsi 研究系
Yen Fu 嚴復
Yen-hsia-tung 烟霞洞
Yen Hui 顏回
Yen Hui-ch'ing 顏惠慶
Yen Jo-chü 閻若璩
yen-lun 言論
yu-chih cheng-chih 幼稚政治
yu-sheng lieh-pai 優勝劣敗

Yü Ch'en-tzu 雨塵子
Yü Jih-chang 余日章
yü min hsiu-hsi ti jen-cheng 與民休息
    的仁政
Yü P'ing-po 俞平伯
Yü Yu-jen 于右任
Yüan Mei 袁枚
Yüan Shih-k'ai 袁世凱

Index

Abbott, Lyman, 54, 55n
Abend, Hallett, 243n
Academia Sinica, 277, 279, 311, 341
Ai Ssu-ch'i, 363, 364
American Association for International
  Conciliation, 60
American Civil Liberties Union, 277
Anarchism, 123, 182
Anderson, J. G., 219
Anfu Clique, 182, 193, 202
Anfu Club (Anfu Clique), 177
Angell, Sir Norman, 55, 59
Anti-Americanism, 306n, 362
Anti-Manchu sentiment, 21n, 23, 28,
  229
Association of Cosmopolitan Clubs, 53,
  60
Authoritarianism and democracy,
  debate on (1933–1935), 259–274
Autocracy. See Authoritarianism

Balfour, David, 159n
Bentham, Jeremy, 28n
Bergson, Henri, 133, 138, 157, 158, 167
Björnson, Björnstjerne, 337
Bland, J. O. P., 66
Bloomsbury, 225
Bolshevik Revolution, 123, 153, 296
Bosanquet, Bernard, 47
Boxer Indemnity Scholarship Program,
  27, 35–36, 79, 80n
Bradley, Francis Herbert, 47
Brandes, Georg, 94, 337
Brieux, Eugene, 93
Brinton, Crane, 338
British Boxer Indemnity Committee,
  216
British Labor Party, 299, 303
Browning, John, 44
Bryan, William Jennings, 57, 159n
Buddhism: and Neo-Confucianism,
  14–16, 96, 164; influence on Hu Shih,
  17–18; and Liang Sou-ming,
  137–138; Hu Shih's view of, 162,
  164, 225–226
Bull Moose Party, 52
Burr, Lincoln, 49
Byron, George Gordon, 103, 225

Canton, Hu Shih's visit to (1935), 286
Carlyle, Thomas, 58, 214
Carnegie Endowment, 55
Castelnuevo, 181n
Cavour, Camillo di, 352
CCP (Chinese Communist Party), 169,
  179, 207, 249. See also Ch'en
  Tu-hsiu, Hu Shih, Li Ta-chao,
  Marxism-Leninism
CCP attack on Hu Shih, 312, 320–321,
  358–368; Hu Shih's evaluation of,
  366–367
Chang Chia-shen. See Chang Chün-mai
Chang Chien, 25, 174n, 199
Chang Chün-mai: in Europe (1919),
  129n, 145; as student of Eucken's,
  145, 157; as exponent of
  neo-traditionalism, 146–150; on
  "spiritual civilization," 147–148;
  as student of Bergson's, 157;
  mentioned, 151, 159, 204n
Chang Hsi-jo, 34n, 359
Chang Hsi-lü, 248n
Chang Hsün, 174
Chang Huan-lun, 5n, 7n, 22
Chang Loy, 356, 357
Chang P'eng-ch'un, 356, 357
Chang Ping-lin, 23n, 78
Chang Po-ling, 357
Chang Shih-chao, 30n
Chang Tsai, 19
Chang Tso-lin, 202, 222, 223
Chang Tung-sun, 167, 168
Chang Wei-tz'u: and The Weekly
  Critic, 180; signs "Our Political
  Proposals," 190n; and The
  Endeavor, 205; mentioned, 194,
  219, 236n
Chao Ch'i, 68n
Chao Yuen-ren (Y. R. Chao), 80n
Chekov, Anton, 87
Ch'en Cheng-shih, 356
Ch'en Chi-t'ang, 286–287, 288
Ch'en Chih-mai, 311n
Ch'en Heng-che, Miss, 80n
Ch'en Kuo-fu, 239
Ch'en Mao-k'ang, 356
Ch'en Po-sha, 158
Ch'en Te-cheng, 240–241

Ch'en Tu-hsiu: and literary revolution, 76, 78, 85–86; as member of Peita group, 78; on materialist view of history, 106–108; on democracy and science, 110–111; on social continuity, 112; and *The Weekly Critic*, 123, 180; conversion to Marxism-Leninism, 127, 184–185; on participation in politics, 176n, 180; his understanding of politics, 178; arrested (1919), 181, 184; signs Manifesto of the New Youth Society, 183; accepts Dewey's gradualism, 183–184; leaves Peking, 184; edits *The New Youth* in Shanghai and Canton, 184; breaks with Hu Shih, 184–187; final admonition to Hu Shih, 186; arrested (1932), 186n, 278n; as secretary-general of CCP, 207, 223; mentioned, 89, 90, 128, 214, 237, 299n, 321, 360, 362

Ch'en Wang-tao, 184, 185
Cheng Chen-to, 363
Cheng-chung School (Cheng-chung hsüeh-t'ang), 22n, 24, 31
Cheng-li kuo-ku (systematizing the national heritage), 161–163, 165–166, 343
Ch'eng-Chu School, 14, 31. *See also* Neo-Confucianism
Ch'eng Hao, 14
Ch'eng I, 14, 48, 230
Ch'eng I-ch'uan. *See* Ch'eng I
Ch'eng I-tsao, 356
Ch'eng T'ien-fang, 122n
Ch'eng Ts'ang-p'o, 244n
Chi-hsi hsien, 4–6, 10–12, 303
Chiang Fang-chen, 129n, 204n
Chiang Kai-shek: as cultural nationalist, 230; warns political critics, 243; and Hu Shih's ambassadorship, 295; and suppression of dissent, 302; and presidential election of 1947, 305–306; Hu Shih's opinion of in 1948, 309; his critique of liberalism, 319–320; his evaluation of Hu Shih's contribution, 344–345; mentioned, 222, 277, 290, 294, 298, 299, 303, 310, 312n, 327, 361, 365
Chiang Meng-lin. *See* Chiang Monlin
Chiang, Mme. *See* Soong Mei-ling
Chiang Monlin: as revolutionary

journalist, 30n; as student of Dewey's, 46; as Minister of Education, 242, 244; as chancellor of Peita, 245; appointed secretary-general of Executive Yuan, 296, 297; mentioned, 157n, 226, 257n
Chiang Po-li. *See* Chiang Fang-chen
Chiang T'ing-fu: on autocracy and revolution, 259–260; on China's lack of nationhood, 281; and KMT, 297; and United Nations, 311n; and China Lobby, 311n; mentioned, 266, 279n
Chiang Tung-hsiu (wife of Hu Shih), 11–12, 352–354
Ch'ien Hsüan-t'ung, 78, 85–86, 184n
Ch'ien I-ku. *See* Ch'ien Hsüan-t'ung
Ch'ien Ta-hsin, 165
Ch'ien Tuan-sheng, 265, 266, 297–298, 359
Chih-chih. *See* "Extension of knowledge"
Chih-Feng War, 202
China Foundation for the Promotion of Education and Culture, 239–240, 341
China Lobby, 311n
China National Institute (Chung-kuo kung-hsüeh), 24–26, 33–34, 239, 367; Hu Shih accepts presidency of, 224; Hu Shih ousted from, 245.
China Weekly Review, The, 279n
China's Destiny, 319
Chinese Communist Party. *See* CCP
Chinese League for the Protection of Civil Rights (Chung-kuo min-ch'üan pao-chang t'ung-meng), 277–279
Chinese liberalism. *See* Liberalism in China
Chinese Renaissance, The, 279
Chinese Renaissance, 289, 314. *See also* Hu Shih, views on Chinese and Western cultures
Chinese Students' Alliance, 53
Ching-t'ien (well-field) system, 5n, 136n, 166
Ching-yeh hsün-pao. See *The Struggle*
Ch'ing Scholarship. *See* Han Learning
Chiu Ch'ang-yün, 356
Chou En-lai, 360
Chou Hou-k'un, 356
Chou I-ch'un, 204n

Index

Chou Sheng-yu, 21n
Chou Shu-jen. *See* Lu Hsün
Chou Tse-ch'i, 356
Chou Tso-jen, 78, 87n, 185, 285, 359
Chou Yang, 363
Chu Ch'i-chih, 356
Chu Chia-hua, 296
Chu Ching-nung, 190n
Chu Hsi, 14, 15, 16n, 17, 68n, 149n,
 189, 230
Chuang-tzu, 261
Chung-kuo kung-hsüeh. *See* China
 National Institute
Chung-kuo min-ch'üan pao-chang
 t'ung-meng. *See* Chinese League for
 the Protection of Civil Rights
Chung-kuo wen-t'i (China's problems),
 236n
Chung-t'un, 7n
Civil War (1946–1949), 296, 298–301,
 303, 308, 310
Classic of Poetry (Shih ching), 82n
Collegiate League to Abolish
 Militarism, 59
Columbia University, 11, 34n, 42–43,
 50, 54, 225, 236, 296, 328
Comintern, 207
Commercial Press, 21
Communications Clique (Chiao-t'ung
 hsi), 186n
Compilation and Translation Commit-
 tee of the China Foundation, 245
Confucianism: and individualism, 95–
 98; and gentry culture, 321; political
 theory of, 324–325, 328. *See also*
 Chang Chün-mai; Hu Shih, views
 on Chinese and Western cultures;
 Liang Ch'i-ch'ao; Liang Sou-ming;
 Neo-Confucianism
Confucius, 15, 96, 103, 144, 164, 189,
 230
Confucius' birthday, celebration of
 under KMT, 230, 282, 283–284
Consensus, 119–120, 335–336
*Contemporary Review, The (Hsien-tai
 p'ing-lun)*, 206
Cornell Cosmopolitan Club, 52–53
Cornell University, 11, 34n, 40–42, 49,
 55, 60, 8on, 328, 352
Cosmopolitanism, 57–61, 208, 287, 315,
 317, 321, 334. *See also* Hu Shih,
 political opinions

Creighton, James E., 42, 47
Crescent, The (Hsin yüeh), 206, 224–
 225, 233, 236, 241, 245, 247, 297, 314
Crick, Bernard, 324, 332, 336n
Cultural Revolution, 327, 367

Darwin, Charles, 24, 28n
Darwinism, 27–28, 211
Daudet, Alphonse, 87
Debs, Eugene, 52n
Decatur, Stephen, 58
December 9 Movement, 255; Hu Shih's
 response to, 256–257
Democracy. *See* Hu Shih, political
 opinions
Democratic League, 297, 304
*Democratic Weekly, The (Min-chu
 chou-k'an)*, 297
Descartes, René, 28n, 352
Dewey, John: influence on Hu Shih,
 45–51, 111–121, 334, 335–336; as
 political activist, 54, 64; views on
 force and violence, 59; and Hu
 Shih's theory of "social immortality,"
 118; on differences between China
 and the West, 120–121; in China
 (1919–1921), 121–122; lectures on
 social and political philosophy
 published in *The New Youth*, 183;
 on the political influence of the
 intellectual minority, 201–202; on
 liberalism and warlordism, 221; and
 the theory of knowledge and action,
 235; definition of liberalism, 328;
 social philosophy of, 332; on the
 prerequisites to a modern political
 order, 335; on the need for concrete
 analyses of social conditions, 340,
 342; mentioned, 42, 44, 67, 138,
 184n, 242, 323, 325, 329, 341. *See also*
 Hu Shih, intellectual reform;
 Pragmatism
Dickens, Charles, 161
Dismissal of Hai Jui, The, 367
Dobson, W. A. C. H., 68n
Doll's House, A, 91, 93
*Dream of the Red Chamber, The
 (Hung-lou meng)*, 162, 363
Dreisch, Hans Adolph, 158
Dumas, Alexandre, 161

Eddy, Sherwood, 219

Edman, Irwin, 115
Eight-legged essay, 20
Elitism: and gentry society, 281–282; and Confucianism, 324, 336, 343; and KMT, 336; and CCP, 336. See also Hu Shih, political opinions
Endeavor, The (Nu-li chou-pao), 150, 188–189, 193, 195, 196, 197, 198, 200, 202–203, 204n, 205, 209, 210, 218, 224, 233, 247, 359
Enemy of the People, An, 91, 93
Enlightenment, European, and Chinese Renaissance, 315–317, 318
Eucken, Rudolf Christoph, 133, 138, 157
Evolution and Ethics, 26–27
Examination system, 20, 22
Experimentalism, 182, 335. See also Dewey, John; Hu Shih, intellectual reform; Pragmatism
Expertise in government, 235–238, 264, 271–272, 339–340, 343, 367. See also Hu Shih, political opinions
"Extension of knowledge" (chih-chih), 16, 96–97, 165

Fabians, 225, 236, 269, 322
Fan Chen, 18, 19n, 30, 117
Federalism, 195–196, 252
Fédération Internationale des Etudiants, "Corda Fratres" (F. I. d. E.), 52–53, 55–57, 355
Feng Shun-ti (Hu Shih's mother), 7–13 passim, 103, 180, 351–353, 354
Feng Tzu-yu, 30n
Feng Yü-hsiang, 357
Franke, O., 219
Franklin, Benjamin, 90
Free China (Tzu-yu Chung-kuo), 312n
French Revolution, 296
Fu Ssu-nien, 76n, 186n, 298

Gannett, Lewis, 12, 345
Gay, Peter, 315–316, 317
Genesis, 314
Gentry (shih-ta-fu), 281–282
Ghosts, 93
Gibbon, Edward, 352
Gladden, Washington, 54, 58n
Gladstone, William E., 159n
Golden Rule, 343

"Good Men Cabinet" (1922), 203–204, 223, 359
Goodnow, Dr. Frank J., 66
Gorki, Maxim, 87, 181n
Great Illusion, The, 55
Guide Weekly, The (Hsiang-tao chou-pao), 214, 359
Gunther, John, 294

Han Fei, 163, 164
Han-hsüeh. See Han Learning
Han Learning, 5, 16n, 122, 165–166, 167
Han Yü, 14, 83
Harvard University, 80n, 265, 296
Haskell Lectures, 279
Hauptmann, Gerhart, 93
Hedda Gabler, 93
Hedin, Sven, 86n, 219
Hegel, Georg Wilhelm Friedrich, 211
Hiram Corson Browning Prize, 40n
Hobbes, Thomas, 28n, 352
Hobhouse, Leonard T., 327–328, 329
Hornbeck, Stanley, 295
Hou Mao-ch'ing, 356
Hsiang-tao chou-pao. See The Guide Weekly
Hsiao-hsüeh, 18
Hsien-tai p'ing-lun. See The Contemporary Review
Hsin ch'ing-nien. See The New Youth
Hsin-min ts'ung-pao, 21, 23, 28
Hsin shih-chi pao, 30n
Hsin yüeh. See The Crescent
Hsiung Hsi-ling, 25, 65
Hsu, Jabin. See Hsü Chien-p'ing
Hsü Chien-p'ing, 356, 357
Hsü Chih-mo, 194, 218, 225, 232, 236n
Hsü Hsin-liu, 129n
Hsü Pao-huang, 190n
Hsü Shih-ch'ang, 65, 202
Hsü Tzu-ming, 312n
Hsüan-t'ung Emperor, The. See P'u-i
Hsüeh-heng, 80n
Hsüeh-hsi, 363, 364
Hsün-tzu, 31, 163, 164
Hu Ch'uan, 4–8, 11, 12–14, 17, 19n
Hu Ch'un-ch'iao, 5n
Hu Feng, 366n
Hu Han-min, 166–167
Hu Hsüan-ming, 357
Hu Hung-chui, 7n, 9, 20, 24

Hu Hung-chün, 7n, 9, 20
Hu Hung-hsing, 7n
Hu Hung-p'i, 7n, 20
Hu K'uang-chung, 5n
Hu P'ei-hui, 5n
Hu P'u-chai. *See* Hu K'uang-chung
Hu Shih: schooling in Shanghai, 20–
    26; changes name to Hu Shih, 27;
    wins Boxer Indemnity Scholarship,
    36–37; at Cornell, 41–42; at
    Columbia, 42–43; and international
    student movement, 53–57, 356;
    returns to China, 75; and *The
    New Youth*, 75–76, 78, 185–188; as
    member of Peita group, 78; breaks
    with Ch'en Tu-hsiu, 184–187;
    relationship with Ch'en Tu-hsiu
    and Li Ta-chao compared, 186n;
    and *The Endeavor*, 188–189, 205–
    206; writes "Our Political
    Proposals," 189–190; and returned
    students, 204n; trip to Europe
    and America (1926–1927), 217–
    218, 222; his life in Peking in
    1920s, 219–220; and *The Crescent*,
    225–226; and P'ing she, 236n; edits
    The Independent Critic, 247; and
    League for the Protection of Civil
    Rights, 277–279; envoy to U.S.
    (1936), 293–294; ambassador to
    U.S. (1937–1942), 294–295, 361;
    chancellor of Peita, 296, 301–302,
    306n; and Democratic League,
    297n; and Mao Tse-tung, 299n;
    and election of 1947, 305–306; final
    departure from Peking, 308–309,
    365n; and China Lobby, 311n;
    returns to Taiwan (1958), 311–313;
    and Academia Sinica, 311, 313
    family background and early educa-
    tion: mother's influence on, 10–12,
    352–354; marriage, 11–12, 352–354;
    father's influence on, 13, 17; influ-
    ence of Buddhism, 17; influenced
    by Neo-Confucian skepticism, 17–
    18; influenced by Liang Ch'i-ch'ao,
    26, 28–29; influenced by Yen Fu,
    26; and Darwinism, 26–28; influ-
    ence of home life on his social
    opinions, 32, 100, 352
    character and personality, 40, 116;
    optimism, 44–45, 70, 258, 289,
    294, 326, 347; pacifism, 58–59, 68,
    254; emotional detachment, 70,
    208, 322, 338; self-appraisal in
    1914, 40; self-appraisal in 1915,
    64; self-appraisal in 1926, 218;
    self-appraisal in 1948, 309; his
    estimate of his own role, 343
    appraisal of the Chinese situation:
    before 1917, 64, 66–67; sentiments
    on returning to China (1917), 75;
    on the analysis of China's prob-
    lems, 124–126; his understanding
    of May Fourth, 176–179; views on
    Sino-Japanese crisis (1931–1937),
    250–254; views on the civil war
    (1946–1949), 298, 299–301, 310–311;
    an evaluation of his understanding
    of Chinese conditions, 334, 339–343
    the Literary Revolution: discovers
    vernacular fiction, 19–20; formu-
    lates program for literary reform,
    79–80; the program, 81–82; his
    attitude toward Literary Revolu-
    tion, 85–86; views on the purposes
    of literature, 87–88; on literature
    as a vehicle for social reform and
    the importation of foreign ideas,
    90
    social criticism and social reform:
    early criticism of Chinese society,
    30–33; "social immortality," 33,
    103–104, 116–118, 352; formulation
    of reform program, 67–70; grad-
    ualism, 68–70, 126–127; "Ibsenism,"
    93–95, 98, 215, 312; individualism,
    93–99, 106, 108, 112, 115–116, 127,
    322, 325, 327, 329, 337, 338, 342; on
    the division of labor, 97, 343; and
    the family system, 99–102
    intellectual reform: skepticism and
    the critical attitude, 101–102, 108–
    111, 112, 230–231, 312, 325, 326–
    327, 328; on science and the
    scientific method, 104, 112, 151,
    288; on the importance of
    scientific education, 157–158; prag-
    matism, 42–43, 46–51, 111–121,
    118–120, 209, 334, 336, 340, 342;
    rationalism, 117, 153–156, 287,
    290, 326, 334–335
    views on Chinese and Western
    cultures: on the introduction of

Western ideas, 124–125; as exponent of cultural synthesis, 136, 160–161; on "spiritual" vs. "materialistic" civilization, 151–156; on the European Renaissance, 159–160, 212, 318–319; on problems of cultural conflict, 160–161; and *cheng-li kuo-ku*, 161–163, 343; his interpretation of China's intellectual history, 163–166; on the Chinese Renaissance, 164–165, 289, 318; on the Han Learning, 165–166; and "total" westernization, 285–286, 287–289; on modernization vs. westernization, 287; on cultural inertia, 288; and scholarship, 341–342

political opinions: his understanding of the nature of politics, 51–63, 178, 180, 251, 322–323, 325, 328–329; views on the student movement, and on intellectuals and politics, 54, 61–62, 175–176, 215, 249–250, 255–257, 301–302, 304–308, 344; on revolutionary and evolutionary change, 33–34, 51, 70–71, 227–228, 342–343; assessment of the accomplishments of the revolution, 257–259; on "fundamental solutions" (the debate with Li Ta-chao on "Problems and Isms," 1919), 181–183, 189, 208–210, 280–281; critique of Marxism, 125, 127–128, 211; his understanding of democracy, 77n, 178, 197–198, 212–213, 238, 266–272, 308, 326, 328, 334; on the competence of the people for self-government, 238, 261, 267–270, 337; democracy and socialism, 212–213; on representative government, 271–272; democracy in China, 295, 333; liberalism, 213, 262–263, 274, 308, 329–336; on "government with a plan," 67–68, 193–195, 204n, 325, 333; on authoritarianism, 232, 235, 266; on "*wu-wei* government," 261–264, 283, 332; and federalism, 195–196, 252; and constitutionalism, 192, 203, 233, 275–277, 304; respect for law, 276, 277–278, 302–303; respect for established authority, 198–199, 226, 275, 276, 330; asserts the right to dissent, 274, 278n, 329, 336; distrust of partisanism, 200–201, 272–274; on public opinion and consensus, 119–120, 189, 193, 201, 251–252, 334–335; and "government by good men," 191–193, 204n; on government by experts, 236–238, 264, 269–270, 339–340; elitism, 196–197, 238, 270, 272, 281–282, 288, 336–337, 343–344; on nationalism and cosmopolitanism, 57–61, 168–169, 222, 230, 282–287, 322, 334; and imperialism, 210, 213–215, 226–227, 246–247, 257n, 307, 359, 360, 361, 365

and KMT: criticism of KMT program, 226, 229–231, 234–238, 245, 275–277; friends in KMT government, 226, 240, 244; troubles with KMT government (1929–1930), 239–245; and T. V. Soong, 244n, 295; on KMT's loss of intellectuals' support, 245; opinion of Sun Yat-sen in 1930s, 274–275; on New Life Movement, 283; supports KMT after 1937, 293, 300–301, 309; Chiang Kai-shek's opinion of him, 344–345

and CCP: his understanding of CCP, 298–299, 300, 303–304, 310, 360; CCP attack on, 312, 320–321, 358–368

and U.S.: his appreciation of America, 40–41, 43–45; American influence on, 157, 201, 332, 335–337; prestige in U.S., 294, 302, 306–307; and anti-Americanism, 306

sense of history, 108, 315, 317, 326–327, 335

world view, 103–106, 325–326

transcendent vision, 330, 338, 347

Hu Shih ssu-hsiang p'i-p'an (A critique of Hu Shih's thought), 367

Hu Shih yü kuo-yün (Hu Shih and the nation's destiny), 312n, 320

Hu Ssu-tu, 9n, 359, 360–361

Hu T'ieh-hua. *See* Hu Ch'uan

Hu Tsai-p'ing. *See* Hu P'ei-hui

Hu Tsu-wang, 102n

Index

Hua-t'ung Public School (Hua-t'ung kung-hsüeh), 34
Huang Hsing, 174n
Hui-chou prefecture, 4, 5
Hui-tzu, 163
Hundred Flowers Campaign, 366
Hung-lou meng. See *The Dream of the Red Chamber*
Huxley, Thomas Henry, 26, 48, 90, 117, 164, 341

Ibsen, Henrik, 91, 93–95, 215, 337
"Ibsenism." *See* Hu Shih, social criticism and social reform
Imperialism: and CCP, 207–208; and KMT, 220–221. *See also* Hu Shih, political opinions
Independent Critic, The (Tu-li p'ing-lun), 186n, 247–248, 259, 274, 276, 281, 297, 300, 311n, 360
Individualism, 324–325, 327, 329, 337, 338, 342; Liang Ch'i-ch'ao on, 91–92; and Confucianism, 95–98; Liang Sou-ming on, 140–142. *See also* Hu Shih, social criticism and social reform
Institute of Pacific Relations, 279
"Investigation of things" (*ko-wu*), 16, 165

James, William: his theory of truth, 114; Hu Shih's estimate of, 114; on intellectual continuity, 118; and meliorism, 126; mentioned, 48, 49, 138
Jao Meng-k'an, 225
Jefferson, Thomas, 299, 303, 335
Jen Hung-chün, 80n, 218
Jen-min jih-pao, 363, 367
Jen Shu-yung. *See* Jen Hung-chün
Jen Tsai-t'ang, 288
Jesus, 103
Joffe, Adolf, 219
Johnson, Nelson T., 254

K'ai-chih lu yüeh-k'an, 30n
K'ang Yu-wei, 131, 133, 173–174, 177
Kant, Immanuel, 28n, 167, 343, 352
Kao I-han: as member of Peita group, 78; and *The Weekly Critic*, 180; translates Dewey's lectures, 183; signs "Our Political Proposals," 190;

and *The Endeavor*, 205; mentioned, 181n, 184, 219, 359
Kao Lu, 204n
Kao-tzu, 32
Keikoku Bidan, 37
"Kindergarten government," Hu Shih's theory of, 261, 267–270
Kipling, Rudyard, 87
KMT (Kuomintang), 169, 179, 207, 220–221, 225, 229; ideology of, 221; and cultural nationalism, 229–230; 282–287, 319–320; and suppression of dissent, 222, 275, 298, 302, 312n; and student nationalism, 249, 255; opposed by advocates of authoritarian government, 264–265; and "Period of political tutelage," 231–232; and assassination of Yang Ch'üan, 279; Constitution of 1947, 304; and self-strengtheners, 286–287. *See also* Hu Shih, Sun Yat-sen
KMT-CCP Alliance, 207, 220, 222; Hu Shih's evaluation of, 231
Knowledge and action, Hu Shih's dispute with Sun Yat-sen on, 234–238
Ko-ming chün (The revolutionary army), 23–24
Ko-wu. See "Investigation of things"
K'o-hsüeh yü jen-sheng-kuan. See *Science and the Philosophy of Life*
K'o-pao, 30n
Kommunist, 364
Koo, V. K. Wellington, 186n, 203, 204, 297, 345
Kropotkin, Pëtr Alekseevich, 133, 189
Ku Chieh-kang, 162, 341, 359, 362
Ku Wei-chün. *See* Koo, V. K. Wellington
Ku Yen-wu, 158, 165
Kuang-hua University, 224, 239
Kuling Conference (1937), 290, 293
Kung, H. H., 357
Kung-sun Lung, 163
Kuo-hsüeh chi-k'an (Sinological quarterly), 188n
Kuo-min-pao yüeh-k'an, 30n
Kuo Mo-jo, 359, 363, 365
Kuomintang. *See* KMT

"La Jeunesse." See *The New Youth*
Laissez-faire liberalism, 194, 212–213, 262–263

Index

Lan Chih-hsien, 182
Lao She, 363
Lao-tzu, 103
Laski, Harold, 225, 236, 237, 325
Latourette, K. S., 219
League of Nations, Hu Shih's confidence in, 251, 294
Legge, James, 68n, 149n
Lei Chen, 312n
Lenin, 232, 364
Leninism, and KMT, 229
Leslie's Illustrated Magazine, 39
L'Esprit des lois, 26
Levenson, Joseph R., 119n
Li (Principle), 15, 97
Li-hsüeh (Study of Principle), 14. *See
also* Neo-Confucianism
Li I-shan, 288
Li Po, 35, 103
Li Shih-tseng, 30n, 204n
Li-shih yen-chiu, 364
Li Ta-chao: as member of Peita group,
78; and *The Weekly Critic*, 123,
180; sponsors Marxist study groups
at Peita, 123; conversion to Marxism-
Leninism, 127; signs manifesto of
the New Youth Society, 183; and
The New Youth, 184n; on the
dangers of political opportunism,
186n; his relationship with Hu Shih,
186n; arrest and execution, 186n,
223; signs "Our Political Proposals,"
190, 210; and Mao Tse-tung, 299n;
mentioned, 128, 213, 219, 321, 365
Li Tsung-jen, 305
Li Yüan-hung, 202, 203
Liang Ch'i-ch'ao: early influence on
Hu Shih, 23, 26, 28–29; as a nationalist, 57; participates in government of Yüan Shih-k'ai, 65; on
individualism, 91–92; as exponent of
neo-traditionalism, 128, 131–135; in
Europe (1919), 129–130; on evolutionism, 133; and attack on Western
materialism, 134, 152; as Confucian
evangelist, 134–135, 144; compared to
Liang Sou-ming, 135–136, 144–145;
influence on Liang Sou-ming, 142–
143; on proper role of science, 151;
influenced by European pessimism
and Marxist analyses, 156–157, 211;
opposes Manchu restoration (1917),

174; Hu Shih's criticism of his
political involvement, 189; and
Research Clique, 190n; mentioned,
21, 95, 121, 150, 160, 199, 325, 327,
360
Liang Shih-ch'iu, 225, 236n
Liang Sou-ming: as exponent of neo-
traditionalism, 135-145; compared to
Liang Ch'i-ch'ao, 135–136, 144–145;
influence of Buddhism on, 137–138;
his theory of cultural diversity, 138–
140; on Western concepts of individualism and law, 140–142; and
Confucianism, 142–144; signs "Our
Political Proposals," 190; mentioned,
150, 163, 168, 359
Liao Chung-k'ai, 166–167
Liberalism: and intellectual elitism,
196–197; Hu Shih's use of term, 213;
and divided opinion, 273–274; and
consensus, 274; and Mao Tse-tung,
299n; Hobhouse on, 327–328; Dewey
on, 328; Hu Shih's understanding of,
328; as theory of public life, 329,
330–331; empirical bases of, 331; and
revolution, 340, 343, 345. *See also* Hu
Shih, political opinions; Laissez-
faire liberalism; Liberalism in China
Liberalism in China, 315–316, 319, 325;
as expressed in "Our Political
Proposals," 190; Dewey's assessment
of, 221; Chiang Kai-shek's critique
of, 319–320; relevance of, 323, 329–
330; as an abstraction, 344; and
Confucianism, 344; failure of, 345.
See also Dewey, John; Hu Shih,
political opinions
Library of Congress, 296
Lin Ch'ang-min, 190n, 204n
Lin Shu, 131, 161
Lin Tsung-meng. *See* Lin Ch'ang-min
Lin Yutang, 279n
Ling Tao-yang, 356
Literary Revolution: genesis of, 76–77,
78–79; Hu Shih's rationale for, 81–
83; democratic significance of, 83–85;
Hu Shih's tentative attitude toward,
85–86; Ch'en Tu-hsiu's views on
historical causes of, 107–108; Hu
Shih's views on historical causes of,
108. *See also* Hu Shih
Liu Ch'ung-chieh, 129n

Liu Fu, 184n
Liu Tsung-yüan, 83
Liu Tzu-k'ai. *See* Liu Ch'ung-chieh
Liu Yung-fu, 8
Lo Chia-lun, 91
Lo Erh-kang, 248n, 341, 359
Lo Lung-chi: and *The Crescent*, 225; political essays of, 236n; and Democratic League, 297; mentioned, 236n, 359
Lo Wen-kan, 190n, 203–204
Lochner, Louis P., 55
Locke, John, 352
London School of Economics, 236
Lu Hsün: and Peita group, 78; on *The New Youth*, 185–186; in exile in Shanghai, 223; criticizes Crescent group, 225; mentioned, 365
Lun-yü, 149n
Lung-men Academy, 6, 19
Lytton Commission, 252

Ma Chün-wu, 25, 275n
Ma Ho. *See* Ma Chün-wu
Mach, Ernst, 364
Manifesto of the New Youth Society (1919), 183, 189, 200
Mansfield, Katherine, 225
Mao I, 11
Mao Tse-tung: Hu Shih's telegram to (1945), 298–299; and Hu Shih, 299n; mentioned, 308, 321, 327
Marco Polo Bridge incident, 290
Marshall mission, 301
Marx, Karl, 189
Marxism-Leninism, 111, 123, 182, 183; influence on Ch'en Tu-hsiu, 107; Hu Shih's critique of, 211; vogue for in China, 211–212; Sun Yat-sen's reservations on, 229; critique of pragmatism, 364n
Maupassant, Guy de, 76, 87
May Fourth Movement, 121, 123, 169, 307, 317, 319, 341, 361; Hu Shih's understanding of its significance, 176–179; Dewey's reaction to, 178–179
May 30 Incident (1925), 214; Hu Shih's reaction to, 215
Mei-chi School (Mei-chi hsüeh-t'ang), 22

Mei-chou p'ing-lun. See The Weekly Critic
Mei I-ch'i, 256, 257
Mei Kuang-ti, 80n
Mei, Y. C. *See* Mei I-ch'i
Meisner, Maurice, 186n, 209n
Mencius: on human nature, 31–32; on filialism, 32; and individualism, 95, 98–99; on *ching-t'ien* system, 166; on the obligations of the ruler, 329; mentioned, 68n, 164, 230, 283
Michels, Robert, 272
Mill, John Stuart, 26, 325
Min-kuo jih-pao. See Republican Daily News
Min-pao, 21
Mo-tzu, 59, 136n, 163
Montesquieu, 26
Morley, John Viscount, 11–12, 352
Mosca, Gaetano, 272
Mukden incident (1931), 245
Murobushi Kōshin, 246

Nankai University, 296, 357
Nasmyth, George, 55, 58
National Assembly (1947), Hu Shih's role in, 304–306
National Education Conference (1928), 239
Nationalism, 169, 207, 215, 216, 249. *See also* Hu Shih, political opinions
Nationalist Clique (Kuo-min hsi), 186n
Nationalist Party. *See* KMT
Neo-Confucianism, 14–17, 19, 31, 96, 164–165, 234. *See also* Ch'eng-Chu School, Chu Hsi, *Li-hsüeh*
Neo-traditionalism: expounded by Liang Ch'i-ch'ao, 131–135; expounded by Liang Sou-ming, 135–145; expounded by Chang Chün-mai, 146–150
New China National Institute, 26, 34
New Culture Movement, 88, 111, 121–122, 177, 299n, 345; Hu Shih's evaluation of its significance, 229–230; Hu Shih's estimate of its effect, 259; CCP estimate of Hu Shih's contribution to, 365
New Life Movement, 230, 282–283, 327; Hu Shih's reaction to, 283
New York Times, The, 243n, 244, 294, 295

New Youth, The (Hsin ch'ing-nien),
75–76, 80n, 85, 87n, 89–90, 91, 93,
121, 122, 188, 206, 361; apolitical
policy of, 176; becomes outlet for
Marxist opinion, 184; closed down
by French police in Shanghai, 186
New Youth group, 180; rift in, 184–187
Newman, Cardinal John H., 75n
Newton, Isaac, 352
Nietzsche, Friedrich, 110, 138
Nobel Prize: for peace, 55; for litera-
ture, 86n
North China Herald, The, 244
Northern Expedition, 216
Nu-li chou-pao. See *The Endeavor*

On Compromise, 11, 352
On Liberty, 26
"On the New People" ("Hsin min
shuo"), 28
Orth, Samuel P., 52
"Our Political Proposals," 199, 227,
233; drafted by Hu Shih, 189–190;
translation of sections 1–4, 191–193;
CCP critique of, 210
Outlook, The, 55n, 66n
Oxford Movement, 75n

Pai-hua: as literary medium, 80, 86–
87; Hu Shih's early poems in, 80–81
Pai-hua literature, 220; models for, 20,
76n; Hu Shih's theory of the history
of, 82–83
Pai-hua movement, 131, 162, 230, 342,
362. *See also* Hu Shih, Literary
Revolution
Paine, Thomas, 335
Pan, Quentin. *See* P'an Kuang-tan
P'an Kuang-tan, 225
P'an Wen-huan, 356
Pareto, Vilfredo, 272
Paris Peace Conference (1919), 129,
176
"Peiping rape case," 306n
Peirce, C. S., 48
Peita, 43, 137, 224, 255, 306, 309, 312n,
313, 341, 361, 362, 363, 366, 367; as
center of new thought, 77–78;
Marxist study groups established at,
123, 207; Hu Shih returns to (1931),
245; postwar, 296, 301–302

Peking: as center of new thought, 77–
78; loses preeminence, 223
Peking National University. *See* Peita
Peking Union Medical College, 223
P'ing she (P'ing society), 236n
Pitt, William, 352
Plato, 167
Political Study Clique (Cheng-hsüeh
hsi), 186n
Pragmatism: Hu Shih's understanding
of, 46–51; as universal methodology,
47, 120–121; and Neo-Confucianism,
49–50; and anti-traditionalism, 114–
115; and religious skepticism, 115–
117; Dewey's beliefs contrasted to
Hu Shih's, 116–121; and rationalism,
117; attitude toward the past, 118–
121; assumption of consensus, 119–
120; popularity in China, 121. *See
also* Dewey, John; Hu Shih, intellectual reform; Liberalism
Pre-Raphaelites, 225
Princeton University, 311
Principle. *See Li, Li-hsüeh*
"Problems and Isms." *See* Hu Shih,
political opinions
Progressivism (U.S.), 43, 332, 336
P'u-i (The Hsüan-t'ung Emperor), 173–
174, 219
Public opinion, 196, 199, 201. *See also*
Hu Shih, political opinions

Rationalism. *See* Hu Shih, intellectual
reform
Renaissance, European, 212; and
Chinese Renaissance, 317–319
*Republican Daily News (Min-kuo jih-
pao),* 223, 241
Research Clique (Yen-chiu hsi), 186n,
190n
Returned students, 122, 204n, 354, 362,
366
Revolution of 1911, 51, 92, 243, 257–
258, 281, 325
*Revolutionary Army, The. See Ko-ming
chün*
Roosevelt, Franklin D., 269, 295
Roosevelt, Theodore, 52, 59, 337
Rousseau, J.-J., 28n, 330–331
Rotours, Robert des, 219
Russell, Bertrand, 46, 138
Russo-Japanese War, 21n, 22–23, 79

Sakyamuni, 103
San-kang wu-lun. See Three Bonds
    and Five Relationships
Sanger, Margaret, 219
Santayana, George, 335
Schopenhauer, Arthur, 137n
Schwartz, Benjamin I., 84n
Science: Liang Ch'i-ch'ao's attack on,
    132–133; defined by Chang Chün-
    mai, 146–147; promoted by Hu Shih
    and Ting Wen-chiang, 157–158
Science and the philosophy of life,
    debate on (1923), 104, 150–151
Science and the Philosophy of Life
    (K'o-hsüeh yü jen-sheng-kuan), 150n
Science Society of China, 80n
Seignobos, Charles, 90
Self-cultivation, Hu Shih's rejection of,
    98–99
Self-strengtheners, 286, 288
Shameen Massacre, 214–215
Shang-chuang, 4, 9, 12
Shanghai: in 1890s, 4; Hu family
    business in, 9; in 1900s, 21, 31; Hu
    Shih's reaction to in 1917, 175; in
    late 1920s, 224; battle for (1949), 310
Shantung, 62
Shantung Provincial University, 363
Shao Li-tzu, 30n, 223
Shao Yu-lien, 7
Shaw, George Bernard, 322
Shelley, Percy Bysshe, 314
Shen-chou jih-pao, 30n
"Shen-mieh lun," 18, 19n
Shen-pao, 21
Shen Yin-mo, 184n, 361
Shih-chi, 83
Shih-pao, 21, 23
Shih-shih hsin-pao, 21, 243–244
Shimonoseki, Treaty of, 8
Shu ching, 159n
Shui-ching chu, 296
Shui-hu chuan, 20, 79n
Sichel, Edith, 319n
Sino-Japanese War (1894–1895), 8
Sino-Japanese War (1937–1945), 30n,
    290, 293–295
Siren, Osvald, 219
Smedley, Agnes, 225
Smith, Adam, 352
Smith, Goldwin, 60
Snow, Edgar, 279n, 299n

Socialism, 123; Hu Shih's understand-
    ing of, 212–213. See also Chang
    Chün-mai, Sun Yat-sen
Soong Ch'ing-ling, 244n, 277, 278–279
Soong Mei-ling, 244n
Soong, T. V.: and Hu Shih, 244, 357;
    character of, 244n; in Washington
    during World War II, 295; and
    China Lobby, 311n; and interna-
    tional student movement, 356, 357;
    mentioned, 226
Soviet Union, 152, 364; Hu Shih's
    admiration for, 194, 232, 280
Spencer, Herbert, 117, 263, 352
Spinoza, Baruch, 352
Spiritual civilization: claimed for China
    by Chang Chün-mai, 147–148; Hu
    Shih's views on, 151–156
Spring and Autumn Annals (Ch'un-
    ch'iu), 103
Ssu-ma Kuang, 18, 30, 117
Strindberg, August, 87, 93, 181n
Struggle, The (Ching-yeh hsün-pao),
    29–30, 34, 79
Stuart, John Leighton, 299n, 306, 309,
    310
Student movement, 53–54, 215, 249,
    255–257, 289, 298, 301–302
Su-pao, 23n, 30n
Suffragette movement, 54, 100
Sun Ch'uan-fang, 218
Sun Chung-shan. See Sun Yat-sen
Sun Fo, 240, 242, 305
Sun, Mme. See Soong Ch'ing-ling
Sun Yat-sen: program of, 220–221;
    concept of political tutelage, 231;
    and democracy, 231, 233; elitist tend-
    encies, 233–234; theory of knowledge
    and action, 234–235; on administra-
    tive competence and popular sover-
    eignty, 270–271; and Five Power
    Constitution, 273; Hu Shih's views
    on, 274–275; mentioned, 21, 25, 33,
    65, 179, 184, 207, 239, 277, 327
Sun Yat-sen University, 286
Sung Che-yüan, 255
Sung scholarship, 5, 6. See also Neo-
    Confucianism
"Systematizing the national heritage."
    See Cheng-li kuo-ku

Ta-kung pao, 361, 362

Ta-t'ung jih-pao, 30n
Taft, William Howard, 52
Tai Chen, 5, 165
Taiping Rebellion, 4n, 5–6, 341
Taiwan Province, 7–8, 311, 320
Taiwan, Republic of, 8
T'ang Erh-ho, 190n, 203
T'ang Ming-tsung, 232
T'ang Yüeh-liang, 356, 357
Tangku Truce, 252
Tanizaki Junichiro, 140n
Tao, 261
Tao-te ching, 59, 261
T'ao Chih-hsing, 190n
T'ao Lü-kung. *See* T'ao Meng-ho
T'ao Meng-ho: as member of Peita group, 78; in Europe (1919), 130; signs "Our Political Proposals," 190; and returned students, 204n; and *The Endeavor,* 205; accepts Marxist analyses of postwar Europe, 212; mentioned, 91, 185, 219, 359
Taoism, 86
Teleshëv, 76
Tennyson, Alfred, 58, 103
Three Bonds and Five Relationships, 114
"Three Hus of Chi-hsi," 5, 122
Ting Hsi-lin, 236n
Ting Jih-ch'ang, 6
Ting Tsai-chün. *See* Ting Wen-chiang
Ting Wen-chiang: in Europe (1919), 129n, 130; as defender of science, 150, 157–158; on crisis in postwar Europe, 158–159, 211–212; on Han Learning, 166; and *The Endeavor,* 188–189; signs "Our Political Proposals," 190; and elitism, 196–197, 265; and returned students, 204n; edits *The Endeavor,* 205; on Japan, 222; on the student movement, 255; advocates authoritarianism, 260, 265–266, 267
"Total" westernization, 285–286, 287–289
Ts'ai Yüan-p'ei: as chancellor of Peita, 78; appreciation of Hu Shih, 121–122; and anarchism, 123; signs "Our Political Proposals," 190; and returned students, 204n; and KMT, 223, 239; and League for the

Protection of Civil Rights, 277; mentioned, 226, 244
Ts'ao Chan, 162
Ts'ao Ju-lin, 192
Ts'ao K'un, 202, 204–205
Tsiang, T. F. *See* Chiang T'ing-fu
Tsinghua University, 145, 224, 255, 256n, 259, 296, 297, 357, 367
Tso chuan, 103
Tsou Jung, 23–24
Tsou Lu, 30n, 286
Tsur, Y. T. *See* Chou I-ch'un
Tu Fu, 103
Tu-li p'ing-lun. See The Independent Critic
Tuan Ch'i-jui, 65, 71, 174, 177, 179, 189, 192, 202, 223
Tun-huang manuscripts, 218, 225–226
Tung-lin group, 258
Tung-nan University, 190n
Tung Pi-wu, 298, 299
T'ung-meng hui, 21, 33, 325
Twenty-One Demands, 61
Tzu-chih t'ung-chien, 13, 18
Tzu-yu Chung-kuo. See Free China

UNESCO, London Conference (1945), 296
United Front, 289, 360
United Nations, San Francisco Conference (1945), 296, 298
University Council, 277
University of Chicago, 245, 279
University of Hong Kong, 286·
University of Wisconsin, 53, 236, 312n
Utopian anarchism, 98

Van Slyke, Lyman P., 136n
Vernacular fiction, 19–20, 119, 341. *See also* Literary Revolution, *Pai-hua*
Versailles, Treaty of, 176
Villard, Oswald Garrison, 59
Voltaire, 164, 352

Waley, Arthur, 149n
Wang, C. T. *See* Wang Cheng-t'ing
Wang Ch'ang-hsin, 204n
Wang Cheng, 190n
Wang Cheng-fu, 356

Wang Cheng-t'ing, 294
Wang Chih-ch'un, 21n
Wang Ching-wei, 240, 283–284
Wang Ch'ung, 164
Wang Ch'ung-hui: as revolutionary journalist, 30n; signs "Our Political Proposals," 190n; and "Good Men Cabinet," 203–204; and returned students, 204n; president of Judicial Yuan, 240, 244; mentioned, 226
Wang Hung-cho, 356
Wang Keng, 357
Wang Liang-ch'ou. See Wang Ch'ung-hui
Wang Mang, 167
Wang Nien-sun, 165
Wang Po-ch'iu, 190n
Wang Shou-jen. See Wang Yang-ming
Wang, Y. C., 250n
Wang Yang-ming: on knowledge and action, 234–235; mentioned, 31–32, 158
Wang Yin-chih, 165
Warlordism, 71, 190–191, 195, 202–203
Waseda University, 145
Washington Conference, 157n
Washington, George, 23, 103
Watson, Burton, 261
Wedemeyer mission, 307n
Weekly Critic, The, 123, 180–182
Wei Tao-ming, 295, 297
Wei Wen-pin, 357
Well-field system. See Ching-t'ien system
Wen I-to, 225, 297
Weng Wen-hao, 256n, 297, 310
Whitehead, Alfred North, 46
Wilde, Oscar, 90
Williams, Edith, 100, 352
Wilson, Woodrow, 39, 52, 57, 332, 336, 337
Woodbridge, Frederick, 49
Woolf, Virginia, 225
Wordsworth, William, 225
World Peace Foundation, 55

World War I: influence on Hu Shih, 58–59; Liang Ch'i-ch'ao's appraisal of its consequences, 131–132
Wu Chih-hui, 30n, 123, 150n, 152, 226
Wu Ching-lien, 204
Wu Han, 367–368
Wu Nan-hsien, 256n
Wu P'ei-fu, 202, 204, 218, 345
Wu Ta-ch'eng, 6
Wu-wei, 261
"Wu-wei government," Hu Shih's theory of, 261–264, 269, 281n, 283
Wuhan Government, 222
Wundt, Wilhelm, 147n

Yale University, 245
Yang Ch'üan: and Hu Shih, 34n, 80n, 277, 279n; and Ts'ai Yüan-p'ei, 277; and League for the Protection of Civil Rights, 277, 278–279; assassination of, 279; mentioned, 289
Yang Hsing-fo. See Yang Ch'üan
Yang Wei-hsin, 129n
Yano Fumio, 37
Yeh Ch'eng-chung, 22n
Yeh Ching-hsin, 204n
Yeh Ch'ing, 359, 360
Yeh Kung-ch'ao, 236n
Yeh Shu-heng. See Yeh Ching-hsin
Yellow Emperor, The, 23, 320
Yen Fu, 26, 84, 92, 117, 325
Yen Hui, 144
Yen Hui-ch'ing, 203
Yen Jo-chü, 165
Yenching University, 255, 258n, 296, 309
Yü Ch'en-tzu, 37n
Yü Jih-chang, 357
Yü P'ing-po, 162, 341, 359, 363
Yü Yu-jen, 30n
Yüan Mei, 37
Yüan Shih-k'ai, 65–66, 68, 71, 174, 189, 202, 233
Yui, David. See Yü Jih-chang

Zen, H. C. See Jen Hung-chün

Harvard East Asian Series

1. *China's Early Industrialization: Sheng Hsuan-huai (1844–1916) and Mandarin Enterprise.* By Albert Feuerwerker.
2. *Intellectual Trends in the Ch'ing Period.* By Liang Ch'i-ch'ao. Translated by Immanuel C. Y. Hsü.
3. *Reform in Sung China: Wang An-shih (1021–1086) and His New Policies.* By James T. C. Liu.
4. *Studies on the Population of China, 1368–1953.* By Ping-ti Ho.
5. *China's Entrance into the Family of Nations: The Diplomatic Phase, 1858–1880.* By Immanuel C. Y. Hsü.
6. *The May Fourth Movement: Intellectual Revolution in Modern China.* By Chow Tse-tsung.
7. *Ch'ing Administrative Terms: A Translation of the Terminology of the Six Boards with Explanatory Notes.* Translated and edited by E-tu Zen Sun.
8. *Anglo-American Steamship Rivalry in China, 1862–1874.* By Kwang-Ching Liu.
9. *Local Government in China under the Ch'ing.* By T'ung-tsu Ch'ü.
10. *Communist China, 1955–1959: Policy Documents with Analysis.* With a foreword by Robert R. Bowie and John K. Fairbank. (Prepared at Harvard University under the joint auspices of the Center for International Affairs and the East Asian Research Center.)
11. *China and Christianity: The Missionary Movement and the Growth of Chinese Antiforeignism, 1860–1870.* By Paul A. Cohen.
12. *China and the Helping Hand, 1937–1945.* By Arthur N. Young.
13. *Research Guide to the May Fourth Movement: Intellectual Revolution in Modern China, 1915–1924.* By Chow Tse-tsung.
14. *The United States and the Far Eastern Crises of 1933–1938: From the Manchurian Incident through the Initial Stage of the Undeclared Sino-Japanese War.* By Dorothy Borg.
15. *China and the West, 1858–1861: The Origins of the Tsungli Yamen.* By Masataka Banno.
16. *In Search of Wealth and Power: Yen Fu and the West.* By Benjamin Schwartz.
17. *The Origins of Entrepreneurship in Meiji Japan.* By Johannes Hirschmeier, S.V.D.
18. *Commissioner Lin and the Opium War.* By Hsin-pao Chang.
19. *Money and Monetary Policy in China, 1845–1895.* By Frank H. H. King.
20. *China's Wartime Finance and Inflation, 1937–1945.* By Arthur N. Young.
21. *Foreign Investment and Economic Development in China, 1840–1937.* By Chi-ming Hou.
22. *After Imperialism: The Search for a New Order in the Far East, 1921–1931.* By Akira Iriye.

23. *Foundations of Constitutional Government in Modern Japan, 1868–1900.* By George Akita.
24. *Political Thought in Early Meiji Japan, 1868–1889.* By Joseph Pittau, S.J.
25. *China's Struggle for Naval Development, 1839–1895.* By John L. Rawlinson.
26. *The Practice of Buddhism in China, 1900–1950.* By Holmes Welch.
27. *Li Ta-chao and the Origins of Chinese Marxism.* By Maurice Meisner.
28. *Pa Chin and His Writings: Chinese Youth Between the Two Revolutions.* By Olga Lang.
29. *Literary Dissent in Communist China.* By Merle Goldman.
30. *Politics in the Tokugawa Bakufu, 1600–1843.* By Conrad Totman.
31. *Hara Kei in the Politics of Compromise, 1905–1915.* By Tetsuo Najita.
32. *The Chinese World Order: Traditional China's Foreign Relations.* Edited by John K. Fairbank.
33. *The Buddhist Revival in China.* By Holmes Welch.
34. *Traditional Medicine in Modern China: Science, Nationalism, and the Tensions of Cultural Change.* By Ralph C. Croizier.
35. *Party Rivalry and Political Change in Taishō Japan.* By Peter Duus.
36. *The Rhetoric of Empire: American China Policy, 1895–1901.* By Marilyn B. Young.
37. *Radical Nationalist in Japan: Kita Ikki, 1883–1937.* By George M. Wilson.
38. *While China Faced West: American Reformers in Nationalist China, 1928–1937.* By James C. Thomson, Jr.
39. *The Failure of Freedom: A Portrait of Modern Japanese Intellectuals.* By Tatsuo Arima.
40. *Asian Ideas of East and West: Tagore and His Critics in Japan, China, and India.* By Stephen N. Hay.
41. *Canton under Communism: Programs and Politics in a Provincial Capital, 1949–1968.* By Ezra F. Vogel.
42. *Ting Wen-Chiang: Science and China's New Culture.* By Charlotte Furth.
43. *The Manchurian Frontier in Ch'ing History.* By Robert H. G. Lee.
44. *Motoori Norinaga, 1730–1801.* By Shigeru Matsumoto.
45. *The Comprador in Nineteenth Century China: Bridge between East and West.* By Yen-p'ing Hao.
46. *Hu Shih and the Chinese Renaissance: Liberalism in the Chinese Revolution, 1917–1937.* By Jerome B. Grieder.